THE NEW **HENRY GIROUX** READER

"The connections between power, politics, and education can be elusive at times, which is intentional on the part of the powers that be. But Giroux has never been fooled or scared to make the connections that explain power and the injustice inflicted on the most vulnerable. Giroux's body of work is clear, concise, razor sharp, and aimed not only at examining power itself, but also its impact on human life. *The New Henry Giroux Reader* is indispensable for anyone interested in understanding and undoing this American horror story we are all living."
—Bettina L. Love, *Associate Professor, The University of Georgia, Department of Educational Theory & Practice*

"These are times when public intellectuals of the caliber of Henry Giroux are much needed but unfortunately quite rare. This is a timely book, superbly edited, and cleverly organized, designed not to please readers with niceties and wishful thinking, but to engage them with difficult ideas and encourage reflection and action to resist and change. Giroux has an uncanny ability to walk the critical tightrope required to simultaneously point to the terror and violence of contemporary societies while providing ideas and metaphors that could make many readers uncomfortable—but, more importantly, hopeful. This book presents Giroux's pioneering key texts in public pedagogy, cultural studies, youth studies, higher education, media studies, and critical theory, showing his original and challenging perspectives without prescriptive nostalgia or sentimentalism. This is a book that we need to read and discuss, not in search of recipes or easy solutions, but because it will help each of us to explore our individual and social responses in these troubled times and imagine what we can do to more effectively to assume our responsibilities as teachers, students, citizens, and activists."
—Gustavo E. Fischman, *Professor, Mary Lou Fulton Teachers College, Arizona State University*

"Henry Giroux is one of the preeminent (and most prolific) cultural theorists of neoliberalism, investigating the most urgent issues of our contemporary world not only through the lens of moral outrage about what is happening to the planet and the people, but with a razor-sharp intellect that recognizes that our extraordinary time requires new ways of understanding—not just of rehashing and reworking—old concepts in the search for a different world. When Gramsci's "optimism of the will" becomes active, it will be because Henry Giroux's "pessimism of the intellect" has provided us with the conceptual tools to become democratic citizens. This collection, which spans Giroux's entire career, shows the scope and depth of what real intellectual work looks like. If we are to avoid the suicidal consequences of neoliberal capitalism, it will be because of the belief in public pedagogy that writers such as Giroux embody. His hope for another world is organically part of his intellectual project, not just an abstract wish."
Sut Jhally, *Professor of Communication, University of Massachusetts; Founder and Executive Director, Media Education Foundation*

THE NEW **HENRY GIROUX** READER

THE NEW **HENRY**
GIROUX
READER

THE NEW HENRY GIROUX READER

The Role of the Public Intellectual in a Time of Tyranny

HENRY GIROUX
MCMASTER UNIVERSITY

Introduced and Edited by
JENNIFER A. SANDLIN
ARIZONA STATE UNIVERSITY

&

JAKE BURDICK
PURDUE UNIVERSITY

Myers
Education
Press

GORHAM, MAINE

Published by Myers Education Press, LLC
P.O. Box 424 Gorham, ME 04038

Myers Education Press is an academic publisher specializing in books, e-books and digital content in the field of education. All of our books are subjected to a rigorous peer review process and produced in compliance with the standards of the Council on Library and Information Resources.

Library of Congress Cataloging-in-Publication Data available from Library of Congress.

13-digit ISBN 978-1-9755-0075-7 (paperback)
13-digit ISBN 978-1-9755-0074-0 (hard cover)
13-digit ISBN 978-1-9755-0076-4 (library networkable e-edition)
13-digit ISBN 978-1-9755-0077-1 (consumer e-edition)

Printed in the United States of America.

All first editions printed on acid-free paper that meets the American National Standards Institute Z39-48 standard.

Books published by Myers Education Press may be purchased at special quantity discount rates for groups, workshops, training organizations and classroom usage. Please call our customer service department at 1-800-232-0223 for details.

Cover design by Sophie Appel

Visit us on the web at www.myersedpress.com to browse our complete list of titles.

≳ CONTENTS ≲

SECTION III: Neoliberalism and the Phantasmagoria of the Social: Post-9/11 Politics, the Decline of the Public Sphere, and the Decay of Humanity

SECTION IV: No Way Out: The Devouring of Higher Education

SECTION V: Radicalizing Hope: Public Intellectualism, The Vitalism of Education, and the Promise of Democracy

ACKNOWLEDGMENTS

We gratefully acknowledge the permission to reprint from the respective copyright holder.

Chapter 1. Giroux, Henry A. (1983). Theories of Reproduction and Resistance in the New Sociology of Education: A Critical Analysis, *Harvard Educational Review,* 53(3), 257-293. http://www.harvardeducationreview

Chapter 2. Giroux, Henry A. (1988). Border Pedagogy in the Age of Postmodernism. *The Journal of Education, 170*(3), pp. 162-181.

Chapter 3. Giroux, Henry A. (1994). Doing Cultural Studies: Youth and the Challenge of Pedagogy, *Harvard Educational Review, 64*(3), 278-308. http://www.harvardeducationalreview.org

Chapter 4. Giroux, Henry A. (2000). Public Pedagogy and the Responsibility of Intellectuals: Youth, Littleton, and the Loss of Innocence. *jac, 20*(1), 9-24.

Chapter 5. Giroux, Henry A. (2001). Breaking into the Movies: Pedagogy and the Politics of Film. *jac 21*(3), 584-598.

Chapter 6. Giroux, Henry A. (2003). Neoliberalism and the Disappearance of the Social in Ghost World. *Third Text, 17*(2), 151-161. Copyright © *Third Text,* reprinted by permission of Taylor & Francis Ltd, http://www.tandfonline.com on behalf of *Third Text.*

Chapter 7. Giroux, Henry A. (2004). Education After Abu Ghraib: Revisiting Adorno's Politics of Education (2004) *Cultural Studies, 18*(6), 779-815. Reprinted with permission of *Cultural Studies* and Taylor & Francis. For more information see https://www.tandfonline.com/loi/rcus20 and http://www.tandfonline.com

Chapter 8. Giroux, Henry A. (2005). "The Terror of Neoliberalism: Rethinking the Significance of Cultural Politics." *College Literature,* 32:1, 1-19. Copyright © Johns Hopkins University Press and West Chester University.

Chapter 9. Giroux, Henry A. (2017). White Nationalism, Armed Culture and Violence in the Age of Donald Trump. *Philosophy and Social Criticism, 43*(9), 887-910. Reprinted with permission of *Philosophy and Social Criticism* and SAGE Publications.

Chapter 10. Giroux, Henry A. (1999). "Vocationalizing Higher Education: Schooling and the Politics of Corporate Culture." *College Literature, 26*(3), 147-161. Copyright © Johns Hopkins University Press and West Chester University.

Chapter 11. Giroux, Henry A. (2003). Youth, Higher Education and the Crisis of Public Time: Educated Hope and the Possibility of a Democratic Future. *Social Identities, 9*(2), 141-168. https://www.tandfonline.com/loi/csid20 and www.tandfonline.com

Chapter 12. Giroux, Henry A. (2008). The Militarization of U.S. Higher Education after 9/11. *Theory, Culture, & Society, 25*(5), 56-82. .

Chapter 13. Giroux, Henry A. (2002). Democracy, freedom, and justice after September 11th: Rethinking the role of educators and the politics of schooling. *Teachers College Record, 104*(6), 1138-1162. Copyright *Teachers College Record*.

Chapter 14. Giroux, Henry A. (2004). Cultural Studies, Critical Pedagogy, and the Responsibility of Intellectuals. *Communication and Critical/Cultural Studies, 1*(1), 59–79. Copyright © National Communication Association.

Chapter 15. Giroux, Henry A. (2012). Gated Intellectuals and Fortress America: Towards a Borderless Pedagogy in the Occupy Movement. *Policy Futures in Education 10*(6), 728-733. *Policy Futures in Education* and SAGE Publications.

Chapter 16. Henry Giroux on Zombie Politics: Bill Moyers Interviews Henry Giroux. Moyers & Company, November 22, 2013, https://billmoyers.com/segment/henry-giroux-on-zombie-politics/

Chapter 17. Giroux, Henry A. (2017, September 9). Charlottesville, Neo-Nazis and the Challenge to Higher Education. *Truthdig.com*, https://www.truthdig.com/articles/charlottesville-neo-nazis-challenge-higher-education/

Chapter 18. Giroux, Henry A. (2017, December 3). Gangster Capitalism and Nostalgic Authoritarianism in Trump's America. *Salon.com*, https://www.salon.com/2017/12/03/gangster-capitalism-and-nostalgic-authoritarianism-in-trumps-america/

⋛ FOREWORD ⋚

Antonia Darder

The philosophers have only interpreted the world, in various ways.
The point, however, is to change it.
—Karl Marx

Not everything that is faced can be changed,
but nothing can be changed until it is faced.
—James Baldwin

A revolutionary writer for social change is one of the first thoughts that comes to mind as I reflect on the writings of Henry Giroux. Throughout his creative life as teacher, public intellectual, and writer, the focus of his labor has never strayed. With each unfolding generation of ideas, Henry has waged battle gallantly against the political and pedagogical forces of capital that distort our humanity. He names the decaying and loveless culture of competition, individualism, and instrumentalization and the alienating aspirations foisted onto working people. Adamantly loyal to Baldwin's words—*nothing can be changed until it is faced*—Giroux's writing unveils the social and political atrocities of the state, by giving voice to the contemptable ethos of neoliberal times.

Working Class Mentor

I found a mentor and a guide,
someone who understood that learning could be liberatory.
—bell hooks

I first met Henry when I was a graduate student and single mom of three children, aching to understand the oppressive conditions that had shaped my life and struggling to find my way in the world, so that I might, as Eldridge Cleaver so rightly noted, *be part of the solution*, rather than part of the problem. In Henry, I found a fierce critic and pointed mentor who consistently pushed at the edges of my comprehension, demanding precision and sober engagement of the structural inequalities that produce human suffering in the world. Henry's own personal struggles as a working-class kid with a troubled family life echoed my own pathos, in ways that I have only more recently come to better understand, deeply respect, and appreciate, as a possible source for an uncanny capacity to walk the fires of indignation and rage to explicitly and unambiguously name the repulsive greed and necrophilic ethos that threaten our humanity and our planet.

Henry's working-class values were certainly obvious in his mentoring of students, which mixed a down-to-earth, tough-guy demeanor with no-nonsense expectations, and always with a smattering of music. At the time, it was Tracy Chapman, Ella Fitzgerald, and Sarah Vaughn who were captivating his ear. The first time I heard him speak at a conference in Irvine in the summer of 1987, I was preparing to write my dissertation proposal. After speaking with him, I was on fire! His politics, strength, and generosity transfixed my being. I knew almost instantly this was the mentor and guide I had been seeking.

Engaging the intellect of Henry Giroux during my doctoral studies, and for many years after, was both terrifying and deeply inspiring. As I traveled his books and articles—always armed with a dictionary at my side—Henry's writings helped me to forge an intensively grounded political sensibility within me—one that drew heavily on my working-class passion and the precarious world in which I lived. Furthermore, it was through Giroux's writings that I developed the language necessary to forge a more coherent political discourse—one in sync with the revolutionary commitment and solidarity I embraced as a colonized woman of color in the U.S.

Hence, the spirit of Henry's uncompromising stance in unveiling the hegemony of our times was vital to my theoretical formation; as it still remains vital to the formation of a new generations of educational scholars, who seek the radical language and political clarity so absent in most of the literature in our field. Along with Paulo Freire's ideas and those of other radical scholars, Henry Giroux's writings have initiated so many into an intellectual lineage of revolutionary formation that demands presence, rigor, persistence, actions, and a willingness to risk—traits that define the fearless public intellectual.

Fearless Public Intellectual

If you are silent about your pain,
they'll kill you and say you enjoyed it.
—Zora Neale Hurston

As a public intellectual and critical educational philosopher, Giroux has been relentless and fearless in divulging the brutality of advanced capitalism and the fascistic political antics of the right. In tandem, he exposes the hypocrisy and destructiveness of liberal centrists who play both camps—enacting unjust neoliberal pursuits, while promoting civil rights nostalgia. With his mighty pen, Giroux has skillfully fashioned critical assertions about the pervasive conditions that assault the everyday lives of children, youth, women, racialized communities, and working-class populations in the United States and around the world. Few radical theorists have been so relentless in their argumentation against the treachery of a world where the interests of capital predominate, while the distance between the rich and poor expands, rising police shootings of Black youth persist, citizens of color undergo staggering levels of incarceration, anti-immigrant sentiments fuel draconian border policies that separate children from family, a state apparatus sanctions contemporary fascism, and a nihilistic political economy strips away any sense of common decency.

I want to argue here that Giroux represents the very meaning of what Gramsci meant by an organic intellectual—generous and expansive, as well as acerbic and unrelenting should the occasion require such a response. This is a man who has never been a shrinking violet or ever hesitated to pierce through the heart of social reform practices that function to perpetuate the exploitation, domination, and disempowerment of the majority of the world's population. Yet, despite his success as an unrivaled social critic in education and the recipient of an endowed academic chair and a multitude of awards, Giroux has never strayed from indignation in the face of injustice and the oppressive conditions he witnessed growing up in his neighborhood. In his profound articulations of the ravages of neoliberalism and the indignities of racism and sexism upon the lives of ordinary people are the embodied sensibilities of his lived history as a poor working-class white kid, growing up amid social and material chaos. Early on, he witnessed the injustices experienced by impoverished working class men and women, both in his own life and on the streets of his neighborhood—people who never stood a fighting chance against the intersecting forces of poverty, patriarchy, and racism.

As such, the brutal consequences of the disempowering structures of schooling and society have never existed for Henry as mere abstractions—as is often the case even among leftist intellectuals—but rather, these became the impetus for struggle, fueling his determination to uproot the vicious lies of society's official transcripts, meant to silence and undermine the humanity of all those perceived as "other" in the neoliberal landscape of American life. As an organic intellectual, Giroux has been a consummate public voice, chronicling growing political debacles within schools and society, in ways that echo the deep pedagogical sensibilities of an educator who has known the bodily pains of injustice and, as such, has had to endure the many conflicts, contradictions, and complexities of what it means to be a radical democratic citizen amid the rubble of revolutionary dreams.

Giroux's writing also reflects a robust intimacy with radical democracy, informed by a deep critical awareness of the power of solidarity, the historical necessity for a politics of the common good, and our indisputable right to participate as full historical subjects within the public sphere. As an unfaltering proponent for democratic life, Giroux has been a stubborn and unremitting advocate for schools and universities as key public

XVI   THE NEW HENRY GIROUX READER

democratic spaces for the evolution of voice, dialogue, civic participation, solidarity and human liberation. Moreover, for Giroux—as can be the case with working class public intellectuals—surviving conditions of exploitation gave concrete meaning to his political formation and his fierce engagement with the necrophilic cultural mores that have robbed so many men and women of their lives and their right to exist. I would argue here that it was precisely through such a dialectical process of the personal and political, which Paulo Freire called *radicalization*, that Giroux came to profoundly comprehend the power of language as an effective political weapon for transforming the world, in that it is also linked to the evolution of political consciousness and fundamentally undergirds the manner in which we make sense of our world.

A key trait of an effective public intellectual on the left can be linked to the manner in which his or her writings and oration provide a language and conceptual clarity that educators, activists, organizers, artists, and independent media producers can use to make sense of the political and pedagogical complexities surrounding schools, universities, communities, and societies. This entails a courageous process of connecting the dots in the reading of power, by unveiling inequalities, acknowledging suffering, and moving collectively toward the concrete transformation of social and material conditions. In this sense, Giroux has displayed an extraordinary capacity to write and speak in ways that are accessible, without losing the power and complexity of his analysis. I have never been at one of his lectures where people have left untouched—whether they agreed with him or not. Moreover, beyond being an avid reader of Giroux, I have also been a student and comrade of this complex human being. In the process, we have fought, struggled, and learned together to respect the diversity in our perspectives, as much as the commonality of our working-class sensibilities and uncompromising political commitment to the making of a more just world. With Giroux, I personally underwent a political formation that taught me to remain ever cognizant and vigilant of the treachery of cultural hegemony and the multidimensionality of oppression and its expressions. And, it is just this human talent—to stop people in their tracks and motivate us to think outside our commonsensical boxes and conditioned ideologies—that best defines an organic intellectual committed to changing the world.

Over the last forty years, the brilliance and power of Henry Giroux's writings are undeniable, despite whatever criticisms may have been, rightly or wrongly, issued against his ideas and his methods of engagement. Moreover, Henry is, indeed, *a force of nature*, for anyone who knows the man cannot fail to recognize the restless, impatient, and tenacious spirit of his razor-sharp mind, where his yearning for liberation births an intellectual force that simply refuses to be silenced or contained. It is, in fact, this uncompromising dimension responsible for his piercing scholarship, prolific craftsmanship, and deeply determined intellect that has often caused feelings of intimidation and insecurity among those who attempt to spar with the eloquence of his force.

Hence, I believe this towering public intellectual has not only been grossly misunderstood, but unfortunately has remained unrecognized, given his fierce political commitment. In an academic climate that is far more comfortable with mediocrity and ad nauseam debates—which not only reap little societal change (despite all the social justice rhetoric of our times) but more often than not sustain the oppressive antics of the money Gods—it is not surprising that Giroux has been seen by many as a perpetual thorn-in-the-side, ornery and resolute. Yet, what most seem to have missed here is the profoundly sensitive heart, enduring lucidity, and rare love for life that have propelled his tenacious unwillingness to abandon revolutionary principles and fueled an intrepid political spirit that refuses to ignore the thirst for justice.

Finally, it should be noted here that there is no desire to elevate Henry Giroux to objectified or infallible icon, but rather to argue that behind the fury of his scholarship exists an extraordinary human being—warts and all—who has suffered long and hard to remain steadfast as a faithful contemporary messenger of revolutionary dreams. For those of us who have endured our own inner and outer political struggles, there can be nothing but abiding admiration for a working-class intellectual who has refused to be coopted or seduced by the trappings of the academic circus.

Emissary of Justice

If you are neutral in situations of injustice,
you have chosen the side of the oppressor.
—Desmond Tutu

As one of the most prolific contemporary philosophers of education on the left, Giroux's powerful ideas reverberate radical political sensibilities and an unwavering commitment to labor on the side of justice. This volume of his writings demonstrates his ample contributions to a variety of fields, drawing on the works of Karl Marx and Paulo Freire, as well as the works of theorists from cultural studies, postcolonial studies, feminism, Black studies, political science, sociology, and critical philosophy. His numerous books and articles have persistently warned readers of the glaring anti-democratic inclinations at work in the neoliberal era. As such, he has forcefully advocated for youth, workers, the poor, and the racialized, while railing against the imperialistic tenets of militarism and religious fundamentalism. Whether engaging questions of the media's assault on youth or the consuming of children by corporatized innocence or the wretched spectacle produced in response to Hurricane Katrina or the horrific transformation of the university as a training ground for corporate greed and the national security state or the impact of political economic forces producing globalized entropy, Giroux has not minced words nor trod lightly in his exposés of life under the tyranny of neoliberalism.

In the process, Giroux has shed a bright light on questions of critical pedagogy, youth studies, media studies, and cultural studies. His incomparable ease with writing both scholarly and journalistic portrayals of the chaos and unconscionable destruction of neoliberalism has led to the crafting of a multitude of incisive treatises that at their core aim unapologetically to call for the transformation of the world. Rich and strikingly incisive, Giroux's ideas penetrate the deception and mythology of economic Darwinism and the shameful historical and political dynamics of a homogenizing social order that persists in destroying the planet, despite all claims to the contrary.

As we have arrived at each new, appalling development of the last four decades under neoliberalism, Giroux's passionate voice has issued clarion calls that boldly unveil a growing disdain for democratic life among the powerful elite—a ruthless disdain that has made a mockery of civil society and now seeks to destroy all vestiges of liberal democracy. Whether speaking out against hegemonic schooling, the destructive mythology of the Iraq war, the blinding patriotism of responses to 9/11, the mortgage debacle, the culture industry's predatory utility of youth, the mass incarceration and police violence against men and women of color, or the despotic debauchery of the Trump administration, Giroux's ever-evolving ideas have remained staunchly resolute and committed to radical possibilities and the promise of collective movement for transforming the world. From such a commitment, he has posited hard-hitting and persistent critiques fueled by brilliant insights, a devotion to freedom, and an unmistaken sense of radical hope, despite the magnitude of assaults to our human dignity and our inalienable rights as cultural citizens of the world.

As one sifts through the vast archive that is Henry Giroux's writings, one cannot miss his steadfast fidelity to a revolutionary vision—a vision to which he has remained faithful throughout the years. Through his evolution as a theorist, Giroux has utilized, in creative and imaginative ways, a powerful intellectual history mobilized by the works of Marxists, critical theorists, anti-colonial writers, feminists, and cultural studies writers. Yet, despite drawing on insights and conclusions from a great variety of authors, Giroux's work has remained unmistakably current and creatively innovative—never shallow or derivative. With each new offering to the field, Giroux reveals powerful insights and brings greater analytical clarity to much needed connections—connections that could mobilize us further democratically, toward revolutionary struggles on the ground and in our everyday lives.

Undoubtedly, Giroux is reminiscent of the organic intellectual of which Gramsci wrote, and the radical intellectual committed to changing the world, as Marx maintained. Throughout the last four decades, Henry Giroux has consistently concerned himself foremost with unveiling the contemporary horrors of neoliberalism, rather than posturing and pontificating dogma devoid of life and detached from the everyday pain that strips us of self-determination and annuls our political participation. It is precisely for these reasons that in Giroux's writing we find an unrelenting analytical force that weaves beautifully crafted and complex political narratives that bare open the wretched wounds of capital and the impunity of the state. As a remarkably gifted writer—as this outstanding collection illustrates—Giroux critically navigates through chaotic and shrouded entanglements of hegemonic treachery to illuminate emancipatory paths with profound and evolving critical readings of the world—readings anchored in an emancipatory pedagogy, deliberately and conscientiously forged in solidarity and radical hope, knowing at the very core of his being that another world is indeed possible!

REFLECTIONS ON HENRY GIROUX'S LIFE AND WORK

Henry Giroux and the Enduring Spirit of Resistance

PETER MCLAREN, CHAPMAN UNIVERSITY,
NORTHEAST NORMAL UNIVERSITY (CHINA)

The ideas that Henry Giroux has cultivated have profoundly influenced academic and activist life for the past 40 years, and, assuming the human race survives, the effects of his work will be felt by generations to come. Giroux's unwillingness to barricade his work within the frosty precincts of the academy is of one piece with his unflagging struggle to challenge democracy to live up to its name. Henry Giroux has achieved such prominence as a public intellectual that his work—which can be crudely summarized as the prosecution of injustice wherever and whenever it raises its ugly head out of the swampland of corporate contrivance—has taken on world-historical significance, mainly (but not exclusively) among educators, who have responded to Giroux's call for resistance and transformation as a way to dampen the speed of the neoliberal assault, an assault that puts the survival of humanity under a persistent question mark. While Giroux's work has never ceased to be important since he first began publishing in the late 1970s, the social, economic, cultural, and geopolitical forces at work today—culminating in a reactionary social infrastructure and institutional petrification—have given it a singular urgency, especially at this particular historical moment when a parasitical vigilante populism is masquerading as revenge against governing elites on a scale never envisaged by mainstream critics. And at a time when sanity has been lost in the drumbeat of partisan name-calling, duplicity, and embargo on truth, the world appears to be on a trajectory toward a smoking, bombed-out brickyard. In an intellectual climate overflowing with faux-revolutionaries whose *trompe l'œil* revolutions never make it past constructing a personal webpage, Giroux's unbounded insights are widely engaged by a worldwide audience of embattled intellectuals and activists, encapsulating the spirit of struggle that marked his formative years in the 1960s—a spirit that has

THE NEW HENRY GIROUX READER

never faltered and has remained steadfast, politically coherent, and loyal to the cause of the subaltern classes.

While there is no inexorable determination at work here, there are signs that we are already on the brink of catastrophe. The cycle of Sisyphus has seen regime after regime in American politics become more emboldened in defending the tyrannies of concentrated wealth (most commonly referred to as corporations). Its current form is a post-democratic authoritarian populism where the center-right and center-left have melded together like dinosaur bones in a tar pit. Despite some important differences on cultural, moral, and ideological issues, they have been equally determined to insulate themselves against the demands of the popular majorities in all but rhetorical proclamations. The mainstream media evince a spirit co-opted by the corporations that own them, spawning in the process a faction-ridden media seized with a regrettable penchant for manipulation that continues to exploit the prejudices and predilections of their audiences. And it has created a world where "freedom" has come to mean the freedom to exploit others, the free exchange of inaccurate information, the freedom to wage imperialist wars, and to enter into "free" trade agreements that stipulate technological innovations designed not to create but to decimate jobs. Whether the political terrain at this moment has birthed a pan-fascist ideological visionary or a simple-minded narcissist populated by ego-driven incompetence and absent of political acumen misses Giroux's lessons on theory and resistance which, written long before the Trump era, illustrate how society's economic, institutional, cultural, and ideological arrangements, while self-consolidating, are not completely deterministic, requiring the popular majorities to slash through dense and seemingly intractable ideological terrain designed to win the consent of the people. In order to prevent such arrangements from fulfilling their reproductive role as birthing centers for sentinels of the liberal-democratic hegemony, conditions need to exist for the popular majorities to critique and transform their lives through what Giroux calls languages of critique and possibility. Giroux's work reveals that the hegemony of the right is not an unshatterable wall that condemns any opposition to be obsequiously inactive. Sometimes small acts contribute to the building of large social movements. It is in taking up this idea that Giroux's work forms a bridgehead from the *what is* to the *what could be*. Democracy, in this instance, can move beyond its function as a titular power beholden to corporations, consecrating with a callous indifference the powers of the state, and be repristinated as a real force for justice. More than a salutary purge of liberal progressivism, Giroux's work advocates a complete transformation of democracy. The type of democracy envisioned by Giroux comes in forms that cannot be decreed from above—such as something envisioned by an elbow-patched university Don over a cigar and cognac or by a vanguard party of hardened leftists sitting under portraits of Lenin. For Giroux, democracy can only be built by the protagonistic participation of the people, whose dignity, fortitude, and political coloration he has never failed to respect and admire since his formative years as a working-class youth growing up in Smith Hill, Rhode Island.

It's possible to trace Giroux's early work in the areas of critical theory and resistance to his current writings on various manifestations of neoliberalism infused with the fatalistic determination of the surveillance state, American fascism, and the struggle to create a radical democracy able to live up to the tenets of justice for which it professes to serve as its global guardian. There is a clear coherence between his early work and more recent works on youth culture, capitalism, and the surveillance state, which is not to mean that he has stayed in one place. Far from it. The range of topics that fleck the firmament of Giroux's work has addressed innumerable events, all of which cohere around the importance of attending to the practicalities of everyday life while building forms of solidarity and social justice under all forces that hold such justice under siege. What has always been consistent in Giroux's exemplary analyses of social life has been his inbuilt dialectics, persistently illuminating why any personal struggle must at one and the same time be a social struggle—a struggle to name, critique, and engage the world.

Giroux's work in cultural studies refuses to entertain an affiliative liaison with identity politics, preoccupied with the postmodern absence of intrinsicality in identity formations or the freeplay of signifying slippages at a microcapillary level—he recognized that this was an academic move that does little to disrupt the world of fully paid-up capitalists, a world in which resistance becomes another form of carefully packaged neoliberalism with just enough illustrious academic élan to give it the aura of the avant-avant-garde, with theory becoming an end in itself. Giroux's abiding relationship with Freire's emphasis on praxis ensured that Giroux would have none of this.

Given Giroux's singular prominence on the world stage, we should not be induced to forget his early indebtedness to the work of Freire and the Frankfurt School that was burgeoning under a white heat in the 1970s and 1980s, nor the way in which he drew upon and augmented with his own unique creativity theories developed out of what was then the new field of cultural studies, British attempts to develop a sociology of knowledge, as well as advances in literary theory, feminist studies, and theories of resistance that emerged from the Birmingham School of Contemporary Cultural Studies. This was a project that, in the hands of Giroux, not only bit into the speed of the corporatization of education that left public schools to face disintegration, but provided a critical alternative. In so doing, Giroux did more than rejuvenate pedagogical theory: he reinvented it. In fact, next to Freire, it is difficult to think of any other educator who has done more to redefine the meaning of education and contribute to its transformation than Giroux.

Giroux's work constitutes a humanist dialectics of the concrete, where theories of resistance (and as resistance) possess an intentionality that enables the wider project of creating a democratic public sphere—a counterpublic sphere—with the potential to encourage many to traverse the cluttered pathway from docility to insurgency; over time, it would come to serve as a space of possibility with more appeal for those who frequent local diners and truck stops, who are educators, musicians, artists, teachers, and workers than for those who spend their weekends blustering about the death of meaning at art house openings and whose political coloration is more akin to what hijinks occur on the catwalk at Prada's runway shows than the grim architecture of structural exploitation. Giroux's refusal to be trapped within economic deterministic versions of Marxist theories and his commitment to fighting injustice through multi-terraced forms of resistance have left a profound and courageous legacy for new generations of intellectuals and activists to take up. Despite coordinated efforts by those on the right and the specialized moneyed class to impede his investigations, not by full-scale hostilities but by a grim indifference or academic gamesmanship, Giroux's work has continued to defy the sacred cows of the academy, reached out across the globe, and offered the most penetrating analysis of how corporate capitalism, armed with new technologies enabling new forms of *Weltanschauungskrieg*, has become compelled by some portentous force of political amnesia and obsession with heritage and birthright, to become the equivalent of fascism, leading to an inanition of hope so necessary for the realization of an inclusive democracy where people are obliged to sell their labor power to make ends meet. Giroux keeps hope alive not by promoting concord and harmony, but by parrying the most devastating effects of capital and thinking through the dark webs of deceit engineered in line with the apologists for neoliberalism. Giroux's alternative of direct, participatory democracy is built upon the constructive energy of popular participation and social justice, a participation that refuses to be corralled by the dictatorship of any party. The popular majorities can never be made into a formal, static, or bureaucratic category. Giroux sets himself against the negative inheritance of revolutions that turned themselves into their opposite, for there is nothing more important for Giroux than exercising the best of our social heritage: the development of the potentialities of human beings through popular participation—a protagonistic, participatory praxis—in the creation of a democratic public sphere.

Knowing Henry Giroux

SHIRLEY R. STEINBERG, UNIVERSITY OF CALGARY

I wanted to be a vet. A science major at The University of Southern Maine, Henry Giroux was the high scorer on the basketball team (Giroux, interviewed by Steinberg, 2019). After a dispute with his coach, he quit the team in his second year. His science professor made an explicit remark about Henry in class, noting that he couldn't imagine a scholarship player quitting the team. Henry abruptly switched his coursework to social studies, a teaching major: *I love kids, that was my theory. I'll be a teacher the rest of my life, that'll be great.* Teaching high school in the late 1960s, Henry taught electives based on alienation. *It was an amazing experience, the experience felt right, but I had no language through which to filter it. Someone asked me: "Well theoretically, how do you explain what you're doing and why it matters?"* A theorist in search of his theory, Giroux balanced his teaching with his search for ways in which to understand not only his teaching, but his fervor.

While teaching high school, he used a variety of books, always supplementing them with a number of films and other sources, meshed with the culture of the young people he was teaching. As he put it, *I was trying to figure out how to pedagogically work within an institution as an isolated teacher, yet still be able to change the conditions of my own teaching, to broaden the possibilities of a lived style. I used to rent films, radical films. We discussed how things were represented, how they challenged our understanding of the world, and what it meant to challenge the messages they presented.*

I would buy books, five or six at a time and just put them in the library, I wouldn't assign any books. That way I got beyond the ban on certain books. I used readers like "Women in a Sexist Society," and other books that some parents complained about. I once had to defend some material in front of the school board. Material that focused on a critique of Henry Miller...luckily, I won that battle. Knowing how to make something meaningful in order to make it critical and transformative has always been crucial for my pedagogy. The other challenge was to find ways in which to deal with materials without the resources needed.

Inspired by mentors who grasped both his politics and his demand for answers, teaching led to Giroux's completing his doctorate at Carnegie Mellon in 1977. Acutely aware of his aversion to right-wing tropes of the day, he understood that theory was informed by understanding both power and culture, his work was politicized in every way. *I was always interested in culture, I always saw culture as a kind of breeding ground for how people began to understand the relationship with themselves, with others, and how they defined themselves.* Analysis of culture stimulated his early writings, film reviews for *Cineaste* and other magazines at the time. Informed by György Lukács, finding Althusser, and becoming immersed in Gramsci, Henry understood that the late 1970s had become *a classic moment to begin to talk about what I call cultural positivism and how culture was bearing down on education in a way that had to be challenged* (Giroux, 1979). His work in cultural studies was given an international launch in North American educational circles through *Cultural Studies*, a collection of essays edited by Larry Grossberg for Routledge, taken from the journal of the same name (Grossberg et al., 1992). In 1991, Henry published *Border Crossings: Cultural Workers and the Politics of Education* (Giroux, 1991), arguably the most influential book in education at the time, and the first to bring cultural studies to education in a set of essays that literally crossed borders and linked pedagogy to culture, politics, and postmodernism.

It was during this moment that Joe Kincheloe and I proposed a book series to a group of educational publishers, all asking for a hook: what could we do that hadn't been done before? During a serendipitous moment at the University of Miami in Oxford, Ohio, Joe invited Henry to write the first book of the series. Henry, with unbounded generosity, agreed, and *Living Dangerously: Multiculturalism and the Politics of Difference* (Giroux, 1993) launched our series. Years later, our editor noted to us that without Giroux's contribution, the series would never have been published. The book introduced notions of identity, power, politics, and culture to educators, demystifying cultural studies and employing it to expose the ways in which being takes place within cultural contexts of knowing...indeed, an emancipatory and cultural conversation had made its way into faculties of education.

Giroux intellectualized education, he politicized it, and he criticalized it. Refusing to allow cultural studies to remain embedded within literary theory and faculties of English, he granted us access and invited us to participate. Not only was he prolific during these early years of cultural studies and education, but his global influence was threaded throughout students, colleagues, international institutions, and educational discourse. Henry brought educators into the discussion. His work on youth exceeded all curricular and behavioral models: *I tried to integrate the question of education into youth studies, because I felt that they were ignored by everyone.*

I wanted to find concrete examples of notions of vulnerability that raised ethical issues. When you are talking about kids, you can't just say that they are failing, you have to assume a sense of individual responsibility. From there I took up the question of public pedagogy.

The father of three, Henry was *the* ever-vigilant parent/researcher. When his boys developed a passion, he watched and listened, then he wrote. In the 1990s, both Joe Kincheloe and I were at Penn State University with Henry (who was instrumental in bringing us there). Friendship opened into long parenting discussions with both Susan and Henry, our mob of kids interacting and all of them becoming our mentors. The stimulation our offspring brought us catapulted us to the personal level within cultural studies. Family trips were infused by cultural observations, and I am convinced we were all better parents as we began living cultural studies. Henry was the first in our field to sophisticate and interrogate the notion of play within the postmodern context. The ways in which he conceptualized the importance of youth studies informed my own dissertation topic and led to my own eventual work within the field. Henry was there to open the gates into the study of the new youth...the disenfranchised and abandoned young people populating our lives. He called to attention those of us who could possibly give a damn, naming the societal destruction of our most valuable yet, in his words, disposable citizenry. Insisting that the political must consistently inform and haunt us, his vitriol and furor over the Columbine shootings (Giroux, 2000) enlightens youth studies decades later. His discussion of *Kids* and *Fight Club* (Giroux, 2001), introduced a nuanced and sophisticated model of film analysis that continues to interrogate and predict, opening a dystopic vision of what youth-hood may be.

Titles are often bandied about, many of them undeserved; however, when presented with the notion of a public intellectual, it is difficult for me to name anyone more exemplary than Giroux. His writings stand as a library for the politically engaged. His charismatic presentation style, extemporaneous and suffering no fools, hypnotizes, infuriates, and instructs. The media Giroux creates evokes a multi-sensory/leveled response in the audience, bringing to mind a favorite, *Mickey Mouse Monopoly: Disney, Childhood and Corporate Power* (Media Education Foundation, 2002). Critical teacher educators will smile as they recall student reactions to previewing this in-your-face film in class. While the film contains statements from several academics, it is Giroux's words and distinct condemnation of Disney pedagogies gone mad that are most memorable. My own experience in using the film in large lecture classes notes that there are two distinct groups of viewers: those who nod in agreement, furiously writing notes; and whose who are the angry and insulted defenders of capital and all things white and male. Most definitely worth the popcorn.... Henry's discussion of his book *The Mouse That Roared: Disney and the End of Innocence* (1999), relates the anger of those who attacked his book, asking him if there was nothing better he could do than bash Disney. He counters these comments with his observations of power, pedagogy, Disney capital, and politics. He notes that at least 80% of radio interviews based on the book were angry. Great way to wake up our students.

The New Henry Giroux Reader contains some of my favorite works taking up cultural studies, the political, the popular, and the critical. The collection spans several decades of articles that laid the groundwork for what we now take for granted, the inclusion of cultural studies within the theories and frameworks of critical pedagogies. As the personal is political, and the personal is influenced by the culture(s) we are exposed to, we are presented with myriad ways in which to consider, read, and internalize the notions of power, privilege, and capital within our own lives and those we touch. Giroux led the way and continues to usher us along in the conversation.

And me, I'm damn glad he decided not to be a vet.

References

Giroux, H. A. (1979). "Schooling and the Culture of Positivism: Notes on the Death of History." *Educational Theory*, 29(4).

Giroux, H. A. (1991). *Border Crossings: Cultural Workers and the Politics of Education*. New York: Routledge.

Giroux, H. A. (1993). *Living Dangerously: Multiculturalism and the Politics of Difference*. New York: Peter Lang.

Giroux, H. A. (1999). *The Mouse That Roared: Disney and the End of Innocence*. Lanham, MD: Rowman & Littlefield.

Giroux, H. A. (2000). "Public Pedagogy and the Responsibility of Intellectuals: Youth, Littleton, and the Loss of Innocence." *JAC*, 20(1).

Giroux, H. A. (2001). "Breaking into the Movies: Pedagogy and the Politics of Film." *JAC*, 9(6).

Grossberg, L., Nelson, C., & Treichler, P. (eds.). (1992). *Cultural Studies*. New York: Routledge.

Media Educational Foundation. (2002). *Mickey Mouse Monopoly: Disney, Childhood, and Corporate Power*. Miguel Picker, Director. Chyng Sun, Writer.

Steinberg, S. R. (2019). "An Interview with Henry A. Giroux." In S.R. Steinberg & B. Down (eds.), *Sage International Handbook of Critical Pedagogies*. London: Sage Publishing.

Radicalizing Hope

Public Intellectualism, the Vitalism of Education, and the Promise of Democracy

WILLIAM AYERS, DISTINGUISHED PROFESSOR OF EDUCATION (RETIRED), UNIVERSITY OF ILLINOIS AT CHICAGO

During months of illness and self-destructive despair, the post-impressionist painter Paul Gauguin created a huge work on a length of jute fiber that he considered his ultimate artistic statement, his masterpiece. The sprawling panorama includes worshippers and gods: cats, birds, and a tranquil-looking goat; an idol with a benevolent expression and uplifted hands; a figure plucking fruit; and a shrunken hag with an intense eye—all surrounded by scenery that conjures up the dense and riotous groves of his adopted Tahiti or the Marquesas Islands, or possibly a marvelously imagined Garden of Eden. He scrawled the title of the work in bold on top of the image; translated into English it asks three questions: "Where Do We Come From? What Are We? Where Are We Going?" At its completion in 1897, Gauguin attempted suicide.

Where do we come from? What are we? Where are we going?

These questions were flecked with fear and tinged with alarm and turmoil for Gauguin, coming to him in the whirlwind and flux of early modernity. But they are, indeed, perennial and persistent questions—confusion standing side by side with imagination and creativity, dread linked arm in arm with hope. For Henry Giroux, one of the most influential and original cultural theorists in the world, those fundamental questions—and others like them—are as generative as they are provocative, and they spark for him what Emily Dickinson called the "slow fuse of possibility."

Henry Giroux's vast body of work is powered by his prodigious curiosity, his unlimited fascination with life as it's actually lived, and his enthusiastic engagement with humanity— the many artifacts created by human beings, including language, culture, philosophy, science, the humanities, and the various arts. The rhythm of his writing and his teaching, his scholarship and public interventions themselves are instructive: he opens his eyes and pays attention, not once but again and again and again; he is genuinely astonished by the beauty he sees all around as well as the unnecessary pain and suffering in every direction; he speaks up and acts out; he reflects and rethinks; and then he starts over, taking it from the top—pay attention; be astonished; act; doubt. Repeat!

Henry Giroux asks the big moral questions in all of his work, allows them to simmer and flare, and then asks the next question, and the next: How do we see ourselves and our problems/challenges/potentials? How can we connect our various quests for purpose and meaning in our own lives with the practical search for a better world for all? Where are we on the clock of the universe? What does this political moment offer or demand of us? How can we live with one foot in the mud and muck of the world as it is while the other foot stretches toward a possible world, a place that could be but is not yet? How can we transform ourselves in ways that make us worthy of the profound social changes we desire and need? And how can we build within ourselves the thoughtfulness, compassion, and courage to embark on a mission of repair and transformation?

His unstinting willingness to pursue these questions to the far horizons has made Henry Giroux an inspiration and a guide to generations of students, activists, scholars, and engaged citizens. He's never mindlessly followed the rules or driven along thoroughfares already laid out and well-worn, but has, rather, always jumped the barriers and headed off-road, pursuing his singular passions and projects, his own ethical ambitions. His willingness to dance out on a limb, to challenge rather than to confirm what the powerful or the conventional have to say, his active and conscious resistance to orthodoxy or dogma or easy formulas of any kind mark him as an engaged intellectual and a propulsive teacher.

Henry Giroux knows that challenging unjust power always involves exposing that power, because the evidence of power is precisely (if paradoxically) its invisibility. He takes on the task of stripping away power's convenient pretense of innocence—its propagandistic insistence on its own inevitability—shaking us awake and inviting us to peek behind the curtain. In the process he illuminates the conflicts and contradictions that characterize this political moment: militarism and the militarization of culture, imperialism and its attendant degradation of the humanity of the conqueror as well as the conquered, structural racism and the willful blindness promoted by white supremacy, the criminalization of youth, consumerism and the destruction of the public square, the creation of "disposable" populations by the predatory and the powerful, the fracturing and atomization of social life. Giroux explains that the current moment is neither immutable nor inescapable, that its imperfections are cause for general alarm—in fact, for the exploited and the oppressed the status quo is itself an ongoing act of violence.

Giroux dives into the wreckage with courage and hope, swimming fiercely toward a distant and often indistinct shore. His energetic efforts speak to youth, students, educators, and anyone searching for a way to reclaim and vitalize democratic public life. He is a deeply ethical thinker whose work is informed by the learned desire to write what Foucault called "a history of the present."

The fate of youth, both here and throughout the world, is a major focus, for it's in the bodies and the minds of young people that Giroux uncovers the most pernicious effects of social control, as well as the greatest hopes for a world in balance, a place powered by love. His work is a sustained act of inter-generational solidarity—a promise to young people to stand shoulder-to-shoulder with them in their struggles to claim their own agency and discover a meaningful place in a social, political, cultural landscape that too often denies them a role in shaping their own futures. A new world is in the making, and the youth are citizens of a country that does not yet exist—they are the pioneers and cartographers of that new terrain, and Henry Giroux walks with them.

Education for free people is powered by a particularly precious and fragile ideal: every human being is of infinite and incalculable value; each a work in progress and a force in motion; each a unique intellectual, emotional, physical, spiritual, moral, and creative force; each born equal in dignity and rights; each endowed with reason and conscience and agency; each deserving a dedicated place in a community of solidarity as well as a vital sense of brotherhood and sisterhood, recognition, and respect. Embracing that basic ethic and spirit, Giroux recognizes that the fullest development of each individual—given the tremendous range of ability and the delicious soup of race, ethnicity, points of origin, and background—is the necessary condition for the full development of the entire community and, conversely, that the fullest development of all is essential for the full development of each. To the extent that people reflect upon their lives and become more conscious of themselves as actors in the world—conscious, too, of the vast range of alternatives that can be imagined and expressed in any given situation—they become capable of inserting themselves as subjects in history, constructors of the human world, and they recreate themselves, then, as free human beings.

For Henry Giroux, hope and fierce collective determination are choices; confidence is a politics. He never minimizes the horror, nor is he sucked into its thrall. Hope for Giroux is the antidote to cynicism and despair; it's the capacity to notice or invent alternatives; it's nourishing the precious sense that standing directly against the world as such is a world that could be or should be, and that whatever is the case stands side by side with what could be or should be the case. Each of us is, of course, immersed in what is, the world as such. In order to link arms and rise up, we need a combination of somethings: seeds, surely; desire, perhaps; a vision of community and possibility; necessity and even, at times, desperation; willful enthusiasm and an acceptance that there are no guarantees whatsoever.

Imagination is indispensable in these efforts and pursuits because it "ignites Dickinson's slow fuse of possibility." More process than product, more stance than conclusion, engaging the imagination involves the dynamic work of igniting that fuse, mapping the world as it really is, and then purposely stepping outside and leaning toward a possible world.

Without a vital sense of possibility, we cannot adequately oppose injustice; we cannot act freely; we cannot inhabit the most vigorous moral spaces. And as Giroux illustrates again and again, we are never freer, all of us and each of us, than when we refuse the situations before us as settled and certain and determined—the absolute end of the matter—and break the chains that entangle us, launching ourselves toward the imaginable.

The Work of Henry Giroux

Exposing An American Horror Story

JAKE BURDICK AND JENNIFER A. SANDLIN

Our first encounters with Henry Giroux's work were in graduate school. I (Jenny) first encountered him as a graduate student in adult education. I was embarking on my dissertation in the late 1990s and was interested in how curricular ideologies were transmitted and contested through educational practices, and particularly I was concerned with how assumptions about work and education undergirding adult literacy and welfare policy initiatives are played out in classroom settings. I gravitated towards theory and literature in the sociology of education, especially that literature examining the tension between the roles that educational programs play in the reproduction of inequality and the potential of education to help engender social change. Henry Giroux's work on hidden curriculum, the politics of schooling, and reproduction and resistance theory—especially his *Ideology, Culture, and the Process of Schooling* (1981), *Theory and Resistance in Education: A Pedagogy for the Opposition* (1983a), and *Social Education in the Classroom: The Dynamics of the Hidden Curriculum* (1979, with Anthony Penna) were fundamental to shaping my dissertation work and my emerging philosophy about education, both formal and informal. Quoting from my dissertation, I wrote that "this critical research has taught us that education always operates in someone's interests. Giroux (1983a) states that 'the commonsense values and beliefs that guide and structure classroom practice are not a priori universals, but social constructions based on specific normative and political assumptions' (p. 46)." These are such taken-for-granted notions for me now, but when I first encountered Giroux's work, they completely shifted the way I began to view education, opening up an entirely new world of politics and power beneath the 'neutral' surface of educational endeavors, helping me to connect the world inside the adult literacy classroom (teachers, students, curricula both formal and hidden) with the world outside of the classroom (policy, political rhetoric, popular discourse, and popular culture representations of 'women on welfare'), issues that anticipated my own move later in my career to studying public pedagogy while continuing to take up Giroux's work.

Similarly, my (Jake's) introduction to Henry Giroux's work was in a voracious reading of *Pedagogy and the Politics of Hope* (1997) for a graduate course in critical theory, and, as in all good horror stories, that encounter, like Jenny's, was as portentous as it was ominous[1]. For me, Giroux's work in that book illustrated two crucial points with a tenacious clarity: the vastness of education's capacity as a force for cultural reproduction and the extent to which all facets of culture enact pedagogical force. In the case of the former, in all of his work, Giroux has sought to illuminate the penumbras created by the endlessly flickering pedagogies of ideological control, particularly the ways in which market logics have braided themselves into the warp of culture, producing capitalist subjectivities under the guises of innocuity, normality, and, in its most inventively insidious moments, resistance. Throughout much of this text, Giroux leveled his analyses at classroom spaces, illustrating their roles in both maintaining recalcitrant hegemonic formations and creating the possibility for spaces beyond both orthodoxic and heterodoxic approaches, spaces of agentic action. As I read, the application of Giroux's careful analyses (particularly those in his essay *Ideology and Agency in the Process of Schooling*) clearly cohered to spaces—popular, political, and identificatory—beyond the classroom and its then-growing (now nearly complete) antagonisms toward democratic intellectual engagement. Thus, on reflection, it is less than surprising that his first published mention of the phrase *public pedagogy* appeared the following year (Giroux, 1998), charting the course for much of his writing across his career, as well as illustrating to scholars, activists, and teachers across the globe (ourselves clearly included) that education cannot, and ethically should not, be reduced to a synonym for schooling.

For Giroux, capitalism—and later, neoliberalism—has always been in the business of producing the subjectivities it needs to sustain its necrotic hunger. We sought out more of his work, feeling that his writing and teaching enacted a kind of unveiling[2] that moved beyond illumination and into a space of augury, yet this prophetic was grounded not in mysticism but, rather, engaged analysis and theorizing, a form of knowing the future via critically reading the present (Purpel & McLaurin, 2004). Most memorably, we read *Disturbing Pleasures* (1994), *The Mouse that Roared* (1999), *Breaking into the Movies* (2001), *Neoliberalism and the Disappearance of the Social in Ghost World* (2003a, this collection), *Education after Abu Ghraib* (2004b, this collection), and *The Terror of Neoliberalism* (2004b), all of which brought his earlier work into conversation with the greater field of cultural studies, illustrated the multifarious, often malevolent, ways in which the political is innately and pervasively pedagogical. As we detail later in this introduction, the *Ghost World* article serves as a sea change in Giroux's thought—an exhortation that forcefully illustrates Giroux's capacity as a public intellectual as he illustrates the ethical need for radical intellectuals to focus their work directly on the nightmares among us. In our scholarly work in public pedagogy (Sandlin, O'Malley, & Burdick, 2010), our classroom practice as critical educators, and in the thankful act of editing this volume, we work to heed Giroux's call while listening raptly for more.

In devising a structure for this collection and simply in our efforts to understand holistically Henry Giroux's extensive body of work, a metaphor emerged early in the process, and it gained significance the more we worked. In our review of Giroux's work, we saw a predominance of metaphors and images that articulated *death* as the inevitable effect of neoliberalism and its invasion of cultural policy. Entropy, violence, even zombies (Giroux, 2010) permeate Giroux's body of work, coalescing around the central notion that market ideologies are anathema to human life, both psychically and materially. As we pushed this conceptualization further and stretched it across the historical markers against which Giroux has written, we began to read the collective work as the charting of a *horror story*, with his early pieces, such as those collected in Section I of this Reader, signaling the emerging sense that an unnatural, maledicted state of affairs has started to stain the fabric of social life. As Reagan and Thatcher's neoliberal legacy entered its full contagion bloom in the late 1990s and early 2000s, Giroux's interests shifted to cultural studies and public pedagogy (Section II), documenting a virulent escalation of this unease across educative spaces. Section III takes up the shift in Giroux's work heralded by the fallout of 9/11 and the subsequent interbraiding of nationalist, neoliberal, and neoconservative discourses into the abhorrent doctrine that would become Trump's Right—what we are calling the *phantasmagoria* of our present moment. As in the last act of any horror film, Section IV documents the closing in of the darkness and the extinction of the light, highlighting Giroux's analyses of the foreclosure of higher education as a potential space of resistance due to its wholesale capture via neoliberal interests. The collection concludes (Section V) with the perennial possibility, however challenging, of hope in Giroux's work, collecting his writings on education's vitalist capacity and the spaces of a renewed vigor in activists and intellectuals who refuse to give in to the monstrous. In the remainder of this introduction, we briefly situate this horror story alongside the articles we have selected for each section as well as Giroux's other germane work, detailing the conjuration of the neoliberal moment, the descent of the social into its thrall, and the abject now that Giroux has warned us against throughout his prolific career.

A Sense of the Inexplicable

The word on the street (and in the New York Times) is, or at least was, that after all that effort and gardening, the Ambanis don't live in Antilla. No one knows for sure. People still whisper about ghosts and bad luck, Vastu and feng shui. Maybe it's all Karl Marx's fault. (All that cussing.) Capitalism, he said, "has conjured up such gigantic means of production and of exchange, that it is like the sorcerer who is no longer able to control the powers of the netherworld whom he has called up by his spells."

(A. Roy, 2014)

Giroux's work in the early to mid-1980s was written against the backdrop of a looming, enervating chill. Emanating from the aforementioned rise of neoliberalism via Reagan and Thatcher, the subsequent and purported *end* of the Cold War, the burgeoning dismemberment of U.S. public education via *A Nation at Risk* (NCEE, 1983), the recasting of social gains made in the late 60s and 70s as market demographics, and the lure of a kind of solipsistic political inertia within academic intellectualism, this chill set its pall as omen, a sense that global politics and discourse were simply *not right* and that what seemed like historical progress toward a better social order was merely forestalled. In these early moments of late capitalism (Jameson, 1992), Giroux had already begun to look for a way out. Turning away from the then-*playful* postmodern politics and theorizations, Giroux instead returned to the Frankfurt School's formulation of Marxian analysis, and its "dialectical framework by which to understand the mediations that link the institutions and activities of everyday life with the logic and commanding forces that shape the larger social totality" (Giroux, 1982, p. 19). Looking for a social theory that could illustrate the machinations of larger structural forces within the lives of individuals, Giroux essentially sought to short circuit the radical forms of individualism and self-centeredness that, stemming from Enlightenment logics, now found deep purchase in the bodies and minds of a social order driven by self interest and consumptive ends. And, this theoretical attunement has been a presence throughout all of Giroux's work: "one important measure of the demise of vibrant democracy and the corresponding impoverishment of political life can be found in the increasing inability of a society to translate private troubles to broader public issues" (2009, para. 1).

However, as with all of Giroux's scholarship, even these early works were not simply a call to return to a certain author or theoretical approach; rather, they were a call to rethink these works in the face of new times and challenges. For Giroux, the rising dark of the early 1980s could not be served by either the contemporary theoretical proclivities found in much of the educational scholarship of the time, or a return to any form of Marxian analysis that failed to account for the vicissitudes of the historical moment. Giroux's germinal essay, *Theories of Reproduction and Resistance in the New Sociology of Education* (1983, this collection) is an exemplar piece in illustrating these points, as the emphases of the text simultaneously enact a careful, critically responsive reading of the available work in cultural theory; an exhaustion of that work's interrogative capability within the emerging complexity of global capital; and a comprehensive reworking of the notion of resistance that locates a vigilant form of radical pedagogy as the epicenter of counterhegemonic practice. This pedagogical throughline, and its meanings for education in all possible spaces, as well as the exhaustion of the available approaches (as we detail in the following sections) as a means of finding space to develop this pedagogy, would become hallmarks of Giroux's work—an unwavering commitment to constant recursion, constant motion amid theoretical dispositions to ensure that they too would not become spaces that had been swallowed by the stagnation and zombification of neoliberal times. Giroux seems to have always been ahead—sometimes by mere steps—of the monstrosity that, in the 1980s, had only begun to test its strength.

In this section of the reader, we also elected to include another of what we conceptualize as Giroux's early, massively-influential works; however, this piece comes significantly later chronologically: 1988's *Border Pedagogy in the Age of Postmodernism*. As the title suggests, at this point in his career, Giroux had taken up a postmodern understanding of how pedagogical interventions might inform more robust and ultimately effective critical interventions into the tide of a now-infected, feverish American social scene. However, Giroux's albeit-brief foray into postmodernism carried with it none of the excess and suspect politics that had marred that project; rather, Giroux worked toward:

> . . . a critical postmodernism [that] wants to redraw the map of modernism so as to effect a shift in power from the privileged and the powerful to those groups struggling to gain a measure of control over lives in what is increasingly becoming a world marked by a logic of integration (Dews, 1987). Postmodernism not only makes visible the ways in which domination is being prefigured and redrawn, it also points to the shifting configurations of power, knowledge, space, and time that characterize a world that is at once more global and more differentiated. (Giroux, 1988, p. 162)

At the core of this writing, as with all of his contributions, is pedagogy – in this instance, a *border pedagogy* enacted:

> to address the important question of how representations and practices that name, marginalize, and define difference as the devalued Other are actively learned, interiorized, challenged, or transformed. In addition, such a pedagogy needs to address how an understanding of these differences can be used in order to change the prevailing relations of power that sustain them. (Giroux, 1988, p. 174)

In these early writings, it is abundantly clear (in retrospect, disturbingly so) that Giroux was amassing the theoretical, cultural, and educational technologies available to him in order to address the growing shadows across the American landscape and psyche, and upon understanding the dire complexity and perverse malignancy of these shadows, to rework those tools constantly towards a pedagogy that had a hope of beating them back.

The Emergence of Horror

Capitalist society is and has always been horror without end.

(V. I. Lenin, 1916)

Throughout the 1990s and the early years of the new millennium, Giroux's work would again shift – both in terms of its theoretical commitments and its understanding

of the *site* and *time* of cultural pedagogy. It is at this time that Giroux's work illustrates a constant state of seemingly overflowing the metaphors and social structures
that would contain concepts like *pedagogy*: schools, for Giroux, cannot contain education. Neoliberalism had *trickled down* into nearly all facets of culture. Social life
itself had started a violent and viral form of commodification, particularly across the
minds and bodies of children (Giroux, 2001a). Most importantly, Giroux's analyses
cannot be limited to studies of how educational phenomenon *are* political—rather,
he turns to the political *as pedagogical in and of itself* (Giroux, 2000, 2004c) as a
cultural heuristic. Two germinal texts, both focusing on the politics and pedagogies
of popular culture, are most closely associated with Giroux's work at this time: *The
Mouse that Roared: Disney and the End of Innocence* (1999) and *Breaking into the
Movies: Film and the Culture of Politics* (2001b). In the tradition of Cultural Studies
analyses, both of these texts utilize an array of theories to explicate how the cultural
formations of Disney and film have worked to produce social meanings for the publics that intersect them. Thus, via this strong and enduring turn toward the work of
Cultural Studies, especially in its capacity to bring eclectic and radically interdisciplinary thought to bear on social phenomenon, Giroux identified and began to articulate the concept of *public pedagogy* (Giroux, 1998), likely his most widely utilized
construct and the foundation of both of our own scholarly careers.

Public pedagogy, in its most simple and commonly utilized articulation, names
the collective forms of learning that occur outside of formal institutions of education
(Sandlin, Schultz, & Burdick, 2010). Yet, as the essays in this collection will attest,
Giroux understands the relationships and distinctions of public pedagogy in a way
that manifestly honors its roots in his study of Cultural Studies theorists. To describe
film, cultural edifices, or politics *pedagogical*, for Giroux, illuminates their capacities
for either culturally reproductive or productive trajectories, giving a form of futurity
and consequence for these sites and artifacts. Thus, Giroux obviates the largely vacuous analyses of culture that have proliferated across academic journals and instead
reads public pedagogies as propositions for public life, moving either toward greater
relations of freedom or, as is more often the case in late capitalism, toward the zom-
bified unlife of consumption, violence, and social decay (Giroux, 2010).

Phantasmagorification

> *Lovecraft, in fact, may be the great poet of capital—not because he explicitly deals with
> capital in his texts . . . but because he provides a heightened imagery equal to capital's proto-
> plasmic mutability. Capitalist power can be understood as 'tentacular' rather than pyramidal.*
> (A. Fisher, 2007)

In the late 18th century, Belgian physicist-turned-entertainer Étienne Gaspard Robert—under the stage name "Robertson"—terrorized audiences with his necromantic
acts, bringing horrified audiences into close contact with the waking nightmares

of dancing skeletons, hell-bound monks, and beckoning demons (Barber, 1989). Robertson called these raucous séances *phantasmagoria*, producing the images of undeath and monstrosity via a *magic lantern*, consisting of an oil lamp and curved mirrors, that projected images across smoke in ways theretofore unseen (Barber). A completely immersive experience, the phantasmagoria would also involve locking the audience in for the duration of the show, largely under the cover of complete darkness, as well as the creation of a sinister ambiance via sound effects. Audiences were reportedly overwhelmed with terror at the sight of these images, openly weeping and lashing out at the apparitions before them, racked with physical duress and wholly unaware of the illusion that engulfed them (Barber). Walter Benjamin would take interest in the phantasmagoria, linking the embodied reaction to these manufactured images to the false consciousness of commodity fetishism, suggesting that critical intellectual practice must work to denude the illusory qualities of capitalist culture, "to make the veil, which our collective dream-images impose upon it, directly open to the waking gaze" (Markus, 2001, p. 16). For Benjamin, "culture is the phantasmagoria, as it were, of a second order in which 'the bourgeoisie enjoys its own false consciousness' (Markus, p. 20). Culture, then, becomes the horror show to which individuals affix embodied and emotive energies, and in the time of neoliberal power, particularly in the enervation and desolation of the post-9/11 landscape, the public gaze looks ever away from the smoke and mirrors of capital.

Giroux's scholarship would shift acutely following the September 11, 2001 terrorist attacks and the resulting cultural, economic, and epistemic ruptures that followed. In his writing following 9/11, Giroux illustrated far more expansive and structurally complex articulations of power, politics, and pedagogy, taking on discursive and material educational formations in a scope that could no longer be contained via isolated reviews of media, schooling, or practice. Instead, Giroux locates all of these discourses as a constellation of neoliberal influences on cultural practices, with education as the engine of their reproduction. Within our prior work (Sandlin, O'Malley, & Burdick, 2010), we discuss his piece, *Neoliberalism and the Disappearance of the Social in* Ghost World (2003a, also included in this volume) as the seeming departure from studying film to instead interrogating the greater political arrays *behind* film that have produced a culture so dazzled by the image. Giroux's final analyses of the film largely center on its inabilities as a critical fiction, noting silences around the global forms of youth resistance and any substantive linkage between the private dilemmas of characters and the greater social forces that animate them. In essence, Giroux wants the film to enact a critical pedagogy that it, as a product of the very forces it critiques, cannot. The material violence of 9/11 had become a final rite in opening the portal for neoliberalism's entry into all spaces of daily life, the summoning of the radically anti-human via the interlocking discourses of patriotism, fear, and desire. The billowing smoke and engulfing dust from the collapse of the towers would become the screen across which the modern phantasmagoria would play, a horror show that would serve to distract from the true horrors that work to produce its spectacle. For Giroux, then, critical intellectual interventions could no longer be leveled at the artifacts of culture, but at its very metaphysics, at the larger socioeconomic and necromantic forces that transmogrify humanity into economic husks.

Thus, in this section, we focus on Giroux's post-9/11 work in which he turns his attention to neoliberalism's totalizing capacities and extends his analysis to culture writ large. This analytic shift in Giroux's writing and career (still very much present in his current work) takes up the political on much broader cultural scales, such as the horrific spectacle of Abu Ghraib (Giroux, 2004; this volume), the biopolitical subjugations that characterized the response to Hurricane Katrina (Giroux, 2006b), and purportedly innocuous phenomena like the rise of selfie culture (Giroux, 2015), in a way that illustrates the fundamental relationships between daily life and the greater structures that mediate and animate identities and relationships therein. The section closes with one of Giroux's many intensive critiques of what, at least in the moment of this writing, serves as the most immanent and abject manifestation of the contemporary American horror story: the figure of Donald Trump and his location at the axis of neoliberal and neoconservative's most virulent and violent manifestations (Giroux, 2017, this collection). Within the phantasmagoric moment, Trump exists as a particularly harrowing blight—at once both the horrific image and its projectionist, the spectacle and the danger it serves to obscure—and his election, as abhorrent as it might have seemed, should have been absolutely unsurprising, given the prescient work of intellectuals like Giroux. In his writing, Giroux refers to Trump's ascendance as an era of

> lawlessness . . . evident in the presence of a ruthless market-driven corporate culture marked by an economic and political system mostly controlled by the ruling financial elite. This is a mode of corporate lawlessness and criminogenic culture that not only hoards wealth, income and power but also reproduces a savage casino capitalism through the mechanisms of a national security state, mass surveillance, the arming of local police forces, a permanent war economy and an expansive militarized foreign policy (Giroux, 2017, p. 888)

This is the lawlessness of horror itself—the devouring of the state and its social contracts within the maw of a now-solid phantasmagoric reality. And, as Giroux illustrates in the subsequent section of this reader, the path out of this nightmare is fraught as well.

The Light Fades

The only difference between "propaganda" and "education," really, is in the point of view. The advocacy of what we believe in is education. The advocacy of what we don't believe in is propaganda.

(E. Bernays, 1923)

Throughout his career, Giroux has held up the academy as a crucial space for the development and enactment of *public intellectualism*, valorizing the crucial work of scholars like Said (Giroux, 2004a, 2004d), Bourdieu (Giroux & Searls Giroux, 2004), and Hall (Giroux, 2000) for its capacity to produce cultural criticism outside of institutional walls. For Giroux, these transformative intellectuals have been and will continue to be critical elements in the struggle against market ascendance and its attendant social deformations, as "the violence of neoliberalism can be explained through the existential narratives of those who experience its lived relations as well as through conceptual analyses provided by intellectuals" (Giroux, 2004a, p. 145). Thus, particularly in his later work, Giroux understands the relationship between the public and the intellectuals who serve in the public's interest as one of solidarity and mutual pedagogical exchange. But, as in any horror story, the route that presents a solution—the escape route, the holy symbol, the antidote to the plague—often ends up lost as well, succumbing to the very forces it promised to dispel. In many instances, this is the dolorous reality of American higher education and its promise for the production of a democratic public.

The sweeping privatization of existing universities via corporate partnerships; the crest and subsequent ebb of for-profit higher education; the invasion of anti-intellectual extremist thought on college campuses via speakers like Ben Shapiro; the constant proposals for the eradication of tenure and academic freedom; and the vilification of professors who critique the current cultural order have worked in tandem to produce a landscape that is growingly inhospitable to the species of intellectual work that Giroux forwards. Giroux sees these incursions into higher education as an attack on the fundamental tools needed to foster healthy democratic publics, alerting us even to the eradication of *time* itself under corporate signification. Differentiating between *public* and *corporate* forms of time, he writes

> Divested of any viable democratic notion of the social, corporate time measures relationships, productivity, space, and knowledge according to the dictates of cost efficiency, profit, and a market-based rationality. Time, within this framework, is accelerated rather than slowed down and reconfigures academic labour, increasingly through, though not limited to, new computer generated technologies which are making greater demands on faculty time, creating larger teaching loads, and producing bigger classes. Under corporate time, speed controls and organises place, space, and communication as a matter of quantifiable calculation. (Giroux, 2003b, p. 150)

Thus, the life of faculty becomes, as in all corporate spaces, one of management and being managed and of a productivity that is measured less by its intellectual contribution than its efficiency and page count. Thus, whereas Giroux does not discount the academy comprehensively, the intersecting forces of marketization, ideological management, and militarization have produced difficult terrain for the already-difficult project of critical pedagogy. As such, Giroux – particularly in the Trump era – asks us to cast our gaze more broadly.

A Hope in Hell

He never minimizes the horror, but nor is he sucked into its thrall.

(W. Ayers, this collection).

Concluding this collection, as well as this introduction, we highlight Giroux's inexhaustible call for hope against neoliberalism's hordes. From his early work in problematizing resistance to his contemporary writings on the power of modern activisms, Giroux's work is truly animated by the relentless search for possibility and cultural production within the seemingly unassailable moment of market domination. However, Giroux constantly qualifies the condition of hope—militant (Giroux, 2016), radical (Giroux, 2004e), educated (Giroux, 2003c)—discerning it from the specious sloganism of hope that characterized the Obama campaign. Giroux's is not a refuge from the horror, nor it is a holding place for passivity; rather Giroux offers a hope that characterizes the horror *as horror* and refuses to look away. He writes,

> in this view, hope becomes a discourse of critique and social transformation. Hope makes the leap for us between *critical education*, which tells us what must be changed; *political agency*, which gives us the means to make change; and the *concrete struggles* through which change happens. Hope, in short, gives substance to the recognition that every present is incomplete. (Giroux, 2004e, p. 38)

Giroux's approach offers possibility, but always a possibility that is, in and of itself, radicalized. Hope is never utopic in Giroux's work, as the prospects for a more just horizon as products of deep, vigilant intellectual work that commits to the endlessly iterative work of self-critique and attendant reformation. In this way, Giroux's intellectual career—characterized so readily by his trenchant search for new avenues of critique and pedagogical production—structurally models the work we must do as engaged, *hopeful* subjects of the present moment.

In this final section, we have selected readings that illustrate two key ways in which hope is articulated through Giroux's conceptualization of public intellectual work: the call for academic intellectuals to become critical educators of the public, and Giroux's own work as a public intellectual who engages the public beyond the confines of the academy. In the former work, Giroux first entreats educators and intellectuals to understand the scope and complexity of the moments of horror—understanding an event as traumatic as 9/11 as a harbinger for the structural terrorism that would come in its wake, for example—and then engaging them in acts of responsibility, the ethical and professional obligation[3] to *respond to* the cultural abjection they find. Such as praxis transforms classroom spaces into laboratories of cultural production and engaged forms of critical citizenship, all hallmarks of Giroux's imagination of formal education's undergirding purpose (Giroux, 2002, this collection). In recent years, however, this has not been enough. The tendrils of neoliberalism cannot be addressed in a single location, nor can they be stymied solely via an institution that they have spent the last 40 years eviscerating. Hope, then, needed to find other places of purchase, and Giroux's work began to appear in a multitude of non-academic spaces—including online, independent news sites like *Counterpunch* and *Truthdig* to more mainstream spaces, such as his interview with musician Julien Casablancas in *Rolling Stone* (Doyle, 2016)—much like Said's appearances on national news programs to discuss the situation of Palestine. Again, these are pedagogical moments from Giroux—learnings on how public intellectualism and public pedagogy might function towards discourses of hope.

Final Words

We hope that *The New Henry Giroux Reader*, while unerringly and unflinchingly spinning a tale of collapse, also offers its readers capacities for thinking the social anew, a daylight at the end of the long dark. In the end, that is how we read the work of Henry Giroux—as a call for a far more just, humane, and loving world, but one that necessitates vigilant intellectual and cultural work as a constant to its emergence and maintenance. We are honored to have curated this collection of work that has been so foundational to our development as scholars, intellectuals, and citizens, and we are certain that our readers will find the same challenging inspiration herein.

Notes

1. This introduction is not meant to serve as a comprehensive overview of Giroux's work, particularly since that effort has already been accomplished by Robbins' work in the first iteration of this reader (Giroux, 2006a), as well as in his article, *Searching for Politics with Henry Giroux: Through Cultural Studies to Public Pedagogy and the "Terror of Neoliberalism"* (Robbins, 2009).
2. Here, we use this term to signify the etymology of the word *apocalypse*: an unveiling, suggesting that the world is not end*ing*, but rather has end*ed* for all practical reasons, a meaning that resonates with Giroux's theorizations of the zombification produced under the sign of neoliberalism.
3. Here, we are applying some measure of the Bakhtinian (Bakhtin, 1990) ethics of *answerability* to Giroux's approach.

References

Bakhtin, M. M. (1990). *Art and answerability*. Austin: University of Texas Press.

Barber, T. (1989). Phantasmagorical Wonders: The Magic Lantern Ghost Show in Nineteenth-Century America. *Film History*, 3(2), 73–86.

Bernays, E. (1923). *Crystallizing public opinion* (2004 reprint). Whitefish, MT: Kessinger Publishing.

Doyle, P. (2016). Watch Julian Casablancas talk government corruption with Henry Giroux. *Rolling Stone* [online version]. Retrieved May 31, 2018, from: https://www.rollingstone.com/music/music-news/watch-julian-casablancas-talk-government-corruption-with-henry-giroux-126104/

Fisher, A. (2007). Lovecraft and the weird, part II. Retrieved May 10, 2018, from: http://k-punk.abstractdynamics.org/archives/009407.html

Giroux, H. A. (1981). *Ideology, culture, and the process of schooling*. Philadelphia: Temple University Press.

Giroux, H. A. (1982). Culture and rationality in Frankfurt School Thought: Ideological foundations for a theory of social education. *Theory and Research in Social Education*, 9(4), 17–56.

Giroux, H. A. (1983a). *Theory and resistance in education: A pedagogy for the opposition.* South Hadley, MA: Bergin & Garvey.

Giroux, H. A. (1983b). Theories of reproduction and resistance in the new sociology of education: Toward a critical theory of schooling and pedagogy for the opposition. *Harvard Educational Review, 53*(3), 257–293.

Giroux, H. A. (1988). Border pedagogy in the age of postmodernism. *The Journal of Education, 170*(3), 162–181.

Giroux, H. A. (1994). *Disturbing pleasures: Learning popular culture.* New York: Routledge.

Giroux, H. A. (1997). *Pedagogy and the politics of hope.* Boulder, CO: Westview.

Giroux, H. A. (1998). Public pedagogy and rodent politics: Cultural studies and the challenge of Disney. *Arizona Journal of Hispanic Cultural Studies, 2,* 253–266.

Giroux, H. A. (1999). *The mouse that roared: Disney and the end of innocence.* Lanham, MD: Rowman & Littlefield.

Giroux, H. A. (2000). Public pedagogy as cultural politics: Stuart Hall and the crisis of culture. *Cultural Studies, 14*(2), 341–360.

Giroux, H. A. (2001a). *Breaking into the movies: Film and the culture of politics.* New York: Blackwell.

Giroux, H. A. (2001b). *Stealing innocence: Corporate culture's war on children.* New York, NY: Palgrave Macmillan.

Giroux, H. A. (2001c). *Breaking into the movies: Pedagogy and the politics of film.* JAC, 21, 583–598.

Giroux, H. A. (2001d). Brutalized bodies and emasculated politics: Fight Club, consumerism, and masculine violence. *Third Text, 53,* 31–41.

Giroux, H. A. (2002). Democracy, freedom, and justice after September 11th: Rethinking the role of educators and the politics of schooling. *Teachers College Record, 104*(6), 1138–1162.

Giroux, H. A. (2003a). Neoliberalism and the disappearance of the social in *Ghost World. Third Text, 17,* 151–161.

Giroux, H. A. (2003b). Youth, higher education, and the crisis of public time: Educated hope and the possibility of a democratic future. *Social Identities, 9*(2), 141–168.

Giroux, H. A. (2003c). *Public spaces, private lives.* New York: Rowman & Littlefield.

Giroux, H. A. (2004a). *The terror of neoliberalism.* Boulder, CO: Paradigm.

Giroux, H. A. (2004b). Education after Abu Ghraib. *Cultural Studies, 18,* 779–815.

Giroux, H. A. (2004c). Public pedagogy and the politics of neo-liberalism: Making the political more pedagogical. *Policy Futures in Education, 2*(3–4), 494–503.

Giroux, H. A. (2004d). Edward Said and the politics of worldliness: Toward a "rendezvous of victory". *Cultural Studies ↔ Critical Methodologies, 4*(3), 339–349.

Giroux, H. A. (2004e). When hope is subversive. *Tikkun, 19*(6), 38–39.

Giroux, H. A. (2006a). *The Giroux Reader* (C. G. Robbins, ed.). Boulder, CO: Paradigm.

Giroux, H. A. (2006b) Reading Hurricane Katrina: Race, class, and the biopolitics of disposability. *College Literature, 33*(3), 171–196.

Giroux, H. A. (2009, September 15). The spectacle of illiteracy and the crisis of democracy. *Truthout.* Retrieved March 19, 2018, from: http://www.truthout.org/091509A

Giroux, H. A. (2010). Zombie politics and other late modern monstrosities in the age of disposability. *Policy Futures in Education, 8*(1), 1–7.

Giroux, H. A. (2015). Selfie culture in the age of corporate and state surveillance. *Third Text, 29*(3), 155–164.

Giroux, H. A. (2016). Militant hope in the age of the politics of the disconnect. *Counterpunch,* Retrieved May 21, 2018, from: https://www.counterpunch.org/2016/12/23/militant-hope-in-the-age-of-the-politics-of-the-disconnect/

Giroux, H. A. (2017).White nationalism, armed culture and state violence in the age of Donald Trump. *Philosophy and Social Criticism, 43*(9), 887–910.

Giroux, H. A., & Penna, A. N. (1979). Social education in the classroom: The dynamics of the hidden curriculum. *Theory and Research in Social Education, 7*(1), 21–42.

Giroux, H. A., & Searls Giroux, S. (2004). Academic culture, intellectual courage, and the crisis of politics in an era of permanent war. In H. A. Giroux and S. Searls Giroux, eds., *Take back higher education*, 53–87, New York: Palgrave Macmillan.

Jameson, F. (1992). Postmodernism, or the cultural logic of late capitalism. Durham, NC: Duke University Press.

Lenin, V. I. (1916). *The Military programme of the Proletarian revolution: II.* Retrieved June 12, 2018, from: https://www.marxists.org/archive/lenin/works/1916/miliprog/ii.htm

Markus, G. (2001). Walter Benjamin or the commodity as phantasmagoria. *New German Critique, 83*, 3–42.

National Commission on Excellence in Education. (1983). *A nation at risk: The imperative for educational reform: A report to the Nation and the Secretary of Education.* United States Department of Education. Washington, D.C.: The Commission: [Supt. of Docs., U.S. G.P.O. distributor],

Purpel, D. L., & McLaurin Jr., W. M. (2004). *Reflections on the moral and spiritual crisis in education.* New York: Peter Lang.

Robbins, C. G. (2009). Searching for politics with Henry Giroux: Through cultural studies to public pedagogy and the "terror of neoliberalism". *Review of Education, Pedagogy, and Cultural Studies, 31*(5), 428–478.

Roy, A. (2014). *Capitalism: A ghost story.* Chicago: Haymarket Books.

Sandlin, J. A., O'Malley, M. P., & Burdick, J. (2010). Mapping the complexity of public pedagogy scholarship:1894–2010. *Review of Educational Research, 81*(3), 338–375.

Sandlin, J. A., Schultz, B. D., & Burdick, J. (2010). *Handbook of public pedagogy.* New York, NY: Routledge.

Simon, D. (2013). There are now two Americas. My country is a horror show. *The Guardian*, Retrieved June 12, 2018, from https://www.theguardian.com/world/2013/dec/08/david-simon-capitalism-marx-two-americas-wire

SOCIAL THEORY AND THE STRUGGLE FOR PEDAGOGIES

Sociology of Education,
Critical Pedagogy,
and Border Pedagogy

CHAPTER 1

Theories of Reproduction and Resistance in the New Sociology of Education

A Critical Analysis

1983

In the last decade, Karl Marx's concept of reproduction has been one of the major organizing ideas informing socialist theories of schooling. Marx states that "every social process of production is, at the same time, a process of reproduction . . . . Capitalist production, therefore . . . produces not only commodities, not only surplus-value, but it also produces and reproduces the capitalist relation, on the one side the capitalist, on the other the wage-labourer."[1] Radical educators have given this concept a central place in developing a critique of liberal views of schooling. Moreover, they have used it as the theoretical foundation for developing a critical science of education.[2] Thus far, the task has been only partially successful.

Contrary to the claims of liberal theorists and historians that public education offers possibilities for individual development, social mobility, and political and economic power to the disadvantaged and dispossessed, radical educators have argued that the main functions of schools are the reproduction of the dominant ideology, its forms of knowledge, and the distribution of skills needed to reproduce the social division of labor. In the radical perspective, schools as institutions could only be understood through an analysis of their relationship to the state and the economy. In this view, the deep structure or underlying significance of schooling could only be revealed through analyzing how schools functioned as agencies of social and cultural reproduction—that is, how they legitimated capitalist rationality and sustained dominant social practices.

Instead of blaming students for educational failure, radical educators blamed the dominant society. Instead of abstracting schools from the dynamics of inequality and class-race-gender modes of discrimination, schools were considered central agencies in the politics and processes of domination. In contrast to the liberal view of education as the great equalizer, radical educators saw the objectives of schooling quite differently. As Paul Willis states, "Education was not about equality, but inequality. . . . Education's main purpose of the social integration of a class society could be achieved only by preparing most kids for an unequal future, and by insuring their personal underdevelopment. Far from productive roles in the economy simply waiting to be 'fairly' filled by the products of education, the 'Reproduction' perspective reversed this to suggest that capitalist production and its roles required certain educational outcomes."[3]

In my view, radical educators presented a serious challenge to the discourse and logic of liberal views of schooling. But they did more than that. They also tried to fashion a new discourse and set of understandings around the reproduction thesis. Schools were stripped of their political innocence and connected to the social and cultural matrix of capitalist rationality. In effect, schools were portrayed as reproductive in three senses. First, schools provided different classes and social groups with the knowledge and skills they needed to occupy their respective places in a labor force stratified by class, race, and gender. Second, schools were seen as reproductive in the cultural sense, functioning in part to distribute and legitimate forms of knowledge, values, language, and modes of style that constitute the dominant culture and its interests. Third, schools were viewed as part of a state apparatus that produced and legitimated the economic and ideological imperatives that underlie the state's political power.

Radical reproduction theorists have used these forms of reproduction to fashion a number of specific concerns that have shaped the nature of their educational research and inquiry. These concerns have focused on analyses of the relationships between schooling and the workplace,[4] class-specific educational experiences and the job opportunities that emerge for different social groups,[5] the culture of the school and the class-defined cultures of the students who attend them,[6] and the relationship among the economic, ideological, and repressive functions of the state and how they affect school policies and practices.[7]

Reproduction theory and its various explanations of the role and function of education have been invaluable in contributing to a broader understanding of the political nature of schooling and its relation to the dominant society. But it must be stressed that the theory has not achieved its promise to provide a comprehensive critical science of schooling. Reproduction theorists have overemphasized the idea of domination in their analyses and have failed to provide any major insights into how teachers, students, and other human agents come together within specific historical and social contexts in order to both make and reproduce the conditions of their existence. More specifically, reproduction accounts of schooling have continually patterned themselves after structural-functionalist versions of Marxism which stress that history is made "behind the backs" of the members of society. The idea that people do make history, including its constraints, has been neglected. Indeed, human subjects generally "disappear" amidst a theory that leaves no room for moments of self-creation, mediation, and resistance. These accounts often leave us with a view of schooling and domination that appears to have been pressed out of an Orwellian fantasy; schools are often viewed as factories or prisons, teachers and students alike act merely as pawns and role bearers constrained by the logic and social practices of the capitalist system.

By downplaying the importance of human agency and the notion of resistance, reproduction theories offer little hope for challenging and changing the repressive features of schooling. By ignoring the contradictions and struggles that exist in schools, these theories not only dissolve human agency, they unknowingly provide a rationale for *not* examining teachers and students in concrete school settings. Thus, they miss the opportunity to determine whether there is a substantial difference between the existence of various structural and ideological modes of domination and their actual unfolding and effects.

Recent research on schooling in the United States, Europe, and Australia has both challenged and attempted to move beyond reproduction theories. This research emphasizes the importance of human agency and experience as the theoretical cornerstones for analyzing the complex relationship between schools and the dominant society. Organized around what I loosely label as resistance theory, these analyses give central importance to the notions of conflict, struggle, and resistance.[8]

Combining ethnographic studies with more recent European cultural studies, resistance theorists have attempted to demonstrate that the mechanisms of social and cultural reproduction are never complete and always meet with partially realized elements of opposition.[9] In effect, resistance theorists have developed a theoretical framework and method of inquiry that restores the critical notion of agency. They point not only to the role that students play in challenging the most oppressive aspects of schools but also to the ways in which students actively participate through oppositional behavior in a logic that very often consigns them to a position of class subordination and political defeat.

One of the most important assumptions of resistance theory is that working-class students are not merely the by-product of capital, compliantly submitting to the dictates of authoritarian teachers and schools that prepare them for a life of deadening labor. Rather, schools represent contested terrains marked not only by structural and ideological contradictions but also by collectively informed student resistance. In other words, schools are social sites characterized by overt and hidden curricula, tracking, dominant and subordinate cultures, and competing class ideologies. Of course, conflict and resistance take place within asymmetrical relations of power which always favor the dominant classes, but the essential point is that there are complex and creative fields of resistance through which class- race- and gender-mediated practices often refuse, reject, and dismiss the central messages of the schools.

In resistance accounts, schools are relatively autonomous institutions that not only provide spaces for oppositional behavior and teaching but also represent a source of contradictions that sometimes make them dysfunctional to the material and ideological interests of the dominant society. Schools are not solely determined by the logic of the workplace or the dominant society; they are not merely economic institutions but are also political, cultural, and ideological sites that exist somewhat independently of the capitalist market economy. Of course, schools operate within limits set by society, but they function in part to influence and shape those limits, whether they be economic, ideological, or political. Moreover, instead of being homogeneous institutions operating under the direct control of business groups, schools are characterized by diverse forms of school knowledge, ideologies, organizational styles, and classroom social relations. Thus, schools often exist in a contradictory relation to the dominant society, alternately supporting and challenging its basic assumptions. For instance, schools sometimes support a notion of liberal education that is in sharp contradiction to the dominant society's demand for forms of education that are specialized, instrumental, and geared to the logic of the marketplace. In addition, schools still strongly define their role via their function as agencies for social mobility even though they currently turn out graduates at a faster pace than the economy's capacity to employ them.

Whereas reproduction theorists focus almost exclusively on power and how the dominant culture ensures the consent and defeat of subordinate classes and groups, theories of resistance restore a degree of agency and innovation to the cultures of these groups. Culture, in this case, is constituted as much by the group itself as by the dominant society. Subordinate cultures, whether working-class or otherwise, partake of moments of self-production as well as reproduction; they are contradictory in nature and bear the marks of both resistance and reproduction. Such cultures are forged within constraints shaped by capital and its institutions, such as schools, but the conditions within which such constraints function vary from school to school and from neighborhood to neighborhood. Moreover, there are never any guarantees that capitalist values and ideologies will automatically succeed, regardless of how strongly they set the agenda. As Stanley Aronowitz reminds us, "In the final analysis, human praxis is not determined by its preconditions; only the boundaries of possibility are given in advance."[10]

In this rather brief and abstract discussion, I have juxtaposed two models of educational analysis to suggest that theories of resistance represent a significant advance over the important but limited theoretical gains of reproduction models of schooling. But it is important to emphasize that, in spite of more complex modes of analysis, resistance theories are also marred by a number of theoretical flaws. In part, these flaws stem from a failure to recognize the degree to which resistance theories themselves are indebted to some of the more damaging features of reproduction theory. At the same time, however, resistance theories have too readily ignored the most valuable insights of reproduction theory and, in doing so, have failed to examine and appropriate those aspects of the reproduction model that are essential to developing a critical science of education. Furthermore, despite their concrete differences, resistance and reproduction approaches to education share the failure of recycling and reproducing the dualism between agency and structure, a failure that has plagued educational theory and practice for decades, while simultaneously representing its greatest challenge. Consequently, neither position provides the foundation for a theory of education that links structures and institutions to human agency and action in a dialectical manner.

The basis for overcoming this separation of human agency from structural determinants lies in the development of a theory of resistance that both questions its own assumptions and critically appropriates those aspects of schooling that are accurately presented and analyzed in the reproduction model. In other words, the task facing resistance theorists is twofold: first, they must structure their own assumptions to develop a more dialectical model of schooling and society; and second, they must reconstruct the major theories of reproduction in order to abstract from them their most radical and emancipatory insights.

The remainder of this essay will first discuss three important theories that constitute various dimensions of the reproduction model of schooling: the economic-reproductive model, the cultural-reproductive model, and the hegemonic-state reproductive model. Since reproduction theorists have been the object of considerable criticism elsewhere, I shall focus primarily on the strengths of each of these models, and shall only summarize some of the general criticisms. Second, I shall look at what I generously call neo-Marxist theories of resistance that have recently emerged in the literature on education and schooling, examining their theoretical strengths and weaknesses, while at the same time analyzing how they are either positively or negatively informed by theories of reproduction. Finally, I shall attempt to develop a new theory of resistance and shall briefly analyze its implications for a critical science of schooling.

Schooling and Theories of Reproduction

Economic-Reproductive Model

Within the last fifteen years, the political-economy model of reproduction has exercised the strongest influence on radical theories of schooling. Developed primarily around the work of Samuel Bowles and Herbert Gintis, it has had a major influence on theories about the hidden curriculum,[11] educational policy studies,[12] and a wide range of ethnographic research.[13] At the core of the political-economy approach are two fundamentally important questions. The most important of these focuses on the relationship between schooling and society and asks, How does the educational system function within society? The second question points to a related but more concrete concern regarding the issue of how subjectivities actually get constituted in schools, asking, How do schools fundamentally influence the ideologies, personalities, and needs of students? While theorists who work within this model give different answers, they generally agree on the relationship between power and domination, on the one hand, and the relationship between schooling and the economy on the other.

Power in these accounts is defined and examined primarily in terms of its function to mediate and legitimate the relations of dominance and subordinance in the economic sphere. In this perspective, power becomes the property of dominant groups and operates to reproduce class, gender, and racial inequalities that function in the interests of the accumulation and expansion of capital. This becomes clear in the way economic-reproductive theorists analyze the relations between the economy and schooling.

Central to this position is the notion that schools can only be understood by analyzing the structural effects of the workplace on them. In Bowles and Gintis's work this notion becomes clear through their reliance on what they call the correspondence theory.[14] Broadly speaking, the correspondence theory posits that the hierarchically structured patterns of values, norms, and skills that characterize both the workforce and the dynamics of class interaction under capitalism are mirrored in the social dynamics of the daily classroom encounter. Through its classroom social relations, schooling functions to inculcate students with the attitudes and dispositions necessary to accept the social and economic imperatives of a capitalist economy.

In this view, the underlying experience and relations of schooling are animated by the power of capital to provide different skills, attitudes, and values to students of different classes, races, and genders. In effect, schools mirror not only the social division of labor but also the wider society's class structure. The theoretical construct that illuminates the structural and ideological connection between the schools and the workplace is the notion of the hidden curriculum. This term refers to those classroom social relations that embody specific messages which legitimize the particular views of work, authority, social rules, and values that sustain capitalist logic and rationality, particularly as manifested in the workplace. The power of these messages lies in their seemingly universal qualities—qualities that emerge as part of the structured silences that permeate all levels of school and classroom relations. The social relations that constitute the hidden curriculum provide ideological and material weight to questions regarding what counts as high versus low status knowledge (intellectual or manual), high versus low status forms of social organization (hierarchical or democratic), and, of course, what counts as high versus low status forms of personal interaction (interaction based on individual competitiveness or interaction based on collective sharing). The nature and meaning of the hidden curriculum is further extended through an understanding of how it contributes to the construction of student subjectivities—that is, those conscious and unconscious dimensions of experience that inform student behavior. Consideration of this issue leads into the work of the French social theorist, Louis Althusser.

Althusser also argues that schools represent an essential and important social site for reproducing capitalist relations of production.[15] In agreement with Bowles and Gintis, he argues that the school carries out two fundamental forms of reproduction: the reproduction of the skills and rules of labor power, and the reproduction of the relations of production.

The reproduction of the skills and rules of labor power is defined within the context of the formal curriculum and, in Althusser's terms, includes the kind of "know-how" students need in order to

> read, to write and to add—i.e., a number of techniques, and a number of other things as well, including elements of "scientific" or "literary culture," which are directly useful in the different jobs in production (one instruction for manual workers, another for technicians, a third for engineers, a final one for high management). . . . Children also learn the rules of good behaviour, i.e., the attitude that should be observed by every agent in the division of labor, according to the job he is "destined" for: rules of morality, civic and professional conscience, which actually means rules of respect for the socio-technical divisions of labour and ultimately the rules of the order established by class domination.[16]

Although both Althusser and Bowles and Gintis acknowledge the role that school knowledge plays in the reproductive process, it is not of much significance in their analyses. Domination and the reproduction of the work force as constitutive elements of the schooling process take place primarily "behind the backs" of teachers and students through the hidden curriculum of schooling. But it is at this point that these theorists provide important and differing explanations. Unlike Bowles and Gintis, who situate the hidden curriculum in social relations that are somehow internalized by (read imposed on) students, Althusser attempts to explain this "hidden" process of socialization through a systematic theory of ideology.

Althusser's theory of ideology has a dual meaning, which becomes clear in his analysis of how ruling-class domination is secured in schools. In its first meaning, the theory refers to a set of material practices through which teachers and students live out their daily experiences. Ideology has a material existence in the rituals, routines, and social practices that both structure and mediate the day-to-day workings of schools. This material aspect of ideology is clearly seen, for example, in the architecture of school buildings, with their separate rooms, offices, and recreational areas—each positing and reinforcing an aspect of the social division of labor. Space is arranged differently for the administrative staff, teachers, secretaries, and students within the school building. Further, the ideological nature of the ecology of the school is somewhat obvious in the seating arrangements in university halls, or, for that matter, in the classrooms of many urban schools.

This material aspect of Althusser's notion of ideology corresponds somewhat to Bowles and Gintis's notion of the hidden curriculum in pointing to the political nature and use of space, time, and social processes as they function within specific institutional settings. Similarly, it also points to the class-specific source and control of power that bears down on ideological institutions such as schools—institutions deemed essential, according to Althusser, to the production of ideologies and experiences that support the dominant society.[17]

In the second meaning of Althusser's notion of ideology, the dynamics of the reproductive model unfold. In this sense, ideology is completely removed from any notion of intentionality, producing neither consciousness nor willing compliance. Instead, it is defined as those systems of meanings, representations, and values embedded in concrete practices that structure the unconsciousness of students. The effect of such practices and their mediations is to induce in teachers and students alike an "imaginary relationship . . . to their real conditions of existence."[18] Althusser explains:

> It is customary to suggest that ideology belongs to the region of "consciousness". . . . In truth, ideology has very little to do with "consciousness". . . . It is profoundly unconscious, even when it presents itself in a reflected form. Ideology is indeed a system of representations, but in the majority of cases these representations have nothing to do with "consciousness": they are usually images and occasionally concepts, but it is above all as structures that they impose on the vast majority of men, not via their "consciousness." They are perceived-accepted-suffered cultural objects and they act functionally on one in a process that escapes them. Men "live" their ideologies as the Cartesian "saw" the moon at two hundred paces away: not at all as a form of consciousness, but as an object of their "world"—as their world itself.[19]

The economic-reproductive model gains an added dimension in the work of Christian Baudelot and Roger Establet.[20] Baudelot and Establet also stress that the principal function of the school can only be understood in terms of the role it plays in the production of labor power, the accumulation of capital, and in the reproduction of legitimating ideologies. Once again, schools are tied to the engine of domination and reproduction. But in this case, power does not collapse into an all-encompassing construct of ideological domination. Though still tied to the economic-reproductive model, Baudelot and Establet are not willing to dissolve human agency under the heavy hand of a one-sided notion of domination. Domination, they claim, does manifest itself through the imposition of bourgeois ideology in French schools, but the ideology is sometimes opposed and resisted by working-class youths, particularly at the compulsory levels of schooling.

Several important but underdeveloped theoretical considerations begin to emerge in Baudelot and Establet's model of reproduction. First, schools are not viewed as sites that smoothly socialize working-class students into the dominant ideology. Instead, schools are seen as social sites informed by conflicting ideologies which are rooted, in part, in the antagonistic class relations and structured practices that shape the day-to-day workings of these institutions. But if schools are viewed as sites containing oppositional ideologies, the sources of these ideologies—which fuel student resistance—are to be found not only inside but outside the school as well. That is, the basis for both critique and resistance on the part of working-class students is partly produced through the knowledge and practices made available to them in schools, but the primary historical and material basis for such action is located in oppositional public spheres that exist outside of such institutions.

The question of the location of the basis of resistance leads to Baudelot and Establet's second major insight. They rightly argue that the source of working-class student consciousness cannot be limited to such spheres as the workplace and the school. Working-class student social formations—groups organized around specific cultural experiences, values, and class, gender, and racial relations—with their combination of hegemonic and oppositional ideologies, are primarily formed in the family, the neighborhood, and in the mass- and class-mediated youth cultures.[21] Social classes, in this account, are formed not through the primacy of their determined structural relation to the workplace, but through culture as well. Aronowitz captures this complex dynamic behind the construction of class formations in his comment, "The class's capacity for self-representation is marked by common conditions of life, including, but not limited to, a common relation to the ownership and control of the means of production. Among other things, classes are . . . formed by culture, understood here as modes of discourse, a shared symbolic universe, rituals and customs that connote solidarity and distinguish a class from others."[22]

A third important but underdeveloped insight in Baudelot and Establet's analysis is that ideology is limited neither to the realm of the unconscious nor to a configuration of internalized personality traits. As I have mentioned elsewhere, Bowles and Gintis as well as Althusser have drawn accounts of schooling in which the logic of domination appears to be inscribed without the benefit of human mediation or struggle.[23] Baudelot and Establet modify these positions by giving ideology a more active nature. For them, ideology refers to that part of the realm of consciousness that produces *and* mediates the contradictory relations of capitalism and school life. Consequently, ideology becomes the locus of contradictory consciousness, informed by and containing both dominant and oppositional ideologies. This is evident in the contradictory logic exhibited in certain types of resistance. For example, some working-class students either resist or reject the notion of book learning and other forms of literacy in favor of subversive school behavior and a celebration of physicality and manual labor. In doing so, these students may undermine one of the fundamental ideologies of the school, but they do so at the cost of rejecting the possibility for developing modes of critical literacy that could be crucial to their own liberation.[24]

To summarize, the economic-reproductive model has made several important contributions to a radical theory of education. By focusing on the relationship between schools and the workplace, it has helped to illuminate the essential role that education plays in reproducing the social division of labor. In addition, it has made visible the "structured silences" in liberal theory regarding how the imperatives of class and power bear down on and shape school experience, particularly through the hidden curriculum. Furthermore, this model of reproduction has provided important insights into the class and structural basis of inequality. By rejecting the "blaming the victim" ideology that informs much of the research on inequality, these accounts have blamed institutions such as the schools for inequality, and have traced the failure of such institutions to the very structure of capitalist society. Unfortunately, the economic-reproductive model has failed to capture the complexity of the relationship between schools and such other institutions as the workplace and the family. Within its grimly mechanistic and overly-determined model of socialization there appears little room for developing a theory of schooling that takes seriously the notions of culture, resistance, and mediation. Even where contradictions and mediations are mentioned, they generally disappear under the crushing weight of capitalist domination. As such, these accounts are marred not only by a reductionist instrumentalism regarding the meaning and role of schools, but also by a form of radical pessimism that offers little hope for social change and even less reason for developing alternative educational practices.

Cultural-Reproductive Model

Theories of cultural reproduction are also concerned with the question of how capitalist societies are able to reproduce themselves. Central to these theories is a sustained effort to develop a sociology of schooling that links culture, class, and domination. The mediating role of culture in reproducing class societies is given priority over the study of related issues, such as the source and consequences of economic inequality. The work of Pierre Bourdieu and his colleagues in France represents the most important perspective for studying the cultural-reproductive model.[25]

Bourdieu's theory of cultural reproduction begins with the notion that the logic of domination, whether manifested in schools or in other social sites, must be analyzed within a theoretical framework capable of dialectically linking human agents and dominant structures. Bourdieu rejects functionalist theories that either impute the effects of domination to a single, central apparatus or fail to see how the dominated participate in their own oppression. This rejection becomes clear in Bourdieu's theory of schooling in which he attempts to link the notions of structure and human agency through an analysis of the relationships among dominant culture, school knowledge, and individual biographies.[26] In his attempt to understand the role of culture in linking, first, schools to the logic of the dominant classes, and, second, the dynamics of capitalist reproduction to the subordinate classes, Bourdieu argues against the notion that schools simply mirror the dominant society. Instead, he claims that schools are relatively autonomous institutions that are influenced only indirectly by more powerful economic and political institutions. Rather than being linked directly to the power of an economic elite, schools are seen as part of a larger universe of symbolic institutions that do not overtly impose docility and oppression, but reproduce existing power relations more subtly through the production and distribution of a dominant culture that tacitly confirms what it means to be educated.

Bourdieu's theory of cultural reproduction begins with the assumption that class-divided societies and the ideological and material configurations on which they rest are partially mediated and reproduced through what he calls "symbolic violence." That is, class control is constituted through the subtle exercise of symbolic power waged by ruling classes in order "to impose a definition of the social world that is consistent with its interests."[27] Culture becomes the mediating link between ruling-class interests and everyday life. It functions to portray the economic and political interests of the dominant classes, not as arbitrary and historically contingent, but as necessary and natural elements of the social order.

Education is seen as an important social and political force in the process of class reproduction. By appearing to be an impartial and neutral "transmitter" of the benefits of a valued culture, schools are able to promote inequality in the name of fairness and objectivity. Through this argument Bourdieu rejects both the idealist position, which views schools as independent of external forces, and orthodox radical critiques, in which schools merely mirror the needs of the economic system. According to Bourdieu, it is precisely the relative autonomy of the educational system that "enables it to serve external demands under the guise of independence and neutrality, i.e., to conceal the social functions it performs and so to perform them more effectively."[28]

The notions of culture and cultural capital are central to Bourdieu's analysis of how the mechanisms of cultural reproduction function within schools. He argues that the culture transmitted by the school is related to the various cultures that make up the wider society in that it confirms the culture of the ruling classes while simultaneously disconfirming the cultures of other groups. This becomes more understandable through an analysis of the notion of cultural capital—the different sets of linguistic and cultural competencies that individuals inherit by way of the class-located boundaries of their family. A child inherits from his or her family those sets of meanings, qualities of style, modes of thinking, and types of dispositions that are assigned a certain social value and status in accordance with what the dominant class(es) label as the most valued cultural capital. Schools play a particularly important role in legitimating and reproducing dominant cultural capital. They tend to legitimize certain forms of knowledge, ways of speaking, and ways of relating to the world that capitalize on the type of familiarity and skills that only certain students have received from their family backgrounds and class relations. Students whose families have only a tenuous connection to the dominant cultural capital are at a decided disadvantage. Bourdieu sums up this process:

> The culture of the elite is so near that of the school that children from the lower middle class (and *a fortiori* from the agricultural and industrial working class) can acquire only with great effort something which is *given* to the children of the cultivated classes—style, taste, wit—in short, those aptitudes which seem natural in members of the cultivated classes and naturally expected of them precisely because (in the ethnological sense) they are the *culture* of that class.[29]

By linking power and culture, Bourdieu provides a number of insights into how the hegemonic curriculum works in schools, pointing to the political interests underlying the selection and distribution of those bodies of knowledge that are given top priority.[30] These bodies of knowledge not only legitimate the interests and values of the dominant classes, they also have the effect of marginalizing or disconfirming other kinds of knowledge, particularly knowledge important to feminists, the working class, and minority groups. For example, working-class students often find themselves subjected to a school curriculum in which the distinction between high-status and low-status knowledge is organized around the difference between theoretical and practical subjects. Courses that deal with practical subjects, whether they be industrial arts or culinary arts, are seen as marginal and inferior. In this case, working-class knowledge and culture are often placed in competition with what the school legitimates as dominant culture and knowledge. In the end, working-class knowledge and culture are seen not as different and equal, but as different and inferior. It is important to note that high-status knowledge often corresponds to bodies of knowledge that provide a stepping stone to professional careers via higher education. Such knowledge embodies the cultural capital of the middle and upper classes and presupposes a certain familiarity with the linguistic and social practices it supports. Needless to say, such knowledge is not only more accessible to the upper classes, but also functions to confirm and legitimate their privileged positions in schools. Thus, the importance of the hegemonic curriculum lies in both what it includes—with its emphasis on Western history, science, and so forth—and what it excludes— feminist history, black studies, labor history, in-depth courses in the arts, and other forms of knowledge important to the working class and other subordinate groups.[31]

Thus, schools legitimize the dominant cultural capital through the hierarchically arranged bodies of school knowledge in the hegemonic curriculum, and by rewarding students who use the linguistic style of the ruling class. Certain linguistic styles, along with the body postures and the social relations they reinforce (lowered voice, disinterested tone, non-tactile interaction), act as identifiable forms of cultural capital that either reveal or betray a student's social background. In effect, certain linguistic practices and modes of discourse become privileged by being treated as natural to the gifted, when in fact they are the speech habits of dominant classes and thus serve to perpetuate cultural privileges.

Class and power connect with the production of dominant cultural capital not only in the structure and evaluation of the school curriculum but also in the dispositions of the oppressed themselves, who sometimes actively participate in their own subjugation. This point is central to Bourdieu's theory of cultural reproduction and can be examined more closely through a discussion of his notions of habitat (positions) and habitus (dispositions).[32]

In Bourdieu's most recent writings, he examines the relationship between action and structure through forms of historical action that bring together two histories. The first is the habitat, or *objectified history*, "the history which has accumulated over the passage of time in things, machines, buildings, monuments, books, theories, customs, law, etc."[33] The second refers to the *embodied history* of the habitus, and points to a set of internalized competencies and structured needs, an internalized style of knowing and relating to the world that is grounded in the body itself. Habitus, then, becomes a "matrix of perceptions, appreciations and actions,"[34] "a system of durably acquired schemes of perception, thought and action, engendered by objective conditions but tending to persist even after an alteration of those conditions."[35] The habitus is a product of both socialization and embodied history, and differs for various dominant and subordinate groups within society. As principles inscribed deeply within the needs and dispositions of the body, the habitus becomes a powerful force in organizing an individual's experience and is the central category in situating human agency within practical activity.

It is in the dialectical relationship between institutions as objectified history and the habitus or dispositions of different classes that Bourdieu attempts to fashion a theory of domination and learning. Bourdieu explains the process of domination by arguing that it is often forged through a correlation between a certain disposition (habitus) and the expectations and interests embedded in the position of specific institutions (habitat). Thus, it is in this correspondence between the tacitly inscribed values and ideologies that make up the individual's disposition and the norms and ideologies embedded in the positions characterizing institutions such as schools that the dynamics of domination become manifest. Furthermore, for Bourdieu the notions of habitus and habitat reveal how domination is forged in a logic that draws together those corresponding ideologies and practices that constitute both agents and structures. "The dispositions inculcated by a childhood experience of the social world which, in certain historical conditions, can predispose young workers to accept and even wish for entry into a world of manual labor which they identify with the adult world, are reinforced by work experience itself and by all the consequent changes in their dispositions."[36]

The importance of the notion of habitus to a theory of schooling becomes evident in the expanded theory of learning that it suggests. Bourdieu argues that individuals from different social groups and classes undergo processes of socialization that are not only intellectual but also emotional, sensory, and physical. Learning, in this case, is actively situated in the practical activity of the body, senses, and emotions. It is organized around class-specific cultural practices that inscribe their messages beyond consciousness, in the materiality of the body and the values and dispositions it signifies. Bourdieu explains:

> The principles em-bodied in [the habitus] . . . are placed beyond the grasp of consciousness, and hence cannot be touched by voluntary deliberate transformation, cannot even be made explicit; nothing seems more ineffable, more incommunicable, more inimitable, and, therefore, more precious, than the values given body, *made* body by the transubstantiation achieved by the hidden persuasion of an implicit pedagogy, capable of instilling a whole cosmology, an ethic, a metaphysic, a political philosophy, through injunctions as insignificant as "stand up straight" as "don't hold your knife in your left hand."[37]

Bourdieu's work is significant in that it provides a theoretical model for understanding aspects of schooling and social control that have been virtually ignored in conservative and liberal accounts. Its politicization of school knowledge, culture, and linguistic practices formulates a new discourse for examining ideologies embedded in the formal school curriculum. Similarly, Bourdieu adds a new dimension to analyses of the hidden curriculum by focusing on the importance of the body as an object of learning and social control.[38] In effect, what emerges in this account are the theoretical rudiments of a cultural-reproductive model that attempts to take seriously the notions of history, sociology, and psychology.

Yet, Bourdieu's work is not without some serious theoretical flaws. The most glaring flaws concern the mechanistic notions of power and domination and the overly determined view of human agency that characterizes much of this work. For example, Bourdieu's formulation of the notion of habitus is based on a theory of social control and depth psychology that appears to be fashioned almost exclusively in the logic of domination. The following comment by Bourdieu is representative of this position:

> The uses of the body, of languages, and of time are all privileged objects of social control: innumerable elements of explicit education—not to mention practical, mimetic transmission—relate to uses of the body ("sit up straight," "don't touch") or uses of language ("say this" or "don't say that"). Through bodily and linguistic discipline . . . the choices constituting a certain relation to the world are internalized in the form of durable patternings not accessible to consciousness nor even, in part, amenable to will. Politeness contains a politics, a practical immediate recognition of social classifications and of hierarchies between the sexes, the generations, the classes, etc.[39]

Unfortunately, where the conceptual possibility for resistance does appear in Bourdieu's work—that is, in the mismatch between one's habitus and the position one occupies—the foundation for such action rests not on a notion of reflexivity or critical self-consciousness, but on the incompatibility between two structures—the historical structure of the disposition and the historical structure embodied in the institution. Thus, resistance becomes the outcome of a conflict between two formalistic structures, one situated in the realm of the unconscious and the other situated in the social practices that make up institutions such as schools. The result is that the power of reflexive thought and historical agency are relegated to a minor theoretical detail in Bourdieu's theory of change.

Another theoretical flaw in Bourdieu's work is that culture represents a somewhat one-way process of domination. As a result, his theory suggests falsely that working-class cultural forms and knowledge are homogeneous and merely a pale reflection of dominant cultural capital. Working-class cultural production and its relation to cultural reproduction through the complex dynamics of resistance, incorporation, and accommodation are not acknowledged by Bourdieu. The collapse of culture and class into the processes of cultural reproduction raises a number of significant problems. First, such a portrayal eliminates conflict both within and between different classes, resulting in the loss of such notions as struggle, diversity, and human agency in a somewhat reductionist view of human nature and history. Second, by reducing classes to homogeneous groups whose only differences are based on whether they exercise or respond to power, Bourdieu provides no theoretical opportunity to unravel how cultural domination and resistance are mediated through the complex interface of race, gender, and class. What is missing from Bourdieu's work is the notion that culture is both a structuring and transforming process. David Davies captures this dynamic in his comment: "Culture refers paradoxically to conservative adaptation and lived subordination of classes and to opposition, resistance, and creative struggle for change."[40]

Bourdieu's analyses of schooling also suffer from a one-sided treatment of ideology.[41] While it is useful to argue, as Bourdieu does, that dominant ideologies are transmitted by schools and actively incorporated by students, it is equally important to remember that ideologies are also *imposed* on students, who occasionally view them as contrary to their own interests and either resist them openly or conform to them under pressure from school authorities. In other words, dominant ideologies are not just transmitted in schools nor are they practiced in a void. On the contrary, they are often met with resistance by teachers, students, and parents. Furthermore, it is reasonable to argue that in order to be successful, schools have to repress the production of counter-ideologies. Roger Dale illuminates this process in his discussion of how hegemony functions in schools, writing that "hegemony is not so much about winning approval for the status quo. . . . Rather what seems to be involved is the prevention of rejection, opposition or alternatives to the status quo through denying the use of the school for such purposes."[42] Similarly, it must be noted that schools are not simply static institutions that reproduce the dominant ideology; they are active agents in its construction as well. This is aptly portrayed in an ethnographic study of ruling class schools conducted by Robert Connell and his colleagues. They write:

> The school generates practices by which the class is renewed, integrated and re-constituted in the face of changes in its own composition and in the general social circumstances in which it tries to survive and prosper. (This is an embracing practice, ranging from the school fete, Saturday sport and week-night dinners with parents, to the organization of a marriage market—e.g., inter-school dances—and informal networks in business and the professions, to the regulation of class membership, updating of ideology, and subordination of particular interests to those of class as a whole.) The ruling-class school is no mere agent of the class; it is an important and active part of it. In short, it is organic to its class. Bourdieu wrote a famous essay about the "school as conserver"; we would suggest an equal stress should be laid on the school as constructor.[43]

By failing to develop a theory of ideology that speaks to the way in which human beings dialectically create, resist, and accommodate themselves to dominant ideologies, Bourdieu excludes the active nature of both domination and resistance. In spite of his claims, it is important to argue that schools do not simply usurp the cultural capital of working-class families and neighborhoods. Complex relations develop between the schools and working-class families and they need to be analyzed in terms of the conflicts and struggles that inform them. This point is highlighted in an ethnographic study by R. Timothy Sieber that chronicles the history of a power struggle over an elementary school in New York City.[44]

This study reinforces one aspect of Bourdieu's analysis in revealing that middle-class students, with their respective cultural competencies and experiences, were accorded specific academic privileges and freedoms denied to working-class and Puerto Rican students in the same school. But the more interesting aspect of Sieber's study indicates that the "privileged standing" and educational benefits provided to middle-class students were the outcome of a long struggle between the middle-class segment of the community and its predominantly working-class residents. The predominance of middle-class culture in this school was the outcome of a political struggle, and contrary to Bourdieu's position, was actively and systematically developed "both inside and outside of the school" by middle-class parents.[45]

Finally, there is a serious flaw in Bourdieu's work regarding his unwillingness to link the notion of domination with the materiality of economic forces. There is no insight in Bourdieu's analyses regarding how the economic system, with its asymmetrical relations of power, produces concrete constraints on working-class students. Michel Foucault's notion that power works on the body, the family, sexuality, and the nature of learning itself serves to remind us that the relations of power weigh down on more than just the mind.[46] In other words, the constraints of power are not exhausted within the concept of symbolic violence. Domination as an objective, concrete instance cannot be ignored in any discussion of schooling. For instance, the privileged classes have a relationship to time that enables them to make long-term plans regarding their futures. In contrast, the children of the dispossessed, especially those who are in higher education, often are burdened by economic constraints that lock them into the present and limit their goals to short-term plans. Time is a privation, not a possession, for most working-class students.[47] It is the economic dimension that often plays a crucial role in the decision over whether a working-class student can go to school full or part time, or in some cases can afford to go at all, just as the economic issue is often the determining factor in deciding whether or not a student will have to work part time while attending school. Bourdieu appears to have forgotten that domination has to be grounded in something other than mere ideology, that it also has a material foundation. This is no small matter, because it points to a major gap in Bourdieu's reasoning regarding working-class failure. The internalization of dominant ideology is not the only force that motivates working-class students or secures their failure. Their behaviors, failures, and choices are also grounded in material conditions.

As a result of Bourdieu's one-sided emphasis on ruling-class domination and its attendant cultural practices, it becomes clear that both the concept of capital as well as the notion of class are treated as static categories. In my view, class involves a notion of social relations that are in opposition to each other. It refers to the shifting relations of domination and resistance and to capital and its institutions as they constantly regroup and attempt to reconstruct the logic of domination and incorporation. These oppositions are missing from Bourdieu's analyses.[48] What we are left with is a theory of reproduction that displays little faith in subordinate classes and groups and little hope in their ability or willingness to reconstruct the conditions under which they live, work, and learn. Consequently, most reproduction theories informed by Bourdieu's notion of domination ultimately fail to provide the comprehensive theoretical elements needed for a radical pedagogy.

Hegemonic-State Reproductive Model

Recently Marxist theorists have argued that understanding the role of the State is central to any analysis of how domination operates.[49] Thus, a major concern now among a number of educational theorists focuses on the complex role of state intervention in the educational system.[50] These theorists believe that educational change cannot be understood by looking only at capital's domination of the labor process or the way capitalist domination is reproduced through culture. Neither of these explanations, they claim, has given adequate attention to the underlying structural determinants of inequality that characterize the advanced industrial countries of the West. They argue that such accounts display little understanding of how political factors lead to State interventionist policies that serve to structure and shape the reproductive functions of education.

In spite of the agreement among reproductive theorists about the importance of the State, there are significant differences among them as to what the State actually is, how it works, and what the precise relationship is between the State and capital, on the one hand, and the State and education on the other. Michael Apple captures the complexity of this issue in his review of some of the major questions with which theorists of the State are currently grappling. He writes:

> Does the state only serve the interests of capital or is it more complex than that? Is the State instead an arena of class conflict and a site where hegemony must be worked for, not a foregone conclusion where it is simply imposed? Are schools—as important sites of the State— simply "ideological state apparatuses" (to quote Althusser), ones whose primary role is to reproduce the ideological and "manpower" requirements of the social relations of production? Or, do they also embody contradictory tendencies and provide sites where ideological struggles within and among classes, races, and sexes can and do occur?[51]

It is not my intent to unravel how different theorists of the State deal with these issues.

Instead, I will focus on two major themes. First, I will explore some of the dynamics that characterize the relationship between the State and capitalism. Second, I will explore some of the underlying dynamics at work in the relationship between the State and schooling.

The State and capitalism. One of the major assumptions in Marxist accounts regarding the relationship between the State and capitalism has been developed around the work of the late Italian theorist, Antonio Gramsci.[52] For Gramsci, any discussion about the State had to begin with the reality of class relations and the exercise of hegemony by the dominant classes. Gramsci's dialectical formulation of hegemony as an ever-changing combination of force and consent provides the basis for analyzing the nature of the State in capitalist society.

Hegemony, in Gramsci's terms, appears to have two meanings. First, it refers to a process of domination whereby a ruling class exercises control through its intellectual and moral leadership over allied classes.[53] In other words, an alliance is formed among ruling classes as a result of the power and "ability of one class to articulate the interest of other social groups to its own."[54] Hegemony in this instance signifies, first, a pedagogic and politically transformative process whereby the dominant class articulates the common elements embedded in the worldviews of allied groups. Second, hegemony refers to the dual use of force and ideology to reproduce societal relations between dominant classes and subordinate groups. Gramsci strongly emphasizes the role of ideology as an active force used by dominant classes to shape and incorporate the commonsense views, needs, and interests of subordinate groups. This is an important issue. Hegemony in this account represents more than the exercise of coercion: it is a process of continuous creation and includes the constant structuring of consciousness as well as a battle for the control of consciousness. The production of knowledge is linked to the political sphere and becomes a central element in the State's construction of power. The primary issue for Gramsci centers around demonstrating how the State can be defined, in part, by referring to its active involvement as a repressive and cultural (educative) apparatus.

This brings us directly to Gramsci's definition of the State. Rejecting orthodox Marxist formulations of the State as merely the repressive tool of the dominant classes, Gramsci divides the State into two specific realms: political society and civil society. Political society refers to the state apparatuses of administration, law, and other coercive institutions whose primary, though not exclusive, function is based on the logic of force and repression. Civil society refers to those private and public institutions that rely upon meanings, symbols, and ideas to universalize ruling-class ideologies, while simultaneously shaping and limiting oppositional discourse and practice.

Two issues need to be stressed in conjunction with Gramsci's view of the State. All state apparatuses have coercive and consensual functions; it is the dominance of one function over the other that gives the apparatuses of either political or civil society their defining characteristic. Furthermore, as a mode of ideological control, hegemony—whether it takes place in the schools, the mass media, or the trade unions—must be fought for constantly in order to be maintained. It is not something "that simply consists of the projection of the ideas of the dominant classes into the heads of the subordinate classes."[55] The footing on which hegemony moves and functions has to shift ground in order to accommodate the changing nature of historical circumstances and the complex demands and critical actions of human beings. This view of the function of the State redefines class rule and the complex use of power. Power as used here is both a positive and a negative force. It functions negatively in the repressive and ideological apparatuses of the government and civil society to reproduce the relations of domination. It functions positively as a feature of active opposition and struggle, the terrain on which men and women question, act, and refuse to be incorporated into the logic of capital and its institutions.

In short, Gramsci provides a definition of the State that links power and culture to the traditional Marxist emphasis on the repressive aspects of the State. Gramsci is rather succinct on this issue: "The state is the entire complex of practical and theoretical activities with which the ruling class not only justifies and maintains its dominance, but manages to win the active consent of those over whom it rules."[56]

Gramsci's writings are crucial to an understanding of the meaning and workings of the State and have influenced a wide range of Marxist writers who argue that "all state formations under capitalism articulate class power."[57] The crucial starting point for many of these theorists is a sustained attack on the liberal assumption that the State is a neutral, administrative structure that operates in the interests of the general will. This attack generally takes the form of an historical critique that rejects the liberal notion of the State as a naturally evolving structure of human progress which stands above class and sectional interests. Marxist critics have argued in different ways that the State is a specific set of social relations linked historically to the conditions of capitalist production. In effect, the State is an organization, an embodiment of a changing pattern of class relations organized around the dynamics of class struggle, domination, and contestation. Furthermore, as a set of relations organized around class divisions, the State expresses ideological and economic interests through repressive as well as legitimating institutions. "The State is not a structure, it is an organization; or better, it is a complex of social forms organized so that it inflects all relations and ideas about relations in such a way that capitalist production, and all it entails, becomes thought of as lived and natural."[58]

This leads to a related and important issue concerning the defining features of the State's operation. Theorists such as Nicos Poulantzas have rightly argued that the State and its various agencies, including public schools, cannot be seen merely as tools manipulated at will by the ruling classes.[59] On the contrary, as the concrete representation of class relations, the State is constituted through continuing conflicts and contradictions, which, it can be argued, take two primary forms. First, there are conflicts among different factions of the ruling class, who often represent varied and competing approaches to social control and capital accumulation. But it is important to note that the relative autonomy of the State, secured partly through the existence of competing dominant classes, often tends to obscure what various factions of the ruling class have in common. That is, the State's short-term policies are firmly committed to maintaining the underlying economic and ideological structures of capitalist society. Thus, behind the discourse of diverging political, sectional, and social interests, there is the underlying grammar of class domination and structured inequality. Dominant classes may battle over the size of the military budget, monetary cutbacks in social services, and the nature of the tax structure, but they do not challenge basic capitalist production relations.

The definitive feature of the relative autonomy of the State is to be found, then, not in its chorus of oppositional discourses, but in its structured silences regarding the underlying basis of capitalist society. Moreover, the State is defined less by the interest of any one dominant group than by the specific set of social relations it mediates and sustains. Claus Offe and Volker Ronge summarize this position well: "What the State protects and sanctions is a set of rules and social relations which are presupposed by the class rule of the capitalist class. The State does not defend the interests of one class but the common interests of all members of a capitalist society."[60]

The second defining feature of the State centers around the relationship between the dominant and dominated classes. The State is not only an object of struggle among members of the ruling class, it is also a defining force in the production of conflict and struggle between the ruling class and other subordinate groups. The underlying logic of State formation is situated in the State's dual role of performing the often contradictory tasks of establishing the conditions for the accumulation of capital, on the one hand, and the ideological task of moral regulation on the other. In other words, the State has the task of meeting the basic needs of capital by providing, for instance, the necessary flow of workers, knowledge, skills, and values for the reproduction of labor power.[61] But at the same time, the State has the task of winning the consent of the dominated classes, which it attempts by legitimating the social relations and values that structure the capital accumulation process either through remaining silent about the class interests that benefit from such relations, or through marginalizing or disqualifying any serious critique or alternative to them. Furthermore, the State attempts to win the consent of the working class for its policies by making an appeal to three types of specific outcomes—economic (social mobility), ideological (democratic rights), and psychological (happiness). Philip Corrigan and his colleagues point to this issue in their argument:

> We stress that the State is constructed and fought over. Central to this is a two fold set of historical practices: (i) the constant "rewriting" of history to naturalize what has been, in fact, an extremely changeable set of State relations, to claim that there is, and has always been, one "optimal institutional structure" which is what "any" civilization needs; and (ii) to marginalize (disrupt, deny, destroy, dilute, "help") all alternative forms of State, particularly any which announces any form of organization that established difference at the level of the national social formation (or crime of all crimes!, that established any form of international solidarity along class lines).[62]

The contradictions that arise out of the differences between the reality and the promise of capitalist social relations are evident in a number of instances, some of which directly involve schooling. For example, schools often promote an ideology of social mobility that is at odds with high levels of unemployment and the overabundance of highly qualified workers. Furthermore, the ideology of the work ethic is often contradicted by the increasing number of routinized and alienating jobs. In addition, capitalism's appeal to the satisfaction of higher needs often rests on an image of leisure, beauty, and happiness, the fulfillment of which lies beyond the capabilities of the existing society.

What emerges from this analysis of the relationship between the State and the economy are a number of crucial issues that have a significant bearing on educational policy and practice. First, it is rightly claimed that the State is neither the instrument of any one dominant class faction nor simply a pale reflection of the needs of the economic system. Second, the State is accurately portrayed as a site marked by ongoing conflicts among and between various class, gender, and racial groups. Third, the State is not merely an expression of class struggle, it is primarily an organization that actively defends capitalist society through repressive as well as ideological means. Finally, in its capacity as an ideological and repressive apparatus, the State limits and channels the responses that schools can make to the ideology, culture, and practices that characterize the dominant society. The following section contains a more detailed examination of these issues.

The State and schooling. In order to adequately investigate the relationship between the State and schooling, two questions need to be posed and analyzed. How does the State exercise control over schools in terms of its economic, ideological, and repressive functions? How does the school function not only to further the interests of the State and the dominant classes but also to contradict and resist the logic of capital?

As part of the state apparatus, schools and universities play a major role in furthering the economic interests of the dominant classes. Several theorists have argued that schools are actively involved in establishing the conditions for capital accumulation, and they point specifically to a number of instances in which the State intervenes to influence this process.63 For example, through state-established certification requirements, educational systems are heavily weighted toward a highly technocratic rationality that relies upon a logic drawn primarily from the natural sciences. The effects can be seen in the distinction schools at all levels make between high-status knowledge—usually the "hard sciences"—and low-status knowledge—subjects in the humanities. This bias also puts pressures on schools to utilize methods of inquiry and evaluation that stress efficiency, prediction, and the logic of the mathematical formula. The extent of State intervention is obvious in the favorable political orientation exercised through small- and large-scale government funding for educational research programs. Apple, for instance, illuminates this point:

> The state will take on the large initial cost of basic research and development. It then "transfers" the fruits of it back to the "private sector" once it becomes profitable. The state's role in capital accumulation is very evident in its subsidization of the production of technical/administrative knowledge. . . . Like the economy, examples of this pattern of intervention are becoming more visible. They include the emphasis on competency-based education, systems management, career education, futurism (often a code word for manpower planning),

continued major funding for mathematics and science curriculum development (when compared to the arts), national testing programs. . . . All of these and more signal the sometimes subtle and sometimes quite overt role of state intervention into schooling to attempt to maximize efficient production of both the agents and the knowledge required by an unequal economy.[64]

The rationality that supports state intervention into schools also influences the development of curricula and classroom social relations the success of which is often measured against how well they "equip" different groups of students with the knowledge and skills they will need to perform productively in the workplace. Moreover, beneath the production of this type of curriculum and socialization there is the brute reality that schools function partly to keep students out of the labor force. As Dale points out, "schools keep children off the streets, and insure that for a large part of most days in the year they cannot engage in activities which might disrupt a social context amenable to capital accumulation but are exposed to attempts to socialize them into ways compatible with the maintenance of that context."[65]

State intervention is also manifested in the way policy is formulated outside of the control of teachers and parents. The economic interest underlying such policy is present not only in the rationality of control, planning, and other bureaucratic emphases on rule-following but also in the way in which the State funds programs to handle what Apple calls "negative outcomes" in the accumulation process:

> By defining large groups of children as deviant (slow learners, remedial problems, discipline problems, etc.), and giving funding and legislative support for special teachers and for "diagnosis" and for "treatment" the state will fund extensive remedial projects. While these projects seem neutral, helpful, and may seem aimed at increasing mobility, they will actually defuse the debate over the role of schooling in the reproduction of the knowledge and people "required" by society. It will do this in part by defining the ultimate causes of such deviance as within the child or his or her culture and not due to, say, poverty, the conflicts and disparities generated by the historically evolving cultural and economic hierarchies of the society, etc. This will be hidden from us as well by our assumption that schools are primarily organized as distribution agencies, instead of, at least in part, important agencies in the accumulation process.[66]

One of the major questions pursued by educational theorists studying the State focuses on the relationship between power and knowledge—specifically, how the State "exercises and imposes its power through the production of 'truth' and 'knowledge' about education."[67] Poulantzas, for example, argues that the production of dominant ideologies in the schools is to be found not only in the high-status knowledge and social relations sanctioned by the State bureaucracy but, more importantly, in the reproduction of the mental-manual division. The State appropriates, trains, and legitimates "intellectuals" who serve as experts in the production and conception of school knowledge, and who ultimately function to separate knowledge from both manual work and popular consumption. Behind this facade of credentialized expertise and professionalism lies a major feature of dominant ideology—the separation of knowledge from power. Poulantzas states, "The knowledge-power relationship finds expression in particular techniques of the exercise of power—exact devices inscribed in the texture of the State whereby the popular masses are permanently kept at a distance from the centres of decision making. These comprise a series of rituals and styles of speech, as well as structural modes of formulating and tackling problems that monopolise knowledge in such a way that the popular masses are effectively excluded."[68]

This separation becomes more pronounced in the special status that state certification programs and schools give to curriculum "experts;" the underlying logic of this status suggests that teachers should implement rather than conceptualize and develop curriculum approaches. The knowledge-power relation also finds expression in the active production and distribution of knowledge itself. For instance, one of the main roles of the schools is to valorize mental labor and disqualify manual labor. This division finds its highest representation in forms of tracking, classroom social relations, and other aspects of school legitimation that function to exclude and devalue working-class history and culture. Furthermore, this division between mental and manual labor underlies the school's socializing process which prepares working-class and other students for their respective places in the work force.

Schools, of course, do more than mediate the logic of domination, and this can be seen in the contradictions that emerge around the ideology of democratic rights often reproduced in the school curriculum. Schools play an active role in legitimating the view that politics and power are primarily defined around the issues of individual rights and through the dynamics of the electoral process. Central to this liberal ideology of democratic rights are assumptions that define the political sphere and the role of the State in that sphere. The importance of this ideology as a contradictory part of the hegemonic curriculum cannot be overstated. On the one hand, it functions to separate the issues of politics and democracy from the economic sphere and to displace the notion of conflict from its class-specific social context to the terrain of individual rights and struggle. On the other hand, there is a certain counter-logic in democratic liberal ideology that provides the basis for resistance and conflict. That is, liberal democratic ideology contains concerns for human rights that are often at odds with capitalist rationality, its ethos of commodity fetish, and its drive for profits.

Finally, it must be remembered that the most direct intervention exercised by the State is constituted by law. Though impossible to discuss here in detail, this intervention often takes forms which link schools to the logic of repression rather than ideological domination. One instance of this linkage is that the foundation of school policy is sometimes established in the courts, such as the push towards racial integration of public schooling. Another instance is that school attendance is established through the rule of law and provides the "legal" cement that brings students into the schools. Relatedly, it is the courts, the police, and other state agencies that attempt to enforce involuntary school attendance. Of course, involuntary school attendance does not guarantee student obedience, and in some respects becomes a major issue promoting student resistance, a fact often forgotten by resistance theorists.

In conclusion, it must be emphasized that theories of the State perform a theoretical service by adding to our understanding of how the processes of social and cultural reproduction function in the political sphere. They rightly draw our attention to the importance of the relative autonomy of the State and its apparatuses (such as schools), the contradictory character of the State, and the economic, ideological, and repressive pressures the State exerts on schooling. But it must be acknowledged that, as part of a wider theory of reproduction, hegemonic-state accounts exhibit some major theoretical failings. First, theories of the State focus primarily on macro and structural issues, resulting in a mode of analysis that points to contradictions and struggle, but says little about how human agency works through such conflicts at the level of everyday life and concrete school relations. A second failing is that some theories of the State display little understanding of culture as a relatively autonomous realm with its own inherent counter-logic. For instance, Poulantzas's heavy-handed notion of the school as merely an ideological state apparatus provides no theoretical space for investigating the emergence and dynamics of student counter-cultures as they develop in the interplay of concrete, antagonistic school relations.[69] Culture is, however, both the subject and object of resistance; the driving force of culture is contained not only in how it functions to dominate subordinate groups, but also in the way in which oppressed groups draw from their own cultural capital and set of experiences to develop an oppositional logic. Despite theoretical lip service to the contrary, this dialectical view of culture is often subsumed within a view of power that leans too heavily on the logic of domination in defining culture simply as an *object* of resistance rather than its *source*. In order to obtain a more concrete view of the dynamics of resistance and struggle as they inform subordinate school cultures operating under the ideological and material constraints partly constructed by the State, it is necessary to turn to theories of resistance.

Schooling and Theories of Resistance

The concept of resistance is relatively new in educational theory. The reasons behind this theoretical neglect can be traced partly to the failings of both conservative and radical approaches to schooling. Conservative educators analyzed oppositional behavior primarily through psychological categories that served to define such behavior not only as deviant, but more importantly, as disruptive and inferior—a failing on the part of the individuals and social groups that exhibited it. Radical educators, on the other hand, have generally ignored the internal workings of the school and have tended to treat schools as "black boxes." Beneath a discourse primarily concerned with the notions of domination, class conflict, and hegemony, there has been a structured silence regarding how teachers, students, and others live out their daily lives in schools. Consequently, there has been an overemphasis on how structural determinants promote economic and cultural inequality, and an underemphasis on how human agency accommodates, mediates, and resists the logic of capital and its dominating social practices.

More recently, a number of educational studies have emerged that attempt to move beyond the important but somewhat limited theoretical gains of reproduction theory. Taking the concepts of conflict and resistance as starting points for their analyses, these accounts have sought to redefine the importance of mediation, power, and culture in understanding the complex relations between schools and the dominant society. Consequently, the work of a number of theorists has been instrumental in providing a rich body of detailed literature that integrates neo-Marxist social theory with ethnographic studies in order to illuminate the dynamics of accommodation and resistance as they work through countercultural groups both inside and outside schools.[70]

Resistance, in these accounts, represents a significant critique of school as an institution and points to social activities and practices whose meanings are ultimately political and cultural. In contrast to a vast amount of ethnographic literature on schooling in both the United States and England, neo-Marxist resistance theories have not sacrificed theoretical depth for methodological refinement.[71] That is, recent neo-Marxist studies have not followed the method of merely providing overly-exhaustive descriptive analyses of the internal workings of the school. Instead, they have attempted to analyze how determinant socioeconomic structures embedded in the dominant society work through the mediations of class and culture to shape the antagonistic experiences of students' everyday lives. Rejecting the functionalism inherent in both conservative and radical versions of educational theory, neo-Marxist accounts have analyzed curriculum as a complex discourse that not only serves the interests of domination but also contains aspects which provide emancipatory possibilities.

The attempt to link social structures and human agency in order to explore the way they interact in a dialectical manner represents a significant advance in educational theory. Of course, neo-Marxist resistance theories are also beset with problems, and I will mention some of the more outstanding ones here. Their singular achievement is the primary importance they allot to critical theory and human agency as the basic categories to be used in analyzing the daily experiences that constitute the internal workings of the school.

Central to theories of resistance is an emphasis on the tensions and conflicts that mediate relationships among home, school, and workplace. For example, Willis demonstrates in his study of the "lads"—a group of working class males who constitute the "counterculture" in an English secondary school—that much of their opposition to the labels, meanings, and values of the official and hidden curriculum is informed by an ideology of resistance, the roots of which are in the shop-floor cultures occupied by their family members and other members of their class.[72] The most powerful example of this mode of resistance is exhibited by the lads in their rejection of the primacy of mental over manual labor. Not only do the lads reject the alleged superiority of mental labor, they also reject its underlying ideology that respect and obedience will be exchanged for knowledge and success. The lads oppose this ideology because the counter-logic embodied in the families, workplaces, and street life that make up *their* culture points to a different and more convincing reality. Thus, one major contribution that has emerged from resistance studies is the insight that the mechanisms of reproduction are never complete and are always faced with partially realized elements of opposition.

Furthermore, this work points to a dialectical model of domination, one that offers valuable alternatives to many of the radical models of reproduction analyzed previously. Instead of seeing domination as simply the by-product of external forces—for example, capital or the State—resistance theorists have developed a notion of reproduction in which working-class subordination is viewed not only as a result of the structural and ideological constraints embedded in capitalist social relationships, but also as part of the process of self-formation within the working class itself.

One key issue posed by this notion of domination is the question, How does the logic that promotes varied forms of resistance become implicated in the logic of reproduction? For example, theories of resistance have attempted to demonstrate how students who actively reject school culture often display a deeper logic and view of the world that confirms rather than challenges existing capitalist social relations. Two illustrations demonstrate this point. Willis's lads rejected the primacy of mental labor and its ethos of individual appropriation, but in doing so they closed off any possibility of pursuing an emancipatory relationship between knowledge and dissent. By rejecting intellectual labor, the lads discounted the power of critical thinking as a tool of social transformation.[73]

The same logic is displayed by the students in Michelle Fine's study of drop outs from alternative high schools in New York City's South Bronx.[74] Fine had assumed that the students who dropped out of these schools were victims of "learned helplessness," but she discovered instead that they were the most critical and politically astute students in the alternative schools: "Much to our collective surprise (and dismay) the drop outs were those students who were most likely to identify injustice in their social lives and at school, and most ready to correct injustice by criticizing or challenging a teacher. The drop outs were least depressed, and had attained academic levels equivalent to students who remained in school."[75] There is a certain irony here: while such students were capable of challenging the dominant ideology of the school, they failed to recognize the limits of their own resistance. By leaving school, these students placed themselves in a structural position that cut them off from political and social avenues conducive to the task of radical reconstruction.

Another important and distinctive feature of resistance theories is their emphasis on the importance of culture and, more specifically, cultural production. In the concept of cultural production we find the basis for a theory of human agency, one that is constructed through the active, ongoing, collective medium of oppressed groups' experiences. In a more recent work, Willis elaborates on this issue, arguing that the notion of cultural production insists on the active, transformative natures of cultures and on the collective ability of social agents, not only to think like theorists, but to act like activists. Life experiences, individual and group projects, secret illicit and informal knowledge, private fears and fantasies, the threatening anarchic power arising from irreverent association . . . are not merely interesting additions. . . . These things are central: determined but also determining. They must occupy, fully fledged in their own right, a vital theoretical and political transformative stage in our analyses. This is, in part, the project of showing the capacities of the working class to gener-ate albeit ambiguous, complex, and often ironic, collective and cultural forms of knowledge not reducible back to the bourgeois forms and the importance of this as one of the bases for political change.[76]

As Willis suggests, theories of resistance point to new ways of constructing a rad-ical pedagogy by developing analyses of the ways in which class and culture combine to offer the outlines for a "cultural politics." At the core of such a politics is a semi-otic reading of the style, rituals, language, and systems of meaning that inform the cultural terrains of subordinate groups. Through this process, it becomes possible to analyze what counter-hegemonic elements such cultural fields contain, and how they tend to become incorporated into the dominant culture and subsequently stripped of their political possibilities. Implicit in such an analysis is the need to develop strate-gies in schools in which oppositional cultures might be rescued from the processes of incorporation in order to provide the basis for a viable political force. An essential element of such a task, which has been generally neglected by radical educators, is the development of a radical pedagogy that links a politics of the concrete not just with the processes of reproduction but also with the dynamics of social transforma-tion. The possibility for such a task already exists and is present in the attempt by resistance theorists to view the cultures of subordinate groups as more than simply the by-product of hegemony and defeat.[77]

Another important feature of resistance theory is a deeper understanding of the notion of relative autonomy. This notion is developed through a number of analyses that point to those nonreproductive moments that constitute and support the critical notion of human agency. As I have mentioned, resistance theory assigns an active role to human agency and experience as key mediating links between structural determinants and lived effects. Consequently, there is the recognition that different spheres or cultural sites—schools, families, mass media—are governed by complex ideological properties that often generate contradictions both within and among them. At the same time, the notion of ideological domination as all-encompassing and unitary in its form and content is rejected, and it is rightly argued that dominant ideologies themselves are often contradictory, as are different factions of the ruling classes, the institutions that serve them, and the subordinate groups under their control.

In considering the weaknesses in theories of resistance, I will make several crit-icisms which represent starting points for the further development of a critical the-ory of schooling. First, although studies of resistance point to those social sites and "spaces" in which the dominant culture is encountered and challenged by subordinate groups, they do not adequately conceptualize the historical development of the conditions that promote and reinforce contradictory modes of resistance and struggle. What is missing in this perspective are analyses of those historically and culturally mediated factors that produce a *range* of oppositional behaviors, some of which constitute resistance and some of which do not. Put simply, not all oppositional behavior has "radical significance," nor is all oppositional behavior a clear-cut response to domination. The issue here is that there have been too few attempts by educational theorists to understand how subordinate groups embody and express a combination of reactionary and progressive behaviors—behaviors that embody ideologies both underlying the structure of social domination and containing the logic necessary to overcome it.

Oppositional behavior may not be simply a reaction to powerlessness, but might be an expression of power that is fueled by and reproduces the most powerful grammar of domination. Thus, on one level, resistance may be the simple appropriation and display of power, and may manifest itself through the interests and discourse of the worst aspects of capitalist rationality. For example, students may violate school rules, but the logic that informs such behavior may be rooted in forms of ideological hegemony such as racism and sexism. Moreover, the source of such hegemony often originates outside of the school. Under such circumstances, schools become social sites where oppositional behavior is simply played out, emerging less as a critique of schooling than as an expression of dominant ideology.

This becomes clearer in Angela McRobbie's account of sixth-form female students in England who, by aggressively asserting their own sexuality, appear to be rejecting the official ideology of the school with its sexually repressive emphasis on neatness, passivity, compliance, and "femininity."[78] Their opposition takes the form of carving boyfriends' names on school desks, wearing makeup and tight-fitting clothes, flaunting their sexual preferences for older, more mature boys, and spending endless amounts of time talking about boys and boyfriends. It could be argued that this type of oppositional behavior, rather than suggesting resistance, primarily displays an oppressive mode of sexism. Its organizing principle appears to be linked to social practices informed by the objective of developing a sexual, and ultimately successful, marriage. Thus, it appears to underscore a logic that has little to do with resistance to school norms and a great deal to do with the sexism that characterizes working-class life and mass culture in general. This is not to say that such behavior can simply be written off as reactionary. Obviously, the fact that these young women are acting collectively and attempting to define for themselves what they want out of life contains an emancipatory moment. But in the final analysis, this type of opposition is informed by a dominating, rather than liberating, logic.

This leads to a related issue. Resistance theories have gone too far in viewing schools as institutions characterized exclusively by forms of ideological domination. Lost from this view is an insight provided by theorists who deal with the hegemonic-state reproductive model: the notion that schools are also repressive institutions that use various coercive state agencies, including the police and the courts, to enforce involuntary school attendance. The point here is that resistance theories must recognize that in some cases students may be totally indifferent to the dominant ideology of the school with its respective rewards and demands. Their behavior in school may be fueled by ideological imperatives that signify issues and concerns that have very little to do with school directly. School simply becomes the place where the oppositional nature of these concerns is expressed.

In short, oppositional behaviors are produced amid contradictory discourses and values. The logic that informs a given act of resistance may, on the one hand, be linked to interests that are class- gender- or race-specific. On the other hand, it may express the repressive moments inscribed in such behavior by the dominant culture rather than a message of protest against their existence. To understand the nature of such resistance, we must place it in a wider context to see how it is mediated and articulated in the culture of such oppositional groups. Because of a failure to understand the dialectical nature of resistance, most theories of education have treated the concept somewhat superficially. For instance, when domination is stressed in such studies, the portrayals of schools, working-class students, and classroom pedagogy often appear too homogeneous and static to be taken seriously. When resistance is discussed, its contradictory nature is usually not analyzed seriously, nor is the contradictory consciousness of the students and teachers treated dialectically.[79]

A second weakness in theories of resistance is that they rarely take into account issues of gender and race. As a number of feminists have pointed out, resistance studies, when analyzing domination, struggle, and schooling, generally ignore women and gender issues and focus instead on males and class issues.[80] This has meant that women are either disregarded altogether or are included only in terms that echo the sentiments of the male countercultural groups being portrayed. This raises a number of important problems that future analyses must resolve. One problem is that such studies have failed to account for the notion of patriarchy as a mode of domination that both cuts across various social sites and mediates between men and women within and between different social class formations. The point here, of course, is that domination is not singularly informed or exhausted by the logic of class oppression, nor does it affect men and women in similar ways. Women, though in different degrees, experience dual forms of domination in both the home and the workplace. How the dynamics of these forms are interconnected, reproduced, and mediated in schools represents an important area of continuing research. Another problem is that these studies contain no theoretical room for exploring forms of resistance that are race- and gender-specific, particularly as these mediate the sexual and social divisions of labor in various social sites such as schools. The failure to include women and racial minorities in such studies has resulted in a rather uncritical theoretical tendency to romanticize modes of resistance even when they contain reactionary racial and gender views. The irony here is that a large amount of neo-Marxist work on resistance, although allegedly committed to emancipatory concerns, ends up contributing to the reproduction of sexist and racist attitudes and practices.

A third weakness characterizing theories of resistance, as Jim Walker points out, is that they have focused primarily on overt acts of rebellious student behavior.[81] By so limiting their analyses, resistance theorists have ignored less obvious forms of resistance among students and have often misconstrued the political value of overt resistance. For example, some students minimize their participation in routine school practices while simultaneously displaying outward conformity to the school's ideology, opting for modes of resistance that are quietly subversive in the most immediate sense, but that have the potential to be politically progressive in the long run. These students may use humor to disrupt a class, use collective pressure to draw teachers away from class lessons, or purposely ignore the teacher's directions while attempting to develop collective spaces that allow them to escape the ethos of individualism permeating school life. Each type of behavior can indicate a form of resistance if it emerges out of a latent or overt ideological condemnation of the underlying repressive ideologies that characterize schools in general. That is, if we view these acts as practices involving a conscious or semiconscious political response to school-constructed relations of domination, then these students are resisting school ideology in a manner that gives them the power to reject the system on a level that will not make them powerless to protest it in the future. They have not renounced access to knowledge and skills that may allow them to move beyond the class-specific positions of dead-end, alienating labor that most of the showy rebels will eventually occupy.[82]

What resistance theorists have failed to acknowledge is that some students are able to see through the lies and promises of the dominant school ideology but decide not to translate this insight into extreme forms of rebelliousness. In some cases the reason for this decision may be an understanding that overt rebelliousness may result in powerlessness now and in the future. Needless to say, they may also go through school on their own terms and still face limited opportunities in the future. But what is of major importance here is that any other alternative seems ideologically naive and limits whatever transcendent hopes for the future these students may have.[83]

It is the tension between the present reality of their lives and their willingness to dream of a better world that makes such students potential political leaders. Of course, in some cases students may not be aware of the political grounds of their position toward school, except for a general awareness of its dominating nature and the need to somehow escape from it without relegating themselves to a future they do not want. Even this vague understanding and its attendant behavior portend a politically progressive logic, a logic that needs to be incorporated into a theory of resistance.

A fourth weakness of theories of resistance is that they have not given enough attention to the issue of how domination reaches into the structure of personality itself. There is little concern with the often contradictory relation between understanding and action. Part of the solution to this problem may lie in uncovering the genesis and operation of those socially constructed needs that tie people to larger structures of domination. Radical educators have shown a lamentable tendency to ignore the question of needs and desires in favor of issues that center around ideology and consciousness. A critical psychology is needed that points to the way in which "un-freedom" reproduces itself in the psyche of human beings. We need to understand how dominating ideologies prevent many-sided needs from developing in the oppressed, or, in other words, how hegemonic ideologies function to exclude oppressed groups from creating needs that extend beyond the instrumental logic of the market. I am concerned here with such radical needs as those that represent the vital drive toward new relationships between men and women, the generations, different races, and humanity and nature. More specifically, we need to understand how to substitute radical needs organized around the desire for meaningful work, solidarity, an aesthetic sensibility, eros, and emancipatory freedoms for the egoistic, aggressive, calculable greed of capitalist interests. Alienating need structures— those dimensions of our psyche and personality that tie us to social practices and relationships that perpetuate systems of exploitation and the servitude of humanity—represent one of the most crucial areas from which to address a radical pedagogy.

The question of the historical genesis and transformation of needs constitutes, in my mind, the most important basis for a theory of radical educational praxis. Until educators can point to possibilities for the development "of radical needs that both challenge the existing system of interest and production and point to an emancipated society,"[84] it will be exceptionally difficult to understand how schools function to incorporate people, or what that might mean to the establishment of a basis for critical thinking and responsible action. Put another way, without a theory of radical needs and critical psychology, educators have no way of understanding the grip and force of alienating social structures as they manifest themselves in the lived but often nondiscursive aspects of everyday life.[85]

Toward a Theory of Resistance

Resistance is a valuable theoretical and ideological construct that provides an important focus for analyzing the relationship between school and the wider society. More importantly, it provides a new means for understanding the complex ways in which subordinate groups experience educational failure, pointing to new ways of thinking about and restructuring modes of critical pedagogy. As I have noted, the current use of the concept of resistance by radical educators suggests a lack of intellectual rigor and an overdose of theoretical sloppiness. It is imperative that educators be more precise about what resistance actually is and what it is not, and be more specific about how the concept can be used to develop a critical pedagogy. It is also clear that a rationale for employing the concept needs to be considered more fully. I will now discuss these issues and briefly outline some basic theoretical concerns for developing a more intellectually rigorous and politically useful foundation for pursuing such a task.

In the most general sense, resistance must be grounded in a theoretical rationale that provides a new framework for examining schools as social sites which structure the experiences of subordinate groups. The concept of resistance, in other words, represents more than a new heuristic catchword in the language of radical pedagogy; it depicts a mode of discourse that rejects traditional explanations of school failure and oppositional behavior and shifts the analysis of oppositional behavior from the theoretical terrains of functionalism and mainstream educational psychology to those of political science and sociology. Resistance in this case redefines the causes and meaning of oppositional behavior by arguing that it has little to do with deviance and learned helplessness, but a great deal to do with moral and political indignation.

Aside from shifting the theoretical ground for analyzing oppositional behavior, the concept of resistance points to a number of assumptions and concerns about schooling that are generally neglected in both traditional views of schooling and radical theories of reproduction. First, it celebrates a dialectical notion of human agency that rightly portrays domination as a process that is neither static nor complete. Concomitantly, the oppressed are not seen as being simply passive in the face of domination. The notion of resistance points to the need to understand more thoroughly the complex ways in which people mediate and respond to the connection between their own experiences and structures of domination and constraint. Central categories that emerge in a theory of resistance are intentionality, consciousness, the meaning of common sense, and the nature and value of nondiscursive behavior. Second, resistance adds new depth to the notion that power is exercised on and by people within different contexts that structure interacting relations of dominance and autonomy. Thus, power is never unidimensional; it is exercised not only as a mode of domination, but also as an act of resistance. Last, inherent in a radical notion of resistance is an expressed hope for radical transformation, an element of transcendence that seems to be missing in radical theories of education which appear trapped in the theoretical cemetery of Orwellian pessimism.

In addition to developing a rationale for the notion of resistance, there is a need to formulate criteria against which the term can be defined as a central category of analysis in theories of schooling. In the most general sense, I think resistance must be situated in a perspective that takes the notion of emancipation as its guiding interest. That is, the nature and meaning of an act of resistance must be defined by the degree to which it contains possibilities to develop what Herbert Marcuse termed "a commitment to an emancipation of sensibility, imagination and reason in all spheres of subjectivity and objectivity."86 Thus, the central element of analyzing any act of resistance must be a concern with uncovering the degree to which it highlights, implicitly or explicitly, the need to struggle against domination and submission. In other words, the concept of resistance must have a revealing function that contains a critique of domination and provides theoretical opportunities for self-reflection and struggle in the interest of social and self-emancipation. To the degree that oppositional behavior suppresses social contradictions while simultaneously merging with, rather than challenging, the logic of ideological domination, it does not fall under the category of resistance, but under its opposite—accommodation and conformism.

The value of the concept of resistance lies in its critical function and in its potential to utilize both the radical possibilities embedded in its own logic and the interests contained in the object of its expression. In other words, the concept of resistance represents an element of difference, a counter-logic, that must be analyzed to reveal its underlying interest in freedom and its rejection of those forms of domination inherent in the social relations against which it reacts. Of course, this is a rather general set of standards upon which to ground the notion of resistance, but it does provide a notion of interest and a theoretical scaffold upon which to make a distinction between forms of oppositional behavior that can be used for either the amelioration of human life or for the destruction and denigration of basic human values.

Some acts of resistance reveal quite visibly their radical potential, while others are rather ambiguous; still others may reveal nothing more than an affinity for the logic of domination and destruction. It is the ambiguous area that I want to analyze briefly, since the other two areas are self-explanatory. Recently, I heard a "radical" educator argue that teachers who rush home early after school are, in fact, committing acts of resistance. She also claimed that teachers who do not adequately prepare for their classroom lessons are participating in a form of resistance as well. Of course, it is equally debatable that the teachers in question are simply lazy or care very little about teaching, and that what in fact is being displayed is not resistance but unprofessional and unethical behavior. In these cases, there is no logical, convincing response to either argument. The behaviors displayed do not speak for themselves. To call them resistance is to turn the concept into a term that has no analytical precision. In cases like these, one must either link the behavior under analysis with an interpretation provided by the subjects themselves, or dig deeply into the historical and relational conditions from which the behavior develops. Only then will the interest embedded in such behavior be revealed.

It follows from my argument that the interests underlying a specific form of behavior may become clear once the nature of that behavior is interpreted by the person who exhibits it. But I do not mean to imply that such interests will automatically be revealed. Individuals may not be able to explain the reasons for their behavior, or the interpretation may be distorted. In this case, the interest underlying such behavior may be illuminated against the backdrop of social practices and values from which the behavior emerges. Such a referent may be found in the historical conditions that prompted the behavior, the collective values of a peer group, or the practices embedded in other social sites such as the family, the workplace, or the church. I want to stress that the concept of resistance must not be allowed to become a category indiscriminately hung over every expression of "oppositional behavior." On the contrary, it must become an analytical construct and mode of inquiry that is self-critical and sensitive to its own interests—radical consciousness-raising and collective critical action.

Let us now return to the question of how we define resistance and view oppositional behavior, and to the implications for making such distinctions. On one level, it is important to be theoretically precise about which forms of oppositional behavior constitute resistance and which do not. On another level, it is equally important to argue that all forms of oppositional behavior represent a focal point for critical analysis and should be analyzed to see if they represent a form of resistance by uncovering their emancipatory interests. This is a matter of theoretical preciseness and definition. On the other hand, as a matter of radical strategy, *all* forms of oppositional behavior, whether actually resistance or not, must be examined for their possible use as a basis for critical analysis. Thus, oppositional behavior becomes the object of both theoretical clarification and the subject of pedagogical considerations.

On a more philosophical level, I want to stress that the theoretical construct of resistance rejects the positivist notion that the meaning of behavior is synonymous with a literal reading based on immediate action. Instead, resistance must be viewed from a theoretical starting point that links the display of behavior to the interest it embodies, going beyond the immediacy of behavior to the interest that underlies its often hidden logic, a logic that also must be interpreted through the historical and cultural mediations that shape it. Finally, I want to emphasize that the ultimate value of the notion of resistance must be measured not only by the degree to which it promotes critical thinking and reflective action but, more importantly, by the degree to which it contains the possibility of galvanizing collective political struggle among parents, teachers, and students around the issues of power and social determination.

I will now briefly discuss the value of a dialectical notion of resistance for a critical theory of schooling. The pedagogical value of resistance lies, in part, in the connections it makes between structure and human agency on the one hand and culture and the process of self-formation on the other. Resistance theory rejects the idea that schools are simply instructional sites by not only politicizing the notion of culture, but also by analyzing school cultures within the shifting terrain of struggle and contestation. In effect, this represents a new theoretical framework for understanding the process of schooling which places educational knowledge, values, and social relations within the context of antagonistic relations and examines them within the interplay of dominant and subordinate school cultures. When a theory of resistance is incorporated into radical pedagogy, elements of oppositional behavior in schools become the focal point for analyzing different, and often antagonistic, social relations and experiences among students from dominant and subordinate cultures. Within this mode of critical analysis, it becomes possible to illuminate how students draw on the limited resources at their disposal in order to reaffirm the positive dimensions of their own cultures and histories.

Resistance theory highlights the complexity of student responses to the logic of schooling. Thus, it highlights the need for radical educators to unravel how oppositional behavior often emerges within forms of contradictory consciousness that are never free from the reproductive rationality embedded in capitalist social relations. A radical pedagogy, then, must recognize that student resistance in all of its forms represents manifestations of struggle and solidarity that, in their incompleteness, both challenge and confirm capitalist hegemony. What is most important is the willingness of radical educators to search for the emancipatory interests that underlie such resistance and to make them visible to students and others so that they can become the object of debate and political analysis.

A theory of resistance is central to the development of a radical pedagogy for other reasons as well. It helps bring into focus those social practices in schools whose ultimate aim is the control of both the learning process and the capacity for critical thought and action. For example, it points to the ideology underlying the hegemonic curriculum, to its hierarchically organized bodies of knowledge, and particularly to the way in which this curriculum marginalizes or disqualifies working-class knowledge as well as knowledge about women and minorities. Furthermore, resistance theory reveals the ideology underlying such a curriculum, with its emphasis on individual rather than collective appropriation of knowledge, and how this emphasis drives a wedge between students from different social classes. This is particularly evident in the different approaches to knowledge supported in many working-class and middle-class families. Knowledge in the working-class culture is often constructed on the principles of solidarity and sharing, whereas within middle-class culture, knowledge is forged in individual competition and is seen as a badge of separateness.

In short, resistance theory calls attention to the need for radical educators to unravel the ideological interests embedded in the various message systems of the school, particularly those embedded in its curriculum, systems of instruction, and modes of evaluation. What is most important is that resistance theory reinforces the need for radical educators to decipher how the forms of cultural production displayed by subordinate groups can be analyzed to reveal both their limitations and their possibilities for enabling critical thinking, analytical discourse, and learning through collective practice.

Finally, resistance theory suggests that radical educators must develop a critical rather than a pragmatic relationship with students. This means that any viable form of radical pedagogy must analyze how the relations of domination in schools originate, how they are sustained, and how students, in particular, relate to them. This means looking beyond schools. It suggests taking seriously the counter-logic that pulls students away from schools into the streets, the bars, and the shopfloor culture.[87] For many working- class students, these realms are "real time" as opposed to the "dead time" they often experience in schools. The social spheres that make up this counter-logic may represent the few remaining terrains that provide the oppressed with the possibility of human agency and autonomy. Yet, these terrains appear to represent less a form of resistance than an expression of solidarity and self-affirmation.

The pull of this counter-logic must be critically engaged and built into the framework of a radical pedagogy. Yet, this is not to suggest that it must be absorbed into a theory of schooling. On the contrary, it must be supported by radical educators and others from both inside and outside of schools. But as an object of pedagogical analysis, this counter-logic must be seen as an important theoretical terrain in which one finds fleeting images of freedom that point to fundamentally new structures in the public organization of experience.

Inherent in the oppositional public spheres that constitute a counter-logic are the conditions around which the oppressed organize important needs and relations. Thus, it represents an important terrain in the ideological battle for the appropriation of meaning and experience. For this reason, it provides educators with an opportunity to link the political with the personal in order to understand how power is mediated, resisted, and reproduced in daily life. Furthermore, it situates the relationship between schools and the larger society within a theoretical framework informed by a fundamentally political question, How do we develop a radical pedagogy that makes schools meaningful so as to make them critical, and how do we make them critical so as to make them emancipatory?

In short, the basis for a new radical pedagogy must be drawn from a theoretically sophisticated understanding of how power, resistance, and human agency can become central elements in the struggle for critical thinking and learning. Schools will not change society, but we can create in them pockets of resistance that provide pedagogical models for new forms of learning and social relations—forms which can be used in other spheres more directly involved in the struggle for a new morality and view of social justice. To those who would argue that this is a partisan goal, I would reply that they are right, for it is a goal that points to what should be the basis of all learning—the struggle for a qualitatively better life for all.

Notes

1. Marx, *Capital*, I (Moscow: Progress Publishers, 1969), pp. 531, 532.
2. For a critical analysis of the significance of Marx's notion of reproduction in social theory, see Henri Lebevre, *The Survival of Capitalism*, trans. Frank Bryant (New York: St. Martin's Press, 1973). For a critical review of the literature on schooling that takes the notion of reproduction as its starting point see Michael Apple, *Ideology and Curriculum* (London: Routledge & Kegan Paul, 1979); Henry A. Giroux, *Ideology, Culture and the Process of Schooling* (Philadelphia: Temple Univ. Press, 1981); Geoff Whitty and Michael Young, ed., *Society, State, and Schooling* (Sussex, Eng.: Falmer Press, 1977); Len Barton, Roland Meighan, and Stephen Walker, ed., *Schooling, Ideology and Curriculum* (Sussex, Eng.: Falmer Press, 1980); Samuel Bowles and Herbert Gintis, *Schooling in Capitalist America* (New York: Basic Books, 1977).
3. Willis, "Cultural Production and Theories of Reproduction," in *Race, Class and Education*, ed. Len Barton and Stephen Walker (London: Croom-Helm, 1983), p. 110.
4. Bowles and Gintis.
5. Jean Anyon, "Social Class and the Hidden Curriculum of Work," *Journal of Education*, 162 (1980), 67–92.
6. Pierre Bourdieu and Jean Claude Passeron, *Reproduction in Education, Society, and Culture* (Beverly Hills, Calif.: Sage, 1977).
7. Nicos Poulantzas, *Classes in Contemporary Society* (London: Verso Books, 1978).
8. Representative examples include Michael Apple, *Education and Power* (London: Routledge & Kegan Paul, 1982); Richard Bates, "New Developments in the New Sociology of Education," *British*

Journal of Sociology of Education, 1 (1980), 67–79; Robert W. Connell, Dean J. Ashenden, Sandra Kessler, and Gary W. Dowsett, *Making The Difference* (Sydney: Allen & Unwin, 1982); Geoff Whitty, *Ideology, Politics, and Curriculum* (London: Open Univ. Press, 1981); Henry A. Giroux, *Theory and Resistance in Education* (South Hadley, Mass.: Bergin and Garvey, 1983).

9. Paul Willis, *Learning to Labour* (Lexington: Heath, 1977); Women's Study Group, Centre for Contemporary Cultural Studies, ed., *Women Take Issue* (London: Hutchinson, 1978); David Robins and Philip Cohen, *Knuckle Sandwich: Growing Up in a Working-Class City* (London: Pelican Books, 1978); Paul Corrigan, *Schooling and the Smash Street Kids* (London: Macmillan, 1979); Angela McRobbie and Trisha McCabe, *Feminism for Girls* (London: Routledge & Kegan Paul, 1981); Thomas Popkewitz, B. Robert Tabachnick, and Gary Wehlage, *The Myth of Educational Reform* (Madison, Wis.: Univ. of Wisconsin Press, 1982); Robert B. Everhart, "Classroom Management, Student Opposition, and the Labor Process" in *Ideology and Practice in Schooling,* ed. Michael Apple and Lois Weiss (Philadelphia: Temple Univ. Press, forthcoming); Paul Olson, "Inequality Remade: The Theory of Correspondence and the Context of French Immersion in Northern Ontario," *Journal of Education,* 165 (1983), 75–78.

10. Aronowitz, "Marx, Braverman, and the Logic of Capital," *The Insurgent Sociologist,* 8 (1977), 126–146.

11. Michael Apple, "The Hidden Curriculum and the Nature of Conflict," *Interchange,* 2 (1971), 27–40; Henry A. Giroux and Anthony N. Penna, "Social Education in the Classroom: The Dynamics of the Hidden Curriculum," *Theory and Research in Social Education,* 7 (1979), 21–42: Henry A. Giroux and David Purpel, ed., *The Hidden Curriculum and Moral Education* (Berkeley, Calif.: McCutchan, 1983).

12. Martin Camoy and Henry Levin, *The Limits of Educational Reform* (New York: McKay, 1976); W. Timothy Weaver, *The Contest for Educational Resources* (Lexington, Mass.: Lexington Books, 1982).

13. Kathleen Wilcox and Pia Moriarity, "Schooling and Work: Social Constraints on Educational Opportunity," in *Education: Straitjacket or Opportunity,* ed. James Benet and Arlene Kaplan Daniels (New York: Transaction Books, 1980); Roslyn Arlin Mickelson, "The Secondary School's Role in Social Stratification: A Comparison of Beverly Hills High School and Morningside High School," *Journal of Education,* 162 (1980), 83–112; Jean Anyon, "Social Class and School Knowledge." *Curriculum Inquiry,* 11:1 (1981), 3–42.

14. Bowles and Gintis, p. 131.

15. Althusser, *For Marx* (New York: Vintage Books, 1969), *Reading Capital* (London: New Left Books, 1970), and "Ideology and the Ideological State Apparatuses," in his *Lenin and Philosophy, and Other Essays,* trans. Ben Brewster (New York: Monthly Review Press, 1971)·

16. Althusser, "Ideological State Apparatuses," p. 132.

17. Althusser, "Ideological State Apparatuses," pp. 148–158.

18. Althusser, "Ideological State Apparatuses," p. 162.

19. Althusser, *For Marx,* p. 233.

20. Baudelot and Establet, *L'Ecole Capitaliste en France* (Paris: Maspero, 1971).

21. Hegemonic as it is used here refers to elements of unconsciousness, common sense, and consciousness that are compatible with ideologies and social practices that perpetuate existing practices of domination and oppression. This is discussed in greater detail in Giroux, *Theory and Resistance.*

22. Aronowitz, "Cracks in the Bloc: American Labor's Historic Compromise and the Present Crisis," *Social Text,* 5 (1982), 22–52.

23. See Henry A. Giroux, "Hegemony, Resistance, and the Paradox of Educational Reform," *Interchange,* 12 (1981), 3–26.

24. James Donald, "How Illiteracy Became a Problem and Literacy Stopped Being One," *Journal of Education,* 165 (1983), 35–52.

25. Bourdieu and Passeron, *Reproduction*; Bourdieu, *Outline of a Theory of Practice* (Cambridge, Eng.: Cambridge Univ. Press, 1977). It must be noted that the pioneering work in this area was done by Paulo Freire, *Pedagogy of the Oppressed* (New York: Seabury Press, 1970).

26. Bourdeiu and Passeron, *Reproduction*; Bourdieu, "Symbolic Power," *Critique of Anthropology*, 4 (1979), 77–85.

27. Bourdieu, "Symbolic Power," p. 30.

28. Bourdieu and Passeron, *Reproduction*, p.178.

29. Bourdieu, "The School as a Conservative Force: Scholastic and Cultural Inequalities," in *Contemporary Research in the Sociology of Education*, ed. John Eggleston (London: Methuen, 1974), p. 39.

30. The hegemonic curriculum refers to the way in which "schools are organized around a particular organization of learning and content. . . . The crucial features of this curriculum are hierarchically-organized bodies of academic knowledge appropriated in individual competition" (Connell et al., *Making the Difference*, p. 120). The curriculum is hegemonic in that it functions to exclude large numbers of students who are from subordinate classes. Connell et al. were the first to use the term, while Bourdieu and his associates have demonstrated how the hegemonic curriculum works in France's system of higher education.

31. For an illuminating analysis of this issue see Jean Anyon, "Ideology and United States History Textbooks," *Harvard Educational Review*, 49 (1979), 361–386; and Joshua Brown, "Into the Minds of Babes: A Journey Through Recent Children's History Books," *Radical History Review*, 25 (1981), 127–145.

32. Bourdieu, *Outline of a Theory of Practice*; Bourdieu, "Men and Machines," in *Advances in Social Theory and Methodology*, ed. Karin Knorr-Cetina and Aaron V. Cicourel (London: Routledge & Kegan Paul, 1981).

33. Bourdieu, "Men and Machines," p. 305.

34. Bourdieu, *Outline of a Theory of Practice*, p. 83.

35. Pierre Bourdieu and Jean-Claude Passeron, *The Inheritors: French Students and Their Relation to Culture* (Chicago: Univ. of Chicago Press, 1979).

36. Bourdieu, "Men and Machines," p. 314.

37. Bourdieu, *Outline of a Theory of Practice*, p. 94.

38. It must be stressed that the most important work on the politics of the body is to be found in Maurice Merleau-Ponty, *Phenomenology of Perception* (London: Routledge & Kegan Paul, 1962), esp. pp. 67–199.

39. Bourdieu, "The Economics of Linguistic Exchanges," *Social Science Information*, 16 (1977), 645–668.

40. Davies, *Popular Culture, Class, and Schooling* (London: Open Univ. Press, 1981), p. 60.

41. This is particularly true in Bourdieu and Passeron's *Reproduction*.

42. Dale, "Education and the Capitalist State: Contributions and Contradictions," in *Cultural and Economic Reproduction in Education*, ed. Michael Apple (London: Routledge & Kegan Paul, 1982), p. 157.

43. Robert W. Connell, Dean J. Ashenden. Sandra Kessler, and Gary W. Dowsett, "Class and Gender Dynamics in a Ruling Class School," *Interchange*, 12 (1981), 102–117.

44. Sieber, "The Politics of Middle-Class Success in an Inner-City School," *Journal of Education*, 164 (1981), 30–47.

45. Sieber, p. 45.

46. Foucault, *Power and Knowledge: Selected Interviews and Other Writings*, ed. Colin Gordon (New York: Pantheon, 1980).

47. Noelle Bisseret, *Education, Class Language, and Ideology* (London: Routledge & Kegan Paul, 1979).

48. See esp. Bourdieu, "Cultural Reproduction and Social Reproduction," in *Power and Ideology in Education,* ed. Jerome Karabel and Albert H. Halsey (New York: Oxford Univ. Press, 1979); and Bourdieu and Passeron, *Reproduction.*

49. Some representative examples include Ralph Miliband, *The State in Capitalist Society* (New York: Basic Books, 1969); James O'Connor, *The Fiscal Crisis of the State* (New York: St. Martin's Press, 1973); Nicos Poulantzas, *Political Power and Social Classes* (London: New Left Books, 1973), and *Classes in Contemporary Society*; Goran Therborn, *What Does the Ruling Class Do When it Rules* (London: New Left Books, 1978); Philip Corrigan, ed., *Capitalism, State Formation, and Marxist Theory* (London: Quartet Books, 1980).

50. This is a small but growing and important body of literature. Among the more recent works are Roger Dale, Geoff Easland, and Madeleine Macdonald, ed., *Education and the State,* I and II (Sussex, Eng.: Falmer Press, 1980); Mariam E. David, *The State, the Family, and Education* (London: Routledge & Kegan Paul, 1980); Madan Sarup, *Education, State and Crisis* (London: Routledge & Kegan Paul, 1982); Apple, *Education and Power.*

51. Apple, "Reproduction and Contradiction in Education," in *Cultural and Economic Reproduction in Education,* p. 14.

52. Gramsci, *Selections from Prison Notebooks,* ed. and trans. Quintin Hoare and Geoffrey Smith (New York: International Publishers, 1971).

53. Gramsci, pp. 57–58.

54. Chantal Mouffe, "Hegemony and Ideology in Gramsci," in *Gramsci and Marxist Theory,* ed. Chantal Mouffe (London: Routledge & Kegan Paul, 1979), pp. 182–183. It is important to stress that hegemony is not a static concept; on the contrary, hegemony is an active process realized as an uneven and tenuous situation and outcome through which oppositional forces are either accommodated, constrained, or defeated. The relationship between hegemony and political education is treated extensively in Walter Adamson, *Hegemony and Revolution: A Study of Antonio Gramsci's Political and Cultural Theory* (Berkeley: Univ. of California Press, 1980); see also Philip Wexler and Tony Whitson, "Hegemony and Education," *Psychology and Social Theory,* 3 (1982), 31–42.

55. Kenneth Neild and John Seed, "The Theoretical Poverty or the Poverty of Theory," *Economy and Society,* 8 (1979), 383–416.

56. Gramsci, p. 244.

57. Philip Corrigan, Harvie Ramsey, and Derek Sayer, "The State as a Relation of Production," in *Capitalism, State Formation and Marxist Theory,* ed. Philip Corrigan (London: Quartet Books, 1980), p. 21.

58. Corrigan, Ramsey, and Sayer, p. 10.

59. Poulantzas, *Classes in Contemporary Society.* For an important discussion of Marxist theories of the State and the issue of relative autonomy, see Ralph Miliband, "State Power and Class Interests," *New Left Review,* 138 (1983), 57–68.

60. Offe and Ronge, "Thesis on the Theory of the State," *New German Critique,* 6 (1975), 137–147.

61. Althusser, "Ideological State Apparatuses," pp. 127–186.

62. Corrigan, Ramsey, and Sayer, p. 17.

63. See esp. Martin Carnoy, "Education, Economy and the State"; Roger Dale, "Education and the Capitalist State," in *Cultural and Economic Reproduction in Education.*

64. Apple, *Education and Power,* pp. 54–55.

65. Dale, pp. 146–147.

66. Apple, *Education and Power,* p. 95.

67. James Donald, "Green Paper: Noise of a Crisis," *Screen Education,* 30 (1979), 13–49.

68. Poulantzas, quoted in Donald, "Green Paper," p. 21.

69. Poulantzas, *Classes in Contemporary Society,* pp. 259–270.

70. See, for example, Willis, *Learning to Labour*; McRobbie and McCabe, *Feminism for Girls*; Robins and Cohen, *Knuckle Sandwich*; Dick Hebdige, *Subculture: The Meaning of Style* (London: Methuen, 1980).

71. Representative examples of the ethnographic literature in the United States include Howard Becker, *Boys in White* (Chicago: Univ. of Chicago Press, 1961): Arthur Stinchombe, *Rebellion in a High School* (New York: Quadrangle Books, 1964); Harry Wolcott, *The Man in the Principal's Office: An Ethnography* (New York: Holt, Rinehart and Winston, 1973); George Spindler, ed., *Ethnography of Schooling* (New York: Holt, Rinehart and Winston, 1982). Works from England include David Hargreaves, *Social Relations in a Secondary School* (London: Routledge & Kegan Paul, 1967); Colin Lacey, *Hightown Grammar* (Manchester: Manchester Univ. Press, 1970); Peter Woods, *The Divided School* (London: Routledge & Kegan Paul, 1979); Stephen Ball, *Beachside Comprehensive: A Case Study of Secondary Schooling* (London: Cambridge Univ. Press, 1981).

72. Willis, *Learning to Labour,* pp. 99–116.

73. Willis, *Learning to Labour,* pp. 89–116.

74. Fine, "Examining Inequity: View From Urban Schools," Univ. of Pennsylvania, Unpublished Manuscript, 1982.

75. Fine, p. 6.

76. Willis, "Cultural Production and Theories of Reproduction," p. 114.

77. It is important to stress that the opposition displayed by a subordinate group must be seen not only as a form of resistance but also as an expression of a group's struggle to constitute its social identity.

78. Angela McRobbie, "Working Class Girls and the Culture of Femininity," in *Women Take Issue.*

79. A representative example of the work I am criticizing can be found in Nancy King, "Children's Play as a Form of Resistance in the Classroom," *Journal of Education,* 164 (1982), 320–329; Valerie Suransky, "Tale of Rebellion and Resistance: The Landscape of Early Institutional Life," *Journal of Education* (forthcoming). There is a certain irony in that these articles are organized around the concept of resistance without ever providing a rigorous theoretical definition of what the term means.

80. See, for example, Angela McRobbie, "Settling Accounts with Subcultures," *Screen Education,* 34 (1980), 37 49.

81. Walker, "Rebels With Our Applause: A Critique of Resistance Theories," *Journal of Education* (forthcoming).

82. Willis, *Learning to Labour,* pp. 130–137.

83. See Willis, *Learning to Labour,* chs. 8 and 9; Connell et al., *Making The Difference,* ch. 5.

84. Jean Cohen, review of *Theory and Need in Marx,* by Agnes Heller, *Telos,* 33 (1977), 170–184.

85. For an excellent analysis of the relationship between Marxist theory and psychoanalysis, see the differing interpretations by Richard Lichtman, *The Production of Desire* (New York: Free Press, 1982); and Russell Jacoby, *Social Amnesia* (Boston: Beacon Press, 1973).

86. Marcuse, *The Aesthetic Dimension* (Boston: Beacon Press, 1977).

87. I am indebted to a conversation with Stanley Aronowitz for this insight regarding the idea of counter-logic. For an elaborated analysis of this idea, see his *Crisis in Historical Materialism* (New York: Preager, 1981).

⋛ CHAPTER 2 ⋚

Border Pedagogy in the Age of Postmodernism

1988

You must know who is the object and who is the subject of a sentence in order to know if you are the object or subject of history. If you can't control a sentence you don't know how to put yourself into history, to trace your own origin in country, to vocalize, to use your voice. (Pinon, 1982, p. 74)

We are always living out a story. There is no way to live a storyless . . . life. (Michael Novak, cited in Dienske, 1988, p. 23).

Within the last two decades, the varied discourses known as postmodernism have exercised a strong influence on the nature of intellectual life in and out of the university. As a form of cultural criticism, postmodernism has challenged a number of assumptions central to the discourse of modernism. These include modernism's reliance on metaphysical notions of the subject, its advocacy of science, technology, and rationality as the foundation for equating change with progress, its ethnocentric equation of history with the triumphs of European Civilization, and its globalizing view that the industrialized Western countries constitute "a legitimate center—a unique and superior position from which to establish control and to determine hierarchies" (Richard, 1987/1988, p. 6). From the postmodernist perspective, modernism's claim to authority partly serves to privilege Western, patriarchal culture, on the one hand, while simultaneously repressing and marginalizing the voices of those who have been deemed subordinate and/or subjected to relations of oppression because of their color, class, ethnicity, race, or cultural and social capital. In postmodernist terms, the political map of modernism is one in which the voice of the other is consigned to the margins of existence, recognition, and possibility. At its best, a critical postmodernism wants to redraw the map of modernism so as to effect a shift in power from the privileged and the powerful to those groups struggling to gain a measure of control over their lives in what is increasingly becoming a world marked by a logic of disintegration (Dews, 1987). Postmodernism not only makes visible the ways in which domination is being prefigured and redrawn, it also points to the shifting configurations of power, knowledge, space, and time that characterize a world that is at once more global and more differentiated.

One important aspect of postmodernism is its recognition that, as we move into the 21st century, we find ourselves no longer constrained by modernist images of progress and history. Within an emerging postmodern era, the elements of discontinuity, rupture, and difference provide alternative sets of referents by which to understand modernity as well as challenge and modify it. This is a world in which capital no longer is restricted by the imperatives of nationalism; it is a culture in which the production of electronic information radically alters traditional notions of time, community, and history while simultaneously blurring the distinction between reality and image. In the postmodern age, it becomes more difficult not only to define cultural differences in hegemonic colonialist notions of worth and possibility but also to define meaning and knowledge through the master narratives of "great men." Similarly, the modernist emphasis on totality and mastery has given way to a more acute understanding of suppressed and local histories along with a deeper appreciation for struggles that are contextual and specific in scope. In addition, in the age of instant information, global networking, and biogenetics the old distinction between high and popular culture collapses as the historically and socially constructed nature of meaning can no longer be privileged by universalizing claims to history, truth, or class. All culture is worthy of investigation, and no aspect of cultural production can escape its own history within socially constructed hierarchies of meaning.

Another important aspect of postmodernism is that it provides a series of referents both for problematizing some of the most basic elements of modernism and for redrawing and rewriting how individual and collective experience might be struggled over, understood, felt, and shaped. For example, postmodernism presents itself as a critique of all forms of representations and meanings that claim transcendental and transhistorical status. It rejects universal reason as a foundation for human affairs, and poses as alternative forms of knowing that are partial, historical, and social in nature. In addition, postmodernism points to a world in which the production of meaning has become as important as the production of labor in shaping the boundaries of human existence. In this view, how we are constituted in language is no less important than how we are constructed as subjects within relations of production. The political economy of the sign does not displace political economy, it simply assumes its rightful place as a primary category for understanding how identities are forged within particular relations of privilege, oppression, and struggle. Similarly, postmodernism serves to deterritorialize the map of dominant cultural understanding. That is, it rejects the European tradition as the exclusive referent for judging what constitutes historical, cultural, and political truth. There is no tradition or story that can speak with authority and certainty for all of humanity. In contrast, critical postmodernism argues that traditions should be valued for their attempts to name the partial, the particular, the specific; in this view, traditions demonstrate the importance of constituting history as a dialogue among a variety of voices as they struggle within asymmetrical relations of power. Traditions are not valued for their claims to truth or authority, but for the ways in which they serve to liberate and enlarge human possibilities. Tradition does not represent the voice of an all-embracing view of life; instead, it serves to place people self-consciously in their histories by making them aware of the memories constituted in difference, struggle, and hope. Tradition in postmodern terms is a form of counter-memory that points to the fluid and complex identities that constitute the social and political construction of public life.

Finally, and at the risk of great simplification, a postmodernism of resistance challenges the liberal, humanist notion of the unified, rational subject as the bearer of history. In this view, the subject is neither unified nor can such a subject's action be guaranteed in metaphysical or transhistorical terms. Postmodernism not only views the subject as contradictory and multilayered, it rejects the notion that individual consciousness and reason are the most important determinants in shaping human history. It posits instead a faith in forms of social transformation that understand the historical, structural and ideological limits that shape the possibility for self-reflection and action. It points to solidarity, community, and compassion as essential aspects of how we develop and understand the capacities we have for how we experience the world and ourselves in a meaningful way. More specifically, postmodernism offers a series of referents for rethinking how we are constituted as subjects within a rapidly changing set of political, social, and cultural conditions.

What does this suggest for the way we look at the issue of pedagogy? I believe that by combining the best insights of modernism and postmodernism, educators can deepen and extend what is generally referred to as critical pedagogy. We need to combine the modernist emphasis on the capacity of individuals to use critical reason to address the issue of public life with a critical postmodernist concern with how we might experience agency in a world constituted in differences unsupported by transcendent phenomena or metaphysical guarantees. In that way, critical pedagogy can reconstitute itself in terms that are both transformative and emancipatory. This is not to suggest that critical pedagogy constitutes a monolithic discourse and corresponding set of robotlike methods. In fact, the discourse of critical pedagogy as it has developed over the last decade incorporates a variety of theoretical positions that differ in both methodological focus and ideological orientation (Apple & Beyer, 1988; Giroux & McLaren, 1989; Pinar, 1988).

At its worst, critical pedagogy as a form of educational criticism has been overly shaped by the discourse of modernism. Increasingly reduced to a modernist emphasis on technique and procedure, some versions of critical pedagogy reduce its liberatory possibilities by focusing almost exclusively on issues of dialogue, process, and exchange. In this form, critical pedagogy comes perilously close to emulating the liberal-progessive tradition in which teaching is reduced to getting students to merely express or assess their own experiences (i.e., Shor, 1979). Teaching collapses in this case into a banal notion of facilitation, and student experience becomes an unproblematic vehicle for self-affirmation and self-consciousness. Within this perspective, it is assumed that student experience produces forms of understanding that escape the contradictions that inform them. Understanding the limits of a particular position, engaging its contradictory messages, or extending its insights beyond the limits of particular experiences is lost in this position. This position both over-privileges the notion of student voice and simultaneously refuses to engage its contradictory nature. Moreover, this position lacks any sense of its own political project as a starting point from which to define both the role of the teacher in such a pedagogy and the role that the school should play with respect to the larger society. In this version of critical pedagogy, there is a flight from authority and a narrow definition of politics that abandons the utopian project of educating students to both locate themselves in their particular histories and simultaneously confront the limits of their own perspectives as part of a broader engagement with democratic public life.

At its best, critical pedagogy is developed as a cultural practice that enables teachers and others to view education as a political, social, and cultural enterprise. That is, as a form of engaged practice, critical pedagogy calls into question forms of subordination that create inequities among different groups as they live out their lives. Likewise, it rejects classroom relations that relegate difference as an object of condemnation and oppression, and it refuses to subordinate the purpose of schooling to narrowly defined economic and instrumental considerations. This is a notion of critical pedagogy that equates learning with the creation of critical rather than merely good citizens. This is a pedagogy which links schooling to the imperatives of democracy, views teachers as engaged and transformative intellectuals, and makes the notion of democratic difference central to the organization of curriculum and the development of classroom practice.

In what follows, I want to advance the most useful and transformative aspects of this version of critical pedagogy by articulating a theory of what I call a border pedagogy of postmodern resistance. Within this perspective, the issue of critical pedagogy is located within those broader cultural and political considerations that are beginning to redefine our traditional view of community, language, space, and possibility. It is a pedagogy that is attentive to developing a democratic public philosophy that respects the notion of difference as part of a common struggle to extend the quality of public life. In short, the notion of border pedagogy presupposes not merely an acknowledgment of the shifting borders that both undermine and reterritorialize different configurations of power and knowledge, it also links the notion of pedagogy to a more substantive struggle for a democratic society. It is a pedagogy that attempts to link an emancipatory notion of modernism with a postmodernism of resistance.

Border Pedagogy as a Counter-Text

Border pedagogy offers the opportunity for students to engage the multiple references that constitute different cultural codes, experiences, and languages. This means educating students not only to read those codes critically but also to learn the limits of such codes, including the ones they use to construct their own narratives and histories. Partiality becomes, in this case, the basis for recognizing the limits built into all discourses and necessitates taking a critical view of authority. Within this discourse, a student must engage knowledge as a border-crosser, as a person moving in and out of borders constructed around coordinates of difference and power (Hicks, 1988). These are not only physical borders, they are cultural borders historically constructed and socially organized within maps of rules and regulations that limit and enable particular identities, individual capacities, and social forms. In this case, students cross over into borders of meaning, maps of knowledge, social relations, and values that are increasingly being negotiated and rewritten as the codes and regulations which organize them become destabilized and reshaped. Border pedagogy decenters as it remaps. The terrain of learning becomes inextricably linked to the shifting parameters of place, identity, history, and power.

Within critical social theory, it has become commonplace to argue that knowledge and power are related, though the weight of the argument has often overemphasized how domination works through the intricacies of this relationship (Foucault, 1977b). Border pedagogy offers a crucial theoretical and political corrective to this insight. It does so by shifting the emphasis of the knowledge/power relationship away from the limited emphasis on the mapping of domination to the politically strategic issue of engaging the ways in which knowledge can be remapped, reterritorialized, and decentered in the wider interests of rewriting the borders and coordinates of an oppositional cultural politics. This is not an abandonment of critique as much as it is an extension of its possibilities. In this case, border pedagogy not only incorporates the postmodern emphasis on criticizing official texts and using alternative modes of representation (mixing video, photography, and print), it also incorporates popular culture as a serious object of politics and analysis and makes central to its project the recovery of those forms of knowledge and history that characterize alternative and oppositional Others (Said, 1983). How these cultural practices might be taken up as pedagogical practices has been demonstrated by a number of theorists (Brodkey & Fine, 1988; Cherryholmes, 1988; Giroux & Simon, 1988; Scholes, 1985).

For example, Robert Scholes (1985) develops elements of a "border pedagogy" around the notion of textual power. According to Scholes, texts have to be seen in historical and temporal terms and not treated as a sacred vehicle for producing eternal truths. Instead of simply imparting information to students, Scholes argues that teachers should replace teaching texts with what he calls textuality. What this refers to pedagogically is a process of textual study that can be identified by three forms of practice: reading, interpretation, and criticism, which roughly correspond to what Scholes calls reading within, upon, and against a text. In brief, reading within a text means identifying the cultural codes that structure an author's work. But it also has the pedagogical value of illuminating further how such codes function as part of a student's own attempt "to produce written texts that are 'within' the world constructed by their reading" (p. 27). This is particularly important, Scholes adds, in giving students the opportunity to "retell the story, to summarize it, and to expand it." Interpretation means reading a text along with a variety of diverse interpretations that represent a second commentary on the text. At issue here is the pedagogical task of helping students to analyze texts within "a network of relations with other texts and institutional practices" so as to make available to students "the whole intertextual system of relations that connects one text to others—a system that will finally include the student's own writing" (Scholes, 1985, p. 30). The first two stages of Scholes's pedagogical practice are very important because they demonstrate the need for students to sufficiently engage and disrupt the text. He wants students to read the text in terms that the author might have intended so as not to make the text merely a mirror image of the student's own subjective position, but at the same time he wants students to open the text up to a wide variety of readings so it can be "sufficiently other for us to interpret it and, especially to criticize it" (Scholes, 1985, p. 39). Finally, Scholes wants students to explode the cultural codes of the text through the assertion of the reader's own textual power, to analyze the text in terms of its absences, to free "ourselves from [the] text [by] finding a position outside the assumptions upon which the text is based" (p. 62). Scholes combines the best of postmodern criticism with a notion of modernity in his notion of pedagogy. He wants, on the one hand, to engage texts as semiotic objects, but on the other hand he employs a modernist concern for history by arguing that the point of such an interrogation is to "liberate us from the empirical object—whether institution, even, or individual work—by displacing our attention to its constitution as an object and its relationship to the other objects constituted" (Scholes, 1985, p. 84).

Another example of how a postmodern pedagogy of resistance might inform the notion of border pedagogy can be found in some of the recent work being done on educational theory and popular culture (Giroux & Simon, 1988; Giroux & Simon, 1989). Two important issues are being worked out. First, there is a central concern for understanding how the production of meaning is tied to emotional investments and the production of pleasure. In this view, it is necessary for teachers to incorporate into their pedagogies a theoretical understanding of how the production of meaning and pleasure become mutually constitutive of who students are, how they view themselves, and how they construct a particular vision of their future. Second, rethinking the nature of how students make semantic and emotional investments needs to be theorized within a number of important pedagogical considerations. One such consideration is that the production and regulation of desire must be seen as a crucial aspect of how students mediate, relate, resist, and create particular cultural forms and forms of knowing. Another concern is that popular culture be seen as a legitimate aspect of the everyday lives of students and be analyzed as a primary force in shaping the various and often contradictory subject positions that students take up. Finally, popular culture needs to become a serious object of study in the official curriculum. This can be done by treating popular culture either as a distinct object of study within particular academic disciplines such as media studies or by drawing upon the resources it produces for engaging various aspects of the official curriculum (Simon & Giroux, 1988).

In both of these examples, important elements of a border pedagogy informed by postmodern criticism point to ways in which those master narratives based on white, patriarchal, and class-specific versions of the world can be challenged critically and effectively deterritorialized. That is, by offering a theoretical language for establishing new boundaries with respect to knowledge most often associated with the margins and the periphery of the cultural dominant, postmodern discourses open up the possibility for incorporating into the curriculum a notion of border pedagogy in which cultural and social practices need no longer be mapped or referenced solely on the basis of the dominant models of Western culture. In this case, knowledge forms emanating from the margins can be used to redefine the complex, multiple, heterogeneous realities that constitute those relations of difference that make up the experiences of students who often find it impossible to define their identities through the cultural and political codes of a single, unitary culture.

The sensibility which informs this view of knowledge emphasizes a pedagogy in which students need to develop a relationship of non-identity with respect to their own subject positions and the multiple cultural, political, and social codes which constitute established boundaries of power, dependency, and possibility. In other words, such a pedagogy emphasizes the non-synchronous relationship between one's social position and the multiple ways in which culture is constructed and read. That is, there is no single, predetermined relationship between a cultural code and the subject position that a student occupies. One's class, racial, gender, or ethnic position may influence but does not irrevocably predetermine how one takes up a particular ideology, reads a particular text, or responds to particular forms of oppression. Border pedagogy recognizes that teachers, students, and others often "read and write culture on multiple levels" (Kaplan, 1987, p. 187). Of course, the different subject positions and forms of subjugation that are constituted within these various levels and relations of culture have the potential to isolate and alienate instead of opening up the possibility for criticism and struggle. What is at stake here is developing a border pedagogy that can fruitfully work to break down those ideologies, cultural codes, and social practices that prevent students from recognizing how social forms at particular historical conjunctures operate to repress alternative readings of their own experiences, society, and the world.

Border Pedagogy as Counter-Memory

Postmodernism charts the process of deterritorialization as part of the breakdown of master narratives. It celebrates, in part, the loss of certainty and experience of defamiliarization even as it produces alienation and the displacement of identities

(Deleuze & Guattari, 1986). In opposition to conservative readings of this shifting destabilizing process, I believe that such a disruption of traditional meaning offers important insights for developing a theory of border pedagogy based on a postmodernism of resistance. But this language runs the risk of undercutting its own political possibilities by ignoring how a language of difference can be articulated with critical modernist concerns for developing a discourse of public life. It also ignores the possibilities for developing, through the process of counter-memory, new and emancipatory forms of political identity. In what follows, I address some of the important work being done in radical public philosophy and feminist theory, paying particular attention to the issues of identity and counter-memory. The brief final section of this paper will offer some considerations of how the critical insights of a postmodernism of resistance can be deepened within a theory of border pedagogy.

Postmodernism has launched a major attack on the modernist notion of political universality (Ross, 1988). By insisting on the multiplicity of social positions, it has seriously challenged the political closure of modernity with its divisions between the center and the margins and in doing so has made room for those groups generally defined as the excluded others. In effect, postmodernism has reasserted the importance of the partial, the local, and the contingent, and in doing so it has given general expression to the demands of a wide variety of social movements. Postmodernism has also effectively challenged the ways in which written history has embodied a number of assumptions that inform the discourse of Eurocentrism. More specifically, it has rejected such Eurocentric assumptions as the pretentious claim to "speak" for all of mankind (*sic*) and the epistemological claims to foundationalism.

Laclau (1988) rightfully argues that an adequate approximation of the postmodern experience needs to be seen as part of a challenge to the discourses of modernity, with their "pretension to intellectually dominate the foundation of the social, to give a rational context to the notion of the totality of history, and to base in the latter the project of global human emancipation" (pp. 71-72). But Laclau also points out that the postmodern challenge to modernity does not represent the abandonment of its emancipatory values so much as it opens them up to a plurality of contexts and an indeterminacy "that redefines them in an unpredictable way" (p. 72). Chantal Mouffe (1988) extends this insight and argues that modernity has two contradictory aspects: its political project is rooted in a conception of the struggle for democracy, while its social project is tied to a foundationalism which fuels the process of social modernization under "the growing domination of relations of capitalist production" (p. 32). For Mouffe, the modernist project of democracy must be coupled with an understanding of the various social movements and the new politics that have emerged with the postmodern age. At the heart of this position is the need to rearticulate the tradition of liberty and justice with a notion of radical democracy; similarly, there is a need to articulate the concept of difference as more than a replay of liberal pluralism or a pastiche of diverse strands of interests with no common ground to hold them together.

This is not a liberal call to harmonize and resolve differences, as critics like Elizabeth Ellsworth (1988) wrongly argue, but an attempt to understand differences in terms of the historical and social grounds on which they are organized. By locating differences in a particular historical and social location, it becomes possible to understand how they are organized and constructed within maps of rules and regulations and located within dominant social forms which either enable or disable such differences. Differences only exist relative to the social forms in which they are enunciated, that is, in relation to schools, workplaces, families, as well as in relationship to the discourses of history, citizenship, sex, race, gender, and ethnicity. To detach them from the discourse of democracy and freedom is to remove the possibility of either articulating their particular interests as part of a wider struggle for power or understanding how their individual contradictory interests are developed with historically specific conjunctures. At stake here is the need for educators to fashion a critical politics of difference not outside but within a tradition of radical democracy. Similarly, it is imperative for critical educators to develop a discourse of counter-memory, not as an essentialist and closed narrative, but as part of a utopian project that recognizes "the composite, heterogeneous, open, and ultimately indeterminate character of the democratic tradition" (Mouffe, 1988, p. 41). The pedagogical issue here is the need to articulate difference as part of the construction of a new type of subject, one which would be both multiple and democratic. Chantal Mouffe (1988) is worth quoting at length on this issue:

> If the task of radical democracy is indeed to deepen the democratic revolution and to link together diverse democratic struggles, such a task requires the creation of new subject-positions that would allow the common articulation, for example, of antiracism, antisexism, and anticapitalism. These struggles do not spontaneously converge, and in order to establish democratic equivalences, a new "common sense" is necessary, which would transform the identity of different groups so that the demands of each group could be articulated with those of others according to the principle of democratic equivalence. For it is not a matter of establishing a mere alliance between given interests but of actually modifying the very identity of these forces. In order that the defense of workers' interests is not pursued at the cost of the rights of women, immigrants, or consumers, it is necessary to establish an equivalence between these different struggles. It is only under these circumstances that struggles against [authoritarian] power become truly democratic. (p. 42)

How might the issue of democracy and difference be taken up as part of a border pedagogy informed by a project of possibility? I want to argue that the discourses of democracy and difference can be taken up as pedagogical practices through what Foucault calls the notion of counter-memory. For Foucault (1977a), counter-memory is a practice which "transforms history from a judgment on the past in the name of the present truth to a 'counter-memory' that combats our current modes of truth and justice, helping us to understand and change the present by placing it in a new relation to the past" (pp. 160, 163-164). Counter-memory represents a critical reading of not only how the past informs the present but how the present reads the past. Counter-memory provides a theoretical tool to restore the connection between the language of public life and the discourse of difference. It represents an attempt to rewrite the language of resistance in terms that connect human beings within forms of remembrance that dignify public life while at the same time allowing people to speak from their particular histories and voices. Counter-memory refuses to treat democracy as merely inherited knowledge; it attempts, instead, to link democracy to notions of public life that "afford both agency and sources of power or empowering investments" (De Lauretis, 1987, p. 25). It also reasserts as a pedagogical practice the rewriting of history through the power of student voice. This points to the practice of counter-memory as a means of constructing democratic social forms that enable and disable particular subjectivities and identities; put another way, democracy in this instance becomes a referent for understanding how public life organizes differences and what this means for the ways in which schools, teachers, and students define themselves as political subjects, as citizens who operate within particular configurations of power.

In effect, the language of radical democracy provides the basis for educators not only to understand how differences are organized but also how the ground for such difference might be constructed within a political identity rooted in a respect for democratic public life (Giroux, 1988b). What is being suggested here is the construction of a project of possibility in pedagogical terms which is connected to a notion of democracy capable of mobilizing a variety of groups to develop and struggle for what Linda Alcoff (1988) calls a positive alternative vision. She writes, "As the Left should by now have learned, you cannot mobilize a movement that is only and always against: you must have a positive alternative, a vision of a better future that can motivate people to sacrifice their time and energy toward its realization" (Alcoff, 1988, pp. 418-419). If the notion of radical democracy is to function as a pedagogical practice, educators need to allow students to comprehend democracy as a way of life that consistently has to be fought for, has to be struggled over, and has to be rewritten as part of an oppositional politics. This means that democracy has to be viewed as a historical and social construction rooted in the tension between what Bruce James Smith (1985) calls remembrance and custom. I want to extend Smith's argument by developing remembrance as a form of counter-memory and custom as a form of reactionary nostalgia rooted in the loss of memory.

Custom, as Smith (1985) argues, constructs subjects within a discourse of continuity in which knowledge and practice are viewed as a matter of inheritance and transmission. Custom is the complex of ideologies and social practices that views counter-memory as subversive and critical teaching as unpatriotic. It is the ideological basis for forms of knowledge and pedagogy which refuse to interrogate public forms and which deny difference as a fundamental referent for a democratic society. According to Smith (1985), custom can be characterized in the following manner:

The affection it enjoys and the authority it commands are prescriptive. The behavior of the person of custom is, by and large, habitual. To the question "why?" he [sic] is apt to respond simply, "This is the way it has always been done"... A creature of habit, the person of custom does not reflect upon his condition. To the extent that a customary society "conceives" of its practice, it is likely to see it, says, Pocock, as "an indefinite series of repetitions." If the customary society is, in reality, a fluid order always in the process of adaptation, its continuity and incrementalism give rise to perceptions of changelessness and of the simple repetition of familiar motions. . . . Indeed, . . . custom operates as if it were a second nature . . . Custom is at once both more and less inclusive than remembrance. It includes things that are remembered and things that are forgotten. It is almost a definition of custom that its beginnings are lost. (pp. 15-16)

Remembrance is directed more toward specificity and struggle, it resurrects the legacies of actions and happenings, it points to the multitude of voices that constitute the struggle over history and power. Its focus is not on the ordinary but the extraordinary. Its language presents the unrepresentable, not merely as an isolated voice, but as a subversive interruption, a discursive space, that moves "against the grain" as it occupies "a view. . . carved in the interstices of institutions and in the chinks and cracks of the power-knowledge apparati" (De Lauretis, 1987, p. 25). Remembrance is part of a language of public life that promotes an ongoing dialogue between the past, present, and future. It is a vision of optimism rooted in the need to bear witness to history, to reclaim that which must not be forgotten. It is a vision of public life which calls for an ongoing interrogation of the past that allows different groups to locate themselves in history while simultaneously struggling to make it.

Counter-memory provides the ethical and epistemological grounds for a politics of solidarity within difference. At one level, it situates the notion of difference and the primacy of the political firmly within the wider struggle for broadening and revitalizing democratic public life. At the same time, it strips reason of its universal pretensions and recognizes the partiality of all points of view. In this perspective, the positing of a monolithic tradition that exists simply to be revered, reaffirmed, reproduced, or resisted is unequivocally rejected. Instead, counter-memory attempts to recover communities of memory and narratives of struggle that provide a sense of location, place, and identity to various dominant and subordinate groups. Counter-memory as a form of pedagogical practice is not concerned with simply marking difference as a historical construct; rather, it is concerned with providing the grounds for self-representation and the struggle for justice and a democratic society. Counter-memory resists comparison to either a humanist notion of pluralism or a celebration of diversity for its own sake. As both a pedagogical and political practice, it attempts to alter oppressive relations of power and to educate both teachers and students to the ways in which they might be complicitous with dominant power relations, victimized by them, and how they might be able to transform such relations. Abdul JanMohamed and David Lloyd (1987) are instructive on what counter-memory might mean as part of discourse of critique and transformation:

> Ethnic or gender difference must be perceived as one among a number of residual cultural elements which retain the memory of practices which have had to be and still have to be repressed in order that the capitalist economic subject may be more easily produced. . . . "Becoming minor" is not a question of essence but a question of positions—a subject-position that can only be defined, in the final analysis, in "political" terms, that is, in terms of the effects of economic exploitation, political disfranchisement, social manipulation, and ideological domination on the cultural formation of minority subjects and discourses. It is one of the central tasks of the theory of minority discourse to define that subject-position and explore the strengths and weaknesses, the affirmations and negations that inhere in it. (p. 11)

Remembrance as a form of counter-memory attempts to create for students the limits of any story that makes claims to predetermined endings and to expose how the transgressions in those stories cause particular forms of suffering and hardship. At the same time, remembrance as counter-memory opens up the past not as nostalgia but as the invention of stories, some of which deserve a retelling, and which speak to a very different future—one in which democratic community makes room for a politics of both difference and solidarity, for otherness stripped of subjugation, and for others fighting to embrace their own interests in opposition to sexism, racism, ethnocentrism, and class exploitation. Counter-memory is tied in this sense to a vision of public life that both resurrects the ongoing struggle for difference and situates difference within the broader struggle for cultural and social justice.

Counter-memory provides the basis and rationale for a particular kind of pedagogy but it cannot on its own articulate the specific classroom practices that can be constructed on the basis of such a rationale. The formation of democratic citizens demands forms of political identity which radically extend the principles of justice, liberty, and dignity to public spheres constituted by difference and multiple forms of community. Such identities have to be constructed as part of a pedagogy in which difference becomes a basis for solidarity and unity rather than for hierarchy, denigration, competition, and discrimination. It is to that issue that I will now turn.

Border Pedagogy and the Politics of Difference

If the concept of border pedagogy is to be linked to the imperatives of a critical democracy, as it must, it is important that educators possess a theoretical grasp of the ways in which difference is constructed through various representations and practices that name, legitimate, marginalize, and exclude the cultural capital and voices of subordinate groups in American society.

As part of this theoretical project, a theory of border pedagogy needs to address the important question of how representations and practices that name, marginalize, and define difference as the devalued Other are actively learned, interiorized, challenged, or transformed. In addition, such a pedagogy needs to address how an understanding of these differences can be used in order to change the prevailing relations of power that sustain them. It is also imperative that such a pedagogy acknowledge and critically interrogate how the colonizing of differences by dominant groups is expressed and sustained through representations: in which Others are seen as a deficit, in which the humanity of the Others is either cynically posited as problematic or ruthlessly denied. At the same time, it is important to understand how the experience of marginality at the level of everyday life lends itself to forms of oppositional and transformative consciousness. This is an understanding based on the need for those designated as Others to both reclaim and remake their histories, voices, and visions as part of a wider struggle to change those material and social relations that deny radical pluralism as the basis of democratic political community. For it is only through such an understanding that teachers can develop a border pedagogy, one which is characterized by what Teresa De Lauretis (1987) calls "an ongoing effort to create new spaces of discourse, to rewrite cultural narratives, and to define the terms of another perspective—a view from 'elsewhere'" (p. 25). This suggests a pedagogy in which occurs a critical questioning of the omissions and tensions that exist between the master narratives and hegemonic discourses that make up the official curriculum and the self-representations of subordinate groups as they might appear in "forgotten" or erased histories, texts, memories, experiences, and community narratives.

Border pedagogy both confirms and critically engages the knowledge and experience through which students author their own voices and construct social identities. This suggests taking seriously the knowledge and experiences that constitute the individual and collective voices by which students identify and give meaning to themselves and others and drawing upon what they know about their own lives as a basis for criticizing the dominant culture. In this case, student experience has to be first understood and recognized as the accumulation of collective memories and stories that provide students with a sense of familiarity, identity, and practical knowledge. Such experience has to be both affirmed and critically interrogated. In addition, the social and historical construction of such experience has to be affirmed and understood as part of a wider struggle for voice. But it must also be understood that while past experiences can never be denied, their most debilitating dimensions can be engaged through a critical understanding of what was at work in their construction. It is in their critical engagement that such experiences can be re-made, reterritorialized in the interest of a social imagery that dignifies the best traditions and possibilities of those groups who are learning to speak from a discourse of dignity and self-governance. In her analysis of the deterritorialization of women as Other, Caren Kaplan (1987) astutely articulates this position:

> Recognizing the minor cannot erase the aspects of the major, but as a mode of understanding it enables us to see the fissures in our identities, to unravel the seams of our totalities. . . .We must leave home, as it were, since our homes are often sites of racism, sexism, and other damaging social practices. Where we come to locate ourselves in terms of our specific histories and differences must be a place with room for what can be salvaged from the past and made anew. What we gain is a reterritorialization; we reinhabit a world of our making (here "our" is expanded to a coalition of identities—neither universal nor particular). (pp. 187-188)

Furthermore, it is important to extend the possibilities of the often contradictory values that give meaning to students' lives by making them the object of critical inquiry—and by appropriating in a similarly critical fashion, when necessary, the codes and knowledges that constitute broader and less familiar historical and cultural traditions. At issue here is the development of a pedagogy that replaces the authoritative language of recitation with an approach that allows students to speak from their own histories, collective memories, and voices while simultaneously challenging the grounds on which knowledge and power are constructed and legitimated. Such a pedagogy contributes to making possible a variety of social forms and human capacities which expand the range of social identities that students may carry and become. It points to the importance of understanding in both pedagogical and political terms how subjectivities are produced within those social forms in which people move but of which they are often only partially conscious. Similarly, it raises fundamental questions regarding how students make particular investments of meaning and affect, how they are constituted within a triad of relationships of knowledge, power, and pleasure, and why students should be indifferent to the forms of authority, knowledge, and values that we produce and legitimate within our classrooms and university. It is worth noting that such a pedagogy not only articulates a respect for a diversity of student voices, it also provides a referent for developing a public language rooted in a commitment to social transformation.

Central to the notion of border pedagogy are a number of important pedagogical issues regarding the role that teachers might play within the interface of modern and postmodern concerns that have been taken up in this essay. Clearly, the concept of border pedagogy suggests that teachers exist within social, political, and cultural boundaries that are both multiple and historical in nature and that place particular demands on a recognition and pedagogical appropriation of differences. As part of the process of developing a pedagogy of difference, teachers need to deal with the plethora of voices, and the specificity and organization of differences that constitute any course, class, or curriculum so as to make problematic not only the stories that give meanings to the lives of their students, but also the ethical and political lineaments that inform their students' subjectivities and identities.

In part this suggests a pedagogy which does more than provide students with a language and context by which to critically engage the plurality of habits, practices, experiences, and desires that define them as part of a particular social formation within ongoing relations of domination and resistance. Border pedagogy provides opportunities for teachers to deepen their own understanding of the discourse of various others in order to effect a more dialectical understanding of their own politics, values, and pedagogy. What border pedagogy makes undeniable is the relational nature of one's own politics and personal investments. But at the same time, border pedagogy emphasizes the primacy of a politics in which teachers assert rather than retreat from the pedagogies they utilize in dealing with the various differences represented by the students who come into their classes. For example, it is not enough for teachers to merely affirm uncritically their students' histories, experiences, and stories. To take student voices at face value is to run the risk of idealizing and romanticizing them. The contradictory and complex histories and stories that give meaning to the lives of students are never innocent and it is important that they be recognized for their contradictions as well as for their possibilities. Of course, it is crucial that critical educators provide the pedagogical conditions for students to give voice to how their past and present experiences place them within existing relations of domination and resistance. Central to this pedagogical process is the important task of affirming the voices that students bring to school and challenging the separation of school knowledge from the experience of everyday life (Fine, 1987). But it is crucial that critical educators do more than allow such stories to be heard. It is equally important for teachers to help students find a language for critically examining the historically and socially constructed forms by which they live. Such a process involves more than "speaking" one's history and social formation, it also involves engaging collectively with others within a pedagogical framework that helps to reterritorialize and rewrite the complex narratives that make up one's life. This is more than a matter of rewriting stories as counter-memories, it is what Frigga Haug (1988) and her colleagues call memory-work, a crucial example of how the pedagogical functions to interrogate and retrieve rather than to merely celebrate one's voice. She writes:

> By excavating traces of the motives for our past actions, and comparing these with our present lives, we are able to expand the range of our demands and competences. Admittedly, this is not easy as it sounds. Our stories are expressed in the language we use today. Buried or abandoned memories do not speak loudly; on the contrary we can expect them to meet us with obdurate silence. In recognition of this, we must adopt some method of analysis suited to the resolution of a key question for women; a method that seeks out the un-named, the silent and the absent. Here too, our experience of education maps out a ready-made path of analysis; we have been taught to content ourselves with decoding texts, with search for truth in textual analysis, complemented at best by the author's own analysis. "Re-learning" in this context means seeing what is *not* said as interesting, and the fact that it was not said as important; it involves a huge methodological leap, and demands more than a little imagination. (p. 65)

The different stories that students from all groups bring to class need to be interrogated for their absences as well as their contradictions, but they also need to be understood as more than simply a myriad of different stories. They have to be recognized as being forged in relations of opposition to the dominant structures of power. At the same time, differences among students are not merely antagonistic as Liz Ellsworth (1988) has argued. She suggests not only that there is little common ground for addressing these differences, but that separatism is the only valid political option for any kind of pedagogical and political action. Regrettably, this represents less an insight than a crippling form of political disengagement. It reduces one to paralysis in the face of such differences. It ignores the necessity of exploring differences for the specific, irreducible interests they represent, for the excesses and reactionary positions they may produce, and for the pedagogical possibilities they contain for helping students to work with other groups as part of a collective attempt at developing a radical language of democratic public life. Moreover, Ellsworth's attempt to delegitimate the work of other critical educators by claiming rather self-righteously the primacy and singularity of her own ideological reading of what constitutes a political project appears to ignore both the multiplicity of contexts and projects that characterize critical educational work and the tension that haunts all forms of teacher authority, a tension marked by the potential contradiction between being theoretically or ideologically correct and pedagogically wrong. By ignoring the dynamics of such a tension and the variety of struggles being waged under historically specific educational conditions, she degrades the rich complexity of theoretical and pedagogical processes that characterize the diverse discourses in the field of critical pedagogy. In doing so, she succumbs to the familiar academic strategy of dismissing others through the use of strawman tactics and excessive simplifications which undermine not only the strengths of her own work, but also the very nature of social criticism itself. This is "theorizing" as a form of "bad faith," a discourse imbued with the type of careerism that has become all too characteristic of many left academics.

At stake here is an important theoretical issue that is worth repeating. Knowledge and power come together not merely to reaffirm difference but also to interrogate it, to open up broader theoretical considerations, to tease out its limitations, and to engage a vision of community in which student voices define themselves in terms of their distinct social formations and their broader collective hopes. As teachers we can never inclusively speak *as* the Other (though we may be the Other with respect to issues of race, class, or gender), but we can certainly work *with* diverse Others to deepen their understanding of the complexity of traditions, histories, knowledges, and politics that they bring to the schools. This means, as Abdul JanMohemad and David Lloyd (1987) point out, that educators need to recognize the importance of developing a theory of minority discourse which not only explores the strengths and weaknesses, affirmations and negations that inhere in the subject positions of subordinate groups but also "involves drawing our solidarities in the form of similarities between modes of repression and modes of struggle which all minorities separately experience, and experience precisely as minorities" (JanMohamed & Lloyd, 1987, p. 11). To assume such a position is not to practice forms of gender, racial, or class-specific imperialism as Ellsworth suggests; rather, it is to create conditions within particular institutions that allow students to locate themselves and others in histories that mobilize rather than destroy their hopes for the future.

The theoretical sweep may be broad, the sentiment utopian, but it is better than wallowing in guilt or refusing to fight for the possibility of a better world. Sentimentality is no excuse for the absence of any vision for the future. Like Klee's angel in the painting "Angels Novus," modernity provides a faith in human agency while recognizing that the past is often built on the suffering of others. In the best Enlightenment tradition, reason at least offers the assumption and hope that men and women can change the world in which they live. Postmodernism frays the boundaries of that world and makes visible what has often been seen as unrepresentable. The task of modernity with its faith in reason and emancipation can perhaps renew its urgency in a postmodern world, a world where difference, contingency, and power can reassert, redefine, and in some instances collapse the monolithic boundaries of nationalism, sexism, racism, and class oppression. In a world whose borders have become chipped and porous, new challenges present themselves not only to educators but to all those for whom contingency and loss of certainty do not mean the inevitable triumph of nihilism and despair but rather a state of possibility in which destiny and hope can be snatched from the weakening grasp of modernity. We live in a postmodern world that no longer has any firm—but has ever flexing—boundaries. It is a time when reason is in crisis and new political and ideological conditions exist for fashioning forms of struggle defined in a radically different conception of politics. For educators, this is as much a pedagogical issue as it is a political one. At best, it points to the importance of rewriting the relationship between knowledge, power, and desire. It points as well to the necessity of redefining the importance of difference while at the same time seeking articulations among subordinate groups and historically privileged groups committed to social transformations that deepen the possibility for radical democracy and human survival.

References

Alcoff, L. (1988). Cultural feminism vs. poststructuralism: The identity crisis in feminist theory. *Signs, 13*, 405–436.

Apple, M., & Beyer, L. (Eds.) (1988). *The curriculum: Problems, politics and possibilities.* Albany: State University of New York Press.

Brodkey, L., & Fine, M. (1988). Presence of mind in the absence of body. *Journal of Education, 170*(3), 84–99.

Cherryholmes, C. (1988). *Power and criticism: Poststructural investigations in education.* New York: Teachers College Press.

Deleuze, G., & Guattari, F. (1986). *Toward a minor literature.* Minneapolis: University of Minnesota Press.

De Lauretis, T. (1987). *Technologies of gender.* Bloomington: Indiana University Press.

Dews, P. (1987). *Logics of disintegration.* London: Verso Books.

Dienske, I. (1988). Narrative knowledge and science. *Journal of Learning About Learning, 1*(1), 19–27.

Ellsworth, E. (1988). *Why doesn't this feel empowering? Working through the repressive myths of critical pedagogy.* Paper presented at the Tenth Conference on Curriculum Theory and Classroom Practice, Bergamo Conference Center, Dayton, Ohio, October 26–29, 1988.

Fine, M. (1987). Silencing in the public schools. *Language Arts, 64*(2), 157–174.

Foucault, M. (1977a). *Language, counter-memory, practice: Selected essays and interviews* (D. Bouchard, Ed.). Ithaca: Cornell University

Foucault, M. (1977b). *Power and knowledge: Selected interviews and other writings* (G. Gordon, Ed.). New York: Pantheon.

Giroux, H. (1988a). *Schooling and the struggle for public life.* Minneapolis: University of Minnesota Press.

Giroux, H. (1988b). *Teachers as intellectuals.* Granby, MA: Bergin & Garvey.

Giroux, H., & McLaren, P. (1989). Introduction. In H. Giroux & P. McLaren (Eds.), *Critical pedagogy, the state, and cultural struggle*. Albany: State University of New York Press.

Giroux, H., & Simon, R. (1988). Critical pedagogy and the politics of popular culture. *Cultural Studies, 2*, 294–320.

Giroux, H., & Simon, R. (1989). *Popular culture, schooling, and everyday life*. Bergin & Garvey Press.

Haug, F., et al. (1987). *Female sexualization: A collective work of memory*. London: Verso Press.

Hicks, E. (1988). Deterritorialization and border writing. In R. Merrill (Ed.), *Ethics/aesthetics: Post-modern positions* (pp. 47–58). Washington, DC: Maisonneuve Press.

Jameson, F. (1984). Postmodernism or the cultural logic of late capitalism. *New Left Review, 146*, 53–93.

JanMohamed, A. (1987). Introduction: Toward a theory of minority discourse. *Cultural Critique, 6*, 5–11.

JanMohamed, A., & Lloyd, D. (1987). Introduction: Minority discourse—what is to be done? *Cultural Critique, 7*, 5–17.

Kaplan, C. (1987). Deterritorialisations: The rewriting of home and exile in western feminist discourse. *Cultural Critique, 6*, 187–198.

Kellner, D. (1988). Postmodernism as social theory: Some challenges and problems. *Theory, Culture and Society, 5*(2 & 3), 239–269.

Kellner, D. (in press). Boundaries and borderlines: Reflections on Jean Baudrillard and critical theory. *In From Marxism to postmodernism and beyond: Critical studies of Jean Baudrillard*. Oxford: Polity Press.

Kolb, D. (1986). *The critique of pure modernity: Hegel, Heidegger, and after*. Chicago: University of Chicago Press.

Laclau, E. (1988). Politics and the limits of modernity. In A. Ross (Ed.), *Universal abandon? The politics of postmodernism* (pp. 63–82). Minneapolis: University of Minnesota Press.

Laclau, E., & Mouffe, C. (1985). *Hegemony and socialist strategy*. London: Verso Books.

Lash, S., & Urry, J. (1987). *The end of organized capitalism*. Madison: University of Wisconsin Press.

Lunn, E. (1982). *Marxism and modernism*. Berkeley: University of California Press.

Lyotard, J. (1984). *The postmodern condition*. Minneapolis: University of Minnesota Press.

McLaren, P. (1986). Postmodernism and the death of politics: A Brazilian reprieve. *Educational Theory, 36*, 389–401.

McLaren, P. (1988). *Life in schools*. New York: Longman.

Morris, M. (1988). *The pirate's fiancee: Feminism, reading, postmodernism*. London: Verso Press.

Mouffe, C. (1988). Radical democracy: Modern or postmodern? In A. Ross (Ed.), *Universal abandon? The politics of postmodernism* (pp. 31–45). Minneapolis: University of Minnesota Press.

Peller, G. (1987). Reason and the mob: The politics of representation. *Tikkun, 2*(3), 28–31, 92–95.

Pinar, W. (Ed.), (1988). *Contemporary curriculum discourses*. Scottsdale, AZ: Gorsuch Scarisbrick.

Pinon, N. (1982). La contaminación de La Languaje: Interview with Nelida Pinon. *13th Moon, 6*(1 & 2), 72–76.

Richard, N. (1987/1988). Postmodernism and periphery. *Third Text, 2*, 5–12.

Ross, A. (Ed.). (1988). *Universal abandon? The politics of postmodernism*. Minneapolis: University of Minnesota Press.

Said, E. (1983). Opponents, audiences, constituencies, and community. In H. Foster (Ed.), *The anti-aesthetic: Essays on postmodern culture* (pp. 135–139). Port Townsend, WA: Bay Press.

Scholes, R. (1985). *Textual power*. New Haven: Yale University Press.

Shor, I. (1979). *Critical teaching and everyday life*. Boston: South End Press.

Smith, B. J. (1985). *Politics and remembrance*. Princeton: Princeton University Press.

CULTURE AS PEDAGOGY

Cultural Studies,
Public Pedagogy,
and the Politics of
Popular Culture

CHAPTER 3

Doing Cultural Studies

Youth and the Challenge of Pedagogy

1994

In our society, youth is present only when its presence is a problem, or is regarded as a problem. More precisely, the category 'youth' gets mobilized in official documentary discourse, in concerned or outraged editorials and features, or in the supposedly disinterested tracts emanating from the social sciences at those times when young people make their presence felt by going 'out of bounds,' by resisting through rituals, dressing strangely, striking bizarre attitudes, breaking rules, breaking bottles, windows, heads, issuing rhetorical challenges to the law.[1]

A recent commentary in *The Chronicle of Higher Education* claimed that the field of cultural studies is "about the hottest thing in humanities and social-science research right now, but it's largely peopled by scholars in literature, film and media, communications, and philosophy".[2] Given the popularity of cultural studies for a growing number of scholars, I have often wondered why so few academics have incorporated cultural studies into the language of educational reform. If educators are to take seriously the challenge of cultural studies, particularly its insistence on generating new questions, models, and contexts in order to address the central and most urgent dilemmas of our age, they must critically address the politics of their own location. This means understanding not only the ways in which institutions of higher education play their part in shaping the work we do with students, but also the ways in which our vocation as educators supports, challenges, or subverts institutional practices that are at odds with democratic processes and the hopes and opportunities we provide for the nation's youth. In what follows, I want to explore not only why educators refuse to engage the possibilities of cultural studies, but also why scholars working within a cultural studies framework often refuse to take seriously pedagogy and the role of schools in the shaping of democratic public life.

Educational theorists demonstrate as little interest in cultural studies as cultural studies scholars do in the critical theories of schooling and pedagogy. For educators, this indifference may be explained in part by the narrow technocratic models that dominate mainstream reform efforts and structure education programs. Within such a tradition, management issues become more important than understanding and furthering schools as democratic public spheres.[3] Hence, the regulation, certification, and standardization of teacher behavior is emphasized over creating the conditions for teachers to undertake the sensitive political and ethical roles they might assume as public intellectuals who selectively produce and legitimate particular forms of knowledge and authority. Similarly, licensing and assimilating differences among students is more significant than treating students as bearers of diverse social memories with a right to speak and represent themselves in the quest for learning and self-determination. While other disciplines have appropriated, engaged, and produced new theoretical languages in keeping with changing historical conditions, colleges of education have maintained a deep suspicion of theory and intellectual dialogue and thus have not been receptive to the introduction of cultural studies.[4] Other explanations for this willful refusal to know would include a history of educational reform that has been overly indebted to practical considerations that often support a long tradition of anti-intellectualism. Moreover, educators frequently pride themselves on being professional, scientific, and objective. Cultural studies challenges the ideological and political nature of such claims by arguing that teachers always work and speak within historically and socially determined relations of power.[5] Put another way, educators whose work is shaped by cultural studies do not simply view teachers and students either as chroniclers of history and social change or recipients of culture, but as active participants in its construction.

The resistance to cultural studies may also be due to the fact that it reasserts the importance of comprehending schooling as a mechanism of culture and politics, embedded in competing relations of power that attempt to regulate and order how students think, act, and live.[6] Since cultural studies is largely concerned with the critical relationship among culture, knowledge, and power, it is not surprising that mainstream educators often dismiss cultural studies as being too ideological, or simply ignore its criticisms regarding how education generates a privileged narrative space for some social groups and a space of inequality and subordination for others.

Historically, schools and colleges of education have been organized around either traditional subject-based studies (math education) or into largely disciplinary/administrative categories (curriculum and instruction). Within this type of intellectual division of labor, students generally have had few opportunities to study larger social issues. This slavish adherence to structuring the curriculum around the core disciplinary subjects is at odds with the field of cultural studies, whose theoretical energies are largely focused on interdisciplinary issues, such as textuality and representation refracted through the dynamics of gender, sexuality, subordinated youth, national identity, colonialism, race, ethnicity, and popular culture.[7] By offering educators a critical language through which to examine the ideological and political interests that structure reform efforts in education, such as nationalized testing, standardized curriculum, and efficiency models, cultural studies incurs the wrath of mainstream and conservative educators who often are silent about the political agendas that underlie their own language and reform agendas.[8]

Cultural studies also rejects the traditional notion of teaching as a technique or set of neutral skills and argues that teaching is a social practice that can only be understood through considerations of history, politics, power, and culture. Given its concern with everyday life, its pluralization of cultural communities, and its emphasis on multidisciplinary knowledge, cultural studies is less concerned with issues of certification and testing that it is with how knowledge, texts, and cultural products are produced, circulated, and used. In this perspective, culture is the ground "on which analysis proceeds, the object of study, and the site of political critique and intervention."[9] This in part explains why some advocates of cultural studies are increasingly interested in "how and where knowledge needs to surface and emerge in order to be consequential" with respect to expanding the possibilities for a radical democracy.[10]

Within the next century, educators will not be able to ignore the hard questions that schools will have to face regarding issues of multiculturalism, race, identity, power, knowledge, ethics, and work. These issues will play a major role in defining the meaning and purpose of schooling, the relationship between teachers and students, and the critical content of their exchange in terms of how to live in a world that will be vastly more globalized, high tech, and racially diverse than at any other time in history. Cultural studies offers enormous possibilities for educators to rethink the nature of educational theory and practice, as well as what it means to educate future teachers for the twenty-first century.[11]

At the same time, it is important to stress that the general indifference of many cultural studies theorists to the importance of critical pedagogy as a form of cultural practice does an injustice to the politically charged history of cultural studies, one which points to the necessity for combining self-criticism with a commitment to transforming existing social and political problems. It is not my intention here to replay the debate regarding what the real history of cultural studies is, though this is an important issue. Instead, I want to focus on the importance of critical pedagogy as a central aspect of cultural studies and on cultural work as a pedagogical practice. This suggests analyzing cultural studies for the insights it has accrued as it has moved historically from its previous concerns with class and language to its more recent analysis of the politics of race, gender, identity, and ethnicity. This is not meant to suggest that the history of cultural studies needs to be laid out in great detail as some sort of foundational exegesis. On the contrary, cultural studies needs to be approached historically as a mix of founding moments, transformative challenges, and self critical interrogations.[12] And it is precisely the rupturing spirit that informs elements of its interdisciplinary practice, social activism, and historical awareness that prompts my concern for the current lacunae in cultural studies regarding the theoretical and political importance of pedagogy as a founding moment in its legacy.

In what follows, I want to take up these concerns more concretely as they bear on what Dick Hebdige calls the "problem of youth" and the necessary importance of this issue for educators and other cultural workers.[13] In constructing this line of thought, I begin by making the case that pedagogy must become a defining principle of any critical notion of cultural studies. This position is developed, in part, to expand the meaning and relevance of pedagogy for those engaged in cultural work both in and outside of the university. I then argue for the pedagogical practice of using films about youth not only as legitimate objects of social knowledge that offer representations in which youth can identify their desires and hopes, but also as pedagogical texts that play a formative role in shaping the social identities of youth. Through an analysis of four Hollywood films about youth, I hope to show how the more progressive elements of critical pedagogical work can inform and be informed by cultural studies' emphasis on popular culture as a terrain of significant political and pedagogical importance. I will conclude by developing the implications cultural studies might have for those of us who are concerned about reforming schools and colleges of education.

The Absence of Pedagogy in Cultural Studies

It is generally argued that cultural studies is largely defined through its analysis of culture and power, particularly with regard to its "shifting of the terrain of culture toward the popular" while simultaneously expanding its critical reading of the production, reception, use, and effects of popular texts.[14] Texts in this case constitute a wide range of aural, visual, and printed signifiers; moreover, such texts are often taken up as part of a broader attempt to analyze how individual and social identities are mobilized, engaged, and transformed within circuits of power informed by issues of race, gender, class, ethnicity, and other social formations. All of these concerns point to the intellectual and institutional borders that produce, regulate, and engage meaning as a site of social struggle. Challenging the ways in which the academic disciplines have been used to secure particular forms of authority, cultural studies has opened up the possibility for questioning how power operates in the construction of knowledge while simultaneously redefining the parameters of the form and content of what is being taught in institutions of higher education. In this instance, struggles over meaning, language, and textuality have become symptomatic of a larger struggle over the meaning of cultural authority, the role of public intellectuals, and the meaning of national identity. While cultural studies proponents have provided an enormous theoretical service in taking up the struggle over knowledge and authority, particularly as it affects the restructuring of the curriculum in many colleges and universities, such struggles often overlook some of the major concerns that have been debated by various theorists who work within the diverse tradition of critical pedagogy. This is especially surprising since cultural studies draws its theoretical and political inspiration from feminism, postmodernism, post-colonialism, and a host of other areas that have at least made a passing reference to the importance of pedagogy.

I want to argue that cultural studies is still too rigidly tied to the modernist, academic disciplinary structures that it often criticizes. This is not to suggest that it does not adequately engage the issue of academic disciplines. In fact, this is one of its most salient characteristics.[15] What it fails to do is critically address a major prop of disciplinarity, which is the notion of pedagogy as an unproblematic vehicle for transmitting knowledge. Lost here is the attempt to understand pedagogy as a mode of cultural criticism for questioning the very conditions under which knowledge and identities are produced. Of course, theorists such as Gayatri Spivak, Stanley Aronowitz, and others do engage the relationship between cultural studies and pedagogy, but they constitute a small minority.[16] The haunting question here is, What is it about pedagogy that allows cultural studies theorists to ignore it?

One answer may lie in the refusal of cultural studies theorists either to take schooling seriously as a site of struggle or to probe how traditional pedagogy produces particular social histories, how it constructs student identities through a range of subject positions. Of course, within radical educational theory, there is a long history of developing critical discourses of the subject around pedagogical issues.[17]

Another reason cultural studies theorists have devoted little attention to pedagogy may be due to the disciplinary policing that leaves the marks of its legacy on all areas of the humanities and liberal arts. Pedagogy is often deemed unworthy of being taken up as a serious project; in fact, even popular culture has more credibility than pedagogy. This can be seen not only in the general absence of any discussion of pedagogy in cultural studies texts, but also in those studies in the humanities that have begun to engage pedagogical issues. Even in these works there is a willful refusal to acknowledge some of the important theoretical gains in pedagogy that have gone on in the last twenty years.[18] Within this silence lurks the seductive rewards of disciplinary control, a refusal to cross academic borders, and a shoring up of academic careerism, competitiveness, and elitism. Of course, composition studies, one of the few fields in the humanities that does take pedagogy seriously, occupies a status as disparaging as the field of education.[19] Hence, it appears that the legacy of academic elitism and professionalism still exercises a strong influence on the field of cultural studies, in spite of its alleged democratization of social knowledge.

Cultural Studies and Pedagogy

In what follows, I want to make a case for the importance of pedagogy as a central aspect of cultural studies. In doing so, I first want to analyze the role that pedagogy played in the early founding stages of the Birmingham Centre for Cultural Studies.[20] I then want to define more specifically the central dimensions of pedagogy as a cultural practice. But before I address these two important moments of critical pedagogy as a form of cultural politics, I think it is important to stress that the concept of pedagogy must be used with respectful caution. Not only are there different versions of what constitutes critical pedagogy, but there is also no generic definition that can be applied to the term. At the same time, there are important theoretical insights and practices that are woven through various approaches to critical pedagogy. It is precisely these insights, which often define a common set of problems, that serve to delineate critical pedagogy as a set of conditions articulated within the shifting context of a particular political project. These problems include, but are not limited to, the relationship between knowledge and power, language and experience, ethics and authority, student agency and transformative politics, and teacher location and student formations.

Richard Hoggart and Raymond Williams addressed the issue of pedagogy in a similar manner in their early attempts to promote cultural studies in Britain. As founding figures in the Birmingham Centre for Cultural Studies, Hoggart and Williams believed that pedagogy offered the opportunity to link cultural practice with the development of radical cultural theories. Not only did pedagogy connect questions of form and content, it also introduced a sense of how teaching, learning, textual studies, and knowledge could be addressed as political issues that bring to the foreground considerations of power and social agency. According to Williams, the advent of cultural studies in the 1930s and 1940s emerged directly out of the pedagogical work that was going on in adult education. The specificity of the content and context of adult education provided cultural studies with a number of issues that were to direct its subsequent developments in Birmingham. These included the refusal to accept the limitations of established academic boundaries and power structures, the demand for linking literature to the life situations of adult learners, and the call that schooling be empowering rather than merely humanizing.[21]

For Williams there is more at stake here than reclaiming the history of cultural studies; he is most adamant in making clear that the "deepest impulse [informing cultural studies] was the desire to make learning part of the process of social change itself."[22] It is precisely this attempt to broaden the notion of the political by making it more pedagogical that reminds us of the importance of pedagogy as a cultural practice. In this context, pedagogy deepens and extends the study of culture and power by addressing not only how culture is produced, circulated, and transformed, but also how it is actually negotiated by human beings within specific settings and circumstances. In this instance, pedagogy becomes an act of cultural production, a process through which power regulates bodies and behaviors as "they move through space and time."[23] While pedagogy is deeply implicated in the production of power/knowledge relationships and the construction of values and desires, its theoretical center of gravity begins not with a particular claim to new knowledge, but with real people articulating and rewriting their lived experiences within rather than outside of history. In this sense, pedagogy, especially in its critical variants, is about understanding how power works within particular historical, social, and cultural contexts in order to engage and, when necessary, to change such contexts.[24]

The importance of pedagogy to the content and context of cultural studies lies in the relevance it has for illuminating how knowledge and social identities are produced in a variety of sites in addition to schools. For Raymond Williams, one of the founding concepts of cultural studies was that cultural education was just as important as labor, political, and trade union education. Moreover, Williams believed that limiting the study of culture to higher education was to run the risk of depoliticizing it. Williams believed that education in the broad, political sense was essential not only for engaging, challenging, and transforming policy, but was also the necessary referent for stressing the pedagogical importance of work shared by all cultural workers who engage in the production of knowledge. This becomes clear in Williams's notion of permanent education. He writes:

> This idea [permanent education] seems to me to repeat, in a new and important idiom, the concepts of learning and of popular democratic culture which underlie the present book. What it valuably stresses is the education force of our whole social and cultural experience. It is therefore concerned, not only with continuing education, of a formal or informal kind, but with what the whole environment, its institutions and relationships, actively and profoundly teaches. To consider the problems of families, or of town planning, is then an educational enterprise, for these, also, are where teaching occurs. And then the field of this book, of the cultural communications which, under an old shadow, are still called mass communications, can be integrated, as I have always intended, with a whole social policy. For who can doubt, looking at television or newspapers, or reading the women's magazines, that here, centrally, is teaching, and teaching financed and distributed in a much larger way than in formal education?[25]

Building upon Williams's notion of permanent education, pedagogy in this sense provides a theoretical discourse for understanding how power and knowledge mutually inform each other in the production, reception, and transformation of social identities, forms of ethical address, and "desired versions of a future human community."[26] By refuting the objectivity of knowledge and asserting the partiality of all forms of pedagogical authority, critical pedagogy initiates an inquiry into the relationship between the form and content of various pedagogical sites and the authority they legitimate in securing particular cultural practices.

I want to be more specific about the importance of pedagogy for cultural studies and other emerging forms of interdisciplinary work by analyzing how youth are increasingly being addressed and positioned through the popular media, changing economic conditions, an escalating wave of violence, and the emergence of discourse that Ruth Conniff has aptly called "the culture of cruelty."[27] I will then address, both through theory and through examples of my own teaching, how the pedagogy implicit in a spate of Hollywood films about youth culture reinforces dominant racist and cultural stereotypes, but in so doing also creates the conditions for rewriting such films through diverse critical pedagogical strategies.

Mass Culture and the Representation of Youth(s)

Youth have once again become the object of public analysis. Headlines proliferate like dispatches from a combat zone, frequently coupling youth and violence in the interests of promoting a new kind of causal relationship. For example, "gangsta rap" artist Snoop Doggy Dogg was featured on the front cover of an issue of *Newsweek*.[28] This message is that young Black men are selling violence to the mainstream public through their music. But according to *Newsweek*, the violence is not just in the music—it is also embodied in the lifestyles of the rappers who produce it. The potential victims in this case are a besieged White majority of male and female youth. Citing a wave of arrests among prominent rappers, the story reinforces the notion that crime is a racially coded word for associating Black youth with violence.[29]

The statistics on youth violence point to social and economic causes that lie far beyond the reach of facile stereotypes. On a national level, U.S. society is witnessing the effects of a culture of violence in which

> Close to 12 U.S. children aged 19 and under die from gun fire each day. According to the National Center for Health Statistics, "Firearm homicide is the leading cause of death of high school age children in the United States."[30]

What is missing from these reports is any critical commentary on underlying causes that produce the representations of violence that saturate the mass media. In addition, there is little mention of the high numbers of infants and children killed every year through "poverty-related malnutrition and disease." Nor is the U.S. public informed in the popular press about "the gruesome toll of the drunk driver who is typically White."[31] But the bad news doesn't end with violence.

The representations of White youth produced by dominant media within recent years have increasingly portrayed them as lazy, sinking into a self-indulgent haze, and oblivious to the middle-class ethic of working hard and getting ahead. Of course, what the dominant media do not talk about are the social conditions that are producing a new generation of youth steeped in despair, violence, crime, poverty, and apathy. For instance, to talk about Black crime without mentioning that the unemployment rate for Black youth exceeds 40 percent in many urban cities serves primarily to conceal a major cause of youth unrest. Or to talk about apathy among White youth without analyzing the junk culture, poverty, social disenfranchisement, drugs, lack of educational opportunity, and commodification that shape daily life removes responsibility from a social system that often sees youth as simply another market niche.

A failing economy that offers most youth the limited promise of service-sector jobs, dim prospects for the future, and a world of infinite messages and images designed to sell a product or to peddle senseless violence as another TV spectacle, constitutes, in part, the new conditions of youth. In light of radically altered social and economic conditions, educators need to fashion alternative analyses in order to understand what is happening to our nation's youth. Such a project seems vital in light of the rapidity in which market values and a commercial public culture have replaced the ethical referents for developing democratic public spheres. For example, since the 1970s, millions of jobs have been lost to capital flight, and technological change has wiped out millions more. In the last twenty years alone, the U.S. economy lost more than five million jobs in the manufacturing sector.[32] In the face of extremely limited prospects for economic growth over the next decade, schools will be faced with an identity crisis regarding the traditional assumption that school credentials provide the best route to economic security and class mobility for a large proportion of our nation's youth. As Stanley Aronowitz and I have pointed out elsewhere:

> The labor market is becoming increasingly bifurcated: organizational and technical changes are producing a limited number of jobs for highly educated and trained people-managers, scientific and technological experts, and researchers. On the other hand, we are witnessing the disappearance of many middle-level white collar subprofessions . . . And in the face of sharpening competition, employers typically hire a growing number of low paid, part-time workers. . . . Even some professionals have become free-lance workers with few, if any, fringe benefits. These developments call into question the efficacy of mass schooling for providing the "well-trained" labor force that employers still claim they require.[33]

In light of these shattering shifts in economic and cultural life, it makes more sense for educators to reexamine the mission of the school and the changing conditions of youth rather than blaming youth for the economic slump, the culture of racially coded violence, or the hopelessness that seems endemic to dominant versions of the future.

But rethinking the conditions of youth is also imperative in order to reverse the mean-spirited discourse of the 1980s, a discourse that has turned its back on the victims of U.S. society and has resorted to both blaming and punishing them for their social and economic problems. This is evident in states such as Michigan and Wisconsin, which subscribe to "Learnfare" programs designed to penalize a single mother with a lower food allowance if her kids are absent from school. In other states, welfare payments are reduced if single mothers do not marry. Micky Kaus, an editor at The New Republic, argues that welfare mothers should be forced to work at menial jobs, and if they refuse, Kaus suggests that the state remove their children from them. Illiterate women, Kaus argues, could work raking leaves.[34] There is an indifference and callousness in this kind of language that now spills over to discussions of youth. Instead of focusing on economic and social conditions that provide the nation's youth, especially those who are poor and live on the margins of hope, with food, shelter, access to decent education, and safe environments, conservatives such as former Secretary of Education William Bennett talk about imposing national standards on public schools, creating voucher systems that benefit middle-class parents, and doing away with the concept of "the public" altogether. There is more at work here than simply ignorance and neglect.

It is in the dominant discourse on values that one gets a glimpse of the pedagogy at work in the culture of mean-spiritedness. Bennett, for instance, in his new book, *The Book of Virtues: A Treasury of Great Moral Stories*, finds hope in "Old Mr. Rabbit's Thanksgiving Dinner" in which the rabbit instructs us that there is more joy in being helpful than being helped. This discourse of moral uplift may provide soothing and inspirational help for children whose parents send them to private schools, establish trust-fund annuities for their future, and connect them to the world of political patronage, but it says almost nothing about the culture of compressed and concentrated human suffering that many children have to deal with daily in this country. In part, this can be glimpsed in the fact that over seventy percent of all welfare recipients are children. In what follows, I want to draw from a number of insights provided by the field of cultural studies to chart out a different cartography that might be helpful for educators to address what might be called the changing conditions of youth.

Framing Youth

The instability and transitoriness characteristically widespread among a diverse generation of 18- to 25-year-old youth is inextricably rooted in a larger set of postmodern cultural conditions informed by the following: a general loss of faith in the modernist narratives of work and emancipation; the recognition that the indeterminacy of the future warrants confronting and living in the immediacy of experience; an acknowledgement that homelessness as a condition of randomness has replaced the security, if not misrepresentation, of home as a source of comfort and security; an experience of time and space as compressed and fragmented within a world of images that increasingly undermine the dialectic of authenticity and universalism. For many youth, plurality and contingency—whether mediated through media culture, or through the dislocations spurred by the economic system, the rise of new social movements, or the crisis of representation and authority—have resulted in a new world with few secure psychological, economic, or intellectual markers. This is a world in which one is condemned to wander within and between multiple borders and spaces marked by excess, otherness, and difference. This is a world in which old certainties are ruptured and meaning becomes more contingent, less indebted to the dictates of reverence and established truth. While the circumstances of youth vary across and within terrains marked by racial and class differences the modernist world of certainty and order that has traditionally policed, contained, and insulated such difference has given way to a shared postmodern culture in which representational borders collapse into new hybridized forms of cultural performance, identity, and political agency. As the information highway and MTV condense time and space into what Paul Virilio calls "speed space," new desires, modes of association, and forms of resistance inscribe themselves into diverse spheres of popular culture.[35] Music, rap, fashion, style, talk, politics, and cultural resistance are no longer confined to their original class and racial locations. Middle-class White kids take up the language of gangsta rap spawned in neighborhood turfs far removed from their own lives. Black youth in urban centers produce a bricolage of style fashioned from a combination of sneakers, baseball caps, and oversized clothing that integrates forms of resistance and style later to be appropriated by suburban kids whose desires and identities resonate with the energy and vibrancy of the new urban funk. Music displaces older forms of textuality and references a terrain of cultural production that marks the body as a site of pleasure, resistance, domination, and danger.[36] Within this postmodern culture of youth, identities merge and shift rather than become more uniform and static. No longer belonging to any one place or location, youth increasingly inhabit shifting cultural and social spheres marked by a plurality of languages and cultures.

Communities have been refigured as space and time mutate into multiple and overlapping cyberspace networks. Bohemian and middle-class youth talk to each other over electronic bulletin boards in coffee houses in North Beach, California. Cafes and other public salons, once the refuge of beatniks, hippies, and other cultural radicals, have given way to members of the hacker culture. They reorder their imaginations through connections to virtual reality technologies and produce forms of exchange through texts and images that have the potential to wage a war on traditional meaning, but also run the risk of reducing critical understanding to the endless play of random access spectacles.

This is not meant to endorse a Frankfurt School dismissal of popular culture in the postmodern age.[37] On the contrary, I believe that the new electronic technologies with their proliferation of multiple stories and open-ended forms of interaction have altered not only the pedagogical context for the production of subjectivities, but also how people "take in information and entertainment."[38] Produced from the centers of power, mass culture has spawned in the name of profit and entertainment a new level of instrumental and commodified culture. On the other hand, popular culture offers resistance to the notion that useful culture can only be produced within dominant regimes of power. This distinction between mass and popular culture is not meant to suggest that popular culture is strictly a terrain of resistance. Popular culture does not escape commodification, racism, sexism, and other forms of oppression, but it is marked by fault lines that reject the high/low culture divide while simultaneously attempting to affirm a multitude of histories, experiences, cultural forms, and pleasures. Within the conditions of postmodern culture, values no longer emerge unproblematically from the modernist pedagogy of foundationalism and universal truths, or from traditional narratives based on fixed identities with their requisite structure of closure. For many youths, meaning is in rout, media has become a substitute for experience, and what constitutes understanding is grounded in a decentered and diasporic world of difference, displacement, and exchanges.

The intersection among cultural studies and pedagogy can be made more clear through an analysis of how the pedagogy of Hollywood has attempted in some recent films to portray the plight of young people within the conditions of a postmodern culture. I will focus on four films: *River's Edge* (1986), *My Own Private Idaho* (1991), *Slacker* (1991), and *Juice* (1992). These films are important as arguments and framing devices that in diverse ways attempt to provide a pedagogical representation of youth. They point to some of the economic and social conditions at work in the formation of different racial and economic strata of youth, but they often do so within a narrative that combines a politics of despair with a fairly sophisticated depiction of the alleged sensibilities and moods of a generation of youth growing up amid the fracturing and menacing conditions of a postmodern culture. The challenge for progressive educators is to question how a critical pedagogy might be employed to appropriate the more radical and useful aspects of cultural studies in addressing the new and different social, political, and economic contexts that are producing the twenty-something generation. At the same time, there is the issue of how a politics and project of pedagogy might be constructed to create the conditions for social agency and institutionalized change among diverse sectors of youth.

White Youth and the Politics of Despair

For many youth, showing up for adulthood at the fin de siècle means pulling back on hope and trying to put off the future rather than taking up the modernist challenge of trying to shape it.[39] Popular cultural criticism has captured much of the ennui among youth and has made clear that "what used to be the pessimism of a radical fringe is now the shared assumption of a generation."[40] Cultural studies has helped to temper this broad generalization about youth in order to investigate the more complex representations at work in the construction of a new generation of youth that cannot be simply abstracted from the specificities of race, class, or gender. And yet, cultural studies theorists have also pointed to the increasing resistance of a twenty-something generation of youth who seem neither motivated by nostalgia for some lost conservative vision of America nor at home in the New World Order paved with the promises of the expanding electronic information highway.[41] While "youth" as a social construction has always been mediated, in part, as a social problem, many cultural critics believe that postmodern youth are uniquely "alien," "strange," and disconnected from the real world. For instance, in Gus Van Sant's film *My Own Private Idaho*, the main character, Mike, who hustles his sexual wares for money, is a dreamer lost in fractured memories of a mother who deserted him as a child. Caught between flashbacks of Mom, shown in 8-mm color, and the video world of motley street hustlers and their clients, Mike moves through his existence by falling asleep in times of stress only to awaken in different geographic and spatial locations. What holds Mike's psychic and geographic travels together is the metaphor of sleep, the dream of escape, and the ultimate realization that even memories cannot fuel hope for the future. Mike becomes a metaphor for an entire generation of lower middle-class youth forced to sell themselves in a world with no hope, a generation that aspires to nothing, works at degrading McJobs, and lives in a world in which chance and randomness rather than struggle, community, and solidarity drive their fate.

A more disturbing picture of White, working-class youth can be found in *River's Edge*. Teenage anomie and drugged apathy are given painful expression in the depiction of a group of working-class youth who are casually told by John, one of their friends, that he has strangled his girlfriend, another member of the group, and left her nude body on the riverbank. The group at different times visits the site to view and probe the dead body of the girl. Seemingly unable to grasp the significance of the event, the youth initially hold off from informing anyone of the murder and with different degrees of concern initially try to protect John, the teenage sociopath, from being caught by the police. The youth in *River's Edge* drift through a world of broken families, blaring rock music, schooling marked by dead time, and a general indifference. Decentered and fragmented, they view death, like life itself, as merely a spectacle, a matter of style rather than substance. In one sense, these youth share the quality of being "asleep" that is depicted in *My Own Private Idaho*. But what is more disturbing in *River's Edge* is that lost innocence gives way not merely to teenage myopia, but also to a culture in which human life is experienced as a voyeuristic seduction, a video game, good for passing time and diverting oneself from the pain of the moment. Despair and indifference cancel out the language of ethical discriminations and social responsibility while elevating the immediacy of pleasure to the defining moment of agency. In *River's Edge*, history as social memory is reassembled through vignettes of 1960s types portrayed as either burned-out bikers or as the ex-radical turned teacher whose moralizing relegates politics to simply cheap opportunism. Exchanges among the young people in *River's Edge* appear like projections of a generation waiting either to fall asleep or to commit suicide. After talking about how he murdered his girlfriend, John blurts out, "You do shit, it's done, and then you die." Another character responds, "It might be easier being dead." To which her boyfriend replies, "Bullshit, you couldn't get stoned anymore." In this scenario, life imitates art when committing murder and getting stoned are given equal moral weight in the formula of the Hollywood spectacle, a spectacle that in the end flattens the complex representations of youth while constructing their identities through ample servings of pleasure, death, and violence.

River's Edge and *My Own Private Idaho* reveal the seamy and dark side of a youth culture while employing the Hollywood mixture of fascination and horror to titillate the audiences drawn to these films. Employing the postmodern aesthetic of revulsion, locality, randomness, and senselessness, the youth in these films appear to be constructed outside of a broader cultural and economic landscape. Instead, they become visible only through visceral expressions of psychotic behavior or the brooding experience of a self-imposed comatose alienation.

One of the more celebrated White youth films of the 1990s is Richard Linklater's *Slacker*. A decidedly low-budget film, *Slacker* attempts in both form and content to capture the sentiments of a twenty-something generation of middle-class White youth who reject most of the values of the Reagan/Bush era but have a difficult time imagining what an alternative might look like. Distinctly non-linear in format,

Slacker takes place in a twenty-four-hour time frame in the college town of Austin, Texas. Building upon an anti-narrative structure, *Slacker* is loosely organized around brief episodes in the lives of a variety of characters, none of whom are connected to each other except to provide the pretext to lead the audience to the next character in the film. Sweeping through bookstores, coffee shops, auto-parts yards, bedrooms, and rock music clubs, *Slacker* focuses on a disparate group of young people who possess little hope in the future and drift from job to job speaking a hybrid argot of bohemian intensities and New Age pop-cult babble.

The film portrays a host of young people who randomly move from one place to the next, border crossers with little, if any, sense of where they have come from or where they are going. In this world of multiple realities, youth work in bands with the name "Ultimate Loser" and talk about being forcibly put in hospitals by their parents. One neo-punker even attempts to sell a Madonna pap smear to two acquaintances she meets in the street: "Check it out, I know it's kind of disgusting, but it's sort of like getting down to the real Madonna." This is a world in which language is wedded to an odd mix of nostalgia, popcorn philosophy, and MTV babble. Talk is organized around comments like: "I don't know. . . I've traveled . . . and when you get back you can't tell whether it really happened to you or if you just saw it on TV." Alienation is driven inward and emerges in comments like "I feel stuck." Irony slightly overshadows a refusal to imagine any kind of collective struggle. Reality seems too despairing to care about. This is humorously captured in one instance by a young man who suggests: "You know how the slogan goes, workers of the world, unite? We say workers of the world, relax?" People talk, but appear disconnected from themselves and each other, lives traverse each other with no sense of community or connection. There is a pronounced sense in *Slacker* of youth caught in the throes of new information technologies that both contain their aspiration and at the same time hold out the promise of some sense of agency.

At rare moments in the films, the political paralysis of narcissistic forms of refusal is offset by instances in which some characters recognize the importance of the image as a vehicle for cultural production, as a representational apparatus that can not only make certain experiences available but can also be used to produce alternative realities and social practices. The power of the image is present in the way the camera follows characters throughout the film, at once stalking them and confining them to a gaze that is both constraining and incidental. In one scene, a young man appears in a video apartment surrounded by televisions that he claims he has had on for years. He points out that he has invented a game called a "Video Virus" in which, through the use of a special technology, he can push a button and insert himself onto any screen and perform any one of a number of actions. When asked by another character what this is about, he answers: "Well, we all know the psychic powers of the televised image. But we need to capitalize on it and make it work for us instead of working for it." This theme is taken up in two other scenes. In one short clip, a graduate history student shoots the video camera he is using to film himself, indicating a self-consciousness about the power of the image and ability to control it at the same time. In the concluding scene, a carload of people, each equipped with their Super 8 cameras, drive up to a large hill and throw their cameras into a canyon. The film ends with the images being recorded by the cameras as they cascade to the bottom of the cliff in what suggests a moment of release and liberation.

In many respects, these movies largely focus on a culture of White male youth who are both terrified and fascinated by the media, who appear overwhelmed by "the danger and wonder of future technologies, the banality of consumption, the thrill of brand names, [and] the difficulty of sex in alienated relationships."[42] The significance of these films rests, in part, in their attempt to capture the sense of powerlessness that increasingly affects working-class and middle-class White youth. But what is missing from these films, along with the various books, articles, and reportage concerning what is often called the "Nowhere Generation," "Generation X," "13th Gen," or "Slackers," is any sense of the larger political, racial, and social conditions in which youth are being framed, as well as the multiple forms of resistance and racial diversity that exist among many different youth formations. What in fact should be seen as a social commentary about "dead-end capitalism" emerges simply as a celebration of refusal dressed up in a rhetoric of aesthetics, style, fashion, and solipsistic protests. Within this type of commentary, postmodern criticism is useful but limited because of its often theoretical inability to take up the relationship between identity and power, biography and the commodification of everyday life, or the limits of agency in an increasingly globalized economy as part of a broader project of possibility linked to issues of history, struggle, and transformation.[43]

In spite of the totalizing image of domination that structures *River's Edge* and *My Own Private Idaho*, and the lethal hopelessness that permeates *Slacker*, all of these films provide opportunities for examining the social and cultural context to which they refer in order to enlarge the range of strategies and understandings that students might bring to them to create a sense of resistance and transformation. For instance, many of my students who viewed Slacker did not despair over the film, but interpreted it to mean that "going slack" was viewed as a moment in the lives of young people that, with the proper resources, offered them a period in which to think, move around the country, and chill out in order to make some important decisions about the lives. Going slack became increasingly more oppressive as the slack time became drawn out far beyond their ability to end or control it. The students also pointed out that this film was made by Linklater and his friends with a great deal of energy and gusto, which in itself offers a pedagogical model for young people to take up in developing their own narratives.

Black Youth and the Violence of Race

With the explosion of rap music into the sphere of popular culture and the intense debates that have emerged around the crisis of Black masculinity, the issue of Black nationalism, and the politics of Black urban culture, it is not surprising that the Black cinema has produced a series of films about the coming of age of Black youth in urban America. What is unique about these films is that, unlike the Black exploitation films of the 1970s, which were made by White producers for Black audiences, the new wave of Black cinema is being produced by Black directors and aimed at Black audiences.[44] With the advent of the 1990s, Hollywood has cashed in on a number of talented young Black directors such as Spike Lee, Allen and Albert Hughes, Julie Dash, Ernest Dickerson, and John Singleton. Films about Black youth have become big business—in 1991 *New Jack City* and *Boyz N the Hood* pulled in over 100 million dollars between them. Largely concerned with the inequalities, oppression, daily violence, and diminishing hopes that plague Black communities in the urban war zone, the new wave of Black films has attempted to accentuate the economic and social conditions that have contributed to the construction of "Black masculinity and its relationship to the ghetto culture in which ideals of masculinity are nurtured and shaped."[45]

Unlike many of the recent films about White youth whose coming-of-age narratives are developed within traditional sociological categories such as alienation, restlessness, and anomie, Black film productions such as Ernest Dickerson's *Juice* (1992) depict a culture of nihilism that is rooted directly in a violence whose defining principles are homicide, cultural suicide, internecine warfare, and social decay. It is interesting to note that just as the popular press has racialized crime, drugs, and violence as a Black problem, some of the most interesting films to appear recently about Black youth have been given the Hollywood imprimatur of excellence and have moved successfully as crossover films to a White audience. In what follows, I want briefly to probe the treatment of Black youth and the representations of masculinity and resistance in the exemplary Black film, *Juice.*

Juice (street slang for respect) is the story of four young Harlem African-American youth who are first portrayed as kids who engage in the usual antics of skipping school, fighting with other kids in the neighborhood, clashing with their parents about doing homework, and arguing with their siblings over using the bathroom in the morning. If this portrayal of youthful innocence is used to get a general audience to comfortably identify with these four Black youth, it is soon ruptured as the group, caught in a spiraling wave of poverty and depressed opportunities, turn to crime and violence as a way to both construct their manhood and solve their most immediate problems. Determined to give their lives some sense of agency, the group moves from ripping off a record store to burglarizing a grocery market to the ruthless murder of the store owner and eventually each other. Caught in a world in which the ethics of the street are mirrored in the spectacle of TV violence, Bishop, Quincy, Raheem, and Steel (Tupac Shakur, Omar Epps, Kahalil Kain, and Jermaine Hopkins) decided, after watching James Cagney go up in a blaze of glory in *White Heat*, to take control of their lives by buying a gun and sticking up a neighborhood merchant who once chased them out of his store. Quincy is hesitant about participating in the stick-up because he is a talented disc jockey and is determined to enter a local deejay contest in order to take advantage of his love of rap music and find a place for himself in the world.

Quincy is the only Black youth in the film who models a sense of agency that is not completely caught in the confusion and despair exhibited by his three friends. Trapped within the loyalty codes of the street and in the protection it provides, Quincy reluctantly agrees to participate in the heist. Bad choices have major consequences in this typical big-city ghetto, and Quincy's sense of hope and independence is shattered as Bishop, the most violent of the group, kills the store owner and then proceeds to murder Raheem and hunt down Quincy and Steele, since they no longer see him as a respected member of the group. Quincy eventually buys a weapon to protect himself, and in the film's final scene, confronts Bishop on the roof. A struggle ensues, and Bishop plunges to his death. As the film ends, one onlooker tells Quincy, "You got the juice," but Quincy rejects the accolade ascribing power and prestige to him and walks away.

Juice reasserts the importance of rap music as the cultural expression of imaginable possibilities in the daily lives of Black youth. Not only does rap music provide the musical score that frames the film, it also plays a pivotal role by socially contextualizing the desires, rage, and independent expression of Black male artists. For Quincy, rap music offers him the opportunity to claim some "juice" among his peers while simultaneously providing him with a context to construct an affirmative identity along with the chance for real employment. Music in this context becomes a major referent for understanding how identities and bodies come together in a hip-hop culture that at its most oppositional moment is testing the limits of the American dream. But *Juice* also gestures, through the direction of Ernest Dickerson, that if violence is endemic to the Black ghetto, its roots lie in a culture of violence that is daily transmitted through the medium of television. This is suggested in one powerful scene in which the group watch on television both the famed violent ending of James Cagney's *White Heat*, and the news bulletin announcing the death of a neighborhood friend as he attempted to rip off a local bar. In this scene, Dickerson draws a powerful relationship between what the four youth see on television and their impatience over their own lack of agency and need to take control of their lives. As Michael Dyson points out:

> Dickerson's aim is transparent: to highlight the link between violence and criminality fostered in the collective American imagination by television, the consumption of images through a medium that has replaced the Constitution and the Declaration of Independence as the unifying fiction of national citizenship and identity. It is also the daily and exclusive occupation of Bishop's listless father, a reminder that television's genealogy of influence unfolds from its dulling effects in one generation to its creation of lethal desires in the next, twin strategies of destruction when applied in the black male ghetto.46

While Dyson is right in pointing to Dickerson's critique of the media, he overestimates the importance given in *Juice* to the relationship between Black-on-Black

violence and those larger social determinants that Black urban life both reflects and
helps to produce. In fact, it could be argued that the violence portrayed in *Juice* and
similar films, such as *Boyz N the Hood*, *New Jack City*, and especially *Menace II
Society*, "feeds the racist national obsession that Black men and their community are
the central locus of the American scene of violence."[47]

Although the violence in these films is traumatizing as part of the effort to promote an anti-violence message, it is also a violence that is hermetic, sutured, and
sealed within the walls of the Black urban ghetto. While the counterpart of this
type of violence, in controversial White films such as *Reservoir Dogs* is taken up by
most critics as part of an avant garde aesthetic, the violence in the recent wave of
Black youth films often reinforces for middle-class viewers the assumption that such
violence is endemic to the Black community. The only salvation gained in portray-
ing such inner-city hopelessness is that it be noticed so that it can be stopped from
spreading like a disease into the adjoining suburbs and business zones that form a
colonizing ring around Black ghettoes. Because films such as *Juice* do not self-consciously rupture dominant stereotypical assumptions that make race and crime synonymous, they often suggest a kind of nihilism that Cornel West describes as "the
lived experience of coping with a life of horrifying meaninglessness, hopelessness
and (most important) lovelessness."[48]

Unfortunately, West's notion of nihilism is too tightly drawn and while it may
claim to pay attention to the loss of hope and meaning among Black youth, it fails to
connect the specificity of Black nihilism to the nihilism of systemic inequality, calculated injustice, and moral indifference that operates daily as a regime of brutalization
and oppression for so many poor youth and youth of color in this country. Itabari
Njeri forcefully captures the failure of such an analysis and the problems that films
such as *Juice*, in spite of the best intentions of their directors, often reproduce. Commenting on another coming-of-age Black youth film, *Menace II Society*, he writes:

> The nation cannot allow nearly 50% of black men to be unemployed, as is the case in many
> African-American communities. It cannot let schools systematically brand normal black chil-
> dren as uneducable for racist reasons, or permit the continued brutalization of blacks by
> police, or have black adults take out their socially engendered frustrations on each other and
> their children and not yield despair and dysfunction. This kind of despair is the source of the
> nihilism Cornel West described. Unfortunately, the black male-as-menace film genre often
> fails to artfully tie this nihilism to its poisonous roots in America's system of inequality. And
> because it fails to do so, the effects of these toxic forces are seen as causes.[49]

In both pedagogical and political terms, the reigning films about Black youth that
have appeared since 1990 may have gone too far in producing narratives that employ
the commercial strategy of reproducing graphic violence and then moralizing about
its effects. Violence in these films is tied to a self-destructive-ness and senselessness
that shocks but often fails to inform the audience about either its wider determina-
tions or the audience's possible complicity in such violence. The effects of such films

tend to reinforce for White middle-class America the comforting belief that nihilism as both a state of mind and a site of social relations is always somewhere else—in that strangely homogenized social formation known as "Black" youth.

Of course it is important to note that *Juice* refrains from romanticizing violence, just as it suggests at the end of the film that Quincy does not want the juice if it means leading a life in which violence is the only capital that has any exchange value in African-American communities. But these sentiments come late and are too underdeveloped. One pedagogical challenge presented by this film is for educators and students to theorize about why Hollywood is investing in films about Black youth that overlook the complex representations that structure African-American communities. Such an inquiry can be taken up by looking at the work of Black feminist film makers such as Julie Dash, and the powerful and complex representations she offers Black women in *Daughters of the Dust,* or the work of Leslie Harris, whose film *Just Another Girl on the IRT* challenges the misogyny that structures the films currently being made about Black male youth. Another challenge involves trying to understand why large numbers of Black, urban, male youth readily identify with the wider social representations of sexism, homophobia, misogyny, and gaining respect at such a high cost to themselves and the communities in which they live. Films about Black youth are important to engage in order to understand both the pedagogies that silently structure their representations and how such representations pedagogically work to educate crossover White audiences. Most importantly, these films should not be dismissed because they are reductionist, sexist, or one dimensional in their portrayal of the rite of passage of Black male youth; at most, they become a marker for understanding how complex representations of Black youth get lost in racially coded films that point to serious problems in the urban centers, but do so in ways that erase any sense of viable hope, possibility, resistance, and struggle.

Contemporary films about Black youth offer a glimpse into the specificity of otherness; that is, they cross a cultural and racial border and in doing so perform a theoretical service in making visible what is often left out of the dominant politics of representations. And it is in the light of such an opening that the possibility exists for educators and other cultural workers to take up the relationship among culture, power, and identity in ways that grapple with the complexity of youth and the intersection of race, class, and gender formations.

Combining cultural studies with pedagogical theory would suggest that students take these films seriously as legitimate forms of social knowledge that reveal different sets of struggles among youth within diverse cultural sites. For White youth, these films mimic a coming-of-age narrative that indicts the aimlessness and senselessness produced within a larger culture of commercial stupidification; on the other hand, Black youth films posit a *not* coming-of-age narrative that serves as a powerful indictment of the violence being waged against and among African-American youth. Clearly, educators can learn from these films and in doing so bring these different accounts of the cultural production of youth together within a common project that addresses the relationship between pedagogy and social justice, on the one hand, and democracy and the struggle for equality on the other. These films suggest that educators need to ask new questions, and develop new models and new ways of producing an oppositional pedagogy that is capable of understanding the different social, economic, and political contexts that produce youth differently within varied sets and relations of power.

Another pedagogical challenge offered by these films concerns how teachers can address the desires that different students bring to these popular cultural texts. In other words, what does it mean to mobilize the desires of students by using forms of social knowledge that constitute the contradictory field of popular culture? In part, it means recognizing that while students are familiar with such texts, they bring different beliefs, political understandings, and affective investments to such a learning process. Hence, pedagogy must proceed by acknowledging that conflict will emerge regarding the form and content of such films and how students address such issues. For such a pedagogy to work, Fabienne Worth argues that "students must become visible to themselves and to each other and valued in their differences."[50] This suggests giving students the opportunity to decenter the curriculum by structuring, in part, how the class should be organized and how such films can be addressed without putting any one student's identity on trial. It means recognizing the complexity of attempting to mobilize students' desires as part of a pedagogical project that directly addresses representations that affect certain parts of their lives, and to acknowledge the emotional problems that will emerge in such teaching.

At the same time, such a pedagogy must reverse the cycle of despair that often informs these accounts and address how the different postmodern conditions and contexts of youth can be changed in order to expand and deepen the promise of a substantive democracy. In part, this may mean using films about youth that capture the complexity, sense of struggle, and diversity that mark different segments of the current generation of young people. In this case, cultural studies and pedagogical practice can mutually inform each other by using popular cultural texts as serious objects of study. Such texts can be used to address the limits and possibilities that youth face in different social, cultural, and economic contexts. Equally important is the need to read popular cultural texts as part of a broader pedagogical effort to develop a sense of agency in students based on a commitment to changing oppressive contexts by understanding the relations of power that inform them.

The pedagogical challenge represented by the emergence of a postmodern generation of youth has not been lost on advertisers and market research analysts. According to a 1992 study by the Roper Organization, the current generation of 18- to 29-year-olds have an annual buying power of $125 billion. Addressing the interests and tastes of this generation, "McDonald's, for instance, has introduced hip-hop music and images to promote burgers and fries, ditto Coca-Cola, with its frenetic commercials touting Coca-Cola Classic."[51] Benetton, Esprit, The Gap, and other companies have followed suit in their attempts to identify and mobilize the desires, identities, and buying patterns of a new generation of youth.[52] What appears as a despairing expression of the postmodern condition to some theorists becomes for others a challenge to invent new market strategies for corporate interests. In this scenario, youth may be experiencing the indeterminacy, senselessness, and multiple conditions of postmodernism, but corporate advertisers are attempting to theorize a pedagogy of consumption as part of a new way of appropriating postmodern differences among youth in different sites and locations. The lesson here is that differences among youth matter politically and pedagogically, but not as a way of generating new markets or registering difference simply as a fashion niche.

What educators need to do is to make the pedagogical more political by addressing both the conditions through which they teach and what it means to learn from a generation that is experiencing life in a way that is vastly different from the representations offered in modernist versions of schooling. This is not to suggest that modernist schools do not attend to popular culture, but they do so on very problematic terms, which often confine it to the margins of the curriculum. Moreover, modernist schools cannot be rejected outright. As I have shown elsewhere, the political culture of modernism, with its emphasis on social equality, justice, freedom, and human agency, needs to be refigured within rather than outside of an emerging postmodern discourse.[53]

The emergence of electronic media coupled with a diminishing faith in the power of human agency has undermined the traditional visions of schooling and the meaning of pedagogy. The language of lesson plans and upward mobility and the forms of teacher authority on which it was based has been radically delegitimated by the recognition that culture and power are central to the authority/knowledge relationship. Modernism's faith in the past has given way to a future for which traditional markers no longer make sense.

Cultural Studies and Youth: The Pedagogical Issue

Educators and cultural critics need to address the effects of emerging postmodern conditions on a current generation of young people who appear hostage to the vicissitudes of a changing economic order, with its legacy of diminished hopes on the one hand, and a world of schizoid images, proliferating public spaces, and an increasing fragmentation, uncertainty, and randomness that structures postmodern daily life on the other. Central to this issue is whether educators are dealing with a new kind of student forged within organizing principles shaped by the intersection of the electronic image, popular culture, and a dire sense of indeterminacy.

What cultural studies offers educators is a theoretical framework for addressing the shifting attitudes, representations, and desires of this new generation of youth being produced within the current historical, economic, and cultural juncture. But it does more than simply provide a lens for resituating the construction of youth within a shifting and radically altered social, technological, and economic landscape: it also provides elements for rethinking the relationship between culture and power, knowledge and authority, learning and experience, and the role of teachers as public intellectuals. In what follows, I want to point to some of the theoretical elements that link cultural studies and critical pedagogy and speak briefly to their implications for cultural work.

First, cultural studies is premised on the belief that we have entered a period in which the traditional distinctions that separate and frame established academic disciplines cannot account for the great diversity of cultural and social phenomena that has come to characterize an increasingly hybridized, post-industrial world. The university has long been linked to a notion of national identity that is largely defined by and committed to transmitting traditional Western culture.[54] Traditionally, this has been a culture of exclusion, one that has ignored the multiple narratives, histories, and voices of culturally and politically subordinated groups. The emerging proliferation of diverse social movements arguing for a genuinely multicultural and multiracial society have challenged schools that use academic knowledge to license cultural differences in order to regulate and define who they are and how they might narrate themselves. Moreover, the spread of electronically mediated culture to all spheres of everyday intellectual and artistic life has shifted the ground of scholarship away from the traditional disciplines designed to preserve a "common culture" to the more hybridized fields of comparative and world literature, media studies, ecology, society and technology, and popular culture.

Second, advocates of cultural studies have argued strongly that the role of culture, including the power of the mass media with its massive apparatuses of representation and its regulation of meaning, is central to understanding how the dynamics of power, privilege, and social desire structure the daily life of a society.[55] This concern with culture and its connection to power has necessitated a critical interrogation of the relationship between knowledge and authority, the meaning of canonicity, and the historical and social contexts that deliberately shape students' understandings of accounts of the past, present, and future. But if a sea change in the development and reception of what counts as knowledge has taken place, it has been accompanied by an understanding of how we define and apprehend the range of texts that are open to critical interrogation and analysis. For instance, instead of connecting culture exclusively to the technology of print and the book as the only legitimate academic artifact, there is a great deal of academic work going on that analyzes how textual, aural, and visual representations are produced, organized, and distributed through a variety of cultural forms such as the media, popular culture, film, advertising, mass communications, and other modes of cultural production.[56]

At stake here is the attempt to produce new theoretical models and methodologies for addressing the production, structure, and exchange of knowledge. This approach to inter/post-disciplinary studies is valuable because it addresses the pedagogical issue of organizing dialogue across and outside of the disciplines in order to promote alternative approaches to research and teaching about culture and the newly emerging technologies and forms of knowledge. For instance, rather than organize courses around strictly disciplinary concerns arising out of English and social studies courses, it might be more useful and relevant for colleges of education to organize courses that broaden students' understandings of themselves and others by examining events that evoke a sense of social responsibility and moral accountability. A course on "Immigration and Politics in Fin de Siècle America" could provide an historical perspective on the demographic changes confronting the United States and how such changes are being felt within the shifting dynamics of education, economics, cultural identity, and urban development. A course on the Los Angeles uprisings could incorporate the related issues of race, politics, economics, and education to address the multiple conditions underlying the violence and despair that produced such a tragic event.

Third, in addition to broadening the terms and parameters of learning, cultural studies rejects the professionalization of educators and the alienating and often elitist discourse of professionalism and sanitized expertise. Instead, it argues for educators as public intellectuals. Stuart Hall is instructive on this issue when he argues that cultural studies provides two points of tension that intellectuals need to address:

> First, cultural studies constitutes one of the points of tension and change at the frontiers of intellectual and academic life, pushing for new questions, new models, and new ways of study, testing the fine lines between intellectual rigor and social relevance . . . But secondly . . . cultural studies insists on what I want to call the vocation of the intellectual life. That is to say, cultural studies insists on the necessity to address the central, urgent, and disturbing questions of a society and a culture in the most rigorous intellectual way we have available.[57]

In this view, intellectuals must be accountable in their teaching for the ways in which they address and respond to the problems of history, human agency, and the renewal of democratic civic life. Cultural studies strongly rejects the assumption that teachers are simply transmitters of existing configurations of knowledge. As public intellectuals, academics are always implicated in the dynamics of social power through the experiences they organize and provoke in their classrooms. In this perspective, intellectual work is incomplete unless it self-consciously assumes responsibility for its effects in the larger public culture while simultaneously addressing the most profoundly and deeply inhumane problems of the societies in which we live. Hence, cultural studies raises questions about what knowledge is produced in the university and how it is consequential in extending and deepening the possibilities for democratic public life. Equally important is the issue of how to democratize the schools so as to enable those groups who in large measure are divorced from or simply not represented in the curriculum to be able to produce their own representations, narrate their own stories, and engage in respectful dialogue with others. In this instance, cultural studies must address how dialogue is constructed in the classroom about other cultures and voices by critically addressing both the position of the theorists and the institutions in which such dialogues are produced. Peter Hitchcock argues forcefully that the governing principles of any such dialogic exchange should include some of the following elements:

1) attention to the specific institutional setting in which this activity takes place; 2) self-reflex-ivity regarding the particular identities of the teacher and students who collectively undertake this activity; 3) an awareness that the cultural identities at stake in "other" cultures are in the process-of-becoming in dialogic interaction and are not static as subjects; but 4) the knowl-edge produced through this activity is always already contestable and by definition is not the knowledge of the other as the other would know herself or himself.[58]

Fourth, another important contribution of cultural studies is its emphasis on studying the production, reception, and use of varied texts, and how they are used to define social relations, values, particular notions of community, the future, and diverse definitions of the self. Texts in this sense do not merely refer to the culture of print or the technology of the book, but to all those audio, visual, and electronically mediated forms of knowledge that have prompted a radical shift in the construction of knowledge and the ways in which knowledge is read, received, and consumed. It is worth repeating that contemporary youth increasingly rely less on the technology and culture of the book to construct and affirm their identities; instead, they are faced with the task of finding their way through a decentered cultural landscape no longer caught in the grip of a technology of print, closed narrative structures, or the certitude of a secure economic future. The new emerging technologies that construct and position youth represent interactive terrains that cut across "language and cul-ture, without narrative requirements, without character complexities . . . Narrative complexity [has given] way to design complexity; story [has given] way to a sensory environment."[59] Cultural studies is profoundly important for educators in that it focuses on media not merely in terms of how it distorts and misrepresents reality, but also on how media plays "a part in the formation, in the constitution, of the things they reflect. It is not that there is a world outside, 'out there,' which exists free of the discourse of representation. What is 'out there' is, in part, constituted by how it is represented."[60]

I don't believe that educators and schools of education can address the shifting attitudes, representation, and desires of this new generation of youth within the dominant disciplinary configurations of knowledge and practice. On the contrary, as youth are constituted within languages and new cultural forms that intersect dif-ferently across and within issues of race, class, gender, and sexual differences, the conditions through which youth attempt to narrate themselves must be understood in terms of both the context of their struggles and a shared language of agency that points to a project of hope and possibility. It is precisely this language of difference, specificity, and possibility that is lacking from most attempts at educational reform.

Fifth, it is important to stress that when critical pedagogy is established as one of the defining principles of cultural studies, it is possible to generate a new discourse for moving beyond a limited emphasis on the mastery of techniques and methodol-ogies. Critical pedagogy represents a form of cultural production implicated in and critically attentive to how power and meaning are employed in the construction and organization of knowledge, desires, values, and identities. Critical pedagogy in this sense is not reduced to the mastering of skills or techniques, but is defined as a cultural practice that must be accountable ethically and politically for the stories it produces, the claims it makes on social memories, and the images of the future it deems legitimate. As both an object of critique and a method of cultural production, it refuses to hide behind claims of objectivity, and works effortlessly to link theory and practice to enabling the possibilities for human agency in a world of diminishing returns. It is important to make a distinction here that challenges the liberal and conservative criticism that, since critical pedagogy attempts both to politicize teaching and teach politics, it represents a species of indoctrination. By asserting that all teaching is profoundly political and that critical educators and cultural workers should operate out of a project of social transformation, I am arguing that as educators we need to make a distinction between what Peter Euben calls political and politicizing education.

Political education, which is central to critical pedagogy, refers to teaching "students how to think in ways that cultivate the capacity for judgment essential for the exercise of power and responsibility by a democratic citizenry . . . A political, as distinct from a politicizing education would encourage students to become better citizens to challenge those with political and cultural power as well as to honor the critical traditions within the dominant culture that make such a critique possible and intelligible."[61] A political education means decentering power in the classroom and other pedagogical sites so the dynamics of those institutional and cultural inequalities that marginalize some groups, repress particular types of knowledge, and suppress critical dialogue can be addressed. On the other hand, politicizing education is a form of pedagogical terrorism in which the issue of what is taught, by whom, and under what conditions is determined by a doctrinaire political agenda that refuses to examine its own values, beliefs, and ideological construction. While refusing to recognize the social and historical character of its own claims to history, knowledge, and values, a politicizing education silences in the name of a specious universalism and denounces all transformative practices through an appeal to a timeless notion of truth and beauty. For those who practice a politicizing education, democracy and citizenship become dangerous in that the precondition for their realization demands critical inquiry, the taking of risks, and the responsibility to resist and say no in the face of dominant forms of power.

Conclusion

Given its challenge to the traditional notion of teachers as mere transmitters of information and its insistence that teachers are cultural producers deeply implicated in public issues, cultural studies provides a new and transformative language for education teachers and administrators around the issues of civic leadership and public service. In this perspective, teacher education is fashioned not around a particular dogma, but through pedagogical practices that address changing contexts, creating the necessary conditions for students to be critically attentive to the historical and socially constructed nature of the locations they occupy within a shifting world of representations and values. Cultural studies requires that teachers be educated to be cultural producers, to treat culture as an activity, unfinished and incomplete. This suggests that teachers should be critically attentive to the operations of power as it is implicated in the production of knowledge and authority in particular and shifting contexts. This means learning how to be sensitive to considerations of power as it is inscribed on every facet of the schooling process.

The conditions and problems of contemporary youth will have to be engaged through a willingness to interrogate the world of public politics, while at the same time appropriating modernity's call for a better world but abandoning its linear narratives of Western history, unified culture, disciplinary order, and technological progress. In this case, the pedagogical importance of uncertainty and indeterminacy can be rethought through a modernist notion of the dream-world in which youth and others can shape, without the benefit of master narratives, the conditions for producing new ways of learning, engaging, and positing the possibilities for social struggle and solidarity. Critical educators cannot subscribe either to an apocalyptic emptiness or to a politics of refusal that celebrates the abandonment of authority or the immediacy of experience over the more profound dynamic of social memory and moral outrage forged within and against conditions of exploitation, oppression, and the abuse of power.

The intersection of cultural studies and critical pedagogy offers possibilities for educators to confront history as more than simulacrum and ethics as something other than the casualty of incommensurable language games. Educators need to assert a politics that makes the relationship among authority, ethics, and power central to a pedagogy that expands rather than closes down the possibilities of a radical democratic society. Within this discourse, images do not dissolve reality into simply another text: on the contrary, representations become central to revealing the structures of power relations at work in the public, in schools, in society, and in the larger global order. Pedagogy does not succumb to the whims of the marketplace in this logic, nor to the latest form of educational chic; instead, critical pedagogy engages cultural studies as part of an ongoing movement towards a shared conception of justice and a radicalization of the social order. This is a task that not only recognizes the multiple relationships between culture and power, but also makes critical pedagogy one of its defining principles.

Notes

1. Dick Hebdige, *Hiding in the Light* (New York: Routledge, 1988), pp. 17–18.
2. "Footnotes," *Chronicle of Higher Education*, December 1, 1993, p. A8.
3. I provide a detailed critique of this issue in Henry A. Giroux, *Schooling and the Struggle for Public Life* (Minneapolis: University of Minnesota Press, 1988). See also Stanley Aronowitz and Henry A. Giroux, *Education Still Under Siege* (Westport, CT: Bergin & Garvey, 1993).
4. I take this issue up in detail in Henry A. Giroux, *Disturbing Pleasures: Learning Popular Culture* (New York: Routledge, 1994).

5. Feminist theorists have been making this point for years. For an example of some of this work as it is expressed at the intersection of cultural studies and pedagogy, see the various articles in *Between Borders: Pedagogy and the Politics of Cultural Studies*, ed. Henry A. Giroux and Peter McLaren (New York: Routledge, 1993).

6. The relationship between cultural studies and relations of government are taken up in Tony Bennett, "Putting Policy into Cultural Studies," in *Cultural Studies*, ed. Lawrence Grossberg, Cary Nelson, and Paula Treichler (New York: Routledge, 1992), pp. 23–24.

7. For representative examples of the diverse issues taken up in the field of cultural studies, see Grossberg at al., *Cultural Studies*; Simon During, ed., *The Cultural Studies Reader* (New York: Routledge, 1993).

8. This is especially true of some of the most ardent critics of higher education A representative list includes: William J. Bennett, *To Reclaim a Legacy: A Report on the Humanities in Higher Education* (Washington, DC: National Endowment for the Humanities, 1984); Stephen H. Balch and Herbert London, "The Tenured Left," *Commentary*, 82, No. 4 (1986), 41–51; Lynne V. Cheney, *Tyrannical Machines: A Report on Education Practices Gone Wrong on Our Best Hopes for Setting Them Right* (Washington, DC: National Endowment for the Humanities, 1990); Roger Kimball, *Tenured Radicals: How Politics Has Corrupted Our Higher Education* (New York: Harper & Row, 1990); Dinesh D'Souza, *Illiberal Education: The Politics of Race and Sex on Campus* (New York: Free Press, 1991). For a highly detailed analysis of the web of conservative money, foundations, and ideologies that connect the above intellectuals, see Ellen Messer-Davidow, "Manufacturing the Attack on Liberalized Higher Education," *Social Text, 11*, No. 3 (1993), 40–80.

9. Cary Nelson, Paula Treichler, and Lawrence Grossberg, "Cultural Studies: An Introduction," In Nelson, Treichler, and Grossberg, *Cultural Studies*, p. 5.

10. Bennett, "Putting Policy into Cultural Studies," p. 32.

11. I take up these issues in more detail in Henry A. Giroux, *Border Crossings: Cultural Workers and the Politics of Education* (New York: Routledge, 1992) and in Giroux, *Disturbing Pleasures*.

12. Cary Nelson, "Always Already Cultural Studies," in *Journal of the Midwest Language Association, 24*, No. 1 (1991), p. 32.

13. Hebdige, *Hiding in the Light*, pp. 17–18.

14. Stuart Hall, "What is this 'Black' in Popular Culture?" in *Black Popular Culture*, ed. Gina Dent (Seattle: Bay Press, 1992), p. 22.

15. As a representative example of this type of critique, see any of the major theoretical sources of cultural studies, especially the Centre for Contemporary Cultural Studies at the University of Birmingham [England]. For example, Stuart Hall, "Cultural Studies: Two Paradigms," in *Media, Culture, and Society*, ed. Richard Collins et al. (London: Sage Publications, 1986), pp. 34–48, and Stuart Hall, "Cultural Studies and the Center: Some Problematics and Problems," in *Culture, Media, Language: Working Paper in Cultural Studies*, ed. Stuart Hall et al. (London: Hutchinson, 1980); Richard Johnson, "What is Cultural Studies Anyway?" *Social Text, 6*, No. 1 (1987), 38–40; Meaghan Morris, "Banality in Cultural Studies," *Discourse, 10*, No. 2 (1988), 3–29.

16. See Stanley Aronowitz, *Roll Over Beethoven: Return of Cultural Strife* (Hanover, NH: University Press of New England, 1993); Gayatri C. Spivak, *Outside in the Teaching Machine* (New York: Routledge, 1993). See also a few articles in Grossberg et al., *Cultural Studies*. Also, see various issues of *College Literature* under the editorship of Kostas Mrysiades. It is quite revealing to look into some of the latest books on cultural studies and see no serious engagement of pedagogy as a site of theoretical and practical struggle. In David Punter, ed., *Introduction to Contemporary Cultural Studies* (New York: Longman, 1986), there is one chapter on identifying racism in textbooks. For more recent examples, see: Patrick Brantlinger, *Crusoe's Footprints: Cultural Studies in Britain and America* (New York: Routledge, 1990); Graeme Turner, *British Cultural Studies* (London: Unwin Hyman, 1990); John Clarke, *New Times and Old Enemies* (London: Harper Collins, 1991); Sarah Franklin,

Celia Lury, and Jackie Stacey, eds., *Off-Centre: Feminism and Cultural Studies* (London: Harper Collins, 1991). In neither of the following books published in 1993 is there even one mention of pedagogy: During, *The Cultural Studies Reader*; Valda Blundell, John Shepherd, and Ian Taylor, eds., *Relocating Cultural Studies: Developments in Theory and Research* (New York: Routledge, 1993).

17. While there are too many sources to cite here, see R. W. Connell, D. J. Ashenden, S. Kessler, and G. W. Dowsett, *Making the Difference* (Boston: Allen & Unwin, 1982); Julian Henriques, Wendy Hollway, Cathy Urwin, Couze Venn, and Valerie Walkerdine, *Changing the Subject* (London: Methuen, 1984); James T. Sears, *Growing up Gay in the South: Race, Gender, and Journeys of the Spirit* (New York: Harrington Park Press, 1991); Michelle Fine, *Framing Dropouts* (Albany: State University of New York Press, 1991); Roger I. Simon, *Teaching Against the Grain* (New York: Bergin & Garvey, 1992); James Donald, *Sentimental Education* (London: Verso Press, 1992).

18. For instance, while theorists such as Jane Tompkins, Gerald Graff, Gregory Ulmer, and others address pedagogical issues, they do it solely within the referenced terrain of literary studies. Moreover, even those theorists in literary studies who insist on the political nature of pedagogy generally ignore, with few exceptions, the work that has gone on in the field for twenty years. See, for example, Shoshana Felman and Dori Lamb, *Testimony: Crisis of Witnessing in Literature, Psychoanalysis, and History* (New York: Routledge, 1992); Bruce Henricksen and Thais E. Morgan, *Reorientations: Critical Theories & Pedagogies* (Urbana: University of Illinois Press, 1990); Patricia Donahue and Ellen Quahndahl, eds., *Reclaiming Pedagogy: The Rhetoric of the Classroom* (Carbondale: Southern Illinois University Press, 1989); Gregory Ulmer, *Applied Grammatology* (Baltimore: Johns Hopkins University Press, 1985); Barbara Johnson, ed., *The Pedagogical Imperative: Teaching as a Literary Genre* (New Haven: Yale University Press, 1983).

19. One interesting example of this occurred when Gary Olson, the editor of the *Journal of Advanced Composition*, interviewed Jacques Derrida. He asked Derrida, in the context of a discussion about pedagogy and teaching, if he knew of the work of Paulo Freire. Derrida responded, "This is the first time I've heard his name" (Gary Olson, "Jacques Derrida on Rhetoric and Composition: A Conversation," In *[Inter]views]: Cross-Disciplinary Perspectives on Rhetoric and Literacy*, ed. Gary Olson and Irene Gale [Carbondale: Southern Illinois University Press, 1991], p. 133). It is hard to imagine that a figure of Freire's international stature would not be known to someone in literary studies who is one of the major proponents of deconstructing. So much for crossing boundaries. Clearly, Derrida does not read the radical literature in composition studies, because if he did he could not miss the numerous references to the work of Paulo Freire and other critical educators. See, for instances, C. Douglas Atkins and Michael L. Johnson, *Writing and Reading Differently: Deconstruction and the Teaching of Composition and Literature* (Lawrence: University of Kansas Press, 1985); Linda Brodkey, *Academic Writing as a Social Practice* (Philadelphia: Tempe University Press, 1987); C. Mark Hurlbert and Michael Blitz, eds., *Composition & Resistance* (Portsmouth, NH: Heinemann, 1991).

20. It is worth nothing that the term "cultural studies" derives from the Centre for Contemporary Cultural Studies at the University of Birmingham. Initially influenced by the work of Richard Hoggart, Raymond Williams, and E. P. Thompson, the Centre's ongoing work in cultural studies achieved international recognition under the direction of Stuart Hall in the 1970s and later under Richard Johnson in the 1980s. For a useful history of the Centre written from the theoretical vantage point of one of its U.S. supporters, see Lawrence Grossberg, "The Formations of Cultural Studies: An American in Birmingham," in Blundell et al., *Relocating Cultural Studies*, pp. 21–66.

21. Williams is quite adamant in refuting "encyclopedia articles dating the birth of Cultural Studies from this or that book in the late fifties." He goes on to say that: "the shift of perspective about the teaching of art and literature and their relation to history and to contemporary society began in Adult Education, it didn't happen anywhere else. It was when it was taken across by people with that experience to the Universities that it was suddenly recognized as a subject. It is in these and other similar ways that the contribution of the process itself to social change itself, and specifically to

learning, has happened" (cited in Raymond Williams, "Adult Education and Social Change," *What I Came to Say* [London: Hutchinson-Radus, 1989], pp. 157–166). See also, Raymond Williams, "The Future of Cultural Studies," in *The Politics of Modernism*, ed. Tony Pickney (London: Verso, 1989), pp. 151–162.

22. Williams, "The Future of Cultural Studies," p. 158.

23. John Fiske, *Power Plays, Power Works* (London: Verso Press, 1994), p. 20.

24. Larry Grossberg goes so far as to argue that cultural studies "sees both history and its own practice as the struggle to produce one context out of another, one set of relations out of another." Lawrence Grossberg, "Cultural Studies and/in New World," *Critical Studies in Mass Communications* (Annandale, VA: Speech Communication Association, forthcoming), p. 4.

25. Raymond Williams, *Communications*, rev. ed. (New York: Barnes & Noble, 1967), pp. 14–15.

26. Simon, *Teaching Against the Grain*, p. 15.

27. Ruth Conniff, "The Culture of Cruelty," *The Progressive*, September 16, 1992, pp. 16–20.

28. See the November 29, 1993, issue of *Newsweek*. Of course, the issue that is often overlooked in associating "gangsta rap" with violence is that "gangsta rap does not appear in a cultural vacuum, but, rather, is expressive of the cultural crossing, mixing, and engagement of black youth culture with the values, attitudes, and concerns of the white majority." bell hooks, "Sexism and Misogyny: Who Takes the Rap?" *Z Magazine*, February 1994, p. 26. See also Greg Tate's spirited defense of rap in Greg Tate, "Above and Beyond Rap's Decibels," *New York Times*, March 6, 1994, pp. 1, 36.

29. This is most evident in the popular media culture where analysis of crime in the United States is almost exclusively represented through images of Black youth. For example, in the May 1994 issue of *Atlantic Monthly*, the cover of the magazine shows a Black urban youth, without a shirt, with a gun in his hand, staring out at the reader. The story the image is highlighting is about inner-city violence. The flurry of articles, magazines, films, and news stories about crime produced in 1994 focuses almost exclusively on Black youth, both discursively and representationally.

30. Camille Colatosti, "Dealing Guns," *Z Magazine*, January 1994, p. 59.

31. Holly Sklar, "Young and Guilty by Stereotype," *Z Magazine*, July/August 1993, p. 52.

32. Stanley Aronowitz, "A Different Perspective on Educational Inequality," *The Review of Education/Pedagogy/Cultural Studies* (University Park, PA: Gordon & Breach, forthcoming), p. 15.

33. Aronowitz and Giroux, *Education Still Under Siege*, pp. 4–5.

34. These quotes and comments are taken from a stinging analysis of Kaus in Jonathan Kozol, "Speaking the Unspeakable," Unpublished manuscript (1993). The contexts for Kaus's remarks are developed in Mickey Kaus, *The End of Equality* (New York: Basic Books, 1992).

35. Paul Virilio, *Lost Dimension*, trans. Daniel Moshenberg (New York: Semiotext[e], 1991).

36. Andrew Ross and Tricia Rose, eds., *Microphone Fiends: Youth Music and Youth Culture* (New York: Routledge, 1994), and Jonathan Epstein, ed., *Adolescents and Their Music: If It's Too Loud, You're Too Old* (New York: Garland, 1994).

37. Theodor Adorno and Max Horkheimer, writing in the 1940s, argued that popular culture had no redeeming political or aesthetic possibilities. See Max Horkheimer and Theodor Adorno, *Dialectic of Enlightenment* (New York: Herder & Herder, 1944/1972), especially "The Culture Industry: Enlightenment as Mass Deception," pp. 120–167.

38. Walter Parkes, "Random Access, Remote Control," *Omni*, January 1994, p. 54.

39. This section of the paper draws from Henry A. Giroux, "Slacking Off: Border Youth and Postmodern Education," *Journal of Advanced Composition* (forthcoming).

40. Carol Anshaw, "Days of Whine and Poses," *Village Voice*, November 10, 1992, p. 27.

41. For a critique of the so-called "twenty-something generation" as defined by *Time*, *U.S. News*, *Money*, *Newsweek*, and the *Utne Reader*, see Chris de Bellis, "From Slackers to Baby Busters," *Z Magazine*, December 1993, pp. 8–10.

42. Andrew Kopkind, "Slacking Toward Bethlehem," *Grand Street*, *11*, No. 4 (1992), 183.

43. The contours of this type of criticism are captured in a comment by Andrew Kopkind, a keen observer of slacker culture, in "Slacking Toward Bethlehem," p. 187:

> The domestic and economic relationships that have created the new consciousness are not likely to improve in the few years left in this century, or in the years of the next, when the young slackers will be middle-agers. The choices for young people will be increasingly constricted. In a few years, a steady job at a mall outlet or a food chain may be all that's left for the majority of college graduates. Life is more and more like a lottery – is a lottery – with nothing but the luck of the draw determining whether you get a recording contract, get your screenplay produced, or get a job with your MBA. Slacking is thus a rational response to casino capitalism, the randomization of success, and the utter arbitrariness of power. If no talent is still enough, why bother to hone your skills? If it is impossible to find a good job, why not slack out and enjoy life?

44. For an analysis of Black American cinema in the 1990s, see Ed Guerrero, "Framing Blackness: The African-American Image in the Cinema of the Nineties," *Cineaste, 20,* No. 2 (1993), 24–31.

45. Michael Dyson, "The Politics of Black Masculinity and the Ghetto in Black Film," in *The Subversive Imagination: Artists, Society, and Social Responsibility*, ed. Carol Becker (New York: Routledge, 1994), p. 155.

46. Dyson, "The Politics of Black Masculinity," p. 163.

47. Itabari Njeri, "Untangling the Roots of the Violence Around Us – On Screen and Off," *Los Angeles Times Magazine*, August 29, 1993, p. 33.

48. Cornel West, "Nihilism in Black America," In Dent, *Black Popular Culture*, p. 40.

49. Itabari Njeri, "Untangling the Roots," p. 34.

50. Fabienne Worth, "Postmodern Pedagogy in the Multicultural Classroom: For Inappropriate Teachers and Imperfect Spectators," *Cultural Critique*, No. 25 (Fall, 1993), 27.

51. Pierce Hollingsworth, "The New Generation Gaps: Graying Boomers, Golden Agers, and Generation X," *Food Technology, 47*, No. 10 (1993), 30.

52. I have called this elsewhere the pedagogy of commercialism. See Giroux, *Disturbing Pleasures*.

53. For an analysis of the relationship among modernist schooling, pedagogy, and popular culture, see Henry A. Giroux and Roger I. Simon, "Popular Culture as a Pedagogy of Pleasure and Meaning," in *Popular Culture, Schooling, and Everyday Life*, ed. Henry A. Giroux and Roger Simon (Granby, MA: Bergin & Garvey, 1989), pp. 1–30; Henry A. Giroux and Roger I. Simon, "Schooling, Popular Culture, and a Pedagogy of Possibility," in Giroux and Simon, *Popular Culture*, pp. 219–236.

54. Anyone who has been following the culture wars of the past eight years is well aware of the conservative agenda for reordering public and higher education around the commercial goal of promoting economic growth for the nation while simultaneously supporting the values of Western civilization as a common culture designed to undermine the ravages of calls for equity and multiculturalism. For a brilliant analysis of the conservative attack on higher education, see Ellen Messer-Davidow, "Manufacturing the Attack on Liberalized Higher Education," *Social Text, 11*, No. 3 (1993), 40–80.

55. This argument is especially powerful in the work of Edward Said, who frames the reach of culture as a determining pedagogical force against the backdrop of the imperatives of colonialism. See Edward Said, *Culture and Imperialism* (New York: Alfred A. Knopf, 1993); see also, Donaldo Macedo, *Literacies of Power* (Boulder, CO: Westview Press, 1994).

56. Selective examples of this work include: Carol Becker, ed., *The Subversive Imagination* (New York: Routledge, 1994); Giroux and McLaren, *Between Borders*; Simon, *Teaching Against the Grain*; David Trend, *Cultural Pedagogy: Art/Education/Politics* (Westport, CT: Bergin & Garvey, 1992); James Schwoch, Mimi White, and Susan Reilly, *Media Knowledge: Readings in Popular Culture, Pedagogy, and Critical Citizenship* (Albany: State University of New York Press, 1992); Lawrence Grossberg, *We Gotta Get Out of This Place: Popular Conservatism and Postmodern Culture* (New York: Routledge, 1992). See also, Douglas Kellner, *Media Culture* (New York: Routledge, forthcoming); Jeanne Brady, *Schooling Young Children* (Albany: State University of New York Press, forthcoming).

57. Stuart Hall, "Race, Culture, and Communications: Looking Backward and Forward at Cultural Studies," *Rethinking Marxism, 5*, No. 1 (1992), 11.

58. Peter Hitchcock, "The Othering of Cultural Studies," *Third Text, No. 25* (Winter, 1993–1994), 12.

59. Walter Parkes, "Random Access, Remote Control: The Evolution of Story Telling," *Omni*, January 1994, p. 50.

60. Hall, "Race, Culture, and Communications," p. 14.

61. Peter Euben, "The Debate Over the Canon," *Civic Arts Review, 7*, No. 1 (1994), 14–15.

CHAPTER 4

Public Pedagogy and the Responsibility of Intellectuals

Youth, Littleton, and the Loss of Innocence

2000

> Youth is the last and almost always ignored category in the traditional list of subordinated populations (servants—i.e. racial and colonized minorities, women and children) who, in the name of protection, are silenced. —Lawrence Grossberg

In rhetoric and composition studies, there has been a long legacy of attempting to combine theoretical rigor with social relevance.[1] Within this critical tradition, rhetoric and composition theorists have approached language and writing as a form of cultural production by situating it within a politics that links theory to practice, literacy to social change, and academic discourses to the material relations of power shaping everyday life. Moreover, they have consistently attempted to broaden the meaning of such work by theorizing the primacy of pedagogy as an ethical and political practice within disciplinary formations. Rhetoric and composition theorists have made substantial contributions to broadening students' understanding of the interrelated dynamics of class, race, sexuality, and gender—specifically, the role these forces play in shaping the pedagogical landscape of the classroom and other public spheres. Furthermore, rhetoric and composition studies has coupled an attentiveness to questions of context—especially the importance of beginning where students actually are—with the need to intervene in and change such contexts, particularly those founded on deep inequalities that increasingly regulate the administration and organization of our schools and other institutions. Rhetoric and composition, in this instance, has aligned itself historically with progressive political projects aimed at providing the necessary pedagogical conditions for students both to recognize anti-democratic forms of power and to think critically about using their knowledge and skills to change the oppressive conditions under which they learn and experience daily life.

Unfortunately, as the post-Littleton debate has clearly shown, educators in a variety of fields, including rhetoric and composition studies, have had little to say about how young people increasingly have become the victims of adult mistreatment, greed, neglect, and domination. The question of how young people experience, resist, challenge, and mediate the complex cultural politics and social spaces that mark their everyday lives does not seem to warrant the attention such issues deserve, especially in light of the ongoing assaults on minority youth of color and class that have taken place since the 1980s. Figures of youth and age circulate almost unnoticed. While educators in rhetoric and composition have learned to consider gender, race, class, and sexuality as part of a politics of education, they have not begun to think of youth as a critical category for social analysis or of the politics of youth and its implications for a radical democracy. The category of youth has not yet been factored into a broader discourse on politics, power, and social change.

In what follows, I attempt to address this lacunae in rhetoric and composition studies in particular and in educational theory in general by analyzing the current assault on youth, and I suggest that educators rethink the interrelated dynamics of politics, culture, and power as they increasingly erode those social spaces necessary for providing young people with the intellectual and material resources they need to participate in and shape the diverse economic, political, and social conditions influencing their lives. I also attempt to develop a critical language that both engages youth as a critical category and offers suggestions for the political and pedagogical roles that educators might play in addressing the crisis of youth, which is itself part of the broader crisis of public life, and I maintain that understanding the crisis of youth must be central to any notion of literacy, pedagogy, and cultural politics.

Central to the view developed here is the assumption that any viable notion of cultural politics must make the pedagogical more political because it is through the pedagogical force of culture that identities are constructed, citizenship rights are enacted, and possibilities are developed for translating acts of interpretation into forms of intervention. Pedagogy, in my view, is about putting subject positions in place and linking the construction of agency to issues of ethics, politics, and power. Recognizing the educational force of the cultural sphere also suggests making the political more pedagogical by addressing how agency unfolds within power-infused relations—that is, how the very processes of learning constitute the political mechanisms through which identities are produced, desires mobilized, and experiences take on specific forms and meanings. This broad definition of pedagogy is not limited to what occurs in institutionalized forms of schooling; it encompasses every relationship that young people imagine to be theirs in the world, where social agency is both enabled and constrained across multiple sites and where meanings enter the realm of power and function as public discourses. Cultural politics, in this instance, must include the issue of youth culture and can no longer be abstracted from considerations of what happens to the bodies and minds of young people at a time in history when the state is being hollowed out and policies of surveillance, regulation, and disciplinary control increasingly replace a welfare state that once provided minimal social services (food stamp programs, child nutrition programs, child health programs, funds for family planning) designed to prevent widespread poverty, suffering, and deprivations among large numbers of youth. Children have been made our lowest national priority, a fact that is most evident as social policy in this country has shifted from social investment to a politics of containment.[2] The crisis of youth does not simply reflect the loss of social vision, the ongoing corporatization of public space, and the erosion of democratic life; it also suggests the degree to which youth have been "othered" across a wide range of ideological positions, rendered unworthy of serious analysis as an oppressed group, or deemed to be no longer *at risk* but rather to be *a risk* to democratic public life (see Stephens 13). Indifference coupled with demonization make an unholy alliance that fails to foreground the importance of children's agency and the role that young people can play in shaping a future that will not simply repeat the present, a present in which children are increasingly regarded as a detriment to adult society rather than as a valuable resource.

Three Myths about Youth and Culture[3]

The current discourse about children's culture is indebted theoretically and politically to three seemingly separate but interrelated myths, all of which function to limit democracy, jeopardize the welfare of children, and silence socially engaged scholarship. The first myth rests on the assumption that liberal democracy has achieved its ultimate victory and that the twin ideologies of the market and representative democracy now constitute, with a few exceptions, the universal values of the new global village. On this view, liberal culture becomes synonymous with market culture, and the celebrated freedoms of the consumer are bought at the expense of the freedom of citizens. Little public recognition is given either to the limits that democracies must place on market power or to how corporate culture and its narrow definition of freedom as a private good may actually threaten the well-being of children and democracy itself. In short, the conflation of democracy with the logic of the market cancels out the tension between market moralities and those values of civil society that cannot be measured in strictly commercial terms but are critical to democratic public life. I refer specifically to values such as justice, respect for children, and the rights of citizens as equal and free human beings (see Benhabib 9).

The second is the myth of childhood innocence. According to this myth, both childhood and innocence are perceived as mutually informing aspects of a natural state outside the dictates of history, society, and politics. In this common-sense conception, children are viewed, Marina Warner suggests, as "innocent because they're outside society, pre historical, pre-social, instinctual, creatures of unreason, primitive, kin to unspoiled nature" (57). Marked as innately pure and passive, children are afforded the right to protection but are denied a sense of agency and autonomy. Unable to fathom childhood as a historical, social, and political construction that is enmeshed in relations of power, many adults shroud children in an aura of inno-cence and protection that erases any viable notion of adult responsibility even as it evokes it.[4] In fact, the ascription of innocence, in large part, permits adults to avoid assuming responsibility for their role in setting children up for failure, in abandon-ing them to the dictates of marketplace mentalities, and in removing the supportive and nurturing networks that provide young people with adequate health care, food, housing, and educational opportunities.

The third myth mystifies the workings of an ever-expanding commercial culture that harnesses public dialogue and dissent to market values. This pervasive commer-cial culture is also evident in the obsession with careerism and professionalism and with the isolation of educators from politics and the pressing demands of civic life. This third myth suggests that teaching and learning are no longer linked to finding ways to improve the world; the imperatives of social justice are surrendered to a fatalism that renounces practical politics to accommodate the academic culture of professionalism and the ideology of disinterested scientific investigation. Edward Said insightfully comments on the twin dynamics of accommodation and privatiza-tion that inform the culture of professionalism at all levels of education:

> By professionalism I mean thinking of your work as an intellectual as something you do for a living, between the hours of nine and five with one eye on the clock, and another cocked at what is considered to be proper, professional behavior—not rocking the boat, not straying outside the accepted paradigms or limits, making yourself marketable and above all present-able, hence uncontroversial and unpolitical and "objective." (74)

The increasing isolation of academics and intellectuals from the world around them reflects corporate culture's power to define pedagogy as a technical and instrumen-tal practice rather than as an ethical and political act. Removed from the world of practical politics and everyday life, many educators are all too willing to renounce a sense of culture as an important terrain of politics and struggle. Buttressed by the pressures of professionalism and its attendant calls for neutrality, objectivity, and rationality, this approach offers little room to consider how ideologies, values, and power shape all aspects of the educational process. As British cultural theorist Rich-ard Johnson points out,

> Teaching and learning are profoundly political practices. They are political at every moment of the circuit: in the conditions of production (who produces knowledge? for whom?), in the knowledges and knowledge forms themselves (knowledge according to what agenda? useful for what?), their publication, circulation, and accessibility, their professional and popular uses, and their impacts on daily life. (461)

Moreover, mainstream educational discourse not only ignores the ideological nature of teaching and learning, it also erases culture from the political realm by enshrining it either as a purely aesthetic discourse or as a quasi-religious call to celebrate the "great books" and "great traditions" of what is termed "Western Civilization."[5] In both cases, any attempt to transform the nation's classrooms into places where future citizens learn to critically engage politics (and received knowledge outside of the classroom) is dismissed as either irrelevant or unprofessional.

At first glance, these three powerful myths appear to have little in common; however, I want to propose here that it is impossible to invoke any one myth in any meaningful way without invoking the others. What links these three seemingly disparate mythologies? Quite a lot, I believe: in their deployment, they excuse the adult world from any notion of responsibility toward youth by appealing to a thriving economy, the natural order, or disinterestedness; they reproduce race, class, and cultural hierarchies; and they limit citizenship to a narrowly privatized undertaking. What all three myths ignore is the increasingly impoverished conditions that future generations of youth will have to negotiate. They also ignore the fact that childhood is not a natural state of innocence; it is a historical construction. Childhood is a cultural and political category that has very practical consequences for how adults "think about children and conceive of childhood," and the way in which adults conceive of youth has very real consequences for how children will view themselves (Jenks 123).

The Politics of Innocence

On the one hand, by claiming that childhood innocence is a natural rather than constructed state, adults can safely ignore the power imbalance between themselves and children; furthermore, they can continue to think that children have neither rights nor agency since they exist beyond the pale of adult influence, except when they must be protected from aberrant outside forces.[6] On the other hand, the myth of childhood innocence provides a way of denying the effects of real social problems on children. It is, in other words, a way for adults to shift attention away from the pressing problems of racism, sexism, family abuse, poverty, joblessness, industrial downsizing, and other social factors that have made the end of the twentieth century such a dreadful time not only for many adults but also for many children, who are especially powerless in the face of such forces.[7]

By clinging to the assertion that a thriving free market economy (with its insidious consumer-based appropriation of notions of freedom and choice) provides the greatest good for the greatest number, adult society diminishes, as Henry Jenkins observes, "the role of politics in public life in favor of an exclusive focus on individual experience—on a politics of personal responsibilities and self-interest rather than one of the collective good" (11; see also Berlant). This view makes it all the easier for adult society to transform social problems into individual problems while at the same time downsizing the public sphere, eliminating government-funded safety nets for children, and replacing legislation aimed at social investment with punitive policies whose aim is social containment, discipline, and control. In this approach, the logic of the marketplace blames kids—especially those who are poor, Latino, or black—for their lack of character; it also dismantles social services that help them meet their most basic needs. Without understanding the social experience of actual children, contemporary society confronts the sometimes perilous, though hardly rampant, consequences of drug use and violent behavior by prosecuting young people as adults, stiffening jail sentences for young offenders, and building new prisons to incarcerate them in record numbers.[8]

What complicates the intersection of the myths of innocence, the universalized child, and the democratic pretensions of corporate culture is the way that these myths erase the exploitative relations of class, race, and gender differences even as they reproduce them. The appeal to innocence by conservatives and liberals alike offers protection and security to children who are white and middle-class—that is, the conditions of their innocence are defined within traditional (racial-, class-, and gender-coded) notions of home, family, and community (Berlant 5).

Public reactions to the 1999 killings at Columbine High School indicate that innocence is mediated along racial and class lines, as comments of residents of Littleton, Colorado, which were widely reported in the press, clearly suggest. Patricia Williams, for example, noted that some residents laid claim to a racially-coded legacy of innocence by proclaiming that "it couldn't happen here" or that "this is not the inner city" (9). Williams argues that such comments reflect what she terms "innocence profiling," a practice often directed at privileged white kids who, in spite of their behavior, are presumed too innocent to have their often criminal behavior treated seriously. According to Williams, the two teenage killers, Dylan Klebold and Eric Harris

> seem to have been so shrouded in presumptions of innocence—after professing their love for Hitler, declaring their hatred for blacks, Asians and Latinos on a public Web site no less, downloading instructions for making bombs, accumulating the ingredients, assembling them under the protectively indifferent gaze (or perhaps with the assistance) of parents and neighbors, stockpiling guns and ammunition, procuring hand grenades and flak jackets, threatening the lives of classmates, killing thirteen and themselves, wounding numerous others and destroying their school building—still the community can't seem to believe it really happened "here." Still their teachers and classmates continue to protest that they were good kids, good students, solid citizens. (9)

Williams registers how the myth of innocence works to protect privileged white kids, and her assessment rings true in view of the fact that the national press appeared dumbfounded that these two teenage gunmen from affluent families could have murdered twelve fellow students and a teacher before taking their own lives. One TV reporter at Columbine referred to one of the killers as "a gentleman who drove a BMW" (Milloy C9). Other media accounts emphasized how much promise these boys had and analyzed their criminal behavior largely in psychological terms. They were described as alienated, pressured, and stressed out—terms that are seldom used to describe the behavior of nonwhite youths who commit crimes.

Unlike crimes committed by youth in urban areas, the Columbine massacre prompted an enormous amount of national soul searching over the loss of childhood and the threats faced by white children living in affluent areas. Senate Majority leader Trent Lott called for a national conversation on youth and culture. Sociologist Orlando Patterson challenged the dominant media response to Littleton and the racially-coded notion of innocence that informed it. He asked in an op-ed column in *The New York Times* what the public response would have been if "these two killers had not been privileged whites but poor African-Americans or Latinos?" He responded that "almost certainly the pundits would have felt it necessary to call attention to their ethnicity and class" (A31). Actually, Patterson's comments seem understated. If these young people had been black or brown, they would have been denounced as bearers of a social pathology. Moreover, if brown or black youths had exhibited a previous history of delinquent behavior similar to Harris' and Klebold's (including breaking into a van and sending death threats to fellow students over the Internet), their punishment would have been more than short-term counseling; they would have been roundly condemned and quickly sent to prison. But since white middle-class communities cannot face the consequences of their declining economic and social commitment to youth, such young people generally are given the benefit of the doubt, even when their troubling behavior veers to the extreme. White middle-class children too often are protected by the myth of innocence and considered incapable of exhibiting at-risk behavior. And if they do exhibit deviant behavior, blame is placed on the "alien" influence of popular culture (often synonymous with hip hop) or on other "outside" forces that are removed from the spaces of "whiteness" and affluence.

Innocence in this exclusionary dialogue functions in a highly discriminatory way and generally does not extend its privileges to all children. In the age of Reagan and Clinton, the notion of innocence does not apply to some children, and it is being renegotiated for others.[9] Historically, poor children and children of color have been outside the boundaries of both childhood and innocence and often have been associated with the cultures of crime, rampant sexuality, and drug use. In fact, they are frequently perceived as a threat to the innocence of white middle class youths who inhabit increasingly fortress-like suburbs, shielded from the immorality, violence, and other "dangers" lurking within multi-ethnic cities (see Giroux, *Fugitive Cultures and Channel Surfing*). In dealing with youths whose lives do not fit the Ozzie-and-Harriet-family profile, innocence traditionally invokes its antithesis. In short, the rhetoric of innocence and its promise of support and protection typically have not applied to youths who are poor, black, and brown.

Yet, there is some evidence that the rhetoric of innocence has changed in the 1990s. While minority youth are seen as utterly disposable, today white, suburban youth increasingly face the wrath of adult authorities, the media, and the state (see Males). As Sharon Stephens cogently argues,

> There is a growing consciousness of children *at risk*. But the point I want to make here is that there is also a growing sense of children themselves as *the risk*—and thus of some children as

people out of place and excess populations to be eliminated, while others must be controlled, reshaped, and harnessed to changing social ends. Hence, the centrality of children, both as symbolic figures and as objects of contested forms of socialization, in the contemporary politics of culture. (13)

Although some children are considered to be "at risk," more and more kids are viewed as a major threat to adult society, in spite of the fact that different groups—depending on their class, race, gender, and ethnicity—engender different responses. Innocence is not only race-specific, it is also gendered. The romantic notion of childhood innocence idealizes motherhood at the expense of power and relegates women to the private realm of the home where they assume their duty as primary caretakers of children. As public life is once again separated from the domestic sphere and the role of women continues to be limited to an idealized notion of maternity, mothers are required to maintain the notion of childhood innocence. The ideal of childhood innocence infantilizes women and children at the same time that it reproduces an extreme imbalance of power between adults and children and between men and women.

The growing assault on youth is evident not only in the withdrawal of government-supported services—once created with their interests in mind—but also in the indignities young people suffer on a daily basis. For example, schools increasingly subject youth to random strip searches, place them under constant electronic surveillance (such as the use of cameras in buses) and force them to submit to random drug testing. Young people are denied any dignity or agency, and not just in urban schools. Surveillance, control, and regulation are enjoying a renaissance in the aftermath of the school shootings, as evidenced in the increased demand for armed security guards and metal detectors in affluent suburban schools. The post-Littleton climate normalizes what at another time might have been perceived as an extreme reaction: the Dallas-based National Center for Policy Analysis has issued a statement calling for the arming of public school teachers. Not surprisingly, the media characterized this as a legitimate intervention (Tucker C5).

This erosion of students' civil rights is often coupled with school policies that eliminate recess and sports programs, especially in those schools short of financial resources and supplies—schools largely attended by poor, working-class children. At the same time, young people are increasingly excluded from public spaces outside of schools that once offered them the opportunity to hang out with relative security, work with mentors in youth centers, and develop their own talents and sense of self worth. Like the concept of citizenship itself, recreational space is now privatized as a commercial profit-making venture. Gone are the youth centers, public parks, outdoor basketball courts, or empty lots where young people played stick ball. Play areas are now rented out to the highest bidder, and children are invited to "play" in places where they are "caged in by steel fences, wrought iron gates, padlocks, and razor ribbon wire" (Kelley 44). As public space disappears, new services arise in the privatized sphere to take "care" of youth. In *Framing Youth*, Mike Males insightfully argues that these new "kid-fixing" services have ominous consequences for many young people:

Beginning in the mid-1970s, kid-fixing services erupted to meet the market. They were of two kinds. Prison gates opened wide in the 1980s to receive tens of thousands more poorer teens, three-fourths of them non-white. Confinement of minority youths in prisons increased by 80 percent in the last decade . . . . At the same time, mental health and other treatment centers raked in huge profits therapizing hundreds of thousands more health-insured children . . . . Youth treatment is now a 25 billion dollar per year business with a "record of steady profit growth." (12)

Young people often bear the burden of new, undeserved responsibilities and pressures to "grow up." At the same time, both their freedoms and their constitutional protections and rights as citizens are being restricted. Where, outside of the marketplace, can children locate narratives of hope, semiautonomous cultural spheres, discussions of meaningful differences, and nonmarket based democratic identities?[10]

Although adult caretakers and a number of social commentators recognize the new burdens placed on young people, adult concerns about the ways in which childhood is changing and the new sets of responsibilities it places on youth often are defined through highly selective discourses, those closely tied to the class and racial nature of the young people under discussion. For example, liberal commentators on children's culture, such as Neil Postman and David Elkind, argue that the line between childhood and adulthood is disappearing due to the widespread influence of popular culture and the changing nature of the family. Postman believes that popular culture—especially television and child-friendly technologies such as VCRs and computer games—have undermined, if not corrupted, the nature of childhood innocence.

Indeed, the high melodrama of adolescent life—captured in television's *Dawson's Creek* and the hip cynicism of *South Park* (in which one unfortunate eight-year-old, working-class kid named Kenny dies violently every episode)—does seem to be a far cry from the family drama of the *Brady Bunch* or the innocence of the *Peanuts* cartoon series that raised an earlier white, middle-class generation. Young people's access via the Internet to every kind of pornography and the technologically advanced, hyperreal violence of home video games will alarm adults raised on an occasionally titillating issue of *National Geographic* and the flash of the pinball machine. It seems, however, that Postman mourns not only the loss of childhood innocence but also the Victorian principles of stern, hard-working, white middle-class families unsullied by the postmodern technologies of the visual age. Curiously, Postman's attack on the corrupting influence of popular culture says little about the media's role in presenting an endless stream of misrepresentations of black and poor youth. Nor does Postman analyze the role of corporate culture in trading on the contradictory appeal of childhood innocence to exploit its sexual potential and to position young people as both the subject and the object of commodification. Postman's nostalgic longing for high culture constitutes a modernist dream pitting the culture of print (with its own legacy of racist and sexist imagery) against a visual culture that allegedly promotes self-indulgence along with illiteracy; both cultures morally tarnish young people and condemn them to a passive and demeaned role in public life. Postman directly attributes the loss of childhood innocence to the rise of electronic technologies and the mass appeal of popular culture.

Such a focus conveniently absolves Postman of the need to question the class, gender, and racial coding that informs his view of the American past or to question how the political dynamics of a changing economic climate—rather than popular culture—result in reduced funding for public services for young people while simultaneously eroding their freedoms and their possibilities for the future. Postman largely ignores the fact that popular culture is not only a site of numerous contradictions but is also a site of negotiation for kids. Popular culture is one of the few places where they can speak for themselves, produce alternative public spheres, and represent their own interests. Moreover, it serves as one of the most important sites for recognizing how childhood identities are produced, how affective investments are secured, how desires are mobilized, and how learning can be linked to progressive social change. In many ways, Postman's position is symptomatic of the call from many adults and educators, in the aftermath of the Columbine murders, to censor the Internet, banish violent video games, and restrict online services for young people. Rather than acknowledging that the new electronic technologies allow young people to immerse themselves in crucially important forms of social communication, to produce a range of creative expressions, and to exhibit forms of agency that are both pleasurable and empowering, adults profoundly mistrust the new technologies—all in the name of protecting childhood innocence.[11] Rarely is there a serious attempt to find out what kind of meanings children bring to these new electronic cultures, how these cultures enhance the agency of children, or what youth are actually doing with these new media technologies.[12]

In his work on adolescents, prominent child psychologist David Elkind also points to the loss of childhood innocence, but he places the blame on the changing nature of the American family and on the shrinking opportunities American families offer to most children. He cites the increased responsibilities that children now have to assume with the growing number of two-parent working families, divorced parents, and single-parent families. Elkind also shows his nostalgia for a bygone era that afforded youth greater opportunities to develop their own games, culture, and adolescent activities. For Elkind, the rise of the middle-class "superkid" is a classic example of how children are conditioned to perform tasks similar to those performed by their parents in the outside world—a world marked by shrinking resources, increased competition, and an inflated Horatio Alger notion of achievement (*Hurried* 149–50).

In both critiques of contemporary youth culture, the nostalgia for childhood innocence makes childhood appear largely white, middle class, static, and passive. Children in these discussions are denied any agency and live in dire need of protection from the adult world. As such, youth seem to live outside of the sphere of the political, with all of the implications such a terrain carries for viewing childhood within rather than removed from the varied social, economic, and cultural forces that constitute adult society. More importantly, this selective notion of childhood innocence has almost nothing to say about a generation of poor and black youth who do not have the privilege of defining their problems in such narrow terms and for whom the shrinking boundaries between childhood and adulthood result in a dangerous threat to their well-being and often to their very lives. For example, as the war against youth escalates, politicians such as Texas legislator Jim Pittis have attempted to pass state laws that would apply the death penalty to children as young as eleven. Such laws are aimed at poor kids who live in a world in which their most serious problem is not how to complete excessive amounts of homework. On the contrary, these young people live with the daily fear of being incarcerated and with the ongoing experience of improper nutrition as well as inadequate housing and medical care. Shut out from most state-sponsored social programs and public spaces, Latino and black youth bear the burden of an adult society that increasingly views them as a threat to middle-class life and thus as disposable; or, it reifies them through a commercial logic in search of a new market niche. In this instance, not only is the notion of innocence problematic because of the exclusions it produces, but it has become highly susceptible to the worst forms of commercial appropriation.

The eighteenth century's romantic notion of childhood is losing prominence and is being reinvented, in part, through the interests of corporate capital. The ideal of the innocent child as an "object of adoration," Anne Higonnet observes, has turned all too easily into "the concept of the child as object, and then into marketing of the child as a commodity" (194). Capital has proven powerful enough both to renegotiate what it means to be a child and to expand the meaning of innocence as a commercial and sexual category. The force of capital has overridden or canceled out a legacy of appeals that once prompted adults to enact and to enforce child labor laws, protection from child predators, and educational entitlements for children.

Corporate Culture and the Appropriation of Innocence

> It is time to recognize that the true tutors of our children are not schoolteachers or university professors but filmmakers, advertising executives and pop culture purveyors. Disney does more than Duke, Spielberg outweighs Stanford, MTV trumps MIT.
> —Benjamin Barber

The ascendancy of corporate culture has created conditions in which adults can exhibit what Annette Fuentes calls a "sour, almost hateful view of young people" (21). For example, a 1997 Public Agenda report, *Kids These Days*, echoes adults' growing fears of and disdain for young people. The authors of this report found that two-thirds of the adults surveyed thought that kids today were rude, irresponsible, and wild (Farkas et al. 1-15). Another fifty-eight percent thought that young people will make the world either a worse place or no different when they become adults. Unfortunately, such views are not limited to the findings of conservative research institutes. Former Senator Bill Bradley, a prominent liberal spokesperson, reinforces the ongoing demonization of youth by claiming that the United States is in danger of losing "a generation of young people to a self-indulgent, self-destructive lifestyle" (qtd. in Males 341). This discourse provides a limited number of categories for examining what Henry Jenkins calls "the power relations between children and adults" ("Introduction" 3).

When adults invoke the idea of "childhood innocence" to describe the vulnerability of middle-class kids, they often mention as the central threats molestation, pedophilia, and the sexual dangers of the Internet (see Kincaid). This type of discussion assumes that the threat to the innocence of middle-class youth comes from outside of the social formations they inhabit, from forces outside of their control. I do not mean to suggest that pedophiles and abductors are not real menaces (though the danger they pose is ridiculously exaggerated); I merely want to suggest that the image of the pedophile becomes a convenient referent for ignoring the role that middle-class values and institutional forms actually play in threatening the health and welfare of all children.

This perceived threat to childhood innocence ignores the contradiction between adult concern for the safety of children and the reality of how adults treat children on a daily basis. Most of the violence against children is committed by adults. For example, in 1996 almost two thousand children were murdered by family members or friends (Federal Bureau). Too little is said about both a corporate culture that makes a constant spectacle of children's bodies and the motives of specific industries that have a major stake in promoting such exhibitions. Ann Higonnet touches on this issue in arguing that the sexualization of children is not "a fringe phenomenon inflicted by perverts on a protesting society, but a fundamental change furthered by legitimate industries and millions of satisfied consumers" (153). The point here is not that corporate culture is interested only in either commodifying or sexualizing children in the 1990s; instead, I want to underscore the influence corporate culture now wields pedagogically in redefining the terms through which children's experiences and identities are named, understood, and negotiated. Of course, industries also have constituents to please, and corporate culture's sexualization of children as an advertising gimmick to satisfy consumers and shareholders alike has eroded the lines between childhood and adulthood.

When the public recognizes that children can actually imitate adult behavior, images of working class, Latino, and black kids are often invoked as a media spectacle. Their aberrant behavior is invariably attributed to the irresponsibilities of working mothers, rampant drug abuse, and other alleged corruptions of morality circulating within working-class culture. But little mention is made of the violence that is perpetrated by middle-class values and social formation—such as conspicuous consumption, conformity, snobbery, and ostracism—which reproduces a number of racial, class, and gender exclusions. Nor is much said about how middle-class values legitimate and regulate cultural hierarchies that demean the cultures of marginalized groups and that reinforce racial and economic inequalities among the nation's children. Rather than confront the limitations of middle-class values, conservatives battle against the welfare state, dismantle many important children's services, and promote economic policies and mergers that facilitate corporate downsizing—without facing much resistance from the Democratic party. Moreover, the national media rarely acknowledge or criticize those forces within American culture that chip away at the notion of education as a public good or the disastrous effects such policies might have for working-class families and their children.

Similarly, dominant media represent popular culture as a threat to children's purity while they ignore the corporations that produce and regulate popular culture. Consider the following contradictions: pornography on the Internet is held up as an imminent danger to childhood innocence, yet nothing is said about the corporations and their middle class shareholders who relentlessly commodify and sexualize children's bodies, desires, and identities in the interest of turning a profit. Mainstream media critics who focus on the disappearance of childhood argue endlessly that the greatest threat to childhood innocence comes from rap music, while they ignore the threat from media conglomerates, such as Time-Warner (which produces many rap artists), General Electric, Westinghouse, or Disney (see Derber). Corporate culture's appropriation of childhood innocence and purity is rarely fodder for serious discussion, although corporations such as Calvin Klein trade on the appeal of childhood innocence by exploiting its sexual potential in order to sell cologne, underwear, and jeans. Slick, high-end fashion magazines offer up Lolita-like fourteen-year-olds as the newest supermodels and sex symbols, while in a 1992 photo spread for *Vanity Fair* Madonna appears as a blatantly "erotic baby-woman," wearing blond pigtails and sultry make-up (Higonnet 154-55). In a recent issue of *The New York Times Magazine*, Lynn Hirschberg writes about the boom in Hollywood teen films and casually reports that aspiring actors and actresses can't make it in the industry if they are over twenty years old. Rather than deal critically with the crass objectification and endless exploitation of young people by the Hollywood entertainment industry, Hirschberg treats the story as a straightforward narrative and thus becomes complicitous with the violence Hollywood wages on young teens. In these instances of corporate hustling, the emotional resonance of childhood innocence becomes erotically charged at the same moment that it is recontextualized within the commercial sphere. Many critics view erotic images as further proof that children are under assault. Yet they are less concerned about the ever expanding reach of corporate culture into every facet of children's culture than they are alarmed by the growing sexualization of popular culture, with its celebration of the "smut" produced by gangsta rap, its seeming vindication of a sexually charged music/video industry, and its potential to incite the ever-looming presence of the pedophile.

But the images that create such uneasiness are not limited to the looming threat of pedophiles and rap artists—those deemed as "other" by middle-class culture. On the contrary, the threat to innocence and childhood takes many forms. Commercial culture has removed childhood from the civic discourse of rights, public responsi-bility, and equality and turned it into a commodity; as such, it currently is being renegotiated. For example, an endless array of mass media advertisements reduce innocence to an aesthetic or psychological trope that prompts adults to develop the child in themselves, adopt teen fashions, and buy a range of services designed to make them look younger. This type of infantilization enables adults to identify with youth while it simultaneously empties adulthood of all political, economic, and social responsibilities and educative functions. Too many adults rely on the commer-cial language of self-help and character formation to further their own obsession with themselves, and they ignore the social problems that adults create for young people, especially those who are disadvantaged by virtue of their class, gender, and race. Such indifference allows adults to impose on young people the demands and responsibilities they themselves have abandoned.

At the turn of this century, childhood has not ended as a historical experience and social category; it has simply been transformed into another market strategy and fashion aesthetic to expand the consumer based needs of privileged adults who live within a market culture that has little room for ethical considerations, non-commod-ified spaces, or public responsibilities, especially as they might apply to expanding the conditions and opportunities for young people to become critical citizens in a vibrant democratic society. As Jenkins so aptly observes, childhood innocence no longer inspires adults to fight for the rights of children, enact reforms that suggest an investment in their future, or provide them with "the tools to realize their own political agendas or to participate in the production of their own culture" ("Intro-duction" 30). On the contrary, as the terrain of culture becomes increasingly com-modified, the only type of citizenship that adult society provides for children is that of the consumer.

At the same time, children are expected to act like adults, though different demands are made upon different groups of young people. Asked to shoulder enor-mous responsibilities, children are all too often more than willing to respond by mimicking and emulating adult behaviors that they are then condemned for appro-priating. Of course, when privileged white kids mimic destructive adult behavior, such acts are generally treated as an aberration. Yet, when disadvantaged kids do so, their behavior becomes a social problem for which they are both the root cause and the victims. Conversely, the media and most adults largely ignore those young people who refuse to imitate the social and political indifference of adults and who actually take on a number of important social issues and responsibilities.[13]

Current commentaries on the condition of contemporary youth typically miss the fact that what is changing, if not disappearing, is the productive social bonds between adults and children. Today's embattled concept of childhood magnifies how society addresses and mediates the very notion of sociality itself. This becomes evident in the ways in which childhood is increasingly marketed (especially in the move away from making social investments in children) and in the stepped-up efforts to disempower and contain youth. One consequence is that the appeal to innocence now couples an insidious type of adult infantilization with a ruthless moral indifference to the needs of children, a consequence that promotes the conditions for an endless assault on young people in the media and from all manner of politicians.

Current representations of youth—ranging from representations of kids as a threat to society to images of defenseless teenagers corrupted by the all powerful influence of popular culture—often work to undermine any productive sense of agency among young people and offer few possibilities for analyzing how children experience and mediate relationships between themselves and other children as well as adult society. In the post-Littleton climate, moral panic and fear replace critical understanding and allow media pundits such as Barbara Kantrowitz and Pat Wingert to proclaim in a *Newsweek* article that white suburban youth have a dark side and that youth culture in general represents "'Lord of the Flies' on a vast scale" (39). Such representations not only diminish the complexity of children's lives, they also erase any understanding of how power relations between adults and young people actually work against many children. At the same time, such representations replace the discourse of hope with the rhetoric of cynicism and disdain.

As the current assault on youth expands and extends beyond the inner city, it is accompanied by numerous films, books, and media representations that focus on youth culture in a way that would have appeared socially irresponsible twenty years ago. Films such as *Jawbreaker, Varsity Blues, Ten Things I Hate About You*, and *Cruel Intentions* relentlessly celebrate mindless, testosterone-driven, infantilized male athletes who are at the top of a repressive school pecking order; or they celebrate young high school girls who are vacuous as well as ruthless, arrogant, and sexually manipulative. Films such as *Election* and *Jawbreaker* resonate powerfully with the broader public view that a growing number of white suburban kids are inane, neurotically self-centered, or sexually deviant. These films reinforce the assumption that such kids are in need of medical treatment, strict controls, or disciplinary supervision. Moreover, these attacks complement and further legitimate the racist backlash against minority youth that has gained prominence in American society in the last decade of the twentieth century (see Giroux, *Fugitive Cultures* and *Channel Surfing*). In popular culture, this backlash can be seen in Hollywood films such as *The Substitute, Kids*, and *187*, which are premised on the assumption that brown, black, and poor kids cannot be innocent children and, more seriously, that they are a threat to childhood innocence and society because they embody criminality, corruption, rampant sexuality, and moral degeneracy. In these films, young people are demonized and marked as disposable: they are literally murdered as part of a "cleaning up" operation to make the public schools and urban streets safe for a largely white, middle-class adult population whose well being and security are allegedly under siege.

A contradiction at the heart of the public discourse about children points to a disturbing trend in how adults view their relationships to young people and to the obligations of citizenship, civic duty, and democracy. As the line between childhood and adulthood is renegotiated, the notion of childhood innocence serves as a historical and social referent for understanding that the current moral panic over youth is primarily about the crisis of democratic society itself and its waning interest in offering children the social, cultural, and economic opportunities and resources they need to both survive and prosper in this society. In such a perverse climate, innocence represents more than fertile ground for a media machine that increasingly regulates the cultural face of corporate power. The myth of innocence has become the rhetoric of choice of politicians and academics who rely on it to bash single mothers, gay and lesbian families, the legacy of the 1960s, popular culture, and kids themselves.

While public discourse about the loss of childhood innocence does at times consider youth as a valuable resource to be nurtured and protected, the rhetoric of innocence more frequently works to displace this important sense of adult responsibility and views innocence as quite exclusionary. In doing so, this rhetoric of innocence effectively draws a line between those kids worthy of adult protection and those who appear beyond the pale of adult compassion and concern. Yet, increasingly, those kids who fall under the mantle of adult protection suffer a loss of agency in the name of being protected by adult authority. The notion of innocence in this perspective has little to do with empowering youth, with prompting adults to be more self-critical about how they wield power over young people, or with offering young people supportive environments where they can produce their own cultural experiences, mediate diverse public cultures, and develop a wide range of social affiliations. Innocence has a politics, one defined less by the need for adults to invest in the welfare of young people or to recognize their remarkable achievements than by the widening gap between the public's professed concern about the fate of young people and the sadly deteriorating conditions under which too many live.

When viewed outside of the logic of the market, even the terms of the debate about children seem to rest on deception. From the perspective of the many commentators and politicians who loudly proclaim that innocence is under assault, the welfare of children is not really at stake. Rather, they mourn the loss of a mythical view of nationhood, citizenship, and community, where white middle-class values were protected from the evils of popular culture, the changing nature of the workforce, and the rise of immigration. This narrative provides nothing less than a Biblical account of childhood innocence and its fall in which youth appears as a universalized category, history seems removed from the taint of contradictory forces, and adult society takes on the nostalgic glow of an Andrew Wyeth painting.

This discourse of nostalgia often betrays the bad faith of adults who purportedly act in the interest of young people, as was amply displayed in the post-Littleton controversy over youth, school violence, and popular culture. For example, House majority leader Tom Delay shamelessly used the tragedy to further his own conservative political agenda in a recent television appearance. He argued that one response to the school massacre would be to put God back into the schools. Former Secretary of Education William Bennett used the Littleton tragedy as a platform to denigrate popular culture—specifically a popular youth fad known as Goth culture—and to reinforce the notion that young people who are "different" deserve to be scorned and ridiculed. He seemed to forget that many Littleton students felt that scorn and ridicule contributed to the hostile school environment that exacerbated the killers' pent-up rage. Neither Delay nor Bennett has had much to say about how such attacks further marginalize young people, nor did they acknowledge the ample evidence that suggests that adults in general have little interest in listening to kids' problems in school or in hearing how they construct their experiences outside of traditional societal values. Nor do most adults pay attention to how the culture of the Internet, video games, industrial rock, computerized gladiator matches, and androgynous fashions provide an important resource for young people to develop their own cultural identities and sense of social agency. And neither Delay nor Bennett has had much to say about supporting legislation that would eliminate widespread poverty among children, eradicate children's access to guns, and reverse the mounting expense of building more and more prisons. All three of these troubling issues undermine attempts to increase educational and work opportunities for many young people, especially those from the underclasses. The problem is not merely that no dialogue occurs about how young people are being shaped within the current social order; commentators also refuse to discuss how the basic institutions of adult society increasingly participate in a culture of violence that cares more about profits than about human needs and the public good, whose first casualties are the poor, aged, and children who lack adequate medical care, health insurance, food, clothing, and shelter. While adult society is obsessed with youth, it refuses to deal with what it means to value young people, to invest in their well-being by providing the conditions necessary for them to become successful adults and critical social agents.

Commentators such as Mike Males argue that the late 1990s represent the most anti-youth period in American history. James Wagoner, the president of the social-service organization Advocates for Youth, claims that "young people have been portrayed almost universally as a set of problems to be managed by society: juvenile crime, teen-age pregnancy, drug use" (qtd. in Powers G8). Both men suggest that in the last two decades American society has undergone a profound change in the way that it views young people and in how it treats them.[14] Underlying this shift are a number of social problems—such as racism, poverty, unemployment, and the dismantling of childcare services—that are rarely discussed or critically analyzed. While many adults appear obsessed with young people, they are not concerned with listening to their needs or addressing their problems. How a society treats its young people is reflected in how it balances the tensions between corporate needs and democratic values, on the one hand, and, on the other, the rhetoric of childhood innocence—a rhetoric that often overshadows the reality of despair and suffering that many children face daily.

In what follows, I want to highlight the relationship between the current assault on youth and the responsibility of educators to address this crisis. In doing so, I emphasize the necessity for educators to connect their work to the political task of making research, teaching, and learning part of the dynamic of democratic change itself.

Public Intellectuals and the Challenge of Children's Culture

What do we represent? *Whom* do we represent? Are we responsible? For what and to whom? If there is a university responsibility, it at least begins with the moment when a need to hear these questions, to take them upon oneself and respond, is imposed. This imperative for responding is the initial form and minimal requirement of responsibility.

—Jacques Derrida

The last few decades have been a time of general crisis in university life. Issues regarding the meaning and purpose of higher education, the changing nature of what counts as knowledge in a multicultural society, growing dissent among underpaid adjunct faculty and graduate assistants, the increasing vocationalization of university life (with an emphasis on learning corporate skills), battles over affirmative action, and intensifying struggles over the place of politics in teaching—these issues have exacerbated the traditional tensions both within the university community and between the university and society. In the above quotation, Jacques Derrida raises timely and fundamental questions not only for university teachers but for all educators and cultural workers. In response to the ongoing crisis in the university and to the crisis of university responsibility, I have been concerned with considering the fundamental link between knowledge and power, pedagogical practices and effects, authority and civic responsibility. I have argued elsewhere that the question of what educators teach is inseparable from what it means to invest in public life and to locate oneself in a public discourse (*Border*). Implicit in this argument is the assumption that the responsibility of educators cannot be separated from the consequences of the knowledge they produce, the social relations they legitimate, and the ideologies they disseminate in society. Educational work at its best represents a response to questions and issues posed by the tensions and contradictions of public life and attempts to understand and intervene in specific problems that emanate from the material contexts of everyday existence.

Educators and others must recognize that the political, economic, and social forces that demonize young people in the cultural sphere and reduce funding to public services for youth also affect public schools and universities. The increasing influence of corporate power in commercializing youth culture and in eliminating the noncommercial spheres where youth develop a sense of agency and autonomy is not unrelated to corporate culture's attempts to turn institutions of public and higher education over to the imperatives of the market, a move which devalues notions of social improvement and radically reduces the skills of academic labor. Schools have become a crucial battleground for disciplining and regulating youth, particularly poor urban youth of color. Moreover, the continued devaluation of education as a public good points to the need for educators, students, and other cultural workers to struggle collectively to reclaim such sites as democratic public spheres. Crucial to such a struggle, however, is the recognition that such reclamation cannot be removed from broader economic, cultural, and social struggles that affect the lives of many young people. I am not suggesting that educators should separate the academic and the political, the performance of institutional politics from cultural politics; rather, they must find ways to connect the politics of schooling with political struggles that take place across multiple social spheres and institutions. In this situation, cultural politics must construct itself in response to the demands of the institutional contexts of schooling—in all of their differences—and the broader demands and practical commitments that point to change and resistance in ideological and institutional structures that daily oppress young people.

A progressive cultural politics must challenge the priority of corporate culture's exclusive emphasis on the *private good* and reconnect educational theory and criticism to a notion of the *public good* that links democracy in the sphere of culture with democracy in the wider domain of public history and ordinary life. Broadly defined, cultural politics in this perspective must break down the divide between high and low culture and extend the reach of what counts as a serious object of learning from the library and the museum to the mass media and popular culture. Similarly, cultural politics not only must reconstitute and map how meaning is produced, it also must investigate the connections between discourses and structures of material power, the production of knowledge and the effects it has when translated into daily life. But before educators can retheorize what it means to make connections to popular formations outside of the walls of formal educational institutions, they will have to analyze the force of those institutional and ideological structures that shape their own lives.

Critical educators must address what it means to exercise authority from their own academic locations and experiences while assuming the challenge of putting knowledge to work in shaping a more fully realized democracy. Doing this requires redefining the relationship between theory and practice in order to challenge theory's formalist legacy, a legacy that often abstracts it from concrete problems and the dynamics of power. Theory in this sense is reduced to a form of theoreticism and an indulgence in which the production of theoretical discourse becomes an end in itself, a mere expression of language removed from the possibility of challenging strategies of domination. Rather than bridging the gap between public practices and intellectual debates or implementing political projects that merge strategies of understanding and social engagement, theory often becomes merely an avenue to professional advancement. Cut off from concrete struggles and broader public debates, theory often emphasizes rhetorical mastery and cleverness rather than the politically responsible task of challenging the inertia of common-sense understandings of the world, opening up possibilities for new approaches to social reform, or addressing the most pressing social problems that people have to face.

Similarly, in many liberal and critical approaches to education, the politics of meaning is relevant only to the degree that it is separated from a broader politics of engagement. Reading texts is removed from larger social and political contexts and engages questions of power exclusively within a politics of representation. Such readings largely function to celebrate a textuality that has been reduced to a bloodless formalism and a nonthreatening, or merely accommodating, affirmation of indeterminacy as a transgressive aesthetic. Lost here is any semblance of what George Lipsitz has called a radical political project that "grounds itself in the study of concrete cultural practices" and that understands that "struggles over meaning are inevitably struggles over resources" (621). By failing to connect the study of texts to the interests of expanding the goals of economic justice, children's rights campaigns, radical democratic visions, and opposition to anti-welfare and immigration policies, many educators conceive of politics as largely representational or as abstractly theoretical.[15] They also miss the crucial opportunity to develop connections between analyses of representations and strategies of political engagement—that is, the use of critical readings of texts as "routes to a larger analysis of historical cultural formations" (Johnson 465).

To address the problems of youth, rigorous educational work must respond to the dilemmas of the outside world by focusing on how young people make sense of their possibilities for agency within the power regulated relations of everyday life. The motivation for scholarly work cannot be narrowly academic; such work must connect with what Tony Bennett sees as "'real life' social and political issues in the wider society" (538). This requires, in part, that educators and other cultural workers address the practical social consequences of their work while simultaneously making connections to the often ignored institutional forms and cultural spheres that position and influence young people within unequal relations of power. Moreover, critical educators must begin to recognize that the forms of domination that bear down on young people are both institutional and cultural and that one cannot be separated from the other. Within this approach to cultural politics, the effects of domination cannot be removed from the educational conditions in which such behavior is learned, appropriated, or challenged. Analyzing the relationship between culture and politics in addressing the problems of youth requires that critical educators and cultural workers engage both the symbolic and the material conditions that construct the various social formations in which young people experience themselves and their relations to others. That is, any viable form of cultural politics must address the institutional machineries of power that promote child poverty, violence, unemployment, police brutality, rape, sexual abuse, and racism.

But this is not enough. Educators also must question those cultural pedagogies that produce specific meanings, affective investments, and desires that legitimate and secure acts of domination aimed at young people (see Worsham). Educators must do more than simply interview youth using qualitative research methods. They must become border crossers (without passports), willing to examine the multiple sites and cultural forms that young people produce in order to make their voices heard within the larger society. Ann Powers, a writer for *The New York Times*, has pointed out that as young people have been shut out of the larger society, they have created their own web sites and alternative radio programs, "published their own manifestos in photocopied fanzines, made their own music and shared it on cassette, designed their own fashions and arranged to have them sold in boutiques" (G8). Moreover, Powers has argued that many young women have not watched passively as they are misrepresented in the American cultural landscape as vacuous, sexually predatory, dangerous, and pathological. In response, they have produced a "far-ranging girls' culture" that includes bold young athletes, musicians, filmmakers and writers; and they are invigorating the discourse of women's liberation. In addition, she points out that activist groups like YELL, a youth division of ACT UP, have devised new approaches to safe-sex education (G8). Today's diverse youth culture suggests that educators and others must become attentive to the cultural formations that young people inhabit, while making a serious effort to read, listen, and learn from the languages, social relations, and diverse types of symbolic expression that young people produce.

Jon Katz convincingly argues that "children are at the epicenter of the information revolution, ground zero of the digital world. They helped build it, they understand it as well as, or better than anyone else." Thus, as Katz concludes, "they occupy a new kind of cultural space" (173). This is a particularly important insight in light of the attacks on the media and the call for censoring the Internet that arose after the Littleton massacre. These sites engage the public pedagogically and must be considered seriously as knowledge-producing technologies and spheres that demand new types of learning and critical skills from both young people and adults. Many educators, parents, and adults must redefine their own understanding of the new technologies and the new literacies these technologies have produced. The new media, including the Internet and computer culture, must become serious objects of educational analysis and learning, especially in the elementary and public schools. The social affiliations, groups, and cultural experiences these media produce among young people require legitimation and incorporation into the school curricula as seriously as the study of history, English, and language arts. Students must have opportunities, as Jenkins points out, to form supportive communities around their interest in and use of digital media, just as the schools must make media literacy and media production central to the learning process for young people ("Introduction").

If educators, adults, and others are to take seriously what it means to link academic criticism to public knowledge and strategies of intervention, they will have to reevaluate the relationship between culture and power as a starting point for bearing witness to the ethical and political dilemmas that connect the university to other spheres within the broader social landscape. At issue is the need for critical educators to act on the belief that academic work matters in its relationship to broader public practices and policies. In part, this means that educators must address what Cornel West has called the crisis of vision and meaning that currently characterizes all levels of schooling and culture in the United States. The crisis of vision registers the political, social, and cultural demise of democratic relations and values in American institutions and culture. Due to the pervasive despair among young people as well as the possibility of their resistance, educators and others must link educational work, both within and outside of schools, to "what it means to expand the scope of democracy and democratic institutions," and they must address how the very conditions for democracy are being undermined (West 41-42). Such work may lead to an understanding not just of how power operates in particular contexts, but also of how such knowledge "will better enable people to change the contexts and hence the relations of power" that inform the inequalities undermining any viable notion of democratic participation in a wide variety of cultural spheres, including those that play a powerful role in shaping children's culture (Grossberg, "Cultural Studies" 253).

As we move into the new millennium, educators, parents, and others must reevaluate what it means for children to grow up in a world that has been radically altered by corporate culture and new electronic technologies. At the very least, we must assess how new modes of symbolic and social practice affect the way we think about power, social agency, and youth, and what such changes mean for expanding and deepening the process of democratic education, social relations, and public life. In part, such a challenge requires educators to develop a reinvigorated notion of cultural politics in order to reassess the relationship between texts and contexts, meaning and institutional power, critical reflection and informed action. Progressives need new theoretical tools for addressing how knowledge and power can be analyzed within particular spaces and places, especially as such contexts frame the intersection of language and bodies as they become part of the "process of forming and disrupting power relations" (Patton 183). At the same time, critical educators and cultural workers must develop notions of cultural politics that provide an opportunity for parents, educators, and others to better understand how public discourses about youth have become discourses of control, surveillance, and demonization. If progressives interrogate how power works through such discourses to construct particular social formations, they will discover opportunities to challenge the endless stereotypes and myths that provide a rationale for the kinds of regressive legislative policies that contain young people and undermine much needed social investments in their future.

In the post-Littleton climate, rhetoric and composition educators as well as other academics, public school teachers, students, and parents must organize and address the crisis of vision and meaning that permeates late capitalist societies. This crisis is embodied in the growing ascendancy of corporate power; in the shrinking of non-commodified public spaces; and in the spread of market values that has undermined those elements of care, respect, and compassion for others that must be central to any decent democratic society. West correctly argues that the usurpation of democratic values by market values has resulted in a "creeping Zeitgeist of cold heartedness and mean spiritedness" that he terms the "gangsterization of American culture" (43). Any viable form of pedagogy and cultural politics must recognize how the process of gangsterization reproduces and reinforces the crisis of vision and meaning for many Americans—especially young people, who are struggling to redefine their identities within a set of relations based on notions of solidarity, justice, and equality. Such an approach cannot proceed through a series of empty appeals to innocence or through the ritualistic condemnation of young people. It must take shape as a critical attentiveness to the historical, social, and institutional conditions that produce those structures of power and ideologies that bear down on young people at the level of their everyday existence. At stake here is the recognition that the challenge of youth culture must be addressed with the same theoretical rigor and political awareness that have been accorded to the related issues of race, class, gender, and sexuality. I do not mean to suggest, though, that youth should simply be added to the mantra of race, class, and gender. On the contrary, youth must be viewed as an essential category of understanding for all social movements, both within and outside of the university, that struggle to implement a broad vision of social justice.

Notes

1. This effort is evident in the work that has been published over the years in *JAC*. Also see Berlin; Bizzell; Brodkey; Olson; Olson and Gale; and Crowley.
2. For a brilliant analysis of the history and the struggle over youth since the 1970s, see Grossberg, *We Gotta*.
3. Many of the ideas in this paper draw from my "Public Intellectuals and the Challenge of Children's Culture."
4. The universalized notion of childhood and innocence is dismantled in a range of historical work on childhood. See, Ariès; Jenks; Higonnet. For a history of contemporary youth cultures and history, see Austin and Willard.
5. See, for example, Bloom. For a critique of this position, see Aronowitz and Giroux; Levine.
6. I want to emphasize that in using the general term "adults," I am not suggesting that the relationship between children and adults is defined generationally. On the contrary, while all adults are capable of abusing young people, the central issue of adult power cannot be abstracted from larger class, racial, and gender formations, nor can it be removed from the dynamics of American capitalism itself, which, in my estimation, should be at the forefront of any analysis of the devastating effects many young people have to endure in the United States at the present time.
7. This national tragedy is captured by the national Commission on the Role of the Schools when it acknowledges, "Never before has one generation of American children been less healthy, less cared for, or less prepared for life than their parents were at the same age" (3).
8. See Cole. For a passionate and moving commentary on the plight of children who have been incarcerated with adults, see Lewis.
9. For a brilliant commentary on the plight of children in the Reagan-Clinton era, see Finnegan.
10. Stephens ask a similar question: "What are the implications for society as a whole, if there are no longer social spaces conceived as at least partially autonomous from the market and market-driven politics? Where are we to find the sites of difference, the terrain of social witness, critical leverage, and Utopian vision, insofar as the domain of childhood—or of everyday life or of a semiautonomous realm of culture—is increasingly shot through with the values of the marketplace and the discursive

politics of postmodern global culture? And what happens to the bodies and minds of children in the process?" (10–11)

11. Leland offers one almost hysterical tirade against student use of Internet video games.

12. For an important commentary on the recent public attack on the new electronic media and its effect on youth, especially in light of the Littleton tragedy, see Jenkins, "Testimony."

13. For an excellent commentary on how adults construct a number of myths to suggest kids need to be contained for emulating the worst behaviors of adults, see Males; also see Powers' insightful commentary on the various ways in which young people defy such stereotypes and make an enormous number of diverse contributions to society, exhibiting both their own sense of individual and collective agency and social contributions to the larger world. For a complex rendering of youth that completely undermines many of the stereotypes circulated about youth, see Jenkins, "Introduction."

14. The *Index of Social Health* claims that the social health of children is at its lowest point in twenty-five years (6). See also Hewlett and West.

15. Here I am arguing against those educators who focus on questions of difference almost entirely in terms of identity and subjectivity while ignoring the related issues of materialism and power. See Giroux, *Impure*.

Works Cited

Ariès, Philippe. *Centuries of Childhood: A Social History of Family Life.* New York: Vintage, 1962.

Aronowitz, Stanley, and Henry A. Giroux. *Postmodern Education: Politics, Culture, and Social Criticism.* Minneapolis: U of Minnesota P, 1991.

Austin, Joe, and Michael Nevin Willard, eds. *Generations of Youth: Youth Cultures and History in Twentieth-Century America.* New York: New York UP, 1998.

Barber, Benjamin R. "More Democracy! More Revolution!" *Nation* 26 Oct. 1998: 11+.

Benhabib, Seyla. "The Democratic Moment and the Problem of Difference." *Democracy and Difference.* Ed. Seyla Benhabib. Princeton: Princeton UP, 1996. 3–18.

Bennett, Tony. "Cultural Studies: A Reluctant Discipline." *Cultural Studies* 12.4 (1998): 528–45.

Berlant, Lauren. *The Queen of America Goes to Washington City: Essays on Sex and Citizenship.* Durham: Duke UP, 1997.

Berlin, James A. *Rhetorics, Poetics, and Cultures: Refiguring College English Studies.* Urbana: NCTE, 1996.

Bizzell, Patricia. *Academic Discourse and Critical Consciousness.* Pittsburgh: U of Pittsburgh P, 1992.

Bloom, Harold. *The Western Canon: The Books and School of the Ages.* New York: Harcourt, 1994.

Brodkey, Linda. *Academic Writing as Social Practice.* Philadelphia: Temple UP, 1987.

———. *Writing Permitted in Designated Areas Only.* Minneapolis: U of Minnesota P, 1996.

Cole, David. *No Equal Justice: Race and Class in the American Criminal Justice System.* New York: New P, 1999.

Crowley, Sharon. *Composition in the University: Historical and Polemical Essays.* Pittsburgh: U of Pittsburgh P, 1998.

Derber, Charles. *Corporation Nation: How Corporations Are Taking Over Our Lives and What We Can Do About It.* New York: St. Martin's, 1998.

Derrida, Jacques. "Mochlos; or, The Conflict of the Faculties." *Logomachia: The Conflict of the Faculties.* Ed. Richard Rand. Lincoln: U of Nebraska P, 1992. 1–34.

Elkind, David. *The Hurried Child: Growing Up Too Fast Too Soon.* Reading, MA: Addison, 1981.

———. *Reinventing Childhood: Raising and Educating Children in a Changing World.* Rosemont, NJ: Modern Learning, 1998.

———. "The Social Determination of Childhood and Adolescence." *Education Week* 18.24 (1999):48–50.

Farkas, Steve, et al. *Kids These Days: What Americans Really Think About the Next Generation*. New York: Public Agenda, 1997.

Federal Bureau of Investigation. Uniform Crime Reports for the United States 1996. Washington, DC: FBI, 1997.

Finnegan, William. *Cold New World: Growing Up in a Harder Country*. New York: Random, 1998.

Fuentes, Annette. "The Crackdown on Kids." *Nation* 15/22 June 1998:20–22.

Giroux, Henry A. *Border Crossings: Cultural Workers and the Politics of Education*. New York: Routledge, 1992.

———. *Channel Surfing: Race Talk and the Destruction of Today's Youth*. New York: St. Martin's, 1997.

———. *Fugitive Cultures: Race, Violence, and Youth*. New York: Routledge, 1996.

———. *Impure Acts: The Practical Politics of Cultural Studies*. New York: Routledge, forthcoming.

———. "Public Intellectuals and the Challenge of Children's Culture." *Review of Education/Pedagogy/ Cultural Studies*, forthcoming.

Glenn, Cheryl. *Rhetoric Retold: Regendering the Tradition from Antiquity Through the Renaissance*. Carbondale: Southern Illinois University Press, 1997.

Grossberg, Lawrence. "Cultural Studies: What's in a Name? (One More Time)." *Bringing It All Back Home: Essays on Cultural Studies*. Durham: Duke UP, 1997.

———. *We Gotta Get Out of This Place: Popular Conservatism and Postmodern Culture*. New York: Routledge, 1992.

Hewlett, Sylvia Ann, and Cornell West. *The War Against Parents*. New York: Houghton, 1998.

Higonnet, Anne. *Pictures of Innocence*. New York: Thames and Hudson, 1998.

Hirschberg, Lynn. "Desperate to Seem 16." *The New York Times Magazine* 5 Sept. 1999: 42+.

Index of Social Health. New York: Fordham Institute for Innovation in Social Policy, 1996.

Jenkins, Henry. "Introduction: Child Innocence and Other Myths." *The Childrenss Culture Reader*. Ed. Henry Jenkins. New York: New York UP, 1998.

———. "Testimony on *Marketing Violence to Children*." *The U.S. Senate Committee on Commerce, Science and Transportation*, http: www.senate.gov/ ~commerce/hearings/hearings.html (4 May 1999).

Jenks, Chris. *Childhood*. New York: Routledge, 1996.

Johnson, Richard. "Reinventing Cultural Studies: Remembering for the Best Version." *From Sociology to Cultural Studies: New Perspectives*. Ed. Elizabeth Long. Maiden, MA: Blackwell, 1997. 452–88.

Kantrowitz, Barbara, and Pat Wingert. *"How Well Do You Know Your Kid?" Newsweek* 10 May 1998: 36–40.

Katz, Jon. *Virtuous Reality: How America Surrendered Discussion of Moral Values to Opportunists, Nitwits and Blockheads Like William Bennett*. New York: Random, 1997.

Kelley, Robin D. G. *Yo' Mama's DisFUNKtionall: Fighting the Culture Wars in Urban America*. Boston: Beacon, 1997.

Kincaid, James R. *Child-Loving: The Erotic Child and Victorian Culture*. New York: Routledge, 1992.

Leland, John. "The Secret Life of Teens." *Newsweek* 10 May 1999: 45–50.

Levine, Lawrence W. *The Opening of the American Mind: Canons, Culture, and History*. Boston: Beacon, 1996.

Lewis, Anthony. "Suffer the Children." *The New York Times* 7 July 1997: A15.

Lipsitz, George. "Listening to Learn and Learning to Listen: Popular Culture, Cultural Theory, and American Studies." *American Quarterly* 42.4 (1990): 615–36.

Males, Mike. *Framing Youth: Ten Myths About the Next Generation*. Monroe, ME: Common Courage, 1999.

Milloy, Courtland. "A Look At Tragedy in Black, White." *Washington Post* 2 May 1999: C1+.

National Commission on the Role of the Schools and the Community in Improving Adolescent Health. *Code Blue: Uniting for Healthier Youth.* Washington, DC: National Association of State Boards of Education/American Medical Association, 1990.

Olson, Gary A., ed. *Philosophy, Rhetoric, Literary Criticism: Interviews.* Carbondale: Southern Illinois UP, 1994.

Olson, Gary A., and Irene Gale, eds. *(Inter)Views: Cross-Disciplinary Perspectives on Rhetoric and Literacy.* Carbondale: Southern Illinois UP, 1991.

Patterson, Orlando. "When 'They' are 'Us.'" *The New York Times* 30 April 1999: A31.

Patton, Cindy. "Performativity and Spatial Distinction: The End of AIDS Epidemiology." *Performativity and Performance.* Ed. Andrew Parker and Eve Kosofsky Sedgwick. New York: Routledge, 1995. 173–96.

Postman, Neil. *The Disappearance of Childhood.* New York: Delacorte, 1982.

Powers, Ann. "Who Are These People, Anyway?" *The New York Times* 29 April 1998: G1+.

Said, Edward W. *Representations of the Intellectual: The 1993 Reith Lectures.* New York: Pantheon, 1994.

Stephens, Sharon. "Children and the Politics of Culture in 'Late Capitalism.'" *Children and the Politics of Culture.* Ed. Sharon Stephens. Princeton: Princeton UP, 1995. 3–48.

Tucker, Cynthia. "In Littleton's Wake, We All Turn to Movies." *The Atlanta Journal Constitution* 25 April 1999: C5.

Warner, Marina. *Six Myths of Our Time: Little Angels, Little Monsters, Beautiful Beasts, and More.* New York: Vintage, 1995.

West, Cornel. "America's Three-Fold Crisis." *Tikkun* 9.2 (1994): 41–44.

Williams, Patricia J. "The Auguries of Innocence." *Nation* 24 May 1999: 9.

Worsham, Lynn. "Going Postal: Pedagogic Violence and the Schooling of Emotion." *JAC* 18 (1998): 213–45.

CHAPTER 5

Breaking into the Movies

Pedagogy and the Politics of Film

2001

Without a politically guaranteed public realm, freedom lacks the worldly space to make its appearance.

—Hannah Arendt

My memories of Hollywood films cannot be separated from the attractions that such films had for me as a young boy growing up in the 1950s in Smith Hill, a working-class neighborhood of Providence, Rhode Island. While we had access to the small screen of black-and-white television, it held none of the mystery, fascination, and pleasure that we found in the five or six grand movie theaters that populated the downtown section of Providence. Every Saturday afternoon, my friends and I would walk several miles to the business district, all the while making plans to get into a theater without having to pay. None of us could afford to buy tickets, so we had to be inventive about ways to sneak into the theater without being caught. Sometimes we would simply wait next to the exit doors, and as soon as somebody left the theater we would rush in and bury ourselves in the plush seats, hoping that none of the ushers spotted us. We were not always so lucky. At other times, we would pool our money and have one person buy a ticket. At the most strategic moment, he would open the exit door from the inside and let us in. Generally, we would sit in the balcony so as to avoid being asked for a ticket if the ushers came along and spotted us.

Hollywood film engendered a profound sense of danger and otherness for us. Gaining access to the movies meant we had to engage in illicit behavior, risking criminal charges or a beating by an irate owner if caught. But the fear of getting caught was outweighed by the lure of adventure and joy. Once we got inside the theater we were transported into an event. We were able to participate in a public act of viewing that was generally restricted for kids in our neighborhood because films were too expensive, too removed from the daily experiences of kids too poor to use public transportation, and we were too restless to sit in a movie theater without talking and laughing and allegedly too rough to inhabit a public space meant for family entertainment. Silence in the movie theaters was imposed on us by the fear of being noticed. Yet, the thrill of adventure and the expectation of what was about to unfold before us was well worth the self-imposed discipline (that is, the contained silence and focus that such viewing demanded). Back on the street, the movies enabled a space of dialogue, criticism, and solidarity for us. Movies were a source of shared joy, entertainment, and escape. Although we were too young to realize it at the time, they were a source of knowledge—a source of knowledge that, unlike what we were privy to in school, connected pleasure to meaning. Sometimes we saw as many as three double features in one day. When we left the movie theater, the cinematography and narratives that we had viewed filled our conversations and our dreams. We argued, and sometimes actually fought, over their meaning and their relevance to our lives. Hollywood films took us out of Smith Hill, offered narratives that rubbed against the often rigid identities we inhabited, and offered up objects of desire that both seduced us and also left us thinking that the movies were not about reality but were fantasies, remote from the burdens and problems that dominated our neighborhoods. Film pointed to a terrain of pseudo-freedom located in an inner world of dreams, reinforced by the privatized experience of pleasure and joy offered through the twin seductions of escape and entertainment.

All of these memories of my early exposure to Hollywood films came rushing back to me during a recent visit to Universal Studios in Los Angeles. While I was on one of the tours of the studio lots, the guide attempted to capture the meaning of contemporary film by proclaiming, without hesitation, that the great appeal of film lies in its capacity to "make people laugh, cry, and sit on the edge of their seats." Surely, I believed this as a child, as much as the tourists listening to the guide seemed to believe it almost forty years later. My first reaction was to dismiss the guide's comments as typical of Hollywood's attempt to commodify experience through simplification and reification, relieving pleasure of the burden of thinking (let alone engaging in critique) and positioning the public as passive tourists traveling through the Hollywood dream machine. However, there was something about the guide's comments that warranted more than a simple dismissal. While the mythic fantasy and lure of entertainment demands a challenge to the utterly privatized realm of mass-mediated common sense, it also requires more than the arrogance of theory, which too often refuses to link the pleasure of film-viewing with the workings and structures of the public domain. Film does more than entertain; it offers up subject positions, mobilizes desires, influences us unconsciously, and helps to construct the landscape of American culture. Deeply imbricated within material and symbolic relations of power, film produces and incorporates ideologies that represent the outcome of struggles marked by the historical realities of power and the deep anxieties of the times; it also deploys power through the important role it plays in connecting the production of pleasure and meaning to the mechanisms and practices of powerful teaching machines. Put simply, films both entertain and educate.

In the 1970s, I began to understand, though in a limited way, the constitutive and political nature of film—particularly how power is mobilized through its use of images, sounds, gestures, talk, and spectacle— in order to create the possibilities for people to be educated about how to act, speak, think, feel, desire, and behave. Film provided me with a pedagogical tool for offering students alternative views of the world. Of course, film not only challenged print culture as the only viable source of knowledge; it was an attractive cultural text for students because it was not entirely contaminated by the logic of formal schooling. As a young high school teacher, I too was attracted to film as a way of challenging the constraints imposed by the rigidity of the text-based curriculum. In opposition to the heavy reliance on the lock-step, traditional curriculum,

I would rent documentaries from a local Quaker group in order to present students with a critical perspective on the Vietnam War, poverty, youth-oriented issues, the Cold War, and a host of other social concerns. Film became a crucial text for me, useful as a resource to offset dominant textbook ideologies and invaluable as a pedagogical tool to challenge officially sanctioned knowledge and modes of learning.

The choices I made about what films to show were determined by their overtly educational content. At that point in my teaching experience, I had not figured out that every film played a powerful role pedagogically not only in the schools, but also in the wider culture as well. Nor did I ever quite figure out how my students felt about these films. Far removed from the glamor of Hollywood, these documentary narratives were often heavy-handed ideologically, displaying little investment in irony, humor, or self-critique. Certainly, my own reception of them was marked by ambivalence. The traditional notion that film was either a form of entertainment or the more radical argument that dismissed film as a one-dimensional commodity seemed crass to me. One option that I pursued in challenging these deeply held assumptions was to engage film performatively as a social practice and event mediated within the give and take of diverse public spheres and lived experiences. My students and I discussed the films we viewed both in terms of the ideologies they disseminated and how they worked to move mass audiences and break the continuity of common sense. In addition, film became important to me as a way of clarifying my role as a critical teacher and of broadening my understanding of critical pedagogy, but there was a price to pay for such an approach. Film no longer seemed to offer me pleasure inasmuch as my relationship to it was now largely conceived in narrow, instrumental terms. As a subversive resource to enhance my teaching, I focused on film in ways that seem to ignore how it functioned as a site of affective investment, mobilizing a range of desires while invoking the incidental, visceral, and transitory. Film unconsciously became for me a formalized object of detached academic analysis. I attempted to organize the study of film around important pedagogical issues, but in doing so I did not use theory as a resource to link film to broader aspects of public life— connecting it to audiences, publics, and events within the concrete relations of power that characterized everyday life. Instead, I used theory as a way of legitimating film as a social text, rather than as a site where different possibilities of uses and effects intersect. I wanted students to read film critically, but I displayed little concern with what it meant to do more than examine how a given film as a relatively isolated text was implicated in the production of ideologies. Missing from my approach, then, was any sustained attempt to address how both documentary and popular film might be used pedagogically to prepare students to function as critical agents capable of understanding, engaging, and transforming those discourses and institutional contexts that closed down democratic public life. In addition, by being overly concerned with how film might be used as an alternative educational text, I failed to understand and impart to my students the powerful role that film now played within a visual culture employing new forms of pedagogy, signaling different forms of literacy, and exemplifying a mode of politics in which, as Lawrence Grossberg says, "culture [becomes] a crucial site and weapon of power in the modern world" (*Bringing* 143).

I am not suggesting that films are over burdened by theoretical discourse per se or that they should be removed from the sphere of engaged textual analysis. But I do want to challenge those versions of textuality and theory that isolate film from broader social issues and considerations that structure the politics of everyday realities. Drawing on a distinction that Grossberg makes, I am more interested in theorizing politics than in a politics of theory, which suggests less an interest in theory as an academic discourse than as a resource strategically deployed in relation to particular projects, contexts, and practices that both makes pressing problems visible and offers the tools to expand the promises of a substantive democracy.

At the same time, as film (particularly Hollywood film) becomes more commodified, ubiquitous, and increasingly abstracted from serious forms of critical analysis, it is all the more important to engage the varied theoretical discourses around film studies produced by feminists, mass culture theorists, Marxists, and others. These approaches have performed an important theoretical service in enabling us to understand the aesthetic and political significance of film texts on the one hand, and, on the other, the specific industrial and economic formations that shape how they are produced and consumed.[1] However, while academic film studies dramatically offsets the commonplace assumption that film is either simply about entertainment or not worthy of serious academic analysis, such discourses have often become so narrow as to find no way to talk about film as a public pedagogy or to fully engage how film relates to public life. These discourses often treat film in a manner that is overly formalistic and pretentiously scientific, trapped in a jargon that freezes the worldly dimension of film as a public transcript that links meaning to effect, and forged amidst the interconnecting registers of meaning, desire, agency, and power. The refusal to fully engage film as a public medium that, as Gore Vidal points out, provides both a source of joy and knowledge is all the more problematic, especially since film has become so prevalent in popular and global culture as a medium through which people communicate with each other.

The potency and power of the film industry can be seen in its powerful influence on the popular imagination and public consciousness. Unlike ordinary consumer items, film produces images, ideas, and ideologies that shape both individual and national identities. The power of its reach and the extent of its commodification can be seen as film references are used to sell t-shirts, cups, posters, bumper stickers, and a variety of kitsch. At the same time, however, the growing popularity of film as a compelling mode of communication and form of public pedagogy—a visual technology that functions as a powerful teaching machine that intentionally tries to influence the production of meaning, subject positions, identities, and experience—suggests how important it has become as a site of cultural politics. Herman Gray captures this sentiment in arguing that "culture and the struggles over representation that take place there are not just substitutes for some 'real' politics that they inevitably replace or at best delay; they simply represent a different, but no less important, site in the contemporary technological and postindustrial society where political struggles take place" (6).

As a form of public pedagogy, film combines entertainment and politics, and as I have attempted to argue, lays claim to public memory (though in contested ways given the existence of distinctly varied social and cultural formations). Yet, films are more than "vehicles of public memory." Mining the twin operations of desire and nostalgia, they are also sites of educated hopes and hyper-mediated experiences that connect the personal and the social by bridging the contradictory and overlapping relations between private discourses and public life. While film plays an important role in placing particular ideologies and values into public conversation, it also provides a pedagogical space that opens up the "possibility of interpretation as intervention" (Olson and Worsham 29). As public pedagogy, it makes clear the need for forms of literacy that address the profoundly political and pedagogical ways in which knowledge is constructed and enters our lives in what Susan Bordo calls "an image-saturated culture" (2). For progressive educators, this might mean educating students and others to engage the ethical and practical task of critically analyzing how film functions as a social practice that influences their everyday lives and positions them within existing social, cultural, and institutional machineries of power; it might mean educating students in how the historical and contemporary meanings that film produces align, reproduce, and interrupt broader sets of ideas, discourses, and social configurations at work in the larger society (see Gray 132).

Addressing how we think about film as a public pedagogy and a form of cultural politics is all the more crucial as traditional, if not oppositional, public spheres such as religious institutions, schools, trade unions, and social clubs become handmaidens to neoliberal social agendas that turn such noncommodified public spheres into commercial spaces (see Hill and Montag). The decline of public life demands that we use film as a way of raising questions that are increasingly lost to the forces of market relations, commercialization, and privatization. As the opportunities for civic education and public engagement begin to disappear, film may provide one of the few media left that enables conversations that connect politics, personal experiences, and public life to larger social issues (see Giroux *Public*). Not only does film travel more as a pedagogical form compared to other popular forms (such as television and popular music), but film carries a kind of pedagogical weight that other media do not. Films allow their ideologies to play out pedagogically in a way that a three-minute pop song or a twenty-two minute sitcom cannot do and by doing so offer a deeper pedagogical register for producing particular narratives, subject positions, and ideologies. In addition, young people inhabit a culture in which watching film demands a certain degree of attention, allowing them to enter into its discourse intertextually in a way that they cannot or often refuse to do with television programs and other electronic media. Often a backdrop for a wide range of social practices, television, video games, and popular music are a kind of distracted media that do not offer the pedagogical possibilities that appear relatively unique to the way in which film mobilizes a shared and public space.

Using film in my classes during the last decade, I have come to realize that film connects to students' experiences in multiple ways that oscillate between the lure of film as entertainment and the provocation of film as a cultural practice. On the one hand, many students—feeling powerless and insecure in a society marked by a cutthroat economy, increasing privatization, and a breakdown of all notions of public life—find a sense of relief and escape in the spectacle of film. On the other hand, many students see in the public issues addressed by film culture a connection to public life that revitalizes their sense of agency and resonates with their sense of the importance of the cultural terrain as both an important source of knowledge and of critical dialogue. At best, film offers students an opportunity to connect the theoretical discourses we engage in classes to a range of social issues represented through the lens of Hollywood movies. Reading about youth seems more compelling when accompanied by a viewing of Larry Clark's film *Kids*. Theorizing masculinity in American society becomes more meaningful and concrete when addressed in the context of a film such as *Fight Club*, especially since many students identify with the film and only after seeing and talking about it as part of a critical and shared dialogue do they begin to question their own investment in the film. Film no longer merely constitutes another method of teaching for me, a view I had held as a high school teacher. It now represents a new pedagogical text, one that does not simply reflect culture but actually constructs it, one that signals the need for a radically different perspective on literacy and the relationship between film texts and society. The power and pervasiveness of film not only calls into question its status as a cultural product, but also raises serious questions about how its use of spectorial pleasure and meaning work to put into play people's attitudes and orientations toward others and the material circumstances of their own lives. The importance of film as a form of public pedagogy also raises questions about the educational force of the larger culture. Moreover, it recognizes that the effort to make knowledge meaningful in order to make it critical and transformative requires that we understand, engage, and make accountable those modes of learning that have shaped students' identities outside of school. Of course, there is always the risk of using popular cultural forms such as film as a way of policing students' pleasures and in so doing undermining the sense of joy and entertainment that film provides. As Margaret Miles points out, however, it would be an ethical and a pedagogical mistake to allow students to believe that film is merely about entertainment, or, at the same time, that the pleasure of entertainment is identical to the "learned pleasure of analysis" (14). Scrutinizing the pleasure of entertainment in film, James Snead points out that it never has been enough "to just see a film—and now, more than ever, we need, not just to 'see,' but to 'see through' what we see on the screen" (131). Snead is not denying that students make important affective investments in film; rather, he wants educators to recognize that such investments often work effectively to connect people and power through mechanisms of identification and affect that undermine the energies of critical engagement. Snead's comments suggest that students must think seriously about how film not only gives meaning to their lives but also how it mobilizes their desires in powerful ways. Seeing through film means, in this sense, developing the critical skills to engage how the ideological and affective work together to offer up particular ways of viewing the world in ways that come to matter to individuals and groups. Film assumes a major educational role in shaping the lives of many students, and bell hooks is correct in claiming that the pedagogical importance of film (both in terms of what it teaches and the role that it can play as an object of pedagogical analysis) cannot be underestimated. Hooks' comments about her own use of film is quite instructive:

> It has only been in the last ten years or so that I began to realize that my students learned more about race, sex and class from movies than from all the theoretical literature I was urging them to read. Movies not only provide a narrative for specific discourses of race, sex, and class, they provide a shared experience, a common starting point from which diverse audiences can dialogue about these charged issues (2).

As a teaching form, film often puts into play issues that enter the realm of public discourse, debate, and policy-making in diverse and sometimes dramatic ways—whether we are talking about films that deal with racism, challenge homophobia, or provide provocative representations that address the themes of war, violence, masculinity, sexism, and poverty.

Uniquely placed between the privatized realm of the home and other public spheres, film provides a distinct space in which a range of contradictory issues and meanings enter public discourse sometimes in a subversive fashion that addresses pressing and urgent issues in American society. As a space of translation, film also bridges the gap between private and public discourse, plays an important role in putting particular ideologies and values into public conversation, and offers a pedagogical space for addressing how a society views itself and the public world of power, events, politics, and institutions.

Engaging film as a form of public pedagogy in my recent work, I have not been particularly interested in defending film as an art form. Aside from the residue of nostalgia and elitism that guides this position, it is a view that seems particularly out of date, if not irrelevant, given the important role that popular culture, including film, now plays pedagogically and politically in shaping the identities, values, and broader social practices that characterize an increasingly postmodern culture in which the electronic media and visual forms constitute the most powerful educational tools of the new millennium. Similarly, I have avoided addressing or taking up film within the disciplinary strictures of contemporary media and film studies, which are designed, in part, to legitimate film as a serious academic subject. Thus, I choose not to position my particular approach to discussing film in relation to what is admittedly a vast literature of film theory and response theories. Absent from the analysis I recommend is a sustained focus on those specialized film theories that engage film as a self-contained text or that largely focus on film through the narrow lens of specific theoretical approaches such as semiotics, Lacanian psychoanalysis, or feminist theories of pleasure. Film and media studies are bound up with a complex philosophical debate surrounding the meaning and importance of film theory, and while such work is enormously important I point to these traditions in my classes but do not address them with any depth because of the specialized nature of their focus. At the same time, I often provide students with resources to address such traditions in ways that do justice to the complexity of such work. While this work is enormously important, my aim pedagogically is much more modest. I try to address film more broadly as part of a public discourse, cultural pedagogy, and civic engagement that participates in a kind of ideological framing and works to structure everyday issues around particular assumptions, values, and social relations. I make no claim that there is a direct correlation between what people see, hear, and read and how they act, between the representations they are exposed to and the actual events that shape their lives. However, I do argue that film as a form of civic engagement and public pedagogy creates a climate that helps to shape individual behavior and public attitudes in multiple ways, whether consciously or unconsciously.

The entertainment industry is the second largest export—second only to military aircraft—and it is estimated that 10,000,000 see a successful film in theaters, and millions more see it when it is aired on cable and exported to foreign markets (Asner ix). The film industry is controlled by a very limited number of corporations that exercise enormous power in all major facets of movie-making (production, distribution, and circulation in the United States and abroad) (see McChesney). At the same time, the media is not an unchanging, monolithic bastion of corporate culture and ruling-class power; a critical approach to media and film requires an understanding that film is not monolithic nor are its audiences passive dupes. Films, like other media, work to gain consent and operate within limits set by the contexts in which they are taken up. Moreover, as numerous film scholars have indicated, audiences mediate such films rather than simply inhabit their structures of meaning. In my own writing and teaching, I use film to address a number of important social issues and to address educators, students, and others who want to explore film in their classes and other educational sites as part of an interdisciplinary project aimed at linking knowledge to broader social structures, learning to social change, and student experience to the vast array of cultural forms that increasingly shape their identities and values.

Rather than focus on film theory in my classes, I am more concerned with what it means to situate film within a broader cultural context as well as with the political and pedagogical implications of film as a teaching machine. Theory in this approach is used as a resource to study the complex and shifting relations between texts, discourses, everyday life, and structures of power. Rather than reduce the study of film to an academic exercise rooted in a specific theoretical trajectory, I attempt to analyze film in ways that link texts to contexts, culture to the institutional specificity of power, pedagogy to the politics of representation, affective investments to the construction of particular notions of agency, and learning to public intervention. By taking up a given film intertextually, I attempt to foreground not just questions of meaning and interpretation but also questions of politics, power, agency, and social transformation. The ubiquity and importance of film as a mode of public pedagogy offers educators both an opportunity and a challenge to connect film as a cultural practice to broader public issues, social relations, and institutional formations. How films derive their meanings and how specific claims are made by different audiences on films must be addressed not through the narrow lens of film theory or through the somewhat limited lens of reception theory but through an assemblage of other cultural texts, discourses, and institutional formations. Meaning should not be sutured into a text, closed off from the myriad contexts in which it is produced, circulated, and renegotiated. Nor should the primary signification exist at the expense of engaging material relations of power. On the contrary, a given film becomes relevant as public pedagogy to the degree that it is situated within a broader politics of representation, one that suggests that the struggle over meaning is, in part, defined as the struggle over culture, power, and politics. I purposely avoid in my pedagogical practices focusing exclusively on films as isolated texts, and I also avoid using film in what Doug Kellner refers to as a narrowly and one-sidedly ethnographic approach to audience reception of texts (199). These approaches are important, but they do not necessarily yield a productive way of dealing with film as a form of public pedagogy. Rather, they often fail to address questions of effects because they do not theorize the relationship of meaning to historical and institutional contexts and consequently largely ignore the material and power-saturated relations that structure daily life and provide the context that films both reflect and help to construct. Often missing from such analyses are the ways in which films are located along a circuit of power that connects the political economy and regulation of films with how they function as representational systems implicated in processes of identity formation and consumption.[2] The problem is not that a film can be understood in multiple ways, but that some meanings have a force that other meanings do not; that is, the problem is that some meanings gain a certain legitimacy and become the defining terms of reality because of how well they resonate and align under certain conditions with broader discourses, dominant ideologies, and existing material relations of power.

In my own approach to the pedagogy of cultural politics, I emphasize in my classes that I approach film as a serious object of social, political, and cultural analysis; moreover, as part of an attempt to read films politically, I make it clear that I bring a certain set of assumptions, experiences, and ideas to my engagement with film. At the same time, however, I try to emphasize that in doing so I am not suggesting that my analyses in any way offer interpretations that make a claim to either certainty or finality. Not only do I encourage a critique of my own interpretations and analyses of film, but I also urge students to develop their own positions as part of a critique and engagement with varied positions (including my own) that develop amidst class dialogue and in conjunction with outside readings and critical reviews. The pedagogical challenge in this instance is to make a convincing case, through the very process of autocritique and student engagement, that my analyses of films are necessarily partial, incomplete, and open to revision and contestation. Rather than closing down student participation, my own interpretations are meant to be strategic and positional. I eschew the notion that any type of closure is endemic to my perspective on particular films; at the same time, I use my own position to encourage students to think more critically about their interpretations as they enter into dialogue about films. Critical analysis under such circumstances is not replaced or shut down but expanded by encouraging students to enter into dialogue both with the films and with the interpretations that frame them; thus, students engage the meaning, function, and role of film as a pedagogical, moral, and political practice that can only be understood within a range of theoretically constructed practices, relations, and frameworks. Addressing film within a framework that is both defined and problematized, I try to signal to students the pedagogical value of their taking a position while not standing still.

Film both shapes and bears witness to the ethical and political dilemmas that animate the broader social landscape, and it often raises fundamental questions about how we think about politics and political agency in light of such a recognition. Critique—as both a form of self-analysis and as a mode of social criticism—is central to any notion of film analysis that takes seriously the project of understanding just how cultural politics matters in the everyday lives of people and what it might mean to make interventions that are both critical and transformative. Film can enable people to think more critically about how art may contribute to constructing public spaces that expand the possibilities for both pleasure and political agency, democratic relations, and social justice. At the same time, film as a form of public pedagogy provokes students and others outside of the academy to examine critically how Hollywood film—in spite of its unquestioned fetishization of entertainment, spectacle, and glamour—encourages us to understand (or misunderstand) the wider culture and how it influences us to live our lives.

In every class that I teach, I use films that are not only widely accessible to the public but that also deal with complex and provocative topics that highlight a number of important social issues, problems, and values that provoke the public imaginary and that, in many cases, generate substantial controversy. In addressing film as a form of cultural politics and an important mode of public pedagogy, progressive educators may engage the pedagogical and political practice of film in ways that render due account of the complexities of film culture itself. At the same time, such educators must challenge a voyeuristic reception of films by offering students the theoretical resources necessary to engage critically how dominant practices of representation work to secure individual desires, organize specific forms of identification, and regulate particular modes of understanding, knowledge, and agency. Taking film seriously as a vehicle of public pedagogy means, in part, examining how a given film's practices and values embody relations of power and ideological assumptions— admittedly in contradictory ways—that both mirror and construct the interests, fears, longings, and anxieties of the periods in which it was produced. Accordingly, this insight suggests developing pedagogical practices that promote political engagement, that challenge conventional ways of thinking about film as simply entertainment, and that use film as a cultural text to bridge the gap between the academic discourse of the classroom and those social issues and public concerns that animate the larger society.

As a young boy going to the movies in Providence, Rhode Island, I believed that film only provided the diversion of entertainment. I had no idea that it also played an active role in shaping my sense of agency and offered me a moral and political education that largely went unnoticed and uncontested. Film has been a great source of joy throughout my lifetime.

Now it not only provides pleasure, but it also enables me to think more critically about how power operates within the realm of the cultural and how social relations and identities are forged. All films disseminate ideologies, beckon in sometimes clear and always contradictory ways toward visions of the future, and encourage and stultify diverse ways of being in the world. Most importantly, film constitutes a powerful force for shaping public memory, hope, popular consciousness, and social agency and as such invites people into a broader public conversation. As Miriam Hansen suggests, film offers a horizon of "sensory experience and discursive contestation" and engenders a public space in which knowledge and pleasure intersect, which is no small matter as public life becomes increasingly controlled and regulated, if not militarized (312; see also Giroux, *Public*). It is in this promise of education and sensuality that films become other, gesturing toward public spheres beyond those spaces offered by the presence of film, spaces in which critical dialogue, pleasure, shared interaction, and public participation flourish. Film, in this instance, registers a public dialogue and set of experiences that offer the opportunity to revitalize those democratic public spheres in which the popular intersects with the pedagogical and the political in ways that suggest that film cannot be dismissed simply as a commodity but now has become crucial to expanding democratic relations, ideologies, and identities.

Notes

1. For a representative example of film studies scholarship, see Carroll; Denzin; Gledhill and Williams; Hollows et al.; and Perez. Although their focus is not on cinema, Durham and Kellner provide a very useful perspective through which to understand film within the larger body of theoretical work produced around media and cultural studies.
2. Here I am drawing on the "circuit of culture" paradigm developed by Hall and others in the Culture, Media, and Identities series published by Sage.

Works Cited

Arendt, Hannah. "What Is Freedom?" *Between Past and Future: Eight Exercises in Political Thought.* 1954. Ed. Hannah Arendt. New York: Penguin, 1977. 143–71.

Asner, Edward. Foreword. *The Political Companion to American Film.* Ed. Gary Crowdus. Chicago: Lake View, 1994.

Bordo, Susan. *Twilight Zones: The Hidden Life of Cultural Images from Plato to O.J.* Stanford: University of California Press, 1997.

Carroll, Noël. *Mystifying Movies: Fads and Fallacies in Contemporary Film Theory.* New York: Columbia University Press, 1988.

Denzin, Norman K. *The Cinematic Society: The Voyeur's Gaze.* London: Sage, 1995.

Durham, Meenakshi Gigi, and Douglas M. Kellner, eds. *Media and Cultural Studies: Key Works.* Malden: Blackwell, 2001.

Giroux, Henry A. *Channel Surfing: Racism, the Media, and the Destruction of Today's Youth.* New York: St. Martin's, 1997.

——. *Fugitive Cultures: Race, Violence and Youth.* New York: Routledge: 1996.

——. *Public Spaces, Private Lives: Beyond the Culture of Cynicism.* Lanham: Rowman, 2001.

——. *Stealing Innocence: Youth, Corporate Power, and the Politics of Culture.* New York: Palgrave, 2000.

Gledhill, Christine, and Linda Williams, eds. *Reinventing Film Studies.* London: Arnold, 2000.

Gray, Herman. *Watching Race: Television and the Struggle for "Blackness."* Minneapolis: University of Minnesota Press, 1995.

Grossberg, Lawrence. *Bringing It All Back Home: Essays on Cultural Studies.* Durham: Duke University Press, 1997.

——. "The Cultural Studies' Crossroads Blues." *European Journal of Cultural Studies* 1 (1998): 65–82.

Hall, Stuart, ed. *Representation: Cultural Representations and Signifying Practices.* London: Sage, 1997.

Hansen, Mariam Bratu. "*Schindler's List* is Not *Shoah*: The Second Commandment, Popular Modernism, and Public Memory." *Critical Inquiry* 22 (1996): 292–312.

Hill, Mike, and Warren Montag, eds. *Masses, Classes and the Public Sphere.* London: Verso, 2000.

Hollows, Joanne, Peter Hutchings, and Mark Jancovich, eds. *The Film Studies Reader.* London: Arnold, 2000.

hooks, bell. *Reel to Real: Race, Sex, and Class at the Movies.* New York: Routledge, 1996.

Kellner, Douglas. *Media Culture: Cultural Studies, Identity, and Politics Between the Modern and the Postmodern.* London: Routledge, 1995.

McChesney, Robert W. *Rich Media, Poor Democracy: Communication Politics in Dubious Times.* Urbana: University of Illinois Press, 1999.

Miles, Margaret. *Seeing and Believing: Religion and Values in the Movies.* Boston: Beacon, 1996.

Olson, Gary A., and Lynn Worsham. "Staging the Politics of Difference: Homi Bhabha's Critical Literacy." *JAC* 18 (1998): 361–91.

Perez, Gilberto. *The Material Ghost: Films and Their Medium.* Baltimore: Johns Hopkins University Press, 1998.

Snead, James. *White Screens, Black Images: Hollywood from the Dark Side.* Ed. Colin MacCabe and Cornel West. New York: Routledge, 1994.

Vidal, Gore. *Screening History.* Cambridge: Harvard University Press, 1992.

NEOLIBERALISM AND THE PHANTASMAGORIA OF THE SOCIAL

Post-9/11 Politics,
the Decline of the Public Sphere,
and the Decay of Humanity

CHAPTER 6

Neoliberalism and the Disappearance of the Social in *Ghost World*

2003

The terrible events of September 11th opened up a new possibility for engaging the relationship between the related concepts of the social, the future, and youth. In many ways, the September 11th actions pointed to both the importance of the social in providing crucial public services in order to save lives, put out fires, provide funds for decimated families, and offer some modicum of protection against further terrorist actions. But this reliance on and celebration of public services and public life itself seemed short lived as the Bush administration seized on the insecurities and fears of the populace in order to expand the policing and military powers of the state through a series of anti-terrorist acts that compromised some of the basic freedoms provided by the Bill of Rights. While waging a war in Iraq, Bush and his supporters pushed through political legislation that once again drained projected public surpluses by offering tax breaks approximating 1.3 trillion dollars for the wealthy and major corporations. Tax cuts that mostly benefit the top 1% of the population at a time when 'the financial wealth of the top one percent of households now exceeds the combined wealth of the bottom 95 percent'[1] do more than undermine any pretence to democratic values. Such welfare schemes for the rich also blatantly exhibit the ruthlessness of a society that, on the one hand, allows one American, Bill Gates, to amass 'more wealth than the combined net worth of the poorest 45 percent of American households'[2] and, on the other hand, refuses to provide adequate healthcare to 14 million children. It is difficult to understand how democratic values are deepened and expanded in a society in which, according to the Bureau of Labor Statistics, the typical American now works 350 hours more per year than a typical European – almost nine full weeks. Under such conditions, parents are not only working longer, they are also spending 40% less time with their children than they did 40 years ago.[3] While it is too early to see how this tension between democratic values and market interests will be played out in the larger society, it is crucial to recognise that young people more than any other group will bear the burden and the consequences of this struggle as it bears down on their everyday lives. Rather than being cherished as a symbol of the future, youth are now seen as a threat to be feared and a problem to be contained. The continuity that bridges a pre- and post-September 11th social reality resides in the relationship between a depoliticised public sphere and the current attack on youth. These related crises are best exemplified in various representations of youth that shape the contemporary political landscape of American culture. How a society understands its youth is partly determined by how it represents them. Popular representations, in particular, constitute a cultural politics that shapes, mediates, and legitimises how adult society views youth and what it expects from them. In this sense, such representations, in part, produced and distributed through the mass media in sites such as television, video, music, film, publishing, and theatre, function as a form of public pedagogy actively attempting to define youth through the ideological filters of a society that is increasingly hostile to young people. All of these sites make competing claims on youth and their relation to the social order. At worse, they engage in a politics of representation, whether offered up in Hollywood films, television dramas, magazines, or popular advertisements, that constructs youth in terms that largely serve to demonise, sexualise or commodify them, that is, reduce their sense of agency to the consumerist requirements of supply and demand. Such images not only resonate with larger public discourses that contribute to a moral panic about youth, they also help to legitimise policies aimed at both containing and punishing young people, especially those who are marginalised by virtue of class, gender, race and sexual orientation. At best, such representations define youth in complex ways that not only capture the problems, issues and values that bear down on them, but also illustrate how varied youth in diverse circumstances attempt to negotiate the contradictions of a larger social order.

In what follows, I examine an exemplary independent film, *Ghost World*, as part of a broader attempt to critically engage how popular representations of youth signal a particular crisis – but do so through a discourse of privatisation, which fails to locate youth and the problems they face within the related geographies of the social and political. *Ghost World* is a particularly interesting film because it is sympathetic to the plight of alienated, downwardly mobile, teenage girls and goes to great lengths to let the principal characters speak in a way that gives meaning and affect to their sense of despair, ennui and resistance to the adult world. This attempt at 'authenticity' has won praise from critics and viewers alike, and makes the film all the more important to analyse as a form of public pedagogy that provides a unique opportunity to take up the troubled dynamic between teenage resistance and the privatisation of the social.

Loosely adapted from an underground comic book by Daniel Clowes and directed by Terry Zwigoff, who also directed the 1995 documentary Crumb, *Ghost World* presents a post-senior portrait of two teenage malcontents, Enid (Thora Birch) and

Rebecca (Scarlett Johansson), who are working out of a combination of adolescent angst and resentment that informs both their resistance to a phony middle-class world and their attempts to adjust to it without losing their self-ascribed marginal status. Best friends since elementary school, the lonely, sardonic Enid, and Rebecca, her slightly more conventional companion, negotiate the complex territory between high school graduation and the plunge into adulthood. *Ghost World* also chronicles the story of their increasingly strained friendship.

In the opening scenes of the film, which takes place during their high school graduation ceremony, Enid and Rebecca are clearly out of sync with the boorish world of dominant school culture and the deadness of American suburbia it reflects – a world embodied by testosterone-driven surfer-like athletic drones, obsequious academic climbers and pom-pom waving cheerleaders just waiting to become soccer moms. They snarl through a graduation speech by a classmate in a head brace and wheelchair that begins with the cliché: 'High School is like the training wheels for the bicycle that is life.' While listening to the speech, Enid whispers, 'I liked her so much better when she was an alcoholic and drug addict. She gets in one stupid car crash and suddenly she's Little Miss Perfect.' When their classmates throw their caps in the air and cheer, Enid and Rebecca respond accordingly by giving their fellow students a middle finger, and to bring the point home, Enid throws her cap on the ground, stomps on it, and shouts, 'What a bunch of retards'. Rebecca nods approvingly, making clear their shared and active refusal to buy into a world filled with what Enid calls 'creeps, losers, and weirdos'.

When we meet the adults who touch Enid's life, they seem to give legitimacy to her presumption that most adults are either phonies or simply losers. Her timid dad (Bob Balaban) fits into the latter category. Living with him in a small but comfortable apartment in Los Angeles, Enid seems to be in pain every time he approaches. Not only does he call her 'pumpkin' and mutter imperceptibly practically every time he opens his mouth, he is also about to ask his corny girlfriend, Maxine (Teri Garr), who tries to befriend Enid by involving her in the exciting world of computer retailing, to move in with them. Needless to say, Enid despises her.

The other adult that Enid has to put up with is a gushy, comically drawn, purple-clad performance artist-teacher named Roberta (Illeana Douglas), who is a mix between a hippie left over from the sixties and a recruit from the take-no-prisoners and I-am-always-right and- righteous strand of feminism. Enid is forced to take Roberta's lame art class during the summer in order to officially graduate, and she sits in class rolling her eyes every time Roberta speaks. Roberta operates off the pedagogical assumption that the only way to reach her students is to relate to their lives, speak in terms they understand and help them to 'find themselves'. The problem is that Roberta confuses her own ideological interests with her students' and rather than listen to them she simply rewards those students who feed back to her what she wants to hear. From day one in class, the art teacher rubs Enid the wrong way so she passes time by adding to her repertoire of violent, comic book drawings, which she eventually shows Roberta. Roberta soon displays some interest in Enid and even helps to get her a scholarship to an art school. But her convictions soon go out the window when Roberta receives a lot of flack from the school and community for showing Enid's work – a representation of one of her friend Seymour's racist ads called 'Coon Chicken' – at an art exhibition ironically titled, 'Neighborhood and Community: Art and Dialogue'. As a result of school and community indignation over Enid's artwork, which was, after all, an attempt to foster real dialogue about the community's racist history, Roberta withdraws the art school scholarship and joins the rest of the adult creeps and hypocrites who seem to inhabit Enid's life.

These adults seem to fuel Enid's desire to inflict ridicule and pain on every adult she and Rebecca come across. With high school behind them, Enid and Rebecca hang out in mock 1950s diners and record stores. At first, their friendship is fuelled by their mutual disdain for everyone around them. 'Like totally losers', Enid scoffs and Rebecca fully agrees. Biting sarcasm is interlaced with Enid's comic-like portraits of the various adults they encounter along the way. Nobody appears to escape their sardonic looks, commentaries and visual escapades. When not ridiculing people and indulging their unlimited capacity for scorn, Enid and Rebecca embark on their shared dream of renting an apartment together and putting their lives in order. Somewhat bored, they set up a meeting with a hapless schmuck – Seymour (Steve Buscemi) – whom they discovered in the personal ad section of the local newspaper. Seymour used the ad to solicit a woman he briefly met in an airport. Enid and Rebecca respond to the ad and set up a meeting in a diner, wait for him to show up, and then watch him drink milkshakes as he waits for a woman who never appears.

As the summer unfolds, a strain develops between the two girls, as Rebecca moves into high gear by getting a job working in a local Starbucks-like emporium, earnestly starts looking for an apartment, and uses her free time to spend money in typical consumer-like fashion on cheap wares for her new place. Enid resists, nonetheless, what appears to be her only option. She is less inclined to adapt to an adult world she loathes. She is put off by the colourless neighbourhood in which Rebecca tries to find an apartment, has no interests in shopping for mall goods to clutter the apartment, and just can't seem to bring herself to look for a job in the corporate world that sickens her. The one job she does get is a short-lived stint at a local multiplex. But she is soon fired because she cannot bring herself to either prod customers into buying oversized drinks or suggest to them that the movies they are watching are worth the effort. Rebecca disapproves of Enid's inability to move forward, and Enid is confused by how easily Rebecca adapts to the world they both despised while in high school.

The relationship is further strained as Enid's life takes an unexpected turn when she meets Seymour, the hapless victim of her personal ad prank. While hunting for an apartment together, Enid and Rebecca come across Seymour at a garage sale, where he is selling some of his vintage 78 rpm collection of blues records out of milk crates. Rebecca finds the forty-something Seymour gross, and admits to Enid that she has 'a total boner' for some wholesome-looking young, blond guy who likes to listen to reggae. But Enid is intrigued by Seymour's sad-sack looks, his commitment to old blues music and various collections of Americana, his intelligence, his isolation and his utterly alienated life. Before long, Enid begins to see him less as a pathetic, middle-aged geek than as a poster boy for permanent rebellion. Things soon begin to click between them, especially after Seymour gives Enid his 1931 recording of Skip James's 'Devil Got My Woman'. Enid decides she is going to be a matchmaker for Seymour, with each attempt instituting a series of inevitable disasters. Seymour sees himself as a bad candidate for a relationship with another woman, telling Enid that 'I don't want someone who shares my interests. I hate my interests.' This makes Seymour all the more odd – a mixture of unapologetic loneliness and refreshing honesty, and hence all the more attractive to Enid, who tells Rebecca, 'He's the exact opposite of all the things I hate'. Each 'date' disaster seems to feed their own relationship as they end up spending more time with each other. Enid tells Seymour, 'Only stupid people have healthy relationships'. And Seymour, sharing her own sense of alienation and cynicism counters, 'That's the spirit'. Unfortunately for Enid, Seymour does meet up with the personal ad girl, Dana (Stacy Travis), and the relationship between Seymour and Enid begins to sour. Seymour's new girlfriend represents everything Enid despises. She and Seymour go shopping together and she buys him stonewashed jeans in an attempt to transform him into prototype for an Eddie Bauer ad. Dana works as a real-estate agent, and seems utterly attached to a world that is far too normal and removed from the self-deprecation, misery and disdain that keeps Enid alert to everything that is phony and empty in middle-class suburban life. Moreover, Seymour seems attracted to his new girlfriend's utterly bourgeois lifestyle, though she sees his music and art collection as so much junk, compromising Enid's view of him as an oddball resister. Enid wages a desperate campaign to win Seymour back and rekindle her friendship with Rebecca, but to no avail. And in the end she boards a bus during the middle of the night and leaves both Los Angeles and her adolescence behind her.

Ghost World is an important film about youth, friendship, alienation and survival. Many commentators have named it one of the top 10 films of 2001, if not the best film yet produced about youth. And one critic for *USA Today* actually named it the best film of the year.[4] Some critics have labelled it as the filmic equivalent of *Catcher in the Rye*. Most critics have celebrated the film for its dead-end irony, its hilarious dialogue, and its honest portrayal of the posturing and superiority befitting youth who drape themselves in the cloak of rebellion. Unlike many other youth films of the past decade, *Ghost World* refuses to trade in caricatures, stereotypes or degrading representations of youth. Moreover, *Ghost World* rejects the traditional Hollywood narrative that chronicles teenage rebellion as part of a rite of passage towards a deeper understanding of what it means to join adult society. Instead, the film focuses on the dark side of teenage alienation, exploring the fractures, cracks and chasms that locate teenagers in a space that is fraught with resentment, scorn and critical insight. *Ghost World* gently and movingly attempts to explore in non-condescending terms the pain of broken relationships, the justifiable teenage fear of being trapped in an adult world that offers few rewards and even less fulfilment, and the difficulty of choosing an identity that is both critical of such a world and not so removed from it as to become either marginalised or irrelevant. Moreover, this film rightly appealed to critics who celebrate its refusal to offer a predictable Disney-like solution to the problems teenagers face and its ability to capture, with depth and empathy, the tensions and ambiguities that shape the lives of many teenagers on the margins of a throwaway culture. Underlying almost all of the reviews I have read of this film is an affirmation, if not romanticising, of an alleged kind of 'authenticity' as the ultimate arbiter of the film's worth. *Ghost World* arguably may be, as many critics suggest, one of the most important youth films of the decade – its importance, in part, stemming from its attempt to address how marginalised youth attempt to negotiate, if not resist, a political and social landscape that offers them few hopes and even fewer opportunities to see beyond its ideological and institutional boundaries.

At the same time, *Ghost World* is notable for the way in which it becomes complicitous with a dominant discourse that too easily functions pedagogically, in spite of its emphasis on youth resistance among teenage girls, to depoliticise their rebellion by displacing the realm of the social as a crucial political concept that provides them with a sense of what it might mean to struggle both individually and collectively for a more just and democratic future. The most important pedagogical issues that hold this film together appear to resonate powerfully with a much broader set of discourses and values that increasingly celebrate and romanticise youth rebellion while denying young people 'any significant place within the collective geography of life in the United States'.[5] Irony, pathos, rebellion and gritty dialogue may help to capture the spirit of teenage girls who 'talk back', but such depictions remain utterly privatised and ineffectual unless they are situated within broader social, economic and political forces that provide an opportunity to understand the crisis of youth as part of a broader crisis of labour, political agency, democracy and the future itself.

While *Ghost World* is certainly not a comfort food film about youth for the middle class, it also does nothing to link the current war being waged against youth with any of the political, economic and cultural realities that propelled the smooth-sailing waters of yuppie greed and spectacle of the last 20 years. Nor does it address the poverty of public discourse about youth and the breakdown of civic culture in American life during the same period. Unwilling to do justice to the urgency of the crisis that youth face in the United States, or the complexity of violence, meanings and practices that shape children's lives, *Ghost World* ignores the possibility of a pedagogy of resistance that disrupts and challenges conventional narratives of marginalised youth in ways that exceed its own ideological limits. Enid may live in a world of existential angst, but her anger seems to be so diffuse as to be meaningless. Why is it she displays so little understanding of an economic order in which the future for young people like herself seems to offer up nothing more than the promise of fast-food jobs and low-skilled labour? Why is it that few commentators on the film in the national media point out that both Enid and Rebecca seem to define their sense of agency exclusively around consuming, whether it be housewares or bohemian artefacts? Or, as Cynthia Fuchs points out in a different context:

> Somehow, when young adulthood should be an ample universe of growth and discovery – one that gives kids the chance to learn, contribute, experiment, envision, and carve out a meaningful role in the world – it is instead shrunk into the pinpoint activity of buying and selling. We treat kids contemptuously by herding them into de-skilled, meaningless, low-wage jobs and by taking them seriously only insofar as they might divulge to marketers how they plan on spending their on-average $84 per week.[6]

Why is it that so few critics take note of the fact that Enid and Rebecca live in a society in which the wealthiest nation on earth allows one-third of its children to live in poverty, or inhabit a society that invests more in building prisons for young people than institutions of higher learning? Why is it that audiences watching this film are never given a clue that Enid and Rebecca live in a society that bears down particularly hard on the lives of young people. Consider the statistics: One in six children in the United States – 12.1 million – still live in poverty. Nearly 8.4 million children are without health insurance, 90% of whom have working parents. One in eight children never graduate from high school and 'children under 18 are the fastest growing and largest portion of the population of homeless in America, with an average age of 9 years old'.[7]

Ghost World hammers home the lesson that in a world of high youth unemployment, poverty, incarceration rates and a disintegrating urban education system, youth have only themselves to rely on and only themselves to blame if they fail. Against the constant reminders of a society that tells youth that it neither needs them or wants them, youth are only offered right-wing homilies about relying on their own resources and cunning. Within this notion of nomadic subjectivity and privatized resistance, the dystopian notion that there are no alternatives to the present order reinforces the message that young people should avoid at all costs the prospect of organising collectively in order to address the social, political and economic basis of individually suffered problems. Resistance in this film rarely touches upon the possibility for recovering the ideals of a democratic social order or a robust form of collective intervention. As such, *Ghost World* is defined less by what it says than by what it leaves out. This present absence is precisely what is necessary for engaging *Ghost World* within a broader set of historical and political contexts. And though *Ghost World* lampoons the middle-class mores of a market-driven society, it ends up replicating rather than challenging those privatised utopias and excessively individualistic values that it sets out to critique – a position that both undercuts its progressive implications and begs for more analysis. Resistance as presented in *Ghost World* points approvingly to how insightful and nuanced young people can be about the phoniness and emptiness of adult society, but it refuses to expand and deepen this notion of resistance in order to explore its relationship to the obligations of critical citizenship, the power of collective struggle, or the necessary translation of private troubles into larger public considerations. There is a historical, political and social void in this film that not only isolates and privatises teenage resistance within the narrow confines of an art-film sensibility, but also fails to address the role that adults play in creating many of the problems that young girls such as Enid and Rebecca face on a daily basis. Adults are not simply boorish or phonies. They also pass legislation that denies children the most fundamental and basic services. Adults commit 75% of the murders of youth in America; they also sexually abuse somewhere between 400,000 and 500,000 youths every year. Talking back to adults through the high-powered and clever use of irony and sarcasm points to neither an understanding nor a way of challenging the attacks often waged on young people by adult society.

Enid may strike a blow for a hip teenage aesthetic with her black fingernail polish, excessive makeup, and *de rigueur* combat boots, but these are only the trappings of resistance without any political substance. And Enid and her companion are offered few if any insights into a society marked by massive youth unemployment, the commercialisation and sexualisation of kids, the increasing incarceration of young people – especially those marginalised by virtue of their class and colour – and the collapse of healthcare, decent public education, drug programs and job training for teenagers. These are the problems that real youth face, and it is hard to believe that Enid and Rebecca can appear oblivious to these problems as they get caught in the very dynamics such issues produce. But it is around the relevance of the future for Enid, and by implication for marginalised youth, that the film and many of its critics seems to waver badly. Throughout the film, Enid comes across an older man, sitting on a bench at a bus stop that has been closed down for quite some time. He seems to be there at all hours of the day. One day Enid tells him the bus route has been cancelled and that he is wasting his time, but he simply snarls at her and tells her to leave him alone. But near the end of the film while Enid is approaching the bus stop, a bus mysteriously arrives and the man boards it and is never to be seen again during the film. In part, this symbolises in rather dramatic form the notion that there is a possibility within the realm of the impossible. That as bleak as the future might seem, there is hope. This scene is all the more poignant since, in the last scene in the film, Enid is seen boarding that same mysterious, cancelled bus, uncertain of where she is going or what she is going to face in the future. Making the possible out of the impossible surely opens up the issue of how the future is being shaped for children as we enter the twenty-first century. But with no analysis grounded in the realties of a society that wages a war against children precisely because they embody a notion of the future that calls into question the very nature of adult obligations and responsibilities, *Ghost World* ends up not only romanticising Enid's contempt for the world but offers no sense of how she might find her way in the world without being subject to its most oppressive practices. It is hard to imagine that Enid will hold on to her critical intelligence and biting wit without eventually succumbing to cynicism, and this is where the film reveals its most egregious shortcoming. As refreshing as this film is given the treatment youth have received in a host of popular representations over the last 20 years, it resonates too intimately with a major aim of neoliberalism, which is to 'make politics disappear by, in part, producing cynicism in the population'.[8] Cynicism does more than confirm irony as the last resort of the defeated, it also substitutes resignation and angst for any viable notion of resistance, politics and social transformation. It is precisely on these terms that *Ghost World* both indicts and reflects the very society it attempts to portray through the eyes of alienated teenage girls.

A society that views children as a threat has no way of talking about the social or the future as central to a vibrant democracy. Moreover, such a society often finds it increasingly difficult to address the importance of those non-commodified values and public spaces that keep alive issues of justice, ethics, public opportunities, civic courage and critical citizenship.

Youth do not simply invoke a discourse of political and social responsibility, but make visible the ethical consequences and social costs for losing a language, not to mention real spaces and places informed by the discourse and practices of civic engagement, critical dialogue and social activism. Youth is troubling because it offers itself up as social category that demands a politics of responsibility which rejects the notion that market freedoms absorb every other freedom and in return accentuates, as Lani Guinier observes, the collective gaze of 'atomised individuals operating in their own spheres' . . . [with] no sense of citizenry, no sense of community that is committed to a set of common values that they have to hold each other accountable to'.[9] As I mentioned in the beginning of this essay, if youth in the past 'became the privileged sign and embodiment of the future',[10] this has all changed under the regime of neoliberalism. Youth now symbolises a threat to the social order rather, a population under siege by a dominant order eager to erase its responsibility to a democratic future.

Ghost World displays no interest in examples of youth resistance that are taking place all over the globe. Ironically, many of the youth participating in these struggles – ranging from the anti-sweatshop movement to the protest against global capitalism and the increasing corporatisation of the university – share an aesthetic and distrust of official authority that is not unlike Enid's. What would it take to connect Enid's sense of alienation and despair to those youthful movements of resistance taking place on both the streets and on the school campuses across the globe? Surely, Enid's sense of despair cannot be unrelated to those ideological and institutional forces that substitute standardised testing for critical learning, treat young people largely as consumers rather than engaged citizens, utterly privatise their sense of agency, subject them to increasing forms of surveillance and racial profiling, and increasingly offer them the possibility of dead-end jobs and incarceration rather than a decent education.

As a symbolic register of contemporary culture, *Ghost World* points to these issues but never fully engages them, and by never adequately attending to 'questions of politics, power, and public consciousness'[11] it displaces political issues to the realm of aesthetics and depoliticised forms of transgression. This is not to suggest that *Ghost World* does not offer any real pleasures in its depiction of teenage rebellion. On the contrary, the film offers a richly textured script of sensory experience and comic pleasure that weaves itself into the girls' speech, punkish style, and offhand body language. Pleasure and knowledge intersect in this film in a way that allows students to make a real affective investment in Enid and Rebecca's lives – all the more reason to connect the pleasures of entertainment that the film provides with the 'learned pleasure of [critical] analysis'.[12] *Ghost World* both shapes and bears witness to the ethical and political dilemmas that animate the broader social landscape which structures teenage life. By examining *Ghost World* within an assemblage of dominant texts, discourses and institutionalised forces, it becomes less difficult to recognise the constitutive nature of film and how the latter suggests that the struggle over meaning is, in part, defined as the struggle over culture and power. If youth are viewed as a threat to the larger social order, it becomes necessary to raise pedagogical questions about how *Ghost World* works in diverse ways to both reinforce and challenge this perception. Making the pedagogical more political in this instance not only serves to locate *Ghost World* within a representational politics that bridges the gap between private and public discourses, but also offers students the space 'to break the continuity and consensus of common sense'13 and resist forms of authority that deny the value of political agency, the importance of the social and the possibility of social change. Maybe the value of this film resides not only in what it says but also in the discussions it might provoke about what it ignores – especially given its sympathetic treatment of youthful resistance among teenage girls. Even though Ghost World attempts to empty teenage resistance of any substantial content, it also points to a larger social order that appears imperiled as individuals are unable to translate their privately suffered misery into public concerns and collective action. It is precisely this contradiction within the film that offers up a rich pedagogical terrain for rethinking modes of collective resistance and social agency that challenge neoliberalism's ongoing war against youth and the elimination of those public spaces that reveal the rough edges of social order, disrupt consensus, and point to the need for modes of education and knowledge that link learning to the conditions necessary for developing democratic forms of political agency and civic struggle. In this sense, *Ghost World* offers the promise to redeem itself by invoking the social, even as it attempts to eliminate it and politicize agency just as it dissolves it within the realm of the personal.

Notes

1. Jeff Gates, 'Modern Fashion or Global Fascism?', *Tikkun* 17:1, 2001, p. 30.
2. Doug Henwood, 'Debts Everywhere', *The Nation*, 19 July 1999, p. 12.
3. Charles Handy, *The Hungry Spirit*, Broadway, New York, 1998, p. 17.

4. Mike Clark, '"Ghost World" Charms, "Freddy" Fizzles', *USA Today*, Friday, 28 December 2001, p. 13D.

5. Lawrence Grossberg, 'Why does neo-liberalism hate kids? The war on youth and the culture of politics', *Review of Education/ Pedagogy & Cultural Studies*, 23:2, 2001, pp. 112–13.

6. See, Znet Commentary/ Cynthia Fuchs/Teens atsysop@zmag.org, p 2.

7. These figures are taken from the Children's Defense Fund website, and are available at: http//www.childrensdefense.org/factsfigures_moments.htm Also, see Grossberg, 'Why does neo-liberalism hate kids?', pp. 114–15.

8. Ibid, pp. 127–8.

9. Lani Guinier and Anna Deavere Smith, 'Rethinking Power, Rethinking Theater', *Theater* 31:3 (Winter 2002), p. 40.

10. Grossberg, 'Why does neo-liberalism hate kids?', p. 133.

11. Arif Dirlik, 'Literature/ identity: transnationalism, narrative and representation', *Review of Education/Pedagogy/ Cultural Studies*, Volume 24, Number 3 (2002), p. 212.

12. Margaret Miles, *Seeing and Believing: Religion and Values in the Movies*, Beacon Press, Boston, 1996, p. 14.

13. Gary Olson and Lynn Worsham, 'Staging the politics of difference: Homi Bhabha's critical literacy', *JAC*, 18:3, 1999, p. 11.

CHAPTER 7

Education after Abu Ghraib

Revisiting Adorno's Politics of Education

2004

Inhumanity has a great future.

—Paul Valéry

Warring Images

Visual representations of the war have played a prominent role in shaping public perceptions of the United States' invasion and occupation of Iraq. The initial, much celebrated image that was widely used to represent the war in Iraq captured the toppling of the statue of Saddam Hussein in Baghdad soon after the invasion. The second image, also one of high drama and spectacle, portrayed President Bush in full flight gear after landing on the deck of the USS Abraham Lincoln. The scripted photo-op included a banner behind the President proclaiming 'Mission Accomplished'.

The mainstream media gladly seized upon the first image since it reinforced the presupposition that the invasion was a justified response to the hyped-up threat Saddam's regime posed to the USA and that his fall was the outcome of an extension of American democracy and an affirmation of its role as a beneficent empire, animated by 'the use of military power to shape the world according to American interests and values' (Steel 2004). The second image fed into the scripted representations of Bush as a 'tough', even virile leader who had taken on the garb of a Hollywood warrior determined in his efforts to protect the USA from terrorists and to bring the war in Iraq to a quick and successful conclusion.[1] The narrow ideological field that framed these images in the American media proved impervious to dissenting views, exhibiting a deep disregard for either accurate or critical reporting as well as an indifference to fulfilling its traditional role as a fourth estate, as guardians of

democracy and defenders of the public interest. Slavishly reporting the war as if they
were on the payroll at the Pentagon, the dominant media rarely called into question
either the Bush administration's reasons for going to war or the impact the war was
to have on both the Iraqi people and domestic and foreign policy.

In the spring of 2004, a new set of images challenged the mythic representations
of the Iraqi invasion with the release of hundreds of gruesome photographs and videos documenting the torture of Iraqi prisoners by American soldiers at Abu Ghraib.
They were first broadcast on the television series, *60 Minutes II*, and later leaked
to the press, becoming something of a nightly feature in the weeks and months
that ensued. Abu Ghraib prison was one of the most notorious sites used by the
deposed Hussein regime to inflict unspeakable horrors on those Iraqis considered
disposable for various political reasons, ironically reinforcing the growing perception in the Arab world that one tyrant simply replaced another. In sharp contrast to
the all-too-familiar and officially sanctioned images of good-hearted and stalwart
American soldiers patrolling dangerous Iraqi neighbourhoods, caring for wounded
soldiers or passing out candy to young Iraqi children, the newly discovered photos
depicted Iraqi detainees being humiliated and tortured. The face of the American
invasion was soon recast by a number of sadistic images, including now infamous
photos depicting the insipid, grinning faces of Specialist Charles A. Graner and Pfc.
Lynndie R. England flashing a thumbs up behind a pyramid of seven naked detainees, a kneeling inmate posing as if he is performing oral sex on another hooded male
detainee, a terrified male Iraqi inmate trying to ward off an attack dog being handled
by American soldiers, and a US soldier grinning next to the body of a dead inmate
packed in ice. Two of the most haunting images depicted a hooded man standing on
a box, with his arms outstretched in Christ-like fashion, electric wires attached to his
hands and penis. Another image revealed a smiling England holding a leash attached
to a naked Iraqi man lying on the floor of the prison. Like Oscar Wilde's infamous
picture of Dorian Gray, the portrait of American democracy was irrevocably transformed into its opposite. The fight for Iraqi hearts and minds was now irreparably
damaged as the war on terror appeared to reproduce only more terror, mimicking
the very crimes it claimed to have eliminated.

As Susan Sontag points out, the leaked photographs include both the victims and
their gloating assailants. For Sontag, the images from Abu Ghraib are not only 'representative of the fundamental corruptions of any foreign occupation and its distinctive policies which serve as a perfect recipe for the cruelties and crimes in American
run prisons. . . . [but are also] like lynching pictures and are treated as souvenirs of a
collective action' (Sontag 2004). Reminiscent of photos taken by whites who lynched
blacks after Reconstruction, the images were circulated as trophy shots in order to
be passed around and sent out to friends. For Sontag and others, Abu Ghraib could
not be understood outside of the racism and brutality that accompanied the exercise of nearly unchecked, unaccountable absolute power both at home and abroad.
Similarly, Sidney Blumenthal argues that Abu Ghraib was a predictable consequence

of the Bush administration to fight terrorism by creating a system 'beyond law to defend the rule of law against terrorism'. One consequence of such obscenely ironic posturing, as he points out, is a Gulag

> that stretches from prisons in Afghanistan to Iraq, from Guantanamo to secret CIA prisons around the world. There are perhaps 10,000 people being held in Iraq, 1,000 in Afghanistan and almost 700 in Guantanamo, but no one knows the exact numbers. The law as it applies to them is whatever the executive deems necessary. There has been nothing like this system since the fall of the Soviet Union. (Blumenthal 2004)

As time passed, it became clear that the instances of abuse and torture that took place at Abu Ghraib were extensive, systemic and part of a larger pattern of criminal behavior that had taken place in other prisons in both Iraq and Afghanistan—not to mention the prisons on the homefront.[2] Patterns of mistreatment by American soldiers had also taken place in Camp Bucca, a US-run detention center in southern Iraq as well as in an overseas CIA interrogation center at the Bagram airbase in Afghanistan, where the deaths of three detainees were labelled as homicide by US military doctors.[3]

The most compelling evidence refuting the argument that what happened at Abu Ghraib was the result of the actions of a few isolated individuals who strayed from protocol is spelled out by Seymour Hersh in his 10 May *New Yorker* article in which he analyses the 58-page classified report by Major General Antonio Taguba who investigated the abuses at Abu Ghraib. In the report, Taguba insisted that 'a huge leadership failure' (cited in Hersh 2004a) at Abu Ghraib was responsible for what he described as 'sadistic, blatant and wanton criminal abuses' (cited in Pound & Roane 2004). Taguba not only documented examples of torture and sexual humiliation, he also elaborated on the range of indignities, which included:

> Breaking chemical lights and pouring the phosphoric liquid on detainees; pouring cold water on naked detainees; beating detainees with a broom handle and a chair; threatening male detainees with rape; allowing a military police guard to stitch the wound of a detainee who was injured after being slammed against the wall in his cell; sodomizing a detainee with a chemical light and perhaps a broom stick, and sending military working dogs to frighten and intimidate detainees with threats of attack, and in one instance actually biting a detainee. (cited in Hersh 2004b)

Not only does Taguba's report reveal scenes of abuse more systemic than aberrant, but also tragically familiar to communities of color on the domestic front long subjected to profiling, harassment, intimidation, and brutality by law and order professionals.

The Politics of Delay and Outrage

Responses from around the world exhibited outrage and disgust over the US actions at Abu Ghraib. The rhetoric of American democracy was denounced all over the globe as hypocritical and utterly propagandistic, especially in light of President Bush's 30 April remarks claiming that with the removal of Saddam Hussein, 'there are no longer torture chambers or mass graves or rape rooms in Iraq' (cited in Hajjar 2004). The protracted release of new sets of pictures of US soldiers grinning as they tortured and sexually humiliated Iraqi prisoners at Abu Ghraib further undermined the moral and political credibility of the USA both in the Arab world and around the globe. Restoring one of Saddam Hussein's most infamous torture chambers to its original use reinforced the image of the USA as a dangerous, rogue state with despicable imperial ambitions. As columnist Katha Pollitt puts it,

> The pictures and stories [from Abu Ghraib] have naturally caused a furor around the world. Not only are they grotesque in themselves, they reinforce the pre-existing impression of Americans as racist, cruel and frivolous. They are bound to alienate—further alienate—Iraqis who hoped that the invasion would lead to secular democracy and a normal life and who fear Islamic rule. Abroad, if not here at home, they underscore how stupid and wrong the invasion of Iraq was in the first place, how predictably the 'war of choice' that was going to be a cakewalk has become a brutal and corrupt occupation, justified by a doctrine of American exceptionalism that nobody but Americans believes. (Pollitt 2004)

However, Abu Ghraib did more than inspire moral revulsion; it also became a rallying cry for recruiting radical extremists as well as producing legitimate opposition to the American occupation. At one level, the image of the faceless, hooded detainee, arms outstretched and wired, conjured up images of the Spanish Inquisition, the French brutalization of Algerians and the slaughter of innocent people at My Lai during the Vietnam war. The heavily damaged rhetoric of American democracy now gave way to the more realistic discourse of empire, colonization, and militarization. At another level, the images shed critical light on the often ignored connection between American domination abroad, often aimed at the poor and dispossessed, and at home, particularly against people of colour, including the lynching of American blacks in the first half of the twentieth century and the increasingly brutalizing incarceration of large numbers of youth of colour that continues into the new millennium. Patricia Williams links the criminal abuse of Iraqi detainees at Abu Ghraib prison to a web of secrecy, violation of civil rights, and racist violence that has become commonplace on the domestic front. She writes:

> [I]t's awfully hard not to look at those hoods and think Inquisition; or the piles of naked and sodomized men and think Abner Louima; or the battered corpses and think of Emmett Till . . . This mess is the predictable by-product of any authority that starts 'sweeping' up 'bad guys' and holding them without charge, in solitary and in secret, and presuming them guilty. It flourished beyond the reach of any formal oversight by Congress, by lawyers or by the judiciary, a condition vaguely rationalized as 'consistent with' if not 'precisely' pursuant to the Geneva Conventions. Bloodied prisoners were moved around to avoid oversight by international observers, a rather too disciplined bit of sanitizing. (Williams 2004)

Outrage abroad was matched by often low-keyed, if not crude, responses by those implicated whether in military barracks or Washington offices. For the high priests of 'personal responsibility', it was a study in passing the buck. President Bush responded by claiming that what happened at Abu Ghraib was nothing more than 'disgraceful conduct by a few American troops' (Bush 2004). General Richard Myers, chairman of the Joint Chiefs of Staff, suggested it was the work of a 'handful' of enlisted individuals (quoted in Moniz & Squitieri 2004). However, the claim that the Pentagon was unaware of Abu Ghraib was at odds not only with International Red Cross reports that regularly notified the Pentagon of such crimes, but also it was further contradicted by both the Taguba report as well as by a series of memos leaked to the press indicating that the White House, Pentagon and Justice Department had attempted to justify interrogation practices that violated the federal anti-torture statute two years prior to the invasion.

One such memo was written in August 2002, authored by Assistant Attorney General Jay S. Bybee, head of the Justice Department's Office of Legal Counsel. In it, he argued that in a post-9/11 world any attempt to apply the criminal laws against torture under the Geneva Convention Against Torture undermined Presidential power and should be considered unconstitutional. More specifically, the Bybee memo argued 'on behalf of the Justice Department that the President could order the use of torture' (Lewis 2004). Alberto Gonzales, a high ranking government lawyer, argued in a draft memo to President Bush on 25 January 2002 that the Geneva Conventions are 'quaint', if not 'obsolete' and that certain forms of traditionally unauthorized methods of inflicting physical and psychological pain might be justified under the aegis of fighting the war on terrorism.[4] Anthony Lewis in commenting on the memo states 'Does he believe that any treaty can be dismissed when it is inconvenient to an American government?' (Lewis 2004). In fact, a series of confidential legal memoranda produced by the Justice Department flatly stated that the 'administration is not bound by prohibitions against torture' (Lewis, N. A. 2004). A Defense Department memo echoed the same line in a calculated attempt to incorporate torture as part of normal interrogating procedures in defiance of international protocols. The *Wall Street Journal* reported on 7 June 2004 that these memos sought to assign the President virtually unlimited authority on matters of torture' (Bravin 2004). Exercising a degree of rhetorical licence in defining torture in narrow terms, they ended up legitimizing interrogation practices at odds with both the Geneva Convention Against Torture and the Army's own Field Manual for intelligence, which prohibits 'The use of force, mental torture, threats, insults or exposure to unpleasant and inhumane treatment of any kind'.[5] In reviewing the government's case for torture, Anthony Lewis writes:

> The memos read like the advice of a mob lawyer to a mafia don on how to skirt the law and stay out of prison. Avoiding prosecution is literally a theme of the memoranda . . . Another theme in the memoranda, an even more deeply disturbing one is that the President can order the torture of prisoners even though it is forbidden by a federal statute and by the international

Convention Against Torture, to which the United States is a party . . . the issues raised by the Bush administration's legal assertions in its 'war on terror' are so numerous and so troubling that one hardly knows where to begin discussing them. The torture and death of prisoners, the end result of cool legal abstractions, have a powerful claim on our national conscience . . . But equally disturbing, in its way, is the administration's constitutional argument that presidential power is unconstrained by law. (Lewis 2004, p. 4, p. 6)

Both John Ashcroft and Secretary of Defense Donald Rumsfeld denied any involvement by the Bush administration in either providing the legal sanctions for torture or for creating the conditions that made the abuses at Abu Ghraib possible. Ashcroft refused the Senate Judiciary Committee's request to make public a 2002 Justice Department memo sanctioning high-risk interrogation tactics that may violate the federal anti-torture statute while repeatedly insisting that the Bush administration does not sanction torture. When the Abu Ghraib scandal first broke in the press and reporters started asking him about the Taguba report, Rumsfeld claimed that he had not read it.

When reporters raised questions about Seymour Hersh's charge that Rumsfeld had personally approved a clandestine program known as SAP 'that encouraged physical coercion and sexual humiliation of Iraqi prisoners in an effort to generate more intelligence about the growing insurgency in Iraq', Pentagon spokesman Lawrence Di Rita responded by calling Hersh's article, 'outlandish, conspiratorial and filled with error and anonymous conjecture' (Associated Press 2004). At the same time, Di Rita did not directly rebut any of Hirsh's claims. When confronted directly about the charge that he authorized a secret program that was given the blanket approval to kill, torture and interrogate high-value targets, Rumsfeld performed a semantic tap-dance that would have made Bill Clinton blush. He told reporters: 'My impression is that what has been charged thus far is abuse, which I believe technically is different from torture . . . I don't know if . . . it is correct to say what you just said, that torture has taken place, or that there's been a conviction for torture. And therefore I am not going to address the torture word' (cited in Folkenflik 2004). However, Rumsfeld's contempt for the Geneva Conventions and established military protocol were made public soon after the war on terror was launched in 2001. Disdaining a military machine shaped by the 'old rules', he believed they prevented the military and its leadership from taking 'greater risks' (quoted in Hersh 2004a, p. 41). In 2002, he went so far as to claim that 'complaints about America's treatment of prisoners . . . amounted to "isolated pockets of international hyperventilation"' (quoted in Hersh 2004a, p. 41). It was later reported by a range of news sources, including the *Wall Street Journal* and *Newsweek*, that Rumsfeld had indeed supported interrogation techniques against the Taliban and Iraqi prisoners that violated the Geneva Conventions. As the facts surrounding the abuses emerged belatedly in the dominant media, he admitted he was responsible for the hiding of 'Ghost detainees' from the Red Cross and asserted before a Senate Committee that he would assume the blame for Abu Ghraib, but also refused to resign.

What became clear soon after the scandal of Abu Ghraib went public was that it could not be reduced to the 'failure of character' of a few soldiers, as George W. Bush insisted. Nor could it be seen as behaviour that was antithetical to the values and practices of American democracy. In June 2004, both *The New York Times* and *The Washington Post* broke even more stories documenting the use of torture-like practices by American soldiers who subjected prisoners to unmuzzled military dogs as part of a contest waged to see how many detainees they could make involuntarily urinate out of fear of the dogs and forcing detainees to stand on boxes and sing 'the Star Spangled Banner' in the nude (White and Higham 2004, p. A01). Both tactics took place long before the famous photographs were taken at Abu Ghraib (Zernke and Rohde 2004, p. A11). Far from the 'frat boy pranks' apologists compared the torture to, these acts were designed to inflict maximal damage—performed on detainees whose culture views nudity as a violation of religious principles and associates public nudity with shame and guilt. Equally disturbing is the International Committee of the Red Cross estimate that 70 to 90 percent of the detainees arrested by Coalition troops 'had been arrested by mistake' and had nothing to do with terrorism (Drogin 2004). It gets worse. Since the release of the initial photos, a new round of fresh photographs and film footage of torture from Abu Ghraib and other prisons in Iraq 'include details of the rape and . . . abuse of some of the Iraqi women and the hundred or so children— some as young as 10 years old' (Govern 2004). One account provided by US Army Sergeant Samuel Provance, who was stationed in the Abu Ghraib prison, recalls 'how interrogators soaked a 16-year-old, covered him in mud, and then used his suffering to break the youth's father, also a prisoner, during interrogation' (Govern 2004). An Army investigation also revealed that unmuzzled military police dogs were employed at Abu Ghraib prison as part of a sadistic game used to 'make juveniles—as young as 15 years old—urinate on themselves as part of a competition' (White and Ricks 2004).

The wanton abuse of Iraqi detainees, including children, the ongoing efforts at the highest levels of the Bush administration to establish new legal ground for torture, and the use of private contractors to perform the dirty work of interrogating detainees in order to skirt what is clearly an abdication of civil and military law is evidence of a systemic, widespread collusion with crimes against humanity. In spite of claims by the Bush administration that such abuses are the work of a few rogue soldiers, a number of inquiries by high-level outside panels, especially the four-member Schlesinger panel, have concluded that the Abu Ghraib abuses point to leadership failures at the 'highest levels of the Pentagon, Joint Chiefs of Staff and military command in Iraq' (Schmitt 2004, p. 1). Such reports and the increasing revelations of the extent of the abuse and torture perpetuated in Iraq, Afghanistan and American prisons do more than promote moral outrage at the growing injustices practised by the American government, they also position the USA as one more rogue regime sharing, as an editorial in *The Washington Post* pointed out, the company of former military juntas 'in Argentina and Chile . . . that claim[ed] torture is justified when used to combat terrorism' (*The Washington Post* 2004, p. A01).

In spite of the extensive photographic proof, international and internal reports, and journalistic accounts revealing egregious brutality, racism and inhumanity by US soldiers against Arab detainees, conservative pundits took their cue from the White House, attempting to justify such detestable acts and defend the Bush administration's usurpation of presidential power. Powerful right-wing ideologues such as Rush Limbaugh and Cal Thomas defended such actions as simply a way for young men (sic) to 'blow off some steam', engage in forms of harmless frat hazing, or give Muslim prisoners what they deserve. More offensive than the blasé attitudes of talking-heads was the mantle of moral authority and outrage of politicians who took umbrage with those who dared criticize Bush or his army at a time of war. Former Speaker of the House Newt Gingrich and Republican Senator James Inhofe insisted that calling attention to such crimes not only undermined troop morale in Iraq, but it was also deeply unpatriotic. Inhofe actually stated publicly at a Senate Armed Services Committee hearing that he was outraged by the 'outrage everyone seems to have about the treatment of these prisoners . . . I am also outraged by the press and the politicians and the political agendas that are being served by this . . . I am also outraged that we have so many humanitarian do-gooders right now crawling all over these prisons looking for human rights violations while our troops, our heroes, are fighting and dying' (Solomon 2004). That many of these prisoners were innocent civilians picked up in indiscriminate sweeps by the US military or that US troops were operating a chamber of horrors at Abu Ghraib was simply irrelevant, providing fodder for silencing criticism by labelling it unpatriotic, or scapegoating the 'liberal' media for reporting such injustices. Inhofe provides a prime example of how politics is corrupted by a dangerous ethos of divine right informed by the mythos of American exceptionalism and a patriotic fervour that disdains reasonable dissent and moral critique. Inhofe's arrogant puffery must be challenged both for shutting down dialogue but also brought to task for the egregious way in which it invites Americans to identify with the violence of the perpetrators.

Other conservatives such as Watergate-felon-turned-preacher, Charles Colson, Robert Knight of the Culture and Family Institute, and Rebecca Hagelin, the vice president of the Heritage Foundation, assumed the moral high ground, blaming what happened at Abu Ghraib on the debauchery of popular culture. Invoking the tired language of the culture wars, Colson argued that 'the prison guards had been corrupted by a "steady diet of MTV and pornography"'. Knight argued that the depravity exhibited at Abu Ghraib was modelled after gay porn, which gave military personnel 'the idea to engage in sadomasochistic activity and to videotape in voyeuristic fashion'. Rebecca Hagelin viewed the prison scandal as the outcome of a general moral laxity in which 'our country permits Hollywood to put almost anything in a movie and still call it PG-13' (all these examples are cited in Rich 2004). For those hardwired Bush supporters who wanted to do more than blame Hollywood porn, MTV, prime time television and (not least) gay culture, the scandalous images themselves were seen as the source of the problem because of the offensive nature of their representations and the controversy they generated.

Despite the colossal (and it seems deliberate) misrepresentations of the facts leading to the war with Iraq along with the neo-conservative and Christian fundamentalism driving the Bush presidency and its disastrous policies at home and abroad, Bush's credibility remains intact for many conservatives. Consequently, they ignore the underlying conditions that gave rise to the horrific abuses at Abu Ghraib, removing them from the inventory of unethical and damaging practices associated with American exceptionalism and triumphalism. Thus, they ignore: Bush's disastrous, open-ended war on terrorism and how it has failed to protect the American populace at home while sanctioning wars abroad that have been used as recruiting tools for Islamic terrorists; Bush's doctrine of secrecy[6] and unaccountability; Bush's suspension of basic civil liberties under the USA Patriot Act and his willingness to include some named terrorists under the designation of enemy combatants so as to remove them from the protection of the law; and the Bush administration's all out assault on the social contract and the welfare state.[7] Treating the Bush presidency as sacrosanct—and so unaccountable and beyond public engagement—enables conservatives to conveniently overlook their own complicity in furthering those existing relations of power and politics that make the dehumanizing events of Abu Ghraib possible. Within this apologetic discourse, matters of individual and collective responsibility disappear in a welter of hypocritical and strategic diversions. As Frank Rich puts it,

> the point of these scolds' political strategy—and it is a political strategy, despite some of its adherents' quasireligiosity—is clear enough. It is not merely to demonize gays and the usual rogue's gallery of secularist bogeymen for any American ill but to clear the Bush administration of any culpability for Abu Ghraib, the disaster that may have destroyed its mission in Iraq. If porn or MTV or Howard Stern can be said to have induced a 'few bad apples' in one prison to misbehave, then everyone else in the chain of command, from the commander-in-chief down, is off the hook. If the culture war can be cross-wired with the actual war, then the buck will stop not at the Pentagon or the White House but at the Paris Hilton video, or 'Mean Girls', or maybe 'Queer Eye for the Straight Guy'. (Rich 2004, p. AR1, p. AR16)

When it comes to reconciling barbarous acts of torture and humiliation with the disingenuous rhetoric of democracy so popular among conservatives, the issue of blame can assume a brutalizing character. For instance, a number of conservatives (as well as those responsible for the 11 September 2004 report by the Army's Inspector General) place the causes for abuse at Abu Ghraib at the doorstep of low ranking personnel who, once considered disposable fodder for the war effort, now provide equally talented scapegoats. Powerless to defend themselves against the implied accusation that their working-class and rural backgrounds produced the propensity for sexual deviancy and cruelty in the grand style of the film, *Deliverance*, they merely claimed to be following orders. However, class hatred proved a serviceable means to deflect attention from the Bush administration. How else to explain Republican senator Ben

Campbell's comment that 'I don't know how these people got into our army' (Younge 2004). But class antagonism was not the only weapon in right-wing arsenals. Even more desperate, Ann Coulter blames Abu Ghraib on the allegedly aberrant nature of woman, particularly evident in her assertion that 'This is yet another lesson in why women shouldn't be in the military . . . Women are more vicious than men' (Younge 2004). All of these arguments, as *The New York Times* columnist Frank Rich points out, share in an effort to divert attention from matters of politics and history in order to clear the Bush administration of any wrong doing (Rich 2004). Of course, I am not suggesting that Lynndie England, Sabrina Harman, Jeremy Sivits, Charles Graner Jr., and others should not be held responsible for their actions; rather, my claim is that responsibility for Abu Ghraib does not lay with them alone.

Susan Sontag (2004) has argued that photographs lay down the 'tracks for how important conflicts are judged and remembered. However, at the same time, she makes it very clear that all photographs cannot be understood through one language recognized by all. Photographs are never transparent, existing outside of the 'taint of artistry or ideology' (Sontag 2003). Understood as social and historical constructs, photographic images entail acts of translation necessary to mobilize compassion instead of indifference, witnessing rather than consuming, and critical engagement rather than aesthetic *appreciation or crude repudiation*. Put differently, photographs such as those that revealed the horrors that took place at Abu Ghraib prison have no guaranteed meaning, but rather exist within a complex of shifting mediations that are material, historical, social, ideological and psychological in nature.8

Abu Ghraib Photographs and the Politics of Public Pedagogy

Hence, the photographic images from Abu Ghraib prison cannot be taken up outside of history, politics or ideology. This is not to suggest that photographs do not record some element of reality as much as to insist that what they capture can only be understood as part of a broader engagement over cultural politics and its intersection with various dynamics of power, all of which informs the conditions for reading photographs as both a pedagogical intervention and a form of cultural production.9 Photographic images do not reside in the unique vision of their producer or the reality they attempt to capture. Representations privilege those who have some control over self-representation, and they are largely framed within dominant modes of intelligibility.

The Abu Ghraib photographs are constitutive of both diverse sites and technologies of pedagogy and as such represent political and ethical forms of address that make moral demands and claims upon their viewers. Questions of power and meaning are always central to any discussion of photographic images as forms of public pedagogy. Such images not only register the traces of cultural mythologies that must be critically mediated, they also represent ideological modes of address tied to the limits of human discourse and intelligibility and function as pedagogical practices regarding how agency should be organized and represented. The pictures of abuse at Abu Ghraib prison gain their status as a form of public pedagogy by virtue of the spaces they create between the sites in which they become public and the forms of pedagogical address that both frame and mediate their meaning. As they circulate through various sites including talk radio, computer screens, television, newspapers, the Internet and alternative media, they initiate different forms of address, mobilize different cultural meanings, and offer up different sites of learning. The meanings that frame the images from Abu Ghraib prison are 'contingent upon the pedagogical sites in which they are considered' and their ability to limit or rule out certain questions, historical inquiries, and explanations (DiLeo *et al.* 2004). For example, news programs on the Fox Television Network systematically occlude any criticism of the images of abuse at Abu Ghraib that would call into question the American presence in Iraq. If such issues are raised, they are quickly dismissed as unpatriotic.

Attempts to defuse or rewrite images that treat people as things, as less than human have a long history. Commentators have invoked comparison to the images of lynching of black men and women in the American South and Jews in Nazi death camps. John Louis Lucaites and James P. McDaniel have documented how *Life Magazine* during World War II put a photograph on its cover of a woman gazing pensively at the skull of a Japanese solider sent to her by her boyfriend serving in the Pacific, a lieutenant who when he left to fight in the war 'promised her a Jap' (Lucaites & McDaniel 2004, p. 7). Far from reminding its readers of the barbarity of war, the magazine invoked the patriotic gaze in order to frame the barbaric image as part of a public ritual of mortification and a visual marker of humiliation.

As forms of public pedagogy, photographic images must be engaged ethically as well as socio-politically because they are implicated in history and they often work to suppress the very conditions that produce them. Often framed within dominant forms of circulation and meaning, such images generally work to legitimate particular forms of recognition and meaning marked by disturbing forms of diversion and evasion. This position is evident in those politicians who believe that the photographs from Abu Ghraib are the real problem not the conditions that produced them. Or in the endless commentaries that view the abuses at Abu Ghraib as caused by a few 'bad apples'. Subjecting such public pronouncements to critical inquiry can only emerge within those pedagogical sites and practices in which matters of critique and a culture of questioning are requisite to a vibrant and functioning democracy. But public pedagogy at its best offers more than forms of reading that are critical and relate cultural texts such as photographs to the larger world. Public pedagogy not only defines the cultural objects of interpretation, it also offers the possibility for engaging modes of literacy that are not just about competency but also about the possibility of interpretation as an intervention in the world. Meaning does not rest with the images alone, but with the ways in which images are aligned and shaped by larger institutional and cultural discourses and how they call into play the condemnation of torture (or its celebration), how it came about, and what it means to prevent it from happening again. This is not merely a political issue but also a pedagogical one. Making the political more pedagogical in this instance connects what we know to the conditions that make learning possible in the first place. It creates opportunities to be critical, but also as Susan Sontag notes, to 'take stock of our world, and [participate] in its social transformation in such a way that non-violent, cooperative, egalitarian international relations remain the guiding ideal' (Butler 2002, p. 19). While Sontag is quite perceptive in pointing to the political nature of reading images, a politics concerned with matters of translation and meaning, she does not engage such reading as a pedagogical issue.

As part of a politics of representation, photographic images necessitate both the ability to read critically and utilize particular analytical skills that enable viewers to study the relations between images, discourses, everyday life and broader structures of power. As both the subject and object of public pedagogy, photographs both deploy power and are deployed by power and register the conditions under which people learn how to read texts and the world. Photographs demand an ability to read within and against the representations they present and to raise fundamental questions about how they work to secure particular meanings, desires, and investments. As a form of public pedagogy, photographic images have the potential, though by no means guaranteed, to call forth from readers modes of witnessing that connect meaning with compassion, a concern for others and a broader understanding of the historical and contemporary contexts and relations that frame meaning in particular ways. Critical reading demands pedagogical practices that short-circuit common sense, resist easy assumptions, bracket how images are framed, engage meaning as a struggle over power and politics, and as such refuse to posit reading (especially images) exclusively as an aesthetic exercise but also as a political and moral practice.

What is often ignored in the debates about Abu Ghraib, both in terms of its causes and what can be done about it, are questions that foreground the relevance of critical education to the debate. Such questions would clearly focus, at the very least, on what pedagogical conditions need to be in place to enable people to view the images of abuse at Abu Ghraib prison not as part of a voyeuristic, even pornographic, reception but through a variety of discourses that enable them to ask critical and probing questions that get at the heart of how people learn to participate in sadistic acts of abuse and torture, internalize racist assumptions that make it easier to dehumanize people different from themselves, accept commands that violate basic human rights, become indifferent to the suffering and hardships of others, and view dissent as basically unpatriotic. What pedagogical practices might enable the public to foreground the codes and structures that give photographs their meaning while also connecting the productive operations of photography with broader discourses? For example, how might the images from Abu Ghraib prison be understood as part of a broader debate about dominant information networks that not only condone torture, but also play a powerful role in organizing society around shared fears rather than shared responsibilities? Photographs demand more than a response to the specificity of an image, they also raise fundamentally crucial questions about the sites of pedagogy and technologies that produce, distribute, and frame them in particular ways and what these operations mean in terms of how they resonate with historical and established relations of power and the identities and modes of agency that enable such relations to be reproduced rather than resisted and challenged. Engaging the photographs from Abu Ghraib and the events that produced them would point to the pedagogical practice of foregrounding 'the cultures of circulation and transfiguration within which those texts, events, and practices become palpable and are recognized as such' (Gaonkar and Povinelli 2003, p. 386). For instance, how do we understand the Abu Ghraib images and the pedagogical conditions that produced them without engaging the discourses of privatization, particularly the contracting of military labour, the intersection of militarism and the crisis of masculinity, and the war on terrorism and the racism that makes it so despicable? How might one explain the ongoing evaporation of political dissent and opposing viewpoints in the USA that proceeded the events at Abu Ghraib without engaging the pedagogical campaign of fear mongering adorned with the appropriate patriotic rhetoric waged by the Bush administration? How might we provide a historical context for linking Abu Ghraib to a legacy of racial abuse?

I have spent some time suggesting that there is a link between how we translate images and pedagogy because I am concerned about what the events of Abu Ghraib prison might suggest about education as both the subject and object of a democratic society and how we might engage it differently. What kind of education connects pedagogy and its diverse sites to the formation of a critical citizenry capable of challenging the ongoing quasi-militarization of everyday life, growing assault on secular democracy, the collapse of politics into a permanent war against terrorism, and a growing culture of fear that increasingly is used by political extremists to sanction the unaccountable exercise of presidential power? What kinds of educational practices can provide the conditions for a culture of questioning and engaged civic action? What might it mean to rethink the educational foundation of politics so as to reclaim not only the crucial traditions of dialogue and dissent but also critical modes of agency and those public spaces that enable collectively engaged struggle? How might education be understood both as a task of translation but also as a foundation for enabling civic engagement? What new forms of education might be called forth to resist the conditions and complicities that have allowed most people to submit 'so willingly to a new political order organized around fear?' (Greider 2004, p. 14). What does it mean to imagine a future beyond 'permanent war', a culture of fear and the triumphalism that promotes the sordid demands of empire? How might education be used to question the common sense of the war on terrorism or to rouse citizens to challenge the social, political, and cultural conditions that led to the horrible events of Abu Ghraib? Just as crucially, we must ponder the limits of education. Is there a point where extreme conditions short-circuit our moral instincts and ability to think and act rationally? If this is the case, what responsibility do we have to challenge the reckless violence-as-first-resort-ethos of the Bush administration?

Such questions extend beyond the events of Abu Ghraib, but at the same time, Abu Ghraib provides an opportunity to connect the sadistic treatment of Iraqi prisoners to the task of redefining pedagogy as an ethical practice, the sites in which it takes place, and the consequences it has for rethinking the meaning of politics in the twenty-first century. In order to confront the pedagogical and political challenges arising from the reality of Abu Ghraib, I want to revisit a classic essay by Theodor Adorno in which he tries to grapple with the relationship between education and morality in light of the horrors of Auschwitz. While I am certainly not equating the genocidal acts that took place at Auschwitz with the abuses at Abu Ghraib, a completely untenable analogy, I do believe that Adorno's essay offers some important theoretical insights about how to think about the larger meaning and purpose of education as a form of public pedagogy in light of the Abu Ghraib prison scandal. Adorno's essay raises fundamental questions about how acts of inhumanity are inextricably connected to the pedagogical practices that shape the conditions that bring them into being. Adorno insists that crimes against humanity cannot be simply reduced to the behaviour of a few individuals but often speak in profound ways to the role of the state in propagating such abuses, the mechanisms employed in the realm of culture that silence the public in the face of horrible acts, and the pedagogical challenge that would name such acts as a moral crime against humankind and translate that moral authority into effective pedagogical practices throughout society so that such events never happen again. Of course, the significance of Adorno's comments extend far beyond matters of responsibility for what happened at Abu Ghraib prison. Adorno's plea for education as a moral and political force against human injustice is just as relevant today as it was following the revelations about Auschwitz after World War II. As Roger W. Smith points out, while genocidal acts have claimed the lives of over 60 million people in the twentieth century, 16 million of them have taken place since 1945 (Smith 2004). The political and economic forces fuelling such crimes against humanity—whether they are unlawful wars, systemic torture, practiced indifference to chronic starvation and disease or genocidal acts—are always mediated by educational forces just as the resistance to such acts cannot take place without a degree of knowledge and self-reflection about how to name these acts and to transform moral outrage into concrete attempts to prevent such human violations from taking place in the first place.

Education after Abu Ghraib

In 1967, Theodor Adorno published an essay titled 'Education After Auschwitz'. In it, he asserted that the demands and questions raised by Auschwitz had so barely penetrated the consciousness of people's minds that the conditions that made it possible continued, as he put it, 'largely unchanged'.10 Mindful that the societal pressures that produced the Holocaust had far from receded in post-war Germany and that under such circumstances this act of barbarism could easily be repeated in the future, Adorno argued that 'the mechanisms that render people capable of such deeds' must be made visible (Adorno 1998a, p. 192). For Adorno, the need to come to grips with the challenges arising from the reality of Auschwitz was both a political question and a crucial educational consideration. Adorno recognized that education had to be an important part of any politics that took seriously the premise that Auschwitz should never happen again. As he put it:

> All political instruction finally should be centered upon the idea that Auschwitz should never happen again. This would be possible only when it devotes itself openly, without fear of offending any authorities, to this most important of problems. To do this education must transform itself into sociology, that is, it must teach about the societal play of forces that operates beneath the surface of political forms. (Adorno 1998a, p. 203)

Implicit in Adorno's argument is the recognition that education as a critical practice could provide the means for disconnecting common sense learning from the narrowly ideological impact of mass media, the regressive tendencies associated with hyper-masculinity, the rituals of everyday violence, the inability to identify with others, as well as from the pervasive ideologies of state repression and its illusions of empire. Adorno's response to retrograde ideologies and practices was to emphasize the role of autonomous individuals and the force of self-determination that he saw as the outcome of a moral and political project that rescued education from the narrow language of skills, unproblematized authority and the seduction of common sense. Self-reflection, the ability to call things into question, and the willingness to resist the material and symbolic forces of domination were central to an education that refused to repeat the horrors of the past and engaged the possibilities of the future. Adorno urged educators to teach students how to be critical, to learn how to resist those ideologies, needs, social relations, and discourses that lead back to a politics where authority is simply obeyed and the totally administered society reproduces itself through a mixture of state force and often orchestrated consensus. Freedom in this instance meant being able to think critically and act courageously, even when confronted with the limits of one's knowledge. Without such thinking critical debate and dialogue degenerates into slogans, and politics, disassociated from the search for justice becomes a power grab. Within the realm of education, Adorno glimpsed the possibility of knowledge for self and social formation as well as the importance of pedagogical practices capable of 'influencing the next generation of Germans so that they would not repeat what their parents or grandparents had done' (Hohendahl 1995, p. 51).

Adorno realized that education played a crucial role in creating the psychological, intellectual, and social conditions that made the Holocaust possible, yet he refused to dismiss education as an institution and set of social practices exclusively associated with domination. He argued that those theorists who viewed education simply as a tool for social reproduction had succumbed to the premier supposition of any oppressive hegemonic ideology: nothing can change. To dismiss the political and critical force of pedagogy, according to Adorno, was to fall prey to both a disastrous determinism and a complicitous cynicism. He argues:

For this disastrous state of conscious and unconscious thought includes the erroneous idea that one's own particular way of being—that one is just so and not otherwise—is nature, an unalterable given, and not a historical evolution. I mentioned the concept of reified consciousness. Above all this is a consciousness blinded to all historical past, all insight into one's own conditionedness, and posits as absolute what exists contingently. If this coercive mechanism were once ruptured, then, I think, something would indeed be gained. (Adorno 1998a, p. 200)

Realizing that education before and after Auschwitz in Germany was separated by an unbridgeable chasm, Adorno wanted to invoke the promise of education through the moral and political imperative of never allowing the genocide witnessed at Auschwitz to happen again. For such a goal to become meaningful and realizable, Adorno contended that education had to be addressed as both a promise and project in order to reveal not only the conditions that laid the psychological and ideological groundwork for Auschwitz but also defeat the 'potential for its recurrence as far as people's conscious and unconscious is concerned' (Adorno 1998a, p. 191).

Investigating the powerful role that education played to promote consensus among the public along with the conscious and unconscious elements of fascism, he understood education as more than social engineering and argued that it also had to be imagined as a democratic public sphere. In this context, education would take on a liberating and empowering function, refusing to substitute critical learning for mind-deadening training (Adorno 1998b). At its best, such an education would create the pedagogical conditions in which individuals would function as autonomous subjects capable of refusing to participate in unspeakable injustices while actively working to eliminate the conditions that make such injustices possible. Human autonomy through self-reflection and social critique became for Adorno the basis for developing forms of critical agency as a means of resisting and overcoming both fascist ideology and identification with what he calls the fascist collective. According to Adorno, fascism as a form of barbarism defies all educational attempts at self-formation, engaged critique, self-determination, and transformative engagement. He writes: 'The only true force against the principle of Auschwitz would be human autonomy . . . that is, the force of reflection and of self-determination, the will to refuse participation' (Hohendahl 1995, p. 58). While there is a deep-seated tension in Adorno's belief in the increasing power of the totally administered society and his call for modes of education that produce critical, engaging, and free minds, he still believed that without critical education it was impossible to think about politics and agency, especially in light of the new technologies and material processes of social integration. Similarly, Adorno did not believe that education as an act of self-reflection alone could defeat the institutional forces and relations of power that existed outside of both institutionalised education and other powerful sites of pedagogy in the larger culture, though he rightly acknowledged that changing such a powerful complex of economic and social forces began with the educational task of recognizing that such changes were necessary and could actually be carried out through individual and collective forms of resistance. What Adorno brilliantly understood—though in a somewhat limited way given his tendency, in the end, toward pessimism—was the necessity to link politics to matters of individual and social agency.11 Engaging this relationship, in part, meant theorizing what it meant to make the political more pedagogical; that is, how the very processes of learning constitute the political mechanisms through which identities—both individual and collective—are shaped, desired, mobilized, and experienced, and take on form and meaning within those social formations that provide the educational foundation for constituting the realm of the social.

While it would be presumptuous to suggest that Adorno's writings on education, autonomy, and Auschwitz can be directly applied to theorizing the events at Abu Ghraib prison, his work offers some important theoretical insights for addressing how education might help to rethink the project of politics that made Abu Ghraib possible as well as how violence and torture become normalized as part of the war on terrorism and on those others considered marginal to American culture and life.

Recognizing how crucial education was in shaping everyday life and the conditions that made critique both possible and necessary, Adorno insisted that the desire for freedom and liberation was a function of pedagogy and could not be assumed a priori. At the same time, Adorno was acutely aware that education took place both in schools and in larger public spheres, especially in the realm of media. Democratic debate and the conditions for autonomy grounded in a critical notion of individual and social agency could only take place if the schools addressed their critical role in a democracy. Hence, Adorno argued that the critical education of teachers played a crucial role in preventing dominant power from eliminating the possibility of reflective thought and engaged social action. Such an insight appears particularly important at a time when public education is being utterly privatized, commercialized, and test-driven, or, if they serve underprivileged students of color, turned into disciplinary apparatuses that resemble prisons.12 Public schools are under attack precisely because they have the potential to become democratic public spheres instilling in students the skills, knowledge, and values necessary for them to be critical citizens capable of making power accountable and knowledge an intense object of dialogue and engagement. Of course, the attack on public education is increasingly taking place along with an attack on higher education, particularly the humanities (Giroux and Searls 2004). Everything from affirmative action to academic freedom is up for grabs as neo-conservatives, religious fundamentalists, and hard-core right-wing ideologues such as David Horowitz actively push for state and federal legislation in order to impose political quotas on higher education by making conservative ideology a basis for faculty hires (Piper 2003). They are also actively attempting to introduce 'ideological diversity' legislation that would cut federal funding for colleges and universities that harbor faculty and students that criticize Israel,13 and they incessantly attack curricula and faculty for being too liberal. If Adorno is right about educating teachers to neither forget nor allow horrors such as Auschwitz from happening again, the struggle over public and higher education as a democratic public sphere must be defended against base right wing attacks.

At the same time, how we educate teachers for all levels of schooling must be viewed as more than a technical or credentialized task, it must be seen as a pedagogical practice of both learning and unlearning. Drawing upon Freudian psychology, Adorno believed that educators had to be educated to think critically and avoid becoming the mediators and perpetrators of social violence. This meant addressing their psychological deformations by making clear the ideological, social and material mechanisms that encourage people to participate or fail to intervene in such deeds. Pedagogy, in this instance, was not simply concerned with learning particular modes of knowledge, skills and self-reflection, but also with addressing those dominant sedimented needs and desires that allowed teachers to blindly identify with repressive collectives and unreflectingly mimic their values while venting acts of hate and aggression (Adorno 1998a, p. 192). If unlearning as a pedagogical practice meant resisting those social deformations that shaped everyday needs and desires, critical learning meant making visible those social practices and mechanisms that represented the opposite of self-formation and autonomous thinking so as to resist such forces and prevent them from exercising such power and influence.

Adorno realized far more so than Freud that the range and scope, not to mention the impact of education, had far exceeded the boundaries of public and higher education. Adorno increasingly believed that the media as a force for learning constituted a mode of public pedagogy that had to be criticized for discouraging critical reflection and reclaimed as a crucial force in providing the 'intellectual, cultural and social climate in which a recurrence [such as Auschwitz] would no longer be possible, a climate, therefore in which the motives that led to the horror would become relatively conscious' (1998a, p. 194). Adorno rightly understood and critically engaged the media as a mode of public pedagogy, arguing that they contributed greatly to particular forms of barbarization that necessitated that educators and others 'consider the impact of modern mass media on a state of consciousness' (1998a, p. 196). If we are to take Adorno seriously, the role of the media in inspiring fear of Muslims and hatred of Arabs, suppressing dissent regarding the US invasion and occupation of Iraq, and its determining influence in legitimating a number of myths and lies by the Bush administration, must be addressed as part of the larger set of concerns leading to the horror of Abu Ghraib. The media has consistently refused, for example, to comment critically on the ways in which the USA, in its flaunting of the Geneva Accords regarding torture, was breaking international law, favouring instead the discourse of national security provided by the Bush administration. The media has also put into place forms of jingoism, patriotic correctness, narrow-minded chauvinism, and a celebration of militarization that rendered dissent as treason, and the tortures at Abu Ghraib outside of the discourses of ethics, compassion, human rights and social justice.

Adorno also insisted that the global evolution of the media and new technologies that shrank distances as it eroded face-to-face-contact (and hence the ability to disregard the consequences of one's actions) had created a climate in which rituals of violence had become so entrenched in the culture that 'aggression, brutality and sadism' had become a normalized and unquestioned part of everyday life. The result was a twisted and pathological relationship with the body that not only tends towards violence, but also promotes what Adorno called the ideology of hardness. Hardness, in this instance, referred to a notion of masculinity based on an idea of toughness in which:

> virility consists in the maximum degree of endurance [that] aligns itself all too easily with sadism. . . . [and inflicts] physical pain—often unbearable pain—upon a person as the price that must be paid in order to consider oneself a member, one of the collective . . . Being hard, the vaunted quality education should inculcate, means absolute indifference toward pain as such. In this the distinction between one's pain and that of another is not so stringently maintained. Whoever is hard with himself earns the right to be hard with others as well and avenges himself for whose manifestations he was not allowed to show and had to repress. (Adorno 1998a, pp. 197-8)

The rituals of popular culture—especially reality television programs like *Survivor*, *The Apprentice*, *Fear Factor* and the new vogue of extreme sports—either condense pain, humiliation and abuse into digestible spectacles of violence or serve up an endless celebration of retrograde competitiveness, the compulsion to 'go it alone', the ideology of hardness, and power over others as the central feature of masculinity.14 Masculinity in this context treats lies, manipulation and violence as a sport, a crucial component that lets men connect with each other at some primal level in which the pleasure of the body, pain and competitive advantage are maximized while coming dangerously close to giving violence a glamorous and fascist edge.

The celebration of both violence and hardness (witness the fanfare over Donald Trump's tag-line 'you're fired!') can also be seen in those ongoing representations and images that accompany the simultaneous erosion of security (around health care, work, education) and the militarization of everyday life. The USA has more police, prisons, spies, weapons and soldiers than at any time in its history—coupled with a growing 'army' of the unemployed and incarcerated. Yet, its military is enormously popular as its underlying values, social relations and patriotic, hyper-masculine aesthetic spread out into other aspects of American culture. The ideology of hardness, toughness and hyper-masculinity are constantly being disseminated through a militarized culture that functions as a mode of public pedagogy, instilling the values and the aesthetic of militarization through a wide variety of pedagogical sites and cultural venues.

Flags increasingly appear on storefront windows, lapels, cars, houses, SUVs and everywhere else as a show of support for the expanding interests of empire abroad. Public schools not only have more military recruiters, they also have more military personnel teaching in the classrooms. JROTC programmes are increasingly becoming a conventional part of the school day. Humvee ads offer up the fantasy of military glamour and modes of masculinity, marketed to suggest that ownership of these military vehicles guarantees virility for its owners and promotes a mixture of fear and admiration from everyone else. The military industrial complex now joins hands with the entertainment industry in producing everything from children's toys to video games that both construct a particular form of masculinity and serve as an enticement for recruitment. In fact, over 10 million people have downloaded *American Army*, a free video game the Army uses as a recruitment tool (Thompson 2004, pp. 32-7). From video games to Hollywood films to children's toys, popular culture is increasingly bombarded with militarized values, symbols and images. Such representations of masculinity and violence mimic fascism's militarization of the public sphere where physical aggression is a crucial element of male bonding and violence is the ultimate language, referent, and currency through which to understand how, as Susan Sontag has suggested in another context, politics 'dissolves . . . into pathology' (cited in Becker 1997, p. 28).

Such militarized pedagogies play a powerful role in producing identities and modes of agency completely at odds with those elements of autonomy, critical reflection, and social justice that Adorno privileged in his essay. Adorno's ideology of hardness when coupled with neoliberal values that aggressively promote a Hobbesian world based on fear, the narrow pursuit of individual interests, and an embrace of commodified relations profoundly influence individuals who seem increasingly indifferent towards the pain of others, pit their own ambitions against those of everyone else, and assimilate themselves to things, numb to those moral principles that hail us as moral witnesses and call for us to do something about human suffering. Adorno goes so far as to suggest that the inability to identify with others was one of the root causes of Auschwitz:

> The inability to identify with others was unquestionably the most important psychological condition for the fact that something like Auschwitz could have occurred in the midst of more or less civilized and innocent people. What is called fellow travelling was primarily business interest: one pursues one's own advantage before all else, and simply not to endanger oneself, does not talk too much. That is a general law of the status quo. The silence under the terror was only its consequence. The coldness of the societal monad, the isolated competitor, was the precondition, as indifference to the fate of others, for the fact that only very few people reacted. The torturers know this, and they put it to test ever anew. (Adorno 1998a, p. 201)

Adorno's prescient analysis of the role of education after Auschwitz is particularly important in examining those values, ideologies, and pedagogical forces at work in American culture that suggest that Abu Ghraib is not an aberration as much as an outgrowth of those dehumanizing and demonizing ideologies, values and social relations characteristic of an expanding market fundamentalism, militarism, and nationalism. While these are not the only forces that contributed to the abuses and human rights violations that took place at Abu Ghraib, they do point to how particular manifestations of hypermasculinity, violence, militarization and a jingoistic patriotism are elaborated through forms of public pedagogy that produce identities, social relations and values conducive to both the ambitions of empire and the cruel, inhuman, and degrading treatment of those others who are its victims. What ulti-mately drives the ideological vision behind these practices and gives them a stimulus for abuse and sanctioned brutality is the presupposition that a particular society and its citizens are above the law, indebted only to either God, as John Ashcroft, has insisted, or rightfully scornful of those individuals and cultures who do not deserve to be accorded human rights because they are labelled as part of an evil empire or dismissed as terrorists.[15] The educational force of these ideological practices allow state power to be held unaccountable while legitimizing an 'indifference to the con-cerns and the suffering of people in places remote from our Western metropolitan sites of self -interest' (Bilgrami 2004, p. x).

Adorno believed that the authoritarian tendencies in capitalism were creating individuals who make a cult out of efficiency, suffer from emotional callousness, have a tendency to treat other human beings as things, and reproduce the ultimate expressions of reification under capitalism. The grip that these pathogenic traits had on the German populace then and the American public today can be explained, in part, through the inability of people to recognize that such traits are conditioned rather than determined. In keeping with Adorno's (1998a) reasoning, such traits even when seen as an intolerable given are often posited as an absolute, 'something that blinds itself toward any process of having come into being, toward any insight into our own conditionality'. Adorno's insights regarding the educational force of late capitalism to construct individuals who were cold through and through and incapable of empathizing with the plight of others are theoretically useful in illuminating some of the conditions that contributed to the abuses, murders and acts of torture that took place at Abu Ghraib. Adorno was particularly prescient in forecasting the connection among the subjective mechanisms that produced political indifference and racialized intolerance, the all-encompassing market fundamentalism of neoliberal ideology, and a virulent nationalism that fed on the pieties of theocratic pretentiousness and their relationship to an escalating authoritarianism. What is remarkable about his analysis is that it appears to apply equally well to the United States.

The signals are everywhere. Under the reign of market fundamentalism, cap-ital and wealth have been largely distributed upwards while civic virtue has been undermined by a slavish celebration of the free market as the model for organizing all facets of everyday life. Financial investments, market identities, and commercial values take precedence over human needs, public responsibilities and democratic relations. With its debased belief that profit-making is the essence of democracy, and citizenship defined as an energized plunge into consumerism, market funda-mentalism eliminates government regulation of big business, celebrates a ruthless competitive individualism, and places the commanding political, cultural and eco-nomic institutions of society in the hands of powerful corporate interests, the priv-ileged, and unrepentant religious bigots. Under such circumstances, individuals are viewed as privatized consumers rather than public citizens. As the Bush administra-tion rolls American society back to the Victorian capitalism of the Robber Barons, social welfare is viewed as a drain on corporate profits that should be eliminated, while at the same time the development of the economy is left to the wisdom of the market. Market fundamentalism destroys politics by commercializing public spheres and rendering politics corrupt and cynical.[16]

The impoverishment of public life is increasingly matched by the impoverishment of thought itself, particularly as the media substitutes patriotic cheerleading for real journalism.[17] The cloak of patriotism is now cast over retrograde social policies as well as a coercive unilateralism in which military force has replaced democratic idealism, and war has become the organizing principle of society—a source of pride—rather than a source of alarm. In the face of massive corruption, the erosion of civil liberties, and a spreading culture of fear, the defining feature of politics is its insignificance, reduced to an ideology and practice that celebrates passivity and cynicism while promoting conformity and collective impotence (Bauman 1999). For many, the collapse of democratic life and politics is paid for in the hard currency of isolation, poverty, inadequate health care, impoverished schools and the loss of decent employment (see Phillips 2003). Within this regime of symbolic and material capital, the other—figured as a social drain on the individual and corporate accumulation of wealth—is either feared, exploited, reified or considered disposable but rarely is the relationship between the self and the other mediated by compassion and empathy.[18]

However, market fundamentalism does more than destroy the subjective political and ethical conditions for autonomous political agency or concern for fellow citizens; it also shreds the social order as it threatens destruction abroad. As Cornel West points out:

> Free market fundamentalism—the basic dogma across the globe—is producing obscene levels of wealth and inequality around the world. Market as idol. Corporation as fetish. Acting as if workers are just appendages or some kind of market calculation. Outsourcing here, outsourcing there. Ascribing magical powers to the market and thinking it can solve all problems. When free market fundamentalism is tied to escalating authoritarianism, it results in increasing surveillance of citizens and monitoring of classes at universities and colleges. When it is tied to aggressive militarism, we get not just invasion of those countries perceived to be threats, but a military presence in 132 countries, a ship in every ocean. (West 2004, pp. 19-20)

We also get the privatized armies of mercenaries that take over traditional military functions extending from cooking meals to interrogating prisoners. In Iraq, it has been estimated that 'for every ten troops on the ground . . . there is one contract employee. That translates to 10,000 to 15,000 contract workers, making them the second-largest contingent (between American and Britain) of the "coalition of the willing"' (Hartung 2004, p. 5). Firms such as Erinys and CACI International provide rental Rambos, some of whom have notorious backgrounds as mercenaries-for-hire. One widely reported incident involved two civilian contractors blown up by a suicide bomber in Baghdad in the winter of 2003. Both were South Africans who belonged to a terrorist organization infamous for killing blacks, terrorizing anti-apartheid activists and paying a bounty on the bodies of black activists (Navaer 2004). In Iraq, Steve Stefanowicz, a civilian interrogator employed by CACI International was cited in the Taguba report as having "'allowed and/or instructed" MPs to abuse and humiliate Iraqi prisoners and as giving orders that he knew "equated to physical abuse'" (Shorrok 2004, p. 22). While the Justice Department has opened up a criminal investigation on an unnamed civilian contractor in Iraq, CACI has refused to take action against Stefanowicz, making clear the charge that private contractors are not monitored as closely as military personnel and are not subject to the same Congressional and public oversights and scrutiny. The lack of democratic accountability results in more than bungled services and price gouging by Halliburton, Bechtel, Northrop Grumman and other corporations that have become familiar news, it also results in human rights abuses organized under the logic of rationalizing and market efficiency. Journalist Tim Shorrock claims that 'The military's abuse of Iraqi prisoners is bad enough, but the privatization of such practices is simply intolerable' (Shorrok 2004, p. 22).

The pedagogical implications of Adorno's analysis of the relationship between authoritarianism and capitalism suggests that any viable educational project would have to recognize how market fundamentalism has not only damaged democratic institutions but also the ability of people to identify with democratic social formations and invest in crucial public goods, let alone reinvigorate the very concept of compassion as an antidote to the commodity-driven view of human relationships. Adorno understood that critical knowledge alone could not adequately address the deformations of mind and character put into place by the subjective mechanisms of capitalism. Instead, he argued that critical knowledge had to be reproduced and democratic social experiences put into place through shared values, beliefs, and practices that created inclusive and compassionate communities that make democratic politics possible and safeguard the autonomous subject through the creation of emancipatory needs. Within the boundaries of critical education, students have to learn the skills and knowledge to narrate their own stories, resist the fragmentation and seductions of market ideologies, and create shared pedagogical sites that extend the range of democratic politics. Ideas gain relevance in terms of whether and how they enable students to participate in both the worldly sphere of self-criticism and the publicness of everyday life. Theory and knowledge, in other words, become a force for autonomy and self-determination within the space of public engagement, and their significance is based less on a self-proclaimed activism than on their ability to make critical and thoughtful connections 'beyond theory, within the space of politics itself' (Couldry 2004, p. 15). Adorno's educational project for autonomy recognizes the necessity of a worldly space in which freedom is allowed to make its appearance, a space that is both the condition and the object of struggle for any viable form of critical pedagogy. Such a project also understands the necessity of compassion to remind people of the full humanity and suffering of others, as well as 'the importance of compassion in shaping the civic imagination' (Nussbaum 2003,

p. 11). If Adorno is correct, and I think he is, his call to refashion education in order to prevent inhuman acts has to take as one of its founding tasks today the necessity to understand how free market ideology, privatization, outsourcing, and the relentless drive for commodified public space radically diminishes those political and pedagogical sites crucial for sustaining democratic identities, values, and practices.

Adorno's critique of nationalism appears as useful today as it did when it appeared in the late 1960s. He believed that those forces pushing an aggressive nationalism harboured a distinct rage against divergent groups who stood at odds with such imperial ambitions. Intolerance and militarism, according to Adorno, fuelled a nationalism that became 'pernicious because in the age of international communication and supranational blocks it cannot completely believe in itself anymore and has to exaggerate boundlessly in order to convince itself and others that it is still substantial . . . [Moreover] movements of national renewal in an age when nationalism is outdated, seem to be especially susceptible to sadistic practices' (1998a, p. 203). Surely, such a diagnosis would fit the imperial ambitions of Richard Cheney, Richard Perle, Donald Rumsfeld, Paul Wolfowitz and other neo-conservatives whose dreams of empire are entirely at odds with either a desire to preserve human dignity or respect for international law. Convinced that the US should not only maintain political and military dominance in the post-Cold War world, but prevent any nation or alliance from challenging its superiority, nationalists across the ideological spectrum advocate a discourse of exceptionalism that calls for a dangerous unity at home and reckless imperial ambitions abroad. Belief in empire has come to mean that the US would now shape rather than react to world events and act decisively in using 'its overwhelming military and economic might to create conditions conducive to American values and interests' (Devan 2004). American unilateralism buttressed by the dangerous doctrine of pre-emption has replaced multilateral diplomacy, religious fundamentalism has found its counterpart in the ideological messianism of neo-conservative designs on the rest of the globe, and a reckless moralism that divides the world into good and evil has replaced the possibility of dialogue and debate. Within such a climate, blind authority demands as it rewards authoritarian behaviour so as to make power and domination appear beyond the pale of criticism or change, providing the political and educational conditions for eliminating self-reflection and compassion even in the face of the most sadistic practices and imperial ambitions.

American support for the invasions of Iraq and the Apartheid wall in Israel as well as targeted assassinations and torture are now defended in the name of righteous causes even by liberals such as Niall Ferguson, Paul Berman and Michael Ignatieff, who, like their neo-conservative counterparts, swoon in the illusion that American power can be used as a force for progress, in spite of the official terror and reckless suffering it imposes on much of the world (see, for instance, Ferguson 2004 and Ignatieff 2004). National justification for the most messianic militaristic policies, as indicated by the war in Iraq, are wrapped up in the discourse of democracy and divine mission, an updated version of American exceptionalism, in spite of the toll the war takes on Iraqi lives—mostly children—and young, American soldiers. Then there is the wasted $141 billion being spent on the war that could be used to support life-giving social programmes at home. Even moderately liberal democrats now appeal to an uncritical chauvinism with a fervour that is equally matched by its ability to cheapen the most basic tenets of democracy and deaden in some of its citizens the obligation to be responsible to the suffering and hardships of those others who exist outside of its national borders. Barack Obama, a rising star in the Democratic Party and a keynote speaker at the 2004 Democratic convention, insisted we are 'One America', a moniker that does more to hide contradictions and injustices than to invoke their continuing presence and the necessity to overcome them. Equally important, 'One America' when appealed to outside of a critical examination of the damaging chauvinism that informs such a call ends up reproducing a more liberal, though equally privileged, notion of America's role in the world, a role that seems to have little understanding of what the limits might be or the legacy of human suffering it has produced historically and continues to produce.

The aggressive nationalism that Adorno viewed as fundamental to the conditions that produced Auschwitz have not been laid to rest. Echoes of such jingoistic rhetoric can be heard from neo-conservatives who want to wage a holy war against the non-Western hordes that threaten all things Christian, European and civilized. This virulent nationalism can be heard in the semantic contortions justifying hard and soft versions of empire, often produced by conservative think-tanks and Ivy League intellectuals acting as modern day missionaries for their corporate sponsors. It can be heard in the fundamentalist rhetoric of religious bigots such as Jerry Falwell and Pat Robertson who are fanatically pro-Israel and are waging an incessant propaganda war for Palestinian land in the name of Christian ideals. The discourse of empire can be not only heard but also seen in the tangible presence of 725 US military bases in over 138 foreign countries that circle the globe in order to keep the world safe from democracy (figures cited in Cooper 2004).

The discourse of empire must be deconstructed and replaced in our schools and other sites of pedagogy with new global models of democracy, models grounded in an ethics and morality in which the relationship between the self and others extends beyond the chauvinism of national boundaries and embraces a new and critical understanding of the interdependencies of the world and its implications for citizenship in global democracy. Memory must serve as a bulwark against the discourse of empire, which is often built on the erasure of historical struggles and conflicts. Memory in this instance is more than counter-knowledge, it is a form of resistance, a resource through which to wage pedagogical and political struggles to recover those narratives, traditions and values that remind students and others of the graphic nature of suffering that unfolded in the aftermath of America's claims for a permanent war on terrorism. Appeals to American exceptionalism and the obligations of empire building sound hollow in the face of the monstrosities they produce; yet, such appeals also legitimize a process of othering, demonizing those who are not included by appeals to human dignity, human rights and international law.

At the heart of Adorno's concern with education was the call to create pedagogical practices in which we supplement knowledge with self-criticism. Self and social criticism was for Adorno a crucial element of autonomy, but criticism was not enough. Agency as a political force mattered in that it was not only capable of saying no to abusive power, but also because it could imagine itself as a mechanism for changing the world. As a condition of politics and collective struggle, agency requires being able to engage democratic values, principles, and practices as a force for resistance and hope in order to challenge unquestioned modes of authority while also enabling individuals to connect such principles and values to 'the world in which they lived as citizens' (Said 2004, p. 6). Adorno's plea for education rests on the assumption that human beings make both knowledge and history, rather than it simply washing over them. For Adorno, critical reflection was the essence of all genuine education as well as politics. Ongoing reflection provided the basis for individuals to become autonomous by revealing the human origins of institutions and as such the recognition that society could be open to critique and change. Politics is thus theorized as a practical effort to link freedom to agency in the service of extending the promise of democratic institutions, values, and social relations. The capacity for self-knowledge, self-critique and autonomy becomes more powerful when it is nourished within pedagogical spaces and sites that refuse to be parochial, that embrace difference over bigotry, global democracy over chauvinism, peace over militarism, and secularism over religious fundamentalism. The urgency of such a call can be heard in William Greider's plea for critical education to bring the presidency of George W. Bush to an end:

The only way out of this fog of pretension is painful self-examination by

> Americans—cutting our fears down to more plausible terms and facing the complicated realities of our role in the world. The spirited opposition that arose to Bush's war in Iraq is a good starting place, because citizens raised real questions that were brushed aside. I don't think that most Americans are interested in imperial rule, but they were grossly misled by patriotic rhetoric. Now is the time for sober, serious teach-ins that lay out the real history of US power in the world, and that also explain the positive and progressive future that is possible. Once citizens have constructed a clear-eyed, dissenting version of our situation, perhaps politicians can also be liberated from exaggerated fear. The self-imposed destruction that has flowed from Bush's logic cannot be stopped until a new cast of leaders steps forward to guide the country. (Greider 2004, p. 18)

Teach-ins, reading groups, public debates and film screenings should take place in a variety of sites and spaces for dialogue and learning, and they should focus not simply on the imperial ambitions of the US but also on the dehumanizing practices informed by a political culture in which human life that does not align itself with official power and corporate ideology becomes disposable. The connection between Auschwitz and Abu Ghraib can also be traced in the educational force of popular culture in which pedagogy is disassociated from justice, citizenship is restricted to the obligations of consumerism, and compassion is dissolved in the mechanics of social Darwinism.

As mentioned previously, Abu Ghraib cannot be equated with the genocidal intent of Auschwitz, but the conditions that allowed Americans to commit such abuses on Iraqi detainees harbour the possibilities for atrocious acts of inhumanity, only this time they are dressed up in the rhetoric of advancing the democratic principles of freedom and justice. Adorno believed that education as a democratic force could play a central role in altering the rising tide of authoritarianism on both a national and global level. His call to rethink the value and importance of education as a central element of politics offers an opportunity, especially for educators and other cultural workers, to learn not only from the horrors of Abu Ghraib but also to rethink the value of critical education and public pedagogy as an all important part of politics, the future of public institutions and global democracy itself. In addition, Adorno brilliantly understood that it was not enough to turn the tools of social critique simply upon the government or other apparatuses of domination. Critique also had to come to grips with the affective investments that tied individuals, including critics, to ideologies and practices of domination and how an analysis of the deep structures of domination might help to provide a more powerful critique and healthy suspicion of various appeals to community, the public and the social. Clearly, while it is imperative to reclaim the discourse of community, the commons, and public good as part of a broader discourse of democracy, such terms need to be embraced critically in light of the ways in which they have often served the instruments of dominant power.

Adorno was insistent that education was crucial as a point of departure for imagining both autonomy, recognizing the interdependency of human life, and stopping cycles of violence. Education can help us imagine a world in which violence can be minimized as well as to reject the disparagement, exclusion and abuse of those deemed others in a social order in which one's worth is often measured through the privileged categories of gender, class, race, citizenship and language. Education can also seek to identify and destroy the conditions that provide an outlet for murderous rage, hatred, fear and violence. This requires a pedagogical commitment, in Judith Butler's eloquent phrase,

> to return us to the human where we do not expect to find it, in its frailty and at the limits of its capacity to make sense. We would have to interrogate the emergence and vanishing of the human at the limits of what we can know, what we can hear, what we can see, what we can sense. This might prompt us, affectively to reinvigorate the intellectual projects of critique of questioning, of coming to understand the difficulties and demands of cultural translation and dissent, and to create a sense of the public in which oppositional voices are not feared, degraded or dismissed, but valued for the instigation to a sensate democracy they occasionally perform. (Butler 2004, p. 151)

But under certain circumstances, the limits of education have to be understood. What is difficult to grasp is that simply because one learns to be non-violent as part of a respect for humanity, a visceral repulsion for the suffering of others, or an ethical conception of mutual obligation, outbursts of violence cannot be entirely contained within such a rationality or mode of understanding. Under certain enormously stressful conditions, violence merges with circumstances of extreme social and bodily vulnerability and may appear to be one of the few options available for dealing with those already dismissed as inhuman or disposable.[19] Even more horrible is the possibility that inhuman acts of abuse under incredibly nerve-wracking conditions represent one of the few outlets for pleasure. Is it conceivable that under certain conditions of violence and stress only the unthinkable is imaginable, that the only avenue for the release of pleasure can be attained by extending the logic of violence to those deemed as the other, those undeserving of narration, agency and power? Under certain modes of domination with all of its stress inducing consequences, those who exercise a wanton and dehumanizing power often feel that everything is permissible because all of the rules appear to have broken down. The stress soldiers sometime experience under such circumstances is often satisfied through the raw feel and exercise of power. Abu Ghraib remains, tragically, a terrible site of violence, a site in which an ethics of non-violence seems almost incomprehensible given the tension, anxiety and daily violence that framed both what happened in the prison and in daily life in Iraq. Under these conditions, neither education nor an ethics of peace may be enough to prevent 'fear and anxiety from turning into murderous action' (Butler 2004, p. xviii). Under extreme conditions in which abuse, loss, hardship and dehumanization shape the consciousness and daily routines of one's existence, whether it be for American soldiers working in Abu Ghraib or Israeli soldiers occupying Hebron, violence can undercut the appeal to ethics, critical reflection and all educated sensibilities.[20] This is not to suggest education does not matter much in light of such conditions as much as to suggest, following Adorno's insight, that education that particularly matters must address what it means to prevent the conditions in which violence takes root and develops a life of its own.

As a political and moral practice, education must be engaged not only as one of the primary conditions for constructing political and moral agents, but also as a public pedagogy that is produced in a range of sites and public spheres that constitutes cultural practice as a defining feature of any viable notion of politics. Education after Abu Ghraib must imagine a future in which learning is inextricably connected to social change, the obligations of civic justice, and a notion of democracy in which peace, equality, compassion and freedom are not limited to the nation-state but extended to the international community. Education after Abu Ghraib must take seriously what it might mean to strive for the autonomy and dignity of a global citizenry and peace as its fundamental precondition.

Notes

1. For an interesting comment on how the Bush media team attempted to enhance presidential persona through the iconography of conservative, hyped-up, macho-phallic masculinity, see Goldstein (2003).

2. While I cannot name all of the relevant sources theorizing the ethical nature of torture or its use by the American military, some important recent contributions include: Hersh (2004), Danner (2004a, 2004b) and Lewis (2004).

3. See Pound and Roane (2004). Also see *The Nation* (2004, p. 3). Degrading prisoners at Abu Ghraib had become so pervasive that forced nudity was seen as a commonplace phenomenon by both military personnel and detainees (see Zernike & Rohde 2004, p. A11).

4. The memo can be found online at: http://www.cooperativeresearch.org/entity.jsp?entity=draft_memo_to_the_president_from_alberto_gonzales,_january_25,_2004

5. See chapter 1 of the manual, 'Interrogation and the Interrogator'. Available online: http://www.globalsecurity.org/intell/library/policy/army/fm/fm34-52/chapter1.htm

6. The level of secrecy employed by the Bush administration is both dangerous and absurd. For example, some individuals were shocked to learn that if they wanted to attend a rally hosted by Vice-President Dick Cheney at Rio Rancho Mid-High School in New Mexico the weekend of 30 July 2004, they could not get tickets to the rally unless they signed an endorsement pledging allegiance to President George W. Bush (see Jones 2004, p. 1).

7. I take up many of these issues in greater detail in Giroux (2004).

8. For an excellent discussion of this issue, see Lucaites and McDaniel (2004), pp. 1–28.

9. This issue is taken up brilliantly in Solomon-Godeau (1994).

10. This was first presented as a radio lecture on 18 April 1966, under the title 'Padagogik nack Auschwitz'. The first published version appeared in 1967. The English translation appears in Adorno (1998a).

11. Some might argue that I am putting forward a view of Adorno that is a bit too optimistic. However, I think that Adorno's political pessimism, given his own experience of fascism, which under the circumstances seems entirely justified to me, should not be confused with his pedagogical optimism, which provides some insight into why he could write the Auschwitz essay in the first place. Even Adorno's ambivalence about what education could actually accomplish does not amount to an unadulterated pessimism as much as a caution about recognizing the limits of education as an emancipatory politics. Adorno wanted to make sure that individuals recognized those larger structures of power outside of traditional appeals to education while clinging to critical thought as the precondition but not absolute condition of individual and social agency. I want to thank Larry Grossberg for this distinction. I also want to thank Roger Simon and Imre Szeman for their insightful comments on Adorno's politics and pessimism.

12. On the relationship between prisons and schools, see Giroux (2004).

13. On the intellectual diversity issue, see Lazere (2004), pp. B15–B16.

14. George Smith refers to one programme in which a woman was tied up in a clear box while some eager males 'dumped a few hundred tarantulas onto her . . . you can hear the screaming and crying from her and the witnesses. Some guy is vomiting. This is critical, because emptying the contents of the stomach is great TV. Everyone else is laughing and smirking, just like our good old boys and girls at Abu Ghraib' (Smith 2004).

15. This issue is taken up with great insight and compassion in Lifton (2003).

16. I take up this issue in great detail in Giroux (2003).

17. One of the best books examining this issue is McChesney's (1999) *Rich Media, Poor Democracy*.

18. Constructions of the impoverished other have a long history in American society, including more recent manifestations that extend from the internment of Japanese Americans during World War II to the increasing incarceration of young black and brown men in 2004. Of course, they cannot be explained entirely within the discourse of capitalist relations. The fatal combination of chauvinism, militarism and racism has produced an extensive history of photographic images in which depraved representations such as blacks hanging from trees or skulls of 'Japanese soldiers jammed onto a tank

exhaust pipe as a trophy' depict a xenophobia far removed from the dictates of objectified consumerism (see Lucaites & McDaniel 2004, p. 4, and Bauman (2004).

19. This issue is taken up brilliantly in Bauman (2004).

20. I want to illustrate this point with a comment taken from an Israeli soldier about his experience in Hebron:

> I was ashamed of myself the day I realized that I simply enjoy the feeling of power. I don't believe in it: I think this is not the way to do anything to anyone, surely not to someone who has done nothing to you, but you can't help but enjoy it. People do what you tell them. You know it's because you carry a weapon. Knowing that if you didn't have it, and if your fellow soldiers weren't beside you, they would jump on you, beat the shit out of you, and stab you to death—you begin to enjoy it. Not merely enjoy it, you need it. And then, when someone suddenly says 'No' to you, what do you mean no? Where do you draw the chutzpah from, to say no to me? . . . I remember a very specific situation: I was at a checkpoint, a temporary one, a so-called strangulation checkpoint, it was a very small checkpoint, very intimate, four soldiers, no commanding officer, no protection worthy of the name, a true moonlighting job, blocking the entrance to a village. From one side a line of cars wanting to get out, and from the other side a line of cars wanting to pass, a huge line, and suddenly you have a mighty force at the tip of your fingers, as if playing a computer game. I stand there like this, pointing at someone, gesturing to you to do this or that, and you do this or that, the car starts, moves toward me, halts beside me. The next car follows, you signal, it stops. You start playing with them, like a computer game. You come here, you go there, like this. You barely move, you make them obey the tip of your finger. It's a mighty feeling. It's something you don't experience elsewhere. You know it's because you have a weapon, you know it's because you are a soldier, you know all this, but its addictive. When I realized this . . . I checked in with myself to see what had happened to me. That's it. And it was a big bubble that burst. I thought I was immune, that is, how can someone like me, a thinking, articulate, ethical, moral man—things I can attest to about myself as such. Suddenly, I notice that I am getting addicted to controlling people.

I want to thank Roger Simon for this insight and for his making available to me the transcript from which this quote is taken. See 'Soldiers Speak Out About Their Service in Hebron'. Available at www.shovrimshtika.org

References

Adorno, T. W. (1998a) 'Education after Auschwitz', in his *Critical Models: Interventions and Catchwords*, Columbia University Press, New York.

Adorno, T. W. (1998b) 'Philosophy and teachers', in his *Critical Models: Interventions and Catchwords*, Columbia University Press, New York, pp. 19–36.

Associated Press (2004) 'DOD denies report's claims', *Military.Com*, [online]. Available at: http://www.military.com/NewsContent/0,13319,FL_rumsfeld_051604,00.html

Bauman, Z. (1999) *In Search of Politics*, Stanford University Press, Stanford.

Bauman, Z. (2004) *Wasted Lives*, Polity Press, Cambridge.

Becker, C. (1997) 'The art of testimony', *Sculpture*, March, p. 28.

Bilgrami, A. (2004) 'Foreword' in *Humanism and Democratic Criticism*, E. Said, Columbia, New York, p. x.

Blumenthal, S. (2004) 'This is the new gulag', *The Guardian*, 6 May [online] Available at: www.guardian.co.uk/print/0,38584917539-103677,00.html

Bravin, J. (2004) 'Pentagon report set framework for use of torture', *Wall Street Journal*, 7 June [online] Available at: www.Commondreams.org/cgi-bin/print.cgi?file=/headlines04/0607-01.htm

Bush, G. W. (2004) 'President outlines steps to help Iraq achieve democracy and freedom', Office of the White House Press Secretary, 24 May [online] Available at: http://www.whitehouse.gov/news/releases/2004/05/20040524-10.html

Butler, J. (2002) 'Explanation and exoneration, or what we can hear', *Theory & Event*, vol. 5, no. 4, p. 19.

Butler, J. (2004) *Precarious Life: The Powers of Mourning and Violence*, Verso, London.

Cooper, M. (2004) 'Dissing the Republic to save it: a conversation with Chalmers Johnson', *The LA Weekly*, 2–8 July [online] Available at: www.commondreams.org/views04/0701-12.htm

Couldry, N. (2004) 'In the place of a common culture, what?', *The Review of Education, Pedagogy, and Cultural Studies*, vol. 26, no. 1, p. 15.

Danner, M. (2004a) 'The logic of torture', *The New York Review of Books*, 24 June, pp. 70–74.

Danner, M. (2004b) 'Torture and truth', *The New York Review of Books*, 27 May, pp. 46–50.

Devan, J. (2004) 'The rise of the neo conservatives', *The Straits Times*, 30 March [online] Available at: http://www.straitstimes.asia1.com.sg/columnist/0,1886,145-180171-,00.html

DiLeo, J. R., Jacobs, W. & Lee, A. (2004) 'The sites of pedagogy', *Symploke*, vol. 10, nos. 1–2, p. 9.

Drogin, B. (2004) 'Most "arrested by mistake"', *Los Angeles Times*, 11 May [online] Available at: www.commondreams.org/cgi-bin/print.cgi?file_headlines04/0511-04.htm

Ferguson, N. (2004) *Colossus: The Price of America's Empire*, The Penguin Press, New York.

Folkenflik, D. (2004) 'Dodging using words like "torture"', *BaltimoreSun.Com*, 26 May [online] Available at: http://www.baltimoresun.com/entertainment/tv/bal-to.media26may26,0,7304614.column?coll=bal-artslife-tv

Gaonkar, D. P. & Povinelli, E. A. (2003) 'Technologies of public forms: circulation, transfiguration, recognition', *Public Culture*, vol. 15, no. 3, p. 386.

Giroux, H. A. (2003) *Public Spaces, Private Lives: Democracy Beyond 9/11*, Rowman and Littlefield, Lanham, MD.

Giroux, H. A. (2004) *The Terror of Neoliberalism: The New Authoritarianism and the Attack on Democracy*, Paradigm Press, Denver, CO.

Giroux, H. A. & Searls, S. G. (2004) *Take Back Higher Education*, Palgrave, New York.

Goldstein, R. (2003) 'Bush's basket', *The Village Voice*, 21–27 May [online] Available at: http://www.villagevoice.com/issues/0321/goldstein.php

Greider, W. (2004) 'Under the banner of the "war" on terror', *The Nation*, 21 June, p. 14.

Hajjar, L. (2004) 'Torture and the politics of denial', *In These Times*, 21 June, p. 12.

Hartung, W. D. (2004) 'Outsourcing is hell', *The Nation*, 7 June, p. 5.

Hersh, S. M. (2004a) 'Chain of command', *The New Yorker*, 17 May, p. 40.

Hersh, S. M. (2004b) 'Torture at Abu Ghraib', *The New Yorker*, 10 May, pp. 42–7.

Hohendahl, P. U. (1995) *Prismatic Thought: Theodor Adorno*, University of Nebraska Press, Lincoln, NE.

Ignatieff, M. (2004) *The Lesser Evil: Political Ethics in An age of Terror*, Princeton University Press, Princeton, NJ.

Jones, J. (2004) *Albuquerque Journal*, 30 July, p. 1.

Lazere, D. (2004) 'The contradictions of cultural conservatism in the assault on American Colleges', *Chronicle of Higher Education*, 2 July, pp. B15–B16.

Lewis, A. (2004) 'Making torture legal', *The New York Review of Books*, 15 July, p. 8.

Lewis, A. (2004) 'The US case for torture', *The New York Review of Books*, 15 July, pp. 4–8.

Lewis, N. A. (2004) 'Bush didn't order any breach of torture laws, Ashcroft says', *The New York Times*, 9 June, [online] Available at: www.nytimes.com/2004/06/09/politics

Lifton, R. J. (2003) *Super Power Syndrome: America's Apocalyptic Confrontation with the World*, Thunder Mouth Press, New York.

Lucaites, J. L. & McDaniel, J. P. (2004) 'Telescopic mourning/warring in the global village: decomposing (Japanese) authority figures', *Communication and Critical/Cultural Studies*, vol. 1, no. 1, p. 4.

McChesney, R. W. (1999) *Rich Media, Poor Democracy*, The New Press, New York.

McGovern, R. (2004) 'Not scared yet? Try connecting these dots', *Common Dreams*, 11 August [online] Available at: http://www.commondreams.org/views04/0809-11.htm

Moniz, D. and Squitieri, T. (2004) 'Lawyers raised questions and concerns on interrogations', *USA Today*, 10 June, p. 13A.

Navaer, L. (2004) 'Terrorist mercenaries on US payroll in Iraq War', *Pacific News Service*, 4 May [online] Available at: http://www.mindfully.org/Reform/2004/Terrorist-Mercenaries-US4may04.htm

Nussbaum, M. C. (2003) 'Compassion and terror', *Daedalus*, winter, p. 11.

Phillips, K. (2003) *Wealth and Democracy*, Broadway Books, New York.

Piper, M. C. (2003) 'Schools not teaching pro-Israel views to lose funding: congress to pass 'ideological diversity' legislation', *American Free Press*, 22 April [online] Available at: http://www.picosearch.com/cgi-bin/ts.pl

Pollitt, K. (2004) 'Show and tell in Abu Ghraib', *The Nation*, 24 May, p. 9.

Pound, E. T. and Roane, K. R. (2004) 'Hell on earth', *US News and World Report*, 19 July [online] Available at: www.usnews.com/usnews/issue/040719/usnews/19prison.htm

Rich, F. (2004) 'It was porn that made them do it', *The New York Times*, 30 May.

Said, E. (2004) *Humanism and Democratic Criticism*, Columbia University Press, New York.

Schmitt, E. (2004) 'Defense leaders faulted by panel in prison abuse', *The New York Times*, 24 August, p. 1.

Shorrok, T. (2004) 'CACI and its friends', *The Nation*, 21 June, p. 22.

Smith, G. (2004) 'That's entrail-tainment!' *The Village Voice*, 3 August [online] Available at: www.vilagevoice.com/isues/0431/essay.php

Smith, R. W. (2004) 'American self-interest and the response to genocide', *The Chronicle Review*, 30 July [online] Available at: http://chronicle.com/cgi2-bin/printible.cgi?article=http://chronicle.co

Solomon, N. (2004) 'The coming backlash against outrage', *Common Dreams*, 12 May [online] Available at: www.commondreams.org/cgi-bin/print.cgi?file=views04/0512-05.htm

Solomon-Godeau, A. (1994) *Photography At The Dock*, University of Minnesota Press, Minnesota.

Sontag, S. (2003) *Regarding the Pain of Others*, Farrar, Straus and Giroux, New York.

Sontag, S. (2004) 'Regarding the torture of others: notes on what has been done—and why—to prisoners, by Americans', *The New York Times Sunday Magazine*, 23 May, pp. 26–27.

Steel, R. (2004) 'Fight fire with fire', *The New York Times Book Review*, 25 July, pp. 12–13.

The Nation (2004) 'Editorial, "The Horror of Abu Ghraib"', *The Nation*, 24 May, p. 3.

The Washington Post (2004) 'Editorial, "Legalizing Torture"', *The Washington Post*, 9 June, p. A20.

Thompson, C. (2004) 'The making of an Xbox warrior', *The New York Times Magazine*, 22 August, pp. 32–37.

West, C. (2004) 'Finding hope in dark times', *Tikkun*, vol. 19, no. 4, pp. 19–20.

White, J. and Higham, S. (2004) 'Use of dogs to scare prisoners was authorized', *The Washington Post*, 11 June, p. A01.

White, J. and Ricks, T. E. (2004) 'Iraqi teens abused at Abu Ghraib, report finds', *The Washington Post*, 24 August, p. A01.

Williams, P. J. (2004) 'In kind', *The Nation*, 31 May, p. 10.

Younge, G. (2004) 'Blame the white trash', *The Guardian*, 17 May, [online] Available at: www.commondreams.org/cgi-bin/pring.cgi?file=/views04/0517-03.htm

Zernike, K. and Rohde, D. (2004) 'Forced nudity of Iraqi prisoners is seen as a pervasive pattern, not isolated incidents', *The New York Times*, 8 June, p. A11.

CHAPTER 8

The Terror of Neoliberalism

Rethinking the Significance of Cultural Politics

2005

If there is a class war in America, my side is winning. (Warren Buffet qtd. In Woodward 2004, para. 47)

In 1945 or 1950, if you had seriously proposed any of the ideas and policies in today's standard neo-liberal toolkit, you would have been laughed off the stage or sent off to the insane asylum . . . . The idea that the market should be allowed to make major social and political decisions; the idea that the State should voluntarily reduce its role in the economy, or that corporations should be given total freedom, that trade unions should be curbed and citizens given much less rather than more social protection—such ideas were utterly foreign to the spirit of the time. Even if someone actually agreed with these ideas, he or she would have hesitated to take such a position in public and would have had a hard time finding an audience. (George 1999, para.2)

Just as the world has seen a more virulent and brutal form of market capitalism, generally referred to as neoliberalism, develop over the last thirty years, it has also seen "a new wave of political activism [which] has coalesced around the simple idea that capitalism has gone too far" (Harding 2001, para. 28). Wedded to the belief that the market should be the organizing principle for all political, social, and economic decisions, neoliberalism wages an incessant attack on democracy, public goods, and non-commodified values. Under neoliberalism everything either is for sale or is plundered for profit. Public lands are looted by logging companies and corporate ranchers; politicians willingly hand the public's airwaves over to powerful broadcasters and large corporate interests without a dime going into the public trust; Halliburton gives war profiteering a new meaning as it is granted corporate contracts without any competitive bidding and then bills the U.S. government for millions; the environment is polluted and despoiled in the name of profit-making just as the government passes legislation to make it easier for corporations to do so; public services are gutted in order to lower the taxes of major corporations; schools more closely resemble either malls or jails, and teachers, forced to get revenue for their school by adopting market values, increasingly function as circus barkers hawking everything from hamburgers to pizza parties—that is, when they are not reduced to prepping students to take standardized tests. As markets are touted as the driving force of everyday life, big government is disparaged as either incompetent or threatening to individual freedom, suggesting that power should reside in markets and corporations rather than in governments (except for their support for corporate interests and national security) and citizens. Citizenship has increasingly become a function of consumerism and politics has been restructured as "corporations have been increasingly freed from social control through deregulation, privatization, and other neoliberal measures" (Tabb 2003, 153).

Corporations more and more design not only the economic sphere but also shape legislation and policy affecting all levels of government, and with limited opposition. As corporate power lays siege to the political process, the benefits flow to the rich and the powerful. Included in such benefits are reform policies that shift the burden of taxes from the rich to the middle class, the working poor, and state governments as can be seen in the shift from taxes on wealth (capital gains, dividends, and estate taxes) to a tax on work, principally in the form of a regressive payroll tax (Collins, Hartman, Kraut, and Mota 2004). During the 2002-2004 fiscal years, tax cuts delivered $197.3 billion in tax breaks to the wealthiest 1% of Americans (i.e., households making more than $337,000 a year) while state governments increased taxes to fill a $200 billion budget deficit (Gonsalves 2004). Equally alarming, a recent Congressional study revealed that 63% of all corporations in 2000 paid no taxes while "[s]ix in ten corporations reported no tax liability for the five years from 1996 through 2000, even though corporate profits were growing at record-breaking levels during that period" (Woodard 2004, para.11).

Fortunately, the corporate capitalist fairytale of neoliberalism has been challenged all over the globe by students, labor organizers, intellectuals, community activists, and a host of individuals and groups unwilling to allow democracy to be bought and sold by multinational corporations, corporate swindlers, international political institutions, and those government politicians who willingly align themselves with multinational, corporate interests and rapacious profits. From Seattle to Genoa, people engaged in popular resistance are collectively taking up the challenge of neoliberalism and reviving both the meaning of resistance and the sites where it takes place. Political culture is now global and resistance is amorphous, connecting students with workers, schoolteachers with parents, and intellectuals with artists. Groups protesting the attack on farmers in India whose land is being destroyed by the government in order to build dams now find themselves in alliance with young people resisting sweatshop labor in New York City. Environmental activists are joining up with key sections of organized labor as well as groups protesting Third World debt. The collapse of the neoliberal showcase, Argentina, along with numerous corporate bankruptcies and scandals (notably including Enron), reveals the cracks in neoliberal hegemony and domination. In addition, the multiple forms of resistance against neoliberal capitalism are not limited by a version of identity politics focused exclusively on particularized rights and interests. On the contrary, identity politics is affirmed within a broader crisis of political culture and democracy that connects the militarization of public life with the collapse of the welfare state and the attack on civil liberties. Central to these new movements is the notion that neoliberalism has to be understood within a larger crisis of vision, meaning, education, and political agency. Democracy in this view is not limited to the struggle over economic resources and power; indeed, it also includes the creation of public spheres where individuals can be educated as political agents equipped with the skills, capacities, and knowledge they need to perform as autonomous political agents. I want to expand the reaches of this debate by arguing that any struggle against neoliberalism must address the discourse of political agency, civic education, and cultural politics as part of a broader struggle over the relationship between democratization (the ongoing struggle for a substantive and inclusive democracy) and the global public sphere.

We live at a time when the conflation of private interests, empire building, and evangelical fundamentalism brings into question the very nature, if not the existence, of the democratic process. Under the reign of neoliberalism, capital and wealth have been largely distributed upwards, while civic virtue has been undermined by a slavish celebration of the free market as the model for organizing all facets of everyday life (Henwood 2003). Political culture has been increasingly depoliticized as collective life is organized around the modalities of privatization, deregulation, and commercialization. When the alleged champions of neoliberalism invoke politics, they substitute "ideological certainty for reasonable doubt," and deplete "the national reserves of political intelligence" just as they endorse "the illusion that the future can be bought instead of earned" (Lapham 2004a, 9, 11). Under attack is the social contract with its emphasis on enlarging the public good and expanding social provisions—such as access to adequate health care, housing, employment, public transportation, and education—which provided both a safety net and a set of conditions upon which democracy could be experienced and critical citizenship engaged. Politics has been further depoliticized by a policy of anti-terrorism practiced by the Bush administration that mimics the very terrorism it wishes to eliminate. Not only does a policy of all-embracing anti-terrorism exhaust itself in a discourse of moral absolutes and public acts of denunciation that remove politics from the realm of state power, it also strips community of democratic values by defining it almost exclusively through attempts to stamp out what Michael Leeden, a former counter-terror expert in the Reagan administration, calls "corrupt habits of mind that are still lingering around, somewhere"(qtd. in Valentine 2001, para. 33). The appeal to moral absolutes and the constant mobilization of emergency time coded as a culture of fear configures politics in religious terms, hiding its entanglement with particular ideologies and diverse relations of power. Politics becomes empty as it is reduced to following orders, shaming those who make power accountable, and shutting down legitimate modes of dissent (Giroux 2004).

The militarizing of public space at home contributes to the narrowing of community, the increasing suppression of dissent, and as Anthony Lewis argues, a growing escalation of concentrated, unaccountable political power that threatens the very foundation of democracy in the United States (2002, A15). Authoritarianism marches forward just as political culture is being replaced with a notion of national security based on fear, surveillance, and control rather than a vibrant culture of shared responsibility and critical questioning. Militarization is no longer simply the driving force of foreign policy, it has become a defining principle for social changes at home. Catherine Lutz captures the multiple registers and complex processes of militarization that has extensively shaped social life during the 20th century. She is worth quoting at length:

> By militarization, I mean . . . an intensification of the labor and resources allocated to military purposes, including the shaping of other institutions in synchrony with military goals. Militarization is simultaneously a discursive process, involving a shift in general societal beliefs and values in ways necessary to legitimate the use of force, the organization of large standing armies and their leaders, and the higher taxes or tribute used to pay for them. Militarization is intimately connected not only to the obvious increase in the size of armies and resurgence of militant nationalisms and militant fundamentalisms but also to the less visible deformation of human potentials into the hierarchies of race, class, gender, and sexuality, and to the shaping of national histories in ways that glorify and legitimate military action. (Lutz 2002, 723)

Lutz's definition of militarization is inclusive, attentive to its discursive, ideological, and material relations of power in the service of war and violence. But militarization is also a powerful cultural politics that works its way through everyday life spawning particular notions of masculinity, sanctioning war as a spectacle, and fear as a central formative component in mobilizing an affective investment in militarization. In other words, the politics of militarization, with its emphasis on "social processes in which society organizes itself for the production of violence or the threat thereof." (Kraska 1999, 208), has produced a pervasive *culture* of militarization, which as Kevin Baker insists, "inject[s] a constant military presence in our lives" (2003, 40). As the culture of profit and militarization dominate or seek to eliminate democratic public spheres, self-reflection and collective empowerment are reduced to self-promotion and self-interest, legitimated by a new and ruthless social Darwinism played out nightly on network television as a metaphor for the "naturalness" of downsizing, the celebration of hyper-masculinity, and the promotion of a war of all against all over even the most limited notions of solidarity and collective struggle (Bourdieu 1998).

Under neoliberal domestic restructuring and the foreign policy initiatives of the Washington Consensus, which are motivated by an evangelical belief in free-market democracy at home and open markets abroad, the United States in the last thirty years has witnessed the increasing obliteration of those discourses, social forms, public institutions, and non-commercial values that are central to the language of public commitment, democratically charged politics, and the common good (Giroux 2003). Civic engagement now appears impotent as corporations privatize public space and disconnect power from issues of equity, social justice, and civic responsibility. Financial investments, market identities, and commercial values take precedence over human needs, public responsibilities, and democratic relations (Martin 2002). Proceeding outside of democratic accountability, neoliberalism has allowed a handful of private interests to control as much of social life as possible in order to maximize their personal profit (Chomsky 1999).

Abroad, neoliberal global policies have been used to pursue rapacious free-trade agreements and expand Western financial and commercial interests through the heavy-handed policies of the World Bank, the World Trade Organization (WTO), and the International Monetary Fund (IMF) in order to manage and transfer resources and wealth from the poor and less developed nations to the richest and most powerful nation-states and to the wealthy corporate defenders of capitalism. Third world and semi-peripheral states of Latin America, Africa, and Asia have become client states of the wealthy nations led by the United States. Loans made to the client states by banks and other financial institutions have produced severe dislocations in "social welfare programs such as health care, education, and laws establishing labor standards" (Aronowitz and Gautney 2003, xvi). For example, the restrictions that the IMF and World Bank impose on countries as a condition for granting loans—euphemistically referred to as a program of structural adjustment—not only subject them to capitalist values and dire economic restrictions, but also undermine the very possibility of an inclusive and substantive democracy. The results have been disastrous as evidenced by the economic collapse of countries such as Argentina and Nigeria as well as by the fact that "one third of the world's labor force—more than a billion people—are unemployed or underemployed" (Aronowitz 2003, 30). Tracking twenty-six countries that received loans from the World Bank and the IMF, the *Multinational Monitor* spelled out the conditions that accompanied such loans:

> [c]ivil service downsizing, privatization of government-owned enterprises with layoffs required in advance of privatization and frequently following privatization; [p]romotion of labor flexibility—regulatory changes to remove restrictions on the ability of government and private employers to fire or lay off workers; [m]andated wage reductions, minimum wage reductions of containment, and spreading the wage gap between government employees and managers; and [p]ension reforms, including privatization, that cut social security benefits for workers. (Gray 2001, 7-8)[1]

In the United States, neoliberal policies have created a huge deficit projected at $5 trillion over the next decade due in part to President George Bush's exorbitant tax cuts for the wealthy (to the tune of an estimated $3 trillion if they are made permanent). While the rich get tax cuts, 8.2 million people are out of work and 2.3 million have lost their jobs since 2000; some have simply given up the unpromising task of looking for jobs. Massive subsidies for the rich, coupled with the corporate frenzy for short-term profits at the expense of any social considerations, translate into retrograde economic and social policies celebrated by the advocates of neoliberalism, just as they refuse to address an income gap between rich and poor that is not only the widest it has been since 1929, but also represents the most unequal among all developed nations (Woodard 2004, para. 42).

Neoliberalism has been particularly hard on young people. The incarceration rates have soared for black and brown youth, who have become the targeted population in America's ongoing and intensified war on crime. By almost all measures ranging from health care to job opportunities to getting a decent education, youth of color fare considerably worse than white youth. But all youth, except those who are privileged by class and birth, are feeling the weight of an economic and political system that no longer sees them as a social investment for the future. For example, as Anya Kamenetz points out

> Americans between the ages of 19 and 29 are now twice as likely to be uninsured as either children or older adults. The unemployment rate for people aged 16 to 24 was 16.1 percent as of February 2004, versus 6 percent for the general population. An estimated 900,000 people in this age group gave up and left the work force between 2000 and 2002, meaning a total of 6 million people in that range are dropouts, neither in school, working, nor in the military. By some accounts the age group's jobless rate is more than 80 percent. (Kamenetz 2004, para. 11)

For those students who cannot find work or decide to go directly on to college, massive tuition increases over the past decade—over 47 percent at public four-year colleges—prevent many working and middle-class youth from attending higher education, and those that do are often saddled with enormous debt once they graduate. In addition, a spiraling national debt will place a terrible burden on this generation of young people, and this debt will leave little money for critical needs such as education, health care, the environment, and other crucial public provisions. Moreover, as part of an ongoing effort to destroy public entitlements, the Bush administration has reduced government services, income, and health care; implemented cuts in Medicare and veterans' benefits and trimmed back or eliminated funds for programs for children and for public housing. All of these policies have had and continue to have a crippling affect on youth, disabling any hopes not only for a better future, but also for a life that can rise above the hardships driven by the constant pressure to simply survive. Youth are now viewed as a national burden, more despised and feared than cherished and protected.

The destruction of the welfare state has gone hand-in-hand with the emergence of a prison-industrial complex and a new state that is largely used to regulate, control, contain, and punish those who are not privileged by the benefits of class, color, and gender (Cole 1999). How else to explain a national prison population that has grown from 200,000 in 1973 to slightly over two million in 2004, while "another 4.5 million are on probation and parole" (Calvi 2001, 40). More specifically, neo-liberalism has become complicitous with this transformation of the democratic state into a national security state that repeatedly uses its military and political power to develop a daunting police state and military-prison-education-industrial complex to punish workers, stifle dissent, and undermine the political power of labor unions and progressive social movements (Lutz 2002).

With its debased belief that profit-making is the essence of democracy, and its definition of citizenship as an energized plunge into consumerism, neoliberalism elim-inates government regulation of market forces, celebrates a ruthless competitive indi-vidualism, and places the commanding political, cultural, and economic institutions of society in the hands of powerful corporate interests, the privileged, and unrepentant religious bigots (Peters and Fitzsimons 2001). Neoliberal global policies also further the broader cultural project of privatizing social services through appeals to "personal responsibility as the proper functions of the state are narrowed, tax and wage costs in the economy are cut, and more social costs are absorbed by civil society and the family" (Duggan 2003, 16). As I have mentioned, though it is worth repeating, the hard currency of human suffering permeates the social order as health-care costs rise, one out of five children fall beneath the poverty line, and 43 million Americans bear the burden of lacking any health insurance. As part of this larger cultural project fashioned under the sovereignty of neoliberalism, human misery is largely defined as a function of personal choices and human misfortune is viewed as the basis for criminalizing social problems. Misbehaving children are now put in handcuffs and taken to police stations for violating dress codes. Mothers who test positive for drugs in hospitals run the risk of having their children taken away by the police. Young, poor, black men who lack employment are targeted by the criminal justice system and, instead of being educated or trained for a job, often end up in jail. In fact, a report by United for a Fair Economy states that "One of out three Black males born in 2001 will be imprisoned at some point in their lifetime if current trends continue [and that] in 2000, there were at least 13 states in which there were more African-American men in prison than in college" (Muhammad, et. al. 2004, 20-21). Once released from prison, these young people are consigned to a civic purgatory in which they are "denied the right to vote, parental rights, drivers' licenses, student loans, and resi-dency in public housing—the only housing that marginal, jobless people can afford" (Staples 2004, 7). As stipulated in the Welfare Reform Act of 1996, if convicted on a single drug felony, these youth when released are further punished by a lifetime ban on food stamps and welfare eligibility. Such policies are not only unjust and morally reprehensible, they are symptomatic of a society that has relegated matters of equality and racial justice to the back burner of social concerns. In a market society caught up in "the greed cycle" (Cassidy 2002), addressing persistent injustices gets in the way of accumulating capital and the neoliberal and neoconservative revolution aimed at transforming democracy into a one party, corporate state.

Within the discourse of neoliberalism, democracy becomes synonymous with free markets, while issues of equality, racial justice, and freedom are stripped of any substantive meaning and used to disparage those who suffer systemic deprivation and chronic punishment. Individual misfortune, like democracy itself, is now viewed as either excessive or in need of radical containment. The media, largely consolidated through corporate power, routinely provide a platform for high profile right-wing pundits and politicians to remind us either of how degenerate the poor have become or to reinforce the central neoliberal tenet that all problems are private rather than social in nature. Conservative columnist Ann Coulter captures the latter sentiment with her comment that "[i]nstead of poor people with hope and possibility, we now have a permanent underclass of aspiring criminals knifing one another between having illegitimate children and collecting welfare checks" (qtd. in Bean 2003, para.3). Radio talk show host Michael Savage, too, exemplifies the unabashed racism and fanaticism that emerge under a neoliberal regime in which ethics and justice appear beside the point. For instance, Savage routinely refers to non-white countries as "turd world nations," homosexuality as a "perversion" and young children who are victims of gunfire as "ghetto slime" (qtd. in *Fairness and Accuracy in Reporting* 2003, para. 2, 6, 5).

As Fredric Jameson has argued in *The Seeds of Time*, it has now become easier to imagine the end of the world than the end of capitalism (1994, xii). The breathless rhetoric of the global victory of free-market rationality spewed forth by the mass media, right-wing intellectuals, and governments alike has found its material expression both in an all-out attack on democratic values and in the growth of a range of social problems including: virulent and persistent poverty, joblessness, inadequate health care, apartheid in the inner cities, and increasing inequalities between the rich and the poor. Such problems appear to have been either removed from the inventory of public discourse and social policy or factored into talk-show spectacles in which the public becomes merely a staging area for venting private interests and emotions. Within the discourse of neoliberalism that has taken hold of the public imagination, there is no way of talking about what is fundamental to civic life, critical citizenship, and a substantive democracy. Neoliberalism offers no critical vocabulary for speaking about political or social transformation as a democratic project. Nor is there a language for either the ideal of public commitment or the notion of a social agency capable of challenging the basic assumptions of corporate ideology as well as its social consequences. In its dubious appeals to universal laws, neutrality, and selective scientific research, neoliberalism "eliminates the very possibility of critical thinking, without which democratic debate becomes impossible" (Buck-Morss 2003, 65-66). This shift in rhetoric makes it possible for advocates of neoliberalism to implement the most ruthless economic and political policies without having to open up such actions to public debate and dialogue. Hence, neoliberal policies that promote the cutthroat downsizing of the workforce, the bleeding of social services, the reduction of state governments to police precincts, the ongoing liquidation of job security, the increasing elimination of a decent social wage, the creation of a society of low-skilled workers, and the emergence of a culture of permanent insecurity and fear hide behind appeals to common sense and allegedly immutable laws of nature.

When and where such nakedly ideological appeals strain both reason and imagination, religious faith is invoked to silence dissension. Society is no longer defended as a space in which to nurture the most fundamental values and relations necessary to a democracy but has been recast as an ideological and political sphere "where religious fundamentalism comes together with market fundamentalism to form the ideology of American supremacy" (Soros 2004, 10). Similarly, American imperial ambitions are now legitimated by public relations intellectuals as part of the responsibilities of empire-building, which in turn is celebrated as either a civilizing process for the rest of the globe or as simply a right bestowed upon the powerful. For instance, Ann Coulter speaks for many such intellectuals when she recently argued, while giving a speech at Penn State University, that she had no trouble with the idea that the United States invaded Iraq in order to seize its oil. As she put it, "Why not go to war just for oil? We need oil. Of course, we consume most of the world's oil; we do most of the world's production" (qtd. in Colella 2004, 1). In this worldview, power, money, and a debased appeal to pragmatism always trump social and economic justice. Hence, it is not surprising for neo-conservatives to have joined hands with neoliberals and religious fundamentalists in broadcasting to the world at large an American triumphalism in which the United States is arrogantly defined as "[t]he greatest of all great powers in world history" (Frum and Pearle qtd. in Lapham 2004b, 8).[2]

But money, profits, and fear have become powerful ideological elements not only in arguing for opening up new markets, but also for closing down the possibility of dissent at home. In such a scenario, the police state is celebrated by religious evangelicals like John Ashcroft as a foundation of human freedom. This becomes clear not only in the passage of repressive laws such as the USA Patriot Act but also in the work of prominent neoconservatives such as David Frum and Richard Pearle who, without any irony intended, insist that "[a] free society is not an un-policed society. A free society is a self-policed society" (qtd. in Lapham 2004b, 8). In what could only be defined as an Adam Smith joins George Orwell in a religious cult in California scenario, markets have been elevated to the status of sacrosanct temples to be worshiped by eager consumers while citizens-turned soldiers of the-Army-of-God are urged to spy on each other and dissent is increasingly criminalized.[3]

Political culture, if not the nature of politics itself, has undergone revolutionary changes in the last two decades, reaching its most debased expression under the administration of President George W. Bush. Within this political culture, not only is democracy subordinated to the rule of the market, but corporate decisions are freed from territorial constraints and the demands of public obligations, just as economics is disconnected from its social consequences. Power is increasingly removed from the dictates and control of nation states and politics is largely relegated to the sphere of the local. Zygmunt Bauman captures brilliantly what is new about the relationship among power, politics, and the shredding of social obligations:

> The mobility acquired by "people who invest"—those with capital, with money which the investment requires—means the new, indeed unprecedented . . . disconnection of power from obligations: duties towards employees, but also towards the younger and weaker, towards yet unborn generations and towards the self-reproduction of the living conditions of all; in short the freedom from the duty to contribute to daily life and the perpetuation of the community. . . . Shedding the responsibility for the consequences is the most coveted and cherished gain which the new mobility brings to free-floating, locally unbound capital. (Bauman 1998, 9-10)

Corporate power increasingly frees itself from any political limitations just as it uses its power through the educational force of the dominant culture to put into place an utterly privatized notion of agency in which it becomes difficult for young people and adults to imagine democracy as a public good, let alone the transformative power of collective action. Once again, democratic politics has become ineffective, if not banal, as civic language is impoverished and genuine spaces for democratic learning, debate, and dialogue such as schools, newspapers, popular culture, television networks, and other public spheres are either underfunded, eliminated, privatized, or subject to corporate ownership. Under the aggressive politics and culture of neoliberalism, society is increasingly mobilized for the production of violence against the poor, immigrants, dissenters, and others marginalized because of their age, gender, race, ethnicity, and color. At the center of neoliberalism is a new form of politics in the United States, a politics in which radical exclusion is the order of the day, and in which the primary questions no longer concern equality, justice, or freedom, but are now about the survival of the slickest in a culture marked by fear, surveillance, and economic deprivation. This is a politics that hides its own ideology by eliminating the traces of its power in a rhetoric of normalization, populism, and the staging of public spectacles. As Susan George points out, the question that currently seems to define neoliberal "democracy" is "Who has a right to live or does not" (1999, para. 34).

Neoliberalism is not a neutral, technical, economic discourse that can be measured with the precision of a mathematical formula or defended through an appeal to the rules of a presumptively unassailable science that conveniently leaves its own history behind. Nor is it a paragon of economic rationality that offers the best "route to optimum efficiency, rapid economic growth and innovation, and rising prosperity for all who are willing to work hard and take advantage of available opportunities" (Kotz 2003, 16). On the contrary, neoliberalism is an ideology, a politics, and at times a fanaticism that subordinates the art of democratic politics to the rapacious laws of a market economy that expands its reach to include all aspects of social life within the dictates and values of a market-driven society. More important, it is an economic and implicitly cultural theory—a historical and socially constructed ideology that needs to be made visible, critically engaged, and shaken from the stranglehold of power it currently exercises over most of the commanding institutions of national and global life. As such, neoliberalism makes it difficult for many people either to imagine a notion of individual and social agency necessary for reclaiming a substantive democracy or to be able to theorize the economic, cultural, and political conditions necessary for a viable global public sphere in which public institutions, spaces, and goods become valued as part of a larger democratic struggle for a sustainable future and the downward distribution of wealth, resources, and power.

As a public pedagogy and political ideology, the neoliberalism of Friedrich Hayek (1994) and Milton Friedman (2002) is far more ruthless than the classic liberal economic theory developed by Adam Smith and David Ricardo in the eighteenth and nineteenth centuries. Neoliberalism has become the current conservative revolution because it harkens back to a period in American history that supported the sovereignty of the market over the sovereignty of the democratic state and the common good. Reproducing the future in the image of the distant past, it represents a struggle designed to roll back, if not dismantle, all of the policies put into place over seventy years ago by the New Deal to curb corporate power and give substance to the liberal meaning of the social contract. The late Pierre Bourdieu captures what is new about neoliberalism in his comment that neoliberalism is

> a new kind of conservative revolution [that] appeals to progress, reason and science (economics in this case) to justify the restoration and so tries to write off progressive thought and action as archaic. It sets up as the norm of all practices, and therefore as ideal rules, the real regularities of the economic world abandoned to its own logic, the so-called laws of the market. It reifies and glorifies the reign of what are called the financial markets, in other words the return to a kind of radical capitalism, with no other law than that of maximum profit, an unfettered capitalism without any disguise, but rationalized, pushed to the limit of its economic efficacy by the introduction of modern forms of domination, such as 'business administration', and techniques of manipulation, such as market research and advertising. (Bourdieu 1998, 35)

Neoliberalism has indeed become a broad-based political and cultural movement designed to obliterate public concerns and liquidate the welfare state, and make politics everywhere an exclusively market-driven project (Leys 2001). But neoliberalism does more than make the market "the informing principle of politics" (Duggan 2003, 34), while allocating wealth and resources to those who are most privileged by virtue of their class, race, and power. Its supporting political culture and pedagogical practices also put into play a social universe and cultural landscape that sustain a particularly barbaric notion of authoritarianism, set in motion under the combined power of a religious and market fundamentalism and anti-terrorism laws that suspend civil liberties, incarcerate disposable populations, and provide the security forces necessary for capital to destroy those spaces where democracy can be nourished. All the while, the landscape and soundscape become increasingly homogenized through the spectacle of flags waving from every flower box, car, truck, and house, encouraged and supplemented by jingoistic bravado being broadcast by Fox Television News and Clear Channel radio stations. As a cultural politics and a form of economic domination, neoliberalism tells a very limited story, one that is antithetical to nurturing democratic identities, values, public spaces, and institutions and thereby enables fascism to grow because it has no ethical language for recognizing politics outside of the realm of the market, for controlling market excesses, or for challenging the underlying tenets of a growing authoritarianism bolstered by the pretense of religious piety.

Neoliberal ideology, on the one hand, pushes for the privatization of all non-commodified public spheres and the upward distribution of wealth. On the other hand, it supports policies that increasingly militarize facets of public space in order to secure the privileges and benefits of the corporate elite and ultra-rich. Neoliberalism does not merely produce economic inequality, iniquitous power relations, and a corrupt political system; it also promotes rigid exclusions from national citizenship and civic participation. As Lisa Duggan points out, "Neoliberalism cannot be abstracted from race and gender relations, or other cultural aspects of the body politic. Its legitimating discourse, social relations, and ideology are saturated with race, with gender, with sex, with religion, with ethnicity, and nationality" (2003, xvi). Neoliberalism comfortably aligns itself with various strands of neoconservative and religious fundamentalisms waging imperial wars abroad as well as at home against those groups and movements that threaten its authoritarian misreading of the meaning of freedom, security, and productiveness.

Neoliberalism has to be understood and challenged as both an economic theory and a powerful public pedagogy and cultural politics. That is, it has to be named and critically understood before it can be critiqued. The commonsense assumptions that legitimate neoliberalism's alleged historical inevitability have to be unsettled and then engaged for the social damage they cause at all levels of human existence. Such a recognition suggests identifying and critically examining the most salient and powerful ideologies that inform and frame neoliberalism. It also suggests a need on the part of progressives to make cultural politics and the notion of public pedagogy central to the struggle against neoliberalism, particularly since education and culture now play such a prominent political and economic role in both securing consent and producing capital (Peters 2002). In fact, this implies as Susan Buck-Morss has insisted that "[t]he recognition of cultural domination as just as important as, and perhaps even as the condition of possibility of, political and economic domination is a true 'advance' in our thinking" (2003, 103). Of course, this position is meant not to disavow economic and institutional struggles but to supplement them with a cultural politics that connects symbolic power and its pedagogical practices with material relations of power. Engaging the cultural politics and economics of neoliberalism also points to the need for progressives to analyze how neoliberal policies work at the level of everyday life through the language of privatization and the lived cultural forms of class, race, gender, youth, and ethnicity. Finally, such a project must employ a language of critique and possibility, engagement and hope as part of a broader project of viewing democracy as a site of intense struggle over matters of representation, participation, and shared power.

Central to the critique of neoliberalism is the belief, as Alain Touraine argues, that neoliberal globalization has not "dissolved our capacity for political action" (2001, 2). Such action depends on the ability of various groups—the peace movement, the anti-corporate globalization movement, the human rights movement, the environmental justice movement—within and across national boundaries—to form alliances in which matters of community and solidarity provide a common symbolic space and multiple public spheres where norms are created, debated, and engaged as part of an attempt to develop a new political language, culture, and set of relations. Such efforts must be understood as part of a broader attempt not only to collectively struggle against domination, but also to defend all those social advances that strengthen democratic public spheres and services, demand new rights, establish modes of power sharing, and create notions of social justice adequate to imagining and sustaining democracy on a global level. Consider, for example, the anti-corporate globalization movement's slogan "Another World is Possible!" which demands, as Alex Callinicos insightfully points out, a different kind of social logic, a powerful sense of unity and solidarity.

> Another world—that is, a world based on different social logic, run according to different priorities from those that prevail today. It is easy enough to specify what the desiderata of such an alternative social logic would be—social justice, economic efficiency, environmental sustainability, and democracy—but much harder to spell out how a reproducible social system embodying these requirements could be built. And then there is the question of how to achieve it. Both these questions—What is the alternative to capitalism? What strategy can get us there?—can be answered in different ways. One thing the anti-capitalist movement is going to have to learn is how to argue through the differences that exist and will probably develop around such issues without undermining the very powerful sense of unity that has been one of the movement's most attractive qualities. (Callinicos 2003, 147)

Callinicos's insight suggests that any viable struggle against neoliberal capitalism will have to rethink "the entire project of politics within the changed conditions of a global public sphere, and to do this democratically, as people who speak different political languages, but whose goals are nonetheless the same: global peace, economic justice, legal equality, democratic participation, individual freedom, mutual respect" (Buck-Morss 2003, 4-5). One of the most central tasks facing intellectuals, activists, educators, and others who believe in an inclusive and substantive democracy is the need to use theory to rethink the language and possibilities of politics as a way to imagine a future outside the powerful grip of neoliberalism and the impending authoritarianism that has a different story to tell about the future, one that reinvents the past in the image of the crude exercise of power and the unleashing of unimaginable human suffering. Critical reflection and social action in this discourse must acknowledge how the category of the global public sphere extends the space of politics beyond the boundaries of local resistance. Evidence of such actions can be found in the World Social Forums that took place in 2003 in Porto Alegre, Brazil and in Hyderabad, India in 2004. Successful forms of global dissent can also be observed in the international campaign to make AIDS drugs affordable for poor countries as well as in the international demonstrations against multinational corporations in cities from Melbourne and Seattle to Genoa and New York City. New alliances among intellectuals, students, labor unions, and environmentalists are taking place in the streets of Argentina, the West Bank, and in many other places fighting globalization from above. At the same time, a new language of agency and resistance is emerging among many activists and is being translated into new approaches to what it means to make the pedagogical more political as part of a global justice movement. Politics can no longer exclude matters of social and cultural learning and reproduction in the context of globalization or ignore the ways in which, as Imre Szeman asserts, globalization itself constitutes "a problem of and for pedagogy" (2002, 4). The slogan," Another World is Possible!" reinforces the important political insight that one cannot act otherwise unless one can think otherwise, but acting otherwise demands a new politics in which it is recognized that global problems need global solutions along with global institutions, global modes of dissent, global intellectual collaboration, and global social movements.

Notes

1. *The Multinational Monitor* (2001,7–8). See also Moberg, (2004, 20–21).
2. Here I am quoting David Frum and Richard Pearle cited in Lewis H. Lapham, (2004b, 8). This fascistically inspired triumphalism can be found in a number of recent books churned out to gratify the demands of a much celebrated jingoism. See Farah (2003); Malkin (2002); Bennett (2003).
3. For a rather vivid example of how dissent is criminalized, see Moyers (2004). The program documents how undercover agents from all levels of government are infiltrating and documenting peaceful protests in America.

Works Cited

Aronowitz, Stanley. 2003. *How Class Works: Power and Social Movement*. New Haven: Yale University Press.

Aronowitz, Stanley, and Gautney, H. 2003. "The Debate about Globalization: An Introduction." In *Implicating Empire: Globalization and Resistance in the 21st Century World Order*, ed. Stanley Aronowitz and H. Gautney. New York: Basic Books.

Bauman, Z. 1998. *Globalization: The Human Consequences*. New York: Columbia University Press.

Baker, K. 2003. "We're In the Army Now: The G.O.P.'s Plan to Militarize Our Culture". *Harper's Magazine*, October, 35–46.

Bean, K. 2003. "Coulter's Right-Wing Drag". *The Free Press*, 29 October. Available: http://www.free-press.org/departments/display/20/2003/441 Accessed April 24, 2004.

Bennett, W. J. 2003. *Why We Fight: Moral Clarity and the War On Terrorism*. New York: Regnery.

Bourdieu, P. 1998. *Acts of Resistance: Against the Tyranny of the Market*. New York: Free Press.

Buck-Morss, S. 2003. *Thinking Past Terror: Islamism and Critical Theory on the Left*. London: Verso.

Callinicos, A. 2003. "The Anti-Capitalist Movement After Genoa and New York". In *Implicating Empire: Globalization and Resistance in the 21st Century World Order*, ed. Stanley Aronowitz and H. Gautney. New York: Basic Books.

Calvi. S. J. A. 2001. "The Craze of Incarceration." *The Progressive*, May, 40–44.

Cassidy, J. 2002. "The Greed Cycle: How the Financial System Encouraged Corporations to Go Crazy". *The New Yorker*, 23 September, 72–80.

Chomsky, N. 1999. *Profits Over People: Neoliberalism and Global Order*. New York: Seven Stories Press.

Cole, David. 1999. *No Equal Justice: Race and Class in the American Criminal Justice System*. New York: The New Press.

Colella, K. 2004. "Coulter Uses Humor, Sarcasm in Speech." *The Collegian*, 16 April, 1–2.

Collins, C., C. Hartman, K. Kraut, and G. Mota. 2004. "Shifty Tax Cuts: How They Move the Tax Burden Off the Rich and Onto Everyone Else". *United For a Fair Economy*, 20 April. Available: www.FairEconomy.org Accessed April 24, 2004.

Duggan, L. 2003. *The Twilight of Equality? Neoliberalism, Cultural Politics, and the Attack on Democracy*. Boston: Beacon Press.

Fairness and Accuracy in Reporting. 2003. "Action Alert: GE, Microsoft Bring Bigotry To Life, Hate-Talk Host Michael Savage Hired by MSNBC." February 12. Available: http://www.fair.org/activism/msnbc-savage.html Accessed April 24, 2004.

Farah, Joseph. 2003. *Taking America Back*. New York: WND Books.

Friedman, M. 2002. *Capitalism and Freedom*. Chicago: University of Chicago Press.

George, S. 1999. "A Short History of Neo-Liberalism: Twenty Years of Elite Economics and Emerging Opportunities for Structural Change." *Conference on Economic Sovereignty in a Globalizing World* (March 24–26). Available: http://www.globalexchange.org/campaigns/econo101/neoliberalism.html.pdf Accessed April 24, 2004.

Giroux, H. 2003. *Public Spaces, Private Lives: Democracy Beyond 9/11*. Lanham: Rowman and Littlefield.

———. 2004. *The Abandoned Generation: Democracy Beyond the Culture of Fear*. New York: Palgrave.

Gonsalves, S. 2004. "How to Skin a Rabbit." *The Cape Cod Times*, 20 April. Available: www.commondreams.org/views04/0420-05.htm Accessed April 24, 2004.

Gray, Charlie. 2001. "Dubious Development: The World's Bank's Foray Into Private Sector Investment." *The Multinational Monitor*. September, 1–25.

Harding, J. 2001. "Globalization's Children Strike Back." *Financial Times*, 11 September. Available: http://specials.ft.com/countercap/FT33EJSLGRC.html Accessed April 24, 2004.

Hayek, F. 1994. *The Road to Serfdom*. Chicago: University of Chicago Press.

Henwood, D. 2003. *After the New Economy*. New York: The New Press.

Jameson, F. 1994. *The Seed of Time*. New York: Columbia University Press.

Kamenetz, Anya. 2004. "Generation Debt—The New Economics of Being Young: Student Loaned." *The Village Voice*, 20 April. Available: http://www.villagevoice.com/issues/0416/kamenetz.php Accessed April 24, 2004.

Kotz, D. 2003. "Neoliberalism and the U.S. Economic Expansion of the '90s." *Monthly Review*, April, 15–33.

Kraska, P. B. 1999. "Militarizing Criminal Justice: Exploring the Possibilities." *Journal of Political and Military Sociology*, 27: 205–15.

Lapham, L. 2004a. "Buffalo Dances." *Harper's Magazine*, May, 9–11.

———. 2004b. "Dar al-Harb." *Harper's Magazine*, March, 7–9.

Lewis, A. 2002. Taking Our Liberties. *The New York Times*, 9 August, A15.

Leys, C. 2001. *Market Driven Politics*. London: Verso. 2.

Lutz, C. 2002. "Making War At Home in the United States: Militarization and the Current Crisis." *American Anthropologist* 104: 723–35.

Malkin, Michelle. 2002. *Invasion: How America Still Welcomes Terrorists, Criminals, and Other Foreign Menaces to Our Shores.* New York: Regnery Publishing.

Martin, R. 2002. *Financialization of Daily Life.* Philadelphia: Temple University Press.

Moberg, D. 2004. "Plunder and Profit." *In These Times.* 29 March, 20–21.

Moyers, B. 2004. "Going Undercover/Criminalizing Dissent." *NOW*, 5 March.

Muhammad, D Davis, and B. Leondar-Wright. 2004. *The State of the Dream 2004: Enduring Disparities in Black and White.* Boston: United for a Fair Economy.

Peters, M. A., and P. Fitzsimons. 2001. "Neoliberalism and Social Capital: Re-Inventing Community." *Sites: A Journal for South Pacific Cultural Studies* 37: 32–48.

Peters, M. A. 2002. "Foucault and Governmentality: Understanding the Neoliberal Paradigm of Education Policy." *The School Field*, 12.5/6: 59–80.

Soros, G. 2004. *The Bubble of American Supremacy.* New York: Public Affairs.

Staples, B. 2004. "Growing Up in the Visiting Room." *The New York Times Book Review*, 21 March, 7.

Szeman, I. 2002. "Introduction: Learning to Learn from Seattle." *Review of Education, Pedagogy, and Cultural Studies* 24:1: 1–12.

Tabb, W. 2003. "Race to the Bottom?" In *Implicating Empire: Globalization and Resistance In The 21st Century World Order*, ed. Stanley Aronowitz and H. Gautney. New York: Basic Books.

Tourmaline, A. 2001. *Beyond Neoliberalism.* London: Polity Press.

Valentine, D. 2001. "Homeland Insecurity." *Counterpunch.* Available: www.counterpunch.org/homeland1.html. Accessed April 24, 2004.

Woodard, C. 2004, "Who Really Pays Taxes in America? Taxes and Politics in 2004." Available: http://www.askquestions.org/articles/taxes Accessed April 24, 2004.

CHAPTER 9

White Nationalism, Armed Culture, and State Violence in the Age of Donald Trump

2017

Introduction: The Plague

With Donald Trump's election as president of the United States, the scourge of authoritarianism has returned not only in the toxic language of hate, humiliation and bigotry, but also in the emergence of a culture of war and violence that looms over society like a plague. War has been redefined in the age of global capitalism.[1] This is especially true for the United States. No longer defined exclusively as a military issue, it has expanded its boundaries and now shapes all aspects of society. As Ulrich Beck observes, 'the language of war takes on a new and expansive meaning today . . . The notions on which our worldviews are predicated and the distinctions between war and peace, military and police, war and crime, internal and external security' have collapsed.[2] As violence and politics merge to produce an accelerating and lethal mix of bloodshed, pain, suffering, grief and death, American culture has been transformed into a culture of war.

War culture reaches far beyond the machineries of war that enable the United States to ring the world with its military bases, produce vast stockpiles of weapons, deploy thousands of troops all over the globe, and retain the shameful title of 'the world's preeminent exporter of arms, with more than 50 percent of the global weaponry market controlled by the United States'.[3] War culture provides the educational platforms that include those cultural apparatuses, institutions, beliefs and policies with the capacity to produce spectacles of violence, a culture of fear, military values, hyper-masculine ideologies and armed policies that give war machines their legitimacy, converting them into symbols of national identity, if not honored ideals. Under such circumstances, the national security state replaces any viable notion of social security and the common good. Under the Trump regime, armed power is elevated to the measure of national greatness as war and warriors become the most enduring symbols of American life. As a militarized culture is dragged into the center of political life, fear feeds a discourse of bigotry, insecurity and mistrust adding more and more individuals and groups to the register of repression, disposability and social death. Trump's celebration of militarization as the highest of America's ideals was evident in his speech to a joint session of Congress when he stated that 'To those allies who wonder what kind of friend America will be, look no further than the heroes who wear our uniform'.[4] The irony here lies in the gesture of a helping hand that hides the investment in and threat of an aggressive militarism. Needless to say, such militarism is on full display as Trump endorses policies that transform American society into a police precinct willing to use armed force to contain, control, banish and bar all those at odds with his white supremacist ideology.

Violent lawlessness no longer registers ethical and moral concerns and increasingly has become normalized. How else to explain Trump's comment, without irony or remorse, during a campaign rally in Iowa that he 'could stand in the middle of Fifth Avenue and shoot someone and not lose any voters'? Ruthlessness, narcissism and bullying are the organizing principles of Trump's belief that only winning matters and that everything is permitted to further his reactionary ideological and economic interests. These are the values that underlie his call for 'law and order' – a code for lawlessness that has become normalized with the rise of a police state, accompanied by the withering of civic values. Another register of lawlessness is evident in the presence of a ruthless market-driven corporate culture marked by an economic and political system mostly controlled by the ruling financial elite. This is a mode of corporate lawlessness and criminogenic culture that not only hoards wealth, income and power but also reproduces a savage casino capitalism through the mechanisms of a national security state, mass surveillance, the arming of local police forces, a permanent war economy and an expansive militarized foreign policy.

While it would be irresponsible to underestimate Trump's embrace of neo-fascist ideology and policies, he is not solely responsible for the long legacy of authoritarianism that took on a frontal assault with the election of Ronald Reagan in 1980, embraced by the Third Way politics of the Democratic Party, and solidified under the anti-democratic policies of the Bush–Cheney and Obama administrations. During this period, democracy was sold to the bankers and big corporations propelled by the emergence of a savage neo-liberalism, a ruthless concentration of power by the financial elites, and an aggressive ideological and cultural war aimed at undoing the social contract and the democratic, political and personal freedoms gained in the New Deal and culminating in the civil rights and educational struggles of the 1960s. In the face of Trump's unapologetic authoritarianism, Democratic Party members and the liberal elite are trying to place themselves in the forefront of organized resistance to such dark times. It is difficult not to see such moral outrage and resistance as hypocritical in light of the role they have played in the last 40 years of subverting democracy and throwing minorities of class and color under the bus. Chris Hedges gets it right in revealing such hypocrisy for what it is worth – a carnival act. He writes:

Where was this moral outrage when our privacy was taken from us by the security and surveillance state, the criminals on Wall Street were bailed out, we were stripped of our civil liberties and 2.3 million men and women were packed into our prisons, most of them poor people of color? Why did they not thunder with indignation as money replaced the vote and elected officials and corporate lobbyists instituted our system of legalized bribery? Where were the impassioned critiques of the absurd idea of allowing a nation to be governed by the dictates of corporations, banks and hedge fund managers? Why did they cater to the foibles and utterings of fellow elites, all the while blacklisting critics of the corporate state and ignoring the misery of the poor and the working class? Where was their moral righteousness when the United States committed war crimes in the Middle East and our militarized police carried out murderous rampages? What the liberal elites do now is not moral. It is self-exaltation disguised as piety. It is part of the carnival act.[5]

A blend of neo-liberal orthodoxy, religious fundamentalism, educational repression and an accelerating militarism found its end point in the election of Donald Trump. Trump represents the transformation of politics into a Reality TV show and the belief that the worth of a candidate can be judged only in terms of a mixture of one's value as an entertainer and an advertisement for casino capitalism.[6] Corporate money and the ideology of militarism define Trump's embrace of a war culture. For instance, Trump's cabinet appointments of neo-liberal elites such as Steven Mnuchin to be his Treasury Secretary, Wilbur Ross, a billionaire investor, to head the Commerce Department, and Rex Tillerson, the former ExxonMobil CEO, as Secretary of State make clear that he intends to allow the managers of big banks, hedge funds and other major financial institutions to run the economy. This is an upgraded version of neo-liberalism on steroids which, as Cornel West points out, serves to 'reinforce corporate interests, big bank interest, and to keep track of those of who are cast as peoples of color, women, Jews, Arabs, Muslims, Mexicans, and so forth...So, this is one of the most frightening moments in the history of this very fragile empire and fragile republic.'[7] On the other hand, Trump has filled a number of his Cabinet appointments with a number of generals such as John Kelly as Secretary of Homeland Security, James Mattis as Secretary of Defense, and Army Lieutenant-General H. R. McMaster as his National Security Adviser, all of whom are known as 'warrior thinkers'.

With the election of Donald Trump as president of the United States, the hate-filled discourses of intolerance, chauvinism and social abandonment will creep into the ever-widening spheres of society giving rise to a militarized war culture joined to a totalizing embrace of corporate capitalism. Under Trump, ignorance has been weaponized and will continue to be used to produce a profoundly disturbing anti-intellectualism that leaves little room for critical reflection. It is important to remember that in his various pre-election speeches, Trump's endless lies emptied language of any meaning, giving credence to the charge that he was producing a kind of post-truth in which words did not count for anything any more, especially when informed judgments and facts could no longer be distinguished from opinion and falsehoods. Trump's unending tweets suggest an assault on the ability of the wider public to fit things together in a coherent narrative while avoiding and discrediting those public spheres such as the media and press capable of holding him responsible for what he says.

Emulating the fascist embrace of the cultural spectacle, Trump language became a vehicle for producing sensationalism, emotions, shock and effects that mimicked the performances of tawdry Reality TV. He spoke and continues to speak from a discursive space in which everything can be said, the truth is irrelevant, and informed judgment becomes a liability. Under such circumstances, it is extremely difficult to grasp what he knows about anything, except what is filtered through the narcissistic bubble-like world he inhabits. He steals words and discards their meaning, refusing to own up to them ethically, politically and socially. But there is more at work here than the registers of incoherence, ignorance, civic illiteracy and an attack on civic culture. There is a recklessness in Trump's language that pushes far beyond the bounds of rationality making it receptive to the everyday fears and moral panics characteristic of an earlier period of fascism.

How else to explain his claims that Trump Tower was wiretapped by former President Obama, climate change is a hoax, the media is the 'enemy of the American People', terrorist attacks have taken place that no one knows about because they are covered up by the press, and America's intelligence agencies are no different from Nazis? This whirl-wind of irrationality emulates a fascist style that not only mimics the spectacle and theatricizes politics, it also suggests populist forms that are never far away from the political currency of white supremacy, anti-intellectualism and neo-fascism. What we are witnessing in the age of Trump is the resurgence of fascism in new forms. Both its living memory and distinctiveness are evident in Trump's appeal to racial hatred, social cleansing and disposability along with his use of the symbols and language of ultra-nationalism so as to expand a culture of war and domestic terrorism.

This militarized culture serves to connect the war at home with wars abroad. This is an action-oriented mode of fascist ideology in which all thoughtfulness, critical thinking and dissent are subordinated if not cancelled out by the pleasure quotient and hyped-up sensationalism produced in the fog and fantasy of moral panics, a culture of fear, and the spectacle of violence. Trump's discourse feeds the cultural formation of a right-wing populism that weighs in on the side of a militant racism and a racist militarism. For instance, the only moments of clarity in Trump's discourse are when he uses the toxic vocabulary of hate, xenophobia, racism and misogyny to target those he believes refuse to 'Make America Great Again' or are fearful of his use of historically fascist-tinged slogans such as 'America First'. This is a discourse that feeds off upheaval, political uncertainty and economic precarity through an appeal to authoritarian ideals and policies that offer fraudulently a sense of reassurance and certainty that mitigates radical doubts, feelings of exclusion, anger and anxieties. This might explain why the words 'democracy' and 'equality' were absent from both his inaugural address and his speech to Congress.[8]

I: Unapologetic Racism and the Withering of Civic Life

As Trump's presidency unfolds, it appears that Americans are entering a period in which civic formations and public spheres will be modeled after a state of perpetual warfare. Appeals to war and violence were celebrated rhetorical referents used during Donald Trump's presidential campaign. Not only did he provide a nativist language that targeted the most vulnerable in American society – unauthorized immigrants, Blacks, Muslims and Syrian refugees – he also provoked society's darkest impulses which served to energize a range of extremist racist and anti-Semitic groups including the alt-right, white nationalists and other breeding grounds for a new authoritarianism. There can be little doubt that these anti-democratic and racist tendencies will play a major role in shaping his presidency. The call for regime change, a term used by the White House to designate overthrowing a foreign government, will intensify under Trump's administration. This means a more militant foreign policy. But it also signals a domestic form of regime change as well since this authoritarian neo-liberal government will de-regulate, militarize and privatize everything it can. With this regime change will come the suppression of civil liberties and dissent at home through the expansion of a punishing state that will criminalize a wider range of everyday behaviors, expand mass incarceration and all the while enrich the coffers of the ultra-rich and corporate predators. Trump's hate-filled discourse which has targeted Muslims, any unauthorized immigrants and other people of color has been followed by a surge of white supremacy, anti-Semitism and increasing acts of violence against individuals and groups considered other in the United States. As Chauncey DeVega points out in the website *Salon*:

> Since the election of Donald Trump in November, there have been almost 1,000 reported hate crimes targeting Muslims, Arabs, African-Americans, Latinos and other people of color. At this same moment, there have been terrorist threats against Jewish synagogues and community centers as well as the vandalizing of Jewish cemeteries. These hate crimes have also resulted in physical harm and even death: An Indian immigrant was shot and killed by a white man in Kansas who reportedly told him, 'Get out of my country.' Several days ago a white man shot a Sikh man in Washington state after making a similar comment.[9]

Heidi Beirich, director of the Intelligence Project at the Southern Poverty Law Center, has stated that the increase in hate crimes in the United States can be directly related to Trump's endless hate-filled discourse during the presidential primaries that included 'xenophobic remarks, anti-immigrant remarks, anti-Muslim remarks, racist remarks, trading in anti-Semitic imagery and anti-women comments. Let's not forget that during the campaign there were hate crimes committed – very severe ones in Trump's name.'[10] In addition, such violence has provided legitimation for erasing the history of genocidal brutality waged against Native Americans and Black slaves in the United States and its connection to the memory of Nazi genocide in Europe and the disappearance of critics of fascism in Argentina and Chile in the 1970s. Trump's white supremacist policies not only echo elements of a fascist past, they point to the need to recognize, as Paul Gilroy has observed, 'how elements of fascism appear in new forms', especially as 'the living memory of the fascist period fades'.[11]

What is urgent to recognize is that Americans are entering a historical conjuncture under President Trump in which racism will be a major ideological force for establishing terror as a powerful weapon of governance. Not only did Trump make 'law and order' a central motif of his presidential campaign, he also amplified its meaning in his attacks on the Black Lives Matter movement and his depiction of Black neighborhoods as cauldrons of criminal behavior so that Blacks would be treated as enemy combatants. An especially disturbing sign of a war culture poised to shape every aspect of American life can be found in the militarized racist ideology that provides the common ground and organizing principle for hiring a number of intolerant and racist ideologues to top White House posts. Some of the most egregious thus far being the appointment of Jeff Sessions as Attorney General, Stephen Bannon as chief White House strategist, Mike Pompeo to head the CIA, and Tom Price as Secretary of Health and Human Services, all of whom will promote policies that will further increase the misery, suffering and policing of the vulnerable, sick and poor. Given the vice-president-elect's abysmal record on women's issues, there is little doubt that the war on women's reproductive rights will accelerate under the Trump administration. As NARAL Pro-Choice America Senior Vice-President Sasha Bruce has observed:

> With the selection of Tom Price as Secretary of Health and Human Services, Donald Trump is sending a clear signal that he intends to punish women who seek abortion care. Tom Price is someone who has made clear throughout his career that . . . he wants to punish us for the choices we make for our bodies, our futures, and our families.[12]

The repressive racial state will be intensified and expanded, especially under the ideological and political direction provided by Jeff Sessions. Sessions is a strong advocate of mass incarceration and the death penalty, and is considered a leading spokes- person for the Old South. *The Nation*'s Ari Berman observes that Sessions is a 'white-nationalist sympathizer . . . the fiercest opponent in the Senate of immigration reform, a centerpiece of Trump's agenda, and has a long history of opposition to civil rights, dating back to his days as a US Attorney in Alabama in the 1980s'.[13] Sessions has often used racist language, insults and practices, including opposing the Voting Rights Act and addressing a Black lawyer as 'boy'. He was denied a federal judgeship in the 1980s because his colleagues claimed that he made, on a number of occasions, racist remarks. Sessions has also called organizations such as the ACLU, the NAACP and the National Council of Churches 'un-American' because of their emphasis on civil rights, which he believed was being shoved down the throats of the American public. He was also accused of falsely prosecuting Black political activists in Alabama for voting fraud. Not only does Sessions share Trump's dark vision of minority and foreign-born residents 'as America's chief internal threat', he will also use the power of the Justice Department to issue orders – 'to strengthen the grip of law enforcement, raise barriers to voting and significantly reduce all forms of immigration, promoting what seems to be a long- standing desire to reassert the country's European and Christian heritage'.[14]

Sessions' racism often merges with his religious fundamentalism. As Miranda Blue observes, he has 'dismissed immigration reform as "ethnic politics" and warned that allowing too many immigrants would create "cultural problems" in the country'. Earlier this year, he cherry-picked a couple of Bible verses to claim that the position of his opponents on the immigration issue is 'not biblical'.[15] As Andrew Kaczynski points out, Sessions made his religiously inspired racist principles clear while appearing in 2016 on Matt & Aunie's radio talk show on WAPI. While on the program, Sessions praised Trump's stance on capital punishment by pointing to his '1989 newspaper ads advocating the death penalty for five young men of color accused of raping a jogger in Central Park'.[16] Sessions made these comments knowing full well that the Central Park Five were not only exonerated by DNA evidence after serving many years in jail, but were also awarded a wrongful conviction settlement, which ran into millions of dollars. Moreover, Sessions was aware that Trump had later criticized the settlement calling it a disgrace while suggesting the Central Park Five were guilty of a crime for which they should not have been acquitted in spite of the testimony of convicted felon Matias Reyes, who confessed to raping and attacking the victim.

Sessions' racism was also on full display when he stated in the interview that Trump 'believes in law and order and he has the strength and will to make this country safer'. He then added: 'The biggest benefits from that, really, are poor people in the neighborhoods that are most dangerous where most of the crime is occurring.'[17] Trump's tweets falsely alleging voter fraud in order to defend the ludicrous claim that he won the popular vote are ominous because they suggest that in the future he will allow Sessions to make it more difficult for poor minorities to vote. Under Sessions, a racist militarism will serve as an organizing principle to legitimate a species of ultra-nationalism in order to create a society shaped by white nationalists, one that is eager to restrict the voting rights of minorities and stoke the fear of crime in order to increase the militarized presence of police in the inner cities. As the rhetoric of lawlessness and war is applied to inner cities, they are denied economic and social reforms and are transformed into crime-ridden outposts and war zones subject to military solutions and forms of racial sorting and cleansing. How else to explain Trump's call to deport millions of unauthorized Mexican immigrants as a 'military operation'?

Within the Trump administration, Sessions is far from an anomaly and is only one of a number of prominent officials appointed in the Trump administration who are overtly racist and run the gamut in arguing for a Muslim registry and suppressing voter rights to producing social and economic policies that target immigrants and poor Blacks. For example, Trump's appointment of Stephen Bannon as senior counselor and chief White House strategist is deeply disturbing. Bannon is an incendiary figure who critics as politically diverse as Glenn Beck and Senator Bernie Sanders of Vermont have accused of being a racist, a sexist and an anti-Semite. While the head of Breitbart News, the alt- right's most popular website, Bannon courted white nationalists, neo-Nazi groups and other far-right extremists. In doing so, he not only provided a platform for the alt-right, but he helped to rebrand 'white supremacy [and] white nationalism, for the digital age'.[18]

Bannon is on record as stating that only property owners should vote, saying to his ex-wife that he 'did not want his twin daughters to go to school with Jews', calling conservative commentator Bill Kristol a 'Republican spoiler, renegade Jew', and publishing incendiary headlines on Breitbart's website such as 'Would you rather your child had feminism or cancer?' and 'Birth Control makes women unattractive and crazy'.[19] Richard Cohen, the president of the Southern Poverty Law Center, states that Trump's racist campaign was confirmed with Bannon's appointment.[20]

What we see in Trump and his advisors and appointees is an America that embraces the values and ideals of an ultra-nationalist and militarized white public sphere. Even before Trump took office, the menace of authoritarianism was becoming visible, 'exploding in our face, through racist attacks on school children, the proliferation of swastikas around the country, name-calling, death threats, and a general atmosphere of hate'.[21]

II: Military Mania

Trump's appointment of warmongering, right-wing military personnel to top government posts and his ongoing bombast suggesting the need for a vast expansion of the military-industrial complex signal a further intensification of America's war culture, one that inspired a Forbes article to be published with the headline: 'For the Defence Industry, Trump's win means Happy Days are Here Again'.[22] William D. Hartung makes the latter point clear by citing a speech Trump gave in Philadelphia before the election in which he

> . . . called for tens of thousands of additional troops, a Navy of 350 ships, a significantly larger Air Force, an anti-missile, space-based Star Wars-style program of Reaganesque proportions, and an acceleration of the Pentagon's $1 trillion 'modernization' for the nuclear arsenal . . . [all of which] could add more than $900 billion to the Pentagon's budget over the next decade.[23]

Evidence for an updated and expansive war culture is also visible in Trump's initial willingness to consider including in his administration a cabal of racist neo-conservatives, such as John Bolton and James Woolsey – both of whom believe that 'Islam and the Arab world are the enemy of Western civilization' and are strong advocates of a war with Iran.[24] He has welcomed disgraced military leaders such as David H. Petraeus, former 4-star army general and director of the Central Intelligence Agency; he has appointed as Secretary of Defense retired United States Marine Corps General

James Mattis who opposed closing Guantanamo along with Obama's nuclear treaty with Iran. He was brusquely fired by the Obama administration as the Central Command boss. In a particularly worrisome appointment, Trump chose retired General Michael Flynn to become his National Security Advisor. Flynn was fired by Obama for abusive behavior, has been accused of mishandling classified information, and is a firm supporter of Trump's pro-torture policies.[25] *The New York Times* reported that Flynn, who will occupy 'one of the most powerful roles in shaping military and foreign policy . . . believes Islamist militancy poses an existential threat on a global scale, and the Muslim faith itself is the source of the problem...describing it as a political ideology, not a religion'.[26] In other words, Flynn believes that 1.3 billion Muslims are the enemy of western civilization. He has also claimed 'that Sharia, or Islamic law, is spreading in the United States [it is not]. His dubious assertions are so common that when he ran the Defense Intelligence Agency, subordinates came up with a name for the phenomenon: they called them "Flynn facts".'[27] Twenty-four days after taking up his position as National Security Advisor, it was revealed that Flynn had lied about conversations he had with the Russian ambassador Sergey Kislyak while Obama was still in office, a fact he did not reveal to 'the FBI, White House spokesman, Sean Spicer, and the vice-president, Mike Pence'.[28] He resigned in disgrace once it was discovered that he had covered up his conversation with the Russian ambassador.

Trump's love of the military suggests that he will expand rather than cut back on America's infatuation with its wars. Unsurprisingly, he has asked Congress to provide an additional $54 billion to expand an already bloated military. It goes without saying that he will do nothing to alter a dishonorable foreign policy standard that has propelled the USA into a permanent war status 'for virtually the entire twenty-first century' and since the latter part of 2001 has resulted in 'something like 370,000 combatants and noncombatants [being] killed in the various theaters of operations where U.S. forces have been active'.[29] This is how democracy comes to an end.

Under Trump's leadership, a war culture, a culture of aggression, and state violence will intensify. Not only will there be a suppression of dissent, similar to the police violence used against those protesting the Dakota Access pipeline in Standing Rock, North Dakota, along with the arrests of journalists covering the protests. It is reasonable to assume that under the Trump administration there will also be an intensification of the harassment of journalists similar to what of late happened to the Canadian Ed Ou, a renowned photojournalist who has worked for a number of media sources including *The New York Times* and *Time Magazine*. Ou was recently detained by US border officers while traveling from Canada to the USA to report on the protests against the Dakota Access pipeline. According to Hugh Handeyside:

> Ou was detained for more than six hours and subjected . . . to multiple rounds of intrusive interrogation. [The border officers] questioned him at length about his work as a journalist, his prior professional travel in the Middle East, and dissidents or 'extremists' he had encountered or interviewed as a journalist. They photocopied his personal papers, including pages

from his handwritten personal diary.[30]

In the end, he was refused entry into the USA. The harassment and suppressing of individual dissent are only one register of Trump's authoritarianism. He and Steve Bannon have derided the critical media as 'fake news' and labeled them as the opposition party. Trump's attack on the press is about more than discrediting traditional sources of facts and analysis or collapsing the distinction between the truth and lies, it is also about undermining the public's grip on evidence, facts and informed judgment. Such attacks undermine the freedom of the press, destroy public spheres that make dissent possible and simultaneously infantilize and de-politicize the American public. Given Trump's insistence that protesters who burn the American flag should be jailed or suffer the loss of citizenship, his hostile criticism of the Black Lives Matter movement, and his ongoing legacy of stoking white violence against protesters, it is not unreasonable to assume that his future domestic policies will further legitimate a wave of repression and violence waged against dissenters and the institutions that support them. For instance, his tweeted threats regarding the burning of the American flag can be read as code for threatening dissent, or, worse, unleashing the power of the state on them. How else to explain the motive behind Trump's consideration of Milwaukee Sheriff David Clarke as a potential candidate for secretary of the Department of Homeland Security? Clarke has referred to the Black Lives Matter movement as 'Black Lies Matter' and compared it with ISIS. He has 'proposed that terrorist and ISIS sympathizers in America need to be rounded up and shipped off to Guantanamo, and has stated that "It is time to suspend habeas corpus like Abraham Lincoln did during the civil war" . . . He guessed that about several hundred thousand or even a million sympathizers were in the United States and needed to be imprisoned.'[31] It is difficult to believe that this type of egregious call for repressive state violence and a disregard for the constitution support rather than disqualify somebody for a high-ranking government office.

Expanding what might be called his Twitter battles, Trump has made a number of critical comments regarding what he views as dissenting criticism of either him or his administration. For instance, after Brandon Victor Dixon, the actor in *Hamilton*, the Broadway play, addressed Vice-President-elect Mike Pence, after the curtain call, stating, in part, that 'We are diverse Americans who are alarmed and anxious that your new administration will not protect us, our planet, our children, our parents, or defend us and uphold our inalienable right', Trump tweeted that Pence was harassed by the actor and that Dixon should apologize. Trump also took aim at a *Saturday Night Live* episode in which Alec Baldwin satirized a post-election Trump in the process of trying to figure out what the responsibilities of the presidency entail. Trump tweeted that he watched 'Saturday Night Live last night. It is a totally one-sided, biased show – nothing funny at all. Equal time for us?'

As cyberbully in chief, he has taken to Twitter to launch tirades not only against the cast of the play *Hamilton* and *Saturday Night Live*, but also Chuck Jones, president of United Steelworkers Local 1999. Trump's verbal takedown of the union chief was the result of Jones' accusing Trump of lying about the number of jobs he claimed he saved in Indiana at Carrier Corporation from being shipped to Mexico. Actually, since 350 jobs were slated to stay in the USA before Trump's intervention, the number of jobs saved by Trump was 850 rather than 1,100. To some this may seem like a trivial matter, but Trump's weaponizing of Twitter against critics and political opponents not only functions to produce a chilling effect on critics, but gives legitimacy to those willing to suppress dissent through various modes of harassment and even the threat of violence. Frank Sesno, the director of the School of Media and Public Affairs at George Washington University, is right in stating that 'Anybody who goes on air or goes public and calls out the president has to then live in fear that he is going to seek retribution in the public sphere. That could discourage people from speaking out.'[32] Such actions could also threaten their lives as Chuck Jones found out. After the president called him out, he received an endless stream of harassing phone calls and online insults, some even threatening him and his children. According to Jones, "Nothing that says they're gonna kill me, but, you know, you better keep your eye on your kids . . . We know what car you drive. Things along those lines."[33]

Trump has more than 16 million Twitter followers and has no trouble in mobilizing them to carry out his revenge fantasies against potential enemies. His ongoing exchange and battle with Fox host Megyn Kelly, especially after her questioning of Trump in the first Republican primary debate, provides a vivid example of how he has weaponized his Twitter account. After Trump started attacking her on his Twitter, she told Terry Gross on Fresh Air 'that every tweet he unleashes against you . . . creates such a crescendo of anger', if not danger. She then goes on to spell out the living hell she found herself in as a result of being one of Trump's targets for humiliation and derision. She writes:

> The c-word was in thousands of tweets directed at me – lots of threats to beat the hell out of me, to rape me, honestly the ugliest things you can imagine. But most of this stuff I was able to just dismiss as angry people who are trying to scare me, you know. However, there were so many that rose to the level of 'OK, that one we need to pay attention to', that it did become alarming. It wasn't like I walked down the street in constant fear of someone trying to take my life, but I was very aware of it. The thing I was most worried about was that I have a 7- and a 5- and a 3-year-old, and I was worried I'd be walking down the street with my kids and somebody would do something to me in front of them; they would see me get punched in the face or get hurt.[34]

Between Twitter, Instagram and Facebook, Trump has direct communication with close to 36 million people. I am not convinced that these tweets are simply an impetuous outburst of an adult who has the temperament of a bullying 12-year-old. It seems more probable that his right-wing advisors, including Stephen Bannon, view the tweets as part of a legitimate tool to attack their perceived political foes and in this case the attack was not simply on Jones but on unions that may rebel against Trump's policies in the future. Trump is at war with democracy and his online attacks will take place not only in conjunction with ongoing acts of state repression but also with the production of violence in the culture at large, which Trump will orchestrate as if he is producing a Reality TV show.

At first glance, these responses seem as thoughtless as they are trivial given the issues that Trump should be considering, but Frank Rich may be right in suggesting that Trump's tweets, which amount to an attack on the First Amendment, are part of a strategy engineered by Bannon designed to promote a culture war that riles 'up his base and retains its loyalty should he fail, say, to deliver on other promises, like reviving the coal industry'.[35] In addition, such attacks function to initiate a culture war that serves both to repress dissent and to divert the public from more serious issues, all the while driving up ratings for a supine media that will give Trump unqualified and uncritical coverage. Referring to the Dixon incident, Rich writes:

> It's possible that much of that base previously knew little or nothing about *Hamilton*, but thanks to Pence's visit, it would soon learn in even the briefest news accounts that the show is everything that base despises: a multi-cultural-ethnic-racial reclamation of 'white' American history with a ticket price that can soar into four digits – in other words, a virtual monument to the supposedly politically correct 'elites' that Trump, Bannon, and their wrecking crew found great political profit in deriding throughout the campaign. Pence's visit to *Hamilton* was a sure-fire political victory for Trump even without the added value of a perfectly legitimate and respectful curtain speech that he could trash-tweet to further rouse his culture-war storm troopers. The kind of political theater that Trump and Bannon fomented around *Hamilton* is likely to be revived routinely in the Trump era.[36]

Trump's tweet-trashing embrace of a war culture mimics the often hate-filled discourse and threats of violence in which he engaged during the presidential primary campaign. Only now he has a much broader audience. Americans are already witnessing a growing climate of violence across the United States, spurred on by Trump's previous support of such actions, aimed at Muslims, immigrants, Blacks, foreign students and others deemed expendable by Trump's white ultra-nationalist supporters. Of course, none of this should seem surprising given the long legacy of such violence along with the decline of the Welfare State and the rise of the punishing state since the 1970s. What is distinctive is that the formative culture, organizations and institutions that support such violence have moved from the fringe to the center of American politics.

Where this merging of suppression and violence might lead the United States under Trump is difficult to predict, though in an age of vast inequities, a poisonous economic system, a growing moral blindness, the rise of state violence, and the withering of public trust and life, the future looks ominous. How far Trump might go in using state violence is not clear, but a frightening indication of his views on the illegitimate use of state violence can be glimpsed in a post-election conversation he had with President Rodrigo Duterte of the Philippines. Duterte has been condemned by UN officials and human rights organizations across the globe for conducting a brutal anti-drug campaign in which over 2,000 people have been killed by the police and vigilantes. According to Felipe Villamor of the *Washington Post*, 'Mr. Duterte has led a campaign against drug abuse in which he has encouraged the police and others to kill people they suspect of using or selling drugs'.[37] Villamor goes on to write that Duterte stated that

> Donald J. Trump had endorsed his brutal antidrug campaign, telling Mr. Duterte that the Philippines was conducting it 'the right way.' Mr. Duterte, who spoke with Mr. Trump by telephone . . . said Mr. Trump was 'quite sensitive' to 'our worry about drugs. He wishes me well, too, in my campaign, and he said that, well, we are doing it as a sovereign nation, the right way,' Mr. Duterte said.[38]

It is terrifying to believe that President-elect Trump would endorse such policies. Trump's alleged support of Duterte also raises questions about how much violence he would use in the United States against dissident journalists. For instance, Duterte is a ruthless dictator who has not only savagely instituted a reign of terror in his country; he has also told journalists that "you are not exempted from assassination, if you're a son of a bitch".[39] David Kaye, a UN special rapporteur on freedom of opinion and expression, stated in response to Duterte's threat that 'justifying the killing of journalists on the basis of how they conduct their professional activities can be understood as a permissive signal to potential killers that the murder of journalists is acceptable in certain circumstances and would not be punished.'[40]

III: Landscapes of a War Culture

As Michael Hardt and Antonio Negri presciently acknowledged, the veneration of war in the United States has now reached a dangerous end point, and has become the foundation of politics itself. This is especially true as Americans entered into what is so far one of the most appalling and threatening periods of the 21st century. They write:

> What is specific to our era...is that war has passed from the final element of the sequences of power – lethal force as a last resort – to the first and primary element, the foundation of politics itself. Imperial sovereignty creates...a regime of disciplinary administration and political control directly based on continuous war action. The constant and coordinated application of violence, in other words, becomes the necessary condition for the functioning of discipline and control. In order for war to occupy this fundamental social and political role, war must be able to accomplish a constituent or regulative function: war must become both a procedural activity and an ordering, regulative activity that creates and maintains social hierarchies, a form of biopower aimed at the promotion and regulation of social life.[41]

The violence produced by a war culture has become a defining feature of American society, providing a common ground for the deployment and celebration of violence abroad and at home. At a policy level, an arms industry fuels violence abroad while domestically a toxic gun culture contributes to the endless maiming and deaths of individuals at home. Similarly, a militaristic foreign policy has its domestic counterpart in the growth of a carceral and punishing state used to enforce a hyped-up brand of domestic terrorism, especially against Black youth and various emerging protest movements in the United States.[42] As John Kiriakou makes clear, according to

> . . . [t]he non-profit Marshall Project . . . things will likely change quickly under Sessions. The new attorney general 'helped block broader drug sentencing reform in the Senate this year despite wide bipartisan support, saying it would release "violent felons" into the street.' He will also be tasked with carrying out the new president's policies on private prisons. The Marshall Project noted that candidate Trump told MSNBC's Chris Matthews in June that 'I do think we can do a lot of privatizations and private prisons. It seems to work a lot better.' Just weeks before the election, Geo Group, the second largest private prison corporation in America, hired two former Sessions aides to lobby in favor of outsourcing federal corrections to private contractors.[43]

Since the Nixon era, a 'political culture of hyper punitiveness'[44] has served not only to legitimate a neo-liberal culture in which cruelty is viewed as virtue, but also a racist system of mass incarceration that functions as the default welfare program and chief mechanism to 'institutionalize obedience'.[45] The police state has increasingly targeted poor people of color turning their neighborhoods into war zones, making it difficult for Blacks to distinguish the police from an invading army – all the while serving a corporate state that has no concern whatsoever for the social costs inflicted upon millions as a result of its predatory policies and practices. The persistent killing of Black youth testifies to a long history and domestic terrorism representing 'an unbroken stream of racist violence, both official and extralegal, from slave patrols and the Ku Klux Klan to contemporary profiling practices and present-day vigilantes'.[46] The historical backdrop to the current killing of Black youth, men and women must be coupled with the shameful truth that '11 million Americans cycle through our jails and prisons each year'.[47] Moreover, the United States 'imprisons the largest proportion of people in the world [and] that, with 4% of the global population, it holds 22% of the world's prisoners' and that 70% of these prisoners are people of color.[48] These figures testify not only to the emergence of a police state, but also to a justice system that has a long legacy of being driven by racism.

Under such circumstances, important distinctions between war and civil society collapse as the police function as soldiers, cities are transformed into combat zones, shared responsibilities are replaced by shared fears, the boundaries disappear between innocent and guilty, and public safety is defined increasingly as a police matter. Neo-liberal society has ceded any vestige of democratic ideals to a social formation saturated with fear, suspicion and violence. Americans are terrified by the threat of terrorism and its ensuing violence; yet, they are more than willing to protect laws that privilege the largely unchecked circulation of guns and the toxic militarized culture of violence that amounts to '58 people who die a day because of firearms'.[49]

Acts of intolerable violence have become America's longest-running, non-stop, cinematic production, overloading both the mainstream media and the entertainment industry. Representations of violence saturate American culture as unending coverage appears daily about mass shootings, children shot by gang members, people killed by gun-related injuries, and the police wantonly shooting and often killing unarmed Black people with impunity. All the while, the distinction between moral repulsion and voyeuristic pleasure is blurred.

Violence now acts as both a monstrous political weapon in the service of oppressive relations of power and as a spectacle fueling an aesthetic that floods the culture with what Brad Evans and I have previously described as 'a kind of hallucinatory form of entertainment in which violence provides one of the truly last possibilities for feeling passion, pleasure and a sense of control'.[50] The line has become blurred between real acts of violence and mythical appeals to violence as cleansing and restorative, as is evident in Donald Trump's emotional appeal to his audience's rage and fear. Dystopian violence is now legitimated at the highest level of politics both in its use as a spectacle fueling a presidential campaign that ended with the election of Donald Trump and as a policy of terror, torture and the killing of innocent people initiated most specifically in the murderous rampage of drone warfare. Consequently, politics is now an extension of the culture of war and violence both as spectacle and real, it is a galvanizing and emboldening force in the production of everyday life. Trump now offers his followers an imagined community organized around the symbols of fear and disposability in which the nation is deemed synonymous with a white Christian public sphere.

IV: Normalizing Violence

The normalization of violence in American society is not only about how it is lived and endured, but also about how it becomes the connective tissue for holding together different modes of governance, policies, ideologies and practices. All of these come to resemble military activities. And it is precisely such activities that serve to legitimate the war on terror, the use of mass surveillance, the weaponizing of knowledge, and the merging of a war culture and a warfare state. In the aftermath of the transition from the Welfare State in the 1960s to the current warfare state, the appeal to fear on many political fronts became paramount in order to legitimate a carceral state that increasingly governed through what can be termed the war on crime, especially affecting marginalized citizens, such as poor Blacks.[51]

Violence, however grotesque, has been relegated to the most powerful force mediating human relations and used to address pressing social problems. It is a habitual response by the state in almost every dilemma. Police violence is only one register of the landscape of everyday violence, but at the same time it is an important and visible indication of how violence has been 'dragged into the heart of political life . . . turning [America] into a military state'.[52] The hidden structure of violence is not only on full display in the killing of unarmed Black people; it can also be found in a range of largely invisible sites of brutality that include debtors' prisons for children, racist juvenile courts, schools modeled after prisons, a systemic debt-machine, and municipal governments that function as extortion factories and inflict misery and penury upon the poor.

A sickening brutalism appears to have taken over American society and is partly reflected in various statistics that present a chilling measure of a society slipping into a lethal culture of sanctioned violence. The numbers are staggering and include 'everything from homicides and multiple-victim gang assaults to incidents of self defense and accidental shootings'.[53] In 2015, '36 Americans were killed by guns' on an average day, and 'that excludes most suicides . . . From 2005 to 2015 . . . 301,797 people were killed by gun violence.'[54] What is often not reported in the mainstream media is that more than half of American gun death victims are poor men of color, living in dilapidated segregated neighborhoods far from the gaze of the mainstream media, tourism and the American public.

At a subtler level, the registers of militarization produce both armed knowledge through university research funded by the military–industrial–Pentagon complex and in a growing culture of political purity in which the personal becomes the only politics there is housed within a discourse of *weaponized sensitivity* and *armed ignorance*. Empathy for others extends only as far as recognizing those who mirror the self. Politics has collapsed into the privatized orbits of a crude essentialism that disdains forms of public discourse and the exercise of public deliberation is viewed as irrelevant to fostering a substantive democracy.[55] This was made clear in Trump's repeated support and use of language in the service of violence at his pre-election rallies.

War culture is legitimated ideologically by collapsing public issues into private concerns. This is a powerful pedagogical tool that functions to de-politicize people by de-coupling social problems from the violence inherent in the structural, affective and pedagogical dimensions of neo-liberalism. Capitalism is about both winning at all costs and privileging what Zygmunt Bauman calls a 'society of individual performance and a culture of sink-or-swim individualism [in which individuals are] doomed to seek individually designed and individually manageable solutions to problems generated by society'.56 Not only does the individualization of the social hide capitalism's structural violence, it also collapses politics into the realm of the personal, substituting the discourse of power, racism and class into the vocabulary of a paralysing and depoliticizing notion of therapy, trauma, character and lifestyles, which coexist with rather than displacing iniquitous and oppressive forms of domination.

This mode of individualized politics functions as a weapon of fear that trades off conditions of precarity in order to amplify the personal anxieties, uncertainties and misery produced through life-draining austerity measures and the destruction of the bonds of sociality and solidarity. Abandoned to their own resources, individuals turn to what Jennifer Silva calls a "mood economy" in which they seek relief from their misery and immiseration through "emotional self-management and willful psychic transformation".[57] Trauma and pain become the starting and end points for a politics that mimics a self-help culture in which the task of self-transformation and self-help replaces any attempt at structural transformation and political liberation. The current regime of neo-liberal pedagogy, which hides behind its anonymity, masks a structure of violence and a deeply anti-democratic ethos that maims and contains the critical modes of agency necessary for real change, while "the interaction between people and the state has been reduced to nothing but authority and obedience".[58]

At the same time, neoliberal pedagogy redefines the pathologies of poverty, patriarchy, structural racism, police violence, homophobia and massive inequities in income and power as personal pathologies and shortcomings to be overcome by support groups, safe spaces and other reforms that ignore fighting for what Robin D. G. Kelley calls "models of social and economic justice".[59] This is the politics of an insidious form of learned helplessness that produces a depoliticized passivity and an absorption with the cruel and narcissistic dimensions of a consumer-based society that we see everywhere.

V: Towards a Comprehensive Politics

Any attempt to resist and restructure the intensification of a war culture with its white supremacist, ultra-nationalist underside in the United States necessitates a new language for politics. Such a discourse must be historical, relational, ethical and as comprehensive as it is radical. Historically, the call for a comprehensive view of oppression, violence and politics can be found in the connections that Martin Luther King, Jr., drew near the end of his life, particularly in his speech *Beyond Vietnam: a Time to Break the Silence*.[60] King made it clear that the United States uses "massive doses of violence to solve its problems, to bring about the changes it wanted," and that such violence could not be clearly addressed if limited to an analysis of single issues such as the Vietnam War.[61] On the contrary, he argued that the war at home was an inextricable part of the war abroad and that matters of militarism, racism, poverty and materialism mutually informed each other and cut across a variety of sites. For instance, he understood that poverty at home could not be abstracted from the money allotted to wars abroad and a death-dealing militarism. Nor could the racism at home be removed from those *others* the United States demonized and objectified abroad, revealing in their mutual connection a racism that drove both domestic and foreign policy. For King, "giant triplets of racism, extreme materialism, and militarism" had to be resisted both through a revolution of values and a broad-based, non-violent movement at home aimed at a radical restructuring of American society.[62] One ethical referent for King's notion of a radical restructuring was his moral and political abhorrence over the millions of children killed at home and abroad by a war culture and its ruthless machineries of militarism and violence.

Michelle Alexander has also argued that what we can learn from King is the need to connect the dots among diverse forms of oppression.[63] A totalizing view of oppression allows us to see the underlying ideological and structural forces of the new forms of domination at work in the United States. For instance, Alexander raises questions about the connection between 'drones abroad and the War on Drugs at home'.[64] In addition, she argues for modes of political inquiry that connect a variety of oppressive practices enacted in order to accumulate capital – such as the workings of a corrupt financial industry and Wall Street bankers, on the one hand, and the moving of jobs overseas, the foreclosing of homes, the increase in private prisons, and the caging of immigrants, on the other. Similarly, she calls for 'connecting the dots between the NSA spying on millions of Americans, the labeling of mosques as "terrorist organizations," and the spy programs of the 1960s and 1970s – specifically the FBI and COINTELPRO programs that placed civil rights advocates under constant surveillance, infiltrated civil rights organizations, and assassinated racial justice leaders'.[65] More recently, we have seen the call for such connections emerge from the Black Lives Matter movement and a range of other grass-roots movements whose politics go far beyond an agenda limited to single issues such as the curbing of anti-Black violence. This type of comprehensive politics is exemplified in the policy document *A Vision for Black Lives: Policy Demands for Black Power, Freedom & Justice*, created by the Movement for Black Lives (M4BL), a coalition of over 60 organizations.[66]

It is worth noting that Angela Davis has for years been calling for progressives to build links to other struggles and has talked about how what has happened in Ferguson must be related to what is happening in Palestine. This type of connective politics might raise questions about what the US immigration policies and the racist discourses that inform them have in common with what is going on in authoritarian countries such as Hungary. Another example is illustrated in Davis' asking what happens to communities when the police who are supposed to serve and protect them are treated like soldiers who are trained to shoot and kill? How might such analyses bring various struggles for social and economic justice together across national boundaries? She argues that such connections have to 'be made in the context of struggles themselves. So as you are organizing against police crimes, against police racism you always raise parallels and similarities in other parts of the world [including] structural connections.'[67] Davis' politics embrace what she calls the larger context, and this is clearly exemplified in her commentary about prisons. She writes:

> We can't only think about the prison as a place of punishment for those who have committed crimes. We have to think about the larger framework. That means asking: Why is there such a disproportionate number of Black people and people of color in prison? So we have to talk about racism. Abolishing the prison is about attempting to abolish racism. Why is there so much illiteracy? Why are so many prisoners illiterate? That means we have to attend to the educational system. Why is it that the three largest psychiatric institutions in the country are jails in New York, Chicago, Los Angeles: Rikers Island, Cook County Jail, and L.A. County

Jail? That means we need to think about health care issues, and especially mental health care issues. We have to figure out how to abolish homelessness.[68]

We need a new political vocabulary for capturing the scope and interconnections that comprise the matrix of permanent war and violence that shapes a variety of experiences and spheres in American society, all of which will expand under the Trump presidency. While the current focus on police killings, gun violence, mass shootings and acts of individual bloodshed is important to analyse, it is crucial not to treat these events as isolated categories because by doing so we lose a broader understanding of the ways in which American society is being held hostage to often invisible but formative modes of intolerable violence that are distributed across a range of sites on a daily basis. This is especially true as Americans enter into a historical moment in which the highest reaches of government will be run by a group of officials who support a president who has condoned torture, wants to increase the numbers and power of the police, views Black neighborhoods as manifestations of a criminal culture, staffs his cabinet appointments with racists and views violence as a legitimate tool for dealing with dissent. Noam Chomsky is right in calling Trump, his generals and the Republican Party 'the most dangerous organization in the world'.[69]

Intolerable violence is most visible when it attracts the attention of mainstream media and conforms to the production of what might be called the spectacle of violence, that is, violence that is put on public display in order to shock and entertain rather than inform.[70] Yet, such violence is just the tip of the iceberg and is dependent upon a foundation of lawlessness that takes place through a range of experiences, representations and spaces that make up daily life across a variety of sites and public spaces. Those spaces of lawlessness are on the rise and the dark shadow of authoritarianism is at our doorstep. Yet, such forces cannot be allowed to cancel out the future and promises of a radical democracy.

VI: Militant Hope and the Politics of Resistance

It is worth repeating that at the core of any strategy to resist the further descent of the United States into authoritarianism must be the recognition that stopping Trump without destroying the economic, political, educational and social conditions that produced him will fail. In part a successful resistance struggle must both be comprehensive and at the same time embrace a vision that is as unified as it is democratic.[71] Instead of reacting to the horrors and misery produced by capitalism, it is crucial to call for its end while supporting a notion of democratic socialism that speaks to the needs of those who have been left out of the discourse of democracy under the financial elite. Such a task is both political and pedagogical. Not only do existing relations of power have to be called into question, but notions of neo-liberal common-sense learning have to be disconnected from any viable sense of political agency and notion of civic literacy. Instead of mounting resistance through a range of single issue movements, it is important to bring such movements together as part of a broad-based political formation. Rather than engaging in a politics of shaming, progressives have to produce a discourse in which people can recognize their problems and the actual conditions that produce them. This is not just a political but a pedagogical challenge in which education becomes central to any viable notion of resistance. For instance, climate change can be addressed not simply by listing all the ways in which it is killing the ecosystem, but also how it functions as a public health problem endangering children, the elderly and other vulnerable populations.

The first step in any form of collective resistance is to recognize the seriousness of the threat of the political, social and economic conditions that a Trump administration poses to American democracy, however fragile. Second, while American society may be slipping away into the dark shadows of authoritarianism, it is imperative to think politics anew in order to wage more formidable struggles in the name of economic and social justice. All societies contain sites of resistance and progressives need desperately to join with those who have been written out of the script of democracy to rethink politics, find a new beginning and develop a vision that is on the side of justice and democracy. Hope in the abstract is not enough. We need a form of militant hope and practice that engages with the forces of authoritarianism on the educational and political fronts so as to become a foundation for what might be called hope in action; that is, a new force of collective resistance and a vehicle for anger transformed into collective struggle – a principle for making despair unconvincing and struggle possible. Education must become central to any politics of resistance because it is fundamental to how subjectivities are produced, desire is constructed and behavior takes place. Paulo Freire, the Brazilian educator, was right in insisting that subjectivity is both the material of politics and the platform where the struggle over consciousness and resistance takes place. Antonio Gramsci, the great Italian Marxist, was also right in arguing that at the heart of political struggle is a war of position, a struggle in which matters of education, persuasion, language and consciousness were fundamental to creating the formative culture that made radical change possible. This is a struggle in which inner worlds are made and remade not only under the weight of economic structures but also through the pedagogical mediums of belief, moments of recognition, and identification.

While we may be entering a period of counter-revolutionary change, it must be remembered that such historical moments are as hopeful as they are dangerous. Hope at the moment resides in struggling to reclaim the radical imagination, bringing together an array of disparate, single issue movements, while working to build an expansive broad-based social movement for real symbolic and structural change. Central to such a task is the need to build alternative public spaces that offer fresh educational opportunities to create a new language for political struggle along with new modes of solidarity. At stake here is the need for progressives to make education central to politics itself in order to disrupt the force of a predatory public pedagogy and common sense produced in mainstream cultural apparatuses that serve as glue for the rise of right-wing populism. This is not merely a call for a third political party. Any vision for this movement must reject the false notion that capitalism and democracy are synonymous. Democratic socialism is once again moving a generation of young people. We need to accelerate this movement for a radical democracy before it is too late.

Notes

1. On the origins of the warfare state, see Carl Boggs, *Origins of the Warfare States: World War II and the Transformation of American Politics* (New York: Routledge, 2017).

2. Ulrich Beck, 'The Silence of Words and Political Dynamics in the World Risk Society', *Logos* 1(4) (Fall 2002): 1–18 (1).

3. Denver Nicks, 'The U.S. Is Still No.1 at Selling Arms to the World', *Time Magazine* (26 December 2015), online, accessible @: http://time.com/4161613/us-arms-sales-exports- weapons/ See also Andrew J. Bacevich, *Washington Rules: America's Path to Permanent War* (New York: Metropolitan Books (Henry Holt), 2010).

4. Trump's address to a joint session of Congress can be found in *Mother Jones* New York Bureau, 'Here Are 4,826 Words Donald Trump Included in His Speech', *Mother Jones* (28 February 2017), online, accessible @: http://www.motherjones.com/politics/2017/02/read-full-text-donald-trumps-speech-congress

5. Chris Hedges, 'Donald Trump's Greatest Allies Are the Liberal Elites', *Truthdig* (7 March 2017), online, accessible @: www.truthdig.com/report/item/donald_trumps_greatest_allies_ are_the_liberal_elites_20170305

6. The classic commentary on politics as show business can be found in Neil Postman, *Amusing Ourselves to Death: Public Discourse in the Age of Show Business* (New York: Penguin Books, 2005[1985]).

7. Amy Goodman, 'Cornel West on Donald Trump: This is What Neo-Fascism Looks Like', *Democracy Now* (1 December 2016), online, accessible @: https://www.democracynow.org/ 2016/12/1/cornel_west_on_donald_trump_this

8. Dahlia Lithwick, 'Trump Lays Down His Law', *Slate* (20 January 2017), online, accessible@: http://www.slate.com/articles/news_and_politics/jurisprudence/2017/01/   trump_s_inaugural_address_was_terrifying.html.

9. Chauncey DeVega, 'Trump's Election Has Created "Safe Spaces" for Racists: Southern Poverty Law Center's Heidi Beirich on the Wave of Hate Crimes', *Salon* (8 March 2017), online, accessible @: http://www.salon.com/2017/03/08/trumps-election-has-created-safe-spaces-for-racists-southern-poverty-law-centers-heidi-beirich-on-the-wave-of-hate-crimes/

10. ibid.

11. Paul Gilroy, *Against Race: Imagining Political Culture beyond the Color Line* (Cambridge, MA: the Belknap Press of Harvard University Press, 2000), pp. 145–6.

12. Sasha Bruce, 'NARAL statement on nomination of Tom Price as Secretary of HHS', NARAL Pro-Choice America (16 November 2016), online, accessible @: http://www.prochoiceamerica.org/media/pressreleases/2016/pr11292016_hhssecretarystatement.html?referrer=https://www.google.ca/

13. Ari Berman, 'Jeff Sessions, Trump's Pick for Attorney General, Is a Fierce Opponent of Civil Rights', *The Nation* (18 November 2016), online, accessible @: https://www.thenation.com/article/jeff-sessions-trumps-pick-for-attorney-general-is-a-fierce-opponent-of-civil-rights/

14. Emily Bazelon, 'Department of Justification', *The New York Times* (28 February 2017), online, accessible @: https://www.nytimes.com/2017/02/28/magazine/jeff-sessions-stephen-bannon-justice-department.html

15. Miranda Blue, '12 Reasons Jeff Sessions Should Never Be Attorney General', *Right Wing Watch* (18 November 2016), online, accessible @: http://www.rightwingwatch.org/post/12- reasons-jeff-sessions-should-never-be-attorney-general/

16. Andrew Kaczynski, 'Sen. Sessions: Central Park Five Ad Shows Trump Has Always Believed In Law And Order', *BuzzFeed News* (18 August 2016), online, accessible @: https:// www.buzzfeed.com/andrewkaczynski/sen-sessions-central-park-five-ad-shows-trump-has-alwaysbel?utm_term=.ym71O7vMP#.fuqqeGk9o

17. ibid.

18. Amy Goodman, 'A White Nationalist & Anti-Semite in the Oval Office: Trump Taps Breitbart's Bannon as Top Aide', *Democracy Now* (14 November 2016), online, accessible @: https://www.democracynow.org/2016/11/14/a_white_nationalist_anti_semite_in

19. The Associated Press, 'Conservative Flame-Thrower to Get Key White House Position', *The New York Times* (14 November 2016), online, accessible @: http://www.nytimes.com/aponline/2016/11/14/us/politics/ap-us-trump-bannon.html?_r=0

20. Goodman, 'A White Nationalist & Anti-Semite', online, accessible @: https://www.democracynow.org/2016/11/14/a_white_nationalist_anti_semite_in

21. Rebecca Gould, 'Regime Change Abroad, Fascism at Home: How US Interventions Paved the Way for Trump', *CounterPunch* (29 November 2016), online, accessible @: http://www.counterpunch.org/2016/11/29/regime-change-abroad-fascism-at-home-how-us-interventions-paved-the-way-for-trump/

22. Loren Thompson, 'For the Defence Industry, Trump's Win Means Happy Days Are Here Again', *Forbes* (9 November 2016), online, accessible @: http://www.forbes.com/sites/lorenthompson/2016/11/09/for-the-defense-industry-trumps-win-means-happy-days-are-here-again/#90fe95652f02

23. William D. Hartung, 'A Pentagon Rising: Is a Trump Presidency Good News for the Military-Industrial Complex?', *TomDispatch* (22 November 2016), online, accessible @: http://www.tomdispatch.com/blog/176213/tomgram%3A_william_hartung%2C_trump_for_the_defense/

24. Robbie Martin, 'Trump's Dark Web of Far Right Militarists Who Want to Attack Iran', *The Real News* (28 November 2016), online, accessible @: http://therealnews.com/t2/index.php?option=com_content&task=view&id=31&Itemid=74&jumival=17662

25. Melvin A. Goodman, 'Trump's Campaign of Militarization', *CounterPunch* (23 November 2016), online, accessible @: http://www.counterpunch.org/2016/11/23/trumps-campaign-of-militarization/

26. Matthew Rosenberg and Maggie Haberman, 'Michael Flynn, Anti-Islamist Ex-General, Offered Security Post, Trump Aide Says', *The New York Times* (17 November 2006), online, accessible @: http://www.nytimes.com/2016/11/18/us/politics/michael-flynn-national-security-adviser-donald-trump.html

27. ibid.

28. Lawrence Douglas, 'Lying Got Michael Flynn Fired. But that's What the Trump White House Does Best', *The Guardian* (15 February 2017), online, accessible @: https://www.theguardian.com/commentisfree/2017/feb/15/lying-got-michael-flynn-fired-trump-white-house

29. Andrew Bacevich, 'Trump Loves to Do It, But American Generals Have Forgotten How', *TomDispatch* (29 November 2016), online, accessible @: www.tomdispatch.com/post/176215/tomgram%3A_andrew_bacevich,_the_swamp_of_war/

30. Hugh Handeyside, 'Does What Happened to This Journalist at the US-Canada Border Herald a Darker Trend?', *CommonDreams* (30 November 2016), online, accessible @: http://www.commondreams.org/views/2016/11/30/does-what-happened-journalist-us-canada-border-herald-darker-trend

31. Grace Guarnieri, '4 Hair-Raising Facts About Trump's Potential Homeland Security Pick', *Salon* (29 November 2016), online, accessible @: http://www.alternet.org/election-2016/4-hair-rais-

ing-facts-about-trumps-potential-homeland-security-pick?akid=14939.40823.PgLddF&rd=1&s-rc=newsletter1068046&t=6

32. Michael D. Shear, 'Trump as Cyberbully in Chief? Twitter Attack on Union Boss Draws Fire', *The New York Times* (8 December 2016), online, accessible @: http://mobile.nytimes.com/2016/12/08/us/politics/donald-trump-twitter-carrier-chuck-jones.html

33. Madeline Farber, 'Union Leader Says He's Getting Threats After Donald Trump Attacked Him on Twitter', *Fortune* (9 December 2016), online, accessible @: http://fortune.com/2016/12/08/carrier-union-leader-threats-donald-trump/

34. Terry Gross, 'Megyn Kelly On Trump And The Media: "We're In A Dangerous Phase Right Now"', *Fresh Air* (7 December 2016), online, accessible @: http://www.npr.org/2016/12/07/504622630/megyn-kelly-on-trump-and-the-media-were-in-a-dangerous-phase-right-now See Chris Hedges's informative commentary on this interview at Chris Hedges, 'Demagogue-in-Chief', *TruthDig* 11 December 2016), online, accessible @: http://www.truthdig.com/report/item/demagogue-in-chief_20161211

35. Frank Rich, 'Don't Be Fooled: Donald Trump Will Never Walk Away From His Businesses', *New York Magazine* (30 November 2016), online, accessible @: http://nymag.com/daily/intelligencer/2016/11/donald-trump-will-never-walk-away-from-his-businesses.html

36. ibid.

37. Felipe Villamor, 'Rodrigo Duterte Says Donald Trump Endorses His Violent Antidrug Campaign', *The New York Times* (3 December 2016), online, accessible @: http://www.nytimes.com/2016/12/03/world/asia/philippines-rodrigo-duterte-donald-trump.html

38. ibid.

39. Cited in Iris C. Gonzales, 'Philippines' Duterte Threatens Assassination of Journalists', *New Internationalist Blog* (22 June 2016), online, accessible @: https://newint.org/blog/2016/06/22/philippines-duterte-threatens-assassination-of-journalists/

40. ibid.

41. Michael Hardt and Antonio Negri, *Multitude: War and Democracy in the Age of Empire* (New York: Penguin, 2004), p. 2.

42. See, for instance, the section 'End the War on Black People', in M4BL, 'A Vision for Black Lives: Policy Demands for Black Power, Freedom & Justice' (1 August 2016), online, accessible @: https://policy.m4bl.org/. Also, see Keeanga-Yamahtta Taylor, *From BlackLivesMatter to Black Liberation* (Chicago, IL: Haymarket Books, 2016).

43. John Kiriakou, 'Trump-Sessions: Expect the Worst for Prison Reform', *Reader Supported News* (1 December 2016), online, accessible @: http://readersupportednews.org/opinion2/277-75/40597-focus-trump-sessions-expect-the-worst-for-prison-reform

44. Steve Herbert and Elizabeth Brown, 'Conceptions of Space and Crime in the Punitive Neo-liberal City', *Antipode* 38(4) (2006): 755–77 (757).

45. Steve Martinot, 'Police Torture and the Real Militarization of Society', *CounterPunch* ([11 November 2015), online, accessible @: http://www.counterpunch.org/2015/11/11/police-torture-and-the-real-militarization-of-society/

46. Angela Y. Davis, *Freedom Is a Constant Struggle: Ferguson, Palestine and the Foundations of a Movement*, ed. Frank Barat (Chicago, IL: Haymarket Books, 2016), p. 77.

47. Rebecca Gordon, 'Should Prison Really Be the American Way', *TomDispatch* (25 September 2016), online, accessible @: http://www.tomdispatch.com/blog/176190/

48. ibid.; for a vivid and searing portrayal of the racist nature of the carceral state, see Ava DuVernay's film, *13th*.

49. Cited in Marian Wright Edelman, 'Why Are Children Less Valuable than Guns in America? It is Time to Protect Children', Children's Defense Fund (8 December 2015), online, accessible @: http://www.childrensdefense.org/newsroom/child-watch-columns/childwatchdocuments/WhyAreChildrenLessValuableThanGuns.html?referrer=https://www.google.ca/

50. Brad Evans and Henry A. Giroux, 'Intolerable Violence', *Symploke* 23(1) (2015): 201–23 (201).

51. Jonathan Simon, *Governing through Crime: How the War on Crime Transformed American Democracy and Created a Culture of Fear* (New York: Oxford University Press, 2007).

52. George Monbiot, 'States of War', *Common Dreams* (17 October 2003), online, accessible @: http://www.commondreams.org/scriptfiles/views03/1014-09.htm

53. Jennifer Mascia, '15 Statistics that Tell the Story of Gun Violence This Year', *The Trace* (23 December 2015), online, accessible @: https://www.thetrace.org/2015/12/gun-violence-stats-2015/

54. ibid.

55. The notion of weaponized sensitivity is from Lionel Shriver, 'Will the Left Survive the Millennials?', *The New York Times* (23 September 2016), online, accessible @: http://www.ny times.com/2016/09/23/opinion/will-the-left-survive-the-millennials.html The phrase 'armed ignorance' was coined by my colleague Brad Evans in personal correspondence.

56. Zygmunt Bauman, *Strangers at Our Door* (London: Polity, 2016), pp. 58–9.

57. Jennifer M. Silva, *Coming Up Short: Working-Class Adulthood in an Age of Uncertainty* (New York: Oxford University Press, 2013), p. 10.

58. George Monbiot, 'Neoliberalism – the Ideology at the Root of All Our Problems', *The Guardian*, (15 April 2016), online, accessible @: http://www.theguardian.com/books/2016/apr/15/neoliberalism-ideology-problem-george-monbiot

59. Robin D. G. Kelley, 'Black Study, Black Struggle', *Boston Review* (7 March 2016), online, accessible @: https://bostonreview.net/forum/robin-d-g-kelley-black-study-black-struggle

60. Rev. Martin Luther King, 'Beyond Vietnam: A Time to Break Silence', *American Rhetoric* (n.d.), online, accessible @: http://www.americanrhetoric.com/speeches/mlkatimetobreaksilence.htm

61. ibid.

62. ibid.

63. Michelle Alexander, 'Michelle Alexander on "Getting Out of Your Lane"', *War Times* (28 August 2013), online, accessible @: http://www.war-times.org/michelle-alexander-getting-out-your-lane

64. ibid.

65. ibid.

66. See the statement accessible @: https://policy.m4bl.org/

67. Davis, *Freedom Is a Constant Struggle*, p. 20.

68. ibid.: 23–4.

69. Cited in Deirdre Fulton, 'Those Who Failed to Recognize Trump as "Greater Evil" Made a "Bad Mistake": Chomsky', *CommonDreams* (15 November 2016), online, accessible @: http://www.commondreams.org/news/2016/11/25/those-who-failed-recognize-trump-greater-evil-made-bad-mistake-chomsky

70. Brad Evans and Henry A. Giroux, *Disposable Futures: The Seduction of Violence in the Age of the Spectacle* (San Francisco, CA: City Lights Books, 2015).

71. This issue is taken up in great detail in Michael Lerner, 'Overcoming Trump-ism: A New Strategy for Progressives', *Tikkun* (31 January 2017), online, accessible @: http://www.tikku n.org/nextgen/overcoming-trump-ism-a-new-strategy-for-progressives.

NO WAY OUT

The Devouring of Higher Education

CHAPTER 10

Vocationalizing Higher Education

Schooling and the Politics of Corporate Culture

1999

Corporate Ascendancy is emerging as the universal order of the post-communist world . . . . Our social landscape is now dominated by corporations that are bigger and more powerful than most countries. . . . Our end of the century and the next century loom as the triumphal age of corporations.

(Derber 1998, 3)

The Final Victory of Liberal Democracy?

A recent full-page advertisement for *Forbes 500* magazine proclaims in bold red letters, "Capitalists of the World Unite" (*World Traveler* 1998). Beneath the slogan covering the bottom half of the page is a mass of individuals, representing various countries throughout the world, their arms raised in victory. Instead of workers in the traditional sense, the *Forbes* professionals (three women among them) are distinctly middle-class, dressed in sport jackets, ties, carrying brief cases, or cellular phones. A sea of red flags with their respective national currency emblazoned on the front of each waves above their heads. At the bottom of the picture is text that reads "All hail the final victory of capitalism." At first glance, the ad appears to simply be a mockery of one of Marxism's most powerful ideals. But as self conscious as the ad is in parodying the dream of a workers' revolution, it also reflects another ideology made famous in 1989 by Francis Fukuyama (1989a), who proclaimed "the end of history," a reference to the end of authoritarian communism in East Central Europe, the former Soviet Union, and the Baltic Countries. According to Fukuyama, "the end of history" meant that liberal democracy has achieved its ultimate victory and that the twin ideologies of the market and representative democracy now constitute, with a few exceptions, the universal values of the new global village.

The *Forbes* ad does more than signal the alleged "death" of communism; it also cancels out the tension between market values and those values representative of civil society that cannot be measured in strictly commercial terms but are critical to democracy. I am referring specifically to values such as justice, freedom, equality, health and respect for children, the rights of citizens as equal and free human beings, as well as "respect for the rule of law, for individual rights, for value pluralism, for constitutional guarantees . . . and democratic politics" (Benhabib 1996, 9).

Who are the cheering men (and three women) portrayed in this ad? Certainly not the 43 million Americans who have lost their jobs in the last fifteen years. Certainly not "the people." The *Forbes* ad celebrates freedom, but only in the discourse of the unbridled power of the market. There is no recognition here (how could there be?) of either the limits that democracies must place on such power or how corporate culture and its narrow redefinition of freedom as a private good may actually present a threat to democracy equal to if not greater than that imagined under communism or any other totalitarian ideology. Fukuyama, of course, proved to be right about the fall of communism, but quite wrong about "the universalization of Western liberal democracy as the final form of government" (Fukuyama 1989b, 2). Before the ink was dry genocide erupted in Bosnia-Herzegovina, Moslem fundamentalism swept Algeria, the Russians launched a bloodbath in Chechnya, Serbs launched genocidal attacks against ethnic Albanians in Kosovo, and parts of Africa erupted in a bloody civil war accompanied by the horror of tribal genocide. Even in the United States, with the Cold War at an end, the language of democracy seemed to lose its vitality and purpose as an organizing principle for society. As corporations have gained more and more power in American society, democratic culture becomes corporate culture, the rightful ideological heir to the victory over socialism.[1]

I use the term corporate culture to refer to an ensemble of ideological and institutional forces that function politically and pedagogically both to govern organizational life through senior managerial control and to produce compliant workers, depoliticized consumers, and passive citizens.[2] Within the language and images of corporate culture, citizenship is portrayed as an utterly privatized affair whose aim is to produce competitive self-interested individuals vying for their own material and ideological gain. Reformulating social issues as strictly individual or economic, corporate culture functions largely to cancel out the democratic impulses and practices of civil society by either devaluing them or absorbing such impulses within a market logic. No longer a space for political struggle, culture in the corporate model becomes an all-encompassing horizon for producing market identities, values, and practices. The good life, in this discourse, "is construed in terms of our identities as consumers—we are what we buy" (Bryman 1995, 154). Public spheres are replaced by commercial spheres as the substance of critical democracy is emptied out and replaced by a democracy of goods, consumer life styles, shopping malls, and the increasing expansion of the cultural and political power of corporations throughout the world.

The broader knowledge, social values and skills necessary for creating substantive democratic participation increasingly seem at odds with, and detrimental to corporate moguls, such as Bill Gates, the new cultural heroes and icons of social mobility, wealth, and success personifying the intersection of greed and moral irresponsibility that has become the hallmark of corporate culture. Gates is envied in the business media for accumulating personal wealth worth 50 billion dollars—"more than the combined bottom 40 percent of the U.S. population, or 100 million Americans" (Derber 1997, 12), but little is said about a society that allows such wealth to be accumulated while at the same time over 40 million Americans, including 20 million children, live below the poverty line. Within the world of national politics, conservative policy institutes along with a Republican Congress incessantly argue that how we think about education, work, and social welfare means substituting the language of the private good for the discourse and values of the public good. At the economic level, the ascendancy of corporate culture has become evident in the growing power of mega-conglomerates such as Disney, General Electric, Time-Warner, and Westinghouse to control both the content and distribution of much of what the American public sees.[3]

Accountable only to the bottom-line of profitability, corporate culture and its growing influence in American life have signaled a radical shift in both the notion of public culture and what constitutes the meaning of citizenship and the defense of the public good. For example, the rapid resurgence of corporate power in the last twenty years and the attendant reorientation of culture to the demands of commerce and regulation have substituted the language of personal responsibility and private initiative for the discourses of social responsibility and public service. This can be seen in government policies designed to dismantle state protections for the poor, the environment, working people, and people of color (Kelley 1997a). For example, the 1996 welfare law signed by President Clinton reduces food stamp assistance for millions of children in working families, and a study by the Urban Institute showed that the bill would "move 2.6 million people, including 1.1 million children into poverty" (Edelman 1997, 43-58). Other examples include the dismantling of race-based programs such as the "California Civil Rights Initiative" and the landmark affirmative-action case, Hopwood vs. Texas, both designed to eliminate affirmative action in higher education, the reduction of federal monies for urban development, such as HUD's housing program, the weakening of Federal legislation to protect the environment, and a massive increase in state funds for building prisons at the expense of funding for public higher education.[4]

As a result of the corporate take-over of public life, the maintenance of democratic public spheres from which to organize the energies of a moral vision loses all relevance. As the power of civil society is reduced in its ability to impose or make corporate power accountable, politics as an expression of democratic struggle is deflated, and it becomes more difficult within the logic of self-help and the bottom-line to address pressing social and moral issues in systemic and political terms.

This suggests a dangerous turn in American society, one that both threatens our understanding of democracy as fundamental to our freedom and the ways in which we address the meaning and purpose of education.

Politics, Power, and Corporate Culture

Politics is the performative register of moral action, it is the mark of a civilized society to prevent justice from going dead in each of us, it is a call to acknowledge the claims of humanity to eliminate needless suffering while affirming freedom, equality, and hope. Markets don't reward moral behavior, and as corporate culture begins to dominate public life it becomes more difficult for citizens to think critically and act morally. For instance, what opportunities exist within the logic of privatization and excessive individualism for citizens to protest the willingness of the United States Congress to serve the needs of corporate interests over pressing social demands? I am not referring simply to the power of individuals and groups to limit government subsidies and bail outs which benefit corporate interests, but to curtail those forms of institutional insanity that have severe consequences for the most vulnerable of our citizens—the young, aged, and the poor. For instance, with no countervailing powers, norms, or values in place in civil society to counter corporate power how can the average citizen protest and stop the willingness of Congress to fund B2 Stealth bombers at a cost of $2 billion each, while refusing to allocate 100 million dollars to expand child nutrition programs? A political and moral default that appears all the more shameful given the fact that 26 per cent of children in the United States live below the poverty line (Sidel 1996, xiv). In a society increasingly governed by profit considerations and the logic of the market, where is the critical language to be developed, nourished, and applied for prioritizing public over private democracy, the social good over those market forces that benefit a very small group of investors, or social justice over rampant greed and individualism?

As the rise of corporate culture reasserts the primacy of privatization and individualism, there is an increasing call for people to surrender or narrow their capacities for engaged politics for a market-based notion of identity, one that suggests relinquishing our roles as social subjects for the limited role of consuming subjects. Similarly, as corporate culture extends ever deeper into the basic institutions of civil and political society, there is a simultaneous diminishing of non-commodified public spheres—those institutions engaged in dialogue, education, and learning that address the relationship of the self to public life, social responsibility to the broader demands of citizenship, and the development of public spheres that invest public culture with vibrancy.

History has been clear about the dangers of unbridled corporate power (Baran and Sweezy 1966). The brutal practices of slavery, the exploitation of child labor, the sanctioning of the cruelest working conditions in the mines and sweatshops of America and abroad, and the destruction of the environment have all been fueled by the law of maximizing profits and minimizing costs, especially when there has been no countervailing power from civil society to hold such powers in check. This is not to suggest that capitalism is the enemy of democracy, but that in the absence of a strong civil society and the imperatives of a strong democratic public sphere, the power of corporate culture when left on its own appears to respect few boundaries based on self restraint and those non-commodified, broader human values that are central to a democratic civic culture. John Dewey (1944) was right in arguing that democracy requires work, but that work is not synonymous with democracy.

Struggling for democracy is both a political and educational task. Fundamental to the rise of a vibrant democratic culture is the recognition that education must be treated as a public good and not merely as a site for commercial investment or for affirming a notion of the private good based exclusively on the fulfillment of individual needs. Reducing higher education to the handmaiden of corporate culture works against the critical social imperative of educating citizens who can sustain and develop inclusive democratic public spheres. There is a long tradition extending from Thomas Jefferson to C. Wright Mills that extols the importance of education as essential for a democratic public life. This legacy of public discourse appears to have faded as educational consultants all over America from Robert Zemsky of Stanford to Chester Finn of the Hudson Institute now call for educational institutions to "advise their clients in the name of efficiency to act like corporations selling products and seek 'market niches' to save themselves" and meet the challenges of the new world order (Aronowitz 1998, 32).

In what follows, I want to address the fundamental shift in society regarding how we think about the relationship between corporate culture and democracy. Specifically, I want to argue that one of the most important indications of such a change can be seen in the ways in which we are currently being asked to rethink the role of higher education. Underlying this analysis is the assumption that the struggle to reclaim higher education must be seen as part of a broader battle over the defense of the public good, and that at the heart of such a struggle is the need to challenge the ever-growing discourse and influence of corporate culture, power, and politics. I will conclude by offering some suggestions as to what educators can do to reassert the primacy of higher education as an essential sphere for expanding and deepening the processes of democracy and civil society.

Education and the Rise of the Corporate Manager

In a recent issue of *The Chronicle of Higher Education* (27 March 1998), Katherine S. Mangan reported that there are a growing number of presidential searches "looking for leaders who can bridge business and academe" (1998, A43). According to Mangan, this has resulted in a large number of business-school deans being offered jobs as college or university presidents. The rationale for such actions appears to be that "Business deans are often in a strong position to cultivate corporate contacts . . . [and are] better at translating the academic environment to the outside world" (1998, A44). Mangan's article makes clear that what was once part of the hidden curriculum of higher education—the creeping vocationalization and subordination of learning to the dictates of the market—has become an open, and defining principle of education at all levels of learning.

According to Stanley Aronowitz (1998), many colleges and universities are experiencing financial hard times brought on by the end of the cold war and the dwindling of government financed defense projects coupled with a sharp reduction of state aid to higher education. As a result, they are all too happy to allow corporate leaders to run their institutions, form business partnerships, establish cushy relationships with business-oriented legislators, and develop curricula tailored to the needs of corporate interests. In some cases, this has meant that universities such as the Massachusetts Institute of Technology and the University of California at Irvine have cut deals with corporations by offering to do product research and cede to their corporate backers the patents for resulting inventions and discoveries in return for ample research money.

Further evidence of the vocationalization of higher education can be found in the increasing willingness on the part of legislators, government representatives, and school officials to rely on corporate leaders to establish the terms of the debate in the media regarding the meaning and purpose of higher education. One typical example can be found in the highly publicized pronouncements of Louis Gerstner, Jr. (1998), who is the Chairman and CEO of IBM. In an editorial in *USA Today* (4 March 1998), Gerstner argues that schools should be treated like businesses because when

> U.S. businesses were faced with a stark choice: change or close, they changed. They began to invest in substantial transformation, new methods of production, new kinds of worker training. Most importantly, they continually benchmarked performance against one another and against international competition. . . . And it worked. (Gerstner 1998, 13A)

For Gerstner and many other CEOs, the current success of the capitalist economy is the direct result of the leadership exercised by corporate America. The lesson to be drawn is simple: "Schools are oddly insulated from marketplace forces and the discipline that drives constant adaptation, self-renewal, and a relentless push for excellence" (1998, 13A). Gerstner's argument is instructive because it is so typical, primarily about issues of efficiency, accountability, and restructuring. Corporate organizations such as the Committee for Economic Development, an organization of executives at about 250 corporations, have been more blunt about their interest in education. Not only has the group argued that social goals and services get in the way of learning basic skills, but that many employers in the business community feel dissatisfied because "a large majority of their new hires lack adequate writing and problem-solving skills" (Manegold 1998, A22).

Given the narrow nature of corporate concerns, it is not surprising that when matters of accountability become part of the language of school reform, they are divorced from broader considerations of ethics, equity, and justice. This type of corporate discourse not only lacks a vision beyond its own pragmatic interests, it also lacks a self-critical inventory of its own ideology and its effects on society. But, of course, one would not expect such concerns to emerge within corporations where questions of consequence begin and end with the bottom line. Questions about the effects of downsizing, deindustrialization, and the "trend toward more low-paid, temporary, benefit-free, blue and white-collar jobs and fewer decent permanent factory and office jobs" (Aronowitz and De Fazio 1997, 193) caused by the reforms implemented by companies such as IBM must come from those democratic arenas that business seeks to "restructure." Mega corporations will say nothing about their profound role in promoting the flight of capital abroad, the widening gap between intellectual, technical, and manual labor and the growing class of permanently underemployed in a mass of "deskilled" jobs, the growing inequality between the rich and the poor, or the scandalous use of child labor in third world countries. The onus of responsibility is placed on educated citizens to recognize that corporate principles of efficiency, accountability, and profit maximization have not created new jobs but in most cases have eliminated them (Rifkin 1995; Wolman and Colamosca 1997; Aronowitz and DiFazio 1994; Aronowitz and Cutler 1998). My point, of course, is that such absences in public discourse constitute a defining principle of corporate ideology, which refuses to address—and must be made to address—the scarcity of moral vision that inspires such calls for school reform modeled after corporate reforms implemented in the last decade.

But the modeling of higher education after corporate principles and the partnerships they create with the business community do more than reorient the purpose and meaning of higher education; such reforms also instrumentalize the curricula and narrow what it means to extend knowledge to broader social concerns. Business-university partnerships provide just one concrete example of the willingness of both educators and corporate executives to acknowledge the effects such mergers have on the production and dissemination of knowledge in the interest of the public good. Lost in the willingness of schools such as MIT to sell part of their curricula to the corporations is the ethical consequence of ignoring basic science research that benefits humanity as a whole because such research offers little as a profit-maximizing venture. Ralph Nader recently indicated in a nationally broadcast speech on C-Span that one result of such transactions is that the universities are doing far too little to develop anti-malaria and tuberculosis vaccines at a time when these diseases are once again killing large numbers of people in third world countries; such interventions are viewed as non-profitable investments (Nader 1998). Research guided only by the controlling yardstick of profit undermines the role of the university as a public sphere dedicated to addressing the most serious social problems a society faces. Moreover, the corporate model of research instrumentalizes knowledge and undermines forms of theorizing, pedagogy, and meaning that define higher education as a public rather than as a private good.

Missing from much of the corporate discourse on schooling is any analysis of how power works in shaping knowledge, how the teaching of broader social values provides safeguards against turning citizen skills into simply training skills for the work place, or how schooling can help students reconcile the seemingly opposing needs of freedom and solidarity in order to forge a new conception of civic courage and democratic public life. Knowledge as capital in the corporate model is privileged as a form of investment in the economy, but appears to have little value when linked to the power of self-definition, social responsibility, or the capacities of individuals to expand the scope of freedom, justice, and the operations of democracy (West 1990). Knowledge stripped of ethical and political considerations offers limited, if any, insights into how schools should educate students to push against the oppressive boundaries of gender, class, race, and age domination. Nor does such a language provide the pedagogical conditions for students to critically engage knowledge as an ideology deeply implicated in issues and struggles concerning the production of identities, culture, power, and history. Education is a moral and political practice and always presupposes an introduction to and preparation for particular forms of social life, a particular rendering of what community is, and what the future might hold.

If pedagogy is, in part, about the production of identities then curricula modeled after corporate culture have been enormously successful in preparing students for low skilled service work in a society that has little to offer in the way of meaningful employment for the vast majority of its graduates. If CEOs are going to provide some insight into how education should be reformed, they will have to reverse their tendency to collapse the boundaries between corporate culture and civic culture, between a society that defines itself through the interests of corporate power and one that defines itself through more democratic considerations regarding what constitutes substantive citizenship and social responsibility. Moreover, they will have to recognize that the problems with American schools cannot be reduced to matters of accountability or cost-effectiveness. Nor can the solution to such problems be reduced to the spheres of management and economics. The problems of higher education and public schooling must be addressed in the realms of values and politics, while engaging critically the most fundamental beliefs Americans have as a nation regarding the meaning and purpose of education and its relationship to democracy.

Corporate Culture as a Model of Leadership

As universities increasingly model themselves after corporations, it becomes crucial to understand how the principles of corporate culture intersect with the meaning and purpose of the university, the role of knowledge production for the twenty-first century, and the social practices inscribed within teacher-student relationships. The signs are not encouraging.

In many ways, the cost accounting principles of efficiency, calculability, predictability, and control of the corporate order have restructured the meaning and purpose of education. As I have mentioned previously, many deans are now given the title of CEO, academic programs are streamlined to cut costs, and in many colleges new presidents are actively pursuing ways to establish closer ties between their institutions and the business community. For example, *The New York Times* reports, in what has become a typical story, that at George Mason University, a business oriented president has emphasized technology training in order to "boost the university's financing (by the state legislature) by as much as $25-million a year, provided that George Mason cultivates stronger ties with northern Virginia's booming technology industry" (Mangan 1998, A44). In other quarters in higher education, the results of the emergence of the corporate university appear even more ominous. James Carlin, a multimillionaire insurance executive who now serves as the Chairman of the Massachusetts State Board of Education, recently gave a speech to the Greater Boston Chamber of Commerce. In a statement that highlights his ignorance of the recent history and critical mission of higher education, Carlin argued that colleges need to be downsized just as businesses have in the past decade, tenure should be abolished, and that faculty have too much power in shaping decisions in the university. Carlin's conclusion: "At least 50 percent of all non-hard sciences research on American campuses is a lot of foolishness" and should be banned (Honan 1998, 33). Pointing to the rising costs of higher education, he further predicted that "there's going to be a revolution in higher education. Whether you like it or not, it's going to be broken apart and put back together differently. It won't be the same. Why should it be? Why should everything change except for higher education" (Honan 1998, 33)? Carlin's "revolution" has been spelled out in his call for increasing the work load of professors to four three credit courses a semester, effectively reducing the time such educators might have in doing research or shaping institutional power.

There is more at stake in university reform than the realities and harsh principles of cost cutting. Corporate culture in its reincarnation in the 1980s and 1990s appears to have little patience with non-commodified knowledge or with the more lofty ideals that have defined higher education as a public service. Carlin's anti-intellectualism and animosity toward educators and students alike signal that as higher education comes under the influence of corporate ideologies, universities will be largely refashioned in the image of the new multi-conglomerate landscape. One consequence will be an attempt to curtail academic freedom and tenure. As one business-oriented administrator admitted to Bill Tierney in a conversation about tenure, "We have to focus on the priorities of the . . . school and not the individual. We must industrialize the school, and tenure—academic freedom—isn't part of that model" (1997, 17). Missing from this model of leadership is the recognition that academic freedom implies that knowledge has a critical function, that intellectual inquiry that is unpopular and critical should be safeguarded and treated as an important social asset, and that public intellectuals are more than merely functionaries of the corporate order. Such ideals are at odds with the vocational function that corporate culture wants to assign to higher education.

While the appeal to downsizing higher education appears to have caught the public's imagination at the moment, it belies the fact that such "reorganization" has been going on for some time. In fact, more professors are working part-time and at two-year community colleges than at any other time in the country's recent history. Alison Schneider recently pointed out in *The Chronicle of Higher Education* that "in 1970, only 22 per cent of the professoriate worked part time. By 1995, that proportion had nearly doubled to 41 per cent" (1998, A14). Creating a permanent underclass of part-time professional workers in higher education is not only demoralizing and exploitative for many faculty who inhabit such jobs, such policies increasingly de-skill both part and full-time faculty by increasing the amount of work they have to do, while simultaneously shifting power away from the faculty to the managerial sectors of the university. Corporate culture has invested heavily in leadership from the top as evidenced by the huge salaries many CEOs get in this country. For instance, Citigroup CEO, Stanford Weill made $141.6 million in direct compensation in 1998 while the CEO of Tyco International, L. Dennis Kozolowski, was paid $74.4 million (Abelson 1998, 1). Michael Eisner, the CEO of Walt Disney, Inc., is estimated to have received over $1 billion dollars since he arrived at Disney 14 years ago (Bonin 1998, 70). But the price to pay for such a model of leadership appears to undermine even the weakest image of the university as a public space for creating democratic values, critical teaching communities, and equitable work relations.

Held up to the profit standard, universities and colleges will increasingly calibrate supply to demand, and the results look ominous with regard to what forms of knowledge and research will be rewarded and legitimated. In addition, it appears that populations marked by class and racial subordination will have less access to higher education. As globalization and corporate mergers increase, technologies develop, and cost effective practices expand, there will be fewer jobs for certain professionals resulting in the inevitable elevation of admission standards, restriction of student loans, and the reduction of student access to higher education. Stanley Aronowitz argues that the changing nature of intellectual labor, knowledge production, and the emerging glut of professionals on a global scale undermine mass education as the answer to the growing underemployment of the professional classes. He writes:

> Although the media hypes that millions of new jobs require specialized, advanced knowledge and credentials, the bare truth is that technological change, globalization, and relatively slow growth have reduced the demand for certain professionals . . . . And despite the boom of the middle 1990s, chronic shortages of physicians, accountants and attorneys have all but disappeared. In fact, the globalization of intellectual labor is beginning to effect knowledge industries, with Indian and Chinese engineers and computer designers performing work that was once almost exclusively done in North America and western Europe. And do nonscientists really need credentials signifying they have completed a prescribed program to perform most intellectual labor? If jobs are the intended outcome of a credential, there are few arguments for mass higher education. (Aronowitz 1998, 34-35)

Fewer jobs in higher education means fewer students will be enrolled or have access, but it also means that the processes of vocationalization—fueled by corporate values that mimic "flexibility," "competition," or "lean production" and rationalized through the application of accounting principles—pose the threat of gutting many academic departments and programs that cannot translate their subject matter into commercial gains. Programs and courses that focus on areas such as critical theory, literature, feminism, ethics, environmentalism, post-colonialism, philosophy, and sociology suggest an intellectual cosmopolitanism or a concern with social issues that will be either eliminated or technicized because their role in the market will be judged as ornamental. Similarly, those working conditions that allow professors and graduate assistants to comment extensively on student work, provide small seminars, spend time with student advising, conduct independent studies, and do collaborative research with both faculty colleagues and students do not appear consistent with the imperatives of downsizing, efficiency, and cost accounting (Bérubé 1998, B4-B5).

Education and the Imperatives of Democracy

I want to return to an issue I raised in the beginning of this article where I argued that corporations have been given too much power in this society, and hence the need for educators and others to address the threat this poses to all facets of public life organized around the non-commodified principles of justice, freedom, and equality. Challenging the encroachment of corporate power is essential if democracy is to remain a defining principle of education and everyday life. Part of such a challenge necessitates that educators and others create organizations capable of mobilizing civic dialogue, provide an alternative conception of the meaning and purpose of higher education, and develop political organizations that can influence legislation to challenge corporate power's ascendancy over the institutions and mechanisms of civil society. This project requires that educators, students, and others will have to provide the rationale and mobilize the possibility for creating enclaves of resistance, new public cultures for collective development, and institutional spaces that highlight, nourish, and evaluate the tension between civil society and corporate power while simultaneously struggling to prioritize citizen rights over the consumer rights.

In strategic terms, revitalizing public dialogue suggests that educators need to take seriously the importance of defending higher education as an institution of civic culture whose purpose is to educate students for active and critical citizenship. Situated within a broader context of issues concerned with social responsibility, politics, and the dignity of human life, schooling should be defended as a site that offers students the opportunity to involve themselves in the deepest problems of society, to acquire the knowledge, skills, and ethical vocabulary necessary for what Vaclav Havel calls "the richest possible participation in public life" (1998, 45). Educators, parents, legislators, students, and social movements need to come together to defend higher education as indispensable to the life of the nation because they are one of the few public spaces left where students can learn the power of and engage in the experience of democracy. In the face of corporate takeovers, the ongoing commodification of the curriculum, a project requires educators to mount a collective struggle to reassert the crucial importance of higher education in offering students the skills they need for learning how to govern, take risks, and develop the knowledge necessary for deliberation, reasoned arguments, and social action. At issue here is providing students with an education that allows them to recognize the dream and promise of a substantive democracy, particularly the idea that as citizens they are "entitled to public services, decent housing, safety, security, support during hard times, and most importantly, some power over decision making" (Kelley 1997b, 146).

But more is needed than defending higher education as a vital sphere in which to develop and nourish the proper balance between democratic public spheres and commercial power, between identities founded on democratic principles and identities steeped in forms of competitive, self-interested individualism that celebrate their own material and ideological advantages. Given the current assault on educators at all levels of schooling, it is politically crucial that educators at all levels of involvement in the academy be defended as public intellectuals who provide an indispensable service to the nation. Such an appeal cannot be made merely in the name of professionalism but in terms of the civic duty such intellectuals provide. Intellectuals who inhabit our nation's universities represent the conscience of a society because they shape the conditions under which future generations learn about themselves and their relations to others and the world, but also because they engage in pedagogical practices that are by their very nature moral and political, rather than simply technical. And at their best, such pedagogical practices bear witness to the ethical and political dilemmas that animate the broader social landscape. The appeal here is not merely ethical; it is also an appeal that addresses the materiality of power, resources, access, and politics.

Organizing against the corporate takeover of schools also suggests, especially within higher education, fighting to protect the jobs of full-time faculty, turning adjunct jobs into full-time positions, expanding benefits to part-time workers, and putting power into the hands of faculty and students. Moreover, such a struggle must address the exploitative conditions many graduate students work under, constituting a de facto army of service workers who are underpaid, overworked, and shorn of any real power or benefits (Nelson 1997). Similarly remedial programs, affirmative action, and other crucial pedagogical resources are under massive assault, often by conservative trustees who want to eliminate from the university any attempt to address the deep social inequities, while simultaneously denying a decent education to minorities of color and class. Hence, both teachers and students bear the burden of overcrowded classrooms, limited resources, and hostile legislators. Such educators and students need to join with community people and social movements around a common platform that resists the corporatizing of schools, the roll back in basic services, and the exploitation of teaching assistants and adjunct faculty.

In the face of the growing corporatization of schools, progressive educators at all levels of education should organize to establish both a bill of rights identifying and outlining the range of non-commercial relations that can be used to mediate between higher education and the business world, and to create the institutional conditions for administrators, teachers, and students to inhabit non-commodified public spheres that expand the possibilities for knowledge-power relations that are not exclusively instrumental and market driven. If the forces of corporate culture are to be challenged, progressive educators must also enlist the help of diverse communities, local and federal government, and other political forces to insure that public institutions of higher learning are adequately funded so that they will not have to rely on corporate sponsorship and advertising revenues. How our colleges and universities educate students for the future may provide one of the few opportunities for them to link learning to social considerations, public life, and the spirit of democratic life.

The corporatizing of American education reflects a crisis of vision regarding the meaning and purpose of democracy at a time when "market cultures, market moralities, market mentalities [are] shattering community [and] eroding civic society" (West 1994, 42). Yet such a crisis also represents a unique opportunity for progressive educators to expand and deepen the meaning of democracy—radically defined as a struggle to combine the distribution of wealth, income, and knowledge with a recognition and positive valorizing of cultural diversity—by reasserting the primacy of politics, power, and struggle as a pedagogical task (Fraser 1997). Such a responsibility necessitates prioritizing democratic community, citizen rights, and the public good over market relations, narrow consumer demands, and corporate interests. At stake is not merely the future of higher education, but the nature of democracy itself. Democracy is not synonymous with capitalism, and critical citizenship should offer young people more than simply the promise of becoming consuming subjects. Higher education is one important site where educators, students, and administrators can address the tensions between corporate culture and democratic civic culture by asserting the primacy of democracy and civic courage over the logic of capital, consumerism, and commodification.

Notes

1. Stuart Ewen has traced this trend historically to the emergence in the 19th century of the culture of abundance which allowed "for the flowering of a provocative, somewhat passive, conception of democracy . . . consumer democracy" (1988, 12).

2. The classic dominant texts on corporate culture are Terrance Deal and Alan Kennedy (1982) and Thomas Peterson and Robert Waterman (1982). I also want point out that corporate culture is a dynamic, ever-changing force. But in spite of innovations and changes, it rarely if ever challenges the centrality of the profit motive, or fails to prioritize commercial considerations over a set of values that would call class based system of capitalism into question. For a brilliant discussion of the changing nature of corporate culture in light of the Cultural Revolution of the 1960s, see Thomas Frank (1997).

3. There are many books that address this issue, but some of the most helpful providing hard statistical evidence for the growing corporate monopolization of American society can be found in Derber (1998), Hazen and Winokur (1997), McChesney (1997), Barneouw (1997), Wolman and Colamosca (1997).

4. For a context from which to judge the effects of such cuts on the poor and children of America, see Children's Defense Fund (1998).

Works Cited

Abelson, Reed. 1998. "Silicon Valley Aftershocks." *The New York Times*, 4 April, section 3:1.

Aronowitz, Stanley. 1998. "The New Corporate University." *Dollars and Sense* (March/April): 32–35.

Aronowitz, Stanley, and Jonathan Cutler. 1998. *Post-Work*. New York: Routledge.

Aronowitz, Stanley and William DiFazio. 1994. *The Jobless Future*. Minneapolis: University of Minnesota Press.

_____. 1997. "The New Knowledge Work." In *Education: Culture, Economy, Society*, ed. A. H. Halsey, et al. New York: Oxford University Press.

Baran, Paul, and Paul M. Sweezy. 1966. *Monopoly Capital*. New York: Monthly Review Press.

Barneouw, Erik, et al. 1997. *Conglomerates and the Media*. New York: The New Press.

Benhabib, Seyla. 1996. "The Democratic Moment and the Problem of Difference." In *Democracy and Difference*, ed. Seyla Benhabib. Princeton: Princeton University Press.

Bérubé, Michael 1998. "Why Inefficiency is Good for Universities." *The Chronicle of Higher Education*, 27 March, B4–B5.

Bonin, Liane. 1998. Tragic Kingdom. *Detour Magazine*, April, 69–72.

Bryman, Alan. 1995. *Disney and His Worlds*. New York: Routledge.

Children's Defense Fund. 1998. *The State of America's Children—A Report from the Children's Defense Fund*. Boston: Beacon Press.

Deal, Terrance, and Alan Kennedy. 1982. *Corporate Culture: The Rites and Rituals of Corporate Life*. Reading, MA: Addison-Wesley.

Derber, Charles. 1998. *Corporation Nation*. New York: St. Martin's Press.

Dewey, John. 1944. *Democracy and Education*. New York: The Free Press.

Edelman, Peter. 1997. "The Worst Thing Bill Clinton Has Done." *The Atlantic Monthly*, March, 43–58.

Ewen, Stuart. 1988. *All Consuming Images*. New York: Basic Books.

Frank, Thomas. 1997. *The Conquest of Cool*. Chicago: University of Chicago Press.

Fraser, Nancy. 1997. *Justice Interruptus*. New York: Routledge.

Fukuyama, Francis. 1989a. *The End of History and the Last Man*. New York: Free Press.

_____. 1989b. "The End of History." *The National Interest*, Summer, 3–18.

"GMC CEO Pay." 1998. *USA Today*, 21 April, Section Bl.

Gerstner, Louis V. Jr. 1998. "Public Schools Need To Go the Way of Business." *USA Today*, 4 March, 13A.

Hazen, Dan, and Julie Winokur, eds. 1997. *We the Media*. New York: The New Press.

Havel, Vaclav. 1998. "The State of the Republic." *The New York Review of Books* 45.4: 42–46.

Honan, William H. 1998. "The Ivory Tower Under Siege." *The New York Times*, 4 January, Section 4A, 33.

Kelley, Robin D. G. 1997a. *Yo' Mama's Disfunktional: Fighting the Culture Wars in Urban America*. Boston: Beacon Press.

_____. 1997b. "Neo-Cons of the Black Nation." *Black Renaissance Noir* 1.2: 134–46.

Mangan, Katherine S. 1998. "Corporate Know-How Lands Presidencies for a Growing Number of Business Deans." *The Chronicle of Higher Education*, 27 March, A43 A44.

Manegold, Catherine. S. 1994. "Study Says Schools Must Stress Academics." *The New York Times*, 23 September, A22.

McChesney, Robert W. 1997. *Corporate Media and the Threat to Democracy*. New York: Seven Stories Press.

Nader, Ralph. 1998. "Civil Society and Corporate Responsibility." Speech given to the National Press Club, *C-Span* 2, 25 March.

Nelson, Cary. ed. 1997. *Will Teach for Food: Academic Labor in Crisis*. Minneapolis: University of Minnesota Press.

Peterson, Thomas, and Robert Waterman. 1982. *In Search of Excellence*. New York: Harper and Row.

Rifkin, Jeremy. 1995. *The End of Work*. New York: Putnam.

Sidel, Ruth. 1996. *Keeping Women and Children Last*. New York: Penguin.

Schneider, Alison. 1998. "More Professors Are Working Part Time, and More Teach at 2-Year Colleges." *The Chronicle of Higher Education*, 13 March, A14–A16.

Tierney, Bill. 1997. "Tenure and Community in Academe." *Educational Researcher* 26.8: 17–23.

West, Cornel. 1990. "The New Cultural Politics of Difference." October 53: 93–109.

_____. 1994. "America's Three-Fold Crisis." *Tikkun* 9.2: 41–44.

Wolman, William, and Anne Colamosca. 1997. *The Judas Economy*. Reading, MA: Addison-Wesley Publishing Company, Inc.

World Traveler. 1998. March, 76.

CHAPTER 11

Youth, Higher Education, and the Crisis of Public Time

Educated Hope and the Possibility of a Democratic Future

2003

Children are the future of any society. If you want to know the future of a society look at the eyes of the children. If you want to maim the future of any society, you simply maim the children. The struggle for the survival of our children is the struggle for the survival of our future. The quantity and quality of that survival is the measurement of the development of our society.

—Ngũgĩ wa Thiong'o, 1993, p. 76

Youth and the Crisis of the Future

Any discourse about the future has to begin with the issue of youth because more than any other group youth embody the projected dreams, desires, and commitment of a society's obligations to the future. This echoes a classical principle of modernity in which youth both symbolise society's responsibility to the future and offer a measure of its progress. For most of this century, Americans have embraced as a defining feature of politics that all levels of government would assume a large measure of responsibility for providing the resources, social provisions, security, and modes of education that simultaneously offered young people a future as it expanded the meaning and depth of a substantive democracy. In many respects, youth not only registered symbolically the importance of modernity's claim to progress, they also affirmed the importance of the liberal, democratic tradition of the social contract in which adult responsibility was mediated through a willingness to fight for the rights of children, to enact reforms that invested in their future, and to provide the educational conditions necessary for them to make use of the freedoms they have while learning how to be critical citizens. Within such a modernist project, democracy was linked to the well being of youth, while the status of how a society imagined democracy and its future was contingent on how it viewed its responsibility towards future generations.

But the category of youth did more than affirm modernity's social contract rooted in a conception of the future in which adult commitment and intergenerational solidarity were articulated as a vital public service; it also affirmed those vocabularies, values and social relations central to a politics capable of both defending vital institutions as a public good and contributing to the quality of public life. Such a vocabulary was particularly important for higher education, which often defined and addressed its highest ideals through the recognition that how it educated youth was connected to both the democratic future it hoped for and its claim as an important public sphere.

Yet, at the dawn of the new millennium, it is not at all clear that we believe any longer in youth, the future, or the social contract, even in its minimalist version. Since the Reagan/Thatcher revolution of the 1980s, we have been told that there is no such thing as society and, indeed, following that nefarious pronouncement, institutions committed to public welfare have been disappearing ever since. Those of us who, against the prevailing common sense, insist on the relationship between higher education and the future of democracy have to face a disturbing reversal in priorities with regard to youth and education, which now defines the United States and other regions under the reign of neoliberalism.[1] Rather than being cherished as a symbol of the future, youth are now seen as a threat to be feared and a problem to be contained. A seismic change has taken place in which youth are now being framed as both a generation of suspects and a threat to public life. If youth once symbolised the moral necessity to address a range of social and economic ills, they are now largely portrayed as the source of most of society's problems. Hence, youth now constitute a crisis that has less to do with improving the future than with denying it. A concern for children is the defining absence in almost any discourse about the future and the obligations this implies for adult society. To witness the abdication of adult responsibility to children we need look no further than the current state of children in America who once served as a "kind of symbolic guarantee that America still had a future, which it still believed in, and that it was crucial to America to invest in that future" (Grossberg, 2001, p. 133).

No longer "viewed as a privileged sign and embodiment of the future" (p. 133), youth are now demonised by the popular media and derided by politicians looking for quick-fix solutions to crime, joblessness, and poverty. In a society deeply troubled by their presence, youth prompt a public rhetoric of fear, control, and surveillance, which translates into social policies that signal the shrinking of democratic public spheres, the hijacking of civic culture, and the increasing militarisation of public space. Equipped with police and drug sniffing dogs, though not necessarily teachers or textbooks, public schools increasingly resemble prisons. Students begin to look more like criminal suspects who need to be searched, tested, and observed under the watchful eye of administrators who appear to be less concerned with educating them than with containing their every move. Nurturance, trust, and respect now give way to fear, disdain, and suspicion. In many suburban malls, young people, especially urban youth of colour, cannot shop or walk around without having appropriate identification cards or being in the company of a parent. Children have fewer rights than almost any other group and fewer institutions protecting these rights. Consequently, their voices and needs are almost completely absent from the debates, policies, and legislative practices that are constructed in terms of their needs.

Instead of providing a decent education to poor young people, American society offers them the growing potential of being incarcerated, buttressed by the fact that the US is one of the few countries in the world that sentences minors to death and spends "three times more on each incarcerated citizen than on each public school pupil" (Wokusch, 2002). Instead of guaranteeing them decent schools and a critical education, we house too many of our young people in dilapidated buildings and serve them more standardised tests; instead of providing them with vibrant public spheres, we offer them a commercialised culture in which consumerism is the only obligation of citizenship. But in the hard currency of human suffering, children pay a heavy price in one of the richest democracies in the world: 20 percent of children are poor during the first three years of life and more than 13.3 million live in poverty; 9.2 million children lack health insurance; millions lack affordable child care and decent early childhood education; in many states more money is being spent on prison construction than on education; the infant mortality rate in the United States is the highest of any other industrialised nation. When broken down along racial categories, the figures become even more despairing. For example, "In 1998, 36 percent of black and 34 percent of Hispanic children lived in poverty, compared with 14 percent of white children".[2] In some cities, such as the District of Columbia, the child poverty rate is as high as 45 percent.[3] While the United States ranks first in military technology, military exports, defence expenditures and the number of millionaires and billionaires, it is ranked 18th among the advanced industrial nations in the gap between rich and poor children, 12th in the percentage of children in poverty, 17th in the efforts to lift children out of poverty, and 23rd in infant mortality.[4] One of the most shameful figures on youth as reported by Jennifer Egan, a writer for *The New York Times*, indicates that "1.4 million children are homeless in America for a time in any given year ... and these children make up 40 percent of the nation's homeless population" (2002, p. 35). In short, economically, politically and culturally, the situation of youth in the United States is intolerable and obscene. It is all the more unforgivable since President Bush insisted during the 2000 campaign that "the biggest percentage of our budget should go to children's education". He then passed a 2002 budget in which 40 times more money went for tax cuts for the wealthiest 1 percent of the population than for education (Wokusch, 2002, p. 1). But Bush's insensitivity to American children represents more than a paean to the rich since he also passed a punitive welfare reform bill that requires poor, young mothers to work a 40-hour week while at the same time cutting low-income childcare programmes. It gets worse.

While the United States government aims to spend up to 400 billion dollars on defence, not including the additional 75 billion dollars it has requested to wage a war against Iraq, it allocates only 16 billion dollars to welfare. At the same time that it has passed tax cuts amounting to 723 billion dollars, 50 per cent of which will go to the richest 1 percent of the population, it is slashing 14.6 billion dollars in benefits for veterans, 93 billion in Medicaid cuts, and promoting cuts in student loans, education programmes, school lunches, food stamps, and cash assistance for the elderly, poor, and disabled (see Kuttner, 2003; Ivins, 2003).

Youth have become the central site onto which class and racial anxieties are projected. Their very presence in an age where there is no such thing as society represents both the broken promises of democracy and the violation of a social contract that traditionally at least offered young people the right to decent food, education, health, employment, and other crucial rights fundamental to their survival, dignity, and a decent future. Corporate deregulation and downsizing and a collective fear of the consequences wrought by systemic class inequalities, racism, and a culture of "infectious greed" have created a generation of displaced and unskilled youth who have been expelled from the "universe of moral obligations" (Bauman, 1999a, p. 77). Youth within the economic, political, and cultural geography of neoliberal capitalism occupy a degraded borderland in which the spectacle of commodification exists side by side with the imposing threat of the prison-industrial complex and the elimination of basic civil liberties. As neoliberalism disassociates economics from its social costs, "the political state has become the corporate state" (Hertz, 2001, p. 11). Under such circumstances, the state does not disappear, but, as Pierre Bourdieu has brilliantly reminded us (Bourdieu, 1998; Bourdieu et al., 1999), is refigured as its role in providing social provisions, intervening on behalf of public welfare, and regulating corporate plunder is weakened. The neo-liberal state no longer invests in solving social problems, it now punishes those who are caught in the downward spiral of its economic policies. Punishment, incarceration, and surveillance represent the face of the new state. One consequence is that the implied contract between the state and citizens is broken and social guarantees for youth as well as civic obligations to the future vanish from the agenda of public concern. Similarly, as market values supplant civic values, it becomes increasingly difficult "to translate private worries into public issues and, conversely, to discern public issues in private troubles" (Bauman, 1999b, p. 2). Alcoholism, homelessness, poverty and illiteracy, among other issues, are not seen as social but as individual problems—matters of character, individual fortitude, and personal responsibility. In light of the increased antiterrorism campaign waged by the Bush administration, it becomes easier to militarise domestic space, criminalise social problems, and escape from the responsibilities of the present while destroying all possibilities of a truly democratic future. Moreover, the social costs of the complex cultural and economic operations of this assault can no longer be ignored by educators, parents, and other concerned citizens.

The war against youth, in part, can be understood within those fundamental values and practices that characterise a rapacious, neoliberal capitalism. For many young people and adults today, the private sphere has become the only space in which to imagine any sense of hope, pleasure, or possibility. Culture as an activity in which people actually produce the conditions of their own agency through dialogue, community participation, resistance and political struggle is being replaced by a "climate of cultural and linguistic privatization" (Klein, 1999, p. 177) in which culture becomes something you consume and the only kind of speech that is acceptable is that of the savvy shopper. Neoliberalism, with its emphasis on market forces and profit margins, narrows the legitimacy of the public sphere by redefining it around the related issues of privatisation, deregulation, consumption, and safety. Big government, recalled from exile after September 11th, is now popularly presented as a guardian of security—security not in terms of providing adequate social provisions or a social safety net, but with increasing the state's role as a policing force. The new emphasis on national security has resulted in the ongoing abridgement of basic freedoms and dissent, the criminalisation of social problems, and the prioritising of penal methods over social investments. Ardent consumers and disengaged citizens provide fodder for a growing cynicism and depoliticisation of public life at a time when there is an increasing awareness not just of corporate corruption, financial mismanagement, and systemic greed but also of the recognition that a democracy of critical citizens is being replaced quickly by an ersatz democracy of consumers. The desire to protect market freedoms and wage a war against terrorism at home and against Iraq abroad ironically has not only ushered in a culture of fear but has also dealt a lethal blow to civil freedoms. Resting in the balance of this contradiction is both the fate of democracy and the civic health and future of a generation of children and young people.

Under this insufferable climate of increased repression and unabated exploitation, young people become the new casualties in an ongoing war against justice, freedom, citizenship, and democracy. What is happening to children in America and what are its implications for addressing the future of higher education? Lawrence Grossberg argues that "the current rejection of childhood as the core of our social identity is, at the same time, a rejection of the future as an affective investment" (2001, p. 133). But the crisis of youth not only signals a dangerous state of affairs for the future, it also portends a crisis in the very idea of the political and ethical constitution of the social and the possibility of articulating the relevance of democracy itself; it is in reference to the crisis of youth, the social, and democracy that I want to address the relationship between higher education and the future.

Higher Education and the Crisis of the Social

There is a prominent educational tradition in the United States extending from Thomas Jefferson and W.E.B. Dubois to John Dewey and C. Wright Mills in which the future of the university is premised on the recognition that in order for freedom to flourish in the worldly space of the public realm, citizens had to be educated for the task of self-government. John Dewey, for example, argued that higher education should provide the conditions for people to involve themselves in the deepest problems of society, to acquire the knowledge, skills, and ethical responsibility necessary for "reasoned participation in democratically organised publics".[5] C. Wright Mills (1963) challenged schooling as a form of corporate training and called for fashioning higher education within a public philosophy committed to a radical conception of citizenship, civic engagement, and public wisdom. Education in this context was linked to public life through democratic values such as equality, justice, and freedom, rather than as an adjunct of the corporation whose knowledge and values were defined largely through the prism of commercial interests. Education was crucial to a notion of individual agency and public citizenship, integral to defending the relationship between an autonomous society—rooted in an ever-expanding process of self-examination, critique, and reform—and autonomous individuals, for whom critical inquiry is propelled by the need to engage in an ongoing pursuit of ethics and justice as a matter of public good. In many ways, higher education has been faithful, at least in theory, to a project of modern politics, whose purpose was to create citizens capable of defining and implementing universal goals such as freedom, equality, and justice as part of a broader attempt to deepen the relationship between an expanded notion of the social and the enabling ground of a vibrant democracy.

Within the last two decades a widespread pessimism about public life and politics has developed in the United States. Individual interests now outweigh collective concerns as market ideals have taken precedence over democratic values. Moreover, the ethos of citizenship has been stripped of its political dimensions and is now reduced to the obligations of consumerism. In the vocabulary of neoliberalism, the public collapses into the personal, and the personal becomes "the only politics there is, the only politics with a tangible referent or emotional valence" (Comaroff and Comaroff, 2000, pp. 305–6), and it is within such an utterly personal discourse that human actions are shaped and agency is privatised. Under neoliberalism, hope becomes dystopian as the public sphere disappears and, as Peter Beilharz argues, "politics becomes banal, for there is not only an absence of citizenship but a striking absence of agency" (2000, p. 160). As power is increasingly separated from the specificity of traditional politics and public obligations, corporations are less subject to the control of the state and "there is a strong impulse to displace political sovereignty with the sovereignty of the market, as if the latter has a mind and morality of its own" (Comaroff and Comaroff, 2000, p. 332). Under the auspices of neoliberalism, the language of the social is either devalued or ignored altogether as the idea of the public sphere is equated with a predatory space, rife with danger and disease—as in reference to public restrooms, public transportation, and urban public schools. Dreams of the future are now modelled on the narcissistic, privatised, and self-indulgent needs of consumer culture and the dictates of the alleged free market. Mark Taylor, a social critic turned apologist for the alleged free market, both embodies and captures the sentiment well with his comment:

Insofar as you want to engage in practice responsibly, you have to play with the hand you're
dealt. And the hand we're dealt seems to me to be one in which the market has certainly won
out over other kinds of systems. (Traub, 2000, p. 93)

There is more at stake here than another dominant media story about a left academic
who finally sees the entrepreneurial halo. The narrative points to something much
larger. Samuel Weber has suggested that what seems to be involved in this transformation is "a fundamental and political redefinition of the social value of public
services in general, and of universities and education in particular" (cited in Simon,
2001, pp. 47–48).

Within this impoverished sense of politics and public life, the university is gradually being transformed into a training ground for the corporate workforce, rendering obsolete any notion of higher education as a crucial public sphere in which
critical citizens and democratic agents are formed. As universities become increasingly strapped for money, corporations provide the needed resources for research
and funds for endowed chairs, exerting a powerful influence on both the hiring of
faculty, and how research is conducted and for what purposes. In addition, universities now offer up buildings and stadiums as billboards for brand name corporations
in order to procure additional sources of revenue while also adopting the values,
management styles, cost-cutting procedures, and the language of excellence that
has been the hallmark of corporate culture. Under the reign of neoliberalism and
corporate culture, the boundaries between commercial culture and public culture
become blurred as universities rush to embrace the logic of industrial management
while simultaneously forfeiting those broader values both central to a democracy
and capable of limiting the excesses of corporate power. Although the university has
always had ties to industry, there is a new intimacy between higher education and
corporate culture, characterised by what Larry Hanley calls a "new, quickened sym-
biosis" (2001, p. 103). As Masao Miyoshi points out, the result is "not a fundamental or abrupt change perhaps, but still an unmistakable radical reduction of its public
and critical role" (1998, p. 263). What was once the hidden curriculum of many
universities, "the subordination of higher education to capital" has now become
an open and much celebrated policy of both public and private higher education
(Aronowitz, 1998a, p. 32). How do we understand the university in light of both
the crisis of youth and the related crisis of the social that have emerged under the
controlling hand of neoliberalism? How can the future be grasped given the erosion
of the social and public life over the last twenty years? What are the implications
for the simultaneous corporatisation of higher education in light of these dramatic
changes? Any concern about the future of the university has to both engage and
challenge this transformation while reclaiming the role of the university as a democratic public sphere. In what follows, I want to analyse the university as a corporate
entity within the context of a crisis of the social. In particular, I will focus on how
this crisis is played out not only through the erosion of public space, but through

the less explained issues of public versus corporate time, on the one hand, and the related issues of agency, pedagogy, and public mission, on the other.

Public Time versus Corporate Time

Questions of time are crucial to how a university structures its public mission, the role of faculty, the use of space, student access, and the legitimation of particular forms of knowledge, research, and pedagogy. Time is not simply a question of how to invoke the future, but is also used to legitimate particular social relations and make claims on human behaviour, representing one of the most important battlefields for determining how the future of higher education is played out in political and ethical terms. Time refers not only to the way in which temporality is mediated differently by institutions, administrators, faculty and students, but also how it shapes and allocates power, identities and space through a particular set of codes and interests. But more importantly time is a central feature of politics and orders not merely the pace of the economic, but the time available for consideration, contemplation, and critical thinking. When reduced to a commodity, time often becomes the enemy of deliberation and thoughtfulness and undermines the ability of political culture to function critically.

For the past twenty years, time as a value and the value of time have been redefined through the dictates of neoliberal economics, which has largely undermined any notion of public time guided by non-commodified values central to a political and social democracy. As Peter Beilharz observes,

> time has become our enemy. The active society demands of us that we keep moving, keep con-suming, experience everything, travel, work as good tourists more than act as good citizens, work, shop, and die. To keep moving is the only way left in our cultural repertoire to push away ... meaning ... [and consequently] the prospects, and forms of social solidarity available to us shrink before our eyes. (2000, p. 161)

Without question, the future of the university will largely rest on the outcome of the current struggle between the university as a public space with the capacity to slow time down in order to question what Jacques Derrida calls the powers that limit "a democracy to come" (2000, p. 9) and a corporate university culture wedded to a notion of accelerated time in which the principle of self-interest replaces politics and consumerism replaces a broader notion of social agency. A meaningful and inclusive democracy is indebted to a notion of public time, while neoliberalism celebrates what I call corporate time. In what follows, I want to comment briefly on some of the theoretical and political work performed by each of these notions of time and the implications they have for addressing the future of higher education. Public time as a condition and critical referent makes visible how politics is played out through the unequal access different groups have to "institutions, goods, services, resources, and power and knowledge" (Hanchard, 1999, p. 253). That is, it offers a critical category for understanding how the ideological and institutional mechanisms of higher education work to grant time to some faculty and students and to withhold it from others, how time is mediated differently within different disciplines and among diverse faculty and students, how time can work across the canvas of power and space to create new identities and social formations capable of "intervening in public debate for the purpose of affecting positive change in the overall position and location in society" (Hanchard, 1999, p. 256). When linked to issues of power, identity, ideology, and politics, public time can be an important social construct for orientating the university towards a vision of the future in which critical learning becomes central to increasing the scope of human rights, individual freedom, and the operations of a substantive democracy. In this instance, public time resonates with a project of leadership, teaching, and learning in which higher education seems an important site for investing democratic public life with substance and vibrancy.

Public time rejects the fever-pitch appeals of 'just in time' or 'speed time', demands often made within the context of "ever faster technological transformation and exchange" (Bind, 2000, p. 52), and buttressed by corporate capital's golden rule: 'time is money'. Public time slows time down, not as a simple refusal of technological change or a rejection of all calls for efficiency but as an attempt to create the institutional and ideological conditions that promote long-term analyses, historical reflection, and deliberations over what our collective actions might mean for shaping the future. Rejecting an instrumentality that evacuates questions of history, ethics, and justice, public time fosters dialogue, thoughtfulness, and critical exchange. Public time offers room for knowledge that contributes to society's self-understanding, that enables it to question itself, and seeks to legitimate intellectual practices that are not only collective and non-instrumental but deepen democratic values while encouraging pedagogical relations that question the future in terms that are political, ethical, and social. As Cornelius Castoriadis points out, public time puts into question established institutions and dominant authority, rejecting any notion of the social that either eliminates the question of judgment or "conceals ... the question of responsibility". Rather than maintaining a passive attitude towards power, public time demands and encourages forms of political agency based on a passion for self-governing, actions informed by critical judgment, and a commitment to linking social responsibility and social transformation. Public time legitimates those pedagogical practices that provide the basis for a culture of questioning, one that enables the knowledge, skills, and social practices necessary for resistance, a space of translation, and a proliferation of discourses. Public time unsettles common sense and disturbs authority while encouraging critical and responsible leadership. As Roger Simon observes, public time

> presents the question of the social—not as a space for the articulation of pre-formed visions
> through which to mobilise action, but as the movement in which the very question of the

possibility of democracy becomes the frame within which a necessary radical learning (and questioning) is enabled. (Simon, 2002, p. 4)

Put differently, public time affirms a politics without guarantees and a notion of the social that is open and contingent. Public time also provides a conception of democracy that is never complete and determinate but constantly open to different understandings of the contingency of its decisions, mechanisms of exclusions, and operations of power (Critchley, 2002). Public time challenges neoliberalism's willingness to separate the economic from the social as well as its failure to address human needs and social costs.

At its best, public time renders governmental power explicit, and in doing so it rejects the language of religious rituals and the abrogation of the conditions necessary for the assumption of basic freedoms and rights. Moreover, public time considers civic education the basis, if not the essential dimension, of justice because it provides individuals with the skills, knowledge, and passions to talk back to power while simultaneously emphasising both the necessity to question that accompanies viable forms of political agency and the assumption of public responsibility through active participation in the very process of governing. Expressions of public time in higher education can be found in shared notions of governance between faculty and administration, in modes of academic labour that encourage forms of collegiality tied to vibrant communities of exchange and democratic values, and in pedagogical relations in which students do not just learn about democracy but experience it through a sense of active participation, critical engagement, and social responsibility. The notion of public time has a long history in higher education and has played a formative role in shaping some of the most important principles of academic life. Public time, in this instance, registers the importance of pedagogical practices that provide the conditions for a culture of questioning in which teachers and students engage in critical dialogue and unrestricted discussion in order to affirm their role as social agents, inspect their own past, and engage the consequences of their own actions in shaping the future.

As higher education becomes increasingly corporatised, public time is replaced by *corporate time*. In corporate time, the market is viewed as a "master design for all affairs" (Rule, 1998, p. 30), profit-making becomes the defining measure of responsibility, and consumption is the privileged site for determining value between the self and the larger social order. Corporate time fosters a narrow sense of leadership, agency, and public values and is largely indifferent to those concerns that are critical to a just society but are not commercial in nature. The values of hierarchy, materialism, competition, and excessive individualism are enshrined under corporate time and play a defining role in how it allocates space, manages the production of particular forms of knowledge, and regulates pedagogical relations. Hence, it is not surprising that corporate time accentuates privatised and competitive modes of intellectual activity, largely removed from public obligations and social responsibilities. Divested of any

viable democratic notion of the social, corporate time measures relationships, productivity, space, and knowledge according to the dictates of cost efficiency, profit, and
a market-based rationality. Time, within this framework, is accelerated rather than
slowed down and reconfigures academic labour, increasingly through, though not
limited to, new computer generated technologies which are making greater demands
on faculty time, creating larger teaching loads, and producing bigger classes. Under
corporate time, speed controls and organises place, space, and communication as a
matter of quantifiable calculation. And as Peter Euben observes, under such circumstances a particular form of rationality emerges as common sense:

> When speed rules so does efficient communication. Calculation and logic are in, moral imag-
> ination and reasoned emotions are out. With speed at a premium, shorthand, quantification
> and measurements become dominant modes of thought. Soon we will talk in clichés and call
> it common sense and wisdom. (Euben, 2000, p. 8)

Corporate time maps faculty relationships through self-promoting market agendas and narrow definitions of self-interest. Caught on the treadmill of getting more
grants, teaching larger classes, and producing more revenue for the university, faculty become another casualty of a business ideology that attempts to "extract labour
from campus workers at the lowest possible cost, one willing to sacrifice research
independence and integrity for profit" (Nelson, 2002, p. 717). Under corporatisation, time is accelerated and fragmented. Overworked and largely isolated, faculty
are now rewarded for intellectual activities privileged as entrepreneurial, "measured
largely in the capacity to transact and consume" (Comaroff and Comaroff, 2000,
p. 30). Faculty are asked to spend more time in larger classrooms while they are
simultaneously expected to learn and use new instructional technologies such as
Power Point, the Web, and various multimedia pedagogical activities. Faculty now
interact with students not only in their classes and offices, but also in chat rooms
and through e-mail.

Grounded in the culture of competitiveness and self-interest, corporate time
reworks faculty loyalties. Faculty interaction is structured less around collective solidarities built upon practices that offer a particular relationship to public life than
through corporate imposed rituals of competition and production that conform to
the "narrowly focused ideas of the university as a support to the economy" (Sharp,
2002, p. 280). For instance, many universities are now instituting post-tenure review
as an alleged measure of faculty accountability and an efficient way to eliminate
'deadwood' professors. As Ben Agger points out, what is "especially pernicious is
the fact that faculty are supposed to axe their own colleagues, thus pitting them
against each other and destroying whatever remains of the fabric of academic community and mutuality" (2002, p. 444).

Corporate time also fragments time by redefining academic labour "as part-time
labour versus academic work as full-time commitment and career" (Rhoades, 2001,

p. 143). Under such conditions, faculty solidarities are weakened ever more as corporate time evokes cost-efficient measures by outsourcing instruction to part-time faculty who are underpaid, overworked, denied health benefits, and deprived of any power to shape the conditions under which they work. As Cary Nelson observes,

> As the university citadel of reason has gradually evolved into the campus sweatshop, this instrumentalized view of human beings has become ever more prevalent in higher education. Universities increasingly employ people without health care, without job security, without fundamental rights to due process, and at salaries below a living wage. Administrators increasingly view many of their employees as expendable. (2003, p. 144)

Powerlessness breeds resentment and anger among part-time faculty, and fear and insecurity among full-time faculty, who no longer believe that their tenure is secure. Hence, the divide between part- and full-time faculty is reproduced by the heavy hand of universities as they downsize and outsource under the rubric of fiscal responsibility and accountability, especially in a post 9-11 era. But more is reproduced than structural dislocations among faculty. There is also a large pool of crippling fear, insecurity, and resentment that makes it difficult for faculty to take risks, forge bonds of solidarity, engage in social criticism, and perform as public intellectuals rather than as technicians in the service of corporate largesse.

Leadership under the reign of corporate culture and corporate time has been rewritten as a form of homage to business models of governance. As Stanley Aronowitz points out, "Today ... leaders of higher education wear the badge of corporate servants proudly" (1998, p. 32). Gone are the days when university presidents were hired for intellectual status and public roles. College presidents are now labelled as Chief Executive Officers, and are employed primarily because of their fundraising abilities. Deans of various colleges are often pulled from the ranks of the business world and pride themselves on the managerial logic and cost-cutting plans they adopt from the corporate cultures of Microsoft, Disney, and IBM. Bill Gates and Michael Eisner replace John Dewey and Robert Hutchins as models of educational leadership. Rather than defend the public role of the university, academic freedom, and worthy social causes, the new corporate heroes of higher education now focus their time on selling off university services to private contractors, forming partnerships with local corporations, searching for new patent and licensing agreements, and urging faculty to engage in research and grants that generate external funds. Under this model of leadership the university is being transformed from a place to think to a place to imagine stock options and profit windfalls.

Corporate time provides a new framing mechanism for faculty relations and modes of production and suggests a basic shift in the role of the intellectual. Academics now become less important as a resource to provide students with the knowledge and skills they need to engage the future as a condition of democratic possibilities. In the 'new economy', they are entrepreneurs who view the future as an investment opportunity and research as a private career opportunity rather than as a civic and collective effort to improve the public good. Increasingly academics find themselves being deskilled as they are pressured to teach more service orientated and market based courses and devote less time to their roles either as well-informed, public intellectuals or as "cosmopolitan intellectuals situated in the public sphere" (Agger, 2002, p. 444).

Corporate time not only transforms the university as a democratic public sphere into a space for training while defining faculty as market orientated producers, it also views students as customers, potential workers, and as a source of revenue. As customers, students "are conceptualised in terms of their ability to pay ... and the more valued customers are those who can afford to pay more" (Rhoades, 2001, p. 122). One consequence, as Gary Rhoades points out, is that student access to higher education is "now shaped less by considerations of social justice than of revenue potential" (2001, p. 122). Consequently, those students who are poor and under-serviced are increasingly denied access to the benefits of higher education. Of course, the real problem, as Cary Nelson observes is not merely one of potential decline, but "long term and continuing failure to offer all citizens, especially minorities of class and colour, equal educational opportunities" (Nelson, 2002, p. 713), a failure that has been intensified under the authority of the corporate university. As a source of revenue, students are now subjected to higher fees and tuition costs, and are bombarded by brand name corporations that either lease space on the university commons to advertise their goods or run any one of a number of student services from the dining halls to the university bookstore. Almost every aspect of public space in higher education is now designed to attract students as consumers and shoppers, constantly subjecting them to forms of advertisements mediated by the rhythms of corporate time which keep students moving through a marketplace of brand name products rather than ideas. Such hyper-commercialised spaces increasingly resemble malls, transforming all available university space into advertising billboards, and bringing home the message that the most important identity available to students is that of a consuming subject. As the line between public and commercial space disappears, the gravitational pull of Taco Bell, McDonald's, Starbucks, Barnes and Noble, American Express, and Nike, among others, creates a "geography of nowhere" (taken from Kunstler, 1993), a consumer placelessness in which all barriers between a culture of critical ideas and branded products simply disappear.[6] Education is no longer merely a monetary exchange in which students buy an upscale, lucrative career, it is also an experience designed to evacuate any broader, more democratic notion of citizenship, the social, and the future that students may wish to imagine, struggle over, and enter. In corporate time, students are disenfranchised "as future citizens and reconstitute[d] ... as no more than consumers and potential workers" (Williams, 2001, p. 23).

Corporate time not only translates faculty as multinational operatives and students as sources of revenue and captive consumers, it also makes a claim on how knowledge is valued, how the classroom is to be organised, and how pedagogy is defined. Knowledge under corporate time is valued as a form of capital. As Michael Peters observes, entire disciplines and bodies of knowledge are now either valued or devalued on the basis of their "ability to attract global capital and ... potential for serving transnational corporations. Knowledge is valued for its strict utility rather than as an end in itself or for its emancipatory effects" (Peters, 2002, p. 148). Good value for students means taking courses labelled as 'relevant' in market terms, which are often counterposed to courses in the social sciences, humanities, and the fine arts which are concerned with forms of learning that do not readily translate into either private gain or commercial value. Under the rule of corporate time, the classroom is no longer a public sphere concerned with issues of justice, critical learning, or the knowledge and skills necessary for civic engagement. As training replaces education, the classroom, along with pedagogy itself, is transformed as a result of the corporate restructuring of the university.

As the structure and content of education change, intellectual and pedagogical practices are less identified with providing the conditions for students to learn how to think critically, hold institutional authority accountable for its actions, and act in ways that further democratic ideals. Rather than providing the knowledge and skills for asserting the primacy of the political, social responsibility, and the ethical as central to preparing students for the demands of an inclusive democracy, intellectual practice is subordinated to managerial, technological, and commercial considerations. Not only are classroom knowledge and intellectual practice bought and traded as marketable commodities, but they are also defined largely within what Zygmunt Bauman calls "the culture of consumer society, which is more about forgetting [than] learning" (1998b, p. 81). That is, forgetting that knowledge can be emancipatory, that citizenship is not merely about being a consumer, and that the future cannot be sacrificed to ephemeral pleasures and values of the market. When education is reduced to training, the meaning of self-government is devalued and democracy is rendered meaningless.

What is crucial to recognise in the rise of corporate time is that while it acknowledges that higher education should play a crucial role in offering the narratives that frame society, it presupposes that faculty in particular will play a different role and assume a "different relation to the framing of cultural reality" (Sharp, 2002, p. 275). Many critics have pointed to the changing nature of governance and management structures in the university as a central force in redefining the relationship of the university to the larger society, but little has been said about how the changing direction of the university impacts on the nature of academic activity and intellectual relations (see Sharp, 2002, and Hinkson, 2002, pp. 233–67). While at one level, the changing nature of the institution suggests greater control of academic life by administrators and an emerging class of managerial professionals, it also points to the privileging of those intellectuals in the techno-sciences whose services are indispensable to corporate power, while recognising information as the reigning commodity of the new economy. Academic labour is now prized for how it fuses with capital, rather than how it contributes to what Sharp calls "society's self-understanding" (Sharp, 2002, pp. 284–85). The changing institutional and social forms of the university reject the elitist and reclusive models of intellectual practice that traditionally have refused to bridge the gap between higher education and the larger social order, theory and practice, the academic and the public. Within the corporate university, transformation rather than contemplation is now a fundamental principle for judging and rewarding intellectual practice. Removed from matters of either social justice or democratic possibilities, transformation is defined through a notion of the social that is entirely rooted in privileging the material interests of the market. Higher education's need for new sources of funding neatly dovetails with the inexhaustible need on the part of corporations for new products. Within this symbiotic relationship, knowledge is directly linked to its application in the market, mediated by a collapse of the distinction between knowledge and the commodity. Knowledge has become capital to invest in the market but has little to do with the power of self-definition, civic commitments, or ethical responsibilities that "require an engagement with the claims of others" (Couldry, 2001, p. 17) and with questions of justice. At the same time, the conditions for scholarly work are being transformed through technologies that eliminate face-to-face contact, speed up the labour process, and define social exchange in terms that are more competitive, instrumental, and removed from face-to-face contact.

Electronic, digital, and image-based technologies shape notions of the social in ways that were unimaginable a decade ago. Social exchanges can now proceed without the presence of 'real' bodies. Contacts among faculty and between teachers and students are increasingly virtual, yet these practices profoundly delineate the nature of the social in instrumental, abstract, and commodified terms. As Hinkson and Sharp have pointed out, these new intellectual practices and technological forms are redefining the nature of the social in higher education in ways in which the free sharing of ideas and cooperativeness as democratic and supportive forms of collegiality seem to be disappearing among faculty (Hinkson, 2002, pp. 233–67). This is not just an issue that can be taken up strictly as an assault on academic labour, it also raises fundamental questions about where those values that support democratic forms of solidarity, sharing, dialogue, and mutual understanding are to be found in university life. This is an especially important issue since such values serve as a "condition for the development of intellectual practices devoted to public service" (Hinkson, 2002 p. 259). Within these new forms of instrumental framing and intellectual practice, the ethic of public service that once received some support in higher education is being eliminated and with it those intellectual relations, scholarly practices, and forms of collegiality that leave some room for addressing a democratic and less commodified notion of the social.

In opposition to this notion of corporate time, instrumentalised intellectual practices, and a deracinated view of the social, I want to reassert the importance of academic social formations that view the university as a site of struggle and resistance.

Central to such a challenge is the necessity to define intellectual practice "as part of an intricate web of morality, rigor and responsibility" (Roy, 2001, p. 6) that enables academics to speak with conviction, enter the public sphere in order to address important social problems, and demonstrate alternative models for what it means to bridge the gap between higher education and the broader society. This is a notion of intellectual practice that refuses both the instrumentality and privileged isolation of the academy, while affirming a broader vision of learning that links knowledge to the power of self-definition and the capacities of administrators, academics, and students to expand the scope of democratic freedoms, particularly as they address the crisis of the social as part and parcel of the crisis of both youth and democracy itself. Implicit in this notion of social and intellectual practice is a view of academics as public intellectuals. Following Said, I am referring to those academics who engage in intellectual practices that interpret and question power rather than merely consolidate it, enter into the public sphere in order to alleviate human suffering, make the connections of power visible, and work individually and collectively to create the pedagogical and social conditions necessary for what the late Bourdieu has called "realist utopias".[7] I want to conclude this essay by taking up how the role of both the university as a democratic public sphere and the function of academics as public intellectuals can be further enabled through what I call a politics of educated hope.

Towards a Politics of Educated Hope

If the rise of the corporate university is to be challenged, educators and others need to reclaim the meaning and purpose of higher education as an ethical and political response to the demise of democratic public life. At stake here is the need to insist on the role of the university as a public sphere committed to deepening and expanding the possibilities of democratic identities, values, and relations. This approach suggests new models of leadership based on the understanding that the real purpose of higher education means encouraging people to think beyond the task of simply getting a lucrative job. Beyond this ever-narrowing instrumental justification there is the more relevant goal of opening higher education up to all groups, creating a critical citizenry, providing specialised work skills for jobs that really require them, democratising relations of governance among administrators, faculty, and students, and taking seriously the imperative to disseminate an intellectual and artistic culture. Higher education may be one of the few sites left in which students learn how to mediate critically between democratic values and the demands of corporate power, between identities founded on democratic principles and identities steeped in forms of competitive, atomistic individualism that celebrate self-interest, profit-making, and greed. This view suggests that higher education be defended through intellectual work that self-consciously recalls the tension between the democratic imperatives and possibilities of public institutions and their everyday realisation within a society dominated by market principles. Morrison is right in arguing that

If the university does not take seriously and rigorously its role as a guardian of wider civic freedoms, as interrogator of more and more complex ethical problems, as servant and pre-server of deeper democratic practices, then some other regime or menage of regimes will do it for us, in spite of us, and without us. (Morrison, 2001, p. 278)

Only if this struggle is taken seriously by educators and others can the university be reclaimed as a space of debate, discussion, and at times dissidence. Within such a pedagogical space, time can be unconditionally apportioned to what Cornelius Castoriadis calls "an unlimited interrogation in all domains" (Castoriadis, 1997a, p. 343) of society, especially with regards to the operations of dominant authority and power and the important issues that shape public life, practices ultimately valued for their contribution to the unending process of democratisation.

Higher education should be defended as a form of civic education where teachers and students have the chance to resist and rewrite those modes of pedagogy, time, and rationality that refuse to include questions of judgment and issues of responsibility. Understood as such, higher education is viewed neither as a consumer driven product nor as a form of training and career preparation but as a mode of critical education that renders all individuals fit "to participate in power...to the greatest extent possible, to participate in a common government" (Castoriadis, 1991a, p. 140), to be capable, as Aristotle reminds us, of both governing and being governed. If higher education is to bring democratic public culture and critical pedagogy back to life, educators need to provide students with the knowledge and skills that enable them not only to judge and choose between different institutions but also to create those institutions they deem necessary for living lives of decency and dignity. In this instance, education provides not only the tools for citizen participation in public life, but also for exercising leadership. As Castoriadis insists, "people should have not just the typical right to participate; they should also be educated in every aspect (of leadership and politics) in order to be able to participate" (Castoriadis, 1996, p. 24) in governing society.

Reclaiming higher education as a public sphere begins with the crucial project of challenging corporate ideology and its attending notions of time, which cover over the crisis of the social by dissociating all discussions about the goals of higher education from the realm of democracy. This project points to the important task of redefining higher education as a democratic public sphere not only to assert the importance of the social, but also to reconfigure it so that "economic interests cease to be the dominant factor in shaping attitudes" (Castoriadis, 1991b, p. 112) about the social as a realm devoid of politics and democratic possibilities. Education is not only about issues of work and economics, but also about questions of justice, social freedom, and the capacity for democratic agency, action, and change as well as the related issues of power, exclusion, and citizenship. These are educational and political issues and should be addressed as part of a broader concern for renewing the struggle for social justice and democracy. Such a struggle demands, as the writer Roy points out, that as intellectuals we ask ourselves some very "uncomfortable questions about our values and traditions, our vision for the future, our responsibilities as citizens, the legitimacy of our 'democratic institutions', the role of the state, the police, the army, the judiciary, and the intellectual community" (Roy, 2001, p. 3).

While it is crucial for educators and others to defend higher education as a public good, it is also important to recognise that the crisis of higher education cannot be understood outside the overall restructuring of the social and civic life. The death of the social, the devaluing of political agency, the waning of non-commercial values, and the disappearance of non-commercialised public spaces have to be understood as part of a much broader attack on public entitlements such as healthcare, welfare, and social security, which are being turned over to market forces and privatised so that "economic transactions can subordinate and in many cases replace political democracy" (Newfield, 2002, p. 314).

Against the increasing corporatisation of the university and the advance of global capitalism, educators need to resurrect a language of resistance and possibility, a language that embraces a militant utopianism while constantly being attentive to those forces that seek to turn such hope into a new slogan or punish and dismiss those who dare look beyond the horizon of the given. Hope as a form of militant utopianism, in this instance, is one of the preconditions for individual and social struggle, the ongoing practice of critical education in a wide variety of sites—the attempt to make a difference by being able to imagine otherwise in order to act in other ways. Educated hope is utopian, as Ruth Levitas observes, in that it is understood "more broadly as the desire for a better way of living expressed in the description of a different kind of society that makes possible that alternative way of life" (Levitas, 1993, p. 257). Educated hope also demands a certain amount of courage on the part of intellectuals in that it demands from them the necessity to articulate social possibilities, mediate the experience of injustice as part of a broader attempt to contest the workings of oppressive power, undermine various forms of domination, and fight for alternative ways to imagine the future. This is no small challenge at a time in American history when jingoistic patriotism is the only obligation of citizenship and dissent is viewed increasingly as the refuge of those who support terrorists.

Educated hope as a utopian longing becomes all the more urgent given the bleakness of the times, but also because it opens horizons of comparison by evoking not just different histories but different futures; at the same time, it substantiates the importance of ambivalence while problematising certainty, or as Ricoeur has suggested, it is "a major resource as the weapon against closure" (cited in Bauman, 1998, p. 98). As a form of utopian thinking, educated hope provides a theoretical service in that it pluralises politics by generating dissent against the claims of a false harmony, and it provides an activating presence in promoting social transformation. Derrida has observed in another context that if higher education is going to have a future that makes a difference in promoting democracy, it is crucial for educators to take up the "necessity to rethink the concepts of the possible and the impossible" (Derrida, 2001, p. 7). What Derrida is suggesting is that educated hope provides a vocabulary for challenging the presupposition that there are no alternatives to the existing social order, while simultaneously stressing the dynamic, still unfinished elements of a democracy to be realised.[8]

Educated hope as a form of oppositional utopianism accentuates the ways in which the political can become more pedagogical and the pedagogical more political. In the first instance, pedagogy merges politics and ethics with revitalised forms of civic education that provide the knowledge, skills, and experiences enabling individual freedom and social agency. Making the pedagogical more political demands that educators become more attentive to the ways in which institutional forces and cultural power are tangled up with everyday experience. It means understanding how higher education in the information age now interfaces with the larger culture, how it has become the most important site for framing public pedagogies and authorising specific relations between the self, the other, and the larger society that often shut down democratic visions. Any viable politics of educated hope must tap into individual experiences while at the same time linking individual responsibility with a progressive sense of social agency. Politics and pedagogy alike spring "from real situations and from what we can say and do in these situations" (Badiou, 2001, p. 96). As an empowering practice, educated hope translates into civic courage as a political and pedagogical practice that begins when one's life can no longer be taken for granted. In doing so, it makes concrete the possibility for transforming higher education into an ethical practice and public event that confronts the flow of everyday experience and the weight of social suffering with the force of individual and collective resistance and the promise of an ongoing project of democratic social transformation.

Emphasising politics as a pedagogical practice and performative act, educated hope accentuates the notion that politics is played out not only on the terrain of imagination and desire, but is also grounded in material relations of power and concrete social formations through which people live out their daily lives. Freedom and justice, in this instance, have to be mediated through the connection between civic education and political agency, which presupposes that the goal of educated hope is not to liberate the individual *from* the social—a central tenet of neoliberalism—but to take seriously the notion that the individual can only be liberated *through* the social. Educated hope, if it is to be meaningful, should provide a link, however transient, provisional, and contextual, between vision and critique, on the one hand, and engagement and transformation, on the other. But for such a notion of hope to be meaningful it has to be grounded in a vision and notion of pedagogy that has some hold on the present.

The limits of the utopian imagination are related, in part, to the failure of academics and intellectuals in a variety of public spheres not only to conceive of life beyond profit margins, but also to imagine what pedagogical conditions might be necessary to bring into being forms of political agency that might expand the operations of individual rights, social provisions, and democratic freedoms. Against such failures and dystopian notions, it is crucial for educators to address utopian long-ings as anticipatory rather than messianic, as temporal rather than merely spatial, forward-looking rather than backwards. Utopian thinking in this view is neither a blueprint for the future nor a form of social engineering, but a belief that differ-ent futures are possible. Utopian thinking rejects a politics of certainty and holds open matters of contingency, context, and indeterminacy as central to any notion of agency and the future. This suggests a view of hope based on the recognition that it is only through education that human beings can learn about the limits of the present and the conditions necessary for them to "combine a gritty sense of limits with a lofty vision of possibility" (Aronson, 1999, p. 489). Educated hope poses the important challenge of how to reclaim social agency within a broader discourse of ethical advocacy while addressing those essential pedagogical and political elements necessary for envisioning alternatives to global neoliberalism and its attendant forms of corporate time and its attendant assault on public time and space.

Educated hope takes as a political and ethical necessity the need to address what modes of education are required for a democratic future and further requires that we ask such questions as: what pedagogical projects, resources, and practices can be put into place that would convey to students the vital importance of public time and its attendant culture of questioning as an essential step towards self-representation, agency, and a substantive democracy? How might public time with its imperative to 'take more time', compel respect rather than reverence, critique rather than silence, while challenging the narrow and commercial nature of corporate time? What kinds of social relations necessarily provide students with time for deliberation as well as spaces of translation in which they can critically engage those forms of power and authority that speak directly to them both within and outside of the academy? How might public time, with its unsettling refusal to be fixed or to collapse in the face of corporate time, be used to create pedagogical conditions that foster forms of self and social critique as part of a broader project of constructing alternative desires and critical modes of thinking, on the one hand, and democratic agents of change, on the other? How to deal with these issues is a major question for intellectuals in the academy today and their importance resides not just in how they might provide teachers and students with the tools to fight corporatisation in higher education, but also how they address the need for fundamental institutional change in the ongoing struggles for freedom and justice in a revitalised democracy.

There is a longstanding tradition among critical theorists that pedagogy as a moral and political practice plays a crucial role in constituting the social. Far from innocent, pedagogical practices operate within institutional contexts that carry great power in determining what knowledge is of most worth, what it means for students to know something, and how such knowledge relates to a particular understanding of the self and its relationship both to others and the future. Connecting teaching as knowledge production to teaching as a form of self production, pedagogy presupposes not only a political and ethical project that offers up a variety of human capacities, it also propagates diverse meanings of the social. Moreover, as an articulation of and intervention in the social, pedagogical practices always sanction particular versions of what knowledge is of most worth, what it means to know something, how to be attentive to the operations of power, and how we might construct representations of ourselves, others, and our physical environment. In the broadest sense, pedagogy is a principal feature of politics because it provides the capacities, knowledge, skills, and social relations through which individuals recognise themselves as social and political agents. As Roger Simon points out, "talk about pedagogy is simultaneously talk about the details of what students and others might do together and the cultural politics such practices support" (Simon, 1987, p. 371).

While many critical educators and social theorists recognise that education, in general, and pedagogy, more specifically, cannot be separated from the dual crisis of representation and political agency, the primary emphasis in many of these approaches to critical pedagogy suggests that its foremost responsibility is to provide a space where the complexity of knowledge, culture, values, and social issues can be explored in open and critical dialogue within a vibrant culture of questioning. This position is echoed by Judith Butler who argues, "For me there is more hope in the world when we can question what is taken for granted, especially about what it is to be human" (cited in Olson and Worsham, 2000, p. 765). Bauman goes further, arguing that the resurrection of any viable notion of political and social agency is dependent upon a culture of questioning, whose purpose, as he puts it, is to

> keep the forever unexhausted and unfulfilled human potential open, fighting back all attempts to foreclose and preempt the further unraveling of human possibilities, prodding human society to go on questioning itself and preventing that questioning from ever stalling or being declared finished. (Bauman and Tester, 2001, p. 4)

Central to any viable notion of critical pedagogy is its willingness to take seriously those academic projects, intellectual practices, and social relations in which students have the basic right to raise, if not define questions, both within and outside disciplinary boundaries. Such a pedagogy also must bear the responsibility of being self-conscious about those forces that sometimes prevent people from speaking openly and critically, whether they are part of a hidden curriculum of either racism, class oppression, or gender discrimination or part of those institutional and ideological mechanisms that silence students under the pretext of a claim to professionalism, objectivity, or unaccountable authority. Crucial here is the recognition that a pedagogical culture of questioning is not merely about the dynamics of communication but also about the effects of power and the mechanisms through which it constrains, denies, or excludes particular forms of agency—preventing some individuals from speaking in specific ways, in particular spaces, under specific circumstances. Clearly such a pedagogy might include a questioning of the corporatisation of the educational context itself, the role of foreign policy, the purpose and meaning of the burgeoning prison-industrial complex, and the declining nature of the welfare state. Pedagogy makes visible the operations of power and authority as part of its processes of disruption and unsettlement—an attempt, as Larry Grossberg points out, "to win an already positioned, already invested individual or group to a different set of places, a different organisation of the space of possibilities" (1994, p. 14).

At its best, such a pedagogy is self-reflective, and views its own practices and effects not as pre-given but as the outcome of previous struggles. Rather than defined as either a technique, method, or "as a kind of physics which leaves its own history behind and never looks back" (Bauman and Tester, 2001, p. 20) critical pedagogy is grounded in a sense of history, politics, and ethics which uses theory as a resource to respond to particular contexts, problems, and issues. I want to suggest that as educators we need to extend this approach to critical pedagogy beyond the project of simply providing students with the critical knowledge and analytic tools that enable them to use them in any way they wish. While this pedagogical approach rightly focuses on the primacy of dialogue, understanding, and critique, it does not adequately affirm the experience of the social and the obligations it evokes regarding questions of responsibility and social transformation. Such a pedagogy attempts to open up for students important questions about power, knowledge, and what it might mean for students to critically engage the conditions under which life is presented to them, but it does not directly address what it would mean for them to work to overcome those social relations of oppression that make living unbearable for those youths and adults who are poor, hungry, unemployed, refused adequate social services, and under the aegis of neoliberalism, viewed largely as disposable.

Some educators such as Goldfarb have argued that education should primarily be used to engage students in "the great conversation", enable them to "pay attention to their critical faculties", and provoke informed discussion (Goldfarb, 2002, pp. 345–67). But Goldfarb also believes that education should be free from politics, providing students ultimately with the tools for civic discussion without the baggage of what he calls debilitating ideology. But by denying the relationship between politics and education, Goldfarb has no language for recognising how pedagogy itself is shot through with issues of politics, power, and ideology. In opposition to Goldfarb, I believe that teaching and learning are profoundly political practices, as is evident in the most basic pedagogical and educational concerns, such as: how does one draw attention to the different ways in which knowledge, power, and experience are produced under specific conditions of learning? How are authority and power individually and institutionally distributed in both the university and the classroom? Who produces classroom knowledge and for whom? Who determines what knowledge is included or excluded? What is the agenda that informs the production and teaching of knowledge? What are the social and ideological horizons that determine student access to classrooms, privilege particular forms of cultural capital—ways of talking, writing, acting, dressing, and embodying specific racial, gendered, and class histories? How does one determine how politics is connected to everyday questions of identity, beliefs, subjectivity, dreams, and desires? How does one acknowledge, mediate, or refuse dominant academic values, pressures, and social relations? Goldfarb confuses politics with indoctrination and in doing so has no way of critically analysing how his own intellectual practices are implicated in relations of power that structure the very knowledge, values, and desires that mediate his relations to students and the outside world. Consequently, his willingness to separate education from matters of power and politics runs the risk of reproducing the latter's worst effects. Goldfarb wants to deny the symbiotic relationship between politics and education, but the real issue is to recognise how such a relationship might be used to produce pedagogical practices that condition but do not determine outcomes, that recognise that "the educator's task is to encourage human agency, not mold it in the manner of Pygmalion" (Aronowitz, 1998b, pp. 10–11). A critical education should enable students to question existing institutions as well as to view politics as "a labour aimed at transforming desirable institutions in a democratic direction" (Castoriadis, 1997b, pp.4–5.). But to acknowledge that critical pedagogy is directed and interventionist is not the same as turning it into a religious ritual. Critical approaches to pedagogy do not guarantee certainty or impose a particular ideology, nor should they. But they should make a distinction between a rigorous ethical and scholarly approach to learning implicated in diverse relations of power and those forms of pedagogy that belie questions of responsibility, while allowing dialogue to degenerate into opinion and academic methods into unreflective and damaging ideological approaches to teaching. Rather than deny the relationship between education and politics, it seems far more crucial to engage it openly and critically so as to prevent pedagogical relations from degenerating into forms of abuse, terrorism, or contempt immune from any viable form of self-reflection and analysis.

A pedagogy that simply promotes a culture of questioning says nothing about what kind of future is or should be implied by how and what educators teach; nor does it address the necessity of recognising the value of a future in which matters of liberty, freedom, and justice play a constitutive role. While it is crucial for education to be attentive to those practices in which forms of social and political agency are denied, it is also imperative to create the conditions in which forms of agency are available for students to learn not only to think critically but to act differently. People need to be educated for democracy not only by expanding their capacities to think critically, but also for assuming public responsibility through active participation in the very process of governing and engaging important social problems. This suggests connecting a pedagogy of understanding with pedagogical practices that are empowering and oppositional, practices that offer students the knowledge and skills needed to believe that a substantive democracy is not only possible but is worth both taking responsibility for and struggling over. Feminist and postcolonial theorist Chandra Talpade Mohanty highlights this issue by arguing that pedagogy is not merely about matters of scholarship and what should be taught but also about issues of strategy, transformation, and practice. In this instance, a critical pedagogy should get:

students to think critically about their place in relation to the knowledge they gain and to transform their world view fundamentally by taking the politics of knowledge seriously. It is a pedagogy that attempts to link knowledge, social responsibility, and collective struggle. And it does so by emphasizing risks that education involves, the struggles for institutional change, and the strategies for challenging forms of domination and by creating more equitable and just public spheres within and outside of educational institutions. (1989–90, p. 192)

Any viable notion of critical pedagogy has to foreground issues not only of under-standing but also social responsibility and address the implications the latter has for a democratic society. As Vaclav Havel has noted,

Democracy requires a certain type of citizen who feels responsible for something other than his own well feathered little corner; citizens who want to participate in society's affairs, who insist on it; citizens with backbones; citizens who hold their ideas about democracy at the deepest level, at the level that religion is held, where beliefs and identity are the same. (cited in Berman, 1997, p. 36)

Pedagogy plays a crucial role in nurturing this type of responsibility and suggests that students should learn about the relevance of translating critique and under-standing to civic courage, of translating what they know as a matter of private privilege into a concern for public life. Responsibility breathes politics into educa-tional practices and suggests both a different future and the possibility of politics itself. Responsibility makes politics and agency possible, because it does not end with matters of understanding; it recognises the importance of students becoming accountable for others through their ideas, language, and actions. Being aware of the conditions that cause human suffering and the deep inequalities that generate dread-fully undemocratic and unethical contradictions for many people is not the same as resolving them. If pedagogy is to be linked to critical citizenship and public life, it needs to provide the conditions for students to learn in diverse ways how to take responsibility for moving society in the direction of a more realisable democracy. In this case, the burden of pedagogy is linked to the possibilities of understanding and acting, engaging knowledge and theory as a resource to enhance the capacity for civic action and democratic change.

The future of higher education is inextricably connected to the future that we make available to the next generation of young people. Finding our way to a more human future means educating a new generation of scholars who not only defend higher education as a democratic public sphere, but who also frame their own agency as both scholars and citizen activists willing to connect their research, teaching and service with broader democratic concerns over equality, justice, and an alternative vision of what the university might be and what society might become.

Notes

· 1. For some of excellent critical commentaries on various aspects of neoliberalism and its consequences, see Chomsky (1999); Bourdieu (1998); Bourdieu, et al. (1999); McChesney (1999); Bauman (1998, 2002).

2. These figures are taken from Child Research Briefs, 'Poverty, Welfare, and Children: A Summary of the Data'. Available online at www.child-trends.org.

3. These figures are taken from Childhood Poverty Research Brief 2, 'Child Poverty in the States: Levels and Trends From 1979 to 1998'. Available online at www.nccp.org.

4. These figures largely come from Children's Defense Fund (2002, pp. iv–v, 13).

5. Cited in Hearn (1985), p. 175. The classic statements by Dewey on this subject can be found in Dewey (1997 [1916]); see also Dewey (1954).

6. The most extensive analysis of the branding of culture by corporations can be found in Klein (1999).

7. The ideas on public intellectuals are taken directly from Said (2001, pp. 502–3). For the reference to realist utopias, see Bourdieu (2000, p. 42).

8. Amin has captured this sentiment in his comment: "Neither modernity nor democracy has reached the end of its potential development. That is why I prefer the term 'democratisation', which stresses the dynamic aspect of a still-unfinished process, to the term 'democracy', which reinforces the illusion that we can give a definitive formula for it". See Amin (2001, p. 12).

References

Agger, B. (2002) 'Sociological Writing in the Wake of Postmodernism', *Cultural Studies/Cultural Methodologies*, 2 (4, November).

Amin, S. (2001) 'Imperialization and Globalization', *Monthly Review*, June.

Aronowitz, S. (1998a) 'The New Corporate University', *Dollars and Sense*, (March/April).

———. (1998b) 'Introduction', in P. Freire, *Pedagogy of Freedom*, Lanham: Rowman and Littlefield.

Aronson, R. (1999) 'Hope After Hope', *Social Research*, 66 (2, Summer).

Badiou, A. (2001) *Ethics: An Essay on the Understanding of Evil*, London: Verso.

Bauman, Z. (1998a) *Work, Consumerism, and the New Poor*, Philadelphia: Open University Press.

———. (1998b) *Globalization: The Human Consequence*, New York: Columbia University Press.

———. (1999a) *Work, Consumerism, and the New Poor*, Philadelphia, Open University Press.

———. (1999b), *In Search of Politics*, Stanford, CA: Stanford University Press.

———. (2002) *Society Under Siege*, Cambridge, England: Polity Press.

Bauman, Z. and K. Tester (2001) *Conversations with Zygmunt Bauman*, Malden, MA: Polity Press.

Beilharz, P. (2000) *Zygmunt Bauman: Dialectic of Modernity*, London: Sage.

Berman, P. (1997) 'The Philosopher-King is Mortal', *The New York Times Magazine*, 11 May: 36.

Bind, J. (2000) 'Toward an Ethic of the Future', *Public Culture*, 12 (1).

Bourdieu, P. (1998) *Acts of Resistance; Against the Tyranny of the Market*, New York: The New Press.

———. (2000) 'For a Scholarship with Commitment', *Profession*.

Bourdieu, P. et al. (1999) *The Weight of the World: Social Suffering in Contemporary Society*, Stanford: Stanford University Press.

Castoriadis, C. (1991a) 'The Nature and Value of Equity', *Philosophy, Politics, Autonomy: Essays in Political Philosophy*, New York: Oxford University Press.

———. (1991b) 'The Greek Polis and the Creation of Democracy', *Philosophy, Politics, Autonomy: Essays in Political Philosophy*, New York: Oxford University Press.

———. (1996) 'The Problem of Democracy Today', *Democracy and Nature*, 8 (April).

———. (1997) 'Culture in a Democratic Society, in D. Ames Curtis (ed.), *The Castoriadis Reader*, Malden, MA: Blackwell.

———. (1997b) 'Democracy as Procedure and Democracy as Regime', *Constellations*, 4 (1).

Children's Defense Fund (2002) *The State of Children in America's Union: A 2002 Action Guide to Leave No Child Behind*, Washington, DC: Children's Defense Fund Publication.

Chomsky, N. (1999) *Profit Over People: Neoliberalism and the Global Order*, New York: Seven Stories Press.

Comaroff, J. and J. L. Comaroff (2000) 'Millennial Capitalism: First Thoughts on a Second Coming', *Public Culture*, 12 (2), Duke University Press.

Couldry, N. (2001) 'Dialogue in an Age of Enclosure: Exploring the Values of Cultural Studies', *The Review of Education/Pedagogy/Cultural Studies*, 23 (1).

Critchley, S. (2002) 'Ethics, Politics, and Radical Democracy: The History of a Disagreement', *Culture Machine*, available at www.culturemachine.tees.ac.uk/frm_f1.htm

Derrida, J. (2000) 'Intellectual Courage: An Interview', *Culture Machine*, 2.

———. (2001) 'The Future of the Profession or the Unconditional University', in L. Simmons and H. Worth (eds.), *Derrida Downunder*, Auckland, New Zealand: Dunmore Press.

Dewey, J. (1997 [1916]) *Democracy and Education*, New York: The Free Press.

———. (1954) *The Public and Its Problems*, Columbus: Ohio University Press.

Egan, J. (2002) 'To Be Young and Homeless', *The New York Times Magazine*, 24 March.

Euben, P. (2000) 'Reforming the Liberal Arts', *The Civic Arts Review*, 2 (Summer/Fall).

Goldfarb, J. C. (2002) 'Anti-Ideology: Education and Politics as Democratic Practices', in R. Castronovo and D. Nelson (eds.), *Materializing Democracy*, Durham: Duke University Press.

Grossberg, L. (1994) 'Introduction: Bringing It All Back Home — Pedagogy and Cultural Studies', in H. A. Giroux and P. McLaren (eds.), *Between Borders: Pedagogy and the Politics of Cultural Studies*, New York: Routledge.

———. (2001) 'Why Does Neo-Liberalism Hate Kids' The War on Youth and the Culture of Politics', *The Review of Education/Pedagogy/Cultural Studies*, 23 (2).

Hanchard, M. (1999) 'Afro-Modernity: Temporality, Politics, and the African Diaspora', *Public Culture*, 11 (1, Winter).

Hanley, L. (2001) 'Conference Roundtable', *Found Object*, 10 (Spring).

Hearn, F. (1985) *Reason and Freedom in Sociological Thought*, Boston: Unwin.

Hyman. Hertz, N. (2001) *The Silent Takeover: Global Capitalism and the Death of Democracy*, New York: The Free Press.

Hinkson, J. (2002) 'Perspectives on the Crisis of the University', in J. Hinkson, and G. Sharp (eds.) *Scholars and Entrepreneurism*, Melbourne, Australia: Arena Publications.

Ivins, M. (2003). 'Bush's Sneak Attack on 'Average' Taxpayers', *Common Dreams*, 27 March, available at www.commondreams.org/views03/0327– 04.htm.

Klein, N. (1999) *No Logo*, New York: Picador.

Kunstler, J. H. (1993) *The Geography of Nowhere*, New York: Touchstone.

Kuttner, R. (2003). 'War Distracts from Bush's Budget Cuts.' *Common Dreams*, 26 March, available at www.commondreams.org/views03/0326–10.htm.

Levitas, R. (1993) 'The Future of Thinking About the Future', in J. Bird et al. (eds.), *Mapping the Futures*, New York: Routledge.

McChesney, R. W. (1999) *Rich Media, Poor Democracy: Communication Politics in Dubious Times*, New York: The New Press.

Miyoshi, M. (1998) ' 'Globalization', Culture, and the University', in F. Jameson and M. Miyoshi (eds.), *The Cultures of Globalization*, Durham: Duke University Press.

Mohanty, C. T. (1998–1999). 'On Race and Voice: Challenges for Liberal Education in the 1990s.', *Cultural Critique*, 14 (Winter).

Morrison, T. (2001) 'How Can Values Be Taught in the University?', *Michigan Quarterly Review*, Spring.

Nelson, C. (2002) 'Between Anonymity and Celebrity: The Zero degrees of Professional Identity', *College English*, 64 (6, July).

———. (2003) 'Higher Education and September 11th, in N. Denzin and Y. Lincoln (eds.), *9/11 in American Culture*, New York: Altamira Press.

Newfield, C. (2002) 'Democratic Passions: Reconstructing Individual Agency', in R. Castronovo and D. Nelson (eds.), *Materializing Democracy*, Durham: Duke University Press.

Olson, G. A. and L. Worsham (2000) 'Changing the Subject: Judith Butler's Politics of Radical Resignification', *JAC*, 20 (4).

Peters, M. (2002) 'The University in the Knowledge Economy', in S. Cooper, J. Hinkson and G. Sharp (eds.), *Scholars and Entrepreneurs: The University in Crisis*, North Carlton: Australia, Arena Publications.

Rhoades, G. (2001) 'Corporate, Techno Challenges, and Academic Space', *Found Object*, 10 (Spring).

Roy, A. (2001) *Power Politics*, Cambridge, MA: South End Press.

Rule, J. (1998) 'Markets In their Place', *Dissent*, Winter.

Said, E. (2001) *Reflections on Exile and Other Essays*, Cambridge: Harvard University Press.

Sharp, G. (2002) 'The Idea of the Intellectual and After', in S. Cooper, J. Hinkson and G. Sharp (eds.), *Scholars and Entrepreneurs*, Melbourne, Australia: Arena Publications.

Simon, R. (1987) 'Empowerment as a Pedagogy of Possibility', *Language Arts*, 64 (4, April).

———. (2001) 'The University: A Place to Think?', in H. A. Giroux and K. Myrsiades (eds.), *Beyond the Corporate University*, Lanham, MD: Rowman and Littlefield.

———. (2002) 'On Public Time', Ontario Institute for Studies in Education, unpublished paper.

Thiong'O, N. W. (1993) *Moving the Centre: The Struggle for Cultural Freedoms*, Portsmouth, NH: Heinemann.

Traub, J. (2000) 'This Campus is Being Simulated', *The New York Times Magazine*, 19 November: 93.

Williams, J. L. (2001) 'Franchising the University', in H. A. Giroux and K. Myrsiades (eds.), *Beyond the Corporate University: Culture and Pedagogy in the New Millennium*, Lanham, MD: Rowman and Littlefield.

Wokusch, H. (2002) 'Leaving Our Children Behind', *Common Dreams News Center*, July, www.commondreams.org/views02/0708–08.htm.

Wright Mills, C. (1963) *Power, Politics, and People*, edited by I. L. Horowitz, New York: Oxford University Press.

CHAPTER 12

The Militarization of U.S. Higher Education after 9/11

2008

> War is the motor behind institutions and order. In the smallest of its cogs, peace is waging a secret war. To put it another way, we have to interpret the war that is going on beneath peace; peace is coded war. We are therefore at war with one another; a battlefront runs through the whole of society, continuously and permanently, and it is this battlefront that puts us all on one side or the other. There is no such thing as a neutral subject. We are all inevitably someone's adversary.
>
> (Foucault, 2003: 50–1)

Neoliberalism has been the subject of intense discussion among various left intellectuals within the last few decades, and rightly so (Aronowitz, 2006; Giroux, 2004; Grossberg, 2005; Hardt and Negri, 2004; Harvey, 2005; Ong, 2006; Saad-Filho and Johnston, 2005; Smith, 2005). As a diverse political, economic and educational project, neoliberalism has constructed a grim alignment among the state, finance capital and transnational corporations, while embracing the 'market as the arbiter of social destiny' (Rule, 1998: 31). By extending the domain of economics into politics, neoliberal market rationality now organizes, regulates and defines the basic principles and workings of the state. Gone are the days when the state 'assumed responsibility for a range of social needs' (Steinmetz, 2003: 337). Instead, the state now pursues a wide range of '"deregulations," privatizations, and abdications of responsibility to the market and private philanthropy' (Steinmetz, 2003: 337). As Wendy Brown points out, 'when deployed as a form of governmentality, neoliberalism reaches from the soul of the citizen-subject to educational policy to practices of empire' (2005: 40). Throughout the globe, the forces of neoliberalism are on the march, dismantling the historically guaranteed social provisions provided by the welfare state, defining profit-making as the essence of democracy, imposing rapacious free-trade agreements, saturating non-economic spheres with market rationalities and equating freedom with the unrestricted ability of markets to 'govern economic relations free of government regulation' (Aronowitz, 2003: 101). Transnational in scope, neoliberalism now imposes its economic regime and market values on developing and weaker nations through the heavy-handed policies of the World Bank, the International Monetary Fund (IMF), and the World Trade Organization (WTO). Western financial and commercial interests now manage and transfer resources and wealth from the poor and less developed nations to the richest and most powerful nation-states as well as wealthy corporate defenders of capitalism.

With the dawn of the new millennium, the Gilded Age, with its '"dreamworlds" of consumption, property, and power', has returned with a vengeance (Davis and Monk, 2007: ix). Market rationalities and entrepreneurial subjects are produced within a growing apparatus of social control while a culture of fear and a battered citizenry are the consequences of the militarization of everyday life. As war has become 'the organizing principle of society, and politics merely one of its means or guises' (Hardt and Negri, 2004: 12), the state has been transformed from a social state into a punishing state, reinforcing what neoliberalism and militarism share in common: a hatred of democracy and dissent (Rancière, 2006b). The possibilities of democracy are now answered not with the rule of law, however illegitimate, but with the threat or actuality of violence (Hardt and Negri, 2004: 341). In a post-9/11 world, neoliberalism has been weaponized, and the high-intensity warfare it promotes abroad is replicated in low-intensity warfare at home. While both militarism and neoliberalism have a long history in the United States, the symbiotic relationship into which they have entered and the way in which this authoritarian ideology has become normalized constitute a distinct historical moment. Both neoliberalism and militarism produce particular views of the world and then mobilize an array of pedagogical practices in a variety of sites in order to legitimate their related modes of governance, subject positions, forms of citizenship and rationality (Ferguson and Turnbull, 1999: 197–8). Moreover, the ever-expanding militarized neoliberal state, marked by the interdependence of finance capital, authoritarian order, a vast war machine and a 'culture of force', now serves as a powerful pedagogical influence that shapes the lives, memories and daily experiences of most Americans (Newfield, 2006). While higher education in the United States has long been a major site for producing the neoliberal subject, it is only in the aftermath of 9/11 that the university has also become an intense site of militarization.

There has been increasing concern among academics and progressives over the growing corporatization of the university. Yet the transformation of academia into a 'hypermodern militarized knowledge factory' has been largely ignored as a subject of public concern and critical debate (Armitage, 2005: 221). Such silence has nothing to do with a lack of visibility or covert attempts to inject a military and security presence into both higher education and the broader society. Military symbols, representations, talk and images now dominate the cultural and political landscape (Bacevich, 2005; Boggs, 2005; Coker, 2007; Giroux, 2007; Johnson, 2004, 2006).

But the idea that 'military is to democracy as fire is to water' has been consistently overlooked by the media and most academics, as well as by almost all major politicians under the Bush presidency (Beck, 1996: 78). As a result, a creeping militarism has materialized into a full-fledged coup, fueled by a war on terror, the military occupation of Iraq and Afghanistan, and endless cases of kidnapping, torture, abuse and murder by the US government.

While collaboration between the national security state and higher education developed during the Cold War (Chomsky et al., 1998; Lowen, 1997; Simpson, 1998), the post-9/11 resurgence of patriotic commitment and support on the part of faculty and administrators towards the increasing militarization of daily life runs the risk of situating academia within a larger project in which the militarized narratives, values and pedagogical practices of the warfare state become commonplace (Armitage, 2005; McColm and Dorn, 2005; Nelson, 2004; Perelman, 2005). As the ensemble of institutions, relations, culture and symbols of militarization now loom large in the civic order's 'field of vision and strategic action' (Singh, 2006: 85), it becomes all the more important for higher education to be defended as a vital public sphere crucial for both the education of critical citizens and the defense of democratic values and institutions. Yet faith in social amelioration and a sustainable future appears to be in short supply as neoliberal capitalism performs the multiple tasks of using education to train workers for service sector jobs, creating life-long consumers, constructing citizen-warriors and expanding the production of militarized knowledge, values and research. Given the current threat posed by the national security state to higher education and democracy, I want to engage the question of what role higher education should perform when 'the government has a free hand to do whatever it wants in the name of national security' (Perelman, 2005: 179). More specifically, I want to offer an alternative analysis of the fate of higher education as a democratic public sphere, one that refuses simply to serve the expressed needs of militarization, neoliberalism and the national security state, all of which appear to be pushing the United States towards a new form of authoritarianism. In what follows, I first situate the development of the university as a 'militarized knowledge factory' within the broader context of what I call the *biopolitics of militarization* and its increased influence and power within American society after the tragic events of 11 September 2001. Second, I highlight and critically engage the specific ways in which this militarization is shaping various aspects of university life, focusing primarily on the growth of militarized knowledge and research, as well as the growing influence of the CIA on college campuses. Finally, I offer some suggestions both for resisting the rising tide of militarization and for reclaiming the university as a democratic public sphere.

From Militarism to a Biopolitics of Militarization in a Post-9/11 World

After the events of 9/11, the United States became no longer simply a militarized state but a militarized society. What this means can, in part, be explained by making a broad, though hardly steadfast, distinction between militarism and militarization. Militarism, as John Gillis argues, 'is the older concept, usually defined as either the dominance of the military over civilian authority, or more generally, as the prevalence of warlike values in a society' (1989: 1). Militarism is often viewed as a retrograde concept because it characterizes a society in which military values and beliefs reside exclusively in a ruling group or class; it is also derided for its anti-democratic tendency to either celebrate or legitimate a hierarchy of authority in which civil society is subordinate to military power. Similarly, militarism makes visible the often-contradictory principles and values between military institutions and the more liberal and democratic values of civil society. Militarism as an ideology has deep roots in American society, though it has never had enough force to transform an often-faltering liberal democracy into a military dictatorship.

Militarization suggests less a complete break with militarism—with its celebration of war as the truest measure of the health of the nation and the soldier-warrior as the most noble expression of the merging of masculinity and unquestioning patriotism—than an intensification and expansion of its underlying values, practices, ideologies, social relations and cultural representations. Michael Geyer describes militarization as 'the contradictory and tense social process in which civil society organizes itself for the production of violence' (1989: 79). Catherine Lutz amplifies this definition, defining militarization as:

> ... an intensification of the labor and resources allocated to military purposes, including the shaping of other institutions in synchrony with military goals. Militarization is simultaneously a discursive process, involving a shift in general societal beliefs and values in ways necessary to legitimate the use of force, the organization of large standing armies and their leaders, and the higher taxes or tribute used to pay for them. Militarization is intimately connected not only to the obvious increase in the size of armies and resurgence of militant nationalisms and militant fundamentalisms but also to the less visible deformation of human potentials into the hierarchies of race, class, gender, and sexuality, and to the shaping of national histories in ways that glorify and legitimate military action. (2002: 723)

Both definitions appear to be even more relevant today than in the past, especially in a post-9/11 society in which military 'power is the measure of national greatness, and war, or planning for war, is the exemplary (and only common) project' (Judt, 2005: 16).

The growth of the military model in American life has played a crucial role in the paramilitarizing of the culture, which provides both a narrative and legitimation 'for recent trends in corrections, including the normalization of special response teams, the increasingly popular Supermax prisons, and drug war boot camps' (Kraska, 2001: 10). As the matrix for all relations of power, war in all of its actual and metaphorical modalities spreads the discourse and values of militarization throughout a society that has shifted, as Hardt and Negri argue, from 'the welfare state to the warfare state' (2004: 17). What is new about militarization in a post-9/11 world is that it has become naturalized, serving as a powerful pedagogical force that shapes our lives, memories and daily experiences, while erasing everything critical and emancipatory about history, justice, solidarity and the meaning of democracy (see Laor, 2006). Military power now expands far beyond the realms of producing military knowledge, enshrining military values and waging wars. As a biopolitical force, military power produces identities, goods, knowledge, modes of communication and affective investments—in short, it now bears down on all other aspects of social life and the social order (see Foucault, 2003; Rose, 2007). And, in doing so, it not only undermines the memories of democratic struggles and hope for the possibility of a more democratic future, it also punishes dissent.

As the punishing state replaces the social state, examples of militarized sovereign power are put on full display by an American government that installs torture as integral to its military and clandestine operations, made visible in the public disclosure of the abuse and torture of prisoners at Abu Ghraib in Iraq, Guantanamo Bay in Cuba, Bagram Air Base in Afghanistan and numerous other detention centers around the world (Mayer, 2005). The lethal consequences of the militarized state are also shamelessly visible in the sickening horror of the massacre which took place in Haditha in Iraq (Holland, 2006), and in a politics of 'disappearing' reminiscent of the Latin American dictatorships of the 1970s, in which human beings disappear outside of the boundaries of the law, sanctioned by a ruthless policy of 'extraordinary rendition' that enables the US government to abduct alleged enemies of the state and transport them to other countries to be tortured (Arar, 2006; Gray, 2006). A politics of disposability and exclusion is also manifest in the existence of secret CIA prisons known as 'black sites' (Priest, 2005) and in the abrogation of basic civil rights enacted by the passage of the Military Commissions Act of 2006, which allows people named as 'enemy combatants' to be imprisoned and charged with crimes without the benefit of a lawyer or the right of *habeas corpus*.

What happens when militarism provides the most legitimate framing mechanism for how we relate to ourselves, each other, and the rest of the world? Andrew Bacevich, Chalmers Johnson, Kevin Baker and others claim that the military 'has become the most revered institution in the country' (Baker, 2003: 37), whose importance is repeatedly accentuated by manufactured moral panics about threats from 'evil doers' and by endless terror alerts that are designed to legitimate Bush's notion of a 'war without limits' as a normal state of affairs. Under such circumstances, private insecurities and public fears translate into a kind of 'war fever' in which '[w]ar then becomes heroic, even mythic, a task that must be carried out for the defense of one's nation, to sustain its special historical destiny and immortality of its people' (Rosen, 2002). The spread of war fever carries with it both a kind of paranoid edge, endlessly mobilized by a high-octane culture of fear, government alerts and repressive laws used 'to create the most extensive national security apparatus in our nation's history' (Rosen, 2002), and a masculine politics that refuses to recognize that '[t]he poison that is war does not free us from the ethics of responsibility' (Hedges, 2003:

16). The politics of militarized masculinity finds its highest cultural expression in the kind of celluloid brutality, violence and carnage that characterizes standard Hollywood fare (see Giroux, 2002; Weaver and Carter, 2006). Indeed, the social topography of militarized masculinity is also evident in the return of the warrior male whose paranoia is endlessly stoked by the existence of a feminized culture of critical thinking, a gay subculture and a liberal ideology that exhibits a disrespect for top-down order and unquestioned authority and discipline. Cultural critic Jonathan Rutherford argues that the current militarization of masculinity is part of America's revival of the fascination with war shaped by an older frontier spirit (2005: 622). Such a fascination also harks back to the shadow of fascism that loomed over Europe in the past century and emboldens the message that the warrior spirit revives an authentic manliness in which 'war makes man'.

The new ethos of militarization no longer occupies a marginal place in the American political landscape, and it is reinforced daily by domestic and foreign policies that reveal a country obsessed with war and with the military values, policies and practices that drive it (see Chomsky, 2003). For instance, the military budget request for 2007 totals $462.7 billion, and when 'adjusted for inflation [the 2007 military budget] exceeds the average amount spent by the Pentagon during the Cold War [and] for a military that is one-third smaller than it was just over a decade ago' (Hellman, 2006). The US military budget is:

> . . . almost 7 times larger than the Chinese budget, the second largest spender . . . almost 29 times as large as the combined spending of the six 'rogue states' (Cuba, Iran, Libya, North Korea, Sudan and Syria) who spent [US]$14.65 billion [and is] more than the combined spending of the next 14 nations. (Shah, 2006)

Such immense levels of defense spending by the federal government have grave implications for expanding a US war machine that not only uses massive resources but is:

> . . . devoted to the monopolistic militarization of space, the development of more usable nuclear weapons, and the strengthening of its world-girdling ring of military bases and its global navy, as the most tangible way to discourage any strategic challenges to its preeminence. (Falk, 2003)

The projection of US military force and power in the world can be seen in the fact that the United States owns or rents 737 bases 'in about 130 countries—over and above the 6,000 bases' at home (Sterngold, 2004). Not only does the United States today spend 'approximately as much as the rest of the world combined on its military establishment' (Fukuyama, 2007)—producing massive amounts of death-dealing weapons—but it is also the world's biggest arms dealer, with sales in 2006 amounting to 'about $20.9 billion, nearly double the $10.6 billion the previous year' (Wolf, 2006). What is clear in light of these figures is that militarization is not just a legitimating ideology for the state's coercive power; it is also a source of economic power for US military industries and, unfortunately, a source of employment for significant portions of the labor force. Such high levels of military funding, spending and arms exporting both fail to guarantee security at home and give too much political power to the global producers and merchants of arms such as Lockheed Martin, Boeing, Raytheon and General Dynamics. Moreover, both major political parties have a stake in high military spending, and as reported in *The New York Times* 'the billions that have been supporting the industry are expected to continue unabated, and perhaps even increase' (Wayne, 2006: 7). Chalmers Johnson argues that US imperial ambitions are driven by what he calls 'military Keynesianism, in which the domestic economy requires sustained military ambition in order to avoid recession or collapse' (2007a: 63).

In the current historical conjuncture, 'war has gone from an instrument of politics, used in the last resort, to the foundation of politics, the basis for discipline and control' (Hardt & Negri, 2004: 334). Increasingly, military power and policies are being expanded to address not only matters of defense and security but also problems associated with the entire health and social life of the nation, which are now measured by military values, spending, discipline, loyalty and hierarchical modes of authority. While citizens increasingly assume the role of informer, soldier and consumer willing to enlist in or be conscripted by the totalizing war on terror, militarization has taken a sinister turn in the United States, as it has increasingly been shaped by the forces of empire, violence and neoliberal global capital. As politics is reduced to the imperatives of homeland security and war becomes the major structuring force of society—a source of pride rather than alarm—it becomes all the more crucial to understand how a 'mature democracy is in danger of turning itself into a military state' (Monbiot, 2003). The increasing militarization of American society raises serious questions about what kind of society the United States is becoming, and how higher education might be implicated in what C. Wright Mills once called 'a military definition of reality' (1993: 191).

The Militarized Knowledge Factory: Research, Credentials and the CIA

While the Cold War and Sovietology are gone from the scene, a parallel project is now underway: the launching of large-scale initiatives to create a cadre and set of institutions that penetrate our campuses and link them to national security, military, and intelligence agencies. The aim is nothing less, as Congressional hearings show, than to turn back opposition on our campuses to imperial war, and turn campuses into institutions that will, over the next generation, produce scholars and scholarship dedicated to the so-called war on terror. These programs are part of a broader effort to normalize a constant state of fear, based on the emotion of terror, while criminalizing anti-war and anti-imperial consciousness and action. As in the past, universities, colleges and schools have been targeted precisely because they are charged with both socializing youth and producing knowledge of peoples and cultures beyond the borders of Anglo-America. (Martin, 2005)

Now that the war on terrorism and a gradual erosion of civil liberties have become commonplace, the idea of the university as a site of critical thinking, public service and socially responsible research appears to have been usurped by a manic jingoism and a market-driven fundamentalism that enshrine the entrepreneurial spirit and military aggression as the best means to produce the rewards of commercial success and power. Not only is the militarization of higher education made obvious by the presence of over 150 military-educational institutions in the United States designed to 'train a youthful corps of tomorrow's military officers' in the strategies, values, skills and knowledge of the warfare state, but also, as the American Association of Universities points out, in the existence of hundreds of colleges and universities that conduct Pentagon-funded research, provide classes to military personnel, and design programs specifically for future employment with various departments and agencies associated with the warfare state (Turse, 2004; see also Johnson, 2004: 97–130). The intrusion of the military into higher education is also on full display with the recent announcement by Robert Gates, the Secretary of Defense under George W. Bush, of the creation of what he calls a new 'Minerva consortium', ironically named after the goddess of wisdom, whose purpose is to fund various universities to 'carry out social-sciences research relevant to national security' (Brainard, 2008). Without apology, Gates would like to turn universities into militarized knowledge factories producing knowledge, research, and personnel in the interest of the Homeland (In) Security State. Faculty now flock to the Department of Defense, the Pentagon and various intelligence agencies either to procure government jobs or to apply for grants to support individual research in the service of the national security state. At the same time, as corporate money for research opportunities dwindles, the Pentagon fills the void with millions of dollars in available grants, stipends, scholarships and other valuable financial rewards, for which college and university administrators actively and openly compete. Indeed, the Department of Homeland Security is flush with money:

[It] handles a $70 million dollar scholarship and research budget, and its initiatives, in alliance with those of the military and intelligence agencies, point towards a whole new network of campus-related programs. [For instance,] the University of Southern California has created the first 'Homeland Security Center of Excellence' with a $12 million grant that brought in multidisciplinary experts from UC Berkeley, NYU, and University of Wisconsin-Madison. Texas A&M and the University of Minnesota won $33 million to build two new Centers of Excellence in agrosecurity. . . . The scale of networked private and public cooperation is indicated by the new National Academic Consortium for Homeland Security led by Ohio State University, which links more than 200 universities and colleges. (Martin, 2005)

Rather than being the object of massive individual and collective resistance, the militarization of higher education appears to be endorsed by liberals and conservatives alike. The National Research Council of the National Academies published a report called *Frameworks for Higher Education in Homeland Security* (2006), which argued that the commitment to learning about homeland security is an essential part of the preparation for work and life in the 21st century, thus offering academics a thinly veiled legitimation for building into undergraduate and graduate curricula intellectual frameworks that mirror the interests and values of the warfare state. Similarly, the Association of American Universities argued in a report titled *National Defense Education and Innovation Initiative* (2005) that winning the war on terrorism and expanding global markets were mutually informing goals, the success of which falls squarely on the performance of universities. This group argues, with a rather cheerful certainty, that every student should be trained to become a soldier in the war on terror and in the battle over global markets, and that the universities should do everything they can 'to fill security-related positions in the defense industry, the military, the national laboratories, the Department of Defense and Homeland Security, the intelligence agencies, and other federal agencies' (Martin, 2005).

More and more universities are cooperating with intelligence agencies with few objections from faculty, students and other concerned citizens (Price, 2005). In the aftermath of the 11 September 2001 terrorist attacks, many academics are enthusiastically offering their services for the plethora of expert personnel positions, which according to National Intelligence Director John Negroponte in 2006 were available among the 16 federal intelligence agencies and programs that employ over 100,000 personnel (*USA Today*, 2006). The *Wall Street Journal* claims that the CIA has become a 'growing force on campus' (Golden, 2002), while a November 2002 issue of the liberal magazine *American Prospect* published an article by Chris Mooney calling for academics and the government intelligence agencies to work together. As he put it, 'Academic–intelligence relationships will never be problem free. But at present, the benefits greatly outweigh the costs' (Mooney, 2002). Such collaboration seems to be in full swing at a number of universities. For example, major universities have appointed former CIA officials as either faculty, consultants or presidents. Michael Crow, a former agent, is now president of Arizona State University and Robert Gates, the former Director of the CIA, was until recently president of Texas A&M. The collusion among the Pentagon, war industries and academia in the fields of research and development is evident as companies that make huge profits on militarization and war, such as General Electric, Northrop Grumman and Halliburton, establish crucial ties with universities through their grants, while promoting their image as philanthropic institutions to the larger society (see Roelofs, 2006). As the university is increasingly militarized, it 'becomes a factory that is engaged in the militarization of knowledge, namely, in the militarization of the facts, information and abilities obtained through the experience of education' (Armitage, 2005: 221). The priority given to such knowledge is largely the result of the huge amount of research money increasingly shaping the curricula, programs and departments in various universities around the country. Money flows from the military war machine in the post-9/11 world, and the grants and research funds that the best universities receive are not cheap. In 2003, for example, Penn State received $149 million in research and development awards while the Universities of California, Carnegie Mellon and Texas received $29.8 million, $59.8 million and $86.6 million respectively, and they are not even the top beneficiaries of such funds (see Turse, 2004). The scale, sweep, range and complexity of the interpenetration between academia and military-funded projects is as extensive as it is frightening. Nicholas Turse explains:

> According to a 2002 report by the Association of American Universities (AAU), almost 350 colleges and universities conduct Pentagon-funded research; universities receive more than 60% of defense basic research funding; and the DoD is the third largest federal funder of university research (after the National Institutes of Health and the National Science Foundation). . . . the Department of Defense accounts for 60% of federal funding for university-based electrical engineering research, 55% for the computer sciences, 41% for metallurgy/materials engineering, and 33% for oceanography. With the DoD's budget for research and development skyrocketing, so to speak, to $66 billion for 2004—an increase of $7.6 billion over 2003—it doesn't take a rocket scientist to figure out that the Pentagon can often dictate the sorts of research that get undertaken and the sorts that don't. (Turse, 2004)

Along with the money that comes with such defense-oriented funding is a particular assumption about the importance of ideas, knowledge and information and their relevance to military technologies, objectives and purposes. Of course, this is about more than how knowledge is obtained, shaped and used by different elements of the military-industrial complex; it is also about the kind of pressure that the Department of Defense and the war industries can bring to bear on colleges and universities to orient themselves towards a society in which non-militarized knowledge and values play a minor role, thus removing from higher education its fundamental purpose in educating students to be ethical citizens, learn how to take risks, connect knowledge to power in the interests of social responsibility and justice, and defend vital democratic ideals, values and institutions. In this context, it would be worthwhile to heed the warning of Jay Reed:

> Universities are not only hotbeds of military activity, they are adversely affected by the ethical compromises and threats to academic freedom that accompany a Department of Defense presence. The dream of the University as a place of disinterested, pure learning and research is far from reality as scientists and administrators from across the country are paid directly by the military to sit on Department of Defense scientific advisory boards and perform other research. It is naive to think that an abundance of funding from the military does not affect the projects chosen to be worthy of scientific inquiry. University research is not the result of objective decisions made in the spirit of an enlightened quest for knowledge; rather, these scientists' agendas are determined by the bloodthirsty architects of military strategy. (Reed, 2001)

For instance, the Department of Defense, along with a number of other departments and agencies invested in the process of militarization, largely support two main areas of weaponry: space-based armaments and so-called Future Combat Systems. The space weapons being researched in universities around the country include 'microwave guns, space-based lasers, electromagnetic guns, and holographic decoys' while the future combat weapons include 'electric tanks, electro-thermal chemical cannons, [and] unmanned platforms' (Reed, 2001). Such research is carried out at universities such as MIT, which gets 75 percent of its funds for its robotics program from the Department of Defense. How these funds shape research and development and the orientation of theory towards the production of militarized knowledge is evident in MIT's design and production of a kind of RoboMarine called 'the Gladiator', which is a tactical unmanned ground vehicle containing an MT40G medium machine gun, surveillance cameras, and slots for launching paint balls and various smoke rounds, including 'tear gas, or stingball and flashbang grenades' (Cole, 2003). One Pittsburgh paper called it:

> . . . a remote-controlled 'toy,' [with] some real weapons . . . [and] containers for hand grenades that can be used for clearing obstacles and creating a footpath on difficult terrain for soldiers following behind. It also features what looks like organ pipes to produce smoke, and it has a mount on top for a medium-size machine gun or multipurpose assault weapon. (Shropshire, 2005)

Critical commentary apparently not included. In fact, the Gladiator is designed for military crowd-control capabilities, reconnaissance, surveillance, and direct fire missions. Carnegie Mellon University received a $26.4 million Defense Department grant to build six Gladiator prototypes. The University of Texas received funding from the Department of Defense for its Applied Research Laboratories, which develop in five separate labs everything from Navy surveillance systems to 'sensing systems to support U.S. ballistic missile targeting' (Reed, 2001). MIT, one of the largest recipients of defense research money, has also been using its talented research-oriented faculty and students to develop remote sensing and imaging systems that would 'nullify the enemy's ability to hide inside complex mountain terrains and cityscapes' (Edwards, 2006). Universities around the country are funded to do similar military-oriented research, producing everything from global positioning systems to undersea surveillance technologies.

Another important element of the military-industrial-academic complex that contributes to the growing presence of military values and interests on campuses can be found in the increasing numbers of college degree programs that serve military employees. As part of a new recruiting strategy, the military adjusted its policies so that its spending for educational benefits has spiked in the last few years to more than a 'half a billion dollars a year in tuition assistance for the members of its active-duty force', thus opening up a market for profit and non-profit educational institutions (Blumenstyk, 2006). Some branches such as the Navy are increasing the importance of education by requiring all sailors beginning in 2011 to have 'an associate degree to qualify for promotion to senior enlisted ranks' (Blumenstyk, 2006). Fueled by a desire for more students, tuition money, and a larger share of the market for online and off-campus programs, many universities and colleges are altering their curricula and delivery services to attract the lucrative education market for military personnel. The military's increased interest in education has proven to be such a bonanza for recruiting and retaining soldiers that one Army officer claims: 'The military has turned the entire recruiting force into essentially admissions counselors' (Carnevale, 2006).

The rush to cash in on such changes has been dramatic, particularly for online, for-profit educational institutions such as the University of Phoenix, which has high visibility on the Internet. Other colleges such as Grantham University and the American Military University use military-friendly messages distributed across cyberspace in order to reach this new market of students and potentially large profits. Creating virtual universities has been a boon for colleges willing to provide online courses, distance-education degrees and programs that appeal to military personnel. In some cases, enrollment figures have skyrocketed as colleges tap into this lucrative market. Dan Carnevale, a writer for the *Chronicle of Higher Education*, reports that in 2006 at Touro University International in California 'about 4,000 of its 6,000 students serve in the military. And more than half of the nearly 11,000 students at Grantham University are in the armed forces'. The importance of online education can be seen in the creation of *eArmyU*, which is a partnership between the Armed Forces and higher education that allows enlisted personnel to use tuition assistance money to take online courses through 28 selected colleges. Those colleges that offer traditional classroom instruction rely heavily on setting up satellite campuses on or close to military bases in order to get a profitable share of the market. Some colleges, such as Central Texas, provide both online courses and on-base classroom instruction. For Central Texas, 74 percent of its 63,000 students are members of the active-duty military.

I should like to be very careful about how this expansion of educational benefits to military personnel contributes to the militarization of the academy. I certainly believe that people who serve in the armed services should be given ample educational opportunities, and that for me is not at issue. What I think is problematic is both the nature of these programs and the wider culture of privatization and militarization legitimated by them. With respect to the former, the incursion of the military presence in higher education furthers and deepens the ongoing privatization of education and knowledge itself. Most of the players in this market are for-profit institutions that are problematic not only for the quality of education they offer but also for their aggressive support of education less as a public good than as a private initiative, defined in this case through providing a service to the military in return for a considerable profit. And as this sector of higher education grows, it will not only become more privatized but also more instrumentalized, largely defined as a credentializing factory designed to serve the needs of the military, thus falling into the trap of confusing training with a broad-based education. Catering to educational needs of the military makes it all the more difficult to offer educational programs that would challenge militarized notions of identity, knowledge, values, ideas, social relations and visions. Military institutions radiate power in their communities and often resemble updated versions of the old company towns of 19th-century America—hostile to dissent, cultural differences, people who take risks and any discourse that might question authority. Moreover, the sheer power of the military apparatus, further augmented by its corporate and political alliances and fueled by an enormous budget, provide the Pentagon with a powerful arm-twisting ability capable of bending higher education to its will, an ominous and largely ignored disaster that is in the making in the United States.

One of the more disturbing indications of academe's willingness to accommodate the growing presence and legitimating ideologies of the national security state can be found in the increasing presence of the CIA and other spy agencies on American campuses. Daniel Golden, writing for the *Wall Street Journal* in 2002, noted that in the aftermath of 9/11 an increasing number of faculty and universities—capitalizing on both a new found sense of patriotism and less politicized sense of self-interest—were turning to the 16 intelligence agencies and offering them their services and new recruitment opportunities. Moreover, as universities recognize that the intelligence agencies have deep pockets for funding opportunities, the CIA has benefited from this new receptivity and is reciprocating by 'turning more to universities . . . to develop high-tech gadgets that track down terrorists and dictators' (Searer, 2003). In addition, it is developing more federal scholarship programs, grants and other initiatives in order to attract students for career opportunities and to involve faculty in various roles that address 'security and intelligence goals' (Clayton, 2003). The CIA's cozy relationship with academics has also been reinforced by the agency's increased presence at annual meetings held by academic groups such as the International Studies Association and the American Anthropological Association.

While part of this receptivity by faculty can be attributed to the scramble for research funding, it is only one factor in the equation. At a time when college students are in desperate need of jobs in an increasingly fragile market, the CIA, because of its political prominence in fighting the war on terrorism, is expanding rather than shrinking its employment opportunities and is viewed by many students—who seem to be beating a path to the agency's employment officers—as a promising career choice. Equally important is the upsurge in patriotic correctness following 9/11 coupled with the ongoing right-wing campaign to squelch 'un-American' dissent in the university. Hence, amid the resurgence of political quietism and hyper-patriotism, and growing job insecurities among college graduates, an unparalleled détente has emerged between academia and the CIA at the beginning of the new millennium. This détente is furthered in part by a new generation of academics more favorable to forging a connection with the CIA. A resurgent sense of patriotism has also energized an older generation of closeted pro-CIA faculty, who either formerly worked with the CIA but did so in secrecy or supported efforts for collaborative work between academia and the CIA but were hesitant to make their views public.

One of the most controversial post-9/11 programs sponsored by the CIA is the Pat Roberts Intelligence Scholars Program (PRISP). The program is named after Senator

Pat Roberts, who was the head of the Senate Select Committee on Intelligence under the Bush administration until the takeover of the Senate by Democrats in 2006 (see ThinkProgress.org, 2006). The Roberts Program was designed to train 150 analysts in anthropology, each of whom would receive a $25,000 stipend per year, with a maximum of $50,000 over the two-year period. The program also provided tuition support, loan paybacks and bonuses for the immediate hiring of those candidates considered to have critical skills. In return, each participant in the program agreed to work for an intelligence agency for one-and-a-half times the period covered by the scholarship support. In this case, two years of support would demand that an analyst work for a government intelligence agency for three years. Students who receive such funding cannot reveal their funding source, are not obligated to inform their professors or fellow students that they are being funded for and will work for an intelligence agency, and are required to attend military intelligence camps (for a description of the program, see CIA, 2007). The association of such a program with Senator Roberts seems particularly apt given that Roberts was well-known for siding with the Bush administration on warrantless domestic spying practices, blocking a vote to investigate the practices, consistently stone-walling an investigation into Bush's use of pre-war intelligence to justify the war in Iraq, defending Guantanamo Bay Prison, and refusing to investigate the CIA's complicity in the abuse and torture of detainees. The *Los Angeles Times* in 2006 claimed that 'In a world without Doublespeak, the panel, chaired by GOP Sen. Pat Roberts of Kansas, would be known by a more appropriate name—the Senate Coverup Committee.' It is altogether mystifying what such practices and policies could bring to higher education in order to enhance the sharing of institutional knowledge and foster the intellectual independence of students and faculty.

Nevertheless, criticisms of the Roberts Program have emerged among a few prominent academics, including David Price, David Gibbs and William Martin. Price, an associate professor of anthropology at St. Martin's College in Olympia, Washington, argues that the Roberts Program permits the CIA not only 'to return to its historical practice of operating within universities' but also to revert to its old habit of collecting information on professors, dissenting students, and what goes on in general in the classroom (cited in Glenn, 2005; see also Price, 2004). Professor Price also believes that such programs give authoritarian regimes 'an excuse to forbid all American social scientists to conduct research in those countries on the grounds that they are spies' (cited in Glenn, 2005). Phil Baty writing in the *Times Higher Education Supplement* extends this argument by insisting that such a program places the lives of all anthropologists in the field at risk of physical danger because they might be suspected of being spies and a danger to the people whom they study. Gibbs, an associate professor of history and political science at the University of Arizona, Tucson, argues that any close relationship between the intelligence services and higher education compromises the ability of academia to make power accountable by undermining the possibility of academics to criticize the policies and practices of intelligence agencies. He argues that the secrecy imposed on scholars working for the CIA is antithetical to the notion of the university as a democratic sphere that fosters critique, open dialogue and engaged debate. He also insists that the CIA practices of engaging in disinformation and propaganda tactics, along with its long and continuing history of destabilizing democratic governments, committing human rights abuses, engaging in acts of abduction and torture, and undermining popular democratic movements, put it at odds with any viable notion of what higher education should represent (Gibbs, 2003). At the very least, the research that is supported in many universities under the funding of the intelligence agencies raises serious questions about what kind of relationship there is between these agencies and academia, and whether such a relationship is capable of producing the ends for which it is purportedly espoused in the first place.

Perhaps the most stinging criticisms come from William Martin, whose comments are aimed not merely at the CIA, but at all Homeland Security Programs working in conjunction with higher education. Martin suggests that the government's efforts to redirect general educational funding towards specific programs not only impoverishes universities and renders them increasingly dependent on alternative sources of funding (such as corporations whose financial support also comes with strings attached), but also denies universities the kind of institutional autonomy needed to conduct important research not directly related to governmental goals and values. He writes:

> What these programs signal is thus not simply an attack on academic freedom or even the diversion of education funding into secret intelligence projects. For students and scholars alike these new programs threaten to solidify dangerous institutional changes. Secret military and intelligence agencies will increasingly dictate which languages, religions, and peoples—both beyond and within our borders—will be studied and by whom. New networked centers and programs, created by and tied to federal security funding, will form an academic homeland security complex destined to implement the fear of 'un-American others', all in pursuit of an increasingly profitable and increasingly illusory 'war on terror'. Meanwhile, hidden behind these facades, marches the development of security and intelligence student trainees who report to security agencies and move back and forth, unknown and unobserved, from our classrooms to security agencies. The forgotten exposés of the 1970s demonstrate what these kinds of programs produce: an academy not simply compromised and at risk, but riddled with secret military and intelligence projects, slowly spreading all over the world in service of misguided imperial ambitions. (Martin, 2005)

Martin's argument appears to be lost on a majority of academics. What is overlooked in the growing, enthusiastic collaboration between the military-industrial complex and academe within the context of developing a powerful post-9/11 national security state is that the increasing militarization of higher education is itself a problem that may be even more insidious, damaging and dangerous to the fate of democracy than that posed by terrorists who 'hate our freedoms'. Heretofore, the university has been one of the few remaining sites where genuine criticism, critical scholarship, spirited debate and organized resistance to the abuse of government power could take place.

Conclusion

Higher education should play a particularly important role in opposing not only its own transformation into a 'hypermodern militarized knowledge factory' but also the growing impact of militarization in the larger society. One crucial step in this process is to reclaim higher education as a democratic public sphere, one that provides the pedagogical conditions for students to become critical agents who connect learning to expanding and deepening the struggle for genuine democratization. Students should be versed in the importance of the social contract (in spite of its damaged legacy), provided with classroom opportunities to become informed citizens, and given the resources to understand politics in both historical and contextual terms as part of the broader discourse of civic engagement. Educators have a responsibility to provide rationales for defending higher education as a public sphere while putting into place long-term strategies and policies that resist the ongoing militarization (and corporatization and political homogeneity) of the university. This means refusing to instrumentalize the curriculum, giving the humanities a larger role in educating all undergraduate students, putting into place curricula, programs and courses that stress a critical education over job training, and enabling students to learn how to read the political and pedagogical forces that shape their lives not as consumers and soldiers but as critically engaged citizens.

Educators need to more fully theorize how pedagogy as a form of cultural politics actually constructs particular modes of address, modes of identification, affective investments and social relations that produce consent and complicity in the ethos and practice of neoliberalism and militarization. Clearly, there is a need to refute the notion that neoliberal hegemony and militarization can be explained simply through an economic optic, one that consequently gives the relationship of politics, culture and education scant analysis. Any serious opposition to militarization and neoliberalism will have to engage pedagogy as a form of cultural politics that requires a concern not only with analyses of the production and representation of meaning, but also with how these practices and the subjectivities they provoke are implicated in the dynamics of social power. Pedagogy as a form of cultural politics and governmentality raises the issue of how education might be understood as a moral and political practice that takes place in a variety of sites outside of schools. Pedagogy as defined here is fundamentally concerned with the relations among politics, subjectivities, and cultural and material production, and takes place not only in schools but also through the myriad technologies and locations that produce and shape the educational force of the wider culture. In this instance, pedagogy anchors governmentality in the 'domain of cognition', functioning largely as 'a grid of insistent calculation, experimentation and evaluation concerned with the conduct of conduct' (Dillon, 1995: 330). As Gramsci reminds us, hegemony as an educational practice is always necessarily part of a pedagogy of persuasion, one that makes a claim to 'speak to vital human needs, interests, and desires, and therefore will be persuasive to many and ultimately most people' (Willis, 1999: xiv). Similarly, Lawrence

Grossberg insists that the popular imaginary is far too important as part of a larger political and educational struggle not to be taken seriously by educators. He writes:

> The struggle to win hegemony has to be anchored in people's everyday consciousness and popular cultures. Those seeking power have to struggle with and within the contradictory realms of common sense and popular culture, with the languages and logics that people use to calculate what is right and what is wrong, what can be done and what cannot, what should be done and what has to be done. The popular is where social imagination is defined and changed, where people construct personal identities, identifications, priorities, and possibilities, where people form moral and political agendas for themselves and their societies, and where they decide whether and in what (or whom) to invest the power to speak for them. It is where people construct their hopes for the future in the light of their sense of the present. It is where they decide what matters, what is worth caring about, and what they are committed to. (Grossberg, 2005: 220–1)

Students need to learn more about how the educational force of the culture actually works pedagogically to produce neoliberal and militaristic ideologies, values, and consent—how the popular imagination both deploys power and is influenced by power. They need a better understanding of how neoliberal and militarized discourses, values and ideas are taken up in ongoing struggles over culture, meaning and identity as they bear down on people's daily lives (Kelley, 1997: 108–9). At stake here are a number of pedagogical challenges such as overcoming the deeply felt view in American culture that criticism is destructive, or for that matter a deeply rooted anti-intellectualism reinforced daily through various forms of public pedagogy as in talk radio, newspapers and the televisual info-tainment sectors. Central to such a task is challenging the neoliberal/militarized mode of governmentality that locates freedom in individual responsibility, views military supremacy as central to national identity, celebrates the armed services as the highest expression of national honor and reduces citizenship to a notion of market entrepreneurship. How might educators and others engage pedagogical practices that open up spaces of resistance to neoliberal/militarized modes of governance and authority through a culture of questioning that enables people to resist and reject neoliberal assumptions that reduce masculinity to expressions of military valor, values and battle? What are the implications of theorizing pedagogy and the practice of learning as essential to social change and where might such interventions take place? How might the related matters of experience and learning, knowledge and authority, and history and cultural capital be theorized as part of a broader pedagogy of critique and possibility? What kind of pedagogical practice might be appropriate in providing the tools to unsettle what Michael Dillon calls hegemonic 'domains of cognition' and break apart the continuity of consensus and common sense as part of a broader political and pedagogical attempt to provide people with a critical sense of social responsibility and agency? How might it be possible to theorize the pedagogical importance of the new media and the new modes of political literacy and cultural production they employ, or to

analyze the circuits of power, translation and distribution that make up neoliberalism's vast apparatus of public pedagogy—extending from talk radio and screen
culture to the Internet and print culture? These are only some of the questions that
would be central to any viable recognition of what it would mean to theorize pedagogy as a condition that supports both critique, understood as more than the struggle against incomprehension, and social responsibility as the foundation for forms of
intervention that are oppositional and empowering.

Large numbers of students pass through the hallowed halls of academe, and it
is crucial that they be educated in ways that enable them to recognize creeping militarization and its effects throughout society, particularly in terms of how these effects
threaten 'democratic government at home just as they menace the independence and
sovereignty of other countries' (Johnson, 2004: 291). But students must also recognize how such anti-democratic forces work in attempting to dismantle the university
itself as a place to learn how to think critically and engage in public debate and civic
engagement. In part, this means giving them the tools to fight for the demilitarization of knowledge on college campuses—to resist complicity with the production
of knowledge, information and technologies in classrooms and research labs that
contribute to militarized goals and purposes, which further, to quote Michael Geyer
again, is 'the process by which civil society organizes itself for the production of
violence' (1989: 79). Even so, there is more at stake than simply educating students
to be alert to the dangers of militarization and the ways in which it is redefining the
very mission of higher education. Chalmers Johnson, in his continuing critique of
the threat the politics of empire presents to democracy at home and abroad, argues
that if the United States is not to degenerate into a military dictatorship, a grassroots
movement will have to occupy center-stage in opposing militarization and reclaiming the basic principles of the republic—though he is far from optimistic. He writes:

> The evidence strongly suggests that the legislative and judicial branches of our government
> have become so servile in the presence of the imperial Presidency that they have largely lost
> the ability to respond in a principled and independent manner. . . . So the question becomes, if
> not Congress, could the people themselves restore Constitutional government? A grass-roots
> movement to abolish secret government, to bring the CIA and other illegal spying operations
> and private armies out of the closet of imperial power and into the light, to break the hold
> of the military-industrial complex, and to establish genuine public financing of elections may
> be at least theoretically conceivable. But given the conglomerate control of our mass media
> and the difficulties of mobilizing our large and diverse population, such an opting for popular
> democracy, as we remember it from our past, seems unlikely. (Johnson, 2007b)

Such a task may seem daunting, but if the American people are to choose democracy
over empire, as Johnson puts it, then there is also the crucial need for faculty, students, administrators and concerned citizens to develop alliances for long-term organizations to resist the growing ties among government agencies, corporations and
higher education that engage in reproducing militarized knowledge, which might

require severing all relationships between the university and intelligence agencies and war industries. It also means keeping military recruiters out of public and higher education. One such example can be found in People' Against Militarization (PAMO) of the Ontario Institute for Studies in Education (OISE), which brought faculty, students and community activists together to protest a partnership between OISE and the Atlantis Systems Corporation, a company that provides knowledge, training and simulation equipment for the militaries of a number of countries, including the United States and Saudi Arabia (for more information, see Homes Not Bombs, 2005). PAMO provides a valuable model, proving that such protests can be used to make visible the ongoing militarization of higher education, while also providing strategies indicating how faculty, students and others can organize to oppose it.

Opposing militarization as part of a broader pedagogical strategy in and out of the classroom also raises the question of what kinds of competencies, skills and knowledge might be crucial to such a task. One possibility is to develop a kind of praxis that addresses what I call an oppositional pedagogy of cultural production, one that defines the pedagogical space of learning not only through the critical consumption of knowledge but also through its production for peaceful and socially just ends. What is at stake here is the crucial need for students to learn how to do more than critically engage and interpret print, visual and media texts, as significant as such a task might be as part of their learning experience. This means that, as the forces of militarization increasingly monopolize the dominant media, students, activists and educators must imagine ways to expand the limits of humanities education to enable the university to shape coming generations of cultural producers capable of not only negotiating the old media forms, such as broadcasting and reporting, but also generating new electronic media, which have come to play a crucial role in bypassing those forms of media concentrated in the hands of corporate and military interests. The current monopolization of the media suggests that students will have to be educated in ways that allow them to develop alternative public spheres, where they can produce their own films, videos, music, radio talk shows, newspapers, magazines and other modes of public pedagogy. The militarization of everyday life—from the production of video games to the uncritical analysis of war and violence in the nightly news—must be challenged through alternative media. Examples of this type of oppositional public pedagogy is evident in the work of a wide range of individuals and groups who make cultural politics and public pedagogy central to their opposition to a number of anti-democratic forces, such as militarization and neoliberalism. For instance, the Media Education Foundation (n.d.) produces a range of excellent documentaries and videos for youth, many of which address the militarization of the culture, and the Global Network Against Weapons and Nuclear Power in Space (n.d.) enables songwriters and singers to disseminate music protesting the militarization of space.

In the fight against the biopolitics of militarization, educators need a language of critique, but they also need a language that embraces a sense of hope and collective struggle. This means elaborating the meaning of politics through a language of critique and possibility, on the one hand, and making a concerted effort to expand the space of politics by reclaiming 'the public character of spaces, relations, and institutions regarded as private', on the other (Rancière, 2006a: 299). We live at a time when matters of life and death are central to political sovereignty. While registering the shift in power towards the large-scale production of death, disposability and exclusion, a new biopolitics must also point to notions of agency, power and responsibility that operate in the service of life, democratic struggles and the expansion of human rights. Such struggles must be made visible, and can be found among AIDS workers in Africa, organized labor in Latin America, and Palestinians acting as human shields against Israeli tanks in the West Bank and Gaza. We can also see a biopolitics of resistance and hope at work in a long tradition of anti-militarist struggles in the United States, which have taken place not only in the wider public sphere but also in the military itself (see, for example, the very powerful film, *Sir, No Sir!*, n.d.). Efforts to end violence, speak out against war, and criticize acts of torture and abuse extend from the founding of the nation to the anti-war movements of the 1960s and the new millennium, and include the emergence of groups fighting against global sweatshops, the arms race, wage slavery, racism, child poverty, the rise of an imperial presidency and the ongoing wars in Iraq, Afghanistan and the Middle East. In addressing the militarization of the academy and everyday life, it is also crucial for educators to recognize that power works in myriad ways in the interest of both domination and struggle. In contemporary times, this suggests that educators should pay more attention to how different modes of domination inform each other, so that strategies for resistance can be layered, complex, and yet held together by more generalized notions of hope and freedom. As Jean Comaroff (2007) has recently argued, progressives need a more adequate theory of power and, as I have argued, a more complicated notion of politics. For example, any redemptive biopolitics of demilitarization would have to be understood in relation to an equally powerful biopolitics of capital, raising fundamental questions about how capital in its neoliberal incarnation and militarization in its various forms connect and inform each other on the level of the local, national and global. We might, for instance, raise the question of how neoliberalism, with its fragmenting of democratic solidarities, privatized notions of agency and eviscerated conception of politics, paves the way for the production of militarized subjects, as well as the normalization of military mentalities and moralities, and how these practices affect generations of young people.

Finally, if higher education is to come to grips with the multilayered pathologies produced by militarization, it will have to rethink not merely the space of the university as a democratic public sphere, but also the global space in which intellectuals, educators, students, artists, labor unions, and other social actors and movements can form transnational alliances both to address the ongoing effects of militarization on the world—including war, pollution, massive poverty, the arms trade, growth of privatized armies, civil conflict and child slavery—and to develop global organizations that can be mobilized in the effort to supplant a culture of war with a culture of peace, whose elemental principles are grounded in the relations of economic, political, cultural and social democracy. Militarization poses a serious threat to higher education, but more importantly it threatens to distort the promise of democracy at home and abroad, and the very meaning of democratic politics and the sustainability of human life. Surely it is time for educators to take a stand and oppose the death-dealing ideology of militarization as it lays siege to higher education and spreads insidiously through every aspect of the social order.

References

Arar, Maher (2006) 'The Horrors of "Extraordinary Rendition"', *Foreign Policy in Focus* 18 October, URL (consulted June 2008): http://www.fpif.org/fpiftxt/3636

Armitage, John (2005) 'Beyond Hypermodern Militarized Knowledge Factories', *Review of Education, Pedagogy, and Cultural Studies* 27(3): 219–39.

Aronowitz, Stanley (2003) *How Class Works*. New Haven, CT: Yale University Press.

Aronowitz, Stanley (2006) *Left Turn: Forging a New Political Future*. Boulder, CO: Paradigm.

Association of American Universities (2006) *National Defense Education and Innovation Initiative: Meeting America's Economic and Security Challenges in the 21st Century*, January, URL (consulted June 2008): http://www.aau.edu/reports/ NDEII.pdf

Bacevich, Andrew (2005) *The New American Militarism: How Americans are Seduced by War*. New York: Oxford University Press.

Baker, Kevin (2003) 'We're in the Army Now: The G.O.P.'s Plan to Militarize Our Culture', *Harper's Magazine* October: 35–46.

Beck, Ulrich (1996) *The Reinvention of Politics*. Cambridge: Polity.

Blumenstyk, Goldie (2006) 'The Military Market', *Chronicle of Higher Education* 52 (7 July): A25.

Boggs, Carl (2005) *Imperial Delusions: American Militarism and Endless War*. Denver, CO: Paradigm.

Brainard, Jeffrey (2008) 'U.S. Defense Secretary Asks Universities for New Cooperation', *The Chronicle of Higher Education*, 14 April, URL (consulted August 2008): http://chronicle.com/news/article/4316

Brown, Wendy (2005) *Edgework: Critical Essays on Knowledge and Politics*. Princeton, NJ: Princeton University Press.

Carnevale, Dan (2006) 'Military Recruiters Play Role of College Counselors', *Chronicle of Higher Education* 52 (7 July): A33.

Chomsky, Noam (2003) *Hegemony or Survival: America's Quest for Global Dominance*. New York: Metropolitan Books.

Chomsky, Noam, Laura Nader, Immanuel Wallerstein, Richard C. Lwontin, Richard Ohmann, Howard Zinn et al. (1998) *The Cold War and the University: Toward an Intellectual History of the Postwar Years*. New York: The New Press.

CIA (2007) 'Careers at the CIA: PRISP', URL (consulted June 2008): https://www.cia.gov/careers/jobs/view-all-jobs/pat-roberts-intelligence-scholars-program-prisp.html

Clayton, Mark (2003) 'Higher Espionage', *Christian Science Monitor* 29 April, URL (consulted June 2008): http://www.csmonitor.com/2003/0429/p13s01-lehl.html

Coker, Christopher (2007) *The Warrior Ethos: Military Culture and the War on Terror*. New York: Routledge.

Cole, William (2003) 'Gladiator Robot Looks to Join Marine Corps', *Honolulu Advertiser.com* 7 July, URL (consulted June 2008): http://the.honoluluadvertiser.com/article/2003/Jul/07/mn/mn01a.html

Comaroff, Jean (2007) 'Bare Life: AIDS, (Bio)Politics, and the Neoliberal Order', *Public Culture* 19(1): 197–219.

Committee on Educational Paradigms for Homeland Security, Policy, and Global Affairs (2005) *Frameworks for Higher Education in Homeland Security*. Washington, DC: National Academies Press. URL (consulted June 2008): http://books.nap.edu/catalog.php?record_id=11141#toc

Davis, Mike and Daniel Bertrand Monk (2007) *Evil Paradises*. New York: The New Press.

Dillon, Michael (1995) 'Sovereignty and Governmentality: From the Problematics of the "New World Order" to the Ethical Problematic of the World Order', *Alternatives* 20: 330.

Edwards, John (2006) 'Military R&D 101', *ElectronicDesign.com* 1 September, URL (consulted June 2008): http://www.elecdesign.com/Articles/Index.cfm?AD=1&ArticleID=13281

Falk, Richard (2003) 'Will the Empire Be Fascist?', Transnational Foundation for Peace and Future Research, 23 March, URL (consulted June 2008): http://www.transnational.org/SAJT/forum/meet/2003/Falk_FascistEmpire.html

Ferguson, Kathy E. and Phyllis Turnbull (1999) *O, Say, Can You See? The Semiotics of the Military in Hawai'i*. Minneapolis: University of Minnesota Press.

Foucault, Michel (2003) *Society Must be Defended: Lectures at the Collège de France 1975–1976*. New York: Palgrave.

Fukuyama, Francis (2007) 'The Neocons Have Learned Nothing from Five Years of Catastrophe', *The Guardian* (UK) 31 January, URL (consulted June 2008): http://www.guardian.co.uk/commentisfree/2007/jan/31/comment.usa

Geyer, Michael (1989) 'The Militarization of Europe, 1914–1945', pp. 65–102 in John R. Gillis (ed.) *The Militarization of the Western World*. New Brunswick, NJ: Rutgers University Press.

Gibbs, David N. (2003) 'The CIA is Back on Campus', *Counterpunch* 7 April, URL (consulted June 2008): http://www.counterpunch.org/gibbs04072003.html

Gillis, John R. (1989) 'Introduction', pp. 1–10 in John R. Gillis (ed.) *The Militarization of the Western World*. New Brunswick, NJ: Rutgers University Press.

Giroux, Henry A. (2002) *Breaking into the Movies*. Malden, MA: Basil Blackwell.

Giroux, Henry A. (2004) *The Terror of Neoliberalism*. Boulder, CO: Paradigm.

Giroux, Henry A. (2007) *The University in Chains: Confronting the Military-Industrial-Academic Complex*. Boulder, CO: Paradigm.

Glenn, David (2005) 'Cloak and Classroom', *Chronicle of Higher Education* 25 March: A14.

Global Network (n.d.) 'No Space Wars: Songs for Peace in Space', URL (consulted June 2008): http://www.spinspace.com/cd/artists.html

Golden, Daniel (2002) 'After Sept. 11 CIA Becomes a Growing Force on Campus', *Wall Street Journal* 4 October, URL (consulted June 2008): http://www.mindfully.org/Reform/2002/CIA-Growing-On-Campus4oct02.htm

Gray, Stephen (2006) *Ghost Plane: The True Story of the CIA Torture Program*. New York: St Martin's.

Grossberg, Lawrence (2005) *Caught in the Crossfire: Kids, Politics, and America's Future*. Boulder, CO: Paradigm.

Hardt, Michael and Antonio Negri (2004) *Multitude: War and Democracy in the Age of Empire*. New York: Penguin.

Harvey, David (2005) *A Brief History of Neoliberalism*. New York: Oxford University Press.

Hedges, Chris (2003) *War Is a Force that Gives Us Meaning*. New York: Anchor Books.

Hellman, Christopher (2006) 'The Runaway Military Budget: An Analysis', *FCNL Washington Newsletter* 3 March, URL (consulted June 2008): http://www.fcnl.org/now/pdf/2006/mar06.pdf

Hersh, Seymour (2005) *Chain of Command: The Road from 9/11 to Abu Ghraib*. New York: HarperCollins.

Holland, Joshua (2006) 'The Mystery of the Marine Massacre in Iraq', *AlterNet* 1 June, URL (consulted June 2008): http://www.alternet.org/story/36752

Homes Not Bombs (2005) 'Urgent Action: Protest Against Militarization of OISE', January, URL (consulted June 2008): http://www.homesnotbombs.ca/oiseprotest.htm

Johnson, Chalmers (2004) *The Sorrows of Empire: Militarism, Secrecy, and the End of the Republic.* New York: Metropolitan Books.

Johnson, Chalmers (2006) *Nemesis: The Last Days of the American Republic.* New York: Metropolitan Books.

Johnson, Chalmers (2007a) 'Republic or Empire: A National Intelligence Estimate on the United States', *Harper's Magazine* January: 63–9.

Johnson, Chalmers (2007b) 'Empire v. Democracy: Why Nemesis is at Our Door', *TomDispatch.com* 31 January, URL (consulted June 2008): http://www.commondreams.org/views07/0131-27.htm

Judt, Tony (2005) 'The New World Order', *New York Review of Books* 11(14 July): 14–18.

Kelley, Robin D. G. (1997) *Yo' Mama's Disfunktional!* Boston, MA: Beacon Press.

Kraska, Peter B. (2001) 'The Military-Criminal Justice Blur: An Introduction', pp. 3–13 in Peter B. Kraska (ed.) *Militarizing the American Criminal Justice System.* Boston: Northeastern University Press.

Laor, Yitzhak (2006) 'You Are Terrorists, We Are Virtuous', *London Review of Books* 28 (17 August), URL (consulted June 2008): http://www.lrb.co.uk/v28/n16/print/laor01_.html

Los Angeles Times editorial (2006) 'Advise and Assent', *Los Angeles Times* 19 February, URL (consulted June 2008): http://www.truthout.org/article/la-times-the-senate-coverup-committee

Lowen, Rebecca S. (1997) *Creating the Cold War University: The Transformation of Stanford.* Berkeley: University of California Press.

Lutz, Catherine (2002) 'Making War at Home in the United States: Militarization and the Current Crisis', *American Anthropologist* 104(3): 723–35.

McColm, Greg and Sherman Dorn (2005) 'A University's Dilemma in the Age of National Security', *Thought & Action* (Fall): 163–77.

Martin, William G. (2005) 'Manufacturing the Homeland Security Campus and Cadre', *ACAS Bulletin* 70 (Spring), URL (consulted June 2008): http://acas.prairienet.org/bulletin/bull70-07-martin.html

Mayer, Jane (2005) 'A Deadly Interrogation', *The New Yorker* 14 November, URL (consulted June 2008): http://www.newyorker.com/fact/content/articles/051114fa_fact

Media Education Foundation (n.d.) URL (consulted June 2008): http://www.mediaed.org/about

Mills, C. Wright (1993 [1956]) *The Power Elite.* New York: Oxford University Press.

Monbiot, George (2003) 'States of War: Appeasing the Armed Forces Has Become a Political Necessity for the American President', *The Guardian* (UK) 14 October, URL (consulted June 2008): http://www.commondreams.org/views03/1014-09.htm

Mooney, Chris (2002) 'Good Company: It's Time for the CIA and Scholars to Work Together. Again', *The American Prospect* 18 November, URL (consulted June 2008): http://www.prospect.org/cs/articles?article=good_company

Nelson, Cary (2004) 'The National Security State', *Cultural Studies* 4(3): 357–361.

Newfield, Christopher (2006) 'The Culture of Force', *South Atlantic Quarterly* (Winter): 241–63.

Ong, Aihwa (2006) *Neoliberalism as Exception: Mutations in Citizenship and Sovereignty.* Durham, NC: Duke University Press.

Perelman, Michael (2005) 'The Role of Higher Education in a Security State', *Thought & Action* (Fall): 179–86.

Price, David (2004) *Threatening Anthropology: McCarthyism and the FBI's Surveillance of Activist Anthropologists.* Durham, NC: Duke University Press.

Price, David (2005) 'The CIA's Campus Spies', *Counterpunch* 12–13 March, URL (consulted June 2008): http://www.counterpunch.org/price03122005.html

Priest, Dana (2005) 'CIA Holds Terror Suspects in Secret Prisons', *Washington Post* 2 November: A01.

Rancière, Jacques (2006a) 'Democracy, Republic, Representation', *Constellations* 13(3): 297–307.

Rancière, Jacques (2006b) *Hatred of Democracy*. London: Verso.

Reed, Jay (2001) 'Towards a 21st-century Peace Movement: The University of Texas Connection', *UT-Watch.org* 12 September, URL (consulted June 2008): http://www.utwatch.org/war/ut_military.html

Roelofs, Joan (2006) 'Military Contractor Philanthropy: Why Some Stay Silent', *Counterpunch* 25 January, URL (consulted June 2008): http://www.counterpunch.org/roelofs01252006.html

Rose, Nikolas (2007) *The Politics of Life Itself: Biomedicine, Power, and Subjectivity in the Twenty-first Century*. Princeton, NJ: Princeton University Press.

Rosen, Ruth (2002) 'Politics of Fear', *San Francisco Chronicle* 30 December, URL (consulted June 2008): http://www.commondreams.org/views02/1230–02.htm

Rule, James (1998) 'Markets, in Their Place', *Dissent* (Winter): 29–35. Rutherford, Jonathan (2005) 'At War', *Cultural Studies* 19(5): 622–42.

Saad-Filho, Alfredo and Deborah Johnston (eds.) (2005) *Neoliberalism: A Critical Reader*. London: Pluto.

Searer, Kirsten (2003) 'ASU's Crow Partners with CIA on Research Projects', *The Tribune* 30 March, URL (consulted January 2007): http://license.icopyright.net/user/viewFreeUse.act?fuid=MTU5NTM5

Shah, Anap (2006) 'High Military Expenditures in Some Places', *Global Issues* 9 November, URL (consulted June 2008): http://www.globalissues.org/Geopolitics/ArmsTrade/Spending.asp?p=1

Shropshire, Corilyn (2005) 'The Gladiator Robot's First Public Appearance', *Pittsburgh Post-Gazette* 5 August, URL (consulted June 2008): http://www.primidi.com/2005/08/08.html

Simpson, Christopher (ed.) (1998) *Universities and Empire: Money and Politics in the Social Sciences during the Cold War*. New York: The New Press.

Singh, Nikhil (2006) 'The Afterlife of Fascism', *South Atlantic Quarterly* 105(1): 71–93.

Sir, No Sir! (n.d.) Documentary film, URL (consulted June 2008): http://www.sirnosir.com/

Smith, Neil (2005) *The Endgame of Globalization*. New York: Routledge.

Steinmetz, George (2003) 'The State of Emergency and the Revival of American Imperialism: Toward an Authoritarian Post-Fordism', *Public Culture* 15(2): 323–46.

Sterngold, James (2004) 'After 9/11 US Policy Built on World Bases', *San Francisco Chronicle* 21 March, URL (consulted June 2008): http://www.sfgate.com/cgi-bin/article.cgi?file=/c/a/2004/03/21/MNGJ65OS4J1.DTL&type=printable

ThinkProgress.org (2006) 'Sen. Pat Roberts (R-KS): Chairman of the Senate Cover-up Committee', *ThinkProgress* 8 March, URL (consulted June 2008): http://thinkprogress.org/roberts-coverup/

Turse, Nicholas (2004) 'The Military-Academic Complex', *TomDispatch.com* 29 April, URL (consulted June 2008): http://www.countercurrents.org/us-turse290404.htm

USA Today (2006) 'Spy Chief Discloses Total Number of US Intelligence Personnel', *USA Today* 20 April, URL (consulted June 2008): http://www.usatoday.com/news/washington/2006-04-20-intelligencepersonnel_x.htm

Wayne, Leslie (2006) 'Heady Days for Makers of Weapons', *The New York Times* 26 December: 7.

Weaver, C. Kay and Cynthia Carter (eds.) (2006) *Critical Readings: Violence and the Media*. New York: Open University Press.

Willis, Ellen (1999) *Don't Think, Smile*. Boston, MA: Beacon Press.

Wolf, Jim (2006) 'US Predicts Bumper Year in Arms Sales', *Reuters* 4 December, URL (consulted June 2008): http://www.commondreams.org/headlines06/120507.htm

RADICALIZING

HOPE

Public Intellectualism,
The Vitalism of Education,
and the Promise of Democracy

CHAPTER 13

Democracy, Freedom, and Justice after September 11th

Rethinking the Role of Educators and the Politics of Schooling

2002

This is a difficult time in American history. The tragic and horrific terrorist acts of September 11 suggest a traumatic and decisive turning point in the history of the United States. Some commentators have compared it to the Japanese attack on Pearl Harbor. Others suggest that the history of the twenty-first century will be defined against the cataclysmic political, economic, and legal changes inaugurated by the monstrous events of September 11. Similarly, many people are now aware that, for better or worse, the United States is part of a globalized system, the effects of which cannot be completely controlled.[1] There is also a newfound sense of collective unity organized not only around flag-waving displays of patriotism but also around collective fears and an ongoing militarization of visual culture and public space.

As President Bush declared that the United States is at war, the major television networks capitalized on this militarized notion of patriotism, repeatedly framing their news programs against tag lines such as "America at War," "America Strikes Back," or "America Recovers." Fox News Network delivered a fever-pitch bellicosity that informed much of its ongoing commentaries and reactions to the terrorist bombings, framed nightly against its widely recognized image, "America United." A majority of both the op-ed commentaries in the dominant media and the television commentaries appearing on the major networks, such as ABC, NBC, and CBS, proclaimed their support for government and military action, while giving relatively little exposure to dissenting positions.[2] Many news commentators and journalists in the dominant press have taken up the events of September 11 within the context of World War II, invoking daily the symbols of revenge, retaliation, and war. Against an endless onslaught of images of U.S. jets bombing Afghanistan, amply supplied by the Defense Department, the dominant media connects the war abroad with the domestic struggle at home by presenting numerous stories about the endless ways in which potential terrorists might use nuclear weapons, poison the food supply, or unleash biochemical agents on the American population. The increased fear and insecurity created by such stories simultaneously served to legitimize a host of anti-democratic practices at home, including "the beginnings of a concerted attack on civil liberties, freedom of expression, and freedom of the press,"[3] and a growing sentiment on the part of the American public that people who suggest that terrorism should be analyzed, in part, within the context of American foreign policy should not be allowed "to teach in the public schools, work in the government, and even make a speech at a college."[4] Against this militarization of public discourse, Hollywood and television producers provide both Spielberg-type patriotic spectacles, such as the made-for-television HBO dramatic series, *Band of Brothers*, and Hollywood's uncritical homage to the military in films such as *Behind Enemy Lines*, *Black Hawk Down*, and *Spy Games*. All of these narratives offer romanticized images of military valor and a hyper-masculine, if not over-the-top, patriotic portrayal of war and violence—while hoping to capitalize on the current infatuation with the military experience by raking in big box office receipts.

In this article I illustrate the many ways in which life in post-September 11 America is both a rupture from some of the antigovernment politics that dominated before these tragic events and an uncanny continuity from the pre-September 11 worship of global capitalism and the virtual abandonment of any effort to create greater equality. In showing both these ruptures and continuities, I hope to help educators contemplate the role that public schools might play in facilitating an alternative discourse grounded in a critique of militarism, consumerism, and racism. Such an alternative discourse would redefine democracy as something separate and distinct from the hyper-individualized market-based relations of capitalism and the retrograde appeal to jingoistic patriotism.

In other words, before the attacks on the World Trade Center and the Pentagon, popular perceptions of politics and government were that they were either corrupt or irrelevant. It now appears that the government, especially the military and law enforcement, is a defining feature of American life, both pressing and despairing at the same time.[5] Still, as significant as September 11 might be as a moment of rupture, it is imperative to look at the crucial continuities that either have remained the same or have escalated since the attacks. For instance, prior to September 11th, there was a growing concern with the buildup in racial profiling, the criminalization of social policies, the growth of the prison-industrial complex and multilayered systems of social control and surveillance,[6] and the ongoing attacks by the police against people of color.[7] These trends seemed disturbing before the events of September 11th, but now they have the cloak of official legitimacy, buttressed by the sense of insecurity and fear that, in part, mobilizes the call for patriotism and national security. For instance, little has been reported in the dominant media about the attacks and violence waged against people perceived as Middle Eastern. As Mike Davis observes,

The big city dailies and news networks have shown patriotic concern for the US image abroad by downplaying what otherwise might have been recognized as the good old boy equivalent of *Kristallnacht*. Yet even the fragmentary statistics are chilling. In this six weeks after 11 September, civil rights groups estimate that there were at least six murders and one thousand serious assaults committed against people perceived as "Arab" or "Muslim" including several hundred attacks on Sikhs.[8]

While there has been some resistance in both the media and among diverse groups to the accelerated practice of racial profiling, the American public largely supports the indefinite detention by federal authorities of over 11,000 immigrants, only four of whom, according to Davis, have direct links to terrorist organizations.[9] Already imperiled before the aftershocks of the terrorists attacks, democracy appears even more fragile in this time of crisis as new antiterrorist laws have been passed that make it easier to undermine those basic civil liberties that protect individuals against invasive and potentially repressive government actions. Against a government and media induced culture of fear, "Federal law enforcement is being restructured so that the FBI can permanently focus on the War against Terrorism— meaning that it will largely become an elite immigration police—while a mysterious new Pentagon entity, the Homeland Defense Command, will presumably adopt the Mexican border as a principal battlefield."[10] A further threat to democracy can be found in the recently passed USA Patriot Act of 2001. This legislation increases law enforcement's power to conduct surveillance, never-disclosed wiretaps, and secret searches and detain immigrants indefinitely, and it authorizes the Central Intelligence Agency (CIA) to resume spying on U.S. citizens. The bill also authorizes secret immigration trials, unreviewable military tribunals, and the monitoring of attorney-client conversations. Not only does the bill introduce a broadly defined crime of "domestic terrorism," it also allows people to be interned and tried on the basis of secret evidence. Many conservatives and liberals view these laws as both a violation of the Constitution and a threat to some of the most basic freedoms endemic to a democratic state. For instance, conservative columnist William Safire has referred to the military tribunals as "kangaroo courts," and David Cole, a progressive lawyer, has argued that the Patriot Act "imposes guilt by association on immigrants . . . and resurrects the philosophy of McCarthyism, simply substituting 'terrorist' for 'communist.'" He also argues that "the military tribunals eliminate virtually every procedural check designed to protect the innocent and accurately identity the guilty."[11] The notion of what constitutes a just society is in flux, betrayed in part by the legacy and language of a commercial culture that collapses the imperatives of a market economy and the demands of a democratic society, and a present that makes humanitarian and political goals a footnote to military goals.[12] Instead of seeing the current crisis as a break from the past, it is crucial for educators and others to begin to understand how the past might be useful in addressing what it means to live in a democracy in the aftermath of September 11. This suggests establishing a vision of freedom, equity, education, and justice, as Homi Bhabha points out "informed by civil liberties and human rights, which carries with it the shared obligations and responsibilities of common, collaborative citizenship."[13]

Unity, Civil Liberties, and Patriotism

Official calls for unity, burdened with rage and grief for those killed or injured in the terrorist attacks, waver between agitprop displays of patriotism and a genuine attempt to understand and address the political reality of balancing civil liberties and national security, fear and reason, compassion and anger. The political reality that emerges from the crisis points to a set of choices the American people are being asked to make that include an ongoing military war in Afghanistan, with the possibility of wider military strikes on other Islamic nations, and the demand to sacrifice some basic civil liberties to strengthen domestic security. Of course, Americans have every right to demand that our children, cities, water supply, public buildings, and most crucial public spaces be safe from terrorists. And we must do something in response to such brutal acts of violence. But the demand for security and safety calls for more than military action and the rescinding of basic civil liberties; it also points to larger political issues that demand a diplomatic offensive based on a critical examination of the very nature of our own domestic and foreign policy. Educators have an important role to play in encouraging such an examination of American history and foreign policy among their students and colleagues. Equally important is the need for educators to use their classrooms not only to help students to think critically about the world around them but also to offer a sanctuary and forum where they can address their fears, anger, and concerns about the events of September 11 and how it has affected their lives. The events of September 11 provide educators with a crucial opportunity to reclaim schools as democratic public spheres in which students can engage in dialogue and critique around the meaning of democratic values, the relationship between learning and civic engagement, and the connection between schooling, what it means to be a critical citizen, and the responsibilities one has to the larger world.[14]

Nothing justifies the violence by terrorists committed against those innocent people who died on September 11th. Americans should be unified against that type of terror, and rightly so, but we need to define not only what we are against but also what we stand for as a nation, and how such a project draws from the principles and values that inform the promise of a more fully developed democracy in a global landscape. In a time of crisis, unity is a powerful force, but it is not always innocent, and it must become part of a broader dialogue about how the United States defines itself and its relationship to the rest of the world, particularly to those Western and Middle Eastern societies that reject or are resistant to democratic and egalitarian rule.

If this national crisis has shattered the American sense of alleged complacency and purported self-indulgence, it has also aroused a sense of unity that has sent a chilling message of intolerance towards dissenting opinions about America's role. Early casualties included two journalists, Dan Guthrie, a columnist for the *Daily*

Courier of Grants Pass, Oregon, and Tom Gutting of *The Texas City Sun*, both of whom were fired for criticizing President Bush soon after the terrorist bombings.[15] Equally disturbing was a statement issued by both the chancellor and the trustees of the City University of New York, condemning professors who criticized United States foreign policy at a teach-in.[16] Neither the trustees nor the chancellor attended the teach-in, basing their response on articles that appeared in *The New York Post*. A similar attack occurred by Lynne V. Cheney, wife of the vice president and former chairwoman of the National Endowment for the Humanities, and Scott Rubush, an associate editor of *FrontPage* magazine. Cheney denounced Judith Rizzo, deputy chancellor of the New York City schools when she "said terrorist attacks demonstrated the importance of teaching about Muslim cultures."[17] Rubush, while appearing on National Public Radio in October, argued that four faculty members at the University of North Carolina at Chapel Hill had been critical of American foreign policy and should be fired because "They're using state resources to the practical effect of aiding and abetting the Taliban."[18]

Cheney was also involved in what was one of the most disturbing attacks on people who have dissented against American foreign policy. She and Senator Joseph Lieberman founded an organization called the American Council of Trustees and Alumni, which published the recent report, *Defending Civilization: How Our Universities Are Failing America, and What Can Be Done About It.*[19] This report includes a list of 117 comments made by faculty and students in the wake of September 11 and points to such comments to argue that American campuses are "short on patriotism and long on self-flagellation."[20] The report not only suggests that dissent is unpatriotic but also reveals the names of those academics who are allegedly guilty of such crimes. The report was sent to three thousand trustees, donors, and alumni across the country, urging them to wage a campaign on college campuses to require the teaching of American history and Western civilization and to protest and take actions against those intellectuals who are not loyal to this group's version of patriotism.[21]

Across the United States, a number of professors have been either fired or suspended for speaking out critically about post-September 11 events.[22] Patriotism in this view becomes a euphemism for shutting down dissent, eliminating critical dialogue, and condemning critical citizenship in the interest of conformity and a dangerous departure from what it means to uphold a viable democracy. Needless to say, teachers in both K-12 and higher education are particularly vulnerable to these forms of censorship, particularly if they attempt to engage their students in pedagogical approaches that critically explore the historical, ideological, and political contexts of the attacks and the underlying causes of terrorism, not to mention any controversial subject that calls into question the authority and role of the United States in domestic and foreign affairs. Such censorship shuts down critical inquiry in the schools and prevents students from learning how to distinguish an explanation from a justification. Richard Rothstein, a *New York Times* reporter, is right in arguing that "[T]eachers should be encouraged to explore whether there are specific politics that may give rise to terrorism, without being accused of undermining patriotism and national unity. Students who are not taught to question our policies will be ill-prepared as adults to improve on them."[23]

There is a difference between justifying terrorism and trying to historically contextualize and explain it, and this distinction appears to be lost on those who are quick to argue that academic freedom and civil liberties are expendable in a post-September 11th world.[24] Unfortunately, an unparalleled sense of unity and display of "patriotism" on the part of the American people have also given rise to what some journalists have called a display of "stunning intolerance,"[25] exacerbating an already unrestrained and indiscriminate hatred toward the seven million Americans who are Muslims. In some cases, insults have been replaced by violence, resulting in death, and as the wave of hate speech and incidents escalate, the American people fall prey to the most retrograde and dangerous views. For instance, a Gallop Poll released on October 4, 2001, indicated that "49 percent of the American people said yes to the idea that Arabs, including those who are American citizens, should carry special identification," and "58 percent demand that Arabs, including those who are Americans, should undergo special, more intense security checks in general."

Such views reflect an uncritical notion of "patriotism"[26] and are at odds with the most basic principles of an effective democracy informed by a critical democratic education that encourages, rather than closes down, dialogue, critique, dissent, and social justice. At its best, patriotism means that a country does everything possible to question itself, to provide the conditions for its people to actively engage and transform the policies that shape their lives and others. At its worst, patriotism confuses dissent with treason, arrogance with strength, and brute force as the only exemplar of justice. The main obstacles to justice will not be found in weakening civil liberties, nourishing bellicose calls for revenge, or for drawing lines in the sand between the West and the rest. As George Monblot points out, "[I]t seems that in trying to shout the terrorist out, we have merely imprisoned ourselves. . . [F]ree speech and dissent have now joined terrorism as the business of 'evil does.' If this is a victory for civilization, I would hate to see what defeat looks like."[27]

Ignorance and arrogance are no substitute for reasoned analyses, critical understanding, and an affirmation of democratic principles of justice. Any call for further giving up civil liberties and freedom of speech suggests a dangerous silence about the degree to which civil liberties are already at risk and how the current call for national safety might work to further a different type of terrorism, one not marked by bombs and explosions but by state-supported repression, the elimination of dissent, and the death of both the reality and promise of democracy.

But unreflective patriotism as home-team boosterism runs the risk of not only bolstering the conditions for what Matthew Rothschild, the editor of *The Progressive*, calls The New McCarthyism[28] but also of feeding a commercial frenzy that turns collective grief into profits and reminds us how easy the market converts noble concepts like public service and civic courage into forms of civic vacuity. Frank Rich, an editorial writer for *The New York Times*, calls this trend "Patriotism on the Cheap" and captures its paean to commercialism in the following commentary:

> "9/11" is now free to be a brand, ready to do its American duty and move products. Ground zero, at last an official tourist attraction with its own viewing stand, has vendors and lines to rival those at Disneyland. (When Ashleigh Banfield stops by, visitors wave and smile at the TV camera just as they do uptown at the "Today'" show.) Barnes & Noble offers competing coffee-table books handsomely packaging the carnage of yesteryear. On Gary Condit's Web site, a snapshot of the congressman's own visit to ground zero sells his re-election campaign. NBC, whose Christmas gift to the nation was its unilateral lifting of a half-century taboo against hard-liquor commercials, deflects criticism by continuing to outfit its corporate peacock logo in stars and stripes.[29]

Red, white, and blue flags adorn a plethora of fashion items, including hats, dresses, coats, T-shirts, robes, and scarves. Many corporations now organize their advertisements around displays of patriotism—signaling their support for the troops abroad, the victims of the brutal terrorists acts, and, of course, American resolve—each ad amply displaying its respective corporate or brand-name logo, working hard to gain some cash value by defining commercialism and consumerism as the ultimate demonstration of patriotism.[30] As I point out in more detail in the following sections, in this register, consumerism and the squelching of dissent represent mutually compatible notions of a view of patriotism in which citizenship is more about the freedom to buy than the ability of individuals to engage in "critical public dialogue and broadened civic participation leading (so it is hoped) to far-reaching change."[31] It gets worse.

Moral panic following the September attacks has not only redefined public space as the "sinister abode of danger, death and infection"[32] and fueled the collective rush to "patriotism on the cheap," it also has buttressed the "fear economy." Defined as "the complex of military and security firms rushing to exploit the national nervous breakdown,"[33] the fear economy promises big financial gains for both the defense department, already asking for an additional twenty billion dollar increase from the Bush administration, and the antiterrorist security sectors, primed to terror-proof everything from trash cans and water systems to shopping malls and public restrooms.

Democracy and Capitalism Are Not the Same

Defined largely through an appeal to fear and a call to strengthen domestic security, the space of the social has been both militarized and increasingly commodified. As such, there is little public conversation about connecting the social to democratic values, justice, or what the public good might mean in light of this horrible attack as a moral and political referent to denounce mass acts of violence and to attempt to secure freedom and justice for all people. In fact, since the terrorist attacks on September 11th, the media has largely treated the notions of freedom and security without any reference to how these terms might be taken up as part of a wider set of political, economic, and social interests that were at work before the terrorists wreaked havoc on New York and Washington, DC. In part, this is due to the willingness of the largely dominant media, politicians, and others to substitute jingoistic drum beating for a reasoned analysis of what it would mean to "put public affairs back on the American agenda, to revive people's sense that they have a stake in the way our society is run."[34]

Such questions are crucial to any national conversation about the relationship among security, freedom, and democracy and the future of the United States, but such a task would demand, in part, addressing what vocabularies and practices regarding the space of the social and political were actually in place prior to the events of September 11th and what particular notions of freedom, security, and citizenship were available to Americans—the legacy and influence of which might prevent them in assuming the role of critical and engaged citizens capable of addressing this national crisis. Instead of seeing the current crisis as a break from the past, it is crucial for the American public to begin to understand how the past might be useful in addressing what it means to live in a democracy in the aftermath of the bombings in New York and Washington, DC. Public schools should play a decisive role in helping students configure the boundaries between history and the present, incorporating a critical understanding of those events that are often left out of the rendering of contemporary considerations that define the roles students might play as critical citizens. Of course, this will be difficult since many public schools are overburdened with high-stakes test and harsh accountability systems designed to get teachers to narrow their curriculum and to focus only on raising test scores. Consequently, any struggle to make schools more democratic and socially relevant will have to link the battle for critical citizenship to an ongoing fight against turning schools into testing centers and teachers into technicians.

How we define the social with its attendant notions of freedom and security cannot be separated from a legacy of neoliberalism, in which the space of the social is largely defined through a set of market relations that commodify, privatize, and utterly commercialize the meaning of freedom and security. Construing profit making as the essence of democracy, neoliberalism provides a rationale for a handful of private interests to control as much of social life as possible to maximize their financial investments. Within this growing marketization and privatization of everyday life, market relations as they define the economy are viewed as a paradigm for democracy itself. Capitalism now defines the meaning of freedom, and to paraphrase Milton Friedman profit making is the essence of democracy. Defined almost exclusively through the rhetoric of commercial forces, the social under the economic policies of neoliberalism has undermined the discourses of moral responsibility, democratic values, and political agency. Abstracted from its notion of the social has been the crucial issue of what it means to provide people with the capacities for them to be critical agents, capable of making collectively binding choices and to carry them out as part of the responsibility of translating social issues into collective action and to insist on a language of the public good. Even worse, the privatized notion of the social that has dominated American life for the last twenty years makes it increasingly difficult for people to invest in the notion of the public good as a political idea, or to believe they can be agents of change and that political and ethical values matter, or that democracy as an experience does not appear as surplus and is worth investing in and fighting for.

The discourse of security and freedom prior to the September 11th attacks pointed to a very different notion of the social, one that had very little to do with democratic social relationships, compassion, and noncommodified values. Freedom was largely defined as the freedom to pursue one's own individual interests, largely free of governmental interference, and seemed at odds with a more democratic notion of freedom—which would include, as Edward Said has argued, the "right to a whole range of choices affording cultural, political, intellectual and economic development— [that] ipso facto will lead to a desire for articulation rather than silence."[35] Decoupled from freedom, security within the last twenty years has become synonymous with big government and a debilitating form of dependency. Security traditionally meant investing in a welfare state that provided individuals not only with basic rights but also those social provisions that enabled them to develop their capacities as citizens free from the most basic wants and deprivations. This suggested creating a state that provided a modicum of support and services to make sure people had access to decent health care, food, child care, public schooling, employment, basic financial support, and housing.

Under neoliberal social and economic policies, such notions of security became highly privatized as the welfare state was hollowed out. With the election of Ronald Reagan to the presidency in the 1980s, freedom was defined largely in market terms, removed from questions of equity, and traditional notions of security became a referent point for attacking big government and dismantling the welfare state. The social, in this instance, extending from the Reagan to the Clinton eras, collapsed under the weight of a market philosophy that could only imagine a privatized notion of agency and viewed community as an obstacle to market-based values that stressed excessive individualism, privatization, commercialization, and the bottom line. Under such circumstances, the helping functions of society gave way to the largely policing functions, and the logic of free market exchange undermined those collective structures that fought for social guarantees, public services, and equality of rights. As the social became individualized, uncertainty and fear worked to depoliticize a population that is educated to believe that social problems can only be addressed through private solutions. Within such a climate, shared responsibilities gave way to shared trepidation.

In light of such views and practices, I want to suggest that while the social is being affirmed and reshaped as a result of this terrible tragedy, the terms through which public life and citizenship are being invoked need to be critically engaged within a legacy of neoliberalism that limits profoundly the vocabulary and values available for developing a language of critique and possibility for addressing the responsibilities of critical citizenship and the demands of a democratic society in a time of crisis. For instance, while the role of big government and public services have made a comeback on behalf of the common good, especially in providing crucial services related to public health and safety, President Bush and his supporters remain "wedded to the same reactionary agenda he pushed before the attack."[36] Instead of addressing the gaps in both public health needs and the safety net for workers, young people, and the poor, President Bush is trying to put into law a stimulus plan based primarily on tax breaks for the wealthy and major corporations, while at the same time "pressing for an energy plan that features subsidies and tax breaks for energy companies and drilling in the Arctic wilderness."[37] Investing in children, the environment, and those most in need as well as in crucial public services, once again gives way to investing in the rich and repaying corporate contributors and suggests that little has changed with respect to economic policy, regardless of all the talk about the past being irrevocably repudiated in light of the events of September 11.

The collapse of public life over the last twenty years makes it all the more essential that educators rearticulate a notion of the social at the present time that is framed not only against the recent terrorist attacks on the United States but also in light of the emergence of a market-based philosophy that undermines the promise of democracy, the meaning of critical citizenship, and the importance of public engagement. Crucial to such a debate is the role that educators, educational researchers, theorists, and policy makers might play in intervening both with students and others in an ongoing public conversation about the national crisis arising out of the events of September 11. At the heart of such a debate is the need to decouple a market economy from the notion of democracy, to refuse the neoliberal notion that market relations and profit making constitute the meaning and substance of democracy. Sheldon Wolin has recently argued that we need to rethink the notion of loss and how it impacts the possibility for opening up democratic public life. Wolin points to the need for educators to resurrect and raise questions about "What survives of the defeated, the indigestible, the unassimilated, the 'cross-grained,' the 'not wholly obsolete.'"[38] As I have argued elsewhere, "something is missing" in an age of manufactured politics and pseudo-publics catering almost exclusively to desires and drives produced by the commercial hysteria of the market.[39] What is missing is a language, movement, and vision that refuses to equate democracy with consumerism, market relations, and privatization. In the absence of such a language and the social formation and public spheres that make it operative, politics becomes narcissistic and caters to the mood of widespread pessimism and the cathartic allure of the spectacle. This is especially important for reinvigorating the debate about public education, which in the last few years has been dominated by discourses of testing, privatization, vouchers, and standards. If schools are not to be defined as either training centers for the corporations or as high-stakes testing centers, it is imperative for educators to reassert the discourse of critical citizenship, public participation, and democracy as central to the meaning and purpose of schooling. It part, this means challenging the most basic tenets of neoliberalism, with its central assumption that market relations define the nature of schooling, the social and public life. Or, as Lewis Lapham puts it, democracy cannot be "understood as a fancy Greek name for the American Express Card."[40]

Education and the Challenge of Revitalizing the Democratic Public Life

Since the beginning of the 1980s Americans have lived with a heightened sense of insecurity and uncertainty. The tools that were available in the past to deal with the most basic necessities of life such as healthcare, employment, shelter, and education are increasingly disappearing as the welfare state is attacked in the name of market forces that equate profit making with the essence of democracy and consumption as the ultimate privilege of citizenship.[41]

As the state is increasingly relieved of its welfare-providing functions, it defaults on its capacity to provide people with the most basic social provisions, extending from health care to public transportation, and simultaneously withdraws from its obligation to create those noncommodified public spheres in which people learn the language of ethics, civic courage, democratically charged politics, and collective empowerment. Within such a turn of events, schools are increasingly defined less as a public good than as sites for financial investment and entrepreneurial training—that is, as a private good. As big business comes to play a central role in school reform, public schools are increasingly asked to operate under the imperative to conform to the needs of the market and reflect more completely the interests of corporate culture. Targeted primarily as a source of investments for substantial profits, public schools are under pressure to define themselves as commercial spheres to restructure civic life in the image of market culture and to educate students as consumers rather than as multifaceted social agents.[42]

Public spheres disappear amid a flurry of commercial activity as shopping malls proliferate, outnumbering both secondary high schools and post offices. Increasingly, the vocabulary of a market-based ideology substitutes the discourse of self-reliance and competition for the language of democratic participation, community, and the notion of the public good. One striking example can be seen in the corporate language of schooling, in which notions of competition, self-reliance, and individual choice dominate the discourse of high-stakes testing, the standards movement, the school choice agenda, and the charter school movement. Another example can be seen in many rural towns, where economic growth is tied to a prison-industry complex that promises jobs by building new prisons. Policing and incarceration emerge as part of a larger pattern of social control, dressed up, in part, as strategic growth to reignite the economies of rural towns.[43] Missing from this unfortunate trend is any mention of the horror "at the spectacle of a society in which local officials are

reduced to lobbying for prisons as their best chance for economic growth."[44] Nor
is there any mention in the rhetoric of such economic renewal projects that mostly
white residents are securing their economic dreams on the transit and lockdown of
largely poor African Americans, who make up fully half of the two million Americans currently behind bars in this country.[45] Nor is there any room in this discourse
for recognizing that increasing militarization abroad will mean more militarization
on the domestic front, especially against "vulnerable groups such as immigrants and
communities of color bearing the brunt of the intensified assault on civil liberties."[46]
Utopia now becomes privatized and racialized as social problems are translated
as personal issues and the tools for translating personal considerations into public
issues gradually disappear amid the alleged virtues of corporate competitive values
and the incessant celebration in the media of those individuals who have made it
in the marketplace because of their ability to "go it alone" through the sheer will
of their competitive spirit.[47] As the social is refigured through the privatized lens of
market relations, radical insecurity and uncertainty replace ethical considerations,
social justice, and any viable notion of collective hope.

As those public spaces that offer forums for debating norms, critically engaging
ideas, making private issues public, and evaluating judgements disappear under the
juggernaut of neoliberal policies, it becomes crucial for educators to raise fundamental questions about what it means to revitalize public life, politics, and ethics in ways
that take seriously such values as patriotism, "citizen participation, . . . political obligation, social governance, and community,"[48] especially at a time of national crisis
when such terms become less an object of analysis than uncritical veneration. The
call for a revitalized politics grounded in an effective democracy substantively challenges the dystopian practices of neoliberalism—with its all-consuming emphasis on
market relations, commercialization, privatization, and the creation of a worldwide
economy of part-time workers—against its utopian promises. Such an intervention
confronts educators with the problem as well as the challenge of analyzing, engaging, and developing those public spheres—such as the media, public education, and
other cultural institutions—that provide the conditions for creating citizens who
are equipped to exercise their freedoms, competent to question the basic assumptions that govern political life, and skilled enough to participate in shaping the basic
social, political, and economic orders that govern their lives. It is precisely within
these public spheres that the events of September 11th and military action against
Afghanistan, the responsibility of the media, the civic obligation of educators, and
America's role in the world as a superpower should be debated rather than squelched
in the name of an unthinking patriotism.

Two factors work against such a debate on any level. First, there are very few
public spheres left that provide the space for such conversations to take place. Secondly, it is increasingly difficult for young people and adults to appropriate a critical
language, outside of the market, that would allow them to translate private problems into public concerns or to relate public issues to private considerations. For

many young people and adults today, the private sphere has become the only space in which to imagine any sense of hope, pleasure, or possibility. Market forces focus on the related issues of consumption and safety. Reduced to the act of consuming, citizenship is "mostly about forgetting, not learning."[49] And as social visions of equity and justice cede from public memory, unfettered brutal self-interests combine with retrograde social policies to make security a top domestic priority. One consequence, once again, is that all levels of government are being hollowed out, reducing their role to dismantling the gains of the welfare state as they increasingly construct politics that criminalize social problems and prioritize penal methods over social investments, even as the post-September 11 events have rallied a renewal on the part of many Americans in the importance of big government as a provider of public services, public infrastructures, and public goods. Hence, it is not surprising that the current concern with security, with its implied notions of further militarizing and policing ever more aspects of daily life, is surprisingly disconnected from the disturbing rise of a prison-industrial complex that also prioritizes punishment over rehabilitation, containment over social investment.[50]

For many commentators, the events of September 11th signaled a turn away from the complacency, cynicism, and political indifference that allegedly attested to civic disengagement and the "weak" character of the American public. In this discourse, the focus on character seemed to replace any sense of either the complexity of the American public or how dominant political, cultural, and economic forces have shaped it. Frank Rich, an op-ed writer for *The New York Times* argues that the terrorist acts had revitalized the patriotic spirit of a "country that during its boom became addicted to instant gratification."[51] Rich seems to forget that the luxury of such "gratification" only applied to the top twenty percent of the population. He also ignores the fact that while most Americans exhibit a disinclination to vote or put too much faith in their government, they also have been bombarded by a corporate culture that not only relentlessly commercializes and privatizes noncommodified public spheres but also has almost nothing to say about civic values, civic engagement, or the importance of nonmarket values in enabling people to identify and fight for those public goods and spheres—such as public schools and a noncommercial media—that are essential to any vibrant democracy. When citizenship is reduced to the spectacle of consumerism, it should come as no surprise that people develop an indifference to citizen engagement and participation in democratic public life.[52] In fact, I want to stress once again that when notions of freedom and security are decoupled and freedom is reduced to the imperatives of market exchange, and security is divested from a defense of a version of the welfare state distinguished by its social provisions and "helping functions," not only does freedom collapse into a brutal form of individualism but also the state is stripped of its helping functions while its policing functions are often inordinately strengthened. Even as the foundations of the security state are being solidified through zero-tolerance policies, anti-terrorist laws, soaring incarceration rates, the criminalization of pregnancy, racial profiling, and anti-immigration policies, it is crucial that educators and scholars take up the events of September 11th, not through a one-sided view of patriotism that stifles dissent and aids the forces of domestic militarization but as part of a broader effort to expand the United States' democratic rather than repressive possibilities.

Unlike some theorists who suggest that politics as a site of contestation, critical exchange, and engagement have come to an end or are in a state of terminal arrest, I believe that the current, depressing state of politics points to the urgent challenge of reformulating the crisis of democracy as part of the fundamental crisis of vision, meaning, education, and political agency. If it is possible to gain anything from the events of September 11th, it must be understood as an opportunity for a national coming together and soul searching, a time for expanding democratic possibilities rather than limiting them. Politics devoid of vision degenerates into cynicism and a repressive notion of patriotism, or it appropriates a view of power that appears to be equated almost exclusively with the militarization of both domestic space and foreign policy initiatives. Lost from such accounts is the recognition that democracy has to be struggled over—even in the face of a most appalling crisis of political agency. Educators, scholars and policy makers must redress the little attention paid to the fact that the struggle over politics and democracy is inextricably linked to creating public spheres where individuals can be educated as political agents equipped with the skills, capacities, and knowledge they need not only to actually perform as autonomous political agents but also to believe that such struggles are worth taking up. Central to my argument is the assumption that politics is not simply about power but also, as Cornelius Castoriadis points out, "has to do with political judgements and value choices,"[53] indicating that questions of civic education—learning how to become a skilled citizen—are central to both the struggle over political agency and democracy itself. Finally, there is the widespread refusal among many educators and others to recognize that the issue of civic education—with its emphasis on critical thinking, bridging the gap between learning and everyday life, understanding the connection between power and knowledge, and using the resources of history to extend democratic rights and identities—is not only the foundation for expanding and enabling political agency but also takes place across a wide variety of public spheres through the very force of culture itself,[54] particularly through the growing power of a mass-mediated culture.[55]

For many educational reformers, education and schooling are synonymous. In actuality, schooling is only one site where education takes place. As a performative practice, pedagogy is at work in a variety of educational sites—including popular culture, television and cable networks, magazines, the Internet, churches, and the press—where culture works to secure identities; it does the bridging work for negotiating the relationship between knowledge, pleasure, and values, and renders authority both crucial and problematic in legitimating particular social practices, communities, and forms of power. As a moral and political practice, the concept of public pedagogy points to the enormous ways in which popular and media culture construct the meanings, desires, and investments that play such an influential role in how students view themselves, others, and the larger world. Unfortunately, the political, ethical, and social significance of the role that popular culture plays as the primary pedagogical medium for young people remains largely unexamined by many educators and seems almost exclusively removed from any policy debates about educational reform. Educators also must challenge the assumption that education is limited to schooling and that popular cultural texts cannot be as profoundly important as traditional sources of learning in teaching about important issues framed through, for example, the social lens of poverty, racial conflict, and gender discrimination. This suggests not only expanding the curricula to allow students to become critically literate in those visual, electronic, and digital cultures that have such an important influence on their lives, but it also suggests teaching students the skills to be cultural producers as well. For instance, learning how to read films differently is no less important than learning how to produce films. Within this expanded approach to pedagogy, both the notion of what constitutes meaningful knowledge as well as what the conditions of critical agency might be point to a more expansive and democratic notion of civic education and political agency.

Educators at all levels of schooling need to challenge the assumption that either politics is dead or that any viable notion of politics will be determined exclusively by government leaders and experts in the heat of moral frenzy to impose vengeance on those who attacked the Pentagon and the World Trade Center. Educators need to take a more critical position, arguing that critical knowledge, debate, and dialogue grounded in pressing social problems offer individuals and groups some hope in shaping the conditions that bear down on their lives. Public engagement born of citizen engagement is urgent if the concepts of the social and public can be used to revitalize the language of civic education and democratization as part of a broader discourse of political agency and critical citizenship in a global world. Linking a notion of the social to democratic public values represents an attempt, however incomplete, to link democracy to public action, and to ground such support in defense of militant utopian thinking (as opposed to unadorned militancy) as part of a comprehensive attempt to revitalize the conditions for individual and social agency, civic activism, and citizen access to decision making while simultaneously addressing the most basic problems facing the prospects for social justice and global democracy.

Educators within public schools and higher education need to continue finding ways of entering the world of politics by both making social problems visible and contesting their manifestation in the policy. We need to build on those important critical, educational theories of the past to resurrect the emancipatory elements of democratic thought, while also recognizing and engaging their damaged and burdened historical traditions.[56] We need to reject both neoliberal and orthodox leftist positions, which dismiss the state as merely a tool of repression, to find ways to use the state to challenge, block, and regulate the devastating effects of capitalism. French sociologist Pierre Bourdieu is right when he calls for collective work by educators to prevent the right and other reactionaries from destroying the most precious democratic conquests in the areas of labor legislation, health, social protection, and education.[57] At the very least, this would suggest that educators defend schools as democratic public spheres, struggle against the deskilling of teachers and students, and argue for a notion of pedagogy that is grounded in democratic values rather than those corporate-driven ideologies and testing schemes that severely limit the creative and liberatory potential of teachers and students.

At the same time, such educators must resist the reduction of the state to its policing functions, while linking such a struggle to the fight against neoliberalism and the struggle for expanding and deepening the freedoms, rights, and relations of a vibrant democracy. Postcolonial theorist Samir Amin echoes this call by arguing that educators should consider addressing the project of a more realized democracy as part of an ongoing process of democratization. According to Amin, democratization "stresses the dynamic aspect of a still-unfinished process" while rejecting notions of democracy that are given a definitive formula.[58] Educators have an important role to play here in the struggle to link social justice and economic democracy with the equality of human rights, the right to education, health, research, art, and work.

On the cultural front, teachers as public intellectuals can work to make the pedagogical more political by engaging in a permanent critique of their own scholasticism and promoting a critical awareness to end oppression and forms of social life that disfigure contemporary life and pose a threat to any viable notion of democracy. Educators need to provide spaces of resistance within the public schools and the university that take seriously what it means to educate students to question and interrupt authority, recall what is forgotten or ignored, and make connections that are otherwise hidden, while simultaneously providing the knowledge and skills that enlarge their sense of the social and their possibilities as viable political agents capable of expanding and deepening democratic public life. At the very least, such educators can challenge the correlation between the impoverishment of society and the impoverishment of intellectuals by offering possibilities other than what we are told is possible. Or as Alain Badiou observes, "showing how the space of the possible is larger than the one assigned—that something else is possible, but not that everything is possible."[59] In times of increased domination of public K-12 education and higher education it becomes important, as George Lipsitz reminds us, that educators—as well as artists and other cultural workers—not become isolated "in their own abstract desires for social change and actual social movements. Taking a position is not the same as waging a war of position; changing your mind is not the same as changing society."[60]

Resistance must become part of a public pedagogy that works to position rigorous theoretical work and public bodies against corporate power and the militarization of visual and public space, connect classrooms to the challenges faced by social movements in the streets, and provide spaces within classrooms and other sites for personal injury and private terrors to be transformed into public considerations and struggles. This suggests that educators should work to form alliances with parents, community organizers, labor organizations, and civil rights groups at the local, national, and international levels to better understand how to translate private troubles into public actions, arouse public interest over pressing social problems, and use collective means to more fully democratize the commanding institutional economic, cultural, and social structures of the United States and the larger global order.

In the aftermath of the events of September 11, it is time to remind ourselves that collective problems deserve collective solutions and that what is at risk is not only a generation of minority youth and adults now considered to be a threat to national security but also the very promise of democracy itself. As militarism works to intensify patriarchal attitudes and antidemocratic assaults on dissent, it is crucial for educators to join with those groups now making a common cause against those forces that would sacrifice basic constitutional freedoms to the imperatives of war abroad and militarism at home.

Toward a Politics of Hope

Rather than define the social through the raw emotions of collective rage and the call for retribution, it is crucial at this momentous time in our history that educators set an example for creating the conditions for reasoned debate and dialogue by drawing on scholarly and popular sources as a critical resource to engage in a national conversation about the place and role of the United States in the world, the conditions necessary to invigorate the political and shape public policy, and to break what Homi Bhabha had called "the continuity and the consensus of common sense."[61] Against the often uncomplicated and ideologically charged discourses of the dominant, national media, educators must use whatever relevant resources and theories they can as an important tool for critically engaging and mapping the important relations among language, texts, everyday life, and structures of power as part of a wider effort to understand the conditions, contexts, and strategies of struggle that will enable Americans to be more self-conscious about their role in the world, how they affect other cultures and countries, and what it might mean to assume world leadership without reducing it to the arrogance of power.

The tools of theory emerge out of the intersection of the past and present; they respond to and are shaped by the conditions at hand. Americans need new theoretical tools—a new language—for linking hope, democracy, education, and the demands of a more fully realized democracy. While I believe that educators need a new vocabulary for connecting how we read critically to how we engage in movements for social change, I also believe that simply invoking the relationship between theory and practice, critique and social action will not do. Any attempt to give new life to a substantive democratic politics by educators must also address how people learn to be political agents, what kind of educational work is necessary within what kind of public spaces to enable people to use their full intellectual resources to both provide a profound critique of existing institutions and struggle to create, as Stuart Hall puts it, "what would be a good life or a better kind of life for the majority of people."[62]

As committed educators, we are required to understand more fully why the tools we used in the past often feel awkward in the present, why they fail to respond to problems now facing the United States and other parts of the globe. More specifically, we need to understand the failure of existing critical discourses to bridge the gap between how society represents itself, particularly through the media, and how and why individuals fail to understand and critically engage such representations to intervene in the oppressive social relationships and distorted truths they often legitimatize.

Educators, scholars, and policy makers can make an important contribution politically and pedagogically in the current crisis in revitalizing a language of resistance and possibility, a language that embraces a militant utopianism while constantly challenging those forces that seek to turn such hope into a new slogan or punish and dismiss those who dare look beyond the horizon of the given. Hope, in this instance, is the precondition for individual and social struggle, the ongoing practice of critical education in a wide variety of sites, the mark of courage on the part of intellectuals in and out of the academy who use the resources of theory to address pressing social problems. But hope is also a referent for civic courage and its ability to mediate the memory of loss and the experience of injustice as part of a broader attempt to open up new locations of struggle, contest the workings of oppressive power, and undermine various forms of domination. At its best, civic courage as a political practice begins when one's life can no longer be taken for granted. In doing so, it makes concrete the possibility for transforming hope and politics into an ethical space and public act that confronts the flow of everyday experience and the weight of social suffering with the force of individual and collective resistance and the unending project of democratic social transformation.

Within the prevailing discourses of neoliberalism and militarism that dominate public space, there is little leeway for a vocabulary of political or social transformation, collective vision, or social agency to challenge the ruthless downsizing of jobs, resist the ongoing liquidation of job security, the inadequacy of health care, many public schools and public institutions, and the disappearance of sites from which to struggle against the elimination of benefits for people now hired on a strictly part-time basis. Moreover, against the reality of low-wage jobs, the erosion of social provisions for a growing number of people and the expanding war against young people of color, the market-driven consumer juggernaut continues to mobilize desires in the interest of producing market identities and market relationships that ultimately appear as, Theodor Adorno once put it, nothing less than "a prohibition on thinking itself."[63]

It is against this ongoing assault on the public, and the growing preponderance of a free market economy and corporate culture that turns everything it touches into an object of consumption, that educators and others must offer a critique of American society and the misfortunes it generates out of its obsessive concern with profits, consumption, and the commercial values that underline its market-driven ethos. As part of this challenge, educators should help their students bridge the gap between private and public discourses, while simultaneously putting into play particular ideologies and values that resonate with broader public conversations regarding how a society views itself and the world of power, events, and politics.

Educators cannot completely eliminate the vagaries of a crude patriotism, but we can work against a politics of certainty, a pedagogy of terrorism, and institutional formations that close down rather than open up democratic relations. This requires, in part, that we work diligently to construct a politics without guarantees—one that perpetually questions itself as well as all those forms of knowledge, values, and practices that appear beyond the process of interrogation, debate, and deliberation. Democracy should not become synonymous with the language of the marketplace, oppression, control, surveillance, and privatization.

The challenge to redefine the social within those democratic values that deepen and expand democratic relations is crucial not only to the forms of citizenship we offer students and the larger public but also to how we engage the media, politicians, and others who would argue for less democracy and freedom in the name of domestic security. This is not to suggest that national security is not important. In fact, no country can allow its populations to live in fear, subject to arbitrary and cowardly terrorist acts. But there has to be a balance and a national conversation among the people of this country about the extent of such a threat and what privileges have to be conceded and at what point democracy itself becomes compromised.

Educators have an important role to play making their voices heard both in and outside of the classroom as part of an effort to articulate a vibrant and democratic notion of the social in a time of national crisis. Acting as public intellectuals, they can help create the conditions for debate and dialogue over the meaning of September 11 and what it might mean to rethink our nation's role in the world, address the dilemmas posed by the need to balance genuine security with democratic freedoms, and expand and deepen the possibilities of democracy itself.

Notes

1. Zygmunt Bauman captures this sentiment well in his observation that "Although it has been unnoticed, ignored, or played down by most of us, the truth is that the world is full. The great dream of the West, the dream that there is always a new place to discover, a new land to colonize, has dissolved. The great hope that a nation could wall itself off from the others is likewise over." Zygmunt Bauman, "Global Solidarity," *Tikkun* 17:1 (January/February 2002): 12.
2. On this issue, see Lewis Lapham, "Drums Along the Potomoc," *Harper's Magazine* (November 2001): 35–41; Steve Rendall, "The Op-Ed Echo Chamber," *Extra* (November/December 2001): 14–15; Seth Ackerman, "Network of Insiders," *Extra* (November/December 2001): 11–12.
3. Eric Alterman, "Patriot Games," *The Nation* (October 29, 2001): 10.
4. Cited in the National Public Radio/Kaiser Family Foundation/Kennedy School of Government Civil Liberties Poll. Available online at https://kaiserfamilyfoundation.files.wordpress.com/2001/11/npr008-external-toplines.pdf (November 30, 2001): 8.
5. Carl Boggs argues that in the 1990s, "American society had become more depoliticized, more lacking in the spirit of civic engagement and public obligation, than at any other time in recent history, with the vast majority of the population increasingly alienated from a political system that is com-

monly viewed as corrupt, authoritarian, and simply irrelevant to the most important challenges of our time." In Carl Boggs, *The End of Politics* (New York: Guilford Press, 2000), vii. I also take up this theme in Henry A. Giroux, *Public Spaces, Private Lives: Beyond the Culture of Cynicism* (Lanham: Rowman and Littlefield, 2001).

6. On the growing culture of surveillance, see William G. Staples, *The Culture of Surveillance: Discipline and Social Control in the United States* (New York: St. Martin's Press, 1997).

7. For some excellent sources on the growing repression in American life, see David Garland, *The Culture of Control: Crime and Social Order in Contemporary Society* (Chicago: University of Chicago Press, 2001); Jill Nelson, Police Brutality (New York: Norton, 2000); David Cole, No Equal Justice: *Race and Class in the American Criminal Justice System* (New York: The New Press, 1999).

8. Mike Davis, "The Flames of New York," *New Left Review* 12 (November/December 2001): 48. Davis points out that of the 11,000 being held only 4 have direct connections to bin Laden (p. 49).

9. Davis, op. cit., 49.

10. Davis, op. cit., 50.

11. Both quotes are from David Cole, "National Security State," *The Nation* (December 17, 2001), pp. 4–5.

12. Jonathan Schell, "Seven Million at Risk," *The Nation* (November 5, 2001), p. 8.

13. Homi Bhabha, "A Narrative of Divided Civilizations," *The Chronicle Review, Section 2 of The Chronicle of Higher Education* (September 28, 2001), p. B12.

14. For some excellent examples of such teaching practices, see the special issue of *Rethinking Schools* 16(2), titled, "War, Terrorism, and America's Classrooms."

15. Richard Reeves, "Patriotism Calls Out the Censor," *The New York Times On the Web*, retrieved from www.nytimes.com (October 1, 2001), p. 1.

16. Robin Wilson, "CUNY Chancellor, Trustees Denounce Professors Who Criticized U.S. Policy After Attacks," *The Chronicle of Higher Education*, available at http://chronicle.com/free/2001/10/2001100502n.htm (Friday, October 5, 2001), p. 1.

17. Cited in Richard Rothstein, "Terror Excuses and Explanations," *The New York Times* (October 17, 2001), p. 20.

18. Cited in David Glenn, "The War on Campus: Will Academic Freedom Survive," *The Nation* (December 3, 2001), p. 11.

19. Lieberman has since denounced the report and his role in founding the American Council of Trustees and Alumni. A report in the December 21, 2001, online version of the *Chronicle* counters Lieberman's claim and argues that he was a founding member of the organization. See Thomas Bartlett, "Sen. Lieberman Distances Himself from Report Decrying Campuses' 'Blame America' Attitude," available at http://chronicle.com/daily/2001/12/2001122105n.htm

20. Goldie Blumenstyk, "Group Denounces 'Blame America First' Response to September 11 Attacks," *The Chronicle of Higher Education*, available at http://chronicle.com/free/2001/11/2001111202n.htm (Monday, November 12, 2001), p. 1. For the full report, see Jerry L. Martin's and Anne D. Neal's self-righteously titled book, *Defending Civilization: How Our Universities Are Failing America and What We Can Do About It* (Washington, DC: The American Council of Trustees and Alumni, 2001).

21. For a critical analysis of this report and its political implications for higher education, see Eric Scigliano, "Naming—and Un-Naming—Names," *The Nation* (December 31, 2001), p. 16.

22. David Glenn, "The War on Campus: Will Academic Freedom Survive," *The Nation* (December 3, 2001), pp. 11–14.

23. Richard Rothstein, "Terror, Excuses, and Explanations," *The New York Times* (October 17, 2001), p. 20.

24. One telling sign of the creeping suppression of dissent can be found in an article by Maria Puente in *USA Today*. Puente defines the current public outcry against dissent as simply a matter of confusion

that has its roots in the political correctness movement of the last decade. Hence, she suggests that the suppression of dissenting opinions is nothing more than an overly sensitive response to language and that we have now entered a period that demands that Americans not only be politically correct but also emotionally correct. Implicit in this embarrassing commentary is the assumption that the left is responsible for the current attack on freedom of speech, and that the defense of the latter has nothing to do with either ethical or legal principles. This is the same logic that Rev. Jerry Falwell used in his remarks in which he blamed liberals, homosexuals, abortion supporters, and Hollywood for the terrorist acts of September 11th. See Maria Puente, "Potentially Confusing," *USA Today* (Monday, October 8, 2001), p. 6D.

25. Robin Wilson and Ana Marie Cox, "Terrorist Attacks Put Academic Freedom to the Test," *The Chronicle of Higher Education* (October 5, 2001), p. A12.

26. Cited in Edward Said, "Backlash and Backtrack," online at Lcommdialogue&Lists.psu.edu, p. 1.

27. Cited in Zygmunt Bauman, "Global Solidarity," *Tikkun* 17(1): 14.

28. Matthew Rothschild, "The New McCarthyism," *The Progressive* (January 2002), pp. 18–23.

29. Frank Rich, "Patriotism on the Cheap," *The New York Times* (January 5, 2002), p. A31.

30. This issue was also explored brilliantly by Doug Kellner with respect to the war against Iraq under the senior Bush presidency. See Douglas Kellner, *Media Culture: Cultural Studies, Identity, and Politics Between the Modern and the Postmodern* (New York: Routledge, 1995), especially pp. 213–214.

31. Carl Boggs, The End of Politics (New York: Guilford Press, 2000), vii.

32. Mike David, "The Flames of New York," *New Left Review* 12 (November/December 2001), p. 44.

33. Ibid., p. 45.

34. Willis, "Dreaming of War," 12. I am not suggesting that all of the media is behind the war or presenting simply the standard government line. On the contrary, there has been an enormous amount of dissent in a wide variety of media, especially on the Internet. At the same time, while critical and dissenting voices have been aired even in the dominant print and visual media, this is no way should suggest any reasonable notion of balance.

35. Edward W. Said, "The Public Role of Writers and Intellectuals," *The Nation* 273(9), p. 31.

36. Editorial, "Bush's Domestic War," The Nation (December 31, 2001) p. 3.

37. Ibid.

38. Sheldon Wolin, "Political Theory: From Vocation to Invocation," In Jason Frank and John Tambornino, eds. *Vocations of Political Theory* (Minneapolis: University of Minnesota Press, 2000), 4.

39. Henry A. Giroux, *Public Spaces, Private Lives: Beyond the Culture of Cynicism* (Lanham: Rowman and Littlefield, 2001).

40. Lewis Lapham, "Res Publica," *Harper's Magazine* (December 2001), p. 10.

41. Even Maureen Dowd, a columnist for *The New York Times*, recently claimed that she couldn't take the increasing control of American society by corporate interests, that George W. Bush continues "to give away the store to Big Business . . . [and that] His White House has become a holding company for Big Money and Media Oligarchy—Murdoch, Gates, Case, Eisner, Redstone." See Maureen Dowd, "I Can't Take It Anymore," *The New York Times* (September 9, 2001), p. 19.

42. A more recent analysis of the corporatization of schooling can be found in Kenneth J. Saltman, *Collateral Damage: Corporatizing Public Schools—A Threat to Democracy* (Lanham: Rowman and Littlefield, 2000). See also, Henry A. Giroux, *Stealing Innocence: Corporate Culture's War on Children* (New York: Palgrave Press, 2001).

43. See Peter Kilborn, "Rural Towns Turn to Prisons to Reignite Their Economies," *The New York Times* (August 1, 2001), p. A1.

44. Paul Street, "Prisons and the New American Racism," *Dissent* (Summer 2001), pp. 49–50.

45. Consider that "in the last twenty years the Justice Department's budget grew by 900 percent; over 60 percent of all prisoners are in for non-violent drug crimes; an estimated one-in-three black men between the ages of twenty and twenty-nine are under some type of criminal justice control or sought

on a warrant; nationwide some 6.5 million people are in prison, on parole, or probation. [This suggests] that the United States is an over-policed, surveillance society that uses prison as one of its central institutions." Given the current talk about limiting civil liberties, these figures make such a demand all the more problematic. See Christian Parenti, "The 'New' Criminal Justice System," *Monthly Review* 53:3 (2001), p. 19.

46. Betsy Hartman, "The Return of Relevance" (October 29). Reproduced from sysop@zmag.org

47. Zygmunt Bauman, *The Individualized Society* (London: Polity Press, 2001).

48. Carl Boggs, *The End of Politics* (New York: Guilford Press, 2000), p. ix.

49. Zygmunt Bauman, *Globalization: The Human Consequences* (New York: Columbia University Press, 1998), 82

50. For an excellent commentary on how the current discourse of security undermines some basic civil liberties, see Bruce Shapiro, "All in the Name of Security," *The Nation* (October 21, 2001), pp. 20–21.

51. Frank Rich, "The End of the Beginning," *The New York Times* (Saturday, September 29, 2001), p. A23.

52. For one excellent analysis of this issue, see Ralph Nader, "Corporate Patriotism," available online at www.citizenworks.org (November 10, 2001).

53. Cornelius Castoriadis, "Institution and Autonomy," in Peter Osborne, *A Critical Sense: Interviews with Intellectuals* (New York: Routledge, 1996), 8.

54. Richard Rothstein, an educational columnist for *The New York Times*, argued in a recent commentary that many teachers are unprepared to talk about or respond to the recent terrorist attacks because they are simply unprepared and know nothing about the issues. I am not sure this is entirely true, but I would argue that because schools increasingly model their curriculum on standardized forms of knowledge and largely reduce educators to teach for the test, teachers are ill-prepared to connect what they teach to the broader social issues, or to even see the relevance of connecting learning to the outside world. It is precisely at a time when a national crisis intrudes on the curriculum that we get a sense of the degree to which current educational policies are deskilling teachers. I would argue that most teachers are very interested in these issues, and are very knowledgeable, but are positioned to squelch their own knowledge for the standardized nonsense that now passes for school knowledge. See Richard Rothstein, "Teach Students More Than Where to Put the H in Afghanistan," *The New York Times* National (Wednesday, September 19, 2001), p. A24. Rothstein does provide a web site for teachers and students interested in the recent terrorist attacks. See www.nytimes.com/learning/terrorism

55. See Henry A. Giroux, *Public Spaces, Private Lives: Beyond the Culture of Cynicism* (Lanham, MD: Rowman and Littlefield, 2001).

56. I am referring to work that extends from John Dewey to some of the more prominent contemporary critical educational theorists such as Paulo Freire and Amy Stuart Wells.

57. Pierre Bourdieu, *Acts of Resistance* (New York: Free Press, 1998).

58. Samin Amin, "Imperialization and Globalization," *Monthly Review* (June 2001), p. 12.

59. Alain Badiou, *Ethics: An Essay on the Understanding of Evil* (London: Verso, 1998), 115–116.

60. George Lipsitz, "Academic Politics and Social Change," in Jodi Dean, ed. *Cultural Studies and Political Theory* (Ithaca: Cornell University Press, 2000), 81.

61. Gary Olson and Lynn Worsham, "Staging the Politics of Difference: Homi Bhabha's Critical Literacy," *Journal of Advanced Composition* 18(3) (1999): 11.

62. Stuart Hall cited in Les Terry, "Traveling 'The Hard Road to Renewal'", *Arena Journal*, no. 8 (1997): 55.

63. Theodor W. Adorno, *Critical Models* (New York: Columbia University Press, 1993), 290.

CHAPTER 14

Cultural Studies, Public Pedagogy, and the Responsibility of Intellectuals

2004

Within the last few decades, a number of critical and cultural studies theorists such as Stuart Hall, Lawrence Grossberg, Douglas Kellner, Meghan Morris, Toby Miller, and Tony Bennett have provided valuable contributions to our understanding of how culture deploys power and is shaped and organized within diverse systems of representation, production, consumption, and distribution. Particularly important to such work is an ongoing critical analysis of how symbolic and institutional forms of culture and power are mutually entangled in constructing diverse identities, modes of political agency, and the social world itself. Within this approach, material relations of power and the production of social meaning do not cancel each other out but constitute the precondition for all meaningful practices. Culture is recognized as the social field where goods and social practices are not only produced, distributed, and consumed but also invested with various meanings and ideologies implicated in the generation of political effects. Culture is partly defined as a circuit of power, ideologies, and values in which diverse images and sounds are produced and circulated, identities are constructed, inhabited, and discarded, agency is manifested in both individualized and social forms, and discourses are created, which make culture itself the object of inquiry and critical analyses. Rather than being viewed as a static force, the substance of culture and everyday life—knowledge, goods, social practices, and contexts—repeatedly mutates and is subject to ongoing changes and interpretations.

Following the work of Antonio Gramsci and Stuart Hall, many cultural theorists acknowledge the primacy of culture's role as an educational site where identities are being continually transformed, power is enacted, and learning assumes a political dynamic as it becomes not only the condition for the acquisition of agency but also the sphere for imagining oppositional social change. As a space for both the production of meaning and social interaction, culture is viewed by many contemporary theorists as an important terrain in which various modes of agency, identity, and values are neither prefigured nor always in place but subject to negotiation and struggle, and open for creating new democratic transformations, though always within various degrees of iniquitous power relations. Rather than being dismissed as a reflection of larger economic forces or as simply the "common ground" of everyday life, culture is recognized by many advocates of cultural studies as both a site of contestation and a site of utopian possibility, a space in which an emancipating politics can be fashioned that "consists in making seem possible precisely that which, from within the situation, is declared to be impossible."[1]

Cultural studies theorists have greatly expanded our theoretical understanding of the ideological, institutional, and performative workings of culture, but as important as this work might be, it does not go far enough—though there are some exceptions as in the work of Stanley Aronowitz, bell hooks, and Nick Couldry—in connecting the most critical insights of cultural studies with an understanding of the importance of critical pedagogy, particularly as part of a larger project for expanding the possibilities of a democratic politics, the dynamics of resistance, and the capacities for social agency. For too many theorists, pedagogy often occupies a limited role theoretically and politically in configuring cultural studies as a form of cultural politics.[2] While many cultural studies advocates recognize the political importance of pedagogy, it is often acknowledged in a very limited and narrow way. For instance, when invoked as an important political practice, pedagogy is either limited to the role that oppositional intellectuals might play within academia or reduced almost entirely to forms of learning that take place in schools. Even when pedagogy is related to issues of democracy, citizenship, and the struggle over the shaping of identities and identifications, it is rarely taken up as part of a broader public politics—as part of a larger attempt to explain how learning takes place outside of schools or what it means to assess the political significance of understanding the broader educational force of culture in the new age of media technology, multimedia, and computer-based information and communication networks. Put differently, pedagogy is limited to what goes on in schools, and the role of cultural studies theorists who address pedagogical concerns is largely reduced to teaching cultural studies within the classroom.

Within this discourse, cultural studies becomes available as a resource to educators who can then teach students how to look at the media (industry and texts), analyze audience reception, challenge rigid disciplinary boundaries, critically engage popular culture, produce critical knowledge, or use cultural studies to reform the curricula and challenge disciplinary formations within public schools and higher education. For instance, Shane Gunster has argued that the main contribution cultural studies makes to pedagogy "is the insistence that any kind of critical education must be rooted in the culture, experience, and knowledge that students bring to the classroom."[3] While this is an important insight, it has been argued in enormously sophisticated ways for over fifty years by a host of progressive educators, including

John Dewey, Maxine Greene, and Paulo Freire. The problem lies not in Gunster's unfamiliarity with such scholarship but in his willingness to repeat the presupposition that the classroom is the exclusive site in which pedagogy becomes a relevant object of analysis. If he had crossed the very disciplinary boundaries he decries in his celebration of cultural studies, he would have found that educational theorists such as Roger Simon, David Trend, and others have expanded the meaning of pedagogy as a political and moral practice and extended its application far beyond the classroom while also attempting to combine the cultural and the pedagogical as part of a broader notion of political education and cultural studies.[4]

Many cultural studies theorists, such as Lawrence Grossberg, have rightly suggested that cultural studies has an important role to play in helping educators rethink, among other things, the nature of pedagogy and knowledge, the purpose of schooling, and the impact of larger social forces on schools.[5] And, surely, Gunster takes such advice seriously but fails to understand its limits and in doing so repeats a now familiar refrain among critical educational theorists about connecting pedagogy to the histories, lived experiences, and discourses that students bring to the classroom. In spite of the importance of bringing matters of culture and power to the schools, I think too many cultural studies theorists are remiss in suggesting that pedagogy is primarily about schools and, by implication, that the intersection of cultural studies and pedagogy has little to do with theorizing the role pedagogy might play in linking learning to social change outside of traditional sites of schooling.[6] Pedagogy is not simply about the social construction of knowledge, values, and experiences; it is also a performative practice embodied in the lived interactions among educators, audiences, texts, and institutional formations. Pedagogy, at its best, implies that learning takes place across a spectrum of social practices and settings. As Roger Simon observes, pedagogy points to the multiplicity of sites in which education takes place and offers the possibility for a variety of cultural workers

> to comprehend the full range of multiple, shifting and overlapping sites of learning that exist within the organized social relations of everyday life. This means being able to grasp, for example, how workplaces, families, community and institutional health provision, film and television, the arts, groups organized for spiritual expression and worship, organized sport, the law and the provision of legal services, the prison system, voluntary social service organizations, and community based literacy programs all designate sets of organized practices within which learning is one central feature and outcome.[7]

In what follows, I want to argue that pedagogy is central to any viable notion of cultural politics and that cultural studies is crucial to any viable notion of pedagogy. Moreover, it is precisely at the intersection at which diverse traditions in cultural studies and pedagogy mutually inform each other that the possibility exists of making the pedagogical more political for cultural studies theorists and the political more pedagogical for educators.

Rethinking the Importance of Cultural Studies for Educators

My own interest in cultural studies emerges from an ongoing project to theorize the regulatory and emancipatory relationship among culture, power, and politics as expressed through the dynamics of what I call public pedagogy. Such a project concerns, in part, the diverse ways in which culture functions as a contested sphere over the production, distribution, and regulation of power, and how and where it operates both symbolically and institutionally as an educational, political, and economic force. Drawing upon a long tradition in cultural studies work, I take up culture as constitutive and political, not only reflecting larger forces but also constructing them; in this instance, culture not only mediates history but shapes it. I want to argue that culture is the primary terrain for realizing the political as an articulation and intervention into the social, a space in which politics is pluralized, recognized as contingent, and open to many formations.[8] I also argue that it is a crucial terrain in order to render visible both the global circuits that now frame material relations of power and a cultural politics in which matters of representation and meaning shape and offer concrete examples of how politics is expressed, lived, and experienced. Culture, in this instance, is the ground of both contestation and accommodation, and it is increasingly characterized by the rise of mega-corporations and new technologies that are transforming the traditional spheres of the economy, industry, society, and everyday life. Culture now plays a central role in producing narratives, metaphors, and images that exercise a powerful pedagogical force over how people think of themselves and their relationship to others. From my perspective, culture is the primary sphere in which individuals, groups, and institutions engage in the art of translating the diverse and multiple relations that mediate between private life and public concerns. It is also the sphere in which the translating possibilities of culture are under assault, particularly as the forces of neo-liberalism dissolve public issues into utterly privatized and individualistic concerns.

Central to my work in cultural studies is the assumption that the primacy of culture and power should be organized through an understanding of how the political becomes pedagogical, particularly in terms of how private issues are connected to larger social conditions and collective forces—that is, how the very processes of learning constitute the political mechanisms through which identities are shaped and desires mobilized, and how experiences take on form and meaning within and through collective conditions and those larger forces that constitute the realm of the social. In this context, pedagogy is no longer restricted to what goes on in schools, but becomes a defining principle of a wide ranging set of cultural apparatuses engaged in what Raymond Williams has called "permanent education." Williams rightfully believed that education in the broadest sense plays a central role in any viable form of cultural politics. He writes:

> What [permanent education] valuably stresses is the educational force of our whole social and
> cultural experience. It is therefore concerned, not only with continuing education, of a formal

or informal kind, but with what the whole environment, its institutions and relationships, actively and profoundly teaches. . . . [Permanent education also refers to] the field in which our ideas of the world, of ourselves and of our possibilities, are most widely and often most powerfully formed and disseminated. To work for the recovery of control in this field is then, under any pressures, a priority.[9]

Williams argued that any viable notion of critical politics would have to pay closer "attention to the complex ways in which individuals are formed by the institutions to which they belong, and in which, by reaction, the institutions took on the color of individuals thus formed."[10] Williams also focused attention on the crucial political question of how agency unfolds within a variety of cultural spaces structured within unequal relations of power.[11] He was particularly concerned about the connections between pedagogy and political agency, especially in light of the emergence of a range of new technologies that greatly proliferated the amount of information available to people while at the same time constricting the substance and ways in which such meanings entered the public domain. The realm of culture for Williams took on a new role in the latter part of the twentieth century because the actuality of economic power and its attendant networks of control now exercised more influence than ever before in shaping how identities are produced, desires mobilized, and everyday social relations acquired the force of common sense.[12] Williams clearly understood that making the political more pedagogical meant recognizing that where and how the psyche locates itself in public discourse, visions, and passions provides the groundwork for agents to enunciate, act, and reflect on themselves and their relations to others and the wider social order.

Following Williams, I want to reaffirm the importance of pedagogy in any viable understanding of cultural politics. In doing so, I wish to comment on some very schematic and incomplete elements of cultural studies that I believe are useful not only for thinking about the interface between cultural studies and critical pedagogy but also for deepening and expanding the theoretical and political horizons of critical pedagogical work. I believe that pedagogy represents both a mode of cultural production and a type of cultural criticism that is essential for questioning the conditions under which knowledge is produced, values affirmed, affective investments engaged, and subject positions put into place, negotiated, taken up, or refused. Pedagogy is a referent for understanding the conditions of critical learning and the often hidden dynamics of social and cultural reproduction. As a critical practice, pedagogy's role lies not only in changing how people think about themselves and their relationship to others and the world, but also in energizing students and others to engage in those struggles that further possibilities for living in a more just society. But like any other body of knowledge that is continuously struggled over, pedagogy must constantly enter into dialogue with other fields, theoretical domains, and emerging theoretical discourses. As diverse as cultural studies is as a field, there are a number of insights it provides that are crucial to educators who use critical pedagogy both inside and outside of their classrooms.

First, in the face of contemporary forms of political and epistemological rela-
tivism, a more politicized version of cultural studies makes a claim for the use of
highly disciplined, rigorously theoretical work. Not only does such a position reject
the notion that intellectual authority can only be grounded in particular forms of
social identity, but it also refuses to endorse an increasing anti-intellectualism that
posits theory as too academic and complex to be of any use in addressing important
political issues. While many cultural studies advocates refuse to separate culture
studies from politics or reject theory as too complex and abstract, they also reject
theory as a sterile form of theoreticism and an academicized vocabulary that is as
self-consciously pedantic as it is politically irrelevant. Matters of language, experience, power, ideology, and representation cannot make a detour around theory,
but that is no excuse for elevating theory to an ethereal realm that has no referent
outside of its own obtuseness or rhetorical cleverness. While offering no guarantees,
theory in a more critical perspective is seen as crucial for relating broader issues of
politics and power to the problems that shape everyday life. Moreover, theory in this
view is called upon as a resource for connecting cultural studies to those sites and
spheres of contestation in which it becomes possible to open up rhetorical and pedagogical spaces between the actual conditions of dominant power and the promise of
future space informed by a range of democratic alternatives.[13]

Underlying such a project is a firm commitment to intellectual rigor and a deep
regard for matters of compassion and social responsibility aimed at deepening and
extending the possibilities for critical agency, racial justice, economic democracy, and
the just distribution of political power. Hence, cultural studies theorists often reject
the anti-intellectualism, specialization, and methodological reification frequently
found in other disciplines. Similarly, such theorists also reject both the universalizing
dogmatism of some strands of radical theory and a postmodern epistemology that
enshrines difference, identity, and plurality at the expense of developing more inclusive notions of the social that bring together historically and politically differentiated
forms of struggles. The more progressive strains of cultural studies do not define or
value theory and knowledge within sectarian ideological or pedagogical interests. On
the contrary, these approaches to cultural studies define theorizing as part of a more
generalized notion of freedom, which combines democratic principles, values, and
practices with the rights and discourses that build on the histories and struggles of
those excluded because of class, race, gender, age, or disability. Theory emerges from
the demands posed by particular contexts, and reflects critically upon ways both to
better understand the world and to transform it when necessary. For instance, cultural studies theorist, Imre Szeman, has looked at the ways in which globalization
not only opens up a new space for pedagogy but also "constitutes a problem of and
for pedagogy."[14] Szeman examines the various forms of public pedagogy at work in
the rhetoric of newspapers, TV news shows, financial service companies, advertising
industries, and the mass media, including how such rhetoric fashions a triumphalist
view of globalization. He then offers an analysis of how alternative pedagogies are

produced within various globalization protest movements that have taken place in cities such as Seattle, Toronto, and Genoa—movements that have attempted to open up new modes and sites of learning while enabling new forms of collective resistance. Resistance in this instance is not limited to sectarian forms of identity politics, but functions more like a network of struggles that affirms particular issues and also provides a common ground in which various groups can develop alliances and link specific interests to broader democratic projects, strategies, and tactics. What is particularly important about Szeman's analysis is how such collective struggles and networks are generating new pedagogical practices of resistance through the use of new media such as the Internet and digital video to challenge official pedagogies of globalization.

Second, cultural studies is radically contextual in that the very questions it asks change in every context. Theory and criticism do not become ends in themselves but are always engaged as a resource and method in response to problems raised in particular contexts, social relations, and institutional formations. This suggests that how we respond as educators and critics to the spheres in which we work is conditioned by the interrelationship between the theoretical resources we bring to specific contexts and the worldly space of public-ness that produces distinct problems and conditions particular responses to them. Politics as an intervention into public life is expressed, in this instance, as part of a broader attempt to provide a better understanding of how power works in and through historical and institutional contexts while simultaneously opening up imagined possibilities for changing them. Lawrence Grossberg puts it well in arguing that cultural studies must be grounded in an act of doing, which in this case means "intervening into contexts and power . . . in order to enable people to act more strategically in ways that may change their context for the better."[15] For educators, this suggests that pedagogy *is not* an a priori set of methods that simply needs to be uncovered and then applied regardless of the contexts in which one teaches but is instead the outcome of numerous deliberations and struggles between different groups over how contexts are made and remade, often within unequal relations of power. At the same time, it is crucial for educators to recognize that while they need to be attentive to the particular contexts in which they work, they cannot separate such contexts from larger matters and configurations of power, culture, ideology, politics, and domination. As Meenakshi Gigi Durham and Douglas Kellner observe, "Pedagogy does not elide or occlude issues of power. . . . Thus, while the distinctive situation and interests of the teachers, students, or critics help decide what precise artifacts are engaged, what methods will be employed, and what pedagogy will be deployed, the socio-cultural environment in which cultural production, reception, and education occurs must be scrutinized as well."[16]

The notion that pedagogy is always contextual rightly points to linking the knowledge that is taught to the experiences students bring to their classroom encounters. One implication for such work is that future and existing teachers should be educated about the viability of developing context-dependent learning that takes account of student experiences and their relationships to popular culture and its terrain of pleasure, including those cultural industries that are often dismissed as producing mere entertainment. Despite the growing diversity of students in both public schools and higher education, there are few examples of curriculum sensitivity to the multiplicity of economic, social, and cultural factors bearing on students' lives. Even where there is a proliferation of programs such as ethnic and black studies in higher education, these are often marginalized in small programs far removed from the high status courses such as business, computer science, and Western history. Cultural studies at least provides the theoretical tools for allowing teachers to recognize the important, though not unproblematic, cultural resources students bring to school and the willingness to affirm and engage them critically as forms of knowledge crucial to the production of the students' sense of identity, place, and history. Equally important, the knowledge produced by students offers educators opportunities to learn from young people and to incorporate such knowledge as an integral part of their own teaching. Yet, there is an important caveat that cannot be stated too strongly.

I am not endorsing a romantic celebration of the relevance of the knowledge and experience that students bring to the classroom. Nor am I arguing that larger contexts, which frame both the culture and political economy of the schools and the experiences of students, should be ignored. I am also not suggesting that teaching should be limited to the resources students already have as much as I am arguing that educators need to find ways to make knowledge meaningful in order to make it critical and transformative. Moreover, by locating students within differentiated sets of histories, experiences, literacies, and values, pedagogical practices can be employed that not only raise questions about the strengths and limitations of what students know, but also grapple with the issue of what conditions must be engaged to expand the capacities and skills needed by students to become engaged global citizens and responsible social agents. This is not a matter of making a narrow notion of relevance the determining factor in the curriculum. But it is an issue of connecting knowledge to everyday life, meaning to the act of persuasion, schools and universities to broader public spheres, and rigorous theoretical work to affective investments and pleasures that students use in mediating their relationship to others and the larger world.

Third, the cultural studies emphasis on transdisciplinary work is important because it provides a rationale for challenging how knowledge has been historically produced, hierarchically ordered, and used within disciplines to sanction particular forms of authority and exclusion. By challenging the established academic division of labor, a transdisciplinary approach raises important questions about the politics of representation and its deeply entrenched entanglement with specialization, professionalism, and dominant power relations. The commitment to a transdisciplinary approach is also important because such work often operates at the frontiers of knowledge, prompting teachers and students to raise new questions and develop models of analysis outside of the officially sanctioned boundaries of knowledge and the established disciplines that sanction them. Transdisciplinarity in this discourse serves a dual function. On the one hand, it firmly posits the arbitrary conditions under which knowledge is produced and encoded, stressing its historically and socially constructed nature and deeply entrenched connection to power and ideological interests. On the other hand, it endorses the relational nature of knowledge, inveighing against any presupposition that knowledge, events, and issues are either fixed or should be studied in isolation. Transdisciplinary approaches stress both historical relations and broader social formations, always attentive to new linkages, meanings, and possibilities. Strategically and pedagogically, these modes of analysis suggest that while educators may be forced to work within academic disciplines, they can develop transdisciplinary tools to make established disciplines the object of critique while also contesting the broader economic, political, and cultural conditions that reproduce unequal relations of power and inequities at various levels of academic work. This is a crucial turn theoretically and politically because transdisciplinary approaches foreground the necessity of bridging the work educators do within the academy to other academic fields as well as to public spheres outside of the university. Such approaches also suggest that educators function as public intellectuals by engaging in ongoing public conversations that cut across particular disciplines while attempting to get their ideas out to more than one type of audience. Under such circumstances, educators must address the task of learning the forms of knowledge and skills that enable them to speak critically and broadly on a number of issues to a wide range of publics.

Fourth, in a somewhat related way, the emphasis by many cultural studies theorists on studying the full range of cultural practices that circulate in society opens the possibility for understanding a wide variety of new cultural forms that have become the primary educational forces in advanced industrial societies. This seems especially important at a time when new electronic technologies and the emergence of visual culture as a primary educational force offer new opportunities to inhabit knowledge and ways of knowing that simply do not correspond to the longstanding traditions and officially sanctioned rules of disciplinary knowledge or of the one-sided academic emphasis on print culture. The scope and power of new informational technologies, multimedia, and visual culture warrant educators to become more reflective about engaging the production, reception, and situated use of new technologies, popular texts, and diverse forms of visual culture, including how they structure social relations, values, particular notions of community, the future, and varied definitions of the self and others. Texts in this sense do not merely refer to the culture of print or the technology of the book, but refer to all those audio, visual, and electronically mediated forms of knowledge that have prompted a radical shift in the production of knowledge and the ways in which it is received and consumed. Recently, my own work has focused on the ways in which Disney's corporate culture—its animated films, radio programs, theme parks, and Hollywood blockbusters—functions as an expansive teaching machine which appropriates media and popular culture in order to rewrite public memory and offer young people an increasingly privatized and commercialized notion of citizenship.[17]

Contemporary youth do not simply rely on the culture of the book to construct and affirm their identities; instead, they are faced with the daunting task of negotiating their way through a de-centered, media-based cultural landscape no longer caught in the grip of either a technology of print or closed narrative structures.[18] I do not believe that educators and other cultural workers can critically understand and engage the shifting attitudes, representations, and desires of new generations strictly within the dominant disciplinary configurations of knowledge and practice and traditional forms of pedagogy. Educators need a more expansive view of knowledge and pedagogy that provides the conditions for young people and adults to engage popular media and mass culture as serious objects of social analysis and to learn how to read them critically through specific strategies of understanding, engagement, and transformation. Informing this notion of knowledge and pedagogy is a view of literacy that is multiple and plural rather than singular and fixed. The modernist emphasis on literacy must be reconfigured in order for students to learn multiple literacies rooted in a mastery of diverse symbolic domains. At the same time, it is not enough to educate students to be critical readers across a variety of cultural domains. They must also become cultural producers, especially if they are going to create alternative public spheres in which official knowledge and its one-dimensional configurations can be challenged. That is, students must also learn how to utilize the new electronic technologies, and how to think about the dynamics of cultural power and how it works on and through them so that they can build alternative cultural spheres in which such power is shared and used to promote non-commodified values rather than simply mimic corporate culture and its underlying transactions.

Fifth, cultural studies provocatively stresses analyzing public memory not as a totalizing narrative but as a series of ruptures and displacements. Historical learning in this sense is not about constructing a linear narrative but about blasting history open, rupturing its silences, highlighting its detours, acknowledging the events of its transmission, and organizing its limits within an open and honest concern with human suffering, values, and the legacy of the often unrepresentable or misrepresented. History is not an artifact to be merely transmitted, but an ongoing dialogue and struggle over the relationship between representation and agency. James Clifford is insightful in arguing that history should "force a sense of location on those who engage with it."[19] This means challenging official narratives of conservative educators such as William Bennett, Lynne Cheney, Diane Ravitch, and Chester Finn for whom history is primarily about recovering and legitimating selective facts, dates, and events. A pedagogy of public memory is about making connections that are often hidden, forgotten, or willfully ignored. Public memory in this sense becomes not an object of reverence but an ongoing subject of debate, dialogue, and critical engagement. Public memory is also about critically examining one's own historical location amid relations of power, privilege, or subordination. More specifically, this suggests engaging history, as has been done repeatedly by radical intellectuals such as Howard Zinn and Noam Chomsky, by analyzing how knowledge is constructed through its absences. Public memory as a pedagogical practice functions, in part, as a form of critique that addresses the fundamental inadequacy of official knowledge in representing marginalized and oppressed groups along with, as John Beverly points out, the deep-seated injustices perpetrated by institutions that contain such knowledge and the need to transform such institutions in the "direction of a more radically democratic nonhierarchical social order."[20]

Sixth, cultural studies theorists are increasingly paying attention to their own institutional practices and pedagogies.[21] They have come to recognize that pedagogy is deeply implicated in how power and authority are employed in the construction and organization of knowledge, desires, values, and identities. Such recognition has produced a new self-consciousness about how particular forms of teacher authority, classroom knowledge, and social practices are used to legitimate particular values and interests within unequal relations of power. Questions concerning how pedagogy works to articulate knowledge, meaning, desire, and values not only provide the conditions for a pedagogical self-consciousness among teachers and students but also foreground the recognition that pedagogy is a moral and political practice which cannot be reduced to an a priori set of skills or techniques. Pedagogy instead is defined as a cultural practice that must be accountable ethically and politically for the stories it produces, the claims it makes on public memories, and the images of the future it deems legitimate. As both an object of critique and a method of cultural production, no critical pedagogical practice can hide behind a claim of objectivity but should instead work, in part, to link theory and practice in the service of organizing, struggling over, and deepening political, economic, and social freedoms. In the broadest sense, critical pedagogy should offer students and others—outside of officially sanctioned scripts—the historically and contextually specific knowledge, skills, and tools they need to participate in, govern, and change, when necessary, those political and economic structures of power that shape their everyday lives. Needless to say, such tools are not pre-given but are the outcome of struggle, debate, dialogue, and engagement across a variety of public spheres.

While this list is both schematic and incomplete, it points to some important theoretical considerations that can be appropriated from the field of cultural studies as a resource for advancing a more public and democratic vision of higher education. Hopefully, it suggests theoretical tools for constructing new forms of collaboration among faculty, a broadening of the terms of teaching and learning, and new approaches to transdisciplinary research that address local, national, and international concerns. The potential of cultural studies for developing forms of collaboration that cut across national boundaries is worth taking up.

Where is the Project in Cultural Studies?

Like any other academic field, cultural studies is marked by a number of weaknesses that need to be addressed by educators drawn to some of its more critical assumptions. First, there is a tendency in some cultural studies work to be simply deconstructive, that is, to refuse to ask questions about the insertion of symbolic processes into societal contexts. There is little sense in some deconstructive approaches of how texts, language, and symbolic systems are historically situated and contextualized "within and by a complex set of social, political, economic and cultural forces."[22] As the exclusive focus of analysis, texts get hermetically sealed, removed from the political economy of power relations, and as such, the terrain of struggle is reduced to a struggle over the meanings that allegedly reside in such texts. Any viable form of cultural studies cannot insist exclusively on the primacy of signification over power and, in doing so, reduce its purview to questions of meaning and texts. An obsession in some cases with cultural texts results in privileging literature and popular culture over history and politics. Within this discourse, material organizations and economic power disappear into some of the most irrelevant aspects of culture. Matters of fashion, cultural trivia, isolated notions of performance, and just plain cultural nonsense take on the aura of cultural analyses that yield to the most privatized forms of inquiry while simultaneously "obstructing the formulation of a publicly informed politics."[23] In opposition to this position, cultural studies needs to foreground the ways in which culture and power are related through what Stuart Hall calls "combining the study of symbolic forms and meanings with the study of power," or more specifically the "insertion of symbolic processes into societal contexts and their imbrication with power."[24] Douglas Kellner for years has also argued that any viable approach to cultural studies has to overcome the divide between political economy and text-based analyses of culture.[25] But recognizing such a divide is not the same thing as overcoming it. Part of this task necessitates that cultural studies theorists anchor their own work, however diverse, in a radical project that seriously engages the promise of an unrealized democracy against its really existing forms. Of crucial importance to such a project is rejecting the assumption that theory can understand social problems without contesting their appearance in public life. At the same time, it is crucial to any viable notion of cultural studies that it reclaims politics as an ongoing critique of domination and society as part of a larger search for justice. Any viable cultural politics needs a socially committed notion of injustice if we are to take seriously what it means to fight for the idea of the good society. I think Zygmunt Bauman is right in arguing that "if there is no room for the idea of *wrong* society, there is hardly much chance for the idea of good society to be born, let alone make waves."[26]

Cultural studies advocates need to be more forceful, if not committed, to linking their overall politics to modes of critique and collective action that address the presupposition that democratic societies are never too just or just enough, and such a recognition means that a society must constantly nurture the possibilities for self-critique, collective agency, and forms of citizenship in which people play a fundamental role in critically discussing, administrating, and shaping the material relations of power and ideological forces that forge their everyday lives. Moreover, the struggle over creating an inclusive and just democracy takes many forms, offers no political guarantees, and provides an important normative dimension to politics as a process that never ends. Such a project is based on the realization that a democracy open to exchange, question, and self-criticism never reaches the limits of justice; it is never just enough and never finished. It is precisely the open-ended and normative nature of such a project that provides a common ground for cultural studies theorists to share their differences and diverse range of intellectual pursuits.

Second, cultural studies is still largely an academic discourse and as such is often too far removed from other cultural and political sites where the work of public pedagogy takes place. In order to become a public discourse of any importance, cultural studies theorists will have to focus their work on the immediacy of problems that are more public and that are relevant to important social issues. Such issues might include the destruction of the ecological biosphere, the current war against youth, the hegemony of neo-liberal globalization, the widespread attack by corporate culture on public schools, the ongoing attack on the welfare system, the increasing rates of incarceration of people of color, the increasing gap between the rich and the poor, the increasing spread of war globally, or the dangerous growth of the prison-industrial complex. Moreover, cultural studies theorists need to write for a variety of public audiences, rather than for simply a narrow group of specialized intellectuals. Such writing needs to become public by crossing over into sites and avenues of expression that speak to more general audiences in a language that is clear but not theoretically simplistic. Intellectuals must combine their scholarship with commitment in a discourse that is not dull or obtuse but expands the reach of their audience. This suggests using opportunities offered by a host of public means of expression including the lecture circuit, radio, Internet, interview, alternative magazines, and the church pulpit, to name only a few.

Third, cultural studies theorists need to be more specific about what it would mean to be both self-critical and attentive to learning how to work collectively through a vast array of networks across a number of public spheres. This might mean sharing resources with cultural workers both within and outside of the university such as the various groups working for global justice or those activists battling against the ongoing destruction of state provisions both within and outside of the United States. This suggests that cultural studies become more active in addressing the ethical and political challenges of globalization. As capital, finance, trade, and culture become extraterritorial and increasingly removed from traditional political constraints, it becomes all the more pressing to put global networks and political organizations into play to contend with the reach and power of neo-liberal globalization. Engaging in intellectual practices that offer the possibility of alliances and new forms of solidarity among cultural workers such as artists, writers, journalists, academics, and others who engage in forms of public pedagogy grounded in a democratic project represents a small, but important, step in addressing the massive and unprecedented reach of global capitalism.

Critical educators also need to register and make visible their own subjective involvement in what they teach, how they shape classroom social relations, and how they defend their positions within institutions that often legitimate educational processes based on ideological privileges and political exclusions. Making one's authority and classroom work the subject of critical analysis with students is important, but such a task must be taken up in terms that move beyond the rhetoric of method, psychology, or private interests. Pedagogy in this instance can be addressed as a moral and political discourse in which students are able to connect learning to social change, scholarship to commitment, and classroom knowledge to public life. Such a pedagogical task suggests that educators and cultural theorists define intellectual practice as part of "an intricate web of morality, rigor and responsibility" that enables them to speak with conviction, enter the public sphere in order to address important social problems, and demonstrate alternative models for what it means to bridge the gap between higher education and the broader society.[27] One useful approach is for educators to think through the distinction between a politicizing pedagogy, which insists wrongly that students think as we do, and a political pedagogy, which teaches students by example the importance of taking a stand (without standing still) while rigorously engaging the full range of ideas about an issue. Political pedagogy connects understanding with the issue of social responsibility and what it would mean to educate students not only to engage the world critically but also to be responsible enough to fight for those political and economic conditions that make its democratic possibilities viable. Such a pedagogy affirms the experience of the social and the obligations it evokes regarding questions of responsibility and social transformation by opening up for students important questions about power, knowledge, and what it might mean for them to critically engage the conditions under which life is presented to them and simultaneously work to overcome those social relations of oppression that make living unbearable for those who are poor, hungry, unemployed, deprived of adequate social services, and viewed under the aegis of neo-liberalism as largely disposable. What is important about this type of critical pedagogy is the issue of responsibility as both a normative issue and a strategic act. Responsibility highlights not only the performative nature of pedagogy by raising questions about the relationship that teachers have to students but also the relationship that students have to themselves and others. Central here is the importance for cultural studies educators to encourage students to reflect on what it would mean for them to connect knowledge and criticism to becoming an actor, buttressed by a profound desire to overcome injustice and a spirited commitment to social agency. Political education teaches students to take risks and challenge those with power, and encourages them to be reflexive about how power is used in the classroom. Political education proposes that the role of the public intellectual is not to consolidate authority but to question and interrogate it, and that teachers and students should temper any reference for authority with a sense of critical awareness and an acute willingness to hold it accountable for its consequences. Moreover, political education foregrounds education not within the imperatives of specialization and professionalization, but within a project designed to expand the possibilities of democracy by linking education to modes of political agency that promote critical citizenship and engage the ethical imperative to alleviate human suffering. However, politicizing education silences in the name of orthodoxy and imposes itself on students while undermining dialogue, deliberation, and critical engagement. Politicizing education is often grounded in a combination of self-righteousness and ideological purity that silences students as it imposes "correct" positions. Authority in this perspective rarely opens itself to self-criticism or, for that matter, to any criticism, especially from students. Politicizing education cannot decipher the distinction between critical teaching and pedagogical terrorism because its advocates have no sense of the difference between encouraging human agency and social responsibility and molding students according to the imperatives of an unquestioned ideological position. Politicizing education is more religious than secular and more about training than educating; it harbors a great dislike for complicating issues, promoting critical dialogue, and generating a culture of questioning.

Finally, if cultural studies theorists are truly concerned about how culture operates as a crucial site of power in the modern world, they will have to take more seriously how pedagogy functions on local and global levels to secure and challenge the ways in which power is deployed, affirmed, and resisted within and outside traditional discourses and cultural spheres. In this instance, pedagogy becomes an important theoretical tool for understanding the institutional conditions that place constraints on the production of knowledge, learning, and academic labor itself. Pedagogy also provides a discourse for engaging and challenging the production of social hierarchies, identities, and ideologies as they traverse local and national borders. In addition, pedagogy as a form of production and critique offers a discourse of possibility, a way of providing students with the opportunity to link meaning to commitment and understanding to social transformation—and to do so in the interest of the greatest possible justice. Unlike traditional vanguardists or elitist notions of the intellectual, cultural studies should embrace the notion of rooting the vocation of intellectuals in pedagogical and political work tempered by humility, a moral focus on suffering, and the need to produce alternative visions and policies that go beyond a language of sheer critique. I now want to shift the frame slightly to focus on the implications of the concerns addressed thus far and how they might be connected to developing an academic agenda for teachers as public intellectuals in higher education, particularly at a time when neo-liberal agendas increasingly guide social policy.

The Responsibility of Intellectuals and the Politics of Education

In opposition to the privatization, commodification, and commercialization of everything educational, educators need to define higher education as a resource vital to the democratic and civic life of the nation. At the heart of such a task is the challenge for academics, cultural workers, and labor organizers to join together in opposition to the transformation of higher education into commercial spheres, to resist what Bill Readings has called a consumer-oriented corporation more concerned about accounting than accountability.[28] As Zygmunt Bauman reminds us, schools are one of the few public spaces left where students can learn the "skills for citizen participation and effective political action. And where there is no [such] institution, there is no 'citizenship' either."[29] Public and higher education may be one of the few sites available in which students can learn about the limits of commercial values, address what it means to learn the skills of social citizenship, and learn how to deepen and expand the possibilities of collective agency and democratic life. Defending education at all levels of learning as a vital public sphere and public good rather than merely a private good is necessary to develop and nourish the proper balance between democratic public spheres and commercial power, between identities founded on democratic principles and identities steeped in forms of competitive, self-interested individualism that celebrate selfishness, profit making, and greed. This view suggests that public and higher education be defended through intellectual work that self-consciously recalls the tension between the democratic imperatives and possibilities of public institutions and their everyday realization within a society dominated by market principles. If public and higher education are to remain sites of critical thinking, collective work, and social struggle, public intellectuals need to expand their meaning and purpose. As I have stressed repeatedly, academics, teachers, students, parents, community activists, and other socially concerned groups must provide the first line of defense in protecting public and higher education as a resource vital to the moral life of the nation, and open to people and communities whose resources, knowledge, and skills have often been viewed as marginal. Such a project suggests that educators and cultural studies theorists develop a more inclusive vocabulary for connecting politics to the tasks of civic courage and leadership. In part, this means providing students with the language, knowledge, and social relations to engage in the "art of translating individual problems into public issues, and common interests into individual rights and duties."[30] Leadership demands a politics and pedagogy that refuses to separate individual problems and experience from public issues and social considerations. Within such a perspective, leadership displaces cynicism with hope, challenges the neo-liberal notion that there are no alternative visions of a better society, and develops a pedagogy of commitment that puts into place modes of literacy in which competency and interpretation provide the basis for actually intervening in the world. Leadership invokes the demand to make the pedagogical more political by linking critical thought to collective action, human agency to social responsibility, and knowledge and power to a profound impatience with a status quo founded upon deep inequalities and injustices.

One of the crucial challenges faced by educators and cultural studies advocates is rejecting the neo-liberal collapse of the public into the private, the rendering of all social problems as biographical in nature. The neo-liberal obsession with the private not only furthers a market-based politics which reduces all relationships to the exchange of money and the accumulation of capital, but also depoliticizes politics itself and reduces public activity to the realm of utterly privatized practices and utopias, underscored by the reduction of citizenship to the act of buying and purchasing goods. Within this discourse, all forms of political solidarity, social agency, and collective resistance disappear into the murky waters of a biopolitics in which the demands of privatized pleasures and ready-made individual choices are organized on the basis of marketplace pursuits and desires that cancel out all modes of social responsibility, commitment, and action. The current challenge for intellectuals is to reclaim the language of the social, agency, solidarity, democracy, and public life as the basis for rethinking how to name, theorize, and strategize a new kind of politics, notions of political agency, and collective struggle.

This challenge suggests, in part, positing new forms of social citizenship and civic education that have a purchase on people's everyday lives and struggles. Academics bear an enormous responsibility in opposing neo-liberalism—the most dangerous ideology of our time—by bringing democratic political culture back to life. Part of this effort demands creating new locations of struggle, vocabularies, and subject positions that allow people in a wide variety of public spheres to become more than they are now, to question what it is they have become within existing institutional and social formations, and "to give some thought to their experiences so that they can transform their relations of subordination and oppression."[31] One element of this struggle could take the form of resisting attacks on existing public spheres, such as the schools, while creating new spaces in clubs, neighborhoods, bookstores, trade unions, alternative media sites, and other places where dialogue and critical exchanges become possible. At the same time, challenging neo-liberalism means fighting against the ongoing reconfiguration of the state into the role of an enlarged police precinct designed to repress dissent, regulate immigrant populations, incarcerate youth who are considered disposable, and safeguard the interests of global investors. As governments globally give up their role of providing social safety nets, social provisions, and regulation of corporate greed, capital escapes beyond the reach of democratic control, leaving marginalized individuals and groups at the mercy of their own meager resources to survive. Under such circumstances, it becomes difficult to create alternative public spheres that enable people to become effective agents of change. Under neo-liberalism's reign of terror, public issues collapse into privatized discourses, and a culture of personal confessions, greed, and celebrities emerges to set the stage for depoliticizing public life and turning citizenship and governance into a form of consumerism.

The growing attack on public and higher education in American society may say less about the reputed apathy of the populace than about the bankruptcy of old political languages and orthodoxies and the need for new vocabularies and visions for clarifying our intellectual, ethical and political projects, especially as they work to reabsorb questions of agency, ethics, and meaning back into politics and public life. In the absence of such a language and the social formations and public spheres that make democracy and justice operative, politics becomes narcissistic and caters to the mood of widespread pessimism and the cathartic allure of the spectacle. In addition, public service and government intervention is sneered upon as either bureaucratic or a constraint upon individual freedom. Any attempt to give new life to a substantive democratic politics must address the issue of how people learn to be political agents as well as what kind of educational work is necessary within what kind of public spaces to enable people to use their full intellectual resources to provide a profound critique of existing institutions and to undertake a struggle to make the operation of freedom and autonomy possible for as many people as possible in a wide variety of spheres. As critical educators, we are required to understand more fully why the tools we used in the past feel awkward in the present, often failing to respond to problems now facing the United States and other parts of the globe. More specifically, educators face the challenge posed by the failure of existing critical discourses to bridge the gap between how society represents itself and how and why individuals fail to understand and critically engage such representations in order to intervene in the oppressive social relationships they often legitimate.

Against neo-liberalism, educators, cultural studies theorists, students, and activists face the task of providing a language of resistance and possibility, a language that embraces a militant utopianism while constantly being attentive to those forces that seek to turn such hope into a new slogan or punish and dismiss those who dare to look beyond the horizon of the given. Hope is the affective and intellectual precondition for individual and social struggle, the mark of courage on the part of intellectuals in and out of the academy who use the resources of theory to address pressing social problems. But hope is also a referent for civic courage which translates as a political practice and begins when one's life can no longer be taken for granted, making concrete the possibility for transforming politics into an ethical space and a public act that confronts the flow of everyday experience and the weight of social suffering with the force of individual and collective resistance and the unending project of democratic social transformation.

There is much talk among social theorists about the death of politics and the inability of human beings to imagine a more equitable and just world in order to make it better. I would hope that educators, of all groups, would be the most vocal and militant in challenging this assumption by making clear that the heart of any form of inclusive democracy is the assumption that learning should be used to expand the public good, create a culture of questioning, and promote democratic social change. Individual and social agency becomes meaningful as part of the willingness to think in oppositional, if not utopian, terms "in order to help us find our way to a more human future."[32] Under such circumstances, knowledge can be used for amplifying human freedom and promoting social justice, and not for simply creating profits. The diverse but connected fields of cultural studies and critical pedagogy offer some insights for addressing these issues, and we would do well to learn as much as possible from them in order to expand the meaning of the political and revitalize the pedagogical possibilities of cultural politics and democratic struggles. The late Pierre Bourdieu has argued that intellectuals need to create new ways for doing politics by investing in political struggles through a permanent critique of the abuses of authority and power, especially under the reign of neo-liberalism. Bourdieu wanted scholars to use their skills and knowledge to break out of the microcosm of academia, combine scholarship with commitment, and "enter into sustained and vigorous exchange with the outside world (especially with unions, grassroots organizations, and issue-oriented activist groups) instead of being content with waging the 'political' battles, at once intimate and ultimately, and always a bit unreal, of the scholastic universe."[33]

At a time when our civil liberties are being destroyed and public institutions and goods all over the globe are under assault by the forces of a rapacious global capitalism, there is a sense of concrete urgency that demands not only the most militant forms of political opposition on the part of academics, but new modes of resistance and collective struggle buttressed by rigorous intellectual work, social responsibility, and political courage. The time has come for intellectuals to distinguish caution from cowardice and recognize the ever-fashionable display of rhetorical cleverness as a form of "disguised decadence."[34] As Derrida reminds us, democracy "demands the most concrete urgency . . . because as a concept it makes visible the promise of democracy, that which is to come."[35] We have seen glimpses of such a promise among those brave students and workers who have demonstrated in Seattle, Genoa, Prague, New York, and Toronto. As public intellectuals, academics can learn from such struggles by turning the university and public schools into vibrant critical sites of learning and unconditional sites of pedagogical and political resistance. The power of the existing dominant order resides not only in the economic or material relations of power, but also in the realm of ideas and culture. This is why intellectuals must take sides, speak out, and engage in the hard work of debunking corporate culture's assault on teaching and learning, orient their teaching for social change, connect learning to public life, link knowledge to the operations of power, and allow issues of human rights and crimes against humanity in their diverse forms to occupy a space of critical and open discussion in the classroom. It also means stepping out of the classroom and working with others to create public spaces where it becomes possible not only to "shift the way people think about the moment, but potentially to energize them to do something differently in that moment," to link one's critical imagination with the possibility of activism in the public sphere.[36] This is, of course a small step, but if we do not want to repeat the present as the future or, even worse, become complicit in the dominant exercise of power, it is time for educators to mobilize collectively their energies by breaking down the illusion of unanimity that dominant power propagates while working diligently, tirelessly, and collectively to reclaim the promises of a truly global, democratic future.

Notes

1. Alain Badiou, *Ethics: An Essay on the Understanding of Evil* (London: Verso, 2001), 121.
2. For instance, in a number of cultural studies readers, the issue of critical pedagogy is left out altogether. Typical examples include: Toby Miller, ed. *A Companion to Cultural Studies* (Malden, MA: Blackwell, 2001); Simon During, ed. *The Cultural Studies Reader,* 2nd ed. (New York: Routledge, 1999); John Storey, ed. *What is Cultural Studies?: A Reader* (New York: Arnold Press, 1996).
3. Shane Gunster, "Gramsci, Organic Intellectuals, and Cultural Studies," in Jason Frank and John Tambornino, eds. *Vocations of Political Theory* (Minneapolis: University of Minnesota Press, 2000), 253.
4. See for example, Roger Simon, *Teaching Against the Grain: Texts for a Pedagogy of Possibility* (Westport, CT: Bergin and Garvey, 1992); Henry A. Giroux, *Border Crossings: Cultural Workers and the Politics of Education* (New York: Routledge, 1992); David Trend, *Cultural Pedagogy: Art/Education/Politics* (Westport: Bergin and Garvey, 1992).
5. For instance, see the brilliant, early essay by Grossberg on education and cultural studies in Lawrence Grossberg, "Introduction: Bringin' It all Back Home—Pedagogy and Cultural Studies," in Henry A. Giroux and Peter McLaren, eds. *Border Crossings: Pedagogy and the Politics of Cultural Studies* (New York: Routledge, 1994), 1–25.
6. I take up this issue in greater detail in Henry A. Giroux, *Impure Acts: The Practical Politics of Cultural Studies* (New York: Routledge, 2000); *Stealing Innocence: Corporate Culture's War on Children* (New York: Palgrave, 2000).
7. Roger Simon, "Broadening the Vision of University-Based Study of Education: The Contribution of Cultural Studies" *The Review of Education/Pedagogy/Cultural Studies* 12, no. 1 (1995): 109.
8. On the importance of problematizing and pluralizing the political, see Jodi Dean, "The Interface of Political Theory and Cultural Studies," in *Cultural Studies and Political Theory,* ed. Jodi Dean (Ithaca, NY: Cornell University Press, 2000), 1–19.
9. Raymond Williams, "Preface to Second Edition," *Communications* (New York: Barnes and Noble, 1967), 15, 16.
10. Raymond Williams, "Preface to Second Edition," *Communications* (New York: Barnes and Noble, 1967), 14.
11. See especially, Raymond Williams, *Marxism and Literature* (New York: Oxford University Press, 1977); Raymond Williams, *The Year 2000* (New York: Pantheon, 1983).
12. Williams, *Marxism and Literature*, Ibid.
13. Matthias Fritsch, "Derrida's Democracy to Come," *Constellations* 9, no. 4 (December 2002): 579.
14. Imre Szeman, "Learning to Learn from Seattle," *The Review of Education, Pedagogy, and Cultural Studies* 24, nos 1–2 (2002): 4.
15. Lawrence Grossberg, "Toward a Genealogy of the State of Cultural Studies," in Cary Nelson and Dilip Parameshwar Gaonkar, eds. *Disciplinarity and Dissent in Cultural Studies* (New York: Routledge, 1996), 143.
16. Meenakshi Gigi Durham and Douglas M. Kellner, "Adventures in Media and Cultural Studies: Introducing Key Works," in *Media and Cultural Studies: Key Works,* eds. Douglas M. Kellner and Meenakshi Gigi Durham (Malden, MA: Blackwell, 2001), 29.
17. Henry A. Giroux, *The Mouse that Roared: Disney and the End of Innocence* (Lanham, MD: Rowman and Littlefield, 2000); also see Henry A. Giroux, *Impure Acts* (New York: Routledge, 2000); Henry A. Giroux, *Breaking into the Movies: Film and the Politics of Culture* (Malden, MA: Blackwell, 2002).

18. See, for instance, Meenakshi Gigi Durham and Douglas M. Kellner, eds. *Media and Cultural Studies: Key Works* (Malden, MA: Blackwell, 2001).

19. James Clifford, "Museums in the Borderlands," in *Different Voices,* eds. Carol Becker et al. (New York: Association of Art Museum Directors, 1992), 129.

20. John Beverly, "Pedagogy and Subalternity: Mapping the Limits of Academic Knowledge," in *Social Cartography: Mapping Ways of Seeing Social and Educational Change,* ed. Rolland G. Paulston (New York: Garland, 1996), p. 354.

21. See Henry A. Giroux and Peter McLaren, eds. *Between Borders: Pedagogy and the Politics of Cultural Studies* (New York: Routledge, 1993).

22. Ien Ang, "On the Politics of Empirical Audience Research," in *Media and Cultural Studies: Keyworks,* eds. Meenakshi Gigi Durham and Douglas M. Kellner (Malden, MA: Blackwell, 2001), 183.

23. Arif Dirlik, "Literature/Identity: Transnationalism, Narrative, and Representation," *Review of Education/Pedagogy/Cultural Studies* 24, no. 3 (July–September 2002): 218. One example of such work can be found in Marjorie Garber, *Sex and Real Estate: Why We Love Houses* (New York: Anchor Books, 2000), or even better, Marjorie Garber, *Dog Love* (New York: Touchstone Press, 1997).

24. Stuart Hall, cited in Peter Osborne and Lynne Segal, "Culture and Power: Stuart Hall Interviewed," *Radical Philosophy* 86 (November/December 1997): 24.

25. See, for example, Douglas Kellner, *Media Culture: Cultural Studies, Identity, and Politics* (New York: Routledge, 1995).

26. Zygmunt Bauman, *Society under Siege* (Malden, MA: Blackwell: 2002), 170.

27. Arundhati Roy, *Power Politics* (Cambridge, MA: South End Press, 2001), 5.

28. Bill Readings, *The University in Ruins* (Cambridge, MA: Harvard University Press), 11, 18.

29. Zygmunt Bauman, *In Search of Politics* (Stanford: Stanford University Press, 1999), 170.

30. Zygmunt Bauman, *Society under Siege* (Malden, MA: Blackwell: 2002), 70.

31. Lynn Worsham and Gary A. Olson, "Rethinking Political Community: Chantal Mouffe's Liberal Socialism," *Journal of Composition Theory* 19, no. 2 (1999): 178.

32. Noam Chomsky, "Paths Taken, Tasks Ahead," *Profession* (2000): 34.

33. Pierre Bourdieu, "For a Scholarship of Commitment," *Profession* (2000): 44.

34. Arundhati Roy, *Power Politics* (Boston: South End Press, 2001), 12.

35. Jacques Derrida, "Intellectual Courage: An Interview," trans. Peter Krapp, *Culture Machine* 2 (2000): 9.

36. Lani Guinier and Anna Deavere Smith, "Rethinking Power, Rethinking Theatre: A Conversation Between Lani Guinier and Anna Deavere Smith," *Theater* 31, no. 3 (fall 2001): 34–35.

CHAPTER 15

Gated Intellectuals
and Fortress America

Towards a Borderless Pedagogy
in the Occupy Movement

2012

A group of right-wing extremists in the United States would have the American public believe it is easier to imagine the end of the world than it is to imagine the end of a market society. Comprising this group are the Republican Party extremists, religious fundamentalists such as Rick Santorum, and a host of conservative anti-public foundations funded by billionaires such as the Koch brothers,[1] whose pernicious influence fosters the political and cultural conditions for creating vast inequalities and massive human hardships throughout the globe. Their various messages converge in support of *neoliberal capitalism* and a fortress mentality that increasingly drive the meaning of citizenship and social life. One consequence is that the principles of self-preservation and self-interest undermine, if not completely sabotage, political agency and democratic public life.

Neoliberalism, or *market fundamentalism*, as it is called in some quarters, and its army of supporters cloak their interests in an appeal to 'common sense' while doing everything possible to deny climate change, massive inequalities, a political system hijacked by big money and corporations, the militarization of everyday life, and the corruption of civic culture by a consumerist and celebrity-driven advertising machine. The financial elite, the 1 percent, and the hedge fund sharks have become the highest-paid social magicians in America. They perform social magic by making the structures and power relations of racism, inequality, homelessness, poverty and environmental degradation disappear. And in doing so they employ deception by seizing upon a stripped-down language of choice, freedom, enterprise and self-reliance—all of which works to personalize responsibility, collapse social problems into private troubles, and reconfigure the claims for social and economic justice on the part of workers, poor minorities of color, women and young people as a species of individual complaint. But this deceptive strategy does more. It also substitutes shared responsibilities for a culture of diminishment, punishment and cruelty. The social is now a site of combat, infused with a live-for-oneself mentality, and a space where a responsibility toward others is now gleefully replaced by an ardent, narrow and inflexible responsibility only for oneself.

When the effects of structural injustice become obscured by a discourse of individual failure, human misery and misfortune are no longer the objects of compassion, but rather are met with scorn and derision. In recent weeks, we have witnessed Rush Limbaugh call Georgetown law student Sandra Fluke a 'slut' and 'prostitute'; US Marines captured on video urinating on the dead bodies of Afghanistan soldiers; and the public revelation by Greg Smith, a Goldman Sachs trader, that the company was so obsessed with making money that it cheated and verbally insulted its own clients, mockingly referring to them as 'muppets.'[2] There is also the mass misogyny of right-wing extremists directed against women's reproductive rights, which Maureen Dowd rightly calls an attempt by 'Republican men to wrestle American women back into chastity belts.'[3] These are not unconnected blemishes on the body of *neoliberal* capitalism. They are symptomatic of an infected political and economic system that has lost touch with any vestige of decency, justice and ethics.

Overlaying the festering corruption is a discourse in which national destiny (coded in biblical scripture) becomes a political theology drawing attention away from the actual structural forces that decide who has access to health insurance, decent jobs, quality schooling and adequate health care. This disappearing act does more than whitewash history, obscure systemic inequalities of power, and privatize public issues. It also creates social automatons, isolated individuals who live in gated communities along with their resident intellectuals who excite legions of consumer citizens to engage in a survival-of-the-fittest ritual in order to climb heartlessly up the ladder of *hyper-capitalism*. The gated individual, scholar, artist, media pundit and celebrity—walled off from growing impoverished populations—are also cut loose from any ethical mooring or sense of social responsibility. Such a radical individualism and its shark-like values and practices have become the hallmark of American society. Unfortunately, *hyper-capitalism* does more than create a market-driven culture in which individuals demonstrate no responsibility for the other and are reduced to zombies worried about their personal safety, on the one hand, and their stock portfolios on the other. It also undermines public values, the centrality of the common good, and any political arenas not yet sealed off from an awareness of our collective fate. As democracy succumbs to the instrumental politics of the market economy and the relentless hype of the commercially driven spectacle, it becomes more difficult to preserve those public spheres, dialogues and ideas through which private troubles and social issues can inform each other.

The gated intellectuals, pursuing their flight from social responsibility, become obsessed with the privatization of everything. And, not content to remain supine intellectuals in the service of corporate hacks, they also willingly, if not joyfully, wage war against what is viewed as the ferocious advance of civil society, public values and the social. Gated intellectuals such as Thomas Friedman, George Will, Dinesh D'Souza, Norman Podhoretz, Charles Murray, David Brooks and others voice their support for what might be called a gated or border pedagogy—one that establishes boundaries to protect the rich, isolates citizens from each other, excludes those populations considered disposable, and renders invisible young people, especially poor youth of color, along with others marginalized by class and race. Such intellectuals play no small role in legitimating what David Theo Goldberg has called a form of neoliberalism, that promotes a 'shift from the caretaker or pastoral state of welfare capitalism to the "traffic cop" or "minimal" state, ordering flows of capital, people, goods, public services, and information.'[4]

The gated intellectual works hard to make thinking an act of stupidity, turn lies into truths, build a moat around oppositional ideas so they cannot be accessed, and destroy those institutions and social protections that serve the common good. Gated intellectuals and the institutions that support them believe in societies that stop questioning themselves, engage in a history of forgetting, and celebrate the progressive 'decomposition and crumbling of social bonds and communal cohesion'[5]. Policed borders, surveillance, state secrecy, targeted assassinations, armed guards, and other forces provide the imprimatur of dominant power and containment, making sure that no one can trespass onto gated property, domains, sites, protected global resources and public spheres. On guard against any claim to the common good, the social contract or social protections for the underprivileged, gated intellectuals spring to life in universities, news programs, print media, charitable foundations, churches, think tanks and other cultural apparatuses, aggressively surveying the terrain to ensure that no one is able to do the crucial pedagogical work of democracy by offering resources and possibilities for resisting the dissolution of sociality, reciprocity and social citizenship itself.

The gated mentality of *market fundamentalism* has walled off, if not *disappeared*, those spaces where dialogue, critical reason, and the values and practices of social responsibility can be engaged. The armies of anti-public intellectuals who appear daily on television, radio talk shows and other platforms work hard to create a fortress of indifference and manufactured stupidity. Public life is reduced to a host of babbling politicians and pundits, ranging from Sarah Palin and Rick Santorum to Sean Hannity, all of whom should have their high school diplomas revoked. Much more than providing idiot spectacles and fodder for late-night comics, the assault waged by the warriors of rule enforcement and gated thought poses a dire threat to those vital public spheres that provide the minimal conditions for citizens who can think critically and act responsibly. This is especially true for public education, where the forces of privatization, philanthropy and commodification have all but gutted public schooling in America.[6] What has become clear is that the attack on public schools has nothing to do with their failings; it has to do with the fact that they are public. How else to explain the fact that a number of conservative politicians refer to them as 'government schools'? I think it is fair to say that the massive assault taking place on public education in Arizona, Wisconsin, Florida, Maine and other Republican Party–led states will soon extend its poisonous attack and include higher education in its sights in ways that will make the current battle look like a walk in the park.

Higher education is worth mentioning because for the gated intellectuals it is one of the last strongholds of democratic action and reasoning, and one of the most visible targets along with the welfare state. As is well known, higher education is increasingly being walled off from the discourse of public values and the ideals of a substantive democracy at a time when it is most imperative to defend the institution against an onslaught of forces that are as anti-intellectual as they are anti-democratic in nature. Universities are now facing a growing set of challenges that collectively pose a dire threat to the status of higher education as a sphere rooted in and fostering independent thought, critical agency and civic courage. These challenges, to name but a few, include budget cuts, the downsizing of faculty, the militarization of research, alienation from the broader public (which increasingly looks upon academe with suspicion, if not scorn), and the revising of the curriculum to fit market-driven goals. Many of the problems in higher education can be linked to the evisceration of funding, the intrusion of the national security state, the lack of faculty self-governance, and a wider culture that appears increasingly to view education as a private right rather than a public good. All of these disturbing trends, left unchecked, are certain to make a mockery of the very meaning and mission of the university as a democratic public sphere.

The Occupy Movement and other social movements are challenging many of these anti- democratic and anti-intellectual forces. Drawing connections between the ongoing assault on the public character and infrastructure of higher education and the broader attack on the welfare state, young people, artists, new media intellectuals and others are reviving what critical intellectuals such as C. Wright Mills, Tony Judt, Zygmunt Bauman and Hannah Arendt engaged as 'the social question'—now with a growing sense of urgency in a society that appears to be losing a sense of itself in terms of crucial public values, the common good and economic justice. One of the most important challenges facing educators, the Occupy Movement, young people and others concerned by the fate of democracy is the challenge of providing the public spaces, critical discourses and counter-narratives necessary to reclaim higher education and other public spheres from the civic- and capital-stripping policies of free-market fundamentalism, the authoritarian politicians who deride critical education, and an army of anti-public intellectuals dedicated to attacking all things collective and sustaining. Public values have for decades been in tension with dominant economic and political forces, but the latter's growing fervor for unbridled individualism, disdain for social cohesion and safety nets, and contempt for the public good appear relentless against increasingly vulnerable communal bonds and weakened democratic resistance. The collateral damage has been widespread and includes a frontal assault on the rights of labor, social services and every conceivable level of critical education.

Instead of the gated intellectual, there is a dire need for public intellectuals in the academy, art world, business sphere, media and other cultural apparatuses to move from negation to hope. That is, there is a need to develop what I call a project of democratization and borderless pedagogy that moves across different sites—from schools to the alternative media—as part of a broader attempt to construct a critical formative culture in the United States that enables Americans to reclaim their voices, speak out, exhibit moral outrage, and create the social movements, tactics, and public spheres that will reverse the growing tide of authoritarianism in the United States. Such intellectuals are essential to democracy, even as social well-being depends on a continuous effort to raise disquieting questions and challenges, use knowledge and analytical skills to address important social problems, alleviate human suffering where possible, and redirect resources back to individuals and communities who cannot survive and flourish without them. Engaged public intellectuals are especially needed at a time when it is necessary to resist the hollowing out of the social state, the rise of a governing-through-crime complex, and the growing gap between the rich and poor that is pushing the United States back into the moral and political abyss of the Gilded Age, characterized by what David Harvey calls the 'accumulation of capital through dispossession' which he claims is 'is about plundering, robbing other people of their rights' through the dizzying dreamworlds of consumption, power, greed, deregulation, and unfettered privatization that are central to a neoliberal project.[7]

One particular challenge now facing the Occupy Movement and the growing number of public intellectuals who reject the zombie politics of neoliberalism is to provide a multitude of public and free access forums—such as *Truthout*, *Truthdig*, *AlterNet*, *Counterpunch*, *Salon* and other alternative media spaces, as well as free learning centers where knowledge is produced—in which critically engaged intellectuals are able not only to do the work of connecting knowledge, skills and techniques to broader public considerations and social problems, but also to make clear that education takes place in a variety of spheres that should be open to everyone. It is precisely through the broad mobilization of traditional and new educational sites that public intellectuals can do the work of resistance, engagement, policymaking and supporting a democratic politics. Such spheres should also enable young people not just to learn how to read the world critically, but to be able to produce cultural and social forms that enable shared practices and ideas rooted in a commitment to the common good to evolve. Such spheres provide a sense of solidarity, encourage intellectuals to take risks, and model what it means to engage a larger public through work that provides both a language of critique and a discourse of educated hope, engagement and social transformation, while shaping ongoing public conversations about significant cultural and political concerns. To echo the great sociologist C. Wright Mills, there is a need for public intellectuals who refuse the role of 'sociological bookkeeper', preferring instead to be 'mutinous and utopian' rather than 'go the way of the literary faddist and the technician of cultural chic'. We can catch a glimpse of what such intellectuals do and why they matter in the work of Pierre

Bourdieu, Edward Said, Jacques Derrida and Noam Chomsky, and more recently in a younger generation of intellectuals such as Arundhati Roy, Naomi Klein, Judith Butler, David Theo Goldberg, and Susan Searls Giroux—all of whom have been crucial in helping a generation of young people find their way to a more humane future, one that demands a new politics, a new set of values and a renewed sense of the fragile nature of democracy. In part, this means educating a new generation of intellectuals who are willing to combine moral outrage with analytic skills and informed knowledge in order to hold power accountable and expand those public spheres where ideas, debate, critique and hope continue to matter.

Under the present circumstances, it is time to remind ourselves—in spite of idiotic anti-intellectual statements from Rick Santorum condemning higher education and critical thought itself—that critical ideas matter. Those public spheres in which critical thought is nurtured provide the minimal conditions for people to become worldly, take hold of important social issues, and alleviate human suffering as the means of making the United States a more equitable and just society. Ideas are not empty gestures and they do more than express a free-floating idealism. Ideas provide a crucial foundation for assessing the limits and strengths of our sense of individual and collective agency and what it might mean to exercise civic courage in order not merely to live in the world, but to shape it in light of democratic ideals that would make it a better place for everyone. Critical ideas and the technologies, institutions and public spheres that enable them *matter* because they offer us the opportunity to think and act otherwise, challenge common sense, cross over into new lines of inquiry, and take positions without standing still—in short, to become border crossers who refuse the silos that isolate the privileged within an edifice of protections built on greed, inequitable amounts of income and wealth, and the one-sided power of the corporate state.

Gated intellectuals work not with ideas, but with sound bites. They don't engage in debates; they simply spew off positions in which unsubstantiated opinion and sustained argument collapse into each other. Yet, instead of simply responding to the armies of gated intellectuals and the corporate money that funds them, it is time for the Occupy Movement and other critically thinking individuals to join with the independent media and make pedagogy central to any viable notion of politics. It is time to initiate a cultural campaign in which reason can be reclaimed, truth defended, and learning connected to social change. The current attack on public and higher education by the armies of gated intellectuals is symptomatic of the fear that right-wing reactionaries have of critical thought, quality education and the possibility of a generation emerging that can both think critically and act with political and ethical conviction. Let's hope that as time unfolds and new spaces emerge, the Occupy Movement and others engage in a form of borderless pedagogy in which they willingly and assertively join in the battle over ideas, reclaim the importance of critique, develop a discourse of hope, and occupy many quarters and sites so as to drown out the corporate-funded ignorance and political ideologies that strip history of its meaning, undermine intellectual engagement and engage in a never-ending pedagogy of deflection and disappearance. There has never been a more important time in American history to proclaim the importance of communal responsibility and civic agency, and to shift from a democracy of consumers to a democracy of informed citizens. As Federico Mayor, the former director general of UNESCO, rightly insisted, 'You cannot expect anything from uneducated citizens except unstable democracy.'[8]

The United States has become Fortress America and its gated banks, communities, hedge funds and financial institutions have become oppressive silos of the rich and privileged designed to keep out disadvantaged and vulnerable populations. At the same time, millions of gated communities have been created against the will of their inhabitants who have no passports to travel and are locked into abandoned neighborhoods, prisons and other sites equivalent to human waste dumps. The walls of privilege need to be destroyed and the fortresses of containment eliminated, but this will not be done without the emergence of a new political discourse, a borderless pedagogy, and a host of public spheres and institutions that provide the formative culture, skills and capacities that enable young and old alike to counter the ignorance discharged like a poison from the mouths of those corporate interests and anti-public intellectuals who prop up the authority of Fortress America and hyper-capitalism. It is time for the Occupy Movement to embrace its pedagogical role as a force for critical reason, social responsibility and civic education. This is a call not to deny politics as we know it, but to expand its reach. The Occupy Movement protesters need to become border crossers, willing to embrace a language of critique and possibility that makes visible the urgency of talking about politics and agency not in the idiom set by gated communities and anti-public intellectuals, but through the discourse of civic courage and social responsibility. We need a new generation of border crossers and a new form of border-crossing pedagogy to play a central role in keeping critical thought alive while challenging the further unraveling of human possibilities. Such a notion of democratic public life is engaged in both questioning itself and preventing that questioning from ever stalling or being declared finished. It provides the formative culture that enables young people to break the continuity of common sense, come to terms with their own power as critical agents, be critical of the authority that speaks to them, translate private considerations into public issues, and assume the responsibility of what it means not only to be governed, but to learn how to govern.

If gated intellectuals defend the privileged, isolated, removed and individualized interests of those who decry the social and view communal responsibility as a pathology, then public intellectuals must ensure their work and actions embody a democratic ideal through reclaiming all those sites of possibility in which dialogue is guaranteed, power is democratized, and public values trump sordid private interests. Democracy must be embraced not merely as a mode of governance but, more importantly, as Bill Moyers points out, as a means of dignifying people so they can become fully free to claim their moral and political agency.

Notes

1. Jane Mayer (2010) Covert Operations: the billionaire brothers who are waging a war against Obama, *The New Yorker*, 30 August. http://www.newyorker.com/reporting/2010/08/30/100830fa_fact_mayer .

2. Greg Smith (2012) Why I am Leaving Goldman Sachs, *The New York Times*, 14 March, p. A25.

3. Maureen Dowd (2012) Don't Tread on Us, *The New York Times*, 14 March, p. A25.

4. David Theo Goldberg (2009) *The Threat of Race: reflections on racial neoliberalism*, pp. 338–339. Malden, MA: Wiley-Blackwell.

5. Zygmunt Bauman (2007) Has the Future a Left? *Review of Education/Pedagogy/Cultural Studies*, 2.

6. I take this up in detail in Henry A. Giroux (2012) *Education and the Crisis of Public Values: challenging the assault on teachers, students, and public education.* New York: Peter Lang.

7. A Conversation with David Harvey, *Logos: A Journal of Modern Society & Culture*, 5(1) (2006). http://www.logosjournal.com/issue_5.1/harvey.htm

8. Quoted in Burton Bollag (1998) UNESCO Has Lofty Aims for Higher Education Conference, But Critics Doubt Its Value, *Chronicle of Higher Education*, 4 September, p. A76.

CHAPTER 16

Henry Giroux on Zombie Politics

Bill Moyers Interviews Henry Giroux

2013

BILL MOYERS: Welcome. A very wise teacher once told us, "If you want to change the world, change the metaphor." Then he gave us some of his favorite examples. You think of language differently, he said, if you think of "words pregnant with celestial fire." Or "words that weep and tears that speak." Of course, the heart doesn't physically separate into pieces when we lose someone we love, but "a broken heart" conveys the depth of loss. And if I say you are the "apple of my eye", you know how special you are in my sight. In other words, metaphors cleanse the lens of perception and give us a fresh take on reality. In other words.

Recently I read a book and saw a film that opened my eyes to see differently the crisis of our times, and the metaphor used by both was, believe it or not, zombies. You heard me right, zombies. More on the film later, but this is the book: *Zombie Politics and Culture in the Age of Casino Capitalism.* Talk about "connecting the dots"—read this, and the headlines of the day will, I think, arrange themselves differently in your head—threading together ideas and experiences to reveal a pattern. The skillful weaver is Henry Giroux, a scholar, teacher and social critic with seemingly tireless energy and a broad range of interests. Here are just a few of his books: *America's Education Deficit and the War on Youth, Twilight of the Social, Youth in a Suspect Society, Neoliberalism's War on Higher Education.*

Henry Giroux is the son of working class parents in Rhode Island who now holds the Global TV Network Chair in English and Cultural Studies at McMaster University in Canada. Henry Giroux, welcome.

HENRY GIROUX: Pleasure. It's great to be here.

BILL MOYERS: There's a great urgency in your recent books and in the essays you've been posting online, a fierce urgency, almost as if you are writing with the doomsday clock ticking. What accounts for that?

HENRY GIROUX: Well, for me democracy is too important to allow it to be undermined in a way in which every vital institution that matters from the political process to the schools to the inequalities that, to the money being put into politics, I mean, all those things that make a democracy viable are in crisis.

And the problem is the crisis, while we recognize in many ways is associated increasingly with the economic system, what we haven't gotten yet is that it should be accompanied by a crisis of ideas, that the stories that are being told about democracy are really about the swindle of fulfillment.

The swindle of fulfillment in that what the reigning elite in all of their diversity now tell the American people if not the rest of the world is that democracy is an excess. It doesn't really matter anymore, that we don't need social provisions, we don't need the welfare state, that the survival of the fittest is all that matters, that in fact society should mimic those values in ways that suggest a new narrative.

I mean you have a consolidation of power that is so overwhelming, not just in its ability to control resources and drive the economy and redistribute wealth upward, but basically to provide the most fraudulent definition of what a democracy should be.

I mean, the notion that profit making is the essence of democracy, the notion that economics is divorced from ethics, the notion that the only obligation of citizenship is consumerism, the notion that the welfare state is a pathology, that any form of dependency basically is disreputable and needs to be attacked, I mean, this is a vicious set of assumptions.

BILL MOYERS: Are we close to equating democracy with capitalism?

HENRY GIROUX: Oh, I mean, I think that's the biggest lie of all actually. The biggest lie of all is that capitalism is democracy. We have no way of understanding democracy outside of the market, just as we have no understanding of how to understand freedom outside of market values.

BILL MOYERS: Explain that. What do you mean "outside of market values?"

HENRY GIROUX: I mean, when Margaret Thatcher married Ronald Reagan—

BILL MOYERS: Metaphorically?

HENRY GIROUX: Metaphorically. Two things happened. First, there was this assumption that the government was evil except when it regulated its power to benefit the rich. So it wasn't a matter of smashing the government as Reagan seemed to suggest, it was a matter of rearranging it and reconfiguring it so it served the wealthy, the elites and the corporate, of course, you know, those who run mega corporations. But Thatcher said something else that's particularly interesting in this discussion.

She said there's no such thing as society. There are only individuals and families. And so what we begin to see is the emergence of a kind of ethic, a survival of the fittest ethic that legitimates the most incredible forms of cruelty, that seems to suggest that freedom in this discourse of getting rid of society, getting rid of the social—that discourse is really only about self-interest, that possessive individualism is now the only virtue that matters. So freedom, which is essential to any notion of democracy, now becomes nothing more than a matter of pursuing your own self-interests. No society can survive under those conditions.

BILL MOYERS: So what is society? When you use it as an antithesis to what Margaret Thatcher said, what do you have in mind? What's the metaphor for—

HENRY GIROUX: I have in mind a society in which the wealth is shared, in which there is a mesh of organizations that are grounded in the social contract, that takes seriously the mutual obligations that people have to each other. But more than anything else—I'm sorry, but I want to echo something that FDR once said, when he said that you not only have to have personal freedoms and political freedoms, the right to vote the right to speak, you have to have social freedom. You have to have the freedom from want, the freedom from poverty, the freedom from—that comes with a lack of health care.

Getting ahead cannot be the only motive that motivates people. You have to imagine what a good life is. But agency, the ability to do that, to have the capacity to basically be able to make decisions and learn how to govern and not just be governed—

BILL MOYERS: As a citizen.

HENRY GIROUX: As a citizen.

BILL MOYERS: A citizen is a moral agent of—

HENRY GIROUX: A citizen is a political and moral agent who in fact has a shared sense of hope and responsibility to others and not just to him or herself. Under this system, democracy is basically like the lotto. You know, go in, you put a coin in, and if you're lucky, you win something. If you don't, then you become something else.

BILL MOYERS: So then why when I talk about the urgency in your writing, your forthcoming book opens with this sentence, "America is descending into madness." Don't you think many people will read that as hyperbole?

HENRY GIROUX: Sometimes in the exaggerations there are great truths. And it seems to me that what's unfortunate here is that's not an exaggeration.

BILL MOYERS: Well, madness can mean several things. It can mean insanity. It can mean lunacy. But it can also mean folly, foolishness, you know, look at that craziness over there. Which do you mean?

HENRY GIROUX: I mean, it's certainly not just about foolishness. It's about a kind of lunacy in which people lose themselves in a sense of power and greed and exceptionalism and nationalism in ways that so undercut the meaning of democracy and the meaning of justice that you have to sit back and ask yourself how could the following, for instance, take place?

How could people who allegedly believe in democracy and the American Congress cut $40 billion from a food stamp program, half of which those food stamps go to children? And you ask yourself how could that happen? I mean, how can you say no to a Medicaid program which is far from radical but at the same time offers poor people health benefits that could save their lives?

How do you shut down public schools and say that charter schools and private schools are better because education is really not a right, it's an entitlement? How do you get a discourse governing the country that seems to suggest that anything public—public health, public transportation, public values, you know, public engagement—is a pathology?

BILL MOYERS: Let me answer that from the other side. They would say to you that we cut Medicaid or food stamps because they create dependency. We closed public schools because they aren't working, they aren't teaching. People are coming out not ready for life.

HENRY GIROUX: No, no, that's the answer that they give. I mean, and it's a mark of their insanity. I mean, that's precisely an answer that in my mind embodies a kind of psychosis that is so divorced—is in such denial about power and how it works and is in such denial about their attempt at what I call individualize the social, in other words—

BILL MOYERS: Individualize?

HENRY GIROUX: Individualize the social, which means that all problems, if they exist, rest on the shoulders of individuals.

BILL MOYERS: You are responsible.

HENRY GIROUX: You are responsible.

BILL MOYERS: If you're poor, you're responsible if you're ignorant, you're responsible if—

HENRY GIROUX: Exactly.

BILL MOYERS: —you're sick?

HENRY GIROUX: That's right, that the government—the larger social order, the society has no responsibility whatsoever so that—you often hear this, I mean, if there—I mean, if you have an economic crisis caused by the hedge fund crooks, you know and millions of people are put out of work and they're all lining up for unemployment, what do we hear in the national media? We hear that maybe they don't know how to fill out unemployment forms, maybe it's about character. You know, maybe they're just simply lazy.

BILL MOYERS: This line struck me, "The ideology of hardness and cruelty runs through American culture like an electric current..."

HENRY GIROUX: Yeah, it sure does. I mean, to see poor people, their benefits being cut, to see pensions of Americans who have worked like my father, all their lives, and taken away, to see the rich just accumulating more and more wealth.

I mean, it seems to me that there has to be a point where you have to say, "No, this has to stop." We can't allow ourselves to be driven by those lies anymore. We can't allow those who are rich, who are privileged, who are entitled, who accumulate wealth to simply engage in a flight from social and moral and political responsibility by blaming the people who are victimized by those policies as the source of those problems.

BILL MOYERS: There's a new reality you write emerging in America in no small part because of the media, one that enshrines a politics of disposability in which growing numbers of people are considered dispensable and a drain on the body politic and the economy, not to mention you say an affront on the sensibilities of the rich and the powerful.

HENRY GIROUX: If somebody had to say to me—ask me the question, "What exactly is new that we haven't seen before?" And I think that what we haven't seen before is an attack on the social contract, Bill, that is so overwhelming, so dangerous in the way in which its being deconstructed and being disassembled that you now have as a classic example, you have a whole generation of young people who are now seen as disposable.

They're in debt, they're unemployed. My friend, Zygmunt Bauman, calls them the zero generation: zero jobs, zero hope, zero possibilities, zero employment. And it seems to me when a country turns its back on its young people because they figure in investments not long term investments, they can't be treated as simply commodities that are going to in some way provide an instant payback and extend the bottom line, they represent something more noble than that. They represent an indication of how the future is not going to mimic the present and what obligations people might have, social, political, moral and otherwise to allow that to happen, and we've defaulted on that possibility.

BILL MOYERS: You actually call it—there's the title of the book, *America's Education Deficit and the War on Youth*.

HENRY GIROUX: Oh, this is a war. It's a war that endlessly commercializes kids, both as commodities and as commodifiable.

BILL MOYERS: Example?

HENRY GIROUX: Example being that the young people can't turn anywhere without in some way being told that the only obligation of citizenship is to shop, is to be a consumer. You can't walk on a college campus today and walk into the student union and not see everybody represented there from the local banks to Disneyland to local shops, all selling things.

I mean, it's like the school has become a mall. It imitates the mall. And if you walk into schools as one example, I mean, you look at the buses, there are advertisements on the buses. You walk into the bathroom, there are advertisements above the stalls. I mean, and the curriculum is written by General Electric.

BILL MOYERS: We're all branded—

HENRY GIROUX: They're branded, they're branded.

BILL MOYERS: —everything is branded?

HENRY GIROUX: Where are the public spaces for young people other learn a discourse that's not commodified, to be able to think about non-commodifiable values like trust, justice, honesty, integrity, caring for others, compassion. Those things, they're just simply absent, they're not part of those public spheres because those spheres have been commodified.

What does it mean to go to school all day and just be taking tests and learning how to teach for the test? Their minds are numb. I mean—the expression I get from them, they call school dead time, these kids. Say it's dead time. I call it their dis-imagination zones.

BILL MOYERS: Dis-imagination?

HENRY GIROUX: Yeah, yeah, they rob—it's a form of learning that robs the mind of any possibility of being imaginative. The arts are cut out, right, so the questions are not being raised about what it means to be creative.

All of those things that speak to educating the imagination, to stretching it, the giving kids the knowledge, a sense of the traditions, the archives to take risks, to learn about the world, they're disappearing.

BILL MOYERS: I heard you respond to someone who asked you at a public session the other evening—"What would you do about what you've just described?" And your first response was—start debating societies in high schools all across the country.

HENRY GIROUX: That's right. One of the things that I learned quickly as a result of the internet is I started getting a ton of letters from students who basically were involved in these debate societies. And they're saying like things, "We use your work. We love this work."

And I actually got involved with one that was working with—out of Brown University—they were working with a high school in the inner cities right, and I got involved with some of the students. But then I began to learn as a result of that involvement that these were the most radical kids in the country.

I mean, these were kids who embodied what a critical public sphere meant. They were going all over the country, different high schools, working class kids no less, debating major issues and getting so excited about in many ways winning these debates but doing it on the side of—something they could believe in.

And I thought to myself, "Wow, here's a space." Here's a space where you're going to have a whole generation of kids who could be actually engaging in debate and dialogue. Every working class urban school in this country should put its resources as much as possible into a debate team.

BILL MOYERS: My favorite of your many books is this one, *Zombie Politics and Culture in the Age of Casino Capitalism*. Why that metaphor, zombie politics?

HENRY GIROUX: Because it's a politics that's informed by the machinery of social and civil death.

BILL MOYERS: Death?

HENRY GIROUX: Death. It's a death machine. It's a death machine because in my estimation it does everything it can to kill any vestige of a robust democracy. It turns people into zombies, people who basically are so caught up with surviving that they have no—they become like the walking dead, you know, they lose their sense of agency—I mean they lose their homes, they lose their jobs.

And so this zombie metaphor actually operated at two levels. I mean, at one level it spoke to people who have no visions, who exercise a form of political leadership that extends the politics of what I call war and the machineries of death, whether those machineries are at home or abroad, whether they're about the death of civil liberties or they're about making up horrendous lies to actually invade a country like Iraq.

So this zombie metaphor is a way to sort of suggest that democracy is losing its oxygen, you know, it's losing its vitality, that we have a politics that really is about the organization of the production of violence.

It's losing its soul. It's losing its spirit. It's losing its ability to speak to itself in ways that would span the human spirit and the human possibility for justice and equality.

BILL MOYERS: Because we don't think of zombies as having souls?

HENRY GIROUX: They don't have souls.

BILL MOYERS: Right. You—

HENRY GIROUX: They're driven by lust.

BILL MOYERS: By lust?

HENRY GIROUX: The lust for money, the lust for power.

BILL MOYERS: Well, that's, I guess, why you mix your metaphors. Because you talk about casino capitalists, zombie politics, which you say in the book shapes every aspect—

HENRY GIROUX: Every aspect.

BILL MOYERS: —of society .

HENRY GIROUX: Yeah, at the current moment. This is what—

BILL MOYERS: How so?

HENRY GIROUX: Well, first, let's begin with an assumption. This casino capitalism as we talk about it, right, one of the things that it does that hasn't been done before, it doesn't just believe it can control the economy. It believes that it can govern all of social life. That's different.

That means it has to have its tentacles into every aspect of everyday life. Everything from the way schools are run to the way prisons are outsourced to the way the financial services are run to the way in which people have access to health care, it's an all-encompassing, it seems to me, political, cultural, educational apparatus.

And it basically has nothing to do with expanding the meaning and the substance of democracy itself. What it has to do is expanding—what it means to get—a quick return, what it means to take advantage of a kind of casino logic in which the only thing that drives you is to go to that slot machine and somehow get more, just pump the machine, put as much money as you can into it and walk out a rich man. That's what it's about.

BILL MOYERS: You say that casino capitalist, zombie politics views competition as a form of social combat, celebrates war as an extension of politics and legitimates a ruthless social Darwinism.

HENRY GIROUX: Oh, I mean, it is truly ruthless. I mean, imagine yourself on a reality TV program called "The Survivor", you and I, we're all that's left. The ideology that drives that program is only one of us is going to win. I don't have any respect for you. I mean, all I'm trying to do is beat you. I just want to be the one that's left. I want to win the big prize.

And it seems to me that what's unfortunate is that reality now mimics reality TV. It is reality TV in terms of the consensus that drives it, that the shared fears are more important than shared responsibilities, that the social contract is a pathology because it basically suggests helping people is a strength rather than a weakness.

It believes that social bonds not driven by market values are basically bonds that we should find despicable. But even worse, in this ethic, the market has colonized pleasure in such a way that violence in many ways seems to be the only way left that people can actually experience pleasure whether it's in the popular medium, whether it's in the way in which we militarize local police to become SWAT teams that actually will break up poker games now in full gear or give away surplus material, equipment to a place like Ohio State University, who got an armored tank.

I mean, I guess—I'm wondering what does it mean when you're on a campus and you see an armored tank, you know, by the university police? I mean, this is—everything is a war zone. You know, Senator Graham—when Lindsey Graham, he said—in talking about the terrorist laws, you know these horrible laws that are being put into place in which Americans can be captured, they can be killed and, you know—the kill list all of this, he basically says, "Everybody's a potential terrorist."

I mean, so that what happens here is that this notion of fear and this fear around the notion of security that is simply about protecting yourself, not about social security, not about protecting the commons, not about protecting the environment, turns everybody into a potential enemy. I mean, we cannot mediate our relationships it seems any longer in this culture in ways in which we would suggest and adhere to the notion that justice is a matter of caring for the other, that compassion matters.

BILL MOYERS: So this is why you write that America's no longer recognizable as a democracy?

HENRY GIROUX: No. Look, as the social state is crippled, as the social state is in some way robbed, hollowed out and robbed of its potential and its capacities, what takes its place? The punishing state takes its place.

You get this notion of incarceration, this, what we call the governing through crime complex where governance now has been ceded to corporations who largely are basically about benefiting the rich, the ultra-rich, the big corporations and allowing the state to exercise its power in enormously destructive and limited ways.

And those ways are about militarizing the culture, criminalizing a wide swathe of social behavior and keeping people in check. What does it mean when you turn on the television in the United States and you see young kids, peaceful protestors, lying down with their hands locked and you got a guy with, you know, spraying them with pepper spray as if there's something normal about that, as if that's all it takes, that's how we solve problems? I mean, I guess the question here is what is it in a culture that would allow the public to believe that with almost any problem that arises, force is the first way to address it.

I mean, one has to recognize that in that kind of logic, something has happened in which the state is no longer in the service of democracy.

BILL MOYERS: Well, George Monbiot, who writes for *The Guardian*, wrote just the other day, "It's business that really rules us." And he says, "So I don't blame people for giving up on politics ... When a state-corporate nexus of power has bypassed democracy and made a mockery of the voting process, when an unreformed political funding system ensures that parties can be bought and sold, when politicians of the main ... parties stand and watch as public services are divvied up by a grubby cabal of privateers, what is left of the system that inspires us to participate?"

HENRY GIROUX: I mean, the real question is why aren't we more outraged? Why aren't we in the streets? I mean, that's the central question for the American public. I mean, and I think that question has to address something fundamental and that is what we have, while we have an economic system that in fact has caused a crisis in democracy. What we haven't addressed is the underlying consensus that informs that crisis. What you have is basically a transgression against the very basic ideals of democracy. We have lost what it means to be connected to democracy.

And I think that's coupled with a cultural apparatus, a culture, an educative culture, a mode of politics in which people now have gone through this for so long that it's become normalized. I mean, it's hard to imagine life beyond capitalism. You know, it's easier to imagine the death of the planet than it is to imagine the death of capitalism. I mean—and so it seems to me—

BILL MOYERS: Well, they don't want the death of capitalism. Don't you think people want to be capitalists? Don't you think they want money?

HENRY GIROUX: I'm not sure if they want those things. I mean, I think when you read all the surveys about what's important to people's lives, Bill, actually the things that they focus on are not about, you know, "I want to be like the Kardashian sisters," God forbid, right?

I mean, I think that what—they the same way we want—we need a decent education for our kids, we want real health care. I mean, we want the sense of equality in the country. We want to be able to control the political process so that we're not simply nameless and invisible and disposable.

I mean, they basically—they want women to be able to have the right to have some control over their own reproductive rights. I mean, they're talking about gay rights being a legitimate pursuit of justice.

And I think that what is missing from all of this are the basic, are those alternative public spheres, those cultural formations, what I call a formative culture that can bring people together and give those ideas, embody them in both a sense of hope, of vision and the organizations and strategies that would be necessary at the very least to start a third party, at the very least. I mean, to start a party that is not part of this establishment, to reconstruct a sense of where politics can go.

BILL MOYERS: Well, you write that the liberal center has failed us and for all of its discourse of helping the poor, of addressing inequality, it always ends up on the side of bankers and finance capital, right.

HENRY GIROUX: Are you talking about Obama?

BILL MOYERS: I'm talking about what you say.

HENRY GIROUX: I know, I know. I'm—

BILL MOYERS: But you do, I must be fair and say that you go on in that same chapter of one of these books to say isn't it time we forget trying to pressure Obama to do the right thing?

HENRY GIROUX: Obama to me is symptomatic to me of the liberal center. But the issue is much greater than him. I mean, the issue is in a system that is entirely broken. It's broken.

Elections are bought by big money. The political process is not in the hands of the people. It's in the hands of very few people. And it seems to me we have to ask ourselves what kind of formative culture needs to be put in place in which education becomes central to politics, in which politics can be used to help people to be able to see things differently, to get beyond this system that is so closed, so powerfully normalized.

I mean, the right since the 1970s has created a massive cultural apparatus, a slew of anti-public intellectuals. They've invaded the universities with think tanks. They have foundations. They have all kinds of money. And you know, it's interesting, the war they wage is a war on the mind.

The war on what it means to be able to dissent, the war on the possibility of alternative visions. And the left really has—and progressives and liberals, we have nothing like that. I mean, we always seem to believe that all you have to do is tell the truth.

BILL MOYERS: You shall know the truth, the truth will set you free.

HENRY GIROUX: Yeah, and the truth will set you free. But I'm sorry, it doesn't work that way.

BILL MOYERS: Which brings me to the book you're now finishing and will be published next spring. You call it *The Violence of Organized Forgetting*. What are we forgetting?

HENRY GIROUX: We're forgetting the past. We're forgetting all those struggles that in fact offered a different story about the United States.

BILL MOYERS: How is it organized, this forgetting?

HENRY GIROUX: It's organized because it's systemic. It's organized because you have people controlling schools who are deleting those histories and making sure that they don't appear. In Tucson, Arizona they banished ethnic studies from the curriculum. This is the dis-imagination machine. That's the hardcore element.

BILL MOYERS: The suffocation of imagination?

HENRY GIROUX: The suffocation of imagination. And we kill the imagination by suggesting that the only kind of rationality that matters, the only kind of learning that matters is utterly instrumental, pragmatist.

So what we do is we collapse education into training, and we end up suggesting that not knowing much is somehow a virtue. And I think what's so disturbing about this is not only do you see it in the popular culture with the lowest common denominator now drives that culture, but you also see it coming from politicians who actually say things that suggest something about the policies they'd like to implement.

I mean, I know Rick Santorum is not—is kind of an obvious figure. But when he stands up in front of a body of Republicans and he says, the last thing we need in the Republican party are intellectuals. And I think it's kind of a template for the sort of idiocy that increasingly now dominates our culture.

BILL MOYERS: What is an intellectual? The atmosphere has been so poisoned, as you know, by what you've been describing, that many people bridle when they hear the term intellectual pursuit.

HENRY GIROUX: I mean, yeah, I think intellectuals are—there are two ways we can describe intellectuals. In the most general sense, we can say, "Intellectuals are people who take pride in ideas. They work with ideas." I mean, they believe that ideas matter. They believe that there's no such thing as common sense, good sense or bad sense, but reflective sense.

That ideas offer the framework for what gives us agency, what allows us to read the world critically, what allows us to be literate. What allows us to be civic—civic literacy may be in some ways the high point of what it means to be an intellectual.

BILL MOYERS: Because?

HENRY GIROUX: Because it suggests that how we learn what we learn and what we do with the knowledge that we have is not just for ourselves. It's for the way in which we can expand and deepen the very processes of democracy in general, and address those problems and anti-democratic forces that work against it. Now some people make a living as a result of being intellectuals. But there are people who are intellectuals who don't function in that capacity. They're truck drivers. They're workers.

I grew up in a working class neighborhood. The smartest people I have ever met were in that neighborhood. We read books. We went to the library together. We drank on Friday nights. We talked about Gramsci. We drove to Boston—

BILL MOYERS: Gramsci being the Italian philosopher.

HENRY GIROUX: The Italian philosopher. I mean—

BILL MOYERS: The pessimism of the—

HENRY GIROUX: Of the intellect, and optimism of the will.

BILL MOYERS: Right.

HENRY GIROUX: Right? I mean, we—

BILL MOYERS: You see the world as it is, but then you act as if you can change the world.

HENRY GIROUX: Exactly. I mean, we tried to find ways to both enliven the neighborhoods we lived in. But at the same time, we knew that that wasn't enough. That there was a world beyond our neighborhood, and that world had all kinds of things for us to learn. And we were excited about that. I mean, we drank, danced and talked. That's what we did.

BILL MOYERS: And I assume there were some other more private activities.

HENRY GIROUX: And there was more private activity.

BILL MOYERS: You know, you are a buoyant man. And yet you describe what you call a shift away from the hope that accompanies the living, to a politics of cynicism and despair.

HENRY GIROUX: Yeah.

BILL MOYERS: What leads you to this?

HENRY GIROUX: What leads me to this is something that we mentioned earlier, and that is when you see policies being enacted today that are so cruel and so savage, wiping out a generation of young people, trying to eliminate public schools, eliminating health care, putting endless percentage of black and brown people in jail, destroying the environment and there's no public outrage.

There aren't people in the streets. You know, you have to ask yourself, "Has this market mentality, is it so powerful and that it's become so normalized, so taken for granted that the collective imagination has been so stunted that it becomes difficult to challenge it anymore?" And I think that leads me to despair somewhat. But I've always felt that in the face of the worst tyrannies, people resist.

They're resisting now all over the world. And it seems to me history is open. I believe history is open. I don't believe that we have reached the finality of a system that is so destructive that all we have to do is look at the clock and say, "One minute left." I don't believe in those kinds of metaphors.

We have to acknowledge the realities that bear down on us, but it seems to me that if we really want to live in a world and be alive with compassion and justice, then we need educated hope.

We need a hope that recognizes the problems and doesn't romanticize them, and also recognizes the need for vision, for social organizations, for strategies. We need institutions that provide the formative culture that give voice to those visions and those ideas.

BILL MOYERS: You've talked elsewhere or written elsewhere about the need for a militant, far-reaching social movement to challenge the false claims that equate democracy and capitalism. Now, what do you mean "Militant and Far Reaching Social Movement"?

HENRY GIROUX: I mean, what we do know, we know this. We know that there are people working in local communities all over the United States around particular kinds of issues, whether it be gay rights, whether it be the environment, whether it be, you know the Occupy movement, helping people with Hurricane Sandy. We have a lot of fragmented movements.

And I think we probably have a lot more than we realize, because the press gives them no visibility, as you know. So, we don't really have a sense of the degree to which these—how pronounced these really are. I think the real issue here is, you know, what would it mean to begin to do at least two things?

To say the very least, one is to develop cultural apparatuses that can offer a new vocabulary for people, where questions of freedom and justice and the problems that we're facing can be analyzed in ways that reach mass audiences in accessible language. We have to build a formative culture. We have to do that. Secondly, we've got to overcome the fractured nature of these movements. I mean the thing that plagues me about progressives in the left and liberals is they are all sort of ensconced in these fragmented movements that seem to suggest those movements constitute the totality of the system of oppression that we are facing. And they don't.

Look, we have technologies in place now in which students all over the world are beginning to communicate with each other because they're realizing that the punishing logic of austerity has a certain kind of semblance that a certain normality that, in common ground, that is affecting students in Greece, students in Spain, students in France.

BILL MOYERS: And in this country?

HENRY GIROUX: And in this country. And it seems to me that while I may be too old to in any way begin to participate in this, I really believe that young people have recognized that they've been written out of the discourse of democracy. That they're in the grip of something so oppressive it will take away their future, their hopes, their possibilities and their sense of the future will be one that is less than what their parents had imagined.

And there's no going back. I mean, this has to be addressed. And it will take time. They'll build the organizations. They'll work with the new technologies. And hopefully they'll have our generation to be able to assist in that, but it's not going to happen tomorrow. And it's not going to happen in a year. It's going to as you have to plant seeds. You have to believe that seeds matter.

But you need a different vocabulary and a different understanding of politics. Look, the right has one thing going for it that nobody wants to talk about. Power is global. And politics is local. They float. They have no allegiance to anyone. They don't care about the social contract, because if workers in the United States don't want to compromise, they'll get them in Mexico. So the notion of political concessions has died for this class. They don't care about it anymore. There are no political concessions.

BILL MOYERS: The financial class.

HENRY GIROUX: The financial class.

BILL MOYERS: The one percent.

HENRY GIROUX: The one percent. That's why they're so savage. They're so savage because there's nothing to give up. They don't have to compromise. The power is so arrogant, so over the top, so unlike anything we have seen in terms of its anti-democratic practices, policies, modes of governance and ideology.

That at some point, you know they feel they don't have to legitimate this anymore. I mean, it's because the contradictions are becoming so great, that I think all of a sudden a lot of young people are recognizing this language, this whole language, doesn't work. The language of liberalism doesn't work anymore.

No, let's just reform the system. Let's work within it. Let's just run people for office. My argument would be, you have one foot in and you have one foot out. I'm not willing to give up the school board. I'm not willing to give up all forms of electoral politics. But it seems to me at the local level we can do some of that thing, that people can get elected. They can make moderate changes.

But the real changes are not going to come there. The real changes are going to come in creating movements that are longstanding, that are organized, that basically take questions of governance and policy seriously and begin to spread out and become international. That is going to have to happen.

BILL MOYERS: But here's the contradiction I hear in what you're saying. That if you write about a turning toward despair and cynicism in politics. Can you get movements out of despair and cynicism? Can you get people who will take on the system when they have been told that the system is so powerful and so overwhelming that they've lost their, as you call it, moral and political agency?

HENRY GIROUX: Well let me put it this way. What we often find is we often find people who take for granted the systems that they live in. They take for granted the savagery—the sort of things that you talked about. And it produces two kinds of rage. It produces an inner rage in which people blame themselves.

It's so disturbing to me to see working class, middle class people blaming themselves when these bankers have actually caused the crisis. That's the first issue.

Then you have another expression of that rage, and that rage blames blacks. It blames immigrants. It blames young people. It says, "They're not—" it says about youth, it says, "Youth is not in trouble. They're the problem."

And so, all of a sudden that rage gets displaced. The question is not what do we—the question is not just where's the outrage. The question is how do you mobilize the rage in ways in which it's not self-defeating, and in ways in which it doesn't basically be used to scapegoat other people. That's an educational issue. That should be at the center of any politics that matters.

BILL MOYERS: One of your intellectual mentors, the philosopher Ernst Bloch, said, "We must believe in the principle of hope." And you've written often about the language of hope. What does that mean, the principle of hope and the language of hope, and why are they important as you see it in creating this new paradigm, metaphor that you talk about?

HENRY GIROUX: Yeah, I mean, hope to me is a metaphor that speaks to the power of the imagination. I don't believe that anyone should be involved in politics in a progressive way if they can't understand that to act otherwise, you have to imagine otherwise.

What hope is predicated on is the assumption that life can be different than it is now. But to be different than it is now, rather than romanticizing hope and turning it into something Disney-like, right, it really has to involve the hard work of A) recognizing the structures of domination that we have to face, B) organizing collectively and somehow to change those, and C) believing it can be done, that it's worth the struggle.

That if the struggles are not believed in, if people don't have the faith to engage in these struggles, and that's the issue. I mean, that working class neighborhood that I talked to you about in the beginning of the program, I mean, it just resonates with such a sense of joy for me, the sense of solidarity, sociality.

And I think all the institutions that are being constructed under this market tyranny, this casino capitalism, is just the opposite. It's like that image of all these people at the bus stop, right. And they're all—they're together, but they're alone. They're alone.

BILL MOYERS: If we have zombie politics, if we have as you say, metaphorically, zombies in the high levels of government, zombies in banks and financial centers and zombies in the military, can't you have a zombie population? I mean, you say the stories that are being told through the commercial corporate entertainment media are all the more powerful because they seem to defy the public's desire for rigorous accountability, critical interrogation and openness.

Now if that's what the public wants, why isn't the market providing them? Isn't that what the market's supposed to do? Provide what people want?

HENRY GIROUX: The market doesn't want that at all. I mean, the market wants the people, the apostles of this market logic, I mean, the first rule of the market is make sure you have power that's unaccountable. That's what they want.

And I think that, I mean, what we see is a war on the ability to produce meanings that hold power accountable. A war on the possibility of an education that enables people to think critically, a war on cultural apparatuses that entertain by simply engaging in this spectacle of violence and not producing programs that really are controversial, that make people think, that make people alive through the possibilities of, you know, the imagination itself.

I mean, my argument is the formative culture that produces those kinds of intellectual and creative and imaginative abilities has been under assault since the 1980s in a very systemic way. So that the formative culture that takes its place is a business culture. It's a culture run by accountants, not by visionaries. It's a culture run by the financial services. It's a culture run by people who believe that data is more important than knowledge.

BILL MOYERS: You paint a very grim picture of the state of democracy, and yet you don't seem contaminated by cynicism yourself.

HENRY GIROUX: No, I'm not.

BILL MOYERS: How do we understand that?

HENRY GIROUX: Because I refuse to become a part of it.

Become I refuse to become complicitous. I refuse to say—I refuse to be alive and to watch institutions being handed over to right wing zealots. I refuse to be alive and watch the planet be destroyed.

I mean, when you mentioned—you talk about the collective imagination, you know, I mean that imagination emerges when people find strength in collective organizations, when they find strength in each other.

Believing that we can work together to produce commons in which we can share that raises everybody up and not just some people, that contributes to the world in a way that—and I really don't mean to be romanticizing here, but a world in which, where we recognize is never just enough. Justice is never done. It's an endless struggle. And that there's joy in that struggle, because there's a sense of solidarity that brings us together around the most basic, most elemental and the most important of democratic values.

BILL MOYERS: Henry Giroux, thank you, very much for talking to me.

HENRY GIROUX: Thank you, Bill.

CHAPTER 17

Charlottesville, Neo-Nazis and the Challenge to Higher Education

2017

The march across the University of Virginia campus in the summer of 2017 by a thousand or more white supremacists, neo-Nazis, and other right-wing extremists offered a glimpse of the growing danger of authoritarian movements both in the United States and across the globe, signaling a danger that mimics the increasingly forgotten horrors of the 1930s. The image of hundreds of fascist thugs chanting anti-Semitic, racist, and white nationalist slogans such as "Heil Trump" and later attacking peaceful anti-racist counter-demonstrators makes clear that radical right-wing groups that historically have been on the margins of American society are now more comfortable in public with their nihilistic and dangerous politics. They appear especially emboldened to come out of the shadows because elements of their neo-fascist ideology have found a comfortable if not supportive place at the highest levels of the Trump administration, especially in the initial and telling presence of Steve Bannon, Jeff Sessions, and Stephen Miller, all of whom embrace elements of the nefarious racist ideology that was on full display in Charlottesville.

As is well known, Trump has not only supported the presence and backing of white nationalists and white supremacists, but he has refused to denounce their Nazi slogans and violence in strong political and ethical terms, suggesting his own complicity with such movements. It should surprise no one that David Duke, a former imperial wizard of the Ku Klux Klan, told reporters in the midst of the events that the Unite the Right followers were "going to fulfill the promises of Donald Trump... to take our country back" (Nelson, 2017, para. 2). Nor should it surprise anyone that Trump initially refused to condemn the fascist groups behind the horrifying, shocking images and violence that took place in Charlottesville. His silence made elements of the far-right quite happy (The Editorial Board, *The New York Times*, 2017). For instance, The Daily Stormer, a white supremacist website, issued the following statement: "Refused to answer a question about White Nationalists supporting him. No condemnation at all. When asked to condemn, he just walked out of the room. Really, really good. God bless him" (quoted in The Editorial Board, *The New York Times*, 2017, para. 2).

It appears that the presence of Nazi and Confederate flags along with the horrendous history of millions lost to the Holocaust and slavery, lynchings, church bombings, and the assassination of Black leaders such as Medgar Evers and Martin Luther King, Jr. did little to move Trump to a serious understanding or repudiation of the poisonous historical forces that surfaced in Charlottesville. The demonstration held in Charlottesville by militarized torch-bearing groups of Nazi sympathizers, Ku Klux Klan members, and white nationalists represents a historical moment that captures some of the elements of a past that led to some of the worse crimes in human history. At the risk of falling prey to historical amnesia, the crucial lesson to be learned is that the ideology, values, and institutions of a liberal democracy are once again under assault by those who no longer believe in equality, justice, and democracy. As the historian Timothy Snyder (2017) has observed, it is crucial to remember that the success of authoritarian regimes in Germany and other places succeeded, in part, because they were not stopped in the early stages of their development.

The events in Charlottesville provide a glimpse of authoritarianism on the rise and speak to the dark clouds that appear to be ushering in a new and dangerous historical moment both in the United States and across the globe. While it is problematic to assume that an American-style totalitarianism will soon become the norm in the United States, it is not unrealistic to recognize that the possibility for a return to authoritarianism is no longer the stuff of fantasy or hysterical paranoia, especially since its core elements of hatred, exclusion, racism, and white supremacy have been incorporated into both the highest levels of state power and throughout the mainstream right-wing media. The horrors of the past are real and the fears they produce about the present are the necessary work of both historical memory and the power of civic courage and moral responsibility.

The authoritarian drama unfolding across the United States has many registers and includes the use of state violence against immigrants, right-wing populist violence against mosques and synagogues, and attacks on Muslims, young blacks, and others who do not fit into the vile script of white nationalism. The violence in Charlottesville is but one register of a larger mirror of domestic terrorism and homegrown fascism that is growing in the United States. Trump's irresponsible response to the violence in Charlottesville should surprise no one given the long history of racism in the Republican Party that extends from Nixon's Southern strategy and George W. Bush's treatment of the Black victims of Hurricane Katrina to the current party's efforts at voter suppression. Like many of his fellow Republican extremists, Trump embraces this long legacy of white supremacy, though he elevates it to a new level of visibility in his refusal to expunge its most naked expressions and his open support for its values and policies.

How else to explain his administration's announcement that it would no longer "investigate white nationalists, who have been responsible for a large share of violent hate crimes in the Unites States" (Shatz, 2017, para. 6). How else to explain Trump's willingness to lift restrictions imposed by the Obama administration to provide local police departments with military surplus equipment such as armed vehicles, bullet-proof vests, and grenade launchers (Goldman, 2017). Clearly, such actions accelerate Trump's law and order agenda, escalate racial tensions in cities that are often treated like combat zones, and reinforce a warrior mentality among polices officers. More telling is Trump's presidential pardon of Joe Arpaio, the notorious White suprema-cist and disgraced former sheriff of Maricopa County, Arizona. Not only did Arpaio engage in racial profiling, despite being ordered by the court to decease, he also had a notorious reputation for abusing prisoners in his Tent City, which he once called "a concentration camp" (Arpaio, quoted in Cohn, 2017, para. 14). These inmates were, among other practices, subjected to blistering heat, forced to work on chain gangs, wear pink underwear, and dress in demeaning striped uniforms.

There is more at work here than Trump's endorsement of white nationalism; there is also the sending of a clear message of support for a culture of violence that gives meaning to acts of domestic terrorism. Moreover, there is a clear contempt for the rule of law, and an endorsement not just for racist ideology but also for institu-tional racism and the primacy of the racially-based incarceration state. There is also the chilling implication that Trump would be willing to pardon those who might be found guilty in any upcoming investigations involving Trump and his administra-tion. Trump's law-and-order regime represents a form of domestic terrorism because it is a policy of state violence designed to intimidate, threaten, harm, and instill fear in a particular community. Pardoning Arpaio, Trump signals to his right-wing extremist base and fellow politicians that he justifies state enacted violence against immigrants, especially Latinos. In addition, Trump's language of fear and violence emboldens right-wing extremists and gives them the green light to support legis-lation and ideologies that are profoundly reactionary. For instance, this is evident in attempts on the part of 20 states to criminalize dissent (Johnson, 2017), overtly decry the benefits of higher education, and state without apology that Republicans would support postponing the 2020 election if Trump proposed it (Malka & Lelkes, 2017).

The events in Charlottesville raise serious questions about the role of higher education in a democracy. What role if not responsibility do universities have in the face of widespread legitimized violence? What role does education have at a time when rigorous knowledge is replaced by opinions, the truth is equated with fake news, self-interest replaces the social good, and language operates in the service of violence? Surely, institutions of higher education cannot limit their role to training at a time when democracy is under assault all over the globe. What does it mean for institutions of higher education to define themselves as a public good, a protective space for the promotion of democratic ideals, the social imagination, values, and the imperatives of critically engaged citizenship? As Jon Nixon (2015, para. 10) observes, what does it mean to view and take responsibility for developing education as "a protected space within which to think against the grain of received opinion: a space to question and challenge, to imagine the world from different standpoints and perspectives, to reflect upon ourselves in relation to others and, in so doing, to understand what it means to assume responsibility"?

Surely, with the ongoing attack on civic literacy, truth, historical memory, and justice it becomes all the more imperative for colleges and universities to educate students to do more than learn work based skills. What might it mean to educate them to become intelligent, compassionate, critically engaged citizens fully aware of the fact that without informed citizens there is no democracy? There is much more at stake here than protecting and opening the boundaries of free speech; there is the more crucial imperative of deepening and expanding the formative cultures and public spheres that make a democracy possible.

We live in an age in which there is emerging a relentless attack on the truth, honesty, and the ethical imagination. Under such circumstances, there is a need for educators to reclaim the discourse of democracy and to expand the parameters of civic literacy and courage by teaching students to think critically, embrace civic courage, develop a historical consciousness, hold on to shared responsibilities rather than shared fares, think historically and comprehensively, translate private issues into larger social problems, and learn how to think differently in order to act responsibly. Education is central to politics and such pedagogical practices raise the bar regarding what counts as education in a democracy, especially in societies that appear increasingly amnesiac—that is, countries where forms of historical, political, and moral forgetting are not only willfully practiced but celebrated. All of which becomes all the more threatening at a time when a country such as the United States has tipped over into a social order that is awash in public stupidity and views critical thought as both a liability and a threat. How else to explain the present historical moment with its collapse of civic culture and the future it cancels out? Democracy is always the outcome of ongoing struggles to preserve its ideals, values, and practices. When democracy is taken for granted, justice dies, social responsibility becomes a burden, and the seeds of authoritarianism flourish.

We may be in the midst of dark times, but history is open and resistance is no longer an option but a necessity. Educators have a particular responsibility to address this growing assault on democracy. Any other option is an act of complicity and a negation of what it means for education to matter in an alleged democratic society.

References

Nelson, L. (2017, August 12). "Why we voted for Donald Trump": David Duke explains the white supremacist Charlottesville protests. *Vox*. https://www.vox.com/2017/8/12/16138358/charlottesville-protests-david-duke-kkk

The Editorial Board. (2017, August 13. Editorial: The hate he dares not speak of. *The New York Times*. https://www.nytimes.com/2017/08/13/opinion/trump-charlottesville-hate-stormer.html?ref=opinion&_r=0

Snyder, T. (2017, May 30). On tyranny: Yale historian Timothy Snyder on how the U.S. can avoid sliding into Authoritarianism. *Democracy Now!* https://www.democracynow.org/2017/5/30/on_tyranny_yale_historian_timothy_snyder

Shatz, A. (2017, August 15). Trump set them free. *London Review of Books blog*. https://www.lrb.co.uk/blog/2017/08/15/adam-shatz/trump-set-them-free/

Goldman, A. (2017, August 28). Trump reverses restrictions on military hardware for police. *The New York Times*. https://www.nytimes.com/2017/08/28/us/politics/trump-police-military-surplus-equipment.html?mcubz=3&_r=0

Cohn, M. (2017, August 28). Trump's Arpaio pardon signals to white supremacists: 'I've got your back'. *Truthout*. http://www.truth-out.org/news/item/41753-trump-s-arpaio-pardon-signals-to-white-supremacists-i-ve-got-your-back

Johnson J. (2017, June 20). Since Trump's election, 20 states have moved to criminalize dissent. *Common Dreams*. https://www.commondreams.org/news/2017/06/20/trumps-election-20-states-have-moved-criminalize-dissent

Malka, A., & Lelkes, Y. (2017, August 10). In a new poll, half of Republicans say they would support postponing the 2020 election if Trump proposed it. *The Washington Post*. https://www.washingtonpost.com/news/monkey-cage/wp/2017/08/10/in-a-new-poll-half-of-republicans-say-they-would-support-postponing-the-2020-election-if-trump-proposed-it/?noredirect=on&utm_term=.18727ae24a80

Nixon, J. (2015, February 26). Hannah Arendt: Thinking versus evil. *Times Higher Education*. https://www.timeshighereducation.com/features/hannah-arendt-thinking-versus-evil/2018664.article?page=0%2C0#survey-answer

CHAPTER 18

Gangster Capitalism and Nostalgic Authoritarianism in Trump's America

2017

Just one year into the Donald Trump presidency, not only have the failures of American democracy become clear, but many of the darkest elements of its history have been catapulted to the center of power.[1] A dystopian ideology, a kind of nostalgic yearning for older authoritarian relations of power, now shapes and legitimates a mode of governance that generates obscene levels of inequality, expands the ranks of corrupt legislators, places white supremacists and zealous ideologues in positions of power, threatens to jail its opponents, and sanctions an expanding network of state violence both at home and abroad.

Trump has accelerated a culture of cruelty, a machinery of terminal exclusion, and social abandonment that wages a war on undocumented immigrants, poor minorities of color, and young people. He uses the power of the presidency to peddle misinformation, erode any sense of shared citizenship, ridicule critical media, and celebrate right-wing "disimagination machines" such as Fox News and Breitbart News. Under his "brand of realty TV politics,"[2] lying has become normalized, truthfulness is viewed as a liability, ignorance is propagated at the highest levels of government and the corporate controlled media, and fear-soaked cyclones of distraction and destruction immunize the American public to the cost of human suffering and misery.

Under the Trump administration, culture has been weaponized and is used as a powerful tool of power, misinformation, and indoctrination. James Baldwin in a 1979 *New York Times* essay titled "If Black English Isn't a Language, Then Tell Me, What Is?" writes, "People evolve a language...in order not to be submerged by a reality that they cannot articulate."[3]

This is certainly true for Trump who recognizes that the normalization of state sanctioned lying kills democracy, and destroys the capacity to produce informed judgments. Trump's serial lying is daunting in that it normalizes discourses, "actions, and policies exempt from moral evaluation [and] treated as beyond good and evil."[4] As Hannah Arendt argues in *The Origins of Totalitarianism,* the erasure of truth, facts, and standards of reference further the collapse of democratic institutions because it is "easier to accept patently absurd propositions than the old truths which have become pious banalities. Vulgarity with its cynical dismissal of respected standards and accepted theories carried with it the worst....and [is] easily mistake for courage and a new style of life."[5]

As language is emptied of any meaning, an authoritarian populism is emboldened and fills the airways and the streets with sonic blasts of racism, anti-Semitism, and violence. *New York Times* columnist, Michelle Goldberg rightly observes that Trump makes it difficult to hold onto any sense of what is normal given his relentless attempts to upend the rule of law, justice, ethics, and democracy itself. She writes:

> The country has changed in the past year, and many of us have grown numb after unrelenting shocks. What now passes for ordinary would have once been inconceivable. The government is under the control of an erratic racist who engages in nuclear brinkmanship on Twitter. ... He publicly pressures the Justice Department to investigate his political opponents. He's called for reporters to be jailed, and his administration demanded that a sportscaster who criticized him be fired. Official government statements promote his hotels. You can't protest it all; you'd never do anything else. After the election, many liberals pledged not to "normalize" Trump. But one lesson of this year is that we don't get to decide what normal looks like.[6]

There is more at work here than the kind of crass entertainment that mimics celebratory culture. As Byung-Chul Han argues, "every age has its signature afflictions."[7] Ours is an unprecedented corporate takeover over of the U.S. government and the reemergence of elements of totalitarianism in new forms. At stake here is the power of an authoritarian ideology that fuels a hyperactive exploitative economic order, apocalyptic nationalism, and feral appeals to racial cleansing that produce what Paul Street has called the nightmare of capitalism.[8]

Trump engages in a culture war that militarizes the social media and in doing so creates a politics of diversion while erasing memories of a Fascist past that bears an uncanny and terrifying resemblance to his own worldview. As Zygmunt Bauman observes in *Strangers at Our Door,* Trump's endless racist discourses, taunts, and policies cast Blacks, immigrants, and Muslims as "humans unworthy of regard and respect" and in engaging in the dehumanization of Other shifts major social problems away from the "sphere of ethics to that of threats to security, crime prevention, and punishment, criminality, defense of order, and, all in all, the state of emergency usually associated with the threat of military aggression and hostilities."[9]

Trump makes no apologies for ramping up the police state, imposing racist-inspired travel injunctions, banning transgender people from serving in the military, and initiating tax reforms that further balloon the obscene wealth gap in the United States, all the while using his Twitter feed to entertain his right-wing, white supremacist, and religious fundamentalist base at home with a steady stream of authoritarian comments while showering affection and further legitimation on a range of despots abroad, the most recent being the self-confessed killer, Rodrigo Duterte, President of the Philippines.

According to Felipe Villamor in *The New York Times*, "Mr. Duterte has led a campaign against drug abuse in which he has encouraged the police and others to kill people they suspect of using or selling drugs."[10] Powerful authoritarian leaders such as Russia's Vladimir Putin and China's Xi Jinping appear to pose an especially strong and fawning attraction to Trump, who exhibits little interest in their massive human rights violations. Trump's high regard for white supremacy and petty authoritarianism became clear on the domestic front when he pardoned former Arizona Sheriff Joseph Arpaio, a vicious racist who waged a war against undocumented immigrants, Latino residents, and individuals who did not speak English. Arpaio also housed detainees in an outdoor prison that he called his personal "concentration camp."

As Marjorie Cohn observes, Arpaio engaged in a series of sadistic practices in his outdoor jail in Phoenix that included forcing inmates "to wear striped uniforms and pink underwear", "work on chain gangs," and be subjected to blistering Arizona heat so severe that their "shoes would melt."[11] There is more at work here than Trump legitimating the practices of a monstrous racist; there is also expressed support for both a culture of violence and state sanctioned oppression.

Trump's authoritarianism cuts deeply into the fabric of both government and everyday politics in the United States. For example, despicable and morally reprehensible acts of collaboration with an emergent authoritarianism have created a Republican Party that echoes an eerie resemblance to similar flights of moral and political corruption that characterized the cowardly politicians in power in Vichy France during WWII.

Former conservative commentator Charles Sykes is right to argue that members of the current Republican Party are "collaborators and enablers" and as such are Vichy Republicans who are willingly engaged in a Faustian bargain with an incipient authoritarianism. Corrupted by power and all too willing to turn a blind eye to corruption, stupidity, barbarism and the growing savagery of the Trump administration, Republicans have been all too willing to surrender to Trump's authoritarian ideology, economic fundamentalism, support for religious orthodoxy, and increasingly cruel and mean-spirited policies, which "meant accepting the unacceptable [all the while reasoning] it would be worth it if they got conservative judges, tax cuts, and the repeal of Obamacare."[12]

Alarmingly, they have ignored the criticisms of Trump by high-profile members of their own party. For instance, Senator Bob Corker, the chairman of the Senate foreign relations committee, accused Trump of "debasing the nation," "treating his office like a reality show." Corker warned that Trump may be setting the U.S. "on the path to WWIII."

Egregious examples of political barbarism, state violence, the morally reprehensible, and the utter corruption of politics and democracy have become all too familiar in the first year of Trump's presidency, and the list just keeps growing. Trump's hatred of Muslims and undocumented immigrants is visible in his call to build walls rather than bridges, to invoke shared fears rather than shared responsibilities, to destroy all the public institutions that make democracy possible, and to expand a culture in which self-interest, greed, militarism, and repression expand the ideology, social relations, and practices that breathe life into what might be called gangster capitalism, rather than the less odious notion of a Second Gilded Age.

Trump has no shame and seems to delight in a pornographic display of moral indiscretion that produces waves of not only moral outrage but a constant theater of distraction. Against growing concern over his connection with the Russians, he fires James Comey as head of the FBI. In the face of his failure to pass any of his regressive legislative policies, particularly around health care reform, he insults fellow Republicans in Congress. As the Mueller investigation heats up, he publicly humiliates Jeff Sessions, his own attorney General.

In the interest of political expediency, both Trump and presidential counselor Kellyanne Conway have called for the election of Roy Moore, Republican nominee for the Alabama Senate seat abandoned by Sessions. Moore is a theocratic extremist, religious fundamentalist, homophobe, and accused sexual predator. More than a half dozen women have now accused him of various forms of sexual misconduct when they were teenagers and he was in his 30s. Trump and Conway's defense rested on the morally vacuous claim and obscene rationale that it was necessary to elect Moore to the Senate so Trump would have another Republican Senate vote to pass a tax bill that functions as a wet kiss and wedding gift for the rich. It gets worse. This is not simply politics without a moral referent. It is a politics that embraces *civic regression*, and represents a form of evil one associates with forms of domestic terrorism that characterize totalitarianism.

Trump is the apostle of moral blindness and unchecked corruption. He revels in a mode of governance that merges the idiocy of a never-ending theatrics of self-promotion with a deeply authoritarian politics of contempt, punishment, and humiliation free from any kind of self-reflection or moral evaluation. One under-analyzed example can be seen in his contempt for young people, whether expressed through his attempt to expel over 700,000 Dreamers from the United States, sanction a budget that eliminates or cuts major social provisions for poor and vulnerable youth, or advocate a tax reform bill that will impose massive suffering and hardships on minorities of class and color.[13]

Trump has given new force to the rise of the punishing state with its obsession with security, incarceration, public shaming, and the resuscitation of debtor prisons and the school-to-prison pipeline. Trump's contempt for the lives of young people, his support for a culture of cruelty, and his appetite for destruction and civic catastrophe are more than symptoms of a society ruled almost exclusively by the logic of the market and a "survival of the fittest" ethos, with its willingness if not glee in calling for the separation of economic, political, and social actions from any sense of social costs or consequences. It is about the systemic derangement of democracy and emergence of a politics that celebrates the toxic pleasures of the authoritarian state.

While there is much talk about the influence of Trumpism, there are few analyses that examine its culture of cruelty and politics of disposability, or the role that culture plays in legitimating intolerance and suffering. The culture of cruelty and mechanisms of disposability reach back to the founding of the United States as a settler-colonial society. How else does one explain a long line of state-sanctioned atrocities: the genocide waged against Native Americans in order to take their land, enslavement and breeding of Black people for profit and labor, and the passage of the Second Amendment to arm and enforce white supremacy over those populations? The legacies of those horrific roots of U.S. history are coded into Trumpist slogans about "making America great again," and egregiously defended through appeals to American exceptionalism.

More recent instances indicative of the rising culture of bigoted cruelty and mechanisms of erasure in U.S. politics include the racially motivated drug wars, policies that shifted people from welfare to workfare without offering training programs or child care, and morally indefensible tax reforms that will "require huge budget cuts in safety net programs for vulnerable children and adults."[14] As Marian Wright Adelman points out, such actions are particularly alarming and cruel at a time when "Millions of America's children today are suffering from hunger, homelessness and hopelessness. Nearly 13.2 million children are poor—almost one in five. About 70 percent of them are children of color who will be a majority of our children by 2020. More than 1.2 million are homeless. About 14.8 million children struggle against hunger in food insecure households."[15]

Trump is both a symptom and enabler of this culture, one that enables him to delight in taunting Black athletes, defending neo-Nazis in Charlottesville, and mocking anyone who disagrees with him. This is the face of a kind of Reichian psycho-politics, with its mix of violence, repression, theatrics, incoherency, and spectacularized ignorance. Trump makes clear that the dream of the confederacy is still with us, that moral panics thrive against a culture of rancid racism, "a background of obscene inequalities, progressive deregulation of labour markets and a massive expansion in the ranks of the precariat."[16]

In an age of almost unparalleled extremism, violence, and cruelty, authoritarianism is gaining ground rapidly creating a society in which shared fears and unchecked hatred have become the organizing forces for community. Under the Trump regime, dissent is disparaged as a pathology or dismissed as fake news, while even the slightest compassion for others becomes an object of disdain and subject to policies that increase the immiseration, suffering, and misery of the most vulnerable.

Under the shadow of 9/11, fear has gained a new momentum as more and more individuals and groups are disparaged, labeled as disposable, subject to forms of social and racial cleansing that are in accord with the force of a resurgent white supremacy emboldened by the fact that one of its sympathizers is now the president of the United States. Rejecting the most basic elements of a sustainable democracy, Trumpism has unleashed a rancid populism and racially inspired ultra-nationalism that sustains itself by looking everywhere for enemies while occupying the high ground of political purity and an empty moralism.

In the past, racist Democrats and Republicans did everything they could to cover over any naked expressions of their racism. This is no longer the case. Under Trump, racist discourse and the underlying principles of white supremacy are both encouraged and emboldened. In the midst of the collapse of civil society and the public spheres that make a democracy possible, every line of decency is crossed, every principle of civility is violated, and more and more elements of justice are transformed into an injustice. Trump has become the blunt instrument and Twitter preacher for displaying contempt for the truth, a critical citizenry, and democracy itself. He has anointed himself as the apostle of unchecked greed, unbridled narcissism, and unbridled militarism.[17]

Wedded to creating a culture of civic illiteracy and the plundering of the planet for both his own personal gain and that of his corporate and rich cronies, Trump has done more than assault standards of truth, verification, and evidence, he has opened the door to the dark cave of moral depravity, political corruption, and a dangerous right wing nationalist populism that as Frank Rich observes threatens to have "remarkable staying power" long after Trump is gone.[18]

Gangster capitalism under Trump has reached a new stage in that it is unabashedly aggressive in mounting a war against every institution capable of providing a vision, a semblance of critical agency, and a formative culture capable of creating agents willing to hold power accountable. The American public is witnessing a crisis not merely of politics, but of history, vision, and agency, or what Andrew O'Hehir more pointedly called the acts of a domestic terrorist. This is a politics of domesticated fear, manufactured illusions, and atomizing effects. Trump is the product of a culture long in the making, one fueled by the triumph of finance capital, the legitimation of a rancid individualism and a crippling notion of freedom. In this age of precarity, infantilizing publicity machines, and uncertainty, a sense of collective impotency and fear provides the breeding ground for isolation, the corporate state, and the discourses of inscription, demonization, and false communities.

A culture of immediacy, an economy of profound boredom, instant gratification, and spectacularized violence has created a society of deliberate forgetting and a sadomasochistic culture that thrives on humiliation, revenge, a culture of punitiveness, and an aesthetics of depravity. Trump signifies the death of the radical imagination and the apotheosis of its opposite: a lackluster hatred of thoughtfulness, creativity, and inventiveness. Trump makes clear that capitalism and democracy are not synonymous and that everyone has to be either consumer or a taxpayer.

I think the artist Sable Elyse Smith is right in arguing that ignorance is more than the absence of knowledge or the refusal to know, it is also a form of violence that is woven into the fabric of everyday life by power of massive "disimagination machines." Its ultimate goal is to enable us to not only consume pain and to propagate it, but to relish in it as a form of entertainment and emotional uplift.[19] Ignorance is also the enemy of memory and a weapon in the politics of disappearance and the violence of organized forgetting. It is also about the erasure of what Brad Evans calls "the raw realities of suffering" and the undermining of a politics that is in part about the battle for memory.[20]

Trump within a very short time has legitimated and reinforced a culture of social abandonment, erasure, and terminal exclusion. Justice in this discourse is disposable along with the institutions that make it possible. What is distinctive about Trump is that he defines himself through the tenets of a predatory and cruel form of gangster capitalism, while using its power to fill government positions with what appear to be the walking dead and at the same time produce death-dealing policies. Of course, he is just the overt and unapologetic symbol of a wild capitalism and dark pessimism that have been decades in the making. He is the theatrical, self-absorbed monster that embodies and emboldens a history of savagery, greed, and extreme inequality that has reached its endpoint—a poisonous form of American authoritarianism that must be stopped before it is too late. Trump makes clear that democracy is tenuous and has to be viewed as a site of ongoing contestation, one that demands a new understanding of politics, language, and collective struggle.

Trump's reign of terror will come to an end, but the forces that made Trump possible will not end with his political demise. This means that in the ongoing struggle against authoritarianism, progressives need a language of critique and possibility. This suggests the need for a new vocabulary that refuses to look away, refuses to surrender to the dictates of consumerism, fear, or bigotry. It also suggests a left/progressive movement that does more than say what it is against. It also needs a vision and an ongoing project that enables it to say what it is for.[21] This could take the form of creating a political, economic, and social platform rooted in the principles of democratic socialism.[22]

Ariel Dorfman drawing upon his own memories and experience of authoritarianism under General Augusto Pinochet, the Chilean dictator, speaks to the need for such a language. He writes: "It brings back to me the imaginative enormity that every true demand for radical change insists upon. It catches a missing feeling of our age: the belief that alternative worlds are possible, that they are within reach if we're courageous enough, and smart enough, and daring enough to take control of our own lives."[23]

We get a hint of such a language in the words of the writer Maaza Mengiste, who calls for a discourse of passion, power, responsibility, and justice, one that "will take us from shock and stunned silence toward a coherent, visceral speech, one as strong as the force that is charging at us."[24] In the age of Trump, we need to take seriously the notion that education is at the center of politics—that, as Stuart Hall has consistently stressed, "politics follows culture." For Hall, this meant that addressing oppression cannot rest with an emphasis on economic structures, however important. What was also needed was recognizing how domination worked at the level of belief and persuasion, which suggested that education and consciousness-raising was at the center of politics.

As Hall puts it, "You can't just rest with the underlying structural logic. And so you think about what is likely to awaken identification. There's no politics without identification. People have to invest something of themselves, something that they recognize is of them or speaks to their condition, and without that moment of recognition . . . .you won't have a political movement without that moment of identification."[25]

This suggest a politics that begins both with a vision of what a democratic socialist society might look like and a narrative that makes power visible. This implies a language that is both rigorous theoretically and accessible. Moreover, it means developing a vocabulary that moves people, speaks directly to their problems, allows them to feel compassion for the other, and gives them the courage to talk back. This suggests forging the appropriate pedagogical and symbolic weapons that make knowledge meaningful in order to make it critical and transformative. Rethinking politics means creating a vocabulary that enables us to confront a sense of responsibility in the face of the unspeakable, and to do so with a sense of dignity, self-reflection, and the courage to act in the service of a radical democracy. It also means providing the theoretical tools that enable people to connect private problems with wider social issues.

In the face of Trump's brand of authoritarianism, progressives need a vocabulary that allows us to recognize ourselves as agents, not victims, in the discourse of a radical democratic politics. We need a politics that addresses systemic problems and refuses gangster capitalism's insistence that all problems are personal, an exclusive matter of individual responsibility and privatized solutions. This is not to underplay how difficult it is to acknowledge any viable sense of the outrage and struggle in an age when the power of culture, new digital technologies, social media, and mainstream cultural apparatuses seem almost overwhelming in their deleterious effects on shaping agency, desires, values, and modes of identification. But rather than surrender to such forces, they need to be reworked in the interest of a set of collective and emancipatory modes of communication, social relations, and forms of resistance.

At the same time it is crucial to remember that there is more at stake here than a struggle over meaning. There is also the struggle over power, over the need to create a formative culture that will produce new modes of critical agency and contribute to a broad social movement that can translate meaning into a fierce struggle for economic, political, and social justice. Power is never entirely on the side of domination, and there are numerous examples of resistance cropping up all over the United States. Not only it is evident in youth movements such as Black Lives Matter and the Dreamers, but also middle-aged women in the red states fighting over what Judith

Shulevitz calls "the big issues for the resistance [such as] health care and gerrymandering, followed by dark money in politics, education and the environment."26

Activists are also mobilizing over immigrant rights, mass incarceration, police violence, abolishing nuclear weapons, and environment justice, among other issues. Facing the challenge of fascism will not be easy, but Americans are marching, protesting, and organizing in record-breaking numbers. Hopefully, mass indignation will evolve into a worldwide movement whose power will be on the side of justice rather than impunity, bridges rather than walls, dignity rather than disrespect, and kindness rather than cruelty. What is crucial is that these discrete movements come together under a large political and social formation in order to develop alliances capable of developing in a democratic socialist party, one willing to make resistance a necessity rather than an option.

Notes

1. See, for instance, my forthcoming book, Henry A. Giroux, *American Nightmare: Facing the Challenge of Fascism* (San Francisco: City Lights Books, 2018).
2. John W. Whitehead, "Trump and the Police State," *Counterpunch* (November 2, 2017). Online: https://www.counterpunch.org/2017/11/02/97153/
3. James Baldwin, "If Black English Isn't a Language, Then Tell Me, What Is?" *The New York Times* (July 29, 1979). Online: http://www.nytimes.com/books/98/03/29/specials/baldwin-english.html
4. Zygmunt Bauman, *Strangers at Our Door* (London: Polity, 2016), p. 79.
5. Hannah Arendt, *The Origins of Totalitarianism* (New York: Harcourt, 1968 edition), p. 334.
6. Michelle Goldberg, "Anniversary of the Apocalypse," *The New York Times* (November 6, 2017). Online: https://www.nytimes.com/2017/11/06/opinion/anniversary-trump-clinton-election.html
7. Byung-Chul Han, *The Burnout Society* (Stanford: Stanford University Press, 2015), p. 1.
8. Paul Street, "Capitalism: the Nightmare," *Truthdig* (September 20, 2017). Online: https://www.truthdig.com/articles/capitalism-the-nightmare/
9. Ibid., Bauman, *Strangers at our Door*, pp. 85–86.
10. Felipe Villamor, "Rodrigo Duterte Says Donald Trump Endorses His Violent Antidrug Campaign," *The New York Times* (December 3, 2016). Online: http://www.nytimes.com/2016/12/03/world/asia/philippines-rodrigo-duterte-donald-trump.html
11. Marjorie Cohn, "Trump's Arpaio Pardon Signals to White Supremacists: 'I've Got Your Back.'" *TruthDig*, [August 28, 2017]. Online: http://www.truth-out.org/news/item/41753-trump-s-arpaio-pardon-signals-to-white-supremacists-i-ve-got-your-back
12. Charles J. Sykes "Year One: The Mad King," *The New York Review of Books,* [Nov 10, 2017]. Online: https://www.nybooks.com/daily/2017/11/10/year-one-the-mad-king/
13. Common Dreams Staff, "New Report Details '13 Terrible Things' About Senate GOP Tax Plan," *Common Dreams* (November 21, 2017). Online: https://www.commondreams.org/news/2017/11/21/new-report-details-13-terrible-things-about-senate-gop-tax-plan
14. Marian Wright Edelman, "Why America May Go to Hell," *Huffington Post* (November 17, 2017). https://www.huffingtonpost.com/entry/why-america-may-go-to-hell_us_5a0f4dd4e4b023121e0e9281
15. Ibid.
16. Pankaj Mishra, "What Is Great about Ourselves," *London Review of Books,* [September 21, 2017]. Online: https://www.lrb.co.uk/v39/n18/pankaj-mishra/what-is-great-about-ourselves

17. Tom Engelhardt, "Empire of Madness: Fiddling Through the Smoke in 2025," *TomDispatch.com* (September 21, 2017). Online: http://www.tomdispatch.com/post/176329/tomgram%3A_engelhardt%2C_tweeting_while_the_planet_burns/#more

18. Frank Rich, "After Trump," *The New York Magazine,* [November 13, 2017]. Online: http://nymag.com/daily/intelligencer/2017/11/frank-rich-trumpism-after-trump.html

19. I am drawing here from Cora Fisher, "An Artist's Bond with Her Imprisoned Father: In Sable Elyse Smith's Exhibition Ordinary Violence, the Artist's Father is Both Muse and Specter," *Hyperallergic* (November 11, 2017). Online: https://hyperallergic.com/410947/sable-elyse-smith-ordinary-violence-queens-museum-2017/

20. Brad Evans, "Remembering the 43," *Los Angeles Review of Books Blog* (September 9, 2017). Online: http://blog.lareviewofbooks.org/essays/remembering-43/

21. Jessa Crispin, "Where Have All the Communes Gone?" *In These Times* [September 18, 2017]. Online: http://inthesetimes.com/article/20491/where-have-all-the-communes-gone-left-wing-melancholia-kommune-tumult

22. See for instance, Frances Goldin, Debby Smith, and Michael Steven Smith, eds. *Living in a Socialist USA* (New York: Harper, 2014).

23. Ariel Dorfman, "How to Read Donald Trump on Burning Books But Not Ideas," *TomDispatch* [September 14, 2017]. Online: http://www.tomdispatch.com/blog/176326/tomgram%3A_ariel_dorfman%2C_a_tale_of_two_donalds

24. Maaza Mengiste, "Unheard-of Things," *The Massachusetts Review* 57-1 (2016), p. 89

25. Stuart Hall and Les Back, "In Conversation: At Home and Not at Home", *Cultural Studies*, Vol. 23, No. 4, (July 2009), pp. 680–681.

26. Judith Shulevitz, "Year One: Resistance Research," *The New York Review of Books,* [Nov 9, 2017]. Online: http://www.nybooks.com/daily/2017/11/09/year-one-resistance-research/

Index

> < > <

About the Author, Editors, and Contributors

Henry A. Giroux currently holds the McMaster University Chair for Scholarship in the Public Interest in the English and Cultural Studies Department and the Paulo Freire Distinguished Scholar Professorship in Critical Pedagogy. In 2002, he was named as one of the top fifty educational thinkers of the modern period in *Fifty Modern Thinkers on Education: From Piaget to the Present* as part of Routledge's Key Guides Publication Series. In 2007, he was named by the *Toronto Star* as one of the "12 Canadians Changing the Way We Think." He is a frequent contributor to online sources such as *Truthout, Tikkun, CounterPunch, Truthdig,* and *Salon,* and his research has appeared in numerous academic journals. In all, he has published over 400 scholarly articles. His most recent books include *Neoliberalism's War on Higher Education* (Haymarket, 2014), *The Violence of Organized Forgetting* (City Lights, 2014), *Dangerous Thinking in the Age of the New Authoritarianism* (Routledge, 2015), *America's Addiction to Terrorism* (Monthly Review Press, 2016), *America at War with Itsel* (City Lights, 2017), *The Public in Peril* (Routledge, 2018), and *The Terror of the Unforeseen* (Los Angeles Review of Books, 2019). Giroux is also a member of the Board of Directors at *Truthout.* His website is www. henryagiroux.com.

Antonia Darder is a distinguished international Freirian scholar. She is a public intellectual, educator, writer, activist, and artist. She holds the Leavey Presidential Endowed Chair of Ethics and Moral Leadership at Loyola Marymount University, Los Angeles and is Professor Emerita of Education Policy, Organization, and Leadership at the University of Illinois Urbana Champaign. She also holds a Distinguished Visiting faculty post at the University of Johannesburg, in South Africa. Her scholarship has consistently focused on issues of racism, political economy, social justice, and education. She is the author of numerous books and articles in the field, including *Culture and Power in the Classroom* (20th anniversary edition), *Reinventing Paulo Freire: A Pedagogy of Love; A Dissident Voice: Essays on Culture, Pedagogy, and Power; Freire and Education;* and the forthcoming *The Student Guide to Freire's Pedagogy of the Oppressed.* She is also co-author of *After Race: Racism After Multiculturalism* and co-editor of *The Critical Pedagogy Reader; Latinos and Education: A Critical Reader;* and the *International Critical Pedagogy Reader,* which was awarded the 2015 Alpha Sigma Nu Book Award.

William Ayers, formerly Distinguished Professor of Education and Senior University Scholar at the University of Illinois at Chicago (UIC), has written extensively about social justice and democracy, education and the cultural contexts of schooling, and teaching as an essentially intellectual, ethical, and political enterprise. His books include *A Kind and Just Parent*; *Teaching Toward Freedom*; *Fugitive Days: A Memoir*; *Public Enemy: Confessions of an American Dissident*; *To Teach: The Journey, in Comics*; *Teaching with Conscience in an Imperfect World*; *Race Course: Against White Supremacy*; *and Demand the Impossible!*

Jake Burdick is an Assistant Professor of Curriculum Studies in the College of Education at Purdue University, where he teaches courses in curriculum theory, multicultural education, and qualitative inquiry. Jake's research centers on deepening conceptualizations of education via public pedagogy and theorizing activism as a pedagogical performance. Jake is the co-editor of the *Handbook of Public Pedagogy* (Routledge), *Complicated Conversations and Confirmed Commitments: Revitalizing Education for Democracy* (Educators International Press), and *Problematizing Public Pedagogy* (Routledge). He has published work in *Qualitative Inquiry, Curriculum Inquiry, Review of Research in Education, Review of Educational Research*, and the *Journal of Curriculum and Pedagogy*.

Peter McLaren is Distinguished Professor in Critical Studies and Co-Chair of the Paulo Freire Democratic Project, Donna Ford Attallah College of Educational Studies, Chapman University, and Chair Professor, Northeast Normal University, China. He is the author and editor of 50 books, and his writings have been translated into 30 languages. Instituto McLaren de Pedagogia Critica has been established throughout Baja California, Morelia, Jalisco, Oaxaca, and Chiapas.

Jennifer A. Sandlin is a Professor in the Justice and Social Inquiry Department in the School of Social Transformation at Arizona State University, where she teaches courses on consumption and education, popular culture and justice, and social and cultural pedagogy. Her research focuses on the intersections of education, learning, and consumption, as well as on the theory and practice of public pedagogy. She also investigates sites of public pedagogy and popular culture-based, informal, and social movement activism centered on "unlearning" consumerism. She is currently co-editor of the *Journal of Curriculum and Pedagogy*. Her work has been published in *Journal of Consumer Culture, Adult Education Quarterly, Qualitative Inquiry, International Journal of Qualitative Studies in Education, Curriculum Inquiry*, and *Teachers College Record*. She recently edited, with Jason Wallin, *Paranoid Pedagogies* (Palgrave, 2018); with Peter McLaren, *Critical Pedagogies of Consumption* (Routledge, 2010); with Brian Schultz and Jake Burdick, *Handbook of Public Pedagogy* (Routledge, 2010); with Jake Burdick and Michael O'Malley, *Problematizing Public Pedagogy* (Routledge, 2014); and with Julie Garlen, *Disney, Culture, and Curriculum* (Routledge, 2016) and *Teaching with Disney* (Peter Lang, 2016).

Shirley R. Steinberg is a Research Professor of Critical Youth Studies at the University of Calgary. She is the author and editor of many books in critical pedagogy and cultures, urban and youth culture, and cultural studies. Originally a social/improvisational theatre creator, she has facilitated happenings and flash mobs globally. A regular contributor to CBC Radio One, CTV, *The Toronto Globe and Mail*, *The Montreal Gazette*, and *The Canadian Press*, she is an internationally known speaker and teacher. She is the co-organizer of the International Institute of Critical Pedagogy and Transformative Leadership, which is committed to a global community of transformative educators and community workers engaged in radical love, social justice, and the situating of power within social and cultural contexts, specifically involving youth. Shirley's work focuses on the cultural/social/educational development of youth, as well as critical community involvement. She is concerned with how society views young people, and her work creates an environment in which youth are viewed as positive democratic agents within society. As a Research Chair, she has established an international network of youth and community workers engaged in a critical pedagogical approach to activism and pedagogy. Her work is currently focused on issues of Islamophobia, Empowerment of Women, and Critical Diversity Studies.